THE NATIONAL SECURITY ENTERPRISE

THE NATIONAL SECURITY ENTERPRISE

NAVIGATING THE LABYRINTH

SECOND EDITION

EDITORS

ROGER Z. GEORGE & HARVEY RISHIKOF

In cooperation with the Center for Security Studies,
Edmund A. Walsh School of Foreign Service,
Georgetown University

Georgetown University Press / *Washington, DC*

Library of Congress Cataloging-in-Publication Data

Names: George, Roger Z., 1949- editor. | Rishikof, Harvey, editor. |
    Georgetown University. Center for Security Studies.
Title: The national security enterprise : navigating the labyrinth / Roger Z.
    George and Harvey Rishikof, editors.
Description: Second edition. | Washington, DC : Georgetown University Press,
    2017. | "In cooperation with the Center for Security Studies, Edmund A.
    Walsh School of Foreign Service, Georgetown University" -- Title page. |
    Includes bibliographical references and index. | Description based on
    print version record and CIP data provided by publisher; resource not viewed.
Identifiers: LCCN 2016058221 (print) | LCCN 2016037925 (ebook) | ISBN 9781626164390
    (hc : alk. paper) | ISBN 9781626164406 (pb : alk. paper) | ISBN 9781626164413 (eb)
Subjects: LCSH: National security—United States. | Interagency
    coordination—United States. | Administrative agencies—United States. |
    Executive departments—United States. | Research institutes—United States.
Classification: LCC UA23 (print) | LCC UA23 .N2487 2017 (ebook) | DDC
    355/.033073—dc23
LC record available at https://lccn.loc.gov/2016058221

21 20   9 8 7 6

Printed in the United States of America

Cover design by Faceout Studio. Cover images by Shutterstock and iStock.

To Trudi Rishikof,
whose warmth, support, and love of life
was felt by all who knew her.

We would like to acknowledge the support of our parents—
Lowell Edwin and Elizabeth Zane George and
Issie and Marjorie Cryer Rishikof—
for their encouragement, love, and understanding over a lifetime.

Contents

Illustrations

FIGURES

TABLES

BOXES

Foreword to the First Edition

National security decision making is particularly difficult in this new era of emerging challenges. To develop a comprehensive US national security strategy requires the integration of all elements of American power, many of which reside in an increasingly complex governmental enterprise. What this book describes is a virtual labyrinth of agencies and actors who participate in shaping American national security policy. At the end of the day, however, it is the president and his national security team who must make and implement the critical decisions that will keep the nation secure, prosperous, and at peace.

In my experience, each president seeks to shape his national security decision-making process to suit his own personal style and policy priorities. Every president faces the challenge of organizing the executive branch, working with Congress, and managing the national debate over national security policy, which involves numerous other players. A president also faces the reality that the organizations and institutions through which he must work have their own customs, operational styles, and capabilities. Understanding those strengths and weaknesses is imperative for a president and his advisors if they are to craft successful policies and implement them.

Today the problem is much harder than it was during the Cold War. Then we faced a single overriding challenger, a reality that shaped the world and our policies. The world was tense but had defined lanes of authority. That world is gone. Today's world is anything but tidy. In some respects it is the exact opposite of the Cold War. There is no place on Earth that cannot become tomorrow's crisis. Globalization is eroding borders and individual states' abilities to manage transnational challenges such as financial crises, environmental damage, networked terrorists, and international crime, to name a few. Shaping policies to deal with these transnational threats is daunting, as they—even more than the traditional threats emanating from states—blur the distinctions between foreign and domestic; moreover, they demand the use of more than simply military force or traditional diplomacy. In many cases, problems will require the use of all forms of US power and influence, be it hard military or economic power, persuasive diplomacy, development aid for nation building, or soft power to attract nations and peoples toward seeing the world more like we do. This requires an extraordinary degree of coordination of these instruments across the entire US government.

Today's national security decision makers face four principal challenges. First, they must determine where the lines of authority for dealing with complex contingencies, like Iraq, Afghanistan, or Syria, lie among the national security agencies. No single agency can manage such challenges, and departments must combine their strengths as well as minimize their weaknesses. Understanding the cultures and the capabilities of these agencies is important in crafting effective policies.

Second, today's decision makers are burdened by institutions and organizational habits of mind that were built for the Cold War, not the twenty-first century. These institutional mindsets, often manifested as resistance to new ways of doing business or new missions for which they were not originally established, need to be brought into line with the globalized security agenda we face. Organizational changes are and will be necessary, but so too are flexible organizational cultures that inhabit those organizations.

Third, the composition and concept of the national security team need to be broadened. The Cold War notion of the National Security Council (NSC) team composed only of the secretaries of state and defense, along with the Joint Chiefs of Staff and the director of CIA, is seriously outdated. Periodic adjustments to the composition of the NSC have occurred but may still be insufficient. Perhaps we have reached the point where all cabinet officers should be considered members of the NSC; accordingly, they should attend meetings whenever their agencies' policies and capabilities are involved. Similarly, there may be a need to develop small NSC cells within each department to ensure close cooperation with the NSC staff and other agencies. This could be a useful alternative to constantly expanding the size of the NSC staff, with the danger of it becoming so large as to challenge effective integration of all elements of power.

Fourth, and perhaps most important, national security strategies will succeed or fail depending on whether they are implemented effectively. Too often a brilliant strategy can flounder for lack of resources or agencies' commitment to implementing the president's decisions. There should be a closer link between the NSC staff and the Office of Management and Budget (OMB) to ensure that the resources are available to implement the policy and that agencies have committed their resources to achieve the president's policy objectives. To its credit, this volume is one of the first I have seen that acknowledges the centrality of the resource question and treats the OMB as a key player in the national security enterprise.

These challenges should not be considered overwhelming for the US system. Indeed, no country has been as successful in marshaling its ideas, people, and resources to confront the world's problems as the United States has. By recognizing some of our own shortfalls, Americans can correct and improve on what overall has been a successful national security enterprise. I would expect no less from our twenty-first century's leaders than from those whom I have served in the past.

Lt. Gen. Brent Scowcroft, USAF (Ret.)

Preface

Preparing a second edition of a book on the so-called national security enterprise has been an enterprise in itself. As editors we have selected those scholars and practitioners who we believe are the best at their profession and who understand the national security process by virtue of their practice and study of it. Weaving together such a set of perspectives on agencies as diverse as the National Security Council staff, the Departments of State and Defense, the Central Intelligence Agency (CIA), and the Federal Bureau of Investigation (FBI)—just to name a few—is a huge task. But it was made so much easier by having a truly professional group of authors who practiced collaboration with us as they did while working in government.

In the seven years that have passed since our first edition appeared, we find that there is still a paucity of discussion and detailed analysis regarding the complex organizational and institutional cultures that drive the national security decision-making process. Having been practitioners earlier in our careers, we are familiar with the hidden incentive systems of our agencies, the sometimes parochialism of these organizations, and peculiarities of the often warring "tribes" of the national security bureaucracies.

This second edition was finalized during the Donald Trump transition process, so there is much that is up in the air about how the next president might alter the current interagency process, use his key national security team members, and define American foreign and security priorities. Agencies will respond to their new political masters according to how they view their missions and organizational processes. Appointees are often seen as more interested in pushing their agendas than leading the organizations. Occasionally, political appointees become champions of their organizations; however, typically this can only happen once the new president's team is in place and confident that the careerists are now loyal to the new team and its agenda. In any case, the chemistry among the Trump national security team members, the kind of presidential leadership Donald Trump provides, and the new foreign policy directions will have a major impact on how the many parts of the national security enterprise (NSE) respond and perform.

Writing about organizational cultures is extremely difficult. Readers will find that the chapters approach this topic in different ways, as there was no possibility of asking authors to use a cookie-cutter approach. Given the diversity of the agencies and institutions this book covers, each author had to approach organizational culture in his or her own idiosyncratic fashion. Still, we believe that the whole is greater than the sum of its parts. In this second edition, however, we did strive to consider what has changed about these organizations since the first edition was published, in particular how a decade of war has reshaped the national security enterprise.

No book that involves this many contributors can truly be the result only of its editors. As mentioned earlier, the chapter authors deserve many thanks for committing to this enterprise and producing some unique and insightful contributions. In addition, the volume would not have been possible without past support of Georgetown University's Center for Peace and Security Studies (CPASS) and its Security Studies Program. Don Jacobs of Georgetown University Press has been understanding of some slipped deadlines, an inevitability when so many busy and overcommitted authors are involved. Likewise, the Georgetown University Press staff has helped us expedite the completion of this volume and given it a very professional look. We also want to thank outside reviewers who helped us to sharpen our focus in a number of places. And for a book about bureaucracies, there were indeed a few organizational hurdles, and we appreciate the CIA Publication Review Board and the National Defense University for their speedy reviews of our manuscript.

This book is largely an outgrowth of the editors' teaching experiences at the National War College, which is part of the National Defense University. We have benefited greatly from discussions with our colleagues and have continually been challenged by our students, whose dedication and integrity we admire immensely. A key objective of this institution is to educate future American leaders about the workings of their agencies and institutions in order to improve the formulation and execution of policy. We hope our book contributes to this goal.

As in writing the first edition, both editors have been supported throughout the process by our significant "others"—Cynthia and Dina. Both have tolerated and humored us through the conceptual and writing phases of this enterprise. While it might seem easier to put together a revised version to an already existing volume, we found that our rising expectations for an even better book made us all the more demanding of ourselves and hence harder to live with for those who love us. For their patience we are very grateful.

We would be remiss if we did not single out for special thanks our research assistant extraordinaire, Brittany Albaugh, who was both a contributing author and master of the manuscript preparation. She represents that next generation of national security specialists for whom we hope this book will be useful.

Finally, the editors must acknowledge how much we have learned and benefited from each other. Our intellectual strengths—a lawyer's insistence on logic and evidence along with an analyst's penchant for organization and flow—made the effort more rigorous and rewarding. As during the work on our first edition, our mutual respect and admiration have continued to grow and deepen. This book project is certainly a tribute to an enduring friendship wherever we may be.

Abbreviations

AAFMAA	American Armed Forces Mutual Aid Association
ACA	Arms Control Association
ADD	associate deputy director
AEI	American Enterprise Institute
AFRICOM	US Africa Command
AIPAC	American-Israel Public Affairs Committee
ANSER	Analytic Services
AQAP	al-Qaeda in the Arabian Peninsula
ASD	assistant secretary of defense
AT&L	Acquisition, Technology, and Logistics
ATFC	Afghan Threat Finance Cell
ATO	Air Tasking Order
AUMF	Authorization for the Use of Military Force
BCA	Budget Control Act of 2011
BDA	Banco Delta Asia
BOB	Bureau of the Budget
BRAC	Base Realignment and Closure Commission
BUR	Bottom-Up Review
CA	covert action
CAP	Center for American Progress
CBO	Congressional Budget Office
CBP	Customs and Border Protection
CBRNE	chemical, biological, radiological, nuclear, and explosive
CENTCOM	US Central Command
CI	Central Intelligence Agency
CIS	Citizenship and Immigration Services
CJ	chief justice
CNO	chief of naval operations
COCOM	Combatant Commander
COLA	cost-of-living adjustment
CFR	Council on Foreign Relations
Cointelpro	Counterintelligence Program
COS	chief of station
CPA	Coalition Provisional Authority
CPASS	Center for Peace and Security Studies
CPC	critical priority country
CPG	Contingency Planning Guidance
CRS	Congressional Research Service
CSIS	Center for Strategic and International Studies

DA	Directorate of Analysis
DAD	deputy associate director
DART	disaster assistance response team
DASD	deputy assistant secretary of defense
DATT	defense attaché
DC	Deputies' Committee
DCHA	Democracy, Conflict, and Humanitarian Assistance
DCI	director of central intelligence
DCIA	director of the Central Intelligence Agency
DCID	Director of Central Intelligence Directive
DEA	Drug Enforcement Administration
DHS	Department of Homeland Security
DI	Directorate of Intelligence
DNDO	Domestic Nuclear Detection Office
DNI	director of national intelligence
DO	Directorate of Operations
DOD	Department of Defense
DOE	Department of Energy
DOJ	Department of Justice
DPG	Defense Planning Guidance
DPKO	Department of Peacekeeping Operations
DRI	Diplomatic Readiness Initiative
DSOP	Directorate of Strategic Operations
DTA	Detainee Treatment Act
EO	executive order
EOP	executive office of the president
ESF	Economic Support Funds
ESG	Executive Steering Group
EUCOM	US European Command
ExComm	Executive Committee
F	Office of the Director of Foreign Assistance
FARA	Foreign Agent Registration Act
FCPA	Foreign Corrupt Practices Act
FBI	Federal Bureau of Investigation
FEMA	Federal Emergency Management Agency
FFRDC	federally funded research and development center
FinCen	Financial Crimes Enforcement Network
FISA	Foreign Intelligence Surveillance Act
FISC	Foreign Intelligence Surveillance Court
FJC	Federal Judicial Center
FMF	Foreign Military Financing
FO	field office
FOIA	Freedom of Information Act
FSN	foreign service national
FSO	foreign service officer
FYDP	Future Years Defense Plan
GAO	Government Accountability Office

GPRA	Government Performance and Results Act
GPS	global positioning systems
HASC	House Armed Services Committee
HQ	headquarters
HSC	Homeland Security Council
HSI	Homeland Security Investigations
HSPD	Homeland Security Presidential Directive
HUMINT	human intelligence
IC	intelligence community
ICE	Immigration and Customs Enforcement
IMET	International Military Education and Training
ISAO	information sharing and analysis organization
ISAC	information sharing and analysis center
IT	information technology
IMF	International Monetary Fund
INR	Bureau of Intelligence and Research
IOG	Iraq Operations Group
IPC	interagency policy committees
ISA	International Security Affairs
ISG	Iraq Study Group
ISIL	Islamic State in Iraq and the Levant
ISIS	Institute for Science and International Security
ISIS	Islamic State in Iraq and Syria
ISR	intelligence, surveillance, and reconnaissance
JAG	Judge Advocate General
JCS	Joint Chiefs of Staff
JFCOM	Joint Forces Command
JICC	Joint Intelligence Community Council
JTTF	joint terrorism task force
KKK	Ku Klux Klan
LAAFB	Los Angeles Air Force Base
LDA	Lobbying Disclosure Act
LEGAT	legal attaché
MCA	Military Commission Act
MCC	Millennium Challenge Corporation
MFO	Multinational Force and Observers
NAFTA	North American Free Trade Agreement
NASA	National Aeronautics and Space Administration
NATO	North Atlantic Treaty Organization
NCCIC	National Cybersecurity and Communication Integration Center
NCIJTF	National Cyber Investigative Joint Task Force
NCIX	National Counterintelligence Executive
NCS	National Clandestine Service
NCTC	National Counterterrorism Center
NEC	National Economic Council
NGO	nongovernmental organization
NHSA	National Homeland Security Agency

NIC	National Intelligence Council
NIE	national intelligence estimate
NIM	national intelligence manager
NIO	national intelligence officer
NIP	National Intelligence Program
NIPF	National Intelligence Priorities Framework
NNSA	National Nuclear Security Administration
NORTHCOM	US Northern Command
NPR	National Performance Review
NRO	National Reconnaissance Organization
NRP	National Response Plan
NSA	national security advisor
NSA	National Security Agency
NSB	National Security Branch
NSC	National Security Council
NSCS	National Security Council staff
NSD	National Security Division
NSE	national security enterprise
NSL	national security letter
NSPS	National Security Personnel System
NSS	National Security Strategy
NSPD	National Security Presidential Directive
NSPG	National Security Planning Group
OCIO	Office of the Chief Information Officer
OCO	overseas contingency operation
ODNI	Office of the Director of National Intelligence
OE	operating expense
OFAC	Office of Foreign Assets Control
OFDA	Office of Foreign Disaster Response
OIA	Office of Intelligence and Analysis
OIRA	Office of Information and Regulatory Affairs
OMB	Office of Management and Budget
OPM	Office of Personnel Management
ORH	AOffice of Humanitarian and Reconstruction Affairs
OSD	Office of the Secretary of Defense
OSD	Policy Office of the Under Secretary for Policy
OSS	Office of Strategic Services
P&R	Personnel and Readiness
PACHA	Presidential Advisory Council on HIV/AIDS
PACOM	US Pacific Command
PAD	program associate director
PART	Program Assessment Rating Tool
PBSO	Peacebuilding Support Office
PC	Principals' Committee
PCC	policy coordinating committee
PDASD	principal deputy assistant secretary for defense

PDB	President's Daily Brief
PDD	Presidential Decision Directive
PEPFAR	President's Emergency Plan for AIDS Relief
PMF	Presidential Management Fellows
PNSR	Project on National Security Reform
PPBS	Planning, Programming, Budgeting System
PPD	Presidential Policy Directive
PRC	People's Republic of China
PRT	provincial reconstruction team
PTSD	post-traumatic stress disorder
QDDR	Quadrennial Diplomacy and Development Review
QDR	Quadrennial Defense Review
RA	resident agency
RMO	resource management office
SAC	special agent in charge
SAP	special access programs
SCA	Bureau of South and Central Asian Affairs
SCI	sensitive compartmented information
SCIF	sensitive compartmentalized information facility
S/CRS	State Department coordinator for reconstruction and stabilization
SDGT	Specially Designated Global Terrorist
SDN	Specially Designated Nationals
SES	senior executive service
SIGINT	signals intelligence
SIOP	Single Integrated Operational Plan
SOCOM	US Special Operations Command
SO/LIC	Special Operations and Low-Intensity Conflict
SOUTHCOM	US Southern Command
SRAP	special representative for Afghanistan and Pakistan
S/RPP	Office of Resources, Plans, and Policies
STRATCOM	US Strategic Command
SWIFT	Society for Worldwide Interbank Financial Telecommunications
TEOAF	Treasury Executive Office for Asset Forfeiture
TFFC	Office of Terrorism and Financial Crimes
TFI	Office of Terrorism and Financial Intelligence
TSA	Transportation Security Administration
TSC	Terrorism Screening Center
TFTP	Terrorist Finance Tracking Program
TRANSCOM	US Transportation Command
TTIC	Terrorist Threat Integration Center
UAV	unmanned aerial vehicle
UC	unanimous consent agreement
USAID	US Agency for International Development
USCYBERCOM	US Cyber Command
USD(I)	under secretary for intelligence
USD(P)	under secretary for policy

USIP	US Institute of Peace
USSS	US Secret Service
VA	Veterans Affairs Department
WH	White House
WINEP	Washington Institute for Near East Policy
WMD	weapon of mass destruction
WTO	World Trade Organization

The National Security Enterprise

Institutions, Cultures, and Politics

Roger Z. George and Harvey Rishikof

> In enacting this legislation, it is the intent of Congress to provide the comprehensive program for the future security of the United States; to provide for the establishment of integrated policies and procedures for the departments, agencies, and functions of the Government relating to the national security.
>
> —Public Law 80–253, sec. 2 (1947)

> Every organization has a culture; that is, a persistent, patterned way of thinking about the central tasks of and human relationships within an organization.
>
> —James Q. Wilson, *Bureaucracy*

Organizing the national security process has been a constant feature of the American government. Some seventy years ago, the United States embarked on a fundamentally new way of formulating its foreign and defense policies. It no longer had the luxury of mobilizing the country and its political, military, and economic power to counter threats once war had occurred. Rather, it needed a permanent national security policy framework to identify, deter, and if necessary, defend against international threats to the nation. The National Security Act of 1947, subsequent legislation, and innumerable executive actions of a dozen presidents have built up an elaborate national security process to safeguard Americans. That system, as remarkably flexible as it has been, is no longer satisfactory for the twenty-first century and the many transnational and complex challenges it confronts. Studies (more than two dozen major ones since the designing of the national security system of the 1940s) continue to identify conceptual as well as structural flaws that inhibit effective planning, formulation, and implementation of national security policies. The US Institute of Peace report on the 2010 Quadrennial Defense Review concluded that there was an urgent need to replace the existing national security planning process with one that is more comprehensive, up-to-date, and effective given the new challenges of the twenty-first century.[1] More recently, a longtime follower of the national security process, David Rothkopf, noted that the Obama administration, following the missteps of the George W. Bush team, had also added to the dysfunction of the process.[2] This book is not another study of those structural flaws found in past and current national security systems. Instead, this book's purpose is to examine the specific organizations and cultures of the institutions and agencies that make up the national security enterprise. The book takes a consciously Washington perspective, focusing on the headquarters' mentalities, as most strategic decisions are made inside the Beltway rather than in embassies, commands, or stations; one often hears of the "Washington clock" versus the "Baghdad clock" or the "Aleppo clock." No doubt the people in the field have their own perspectives, but they most often react to Washington and are seldom defining or driving their organizations in the same way that the Washington bureaucrats and politicians can.

The central premise, then, is that the dysfunction often described in the current national security enterprise gives little rigorous attention to the internal organizational cultures that compose it; moreover, no conceptual or structural fix to the current system is likely to succeed unless it understands the organizations and people in that system. In this sense, our book is a gap filler, as there is limited attention to the individual organizations that make up the growing set of agencies of our national security enterprise. To be sure, Graham Allison and Morton Halperin have done some early groundbreaking work on organizational behavior's influence on foreign policy outcomes, but this work is surprisingly brief in its description of those cultures.[3] The most complete discussion of the role of organizational behavior in recent policies is to be found in Amy Zegart's study of the organizational behavior of the Central Intelligence Agency (CIA) and Federal Bureau of Investigation (FBI) during the 9/11 attack; however, this excellent study is far from complete in describing the many other organizations that make up this enterprise.[4] Recent textbooks recognize the impact of culture on the decision-making process, but few provide deep understanding of different agencies and their operation.[5]

The absence of attention to institutional culture is surprising given that many of the government and nongovernment studies of the national security enterprise regularly complain about the parochial nature of the organizations and institutions that make up the system. The 2008 Project on National Security Reform (PNSR) report, to take one example, squarely identifies the problems as being organizational in nature: "The basic deficiency of the current national security system is that parochial departmental and agency interests, reinforced by Congress, paralyze the interagency cooperation even as the variety, speed, and complexity of emerging security issues prevent the White House from effectively controlling the system."[6]

The PNSR notes that in the midst of huge international changes, the National Security Council (NSC) system is still essentially a hierarchically organized structure that relies on the traditional agencies and their disciplines. Such a structure reflects an assumption—perhaps a conviction—that the government is a unitary actor that develops foreign affairs strategies according to a logical process of matching means with ends and developing courses of action that maximize those ends with the use of all elements of power. Such means–ways–ends models may work well to explain how an ideal national security strategy should be developed, but they have little relevance to how governments actually operate. Although traditional academic study of the foreign policy process gives lip service to the role of bureaucracy and organizational culture, it is never the focus of the models. Yet these cultures shape the process of policy deliberation, as well as its execution within the national security enterprise. Out of frustration with and distrust of such behaviors, however, some presidents have ignored or worked outside this system, sometimes to their political detriment.

WHAT IS THE NATIONAL SECURITY ENTERPRISE?

We have adopted the term "national security enterprise" to capture the notion that the enterprise is more than simply the formal government institutions found in the executive branch and Congress. Typically, when reformers speak of the national security system, they mean executive branch departments and separate agencies and the Office of the President with its NSC staff. Many of the reform studies recommend changes in the way the various national security agencies operate, interact with each other, or respond to the president. In a few cases, most recently the 9/11 Commission, reformers have suggested that both executive and congressional branch reforms are needed if the system is to function more effectively.

However, as this book argues, the enterprise is much broader than those two institutions. Imagining that the enterprise is a series of concentric circles, the core functions of government—executive branch departments—make up the nucleus of the national securnity system. However, outside that nucleus lies another layer of the enterprise: the other branches of government. Most significant is Congress, which has sizable foreign affairs and security policy responsibilities, but also influential are the courts, which increasingly have an impact on the formulation and conduct of foreign and national security policies.

Beyond these two levels, however, lies a more informal set of players in the national security enterprise. Those players include the media, which is instrumental in setting the agenda, evaluating the formal players' performance, and publicizing alternative views. This outer ring also includes the think-tank world, where former government officials and nongovernment experts likewise formulate new initiatives alongside their critiques of government as well as act as informal partners with parts of the formal executive branch and congressional players. Similarly, that outside layer contains important lobby groups that provide expertise and represent domestic interest groups with foreign policy objectives as well as foreign groups that hope to influence the legislative process and executive branch policy priorities.

THE ORGANIZATIONAL DIMENSION

The nature of government generally and national security policies in particular has become so complicated that specialized organizations are necessary to fulfill the nation's will. Public policy has become bureaucratized to ensure a rational and orderly administration of the government's responsibilities. Positively seen, a bureaucracy, in the Max Weber sense, is a group of individuals who operate by a set of rules and standards to achieve certain agreed-upon goals; they are expected to be professionals, sometimes technocrats, who hold their positions by virtue of their expertise, education, or training and other unique characteristics of those professions (see box I.1).[7] Be they government lawyers or economists, military officers, diplomats, legislators or lobbyists, or intelligence officers, they were all selected for certain skills. National security professionals bring expertise to the interagency table, but they often carry other organizational, cultural, and professional baggage as well. These professionals are schooled in the correct procedures used to accomplish their specific tasks and rewarded and promoted according to the organizational interests they represent. This is more than "where you sit" determining "where you stand"; it is "how you tick." So, the military officer spends years in training to develop war-fighting methods and understand what a proper civil–military relationship is; or the diplomat masters foreign languages and hones the art of negotiation and report writing; or the intelligence officer develops the skills of operating clandestinely, handling foreign spies, and evaluating raw intelligence reports. Each such

---

BOX I.1
Organizational Culture Defined

An organization, namely, a group of people organized and managed, often hierarchically, to accomplish a specific set of tasks, quickly institutionalizes a way of doing business. This institutionalization of the specialized functions an organization performs begins to form what becomes known as the organizational culture. The founders of any organization have an especially powerful impact on socializing the workforce and developing the norms, values, and practices of organizational cultures. They pass down these values but also become some of the legends and models to which newer members aspire.

An organizational culture is widely seen as a system of shared meaning or values that the organization's membership holds and that distinguishes it from other groups. The essence of an organization is often characterized by the extent to which the organization defines and values its mission, rewards results and risk taking, and pays attention to details or facts and by the way it develops and retains its people.

A dominant culture is one that expresses the core values held and shared by most members of the organization. Subcultures are possible, especially in large organizations containing divisions separated by different missions, locations, or selection processes. A strong culture is one for which the members accept and enforce the values. Such a culture can build cohesion and loyalty but also is more resistant to change than weaker ones are. The organization's process of selecting, training, evaluating, and promoting people tends to keep and reward those who fit the culture and encourage nonconformists to find other work.

---

organization, then, develops special processes and practices that can improve its efficiency and, most important, its reliability. On a permanent basis, we expect our diplomats to represent our government according to certain principles; likewise, we expect our military services to follow the code of military conduct and intelligence officers to conduct espionage overseas under appropriate executive orders.

Such behaviors become routinized and second nature to the professionals within these bureaucracies. They are unquestioned, for the most part, as they seem to have worked in the past to both accomplish the organization's goals and to ensure that the individual is promoted within the system. So, it should come as no surprise that change is not something that organizations always willingly embrace.[8] Bureaucracies are designed to accomplish certain specific organizational tasks using procedures, doctrines, and regulations to achieve certain goals so there is no question as to how they should operate. Although our intent is not to review the extensive literature on organizational behavior, we do accept the principles embedded in those studies that suggest there are certain behaviors many organizations, be they private or public, often exhibit:

- Organizations promote outcomes and decisions that advance their own interests and minimize costs to their operations.
- Agencies try to avoid taking on tasks that are not central to their understanding of their core mission.
- When an agency has more than a single internal culture, conflicts over priorities often occur.
- Senior officials' positions tend to be defined by the combination of their personal views and the culture they represent.
- Successful changes in a culture have to be seen as central to the perceived mission of the agency.

Social scientists have observed such organizational behaviors in virtually all kinds of private and public sector organizations. Whether it is the firm, the foundation, or the foreign service, certain organizational norms flourish. This is the phenomenon that this book will explore. It is important to remember that organizations are made up of both people and processes. As the chapters will document, the different agencies and institutions self-select people who will perform certain operations successfully, but more important, agencies train those people to conduct themselves in certain ways so that these practices become second nature and frame any approach to a problem. To understand the organization, one has to look at the type of people as well as the special skills and processes that they employ to achieve their objectives.

At the outset we acknowledge that the national security enterprise and its many constituent organizations have changed over time. No organization is totally impervious to new missions, tasks, and structural adaptations. However, sometimes the change is not in the right direction or not effective; at other times organizations resist or defeat the intent of those new missions or tasks. It is not fair to criticize our institutions as totally dysfunctional, nor is it correct to say that all the change we see is positive. These chapters will try to describe both the good and the bad of our bureaucracies.

COMMON CHALLENGES

A number of themes addressed in the book represent challenges to the national security enterprise. Each chapter touches on these, and the cumulative effect of our volume is to address them from a variety of perspectives.

First, the 2017 world reflects a set of institutional players that has vastly increased since the 1947 National Security Act. What once was a function largely focused on the president, his secretaries of state and defense, and his military and intelligence advisors is now spread across virtually every department. So, when senior meetings are held on international topics, the range of agencies will span the foreign and security field but also law enforcement agencies and the Department of Homeland Security (DHS); the economic departments of Treasury, Commerce, and Agriculture; or the technical fields of the Centers for Disease Control and Prevention, the National Aeronautics and Space Administration (NASA), or the Office of the Science Advisor. The blending of such different cultures and priorities makes for an unruly interagency process, brings more congressional voices into the discussion as well, and means that even more outside interest groups and experts are interested in what American policies will emerge from the government deliberations. Even within the more traditional agencies, organizational changes are occurring to reflect the new international challenges. For example, the Department of Defense has stood up a cyber command to handle the growing challenge of hostile cyber operations. Likewise, CIA has begun its own major "modernization" plan that will transform its traditional directorates for operations and analysis into multiple fusion "centers," blending the two directorates and establishing a new "digital" directorate to manage its growing cyber requirements.

Second, and related to this first reality, is the very uneven nature of the different agencies' capabilities and interests. Some critics have argued that US foreign policy has become overly militarized, partly as a result of the massive resources and skills of the Pentagon and the relatively underdeveloped resources and capabilities of the State Department and other civilian agencies. Even within the military, the adage that "you fight the war with the army you have" makes it clear that developing resources and capabilities requires time and planning, something that far too few agencies have when an emergency develops and the interagency calls for them to step forward with new programs. The uneven strengths and weaknesses of the players definitely affect policy outcomes, both in how they are decided but also in how they are implemented.

Third, information sharing remains a major challenge for effective decision making and policy implementation. As agencies control information, they can use it to maximize their influence over decisions or undercut those agencies that are bureaucratic opponents. Yet most reform recommendations are adamant that better information sharing is essential to a smoother operation of government. This info-sharing admonition runs counter to the natural stovepiping of organizations. Their hierarchical nature and desire to control information discourage them from sharing. In some cases their reticence is caused by the need-to-know principle, but in others it is driven more by the idea that information is power or by a professional resistance to share based on bureaucratic principles. Moreover, analytics involving information is proving to be a new frontier that is difficult for the government.

In addition, information can be used for bureaucratic purposes to affect policy. As is often the case, "leaks" and unauthorized disclosures based on open source material by the media often seize the headlines and may at times put at risk individuals and national security programs. Balancing First Amendment rights and security needs has now become an even trickier task and has grown even more difficult in this world of cyber and electronic data storage and the curse of "false news." The Wikileaks and Snowden disclosures bring into the discussion the so-called insider threat and reflect both the massive scale and long-term impact such disclosures can have on the operation of American national security policy.

Fourth, priorities are constantly changing. Every four years there is either a new president or a new term that calls for new directions and ideas. Each new administration has approximately 3,000 appointments to harness and direct the executive branch. Congressional elections and changing majorities in the legislative process can also influence the types of initiatives that will be welcomed or opposed. Moreover, the world itself is an unpredictable place. President George W. Bush came into office thinking he would focus on building relationships with the key powers of Russia, China, and India but quickly found his presidency marked by what he felt justified to call the Global War on Terror. Eight years later, President Obama pledged to end the decade of wars in Afghanistan and Iraq, only to be confronted with a metastasizing Islamic extremist movement called Daesh throughout the Middle East.* The Paris, Brussels, and San Bernardino attacks have once again rocketed terrorism to the top of the national security agenda and put the question of homeland security in front of the American and European publics. Moreover, American presidential election campaigns are sure to introduce new foreign policy priorities or perhaps further shifts in American national security strategies.

ORGANIZATION OF THE BOOK

The book is organized to highlight the different domains of the national security enterprise. In the first section we introduce this notion of an enterprise with some history of how the system itself arose and evolved after 1947. The chapters examining the NSC and Office of Management and Budget (OMB) place special attention on the ethos of these professional

---

*The authors have selected the term "Daesh" to describe the terrorist group operating in Syria and Iraq at present because other commonly used terms, like "ISIS" and "ISIL," unfortunately connote the organization's having the features of a state, which the authors do not accept.

staffs, which must provide continuity and yet be responsive to the changing preferences and philosophies of individual presidents.

In the second section we examine the executive policy agencies and departments that make up the bulk of the formal interagency process: the State, Treasury, and Defense Departments, the US Agency for International Development (USAID), and the military services. In the State Department chapter, the author's diplomatic career allows him to examine the unique cultural practices of the foreign service, highlighting its ability to shift priorities to suit presidential agendas and policies but its limited ability to plan for or surge resources to new problems. The USAID chapter also captures some of the limits of this agency, which operates primarily overseas and so far has been unable to carve out a larger interagency role for itself. The two chapters focused on the civilians and military services in the Department of Defense, in contrast, emphasize the well-developed skills of the Office of the Secretary of Defense (OSD) and the military to plan for future contingencies; however, this preparedness comes at the cost of being more rigid and less willing to conduct operations on the fly. The role of the secretary of defense is also examined, providing readers with insights into how differing personalities, operating styles, and philosophies can shape or break the interagency processes. A new chapter on the Department of Treasury explores its emerging role as a critical instrument in foreign policy given its power to freeze the bank accounts of nations, businesses, and individuals and to bring entities to the negotiation table. Some believe this Treasury power should earn it a statutory seat on the NSC as it has proved to be as effective as kinetic actions.

In the third section the book tackles the intelligence and law enforcement agencies—CIA, the Office of the Director of National Intelligence (ODNI), FBI, and DHS—in terms of their distinct roles in supporting the interagency process and in bridging the gaps between domestic and national security policies. The intelligence chapters provide an interesting contrast between the CIA, which has well-established cultural norms, and the twelve-year-old ODNI, which still has little in the way of an established culture. In the FBI and DHS chapters, the stark differences also are readily apparent. The FBI, with its strong tradition of special agents focused on solving crimes, is struggling to become more of a national security agency with new "intelligence" responsibilities. In contrast, DHS has still not established a common culture among the twenty-two agencies combined in 2005 for the purpose of safeguarding Americans at home. Integrating agencies as diverse as the Federal Emergency Management Agency (FEMA), the US Coast Guard, and the US Secret Service to find a common culture remains a work in progress, possibly requiring new authorities as well as legislation.

In the fourth section we explore the different worlds of Congress and the Court. Congress, by virtue of its Article 1 authorities, has a role to play, but it remains one that fluctuates greatly depending on the kind of issues being discussed, the nature of the executive–legislative relationship at the time, and the roles played by important committees and their chairs. Since 9/11 the courts have also played an increasingly significant role in shaping executive branch domestic as well as foreign programs and operations. Courts increasingly can overrule executive branch plans that infringe on Americans' civil liberties; the past decade of court cases has forced presidents to consider how to execute counterterrorism or intelligence-gathering activities and still remain within the law.

In the final section the book explores the impact that outside players like the media, think tanks, and lobbyists have on the formulation and execution of national security policy. In the chapter on lobbyists, the author examines how lobbyists work the "seams" between the legislative and executive branches and enlist allies among special interest groups, industry, supporters in Congress, or policy agencies. The phenomenon of think tanks—of which Washington,

DC, is perhaps the world's capital—is explored by a well-known former think-tank president who describes both the landscape of this world and its variable impact depending on the foreign policy issue; as she makes clear, think-tank agendas range from nonpartisan to full advocacy and are often shaped by the funding and donors' philosophies of government. The final chapter on the media explores how the press is facing more competition from social media as well as a US government far less tolerant of disclosures of classified information than ever before. As the chapter makes clear, the new social media allow government dissenters to themselves become media purveyors, leaving the traditional media sources more as customers than producers of policy exposés.

The differences in organizational culture and style found in these chapters underline the editors' argument that the structure and nature of US bureaucracies and institutions shape the effectiveness and coherence of the national security enterprise. No one group or entity is charged with a grand strategy; each organization is in a way preoccupied with its own professionalism and therefore coordination is difficult. With every new administration a new layer of political actors arrives, somewhat divorced from power and not well versed in how to use the ways and means of institutional power but understanding their goals. During the Cold War there was continuity across administrations—containment, the Marshall Plan, the World Trade Organization (WTO), full-spectrum domination by our military—because the problem set was relatively constant. The new problem set of the twenty-first century—nuclear proliferation, terrorism, failing states, cyber threats, global warming, and the international economic reshuffle—has revealed the weaknesses of the current national security enterprise. These issues do not fit neatly into the repertoires of individual agencies but will necessitate collaboration among many different agencies and organizational cultures.

In the concluding chapter the editors lay out some modest suggestions for creating more collaboration across these very different agencies and cultures. Redesigning the national security enterprise is clearly not a one-time event; rather, it is an ongoing task that must not rely simply on changing the structures, authorities, and procedures for reaching and implementing decisions. Improving the effectiveness of the national security enterprise means understanding what motivates and drives different organizations so that the right incentives can be developed to build collaboration. Hence, greater understanding of those cultures—their strengths and weaknesses as well as their roles and missions—will be an important step in the right direction.

NOTES

1. See the US Institute of Peace review of the Quadrennial Defense Report, a bipartisan panel led by Stephen J. Hadley and William J. Perry. The report, *The QDR in Perspective: Meeting America's National Security Needs in the 21st Century; The Final Report of the Quadrennial Defense Review Independent Panel* (July 2010), warns of an impending all-volunteer force "train wreck" and advocates for new approaches and institutions for national security at www.usip.org/files/qdr/qdrreport.pdf.

2. Jeff Goldberg, "A Withering Critique of the Obama National Security Council," *The Atlantic*, November 12, 2014, www.theatlantic.com/international/archive/2014/11/a-withering-critique-of -president-obamas-national-security-council/382477/.

3. See Morton H. Halperin and Priscilla A. Clapp, *Bureaucratic Politics and Foreign Policy*, 2nd ed. (Washington, DC: Brookings Institution, 2006); and Graham Allison and Philip Zelikow, *The Essence of Decision: Explaining the Cuban Missile Crisis*, 2nd ed. (Boston: Little, Brown, 1999).

4. Amy Zegart, *Spying Blind: The CIA, the FBI, and the Origins of 9/11* (Princeton, NJ: Princeton University Press, 2007).

5. See Steven W. Hook, "The Foreign Policy Bureaucracy," in *U.S. Foreign Policy: The Paradox of Power*, 2nd ed. (Washington, DC: CQ Press, 2008), 162–97; and Howard J. Wiarda, "Bureaucratic Politics: Turf Battles among Agencies," in *Divided America on the World Stage: Broken Government and Foreign Policy* (Washington, DC: Potomac Books, 2009), 257–81. More recent textbooks also describe the "bureaucracies" in a single chapter, devoting a page or two for organizations as complex at the Departments of State and Defense. See, as an example, Jeffrey S. Lantis, *US Foreign Policy in Action: An Innovative Teaching Text* (West Sussex, UK: Wiley-Blackwell, 2013).

6. Project on National Security Reform, *Forging a New Shield* (Washington, DC, November 2008), Executive Summary, 7.

7. For Weber a bureaucracy constituted a professional corps of career officials with formal qualifications organized in a hierarchical pyramid of authority with specific divisions of labor, governed by impersonal, uniform rational rules and procedures so that promotion could be based on the principles of both seniority and performance. Bureaucratic administration is rational since the exercise of control is based on knowledge. See "Bureaucracy," *Encyclopedia Britannica*, http://lilt.ilstu.edu/rrpope/rrpopepwd/articles/bureacracy2.html.

8. Zegart, *Spying Blind*, 45, explains how the organizational cultures resisted change. As Zegart notes, "The internal barriers to organizational change are powerful and deeply entrenched. . . . Employees inside organizations become wedded to habits, thinking, routines, values, norms, ideas, and identities, and these attachments make change difficult."

PART I

The Interagency Process

CHAPTER 1

History of the Interagency Process for Foreign Relations in the United States

Murphy's Law?

Jon J. Rosenwasser and Michael Warner

> Will you please tell me what in hell the State Department has to do in an active theater of war?
> —Question posed to diplomat Robert Murphy in North Africa, 1942

The processes for making and executing foreign policy in the United States have grown more centralized, more rationalized, and more inclusive of multiple institutional viewpoints since World War II. Nevertheless, they remain remarkably dispersed and their coordination dependent on personality and specific circumstance. This situation results in part from the constitutional fragmentation of power between and among the executive and legislative branches of government, reinforced by customs and precedents forged when the geography of two oceans alone provided the Republic significant security and masked institutional limitations. The demands of global engagement in World War II and the Cold War, however, prompted presidents and Congress to experiment with new legal and institutional forms for coordinating policymaking, diplomacy, and military efforts. Chief among these forms have been the National Security Act of 1947 and the National Security Council (NSC) that it created. Reorganizations and reforms within the nation's military, diplomatic, economic, and intelligence arms have also had significant impacts. Since the Cold War the challenges of state disintegration and transnational threats, punctuated by the September 11, 2001, terrorist attacks, have prompted further innovation in the interagency system, from presidential directives on complex emergencies to the creation of the Department of Homeland Security (DHS) and sweeping intelligence reform. The advent of cyberspace as a prominent domain for political, economic, and social action presents the latest set of challenges. Although these have resulted in greater exchange of views and information (and increased cooperation in the field), the difficulties of coordinating the plans and actions of highly independent cabinet departments endure.

ORIGINS OF THE INTERAGENCY PROCESS IN THE UNITED STATES

Veteran diplomat Robert Murphy had a good answer to the question posed to him by an American major general not long after the Anglo-American invasion of North Africa in 1942.

In his memoir Murphy explained that the State Department "had direct responsibility in the preparatory stage leading to the invasion. It was directly concerned in the political decisions inevitably made during the military operations, and will have to deal with the postwar political effects of this campaign. . . . And that is why I am here."[1] Murphy's experience encapsulates a history of interagency relations in American foreign and security policy. He compensated for the irregularity of his formal authorities ("Don't bother going through State Department channels," President Roosevelt had told him) and his scant preparation ("I became aware of my appalling ignorance of military matters") by dint of tireless work, personal grit, and indomitable common sense. By and large his colleagues in the army, navy, State Department, and Office of Strategic Services did likewise, fashioning ways to work together in common cause with their British (and, ultimately, French) allies. Their effort saw its share of missteps and even comic opera episodes, but it worked, if sometimes only by the narrowest of margins.

Before considering the history of the interagency process, it is important to consider a framework for analysis of its form, because form shapes its operation and, ultimately, the resulting policy outcomes. The interagency system can be considered as comprising two dimensions: dynamics and levels. The dynamics of the interagency system are the function of six structural factors: the nature of the threat environment and a state's geostrategic position, constitutional frameworks, leadership proclivities, technology (particularly its military character), and prevailing public management paradigms. As these factors evolve, so does the interagency process. In addition, the interagency process operates at three levels, corresponding to the place (both physical and institutional) at which the interaction occurs. At the strategic level, policy planning and coordination happen in the national capital, where they are dominated by domestic political and institutional dynamics. At the intermediate or operational level, initiatives to implement policy are conceived and managed by a regional or country-level headquarters, influenced by the relationships among that area's principal power brokers. At the tactical level, personnel deployed in the field execute plans (for war, diplomacy, development, trade, etc.) that contribute to those initiatives, in accord with the specific capabilities and authorities allocated to them. At all three levels, states are increasingly conjoined by foreign governments, inter- and nongovernmental actors, and business interests whose objectives may or may not always converge with those of the United States.

The historical circumstances of the United States' founding decisively shaped its interagency process. Born from a revolutionary separation from Great Britain, America has mistrusted central authority at home while recognizing the need for unified leadership abroad. With good reason the Founding Fathers feared tyranny from both kings and the masses. Article I of the Constitution gave Congress explicit powers to "provide for the common Defence," "declare War," "raise and support Armies," "provide and maintain a Navy," and "make Rules for the Government and Regulation of the land and naval Forces," backed by its exclusive power of the purse. Though the Senate held the right to advise the president in appointing certain officers and to approve treaties (with the high bar of a two-thirds majority), these formal powers were essentially passive; the chief executive held the initiative to act or not in the myriad cases and ways of his office.

The president was to serve as commander in chief to represent and advance US interests abroad. Thus, the executive branch naturally assumed primacy in national security affairs. For the nation's first 150 years, the national security establishment comprised the State Department, War Department (for the army), and Navy Department (for the navy and marine corps). All reported directly to the president. His authorities were few but clear: the power to negotiate treaties, to appoint the heads of the several government departments, and to exercise command in war. Once Congress appropriated funds, the president did not have to share these powers or seek approval or advice before he ordered diplomats abroad or the nation's forces into harm's way. Presidents could keep their own counsel or ask aides to help reach decisions; no formal coordinating or decision-making machinery existed under them. The lack of advanced technological or analytical means to amass, analyze, or disseminate information reinforced presidential autonomy. Matters of national importance might well be discussed by the department secretaries forming the cabinet, a body that could be counted on to bring a broad range of experience and political instincts to bear on a topic but rarely offered much in the way of expertise in foreign affairs.

The congressional committee structure, organized around oversight of a defined set of departments, reinforced this separation of institutions. The segmented approach allowed committees to exert influence over the executive branch and to reflect constituent interests. When Congress created committees in 1816, it fashioned one for each of the three main departments: Foreign Relations for the State Department, Military Affairs for the War Department, and Naval Affairs for the Navy Department. Under this model the departments submitted appropriations requests directly to their respective committee of jurisdiction, with little input from the president or his staff. This division of labor suited the strategic landscape of the Republic's early decades and hewed to congressional interests to keep the executive branch fragmented, and thereby constrained. It also led, however, to each tool of national power developing its own institutional narrative, organizational ethos, and operational coda.

Early US foreign policy focused on supporting the nation's westward expansion, winning the Civil War, and protecting trade. The secretaries of state held an enviable position as primus inter pares relative to their fellow cabinet secretaries, as State also discharged diverse domestic duties (for a time these included supervising the census and the US Mint). With notable exceptions, such as Thomas Jefferson and John Quincy Adams, secretaries of state typically had little direct diplomatic experience. Instead, they were selected because of their achievements in business or law—and their support for the president's ticket and party. They generally made up in ability what they lacked in experience.

Secretaries of state oversaw a bifurcated department. The diplomatic service represented the president in foreign capitals, while the consular service promoted opportunities for American business and protected US citizens abroad. Secretaries of state since Jefferson have lodged bureaucratic power with the diplomatic service. Ambassadors and diplomats typically won their appointments through political connections, leading to some very able men and some appalling embarrassments for carrying America's interests overseas.[2] Continuity and competence instead was provided through career staff in Washington. As Dean Acheson observed, by 1940 the real power in the department "had come to rest in the [geographic] division chiefs and the advisers, political, legal, and economic." The result of this "nineteenth-century" arrangement, argued Acheson, was that "most matters that concerned the Department arose from specific incidents or problems and then evolved into policies, rather than beginning as matters of broad decision and ending in specific action. In this way the departmental division having jurisdiction to deal with the incident became the basic instrument for the formulation and execution of policy."[3]

With little impetus for a robust overseas presence as the early American Republic grew, Congress only reluctantly spent money on overseas missions and activities. The foreign service was "traditionally ill-chosen, ill-treated, ill-paid, ill-housed, ill-coordinated, and undermanned."[4] It became a home away from home for the nation's elite, who paid most of their overseas expenses but who also had unambiguous authority to represent the United States in foreign capitals (at least before the telegraph allowed Washington to exert influence directly). In general, diplomacy served as the principal tool of statecraft, unless and until armed conflict erupted, in which case armies and navies were raised and the military departments oversaw the conduct of combat. In short, Congress and the Department of State were preeminent in peace, with the president and the armed services preeminent in war.

The military developed its own organizational ethos. This evolution was based on four enduring characteristics. First, the armed services were small, surging in size and deploying abroad only in wartime. Second, they fought different and independent forms of war; the army fought one kind on land, and the navy another at sea, with little coordination between their methods or objectives. This bifurcation reinforced their unique cultures and operational models.[5] Third, the army and navy, at least in peacetime, were decentralized structures, dominated not by their line commanders but by their several service and support bureaus. Appointed civilians set strategy, policy, and doctrine, while staff officers ran the military service bureaus. This arrangement in the American military not infrequently resulted in inefficiency, unclear command relationships, and friction between the War and Navy Departments.[6] The military's fourth structural feature was its interdependent relationship with technology. Two nineteenth-century inventions provided new opportunities for coordination by shrinking the distance between Washington and the field. Steam power allowed the rapid transport of supplies to far-flung territory. The telegraph, moreover, enabled communication to distant outposts, including ambassadors and military field commanders, to provide policy direction in a matter of minutes.

The three departments—State, War, and Navy—did exchange information and cooperate. They just did so in their own time, on their own terms. Presidents interfered minimally with the departments' autonomy and did not demand that they adopt common strategies or programs. The interagency coordination that occurred was largely at the strategic level in Washington. Presidents created no formal governing or coordinating body. When coordination was necessary, proximity of the departments' headquarters to one another and to the president helped. All three departments occupied buildings on the same (rather large) city block as the White House until after the Civil War and then were colocated until just before World War II in a grand Second Empire structure (naturally dubbed the "State–War–Navy Building") beside the executive mansion.

This system could work well, and it could work poorly. It did both in America's "splendid little war" with Spain in 1898. Goaded to war by the frightful Spanish counterinsurgency campaign in Cuba, President William McKinley and his cabinet ran the affair amateurishly, in effect counting on their proximity and personal familiarity to facilitate and implement decisions. Then–assistant secretary of the navy Theodore Roosevelt, on his own authority, concentrated a fleet near Manila to strike the first blow but waited impotently for weeks for troops to arrive and seize the city. Unprepared for conflict, the army coordinated haphazardly with the navy in Cuba. McKinley found himself forced to acquire from Spain the entire Philippine archipelago, saddled with a counterinsurgency as gruesome as that in Cuba under Spanish rule.[7]

This segmented interagency system began a march toward integration only with the advent of new ideas about public management and organizational planning, introduced with the Progressive Era in the early decades of the twentieth century. President Theodore Roosevelt rooted out the prevailing spoils system and professionalized the civil service. As a result, for example, the State Department transformed its entrance standards, pay, and training. The

Rogers Act (1924) merged the diplomatic and consular services to unify America's overseas presence and introduced competitive standards to select career foreign service officers. The Porter Foreign Service Buildings Act (1926) also provided major upgrades in American missions abroad to reflect the nation's growing international prestige.[8]

Innovations also came to the military, albeit slowly. In the wake of the mishaps in the Spanish–American War, and with the rapid modernization of Europe's militaries, President Theodore Roosevelt's secretary of war, Elihu Root, centralized the army's technical services under his direction and proposed a joint army–navy board to adjudicate interservice differences.[9] Meanwhile, the navy remained highly decentralized, reflecting the deeper tradition of autonomy given to ships at sea and the strength of the naval bureaus.[10] A subtle but important change to the interagency system came with the new thinking in resource management. Up to this period, predominant attention was paid to internal controls to monitor "inputs," that is, money and people, which were exclusively handled between each federal department and its relevant congressional oversight committee. The 1921 Budget Act, which created a new Bureau of the Budget in the White House (the precursor to the Office of Management and Budget) provided the president with greater insight into departments' spending to achieve certain outputs. This advance eased the way for future synergies between and among departments to achieve collectively desired policy outcomes.

The last significant change of the Progressive Era was the creation of public policy centers that straddled academia and government. The Carnegie Endowment for International Peace (1910), the Brookings Institution (1916), and the Council on Foreign Relations (1921), among others, provided independent research and analysis to spawn, test, and refine foreign policy ideas. Over the ensuing decades, these institutions—whether for research or straight advocacy—would proliferate, serving as proving grounds for former and future senior government officials and their ideas.

Coincidental with these Progressive Era reforms were several technological innovations that facilitated communication and amplified the military's power. The radio and the telephone provided leaders with new instruments to reach and control their diplomatic and military representatives in the field while also creating new opportunities to mobilize society (for causes both ill and good). Mechanization, longer-range artillery, and the airplane all allowed the military to deliver greater firepower over greater distances. Chemical weapons (the first weapons of mass destruction) threatened terrifying effects on civilian populations. Together, these technologies compelled further coordination among the instruments of national power to prevent conflict (or manage its dramatically greater consequences if prevention failed).

World War II forced the departments to unprecedented cooperation. The army and navy's development of airpower capabilities during the interwar period led to overlapping roles and missions that eroded the premise that land and naval warfare were separable propositions.[11] While interservice tensions mounted, it became apparent that the nation's far-flung forces could not defeat Nazi Germany and Imperial Japan without tight coordination between them for supplies, logistics, and operations. The imperative to support allies (while keeping neutrals from siding with the Axis) forced generals, admirals, and diplomats like Robert Murphy to work together closely and constantly. Such challenges required the integrated expertise of the State, War, and Navy Departments as well as an array of emergency entities, like the Joint Chiefs of Staff (JCS), and war agencies, such as the Office of Strategic Services, the Office of War Information, and the coordinator for Latin American affairs. Furthermore, the introduction of the atomic bomb as the "ultimate weapon," as Bernard Brodie termed it, gave the world pause to contemplate the devastation that modern war could wreak if events spiraled out of control. The lessons of World War II, the reshaping of international politics thereafter, and this technological Rubicon had a decisive imprint on the interagency process in the United States.

Problems with the nation's diplomatic and military performance, ironically enough, were glaringly obvious to knowledgeable observers as America celebrated victory in 1945. Dean Acheson, at the time an assistant secretary of state, later complained that "the Department had no ideas, plans, or methods for collecting the information or dealing with the problems" created by the need to mobilize resources and wage war on a global scale.[12] Just a few weeks after the Japanese surrender, General of the Army George C. Marshall told Congress that it was only the looming threat of defeat in 1942 that had persuaded the army and navy to stop fighting each other and fight the Axis powers instead.[13] A study prepared contemporaneously for Navy Secretary James Forrestal echoed this lament, applauding the military's adoption after Pearl Harbor of a unified command structure, in which all forces in theater answered to a single regional commander regardless of home service (the harbinger of today's "combatant commander"). The study noted, however, that this innovation broke down as Allied forces neared Japan. No one in Washington selected a supreme commander for the impending assault on the Home Islands, and thus, the army and navy pursued separate invasion strategies. American diplomacy was hardly better coordinated. As one observer remarked, "Many times, when there has been disagreement about a matter of policy, instead of meeting together for common discussion and decision, there have been independent appeals to the President." The report to Forrestal recommended unifying the armed services and creating a national security council to coordinate policy, ideas that would transform America's approach to foreign policy.[14]

A NEW CHARTER

The postwar Soviet menace and America's new global position made the need to coordinate the national security institutions of the US government increasingly obvious. To meet the challenges America made a series of policy choices that endured throughout the ensuing Cold War: maintaining a large standing military deployed around the world, fielding a robust nuclear arsenal to deter general war and destabilize regional incursions, forging security guarantees with allies in Europe and the Pacific, and participating in new institutions to oversee global affairs and trade (e.g., the United Nations, International Monetary Fund [IMF], World Bank, and General Agreement on Tariffs and Trade).

These choices had practical implications for interagency relations. First, the United States needed an integrated approach across the spectrum of conflict, in all domains (land, sea, air, and soon, space). Second, the civilian and diplomatic instruments of power needed to be managed more carefully to properly signal intent and capability to adversaries to deter nuclear war. Finally, Washington needed more precise and capable intelligence to support allies, halt Soviet expansionism, and ensure that Moscow did not gain (or believe it had gained) an edge in military capability.

In part motivated by the chaotic demobilization after World War II, President Harry Truman and the Eightieth Congress set about overhauling the United States' "antiquated defense set-up."[15] The National Security Act of 1947 preserved the traditional diplomatic and military departments but changed the ways in which they related to one another, centralizing power in certain cases, while clarifying roles and responsibilities in others. In large measure the act's core features endure to this day: an NSC in the White House; a secretary of defense to oversee the armed services, with a statutory JCS to provide advice and regional combatant commanders to execute orders under a unified command plan; and a confederated intelligence system to support the parts and the whole. For the next four decades, presidents and Congresses sought to enhance the effectiveness of the components of this system but made little improvement in their collective operation.

National Security Council

The 1947 National Security Act created an NSC (composed of the president, vice president, and secretaries of state and defense) to coordinate foreign and defense policy. This innovation gave the president a mechanism for crisis management. The NSC's size, role, and influence ebbed and flowed depending on each president's proclivity for maintaining a policy-coordinating mechanism separate from his cabinet, his relationships with top advisors (notably the national security advisor), and the national security advisor's interplay with cabinet secretaries (especially the secretaries of state and defense). A small NSC staff, usually fewer than a hundred, focused on high-level formulation and coordination, with brief exceptions overseeing operations under Presidents Eisenhower through Reagan.

The NSC reflected its president's governing style. As the chapter on the NSC in this volume explains in detail, some presidents have wanted their national security advisors to fashion policy, while others wanted theirs to coordinate it. Dwight Eisenhower's NSC functioned like an army staff. John Kennedy's operated less formally, heavily influenced by his brother, Attorney General Robert Kennedy, though Kennedy's selection of Harvard dean McGeorge Bundy as national security advisor elevated the post's institutional stature. Henry Kissinger raised the national security advisor position to its zenith of power and influence under Presidents Richard Nixon and Gerald Ford; he made and directed policy and briefly served concurrently as secretary of state. President Jimmy Carter criticized the Kissinger model and returned power to the departments while maintaining a strong directive voice from his national security advisor, Zbigniew Brzezinski. President Ronald Reagan vacillated among these models before establishing one that would endure under his successors: an advisor focused on coordination, de-confliction, and alignment among competing departmental perspectives, overseeing a staff balanced between politically appointed officials close to the White House staff (and even the president himself) and career civil servants rotated from the departments. President George H. W. Bush's national security advisor, Brent Scowcroft, institutionalized a model of staff directorates covering core regions and cross-cutting challenges that would endure. These directors shepherded issues of presidential and interagency import through a nested set of interagency committees of increasing seniority (the Principals Committee for cabinet secretaries, the Deputies Committee for their deputies, and smaller committees for regional matters and special topics).[16]

The Department of Defense

The National Security Act did not exactly unify the armed services, but it did create a secretary of defense to oversee the army, the navy, and the (now independent) air force. Amendments to the National Security Act in 1949, 1953, and 1958 created the Department of Defense (DOD), clarified the originally amorphous roles of the secretary of defense and the JCS, and provided them with greater authority and staff to manage the armed services and the department itself. The sheer size, expense, political power, and global footprint of the nation's military lent the DOD influence, authority, and staff to manage the armed services and the department itself. The department's acumen and willingness to serve as a staff element for the entire national security system increased DOD's clout in the interagency process during the Cold War, and thus competed with the State Department's historical dominance of foreign policy.

Without unifying concepts, analytic tools, or bureaucratic discipline, however, neither the secretary of defense nor the Joint Chiefs could manage the defense establishment as an integrated whole. In 1961 Secretary Robert McNamara began to change this situation. Having revolutionized management practices at Ford Motor Company, McNamara adopted a three-pronged strategy to enhance civilian control and focus the defense effort. Organizationally, he expanded the Office of the Secretary of Defense (OSD), centralizing decisions on weapons development, forming the Office of Systems Analysis, and elevating the department's comptroller to outrank the military services. Substantively, he infused defense decision making with new analytic techniques (many developed at RAND) whose chief metrics were economy and efficiency rather than military judgment and intuition. Procedurally, and perhaps most important, he initiated the Planning, Programming, Budgeting System (PPBS). This system, managed by civilians in OSD, linked strategic guidance, the services' programs, fiscal constraints, and execution reviews to provide management coherence. Although these reforms did not penetrate the operational side of the armed services (which would fight largely distinct and separate wars in Vietnam), the goal of integrating management of the nation's military was no longer in question.

Department of State

The State Department adjusted with difficulty to the changed world and interagency environment of the Cold War. Secretaries of state, of course, could execute only the authorities delegated to them by the presidents they served. Not all presidents viewed them as did President Truman, who, according to his secretary of state, Dean Acheson, "looked principally to the Department of State in determining foreign policy and—except where force was necessary—exclusively in executing it."[17] Acheson himself may have been the last secretary who could say such a thing about the department. Several of his successors perhaps matched his personal influence in policy circles, but none of them—not even Henry Kissinger or George Shultz—could argue that the department was the unrivaled leader in making and executing foreign policy. This is not to say that the department did not grow in stature and ability in the postwar era. Robert Murphy recalled that State was indeed "woefully unprepared to handle the staggering amount of work imposed on it" at the end of World War II. Its "failure to make preparations for responsibilities in Germany, Japan and elsewhere caused unbelievable administrative confusion" and forced the armed services to step into the vacuum as occupiers and nation-builders.[18] Acheson credited his predecessor, George Marshall, with modernizing the department's governance. Marshall brought a more military-style efficiency to its procedures and decision making and created a policy planning staff to keep deliberations from fixating on the *crise du jour*.[19] Acheson's successor, John Foster Dulles, continued the reforms of the department's organization, personnel system, and culture in the 1950s, better integrating the foreign service and the departmental staffs and seeking to ensure that State's officials had the training to function alongside the military and other agencies of government whose work took them overseas. State's regional bureaus remained the locus of power in the department, but functional bureaus for economic, environmental, and scientific issues became increasingly important. By the 1960s new independent organizations that reported (for a time) directly to the president with a "dotted reporting line" to the secretary of state played ever-larger roles in making and implementing policy, most notably the US Agency for International Development (USAID), the US Information Agency, and the Arms Control and Disarmament Agency. This arrangement elevated development, public diplomacy, and nuclear arms control but created bureaucratic sprawl that complicated coordination of State Department activities and achievement of broader foreign policy objectives.

Intelligence Community

The National Security Act created a new Central Intelligence Agency (CIA), under a director of central intelligence (DCI), that would inform the NSC's deliberations and implement its decisions by covert means if and as directed. As with the JCS, however, congressional concerns in 1947 about possible overreaching and threats to civil liberties proscribed the DCI's influence over intelligence activities in the armed services and other departments. Directors of central intelligence held marginal influence over intelligence activities and policymaking before the tenures of Gen. Walter B. Smith and Allen Dulles (the younger brother of the secretary of state) under Presidents Truman and Eisenhower. The nation thus grew what was essentially a three-part intelligence system (dubbed the "intelligence community" in the 1950s). Most of the money and personnel stayed with the armed services, which dominated the increasingly sophisticated national technical means of monitoring the Soviet Union and other adversaries. Internal security intelligence remained the purview of the Federal Bureau of Investigation (FBI), a national law enforcement agency based in the Justice Department that was hindered as much as helped by the tenure of its long-serving director, J. Edgar Hoover. National-level analytical work and clandestine activities overseas fell almost by default to the CIA, which also performed useful coordination functions and services of common concern for intelligence under its dual role as community leader. Presidents, the departments, and Congress all benefited from this decentralized configuration: each could exercise control over the part they cared about most.

Congress

Capitol Hill largely deferred to the executive branch during the height of the Cold War in the 1950s and 1960s. But the trauma of Vietnam and President Richard M. Nixon's downfall revolutionized Congress's membership, committee structure, and approach to oversight. Motivated by an unpopular war, a younger generation unseated older members and forced several changes in chamber and party caucus rules that devolved power from older committee chairmen to more youthful subcommittee chairmen. The Legislative Reorganization Act of 1970 expanded the staffs of congressional committees and its auxiliary arms, the General Accounting Office (later renamed the Government Accountability Office) and the Congressional Research Service. Similarly, the Congressional Budget and Impoundment Control Act of 1974 gave Congress greater power in reviewing the president's federal budget request and its execution, augmented by creation of another auxiliary arm, the Congressional Budget Office. In addition, the War Powers Resolution of 1974 ostensibly placed a brake on presidential prerogative to unilaterally deploy military power. The Church and Pike Committees' investigations of intelligence community transgressions in Latin America and at home led to the creation of new select committees on intelligence in each chamber, reporting requirements for covert action, and establishment of the Foreign Intelligence Surveillance Court to review collection involving US persons. By the end of the 1970s, Congress had turned into an activist foreign policy actor to counterbalance the "imperial presidency." But although oversight of each tool of national power was more robust, there was little integrated oversight of the entire apparatus.

Nonfederal Actors

The Cold War also saw a proliferation of several important actors outside the US government that shaped and thus contributed to the interagency dialogue. National laboratories and federally funded research and development centers provided the government with independent analyses in niche areas, most notably nuclear weaponry. The government funded substantial university-based education and research in areas including nuclear physics, development economics, and languages. Think tanks and advocacy groups, backed by growing foundations like Ford and MacArthur, sprang up on increasingly specialized topics, from human rights and refugees to international trade and labor rights. In addition, international institutions—the constellation of United Nations organizations, the North Atlantic Treaty Organization (NATO), the IMF, and the World Bank—played an important role in providing the international collective goods of global diplomacy, security, and financial liquidity. The media, building on Edward R. Murrow's pioneering reporting during World War II, also became increasingly sophisticated on foreign policy matters. The net result was an environment in which US departments and agencies benefited from but also were constrained by the knowledge and clout of institutions beyond their control.

DEFENSE REFORMS

By the 1970s the seemingly static security environment dominated by the superpower competition was becoming more complex. A blue-ribbon panel chartered by Congress (and chaired by now-retired diplomat Robert Murphy) noted in 1975 that "the nature of foreign policy problems facing this country has changed dramatically since 1947. So has the nature of international power. Increasingly, economic forces define the strength or weakness of nations, and economic issues dominate the agenda of international negotiation."

Because of this sea change, "no important foreign policy problem now falls within the jurisdiction of a single department."[20] Although the Murphy Commission's recommendations did not prompt an overhaul of the interagency process, they added volume and insight to the growing recognition in Washington that economic dilemmas and the new issues crowding the headlines, like uncertain energy supplies, human rights, international terrorism, and narcotics trafficking, were demanding ever-greater expertise and collaboration across the US government. The interagency process needed new mechanisms to enable such collaboration. At the policy and coordination level in Washington, the fundamental dilemma was balancing expertise with authority. Cabinet secretaries were by nature too busy running and representing their departments to spend the requisite time with each other coordinating government-wide policies. Their employees may have had the time and expertise to do so but lacked the authority to make binding joint decisions for their departments. Someone possessing authority, time, and expertise therefore had to be delegated to attend numerous meetings at the NSC as well as bilateral sessions with counterparts at other agencies—while remaining fully briefed on developments in his or her own department. Without a reserve of bureaucratically astute officers at the deputy or assistant secretary levels, moreover, the process bogged down or failed.[21] Military mishaps in the early 1980s—the abortive Iran hostage rescue mission (1980), the terrorist bombing of a marine barracks and the United States withdrawal from Lebanon (1983–84), and the chaotic Grenada invasion (1983)—highlighted systemic problems. The JCS, with its committee-like structure, institutionally weak chairman, and mediocre staff contingent, gave inadequate and untimely joint advice and direction to the services, the secretary of defense, and the president. At the operational level the regional combatant commanders lacked clear authority over the forces they led, which had of course been raised, trained, and equipped by their home services and still lacked a joint ethos.

The Department of Defense Reorganization Act of 1986 (commonly known as the Goldwater–Nichols Act after its twin sponsors, Senator Barry Goldwater and Representative Bill Nichols) made three broad reforms to meet these challenges. The chairman of the JCS received greater authority (including becoming a member of the NSC) so he could operate independently of the other service chiefs; he was also given a larger staff to handle the range of interservice issues and a more robust analytical capacity to render independent advice. The chain of command was streamlined to give the combatant commanders explicit control over the forces assigned to them, including joint training, logistics, organization, and doctrine. Finally, the act imbued the joint personnel system with greater professionalism.

The act's reforms faced their first test in the 1991 Persian Gulf War to liberate Kuwait from Iraqi occupation, when the Pentagon deployed roughly 500,000 military personnel under the unified command of Gen. H. Norman Schwarzkopf. Swift battlefield victory affirmed the wisdom of compelling the armed services to plan, train, and fight jointly. And yet victory also exposed lingering problems. General Schwarzkopf proved to be a capable field marshal, but he had no plan to deal with the political and humanitarian turmoil in southern Iraq once combat abruptly ceased. Fighting the actual war and holding together the international coalition that had mounted it had consumed the attentions of the NSC and Defense and State Departments for months, and thus, no one in Washington had better ideas for handling the post-conflict dilemmas that Schwarzkopf suddenly (and not unpredictably) faced. In the resulting policy and security vacuum, Iraqi dictator Saddam Hussein and his ruling Ba'athists mercilessly suppressed a Shi'a uprising almost in sight of coalition forces and sowed seeds of fear and distrust of the United States that would be reaped by a coalition foray into the country in 2003. The American military's war-fighting prowess had been greatly improved, but the interagency process in which it functioned still did not afford its integration with the other elements of national power.

AFTER THE COLD WAR

The Persian Gulf War occurred in the midst a larger restructuring of international politics that profoundly affected the interagency process. The collapse of Soviet communism and the Warsaw Pact created a security vacuum in Central Europe that unleashed centrifugal forces in countries (including Yugoslavia, Czechoslovakia, and the Soviet Union itself) where ethnic or religious populations had once been united by oppressive central authority. As the sole superpower the United States now saw itself as perforce the guarantor of international order. A United Nations Security Council no longer divided by the threat of a Soviet veto allowed the United States to play a leading role in peacekeeping and humanitarian missions in places like Somalia, Bosnia, Haiti, and Kosovo. In local and regional crises the revolution in telecommunications technology (which fueled the growth of real-time global media) and increasingly organized advocacy groups provided new public pressure for leaders even in faraway America to take rapid action, despite the risks of hasty responses' unintended consequences.

The shifting terminology used to describe these missions, however, indicated the poor conceptual understanding of their requirements. Were they peacekeeping operations, peace enforcement, post-conflict operations, military operations other than war, or simply lesser but included cases of war? Regardless of the confusion the missions typically shared several elements: a humanitarian cause and rationale; a set of actors who could be tough to categorize as friend or foe, or even as state or non-state; a desire on the part of an international coalition to impose, or create the conditions for, a peace accord; the involvement of multilateral institutions (often the UN) and nongovernmental organizations (mostly providing aid); and persistent coverage by the international news media (the "CNN effect").

Such missions required new institutional postures by American departments and agencies that had long adapted themselves to the imperatives of the Cold War. Diplomacy needed to operate much more proactively to forestall state disintegration that could create destabilizing population flows and violence. The US military needed stronger capabilities for missions such as peacekeeping. The intelligence community needed to watch events in many regions simultaneously and assess the political implications of moves by a wider range of international actors. The Treasury and Commerce Departments, USAID, and the US trade representative needed to support long-term reconstruction efforts and promote the modernization of infrastructures to provide post-conflict stability. And they all increasingly recognized the contributions and technical assistance that globally active nonprofit organizations could offer in austere regions. Although each institution could meet these challenges in individual crises, the underlying interagency process often complicated the integration of their responses at the strategic and operational levels (in the field, as always, the deployed units from across the government often found ways to work together out of necessity).

The administration of President Bill Clinton established new policies for these "peace" missions, which portended important changes for the interagency process. Presidential Decision Directive 25 (PDD-25, "Reforming Multilateral Peace Operations"), issued in 1994, demonstrated the opportunities and limits of reform. PDD-25 provided a framework for evaluating which missions to undertake, sharing costs among departments, compensating for inadequate UN capabilities, maintaining command and control of American forces operating in multilateral operations, supporting congressional oversight, and improving interagency decision-making capacity. But PDD-25 was limited in its impact on the interagency process. It addressed bureaucratic elements (e.g., requiring the Defense Department to take management and financial responsibility for operations undertaken under Chapter VII of the UN Charter) without explaining how the departments would plan or work together. PDD-25 also assumed that crises proceeded in linear and predictable phases, including a combat phase that would be dominated by military imperatives and a separate post-conflict phase in which the State Department and other civilian agencies could take primary responsibility.

Experiences in Haiti and the Balkans led the Clinton administration to update PDD-25 with PDD-56 (on complex contingency operations) in 1996. The new PDD offered a checklist of requirements for undertaking any such operation, but it still assumed that interagency planning was relevant mostly for the post-conflict phase of a crisis, and not for the combat phase or the even-earlier shaping activities to avoid conflict in the first place. In addition, PDD-56 paid little attention to economic and development aspects of national power, and it did not address how the interagency process should operate for missions other than these complex contingencies. In short, interagency coordination remained relatively tangential to the operation of the national security establishment.

SINCE 9/11

The terrorist attacks against New York and Washington on September 11, 2001, marked a watershed for the interagency system. The Global War on Terror declared by President George W. Bush required an interdisciplinary approach. Because terrorism as propagated by al-Qaeda and its affiliates and allies was a transnational plague that incubated in remote and ungoverned spaces in the developing world, many of the diplomatic, military, economic, and intelligence capabilities developed for contingency operations in the 1990s remained highly relevant. The new situation differed, however, in other respects. Terrorists' ability to target Western cities and to exploit American missteps for public relations gains gave new salience to public diplomacy, while conjoining domestic components of security such as critical infrastructure protection and immigration, into foreign policy decision making.

The nation created new institutions to meet the terrorism challenge. Each of them, however, assumed a different model of interagency coordination. To complement the NSC, President George W. Bush formed a Homeland Security Council, with a focus on internal security and protection of the nation's critical infrastructure, including the transportation, financial, and energy sectors. (In 2009 this council was folded back into the NSC.) In 2002 Congress established the Department of Homeland Security, which subsumed some twenty-two federal agencies and 170,000 workers. This step brought together a range of related functions and specialties, although forging a unity of purpose and a shared culture would likely take longer and be more difficult than it was at the DOD.

The intelligence community underwent changes as well, many of them inspired by the Goldwater–Nichols reforms in the Defense Department. The Intelligence Reform and Terrorism Prevention Act of 2004 replaced the DCI with a somewhat more powerful director of national intelligence (DNI) to coordinate the intelligence community's seventeen elements and created the National Counterterrorism Center. The DNI wielded new authorities over budgets and personnel but still shared authority in many areas with the six cabinet departments that hosted intelligence community elements (Defense, State, Treasury, Justice, Energy, and Homeland Security). The director of the CIA continued to have the primary role in some intelligence matters—e.g., covert action—but otherwise, the DNI generally spoke for the entirety of the intelligence community in interagency deliberations. To complement these new institutions, the Bush White House also issued several national strategies and accompanying implementation plans to integrate the government's efforts in terrorism, maritime and aviation security, weapons proliferation, cybersecurity, pandemic illnesses, emergency response, and other areas. These generally served, however, as vehicles for departments and agencies to state their unique roles rather than as means for articulating new cross-cutting approaches or capabilities.

The wars in Afghanistan and Iraq (launched in 2001 and 2003, respectively) highlighted the need for more effective interagency coordination. Both campaigns achieved quick success on the conventional battlefield, demonstrating the virtues of joint operations and clear chains of command, as well as improved national-level intelligence support to battlefield commanders. The transitions between the combat and post-combat phases, however, showed that Washington's ability to conceptualize and integrate military and political planning remained incomplete. In both Afghanistan and Iraq, the military was the only institution on the ground in significant strength, and thus, by default it was responsible for fighting insurgents while providing day-to-day security, building new political structures, and overseeing large-scale economic development projects.

In the wake of the flawed Iraq postwar effort, a number of reforms built on the efforts of the 1990s and also assumed that interagency collaboration was prone to break down after the cessation of major combat operations (i.e., in the "post-conflict phase"). The Senate Foreign Relations Committee in 2004 instigated the creation of coordinator for reconstruction and stabilization at the State Department (known by its acronym S/CRS). The new office, comprising fewer than a hundred predominantly non–State Department personnel, aimed to balance the interagency relationship between the State and Defense Departments. Still, the office's mission—"to lead, coordinate and institutionalize U.S. Government civilian capacity to prevent or prepare for post-conflict situations, and to help stabilize and reconstruct societies in transition from conflict"—had a narrow scope.[22]

For its part the White House issued National Security Presidential Directive (NSPD) 44 in December 2005 to replace the Clinton-era PDD-56 and buttress the State Department's lead role in post-conflict affairs and recovery efforts.[23] The directive provided S/CRS with greater authority to set reconstruction and stabilization strategy, to develop policy and manage program execution, and to coordinate with foreign and nongovernmental organization (NGO) partners. State nonetheless remained outmanned and outplanned by the Defense Department during the George W. Bush administration, a problem lamented even by Secretary of Defense Robert Gates.[24] The Bush administration belatedly began applying more corporate models for interagency management. Global networked communications, the rapid rise in computing power, and the use of collaborative and social networking tools together gave additional evidence that interagency reform was not only necessary to breed integration but inevitable. President Bush's NSPD-60 sought to foster strategic planning through the creation of a policy-coordinating committee comprising senior officials across the national security establishment to focus on longer-term policy and plans.

The administration of President Barack Obama embraced this directive, but the good intention behind it inevitably competed with issues of more immediate consequence for senior-level official attention. The Obama administration instead tried more direct ways of forcing coordination.[25] Secretary of State Hillary Clinton (with presidential endorsement) appointed several special representatives or envoys ("czars") to bridge the departmental efforts on particularly salient issues, such as the Afghan war, Middle East peace efforts, and Sudan.[26] Despite their personal stature these individuals inevitably competed with State's regional bureaus and the ambassadors for influence, as well as with an activist staff at the NSC. The late Richard Holbrooke, special envoy for Afghanistan and Pakistan, found that some White House staffers "saw his efforts to coordinate among various government agencies as encroaching on their turf. . . . It was painful to watch such an accomplished diplomat marginalized and undercut," recalled Clinton.[27] Secretary of Defense Robert Gates questioned the concept that Holbrooke was hired to fulfill: "Personally, I think the idea of high-profile personalities working on sensitive issues outside normal channels is a mistake because it leads to bureaucratic conflict in Washington and confusion abroad as to who speaks for the president."[28] The Obama administration beefed up the NSC's staff and the foreign policy roles of White House aides without conspicuous success at improving coordination. Gates marveled at the political machinations, "insubordination," and swelling size of the NSC's staff.[29] He also complained that the staff had become "an advocate rather than a neutral party" in the policymaking process—a lament echoed in Secretary Clinton's memoir.[30] Both secretaries turned to interpersonal ties and old-fashioned, face-to-face coordination to reach understandings with other parts of government. Clinton called on CIA Director Leon Panetta for help in crafting a strategy to win the "information wars" against al-Qaeda. Their plan soon encountered opposition from other cabinet members. "To clear the air, as had previously been necessary a number of times, I decided to present it directly to the President," she recalled. His surprised response: "I've been asking for this kind of plan for more than a year!"[31] Gates, for his part, lunched with Secretary of Homeland Security Janet Napolitano to find a way for her department to use DOD means to protect America's critical infrastructure from cyber attacks. With the president's support they were briefly able "to part the bureaucratic Red Sea, but the waters soon came crashing back together," and the authorities that Defense had offered went unused.[32]

Cybersecurity and cyber conflict are ushering in a new chapter in the evolution to interagency coordination. Cyberspace has rapidly become vital to global political, economic, military, and social activity as a means to exchange and foster ideas, engage in commerce, wage war, and forge community with like-minded individuals. The volume and diversity of adversary activity in cyberspace has increased exponentially, especially since cyber capabilities are far easier and cheaper to develop than more conventional tools of military power. North Korea's hacking of Sony, allegations of Chinese infiltration of Office of Personnel Management security clearance data, or Russian cyber involvement in the 2016 US presidential election suggest an emerging and dynamic threat environment.[33] Multiple departments and agencies have equities and capabilities in the cyber domain but engage it differently depending on their mission orientation and statutory authorities. The most influential perspectives are those of the Defense Department, which views the cyberspace as a warfighting domain similar to air, sea, ground, and space; the intelligence community, which views it as an expansive arena in which friendly and adversary actors conduct intelligence operations; DHS, which sees it as the web tying together the nation's critical infrastructure; and the FBI, which treats it as a locale where criminals must be pursued and deterred. Constitutional questions of privacy have abounded, especially as certain US programs and capabilities have become public through a series of unauthorized disclosures and consequently prompted sharp public debates and even a presidential commission.[34] In many ways, the debate about the role of the government in securing cyberspace mirrors the debate in the 1920s–40s about how to harmonize the pursuit of airpower across the military services and the regulation of intra- and international commercial and recreational air travel. That debate spawned creation of several agencies, not to mention a separate air force, though the other services retained certain airborne capabilities. The outcome now regarding cyberspace remains far from certain.

For now, the departments and agencies have adapted current structures and processes to address cyber issues rather than seeking more radical change. The George W. Bush administration launched an executive branch–wide Comprehensive National Cybersecurity Initiative (CNCI) to harmonize increased investment in cyber capabilities and designated a cyber coordinator at the White House to focus interagency coordination. The Obama administration adopted the CNCI and created a sub-unified US Cyber Command at the Department of Defense, with its commander initially dual-hatted as the director of the National Security Agency, giving him, for the time being, authority over the different missions of an operational military command equipped to carry out cyberspace operations and a foreign intelligence agency focused on collection and information assurance. President Obama also issued presidential policy directives on discrete aspects of cyber affairs and promoted information sharing about threats with the private sector.[35]

The predominant role of business interests in cyberspace—which is for the most part constructed, owned, and operated by the private sector—is perhaps the key feature of the current interagency dynamic on this topic. The private sector has a direct and immediate stake in virtually every policy and practice that the government implements—even those that might seem strictly "military." For example, the technology sector has had a substantial voice recently regarding changes in encryption policy. Corporations' and privacy advocates' incentive to protect communications has contrasted with national security and law enforcement rationales for seeking access to data created by terrorists and criminals. The technology sector's access to the corridors of power in Washington ensures they will have a seat, at least by proxy, at the interagency table.

Dealing with cyber threats inevitably raises questions about technologies, norms of behavior, and organizational roles that go to the heart of interagency coordination. When the Obama administration wanted to attribute the recent breach of Sony Pictures Entertainment to North Korea, for example, the FBI got the call. Director James B. Comey publicly explained that the incident and the larger implications of cyber conflict amounted to a "vector change" that "blows away traditional notions of, well, this is my area of responsibility, this is your area of responsibility." While it might not always be possible for law enforcement to reach the perpetrators, the bureau could still help the US government impose costs on them; "I thought it was very, very important that we as a government, we as an FBI, said we know who hacked Sony." Director Comey's FBI had added to its law enforcement mission a foreign messaging role. The message: "That there will be consequences for those who use malicious cyber activity to harm Americans or harm American businesses."[36]

THE PAST AND FUTURE OF THE INTERAGENCY PROCESS

The blue-ribbon commission that Robert Murphy chaired in 1975 began its final report by noting "good organization does not ensure successful policy, nor does poor organization preclude it. But steadily and powerfully, organizational patterns influence the effectiveness of government."[37] The comment and the report together marked an implicit retort to the question posed to Murphy in North Africa three decades earlier: "Will you please tell me what in hell the State Department has to do in an active theater of war?" All the departments and agencies involved in national security affairs must work together and complement one another's efforts, even in contexts (like "active theaters of war") when one dominates. Four decades later, it is possible to see how much and how little the US government has learned in terms of addressing the limits in its interagency process. If Murphy's gifted amateurism, which exemplified the careers of so many other senior officials, commanders, and diplomats, is no longer the rule, coordination and integration of departmental plans, processes, and capabilities is still by no means automatic or even routine. Indeed, the practices of recent years almost seem redolent of those of the nineteenth century, during which presidents and their trusted aides made key decisions with minimal or divided input from the national security enterprise.

Modern states need their own interagency processes because international challenges rarely confine themselves to a single dimension of state power. Although the US government is predominantly organized along departmental lines that align to core functions of the state (e.g., the military, diplomacy, and the treasury), the interagency process tries to stitch the seams between those institutions and capabilities. The long and tortuous path of interagency reform illustrates the complexity and difficulty of this task. At the tactical level among elements deployed in the field, coordination and collaboration have steadily increased. At the operational and strategic levels, however, the system has been only modestly adjusted to reflect modern challenges that by their nature require interagency collaboration in policy formulation and operational planning, not just for a presumed post-conflict phase, but as an integral element of US foreign and national security policy.

History suggests that several obstacles will remain in the path of significant changes in the interagency process, which itself will be required to work better and faster in the years ahead. Current organizational models geared around departments and agencies will need to be increasingly flexible to integrate the various tools of national power, particularly at the strategic and operational levels, to cope with new transnational challenges, like the cybersecurity problem now facing every nation. The interagency system must be prepared to affect the entire range of national security missions (not just complex emergencies or stabilization and reconstruction) in all phases of overseas engagement from shaping activities to develop partners and forestall threats, to combat, to post-conflict reconciliation and development. Yet the benefits of significant interagency reform will remain diffused across the national security establishment. Thus, no one department or leader (even the president) is likely to decide that a significant investment of political capital in this endeavor will yield dividends to him or his institution commensurate with the cost (the "tragedy of the commons" problem).

At a time when the interagency system increasingly includes partners beyond the federal government, to include industry, NGOs, foreign powers, and state/local/tribal governments, departmental bureaucracies will probably continue praising the virtue of interagency collaboration in principle but resist ceding their autonomy in practice. The US government rarely goes it alone anymore; a host of actors are increasingly entwined in all American engagements overseas. Departments, however, can and have resisted collaboration with other agencies and actors because it creates interdependencies that seem to threaten successful execution of their own core missions. The departments and agencies of the national security establishment have developed elaborate standard operating procedures, technical standards, and organizational structures to perform missions assigned to them in law and in presidential directives and are leery of reforms that cause uncertainty in meeting these basic requirements. Civil servants, furthermore, see few professional benefits from involvement in interagency activities, which take them out of sight of their day-to-day management and may force them to articulate career-jeopardizing positions that advance the broader national interest but undermine their own department's autonomy.

Reform of the interagency system at the strategic and operational levels has always required White House attention. Organizing and managing by mission, rather than by department, will likely be the main dimension along which the interagency system will adapt, while departments and agencies continue to foster capabilities that have broad utility across multiple operational environments. The NSC staff might need to lead this effort, but unless it undergoes a significant change in organization and emphasis of its own, it could lack the capacity to do so. In any event, and despite the aforementioned success of the "Scowcroft model" of NSC *committees*, devising an effective NSC *staff* model that survives the administration of the president who fashions it will remain problematic. Presidential leadership, moreover, will be needed to foster government-wide changes like a new human capital model that breeds senior leaders versed in multiple government disciplines; a technological infrastructure that enables safe, secure, and reliable communication and interaction across departmental lines; integrated programming, budgeting, and tasking processes; and mechanisms to ensure that plans are implemented and meet performance expectations.

Finally, interagency process reform has always required a sustained partner in Congress. Legislative oversight of the executive branch principally by department enables effective work by committees but complicates development of interagency approaches that overlap committee jurisdictions. Congressional committees since the nineteenth century have preferred to exercise exclusive jurisdiction to maximize their power and influence over the executive branch. Establishing new committees for national security that look across traditional jurisdictions could work, but unless existing committees are disbanded (as the Military and Naval Affairs Committees gave way to the Armed Services Committees in both houses in 1947), such new bodies might only confuse matters. Effective congressional oversight could potentially be achieved by adapting committee jurisdictions, by creating informal rules of procedures that force coordination among the chief oversight committees, or by creating another oversight body. It may take a crisis, or a series of crises, to inspire a model of congressional oversight befitting the challenges of interagency collaboration.

NOTES

1. Robert D. Murphy, *Diplomat among Warriors* (Garden City, NY: Doubleday, 1964), 155.

2. Thomas A. Bailey, *A Diplomatic History of the American People* (New York: Appleton-Century-Crofts, 1958 [1940]), 13.

3. Dean Acheson, *Present at the Creation: My Years in the State Department* (New York: W. W. Norton, 1969), 15.

4. Bailey, *Diplomatic History of the American People*, 11.

5. Of course, there were examples of joint army–navy operations. For example, they jointly defended Baltimore, Plattsburgh, and New Orleans in the War of 1812 and fought together at Forts Henry and Donelson, Vicksburg, and Richmond and Albemarle and Pamlico Sounds in the Civil War. See Allan R. Millett, "The Organizational Impact of Military Success and Failure: An Historical Perspective," in *The Reorganization of the Joint Chiefs of Staff: A Critical Analysis*, ed. Allen R. Millett et al. (Washington, DC: Pergamon-Brassey's, 1986).

6. John Norton Moore and Robert F. Turner, *The Legal Structure of Defense Organization: Memorandum Prepared for the President's Blue Ribbon Commission on Defense Management* (Washington, DC: US Government Printing Office, 1986), 36.

7. Details of all of these points can be found in Michael Blow's *A Ship to Remember: The Maine and the Spanish-American War* (New York: William Morrow, 1992); see also Ernest R. May, *Imperial Democracy: The Emergence of America as a Great Power* (New York: Harper & Row, 1977 [1961]).

8. Bailey, *Diplomatic History of the American People*, 9–10, 14.

9. For a summary of the origins of the Root reforms, see Paul Y. Hammond, *Organizing for Defense: The American Military Establishment in the Twentieth Century* (Princeton, NJ: Princeton University Press, 1961), 12–24.

10. On a more philosophical level, the army's centralization reflected the neo-Hamiltonian view of administration in which control was exerted through clear lines of accountability, whereas the navy's continued decentralization demonstrated its commitment to the neo-Jeffersonians' principle of devolved power.

11. Gordon N. Lederman, *Reorganizing the Joint Chiefs of Staff* (Westport, CT: Greenwood Press, 1999), 7–10.

12. Acheson, *Present at the Creation*, 16.

13. Frederick R. Barkley, "Marshall Urges Unified War Arm," *New York Times*, October 19, 1945.

14. The panel's report was reprinted by the Senate Committee on Naval Affairs in October 1945 as *Unification of the War and Navy Departments and Postwar Organization for National Security* (Washington, DC: Government Printing Office, 1945), 53, 55, 79. For a good summary of the genesis and assumptions of the report, see Douglas Stuart, "Constructing the Iron Cage: The 1947 National

Security Act," in *Affairs of State: The Interagency and National Security,* ed. Gabriel Marcella (Carlisle, PA: Strategic Studies Institute [US Army], 2008), 67–71.

15. Harry S. Truman, *Memoirs*, vol. 2, *Years of Trial and Hope* (Garden City, NY: Doubleday, 1956), 46.

16. A useful summary of the changes in the NSC's structure and procedures is contained in part 2, "Description and Historical Background of the System," of the final report of the Project on National Security Reform, *Forging a New Shield*, November 2008, www.connectusfund.org/resources/project -national-security-reform-report-forging-new-shield. See also the extended discussion on this in Paul D. Miller, "Organizing the National Security Council: I Like Ike's," *Presidential Studies Quarterly* 43, no. 3 (September 2013): 592–606.

17. Acheson, *Present at the Creation*, 734.

18. Murphy, *Diplomat among Warriors*, 451.

19. Acheson, *Present at the Creation*, 213–14.

20. Commission on the Organization of the Government for the Conduct of Foreign Policy [Murphy Commission], *Final Report* (Washington, DC: US Government Printing Office, 1975), 32, 34. The commission was charged by Congress to suggest "a more effective system for the formulation and implementation of the nation's foreign policy"; see Murphy's transmittal letter, dated June 27, 1975, and reprinted as the report's foreword.

21. Miller, "Organizing the National Security Council," 596.

22. Office of the Coordinator for Reconstruction and Stabilization, Frequently Asked Questions, www.state.gov/s/crs/66427.htm.

23. NSPD-44 promoted "improved coordination, planning, and implementation for reconstruction and stabilization assistance for foreign states and regions at risk of, in, or in transition from conflict or civil strife." George W. Bush, "Management of Interagency Efforts Concerning Reconstruction and Stabilization," National Security Presidential Directive 44, December 7, 2005, www.fas.org/irp/offdocs/ nspd/nspd-44.html.

24. Secretary Gates complained in a speech at National Defense University on September 29, 2008, that the State Department and USAID had been "gutted over the last 15 years." See also Robert M. Gates, *Duty: Memoirs of a Secretary at War* (New York: Andrew A. Knopf, 2014), 145.

25. Miller, "Organizing the National Security Council," 603.

26. Hillary Rodham Clinton, *Hard Choices* (New York: Simon & Schuster, 2014), 28.

27. Ibid., 141.

28. Gates, *Duty*, 295.

29. Ibid., 290–92, 587.

30. Ibid., 385; and Clinton, *Hard Choices*, 190, 370, 464.

31. Clinton, *Hard Choices*, 188–190.

32. Gates, *Duty*, 451.

33. Ellen Nakashima, "Chinese Government Has Arrested Hackers It Says Breached OPM Database," *Washington Post*, December 2, 2015, www.washingtonpost.com/world/national-security/chinese -government-has-arrested-hackers-suspected-of-breaching-opm-database/2015/12/02/0295b918-990c -11e5-8917-653b65c809eb_story.html; and Office of the Director of National Intelligence, "Joint DHS and ODNI Election Security Statement," press release, October 7, 2016, www.dni.gov/index.php/news room/press-releases/215-press-releases-2016/1423-joint-dhs-odni-election-security-statement.

34. Review Group on Intelligence and Communications Technologies, *Liberty and Security in a Changing World* (Washington, DC: White House, December 12, 2013), www.whitehouse.gov/sites/ default/files/docs/2013-12-12_rg_final_report.pdf.

35. See the descriptions of Presidential Policy Directives 20 and 41 in ibid.; and Barack Obama, "Promoting Private Sector Cybersecurity Information Sharing," Executive Order, February 13, 2015. This was reinforced by the Cyber Information Sharing Act of 2015, enacted on December 15, 2015.

36. James B. Comey, Director, Federal Bureau of Investigation, remarks at the International Conference on Cyber Security, Fordham University, New York, January 7, 2015, www.fbi.gov/news/ speeches/addressing-the-cyber-security-threat.

37. Murphy Commission, *Final Report*, 1.

CHAPTER 2

The Evolution of the NSC Process

David P. Auerswald

A principal danger at the top level of government is that discussion may be based on a presentation that is one-sided (however earnestly proposed) or that lacks a critical analysis in which all agencies freely participate at the formative stage.

—Robert Cutler, special assistant to the president for national security affairs, Eisenhower administration

The National Security Council (NSC) and the NSC staff, as led by the national security advisor (NSA), serve critical functions at the heart of the interagency national security process. Formal NSC members, and frequently the NSC staff, coordinate security policy across federal agencies. The NSC staff manages the flow of information and policy recommendations between the president and the various departments. At times the staff engages in long-range, strategic thinking. At other times it engages in short-term crisis policy. On occasion the NSC staff has run particularly sensitive security operations. A competent staff, working within a well-functioning NSC system, greatly facilitates the coordination of US government efforts to achieve security goals. A dysfunctional staff and system can bring about disastrous results.[1]

This chapter explores how and why the NSC's structure and process have changed over time. A number of factors combine to explain the evolution of the NSC system. The institutional needs of the president appear to be a consistent reason why the NSC staff generally—and the NSA in particular—has played a central role in national security policy since the Eisenhower administration. The NSC staff belongs to the president, without loyalties or reporting requirements to federal agencies or the legislative branch—a particularly valuable commodity in an international environment characterized by massive and increasingly complex US commitments and a domestic environment characterized by increasingly fragmented political and media conditions. Yet different presidents have used the NSC system, the NSC staff, and the NSA in particular ways. Variations across and within administrations appear to depend on the operating styles of individual presidents and NSAs, and important external events that shock the national security or domestic political systems and create the need for organizational change.

The first section of this chapter reviews the root causes of the NSC system's importance, focusing attention on the institutional needs of the presidency. It then explores the proximate reasons why presidents change the NSC system. In so doing, the chapter documents the main structural and procedural changes that have occurred since the creation of the NSC and its associated staff. Those changes are linked to the management styles and events that confront each administration to include each administration's reaction to its predecessor's NSC system. Finally, the chapter concludes with an assessment of the Obama administration's NSC structure and operating style.

ROOT CAUSES OF THE NSC SYSTEM'S IMPORTANCE

The NSC was established by the National Security Act of 1947 and was placed within the executive office of the president in 1949.[2] There are two components of the NSC that are important for our purposes. First, there are the statutory members of the NSC. These individuals have varied over time but since 1949 have included the president, vice president, secretaries of state and defense, and advisors from the military and intelligence communities (currently the director of national intelligence and the chairman of the Joint Chiefs of Staff). Other senior officials attend NSC meetings in an advisory capacity at the president's discretion but are not statutory members of the NSC. The second component is the NSC staff, which has grown from a handful of people in the late 1940s and 1950s to upward of 200–400 people in recent times, depending on the administration and the counting rules.[3] The NSC staff advises the NSC and the president, but individual staff assistants are not members of the NSC. Any president must decide on how the NSC and the NSC staff will be structured and make decisions. Structural choices include how big the NSC staff is, how staff members are organized into policy directorates, what entities will consider policy decisions, and who will serve on them. Procedural choices include who will chair and attend NSC and staff meetings, what role the NSC will play in executive branch decision making, how frequent meetings will be, etc. Since 1953 the special assistant to the president for national security affairs, now known as the NSA, has directed the NSC staff.

The NSC system contains an intriguing mix of continuity and change over time. It embodies continuity in the sense that the basic role of the NSC staff and key structural elements of the NSC system have remained relatively constant across time, at least from the beginning of the Kennedy administration to the present.[4] Amy Zegart characterizes the post-Eisenhower NSC system as having strong NSAs, powerful and capable NSC staffs, and relatively underutilized formal NSC meetings.[5] Considering each post-Kennedy president, Zegart concludes that "none has successfully altered the system's three essential features."[6]

To explain the continuity identified by Zegart, we would normally begin by examining an agency's culture and norms. Although organizational culture and bureaucratic norms influence a typical federal agency's behavior, this does not appear to be true with the NSC staff. The staff is different for three reasons. First, almost without exception, tenure at the NSC staff lasts no longer than a president's term in office. The NSC staff is in large part re-created out of whole cloth with the transition to a new administration. Often, NSC staff members burn out significantly faster than a four- or eight-year presidential term.[7] Second, the staff represents an ever-changing mix of officials detailed from federal departments, transplanted legislative branch staff, academicians, and think-tank personnel. Third, staff detailed from federal agencies are chosen carefully and asked to set aside their bureaucratic loyalties for the duration of their NSC tenure. As a result, few if any traditions or behavioral norms pass from administration to administration or staff to staff, which prevents the NSC staff from developing the long-term culture prevalent in so many other government agencies and helps distinguish foreign service officers from civil service employees at the State Department, fighter pilots from transport pilots, intelligence community analysts from operators, cavalry soldiers from infantry, or submariners from surface warfare officers. In short, other than sharing a penchant for ambition and hard work, the NSC staffers would be hard-pressed to develop a corporate identity or culture that is distinct from that of the president they serve or the NSA that leads them.

A better explanation for consistent behavior comes from the study of American political and institutional behavior. That literature focuses attention on the incentives confronting presidents when they choose what strategies and tools to use to achieve policy and political objectives.[8] The argument here is that presidents turn to the personnel in the executive office of the president (EOP) in general, and their White House staff in particular, for their most important and sensitive policy initiatives. Presidents cannot rely on anyone else. Federal agencies have preferences and interests that may not align with those of the president, Congress has institutional incentives to counterbalance executive power, and the growth of the federal government's responsibilities has raised public expectations to the point that presidential inaction is tantamount to political suicide. In short, presidents need an entity that will respond to them and only to them if they are to survive politically while advancing US interests. The EOP and White House fit the bill.

It should be no surprise then that the same logic applies to presidential reliance on NSAs and their NSC staffs.[9] Presidents routinely depend on both to develop the country's most important security initiatives because the NSC has advantages for the president that other bureaucratic entities do not. The NSC staff serves at the pleasure of the president and has been part of the EOP since 1949. With one exception, the NSA has had a West Wing office, which puts him or her in close proximity to the president, with the access to match.[10] NSC staff members are not subject to Senate confirmation and cannot be subpoenaed to testify regarding their advice to the president. At the same time, the NSC staff is not beholden to a federal agency for money or influence, preventing the staff from developing institutional loyalties beyond the White House. From a political perspective then, the NSC staff is an attractive tool of presidential power and influence.

The same is true from a policy perspective. The NSC system was created at the beginning of the Cold War, which was a time of dramatically expanded US international commitments. Creating an NSC staff provided the president with a means of coordinating the complex policies and demands associated with those commitments (to say nothing of managing the dramatically expanded federal workforce devoted to defense and security affairs), just as the need for a government response to the Great Depression led to the creation of the EOP in the late 1930s.[11] Indeed, the NSC system was created in 1947 as part of the broader national security reorganization that also created the Defense Department, the air force as a separate military service, and the Central Intelligence Agency (CIA). The reason for such dramatic reforms, noted in one influential 1945 report, was that "the necessity of integrating all these elements into an alert, smoothly working and efficient machine is more important now than ever before. Such integration is compelled by our present world commitments and risks."[12] The NSC system gave presidents tools to meet Cold War challenges and the even more complex trials of the modern post–Cold War era. From a policy perspective then, it is easy to see why the NSC staff and the NSA continue to play a central role in the national security processes of most administrations.

The empirical record supports these intuitions. Consider the size of the NSC staff. From a relatively small number of influential policy advisors in 1960, the NSC staff had grown in size to over a hundred people by the end of the George W. Bush administration.[13] Growth has not been uniform across time, however. Presidents Ford, Carter, and Reagan and both Bush administrations cut the size of the NSC staff at the beginning of their terms, only to add those positions back as time went on, in most cases to surpass the numbers employed by their predecessors. The trend line shows that presidents have increasingly relied on their NSC staffs for national security advice and coordination.

Or consider the choice of NSAs. Most presidents since Eisenhower have picked powerful advisors to lead the NSC staff. The exceptions were Ronald Reagan, whose first four NSAs were considered insufficiently senior, expert, or both, and George W. Bush, whose first NSA was considered too junior relative to the administration's other senior foreign policy players.[14] Those exceptions notwithstanding, presidents have by and large chosen influential experts as their NSAs, consistent with the importance of the NSC staff for vital policy initiatives. Table 2.1 lists NSAs by presidential administration.

Finally, there is evidence to support the idea that few presidents since Eisenhower have used the formal NSC process on a regular basis. Instead, presidents tend to use informal gatherings to reach agreement or coordinate among their core foreign policy team, or they have allowed their NSAs to do so on the president's behalf. Presidents choose an informal route for two main reasons. First, informal meetings have tended to be relatively small compared to formal

Table 2.1. National Security Advisors, 1961–2016

President	National Security Advisor	Dates
John F. Kennedy	McGeorge Bundy	1961–63
Lyndon Johnson	McGeorge Bundy	1963–66
	Walt Rostow	1966–69
Richard Nixon	Henry Kissinger	1969–74
Gerald Ford	Henry Kissinger	1974–75
	Brent Scowcroft	1975–77
Jimmy Carter	Zbigniew Brzezinski	1977–81
Ronald Reagan	Richard Allen	1981–82
	William Clark	1982–83
	Robert McFarlane	1983–85
	John Poindexter	1985–86
	Frank Carlucci	1986–87
	Colin Powell	1987–89
George H. W. Bush	Brent Scowcroft	1989–93
Bill Clinton	Anthony Lake	1993–97
	Samuel Berger	1997–2001
George W. Bush	Condoleezza Rice	2001–5
	Stephen Hadley	2005–9
Barack Obama	James Jones	2009–10
	Tom Donilon	2010–13
	Susan Rice	2013–17

NSC meetings, which is attractive for administrations that have allowed a broad range of agencies to participate in NSC meetings. Second, small group meetings in theory allow the president or the NSA to have better control over debate and any decisions made.[15] For example, Lyndon Johnson preferred informal Tuesday lunches over NSC meetings because the intimate lunch format allowed him to persuade, test, or bluntly intimidate his advisors, just as he had done in one-on-one and small group meetings with his Senate colleagues when he was majority leader.[16] Some presidents (e.g., Clinton) have even chosen to use presidential envoys, and others (e.g., George W. Bush) have designated a lead agency to make policy for particular regions or crises rather than requiring coordination across cabinet agencies. The various informal mechanisms used by presidents to improve their control over security policy are listed in table 2.2.

Table 2.2. Informal, Alternative Security Fora, 1961–Present

President	Forums and Participants
John F. Kennedy	Executive Committee (ExComm)
Lyndon Johnson	Tuesday lunches: POTUS, DOS, DOD, NSA plus the DCI, CJCS, and WH aides at times
Richard Nixon	Kissinger meetings: POTUS and NSA
Jimmy Carter	Friday breakfasts: POTUS, NSA, DOS plus DOD and WH aides at times
Ronald Reagan	National Security Planning Group: POTUS, VP, DOS, DOD, DCI, NSA, WH aides
	"Family Group" lunches: DOS, DOD, DCI, NSA
George H. W. Bush	"Big Eight" meetings: POTUS, VP, NSA, Deputy NSA, WH COS, DOS, DOD, CJCS
	"Inner Circle" meetings: POTUS, NSA, and either DOS or DOD
Bill Clinton	"Foreign Policy Team" meetings: POTUS and various advisors
	Albright-Berger-Cohen (ABC) lunches: DOS, NSA, DOD plus DCI, CJCS, UN ambassador, and VP NSA at times
	Special Envoys (Russia, Balkans, Middle East, etc.): POTUS and various advisors
George W. Bush	Parallel vice presidential NSC process: 15-person VP national security staff
	"Vulcan" meetings in White House: POTUS, VP, DOD, NSA, and their deputies
	Lead Agency: DOD in Iraq
Barack Obama	Almost 50 special envoy positions created between 2009 and early 2015

Note: Abbreviation key: POTUS = president of the United States, VP = vice president, DOS = State Department, DOD = Defense Department, NSA = national security advisor, DCI = director of central intelligence, WH = White House, CJCS = chairman of the Joint Chiefs of Staff, COS = chief of staff

PROXIMATE CAUSES OF CHANGE

Despite continuity in the growth of the NSC staff and informal advisory systems, the empirical record shows significant variation across and within administrations in terms of the NSC system's structure and processes.[17] This is particularly true with regard to the role played by the NSA.[18]

The most common explanation for changes to the NSC system is that each system reflects the incumbent president's personality to include such things as the president's operating style, comfort level with divergent views and disagreement, knowledge of foreign policy, and reactions to previous administrations' policies and procedures.[19] Adherents to this perspective are not limited to academicians. Robert Cutler, President Eisenhower's special assistant for national security affairs, noted, "Fundamentally, the Council is a vehicle for a President to use in accordance with its suitability to his plan for conducting his great office."[20] Colin Powell, President Reagan's final NSA, argued, "At the end of the day, the duty of the National Security Council staff and the assistant is to mold themselves to the personality of the president."[21] Variants of personality-based explanations focus on the operating style of the NSA or the way the NSA meshes with the president and various cabinet members. All are said to help determine the roles and procedures of each NSC staff and the overall structure of the NSC system.

A second proximate cause of change at the NSC is the international and domestic context within which each administration operates. Here the argument is that important external and internal events provide exogenous shocks to the national security system, which creates the need for institutional innovation and organizational change. In this view the NSC remains a relatively static organization until it is confronted with significant international or domestic policy crises, at which time the institution rapidly adjusts. The parallel in biology would be the punctuated evolution of species in response to regional, environmental, or global cataclysms. International failure can be one generator of change, as can be a desire to advance a dramatically new policy agenda. A desire to separate a new administration's tone or policies from those of its predecessor can be another. To see the degree to which personality or context explains change to the NSC system's structure and process, we must review the main developments associated with the NSC and its staff.[22]

Dwight Eisenhower

President Dwight Eisenhower took office at a time of international crisis for the United States. By January 1953 the United States had suffered a series of setbacks in the increasingly frigid Cold War, to include crises in Greece and Turkey; communist control of Bulgaria, Romania, Poland, Hungary, and Czechoslovakia; the Berlin blockade; and the fall of China, to say nothing of the two-year-old and then-stalemated Korean War. The United States appeared to be playing defense in a losing game. At the same time, the United States was at a crossroad when it came to defense spending. The United States could try to match the Soviets and Chinese in terms of conventional forces, at great expense, or it could focus on deterring communist aggression via nuclear weapons, which would save money but be domestically and internationally risky. The new administration chose the latter option but would need discipline and unity to implement it.

President Eisenhower came to the presidency from a long and distinguished military career. He brought a sense of military organization and hierarchical structure to the NSC system. Eisenhower saw the staff as providing systematic support for his cabinet and the statutory NSC participants as working for him.[23] In the words of his national security assistant, "President Eisenhower has made it clear that he regards the Council as a 'corporate' body, consisting of officials who are advising the President in their own right and not simply as the heads of their respective departments."[24] With regard to the NSC staff members, Eisenhower wanted them to thoroughly prepare for each NSC meeting. "Eisenhower transformed the Council into a forum for vigorous discussion against a background of painstakingly prepared and carefully studied papers."[25]

These preferences and events translated into a formal, regularized, predictable NSC system structure and practice. The administration set up a four-stage NSC system.[26] Agencies would come up with policy proposals. The NSC planning board, staffed with assistant secretary–level personnel, would review those proposals twice per week and highlight disagreements between agencies. The NSC, usually chaired by the president, would hold a weekly meeting to consider those proposals. Monitoring the implementation of NSC decisions fell to the operations coordinating board, staffed at the under-secretary level. The NSC staff prepared the background and options papers associated with this process but had no substantive policy role.[27] In sum, the Eisenhower NSC was the epitome of a structured, systematic NSC process, something that the administration thought was needed given both the circumstances confronting it and the personality of the president.

John F. Kennedy

John F. Kennedy came to office wanting a less formal, more diverse NSC system than Eisenhower had. A priority for Kennedy was to have access to multiple sources of information. In the words of Walt Rostow, an NSC staffer under Kennedy and eventual NSA for Lyndon Johnson, President Kennedy "was determined not to be imprisoned by the options the bureaucracies might generate and lay before him."[28] He did not like formal meetings, preferring instead to have private, informal conversations with a variety of experts on his staff, even to the point of calling in relatively junior staffers for consultations on issues within their portfolios.

Kennedy's NSA, McGeorge Bundy, fit well with this style. He was widely regarded as a brilliant strategist, an academician, and a moderate Republican who had known Kennedy for years.[29] He loved the informal give-and-take of academia and the think tank world and brought that style to the White House.[30] The president and Bundy agreed to a large extent on Bundy's role: provide the president with information and act as an honest broker who would accurately represent cabinet members' views. They thought alike and "liked each other immensely."[31]

Kennedy and Bundy structured the NSC staff system in reaction to two external events. Domestically, they were responding to a Senate report that argued the Eisenhower NSC structure was too bureaucratic and slow to respond to international events.[32] Internationally, the Kennedy NSC system was to some extent a reaction to the failed Bay of Pigs invasion at the beginning of the administration's tenure. The administration attributed that failure to the relatively limited information and biased sources available to the president at the time.[33]

Combined with Kennedy's and Bundy's preferences and operating styles, these two events led to a very different NSC system than had existed under President Eisenhower. Kennedy's thirst for information translated into the creation of the White House Situation Room and a relatively flat NSC staff organization in which any staffer was able to go directly to the president if necessary. According to Carl Keysen, a Kennedy NSC staff member, "Kennedy made very clear we were his men, we operated for him, we had direct contact with him."[34] Kennedy's aversion to formal meetings translated into the NSC system essentially being ignored, with only monthly meetings for most of the administration's tenure.[35] During the Cuban Missile Crisis, the NSC was essentially replaced by the less formal Executive Committee. And even the Executive Committee was too large a body for the most sensitive discussions regarding trading Soviet missiles in Cuba for US missiles in Turkey. Indeed, many in the administration, including members of the NSC, did not know about those discussions until after the crisis.

Lyndon B. Johnson

President Lyndon Johnson entered office with a domestically oriented agenda focused on enacting the Great Society program and civil rights legislation. Both were politically charged issues that had the potential to divide the Democratic Party. By themselves, these issues would dominate the full agenda of any president. Unfortunately for Johnson, he also had a deteriorating situation in Vietnam with which to contend. Focusing on Vietnam, however, would take attention away from the domestic agenda. Moreover, Johnson simply had little interest in foreign affairs. The result was that Johnson tried to keep Vietnam off the national radar for as long as possible. Johnson's desire to control the policy agenda, both domestically and internationally, would help shape his administration's NSC system.

Johnson had a very different operating style compared to his predecessor. He was a retail politician who preferred to build coalitions one person at a time rather than engage in long debates in large groups. That translated into a preference for working through his cabinet secretaries individually rather than with the NSC staff or in large meetings. Johnson had a difficult relationship with the NSC staff for another reason: he came from relatively humble roots and distrusted the intellectuals with whom Kennedy had surrounded himself, including NSA Bundy. Johnson did not want the large volume of information Bundy had provided to Kennedy. Nor did he want his NSA to maintain a neutral broker position. He much preferred his NSA to advocate on behalf of the president's preferred policies instead of trying to forge a compromise among the national security agencies. After all, compromise positions could shift attention away from, and derail progress on, his domestic agenda. In that sort of world, the NSC staff increasingly moved from preparing analytical options papers to monitoring the implementation of presidential decisions.

All this translated into a distrust of the formal NSC process greater even than had existed under the Kennedy administration. From the president's perspective, the forum was too big to meet his needs, it provided too few opportunities for individual persuasion and was staffed by individuals that the president did not respect or trust.[36] Yet there were limits to how much Johnson could change the NSC system, at least initially, in that he came to office via the national tragedy of Kennedy's assassination. Keeping the appearance of the Kennedy structure made sense from a political perspective, so Bundy was initially kept on as NSA. That relationship deteriorated, however, to the point where Walt Rostow replaced Bundy. Rostow was much more of a policy advocate than Bundy, which served him well with the president but at times put him at odds with the other NSC members.[37]

At the same time, the NSC staff's influence was downgraded when Rostow was denied the title of NSA. The two main NSC committees, the NSC senior interdepartmental group and the interdepartmental regional group, were both chaired by State Department officials rather than the NSC staff. Finally, even these NSC committees were largely ignored in favor of the much smaller Tuesday lunch discussions listed in table 2.2.[38] The problem, of course, was that the Tuesday lunch meetings did not include NSC staff, so no official records were kept of their discussions or decisions, and the staff had no way to ensure that decisions were implemented across the federal bureaucracy. In short, NSC meetings appeared to be pro forma ratifications of decisions already made by Johnson, particularly when it came to Vietnam.[39]

Richard M. Nixon

The Nixon administration's initial intent was to bring some order back into the informal NSC system of the Kennedy and Johnson years. Henry Kissinger, Nixon's NSA, created nine formal NSC committees, including the Senior Review Group, which previewed policy proposals before NSC meetings, the Washington Special Action Group on Crisis Policy, the Verification Panel on Arms Control Negotiations, the 40 Committee for Covert Operations, the Vietnam Special Studies Group, the Intelligence Committee and the Intelligence Resources

Advisory Committee, the International Energy Review Group, and the Defense Program Review Committee.[40] The staff initially was tasked to produce two types of documents: national security study memoranda to explore long-range strategy and decision memoranda that presented the president with a series of options. The NSC staff grew tremendously under the Nixon administration, from a dozen members to almost fifty-five by the middle of the first term.

This elaborate system was quickly ignored, however, for reasons related to personalities and the administration's ambitious foreign policy agenda. President Richard Nixon's personal style has been well documented elsewhere.[41] To some extent he was a walking contradiction. He has been called secretive, solitary, controlling, and even paranoid but also politically astute and strategically brilliant. He is said to have wanted a structured, formal NSC process, but then he systematically ignored that process because he was unable to personally confront those he disagreed with.[42] Kissinger was and continues to be one of the most influential NSAs ever to have held the office.[43] He and Nixon had a very close working relationship, shared a similar realist worldview, and were both concerned about media leaks (to the point of having some of the NSC staff wiretapped). That said, there was allegedly a significant element of distrust between the two, which bordered on jealousy.

The other reason the formal system was ignored relates to the sensitive nature of the administration's foreign policy agenda. Three issues dominated that agenda: a greatly expanded commitment in Vietnam that had been the undoing of the Johnson administration; the creation of a new, pragmatic relationship with the Soviets, which had implications for many issues, for example, US–Soviet détente allowed the Nixon administration to create a linkage between missile defense and US–Soviet arms control negotiations, which eventually led to the first Strategic Arms Limitation Talks (SALT) agreement; and establishing relations with China, which was a hugely controversial initiative at the time.

That ambitious agenda, combined with Nixon's and Kissinger's suspicion of leaks and their need for control, led them to regularly cut out all other statutory NSC members from important policy deliberations. Kissinger certainly was not the honest broker that Bundy had initially been eight years earlier. Rather, Kissinger was a policy advocate of the first degree. He wound up running several important foreign policy initiatives for the president, including negotiations with the North Vietnamese, arms control with the Soviets, and most famously, the opening to China.[44] Despite early intentions of a highly structured process, the NSC system effectively boiled down to Kissinger and Nixon.

Jimmy Carter

President Carter came to office with the country still recovering from the abuses of the Nixon administration, including Watergate and the secret bombings in Southeast Asia. The national counterreaction to Nixon extended to Nixon's national security policy process in general and the role played by Kissinger in particular. In June 1975 the Commission on the Organization of the Government for the Conduct of Foreign Policy recommended that the NSC staff's role be greatly curtailed.[45] The Carter administration took those recommendations to heart in the design of its NSC system.

There were other reasons to change the Nixon system. President Carter wanted a more inclusive system with balanced input from his cabinet secretaries and himself at the center. This is explained in part by Carter's micromanager personality and in part by conflicts within the cabinet. Carter's NSA, Zbigniew Brzezinski, was an aggressive, opinionated policy advocate, "one of the most controversial national security advisors."[46] He and Secretary of State Cyrus Vance regularly disagreed on foreign policy toward China, Iran, and arms control negotiations, and these disagreements often spilled out into public view. Thus, Brzezinski was not considered an honest broker but was instead seen as someone trying to dominate the foreign policy decision-making process.

For all these reasons, Carter and Brzezinski greatly simplified the NSC system that they inherited from the Nixon administration. The NSC staff was cut in numbers from the mid-fifties down to the thirties. They dropped the junior and senior staff designations that had existed in Nixon's NSC staff.[47] The plethora of NSC committees were replaced by the Policy Review Committee, which reviewed security issues affecting individual agencies and the Special Coordination Committee, which reviewed issues that cut across several agencies.[48] This minimal structure was matched by a minimal use of formal NSC meetings, of which there were only ten during the entire administration.[49] Instead, the president preferred using so-called Friday breakfasts to discuss national security issues, supplemented by a huge number of informal meetings in 1979 on arms control, the Middle East, and eventually, the Iranian hostage crisis.[50] Policymaking was not as concentrated in the Carter White House as it had been in the Nixon administration, but decision authority had by no means devolved out to the cabinet secretaries.

Ronald Reagan

A huge volume of research discusses the personality and operating style of President Ronald Reagan.[51] President Reagan has been characterized as principled and visionary and as an unparalleled communicator, but also as distant, detached, and incurious about policy details. He is said to have wanted a collegial policy process with robust debate among his staff.[52] The administration certainly did not want a repeat of the Brzezinski–Vance feud from the Carter years and the widespread perceptions of disunity within the national security apparatus created by that feud. After all, that disunity and the policy vacillations it created were seen by the Reagan administration as a large reason for the Soviet invasion of Afghanistan and the taking of US hostages in Iran. That said, Reagan was not willing to side with one advisor over another in his own administration; he liked to split the difference when given conflicting recommendations.[53] He also rarely made the effort to become well versed on the details of an issue. He was famous for taking long vacations in California and for working short days when in Washington. The details of governing were left to a troika of White House advisors: Ed Meese, the counselor to the president; James Baker, the chief of staff; and Michael Deaver, deputy chief of staff. For foreign and security policy recommendations, President Reagan relied on the secretaries of state and defense and the director of central intelligence rather than on his NSA.

Reagan vested almost all foreign policy authority in the State Department, which greatly curtailed the power of the NSC staff and the NSA.[54] The administration cycled through six NSAs over two presidential terms. The choice of the first four was consistent with the expressed organizational priorities of the administration; each NSA lacked the experience or knowledge to be an equal to the secretaries of state or defense. In terms of process the first NSA, Richard Allen, was put under the authority of Ed Meese, and was given no direct access to the president.[55] The NSC staff was tasked with providing staff assistance to the cabinet rather than giving direct advice to the president.

The NSC structure reflected the decreased role of the NSC staff. The administration created four NSC committees: defense policy, intelligence, foreign policy, and crisis management.

Agency or department secretaries chaired each committee, with the vice president leading the Crisis Management Committee. There was no leadership role for the NSA or his designee. Sitting above these committees was the National Security Planning Group (NSPG), which contained the statutory and advisory members of the NSC as well as the aforementioned White House troika.[56] The difference between the NSPG and the NSC was that the NSC staff was not allowed to participate in or provide staff support for the NSPG, on the orders of Ed Meese. As a result, there were no minutes taken during meetings and no process existed to disseminate NSPG decisions out to relevant agencies.[57]

The Reagan NSC staff is perhaps best remembered for its genesis of the Iran-Contra scandal. A detailed treatment of the scandal is beyond the scope of this chapter, but a brief review of the policymaking environment in 1983–86 helps explain why the NSC staff was able to run an illegal covert operation.[58] Reagan's second NSA, William Clark, succeeded in regaining some of the authority enjoyed by other NSAs over the protests of Secretary of State Al Haig.[59] Yet in the latter half of 1982 Clark would be confronted with an emerging feud between newly appointed secretary of state George Shultz (who replaced Al Haig in July 1982) and Secretary of Defense Caspar Weinberger, a feud that Clark was powerless to prevent and that threatened to deadlock most major foreign policy and security initiatives. Clark's successor, Col. Robert "Bud" McFarlane, was too junior to break that deadlock, despite attempts to do so via informal "Family Group" lunches.[60] "The result was a virtual free-for-all, in which Shultz, Weinberger, [CIA Director William] Casey, and ultimately, the NSC sought to get to Reagan and sell him on their latest ideas. Getting the president's approval, and then quickly acting on it before opponents of the proposed policy could stop you, was how foreign policy was increasingly made in the mid-1980s."[61] The result was that relatively junior NSC staff members under the direction of McFarlane, and then Vice Adm. John Poindexter, Reagan's fourth NSA, could run a rogue operation seemingly unbeknownst to senior officials across the national security bureaucracy.

The Iran-Contra scandal led to a wholesale change in the Reagan administration's NSC structure and processes, a change that would be amplified during the George H. W. Bush administration. When Frank Carlucci replaced Poindexter as NSA, he reorganized the NSC structure to emphasize reporting requirements in a hierarchical chain of command.[62] He divided the NSC staff into eleven directorates, each led by a senior director. Each directorate had a staff, and each reported to Carlucci, who ran formal NSC meetings. The bitterness between Shultz and Weinberger did not end, but at least Carlucci forced each side to air its differences in a formal setting (and in informal meetings as well).[63] By all accounts the new system was a huge improvement.

George H. W. Bush

George H. W. Bush assumed the presidency under what was arguably the most hostile friendly takeover of any transition in history, despite Bush having served as Reagan's vice president. Bush was a foreign policy realist whereas Reagan had been an idealist. Bush was a pragmatic, traditional conservative whereas Reagan had been more ideologically extreme. Bush was engaged whereas Reagan had been somewhat detached.

Bush had witnessed firsthand the dysfunction of Reagan's NSC and the late attempts by Carlucci and Powell to bring order to that system. And a regularized, orderly process had advantages during a time that included the end of the Cold War, the reunification of Germany, the invasion of Panama, and the first Gulf War, to name just a few of the events during Bush's tenure. The president's experience certainly helped. When it came to foreign and security policy, President Bush was among the most experienced, prepared presidents ever to have served. He had been vice president for eight years and, before that, CIA director, ambassador to the UN, ambassador to China, and two-term member of Congress. He was very hands-on when it came to foreign policy. He is quoted as having said, "I wanted the foreign policy players to know that I was going to involve myself in many of the details of defense, international trade, and foreign affairs policies."[64] He also wanted an extremely collegial team working for him, perhaps in part as a reaction to the bitter divisions on the Reagan NSC. That translated into a White House–centered foreign policy apparatus, with cabinet members chosen who would not challenge the White House, or each other, for primacy.

Bush's NSA, Brent Scowcroft, shared many of the president's foreign policy views and the belief in a White House–centered NSC system. Scowcroft was a true expert when it came to the NSC, having risen to the rank of lieutenant general in the air force and served as a military assistant in the Nixon White House and then as Gerald Ford's NSA. He had been a principal author on the Tower Commission investigation of Iran-Contra. He saw the NSA role as that of a broker (i.e., similar to Bundy) rather than an advocate (à la Brzezinski or Kissinger) or an operator (à la Poindexter). He succeeded in a broker role by gaining the trust of his colleagues, establishing a cooperative NSC process, and maintaining a very close relationship to the president.[65] On the last point, "no other Bush adviser has had more influence on the agenda of American national security policy."[66]

Scowcroft added structure to the NSC system. He created a four-level NSC process. At the top was the formal NSC chaired by the president. Next was the Principals' Committee (PC), comprising the NSC members minus the president. Scowcroft chaired PC meetings. Under the PC was the Deputies' Committee (DC), with participants drawn from the deputy secretary level. The deputy NSA chaired the DC. Further down the hierarchy were a series of eight issue-specific policy coordinating committees (PCCs). Most policy decisions were made at the DC level after being drafted by the various PCCs. Only debates for which consensus could not be reached at the DC level made it to the PC. It was a rare issue that required a formal NSC meeting involving the president.

As elegant as this NSC structure was, the Bush administration developed two alternative informal venues with which to develop policy: the "Big Eight" (see table 2.2) and the "Inner Circle." They existed probably as a result of the shared worldviews and close interpersonal relationships among the main players in the Bush administration and the fast pace of events that confronted the administration in quick succession. In essence, there was no need for a large formal NSC meeting when the president could gather his closest advisors, who also happened to be close friends, and devise a policy initiative.

Bill Clinton

President Bill Clinton came to office having run on a platform of fixing the domestic economy; "It's the economy, stupid," was a campaign mantra. Clinton had virtually no foreign policy experience and an uncomfortable relationship with the uniform military. During the 1992 campaign he had been pilloried for his opposition to the Vietnam War, and his first weeks in office were marred by the controversy over his policy regarding gays in the military. On other issues he was an insatiable consumer of information and a true policy wonk, frequently holding debates late into the night or calling aides and colleagues in the wee hours of the morning to discuss ideas. His political instincts were legendary as were his character flaws. Finally, he was a politician at heart who believed that his personal charisma and persuasive abilities, combined with carefully calculated compromises, could always win the day. He saw political implications in any policy choice.[67]

Upon assuming office Clinton was confronted with a novel set of international challenges. The Cold War was over, peacefully, thanks in part to the Bush administration, but nothing had yet replaced it as a guiding principle to international affairs. Internal conflicts and humanitarian crises were cropping up worldwide. States were breaking apart. The United States was engaged in a humanitarian intervention in Somalia, even while the presidential transition was occurring, but had no overarching rationale for future interventions.

Clinton chose Anthony Lake as his first NSA. Lake was a surprising choice from some perspectives because he did not know Clinton well and believed that politics should be kept out of national security policy, which was the antithesis of the president's view.[68] But that said, Lake and Clinton believed the NSA should be a broker, not a policy advocate, similar to the role Scowcroft had played in the Bush administration. Lake also was well respected and without obvious ideological axes to grind. That fit with Clinton's desire for a collegial staff that would provide him with a diverse set of views.

The Clinton NSC kept the same basic structure of PCs and DCs that was used by the previous administration with changes at the margins. The Clinton team renamed and recast the PCCs as interagency working groups and created new transnational directorates at the NSC staff level on nonproliferation, environmental affairs, global issues, democracy and human rights, transnational threats, and international health, to supplement a series of traditional regional and functional directorates.[69] The NSC staff was expanded to almost double its previous size. Senior NSC staff members were treated as equals to their cabinet-level counterparts.

The administration made three more fundamental changes from the Bush model, two of which can be attributed to the increasingly fuzzy distinction between the domestic and international realms, and the ever-closer relationship between security and economic issues. First, Clinton created the National Economic Council, a coordinating entity similar to the NSC but focused on economic issues. Second, the administration expanded the NSC membership to include the treasury secretary, the president's economic advisor, the White House chief of staff, the UN ambassador, the NSA and his deputy, and the vice president's NSA. Third and finally, the vice president and his staff were given a much more active role in NSC deliberations during the Clinton administration than had existed in the past.[70] These changes meant that the Clinton NSC was larger and more diverse than was the case under Bush, and it was complemented by (or competing with) a parallel economic forum.

The question was how one could find consensus with the large number of participants in policy debates, the president's brainstorming style, and his desire for collegiality. The answer during the first term was that the NSC process was largely ignored in favor of smaller, ad hoc forums. The PC met infrequently. Unstructured foreign policy team meetings often replaced NSC meetings, where no one really drove the discussion and decisions were rarely reached.[71] The administration created several special envoys to deal with specific problems, from Russia to Northern Ireland to the Middle East and the Balkans, which left it unclear who was really making policy for the administration. On many issues, particularly with regard to Somalia, Haiti, and the Balkans, the administration appeared unable to settle on a course of action.

Lake's attitude slowly changed during the latter part of the first term as debate within the administration failed to produce cohesive policies. His role evolved from neutral broker to policy advocate, particularly on North Atlantic Treaty Organization (NATO) enlargement and intervention in Bosnia.[72] A more activist NSA role would continue on selective issues during the second term, when Sandy Berger would take over as NSA.

Samuel Berger was Clinton's first choice as NSA in 1992. At the time, Berger was Clinton's closest foreign policy aide (the two had known each other since 1972), a distinction he would retain throughout the eight years of the administration. Berger deferred to Lake in the first term, however, believing that the more experienced Lake should lead the NSC. Once Berger assumed the NSA duties in 1997, some believed he was "perhaps the most influential national security advisor since Henry A. Kissinger."[73] Berger had many of the same qualities attributed to Scowcroft: an excellent relationship with the secretaries of state (Madeleine Albright) and defense (Bill Cohen) based on trust, Berger's ability to get the job done, and Berger's belief that the policy process should be fair and transparent to those involved.[74]

Berger took a leadership role in the second term, particularly when President Clinton became consumed with impeachment proceedings. Berger developed the "ABC lunches," involving Berger and Secretaries Albright and Cohen, as an informal means of coordinating with State and Defense. He was well-known for frequently reaching out to both secretaries multiple times a day. He also used the PC more frequently than was done in the first term, and his combination of credibility, trustworthiness, and relationship with the president seemed to succeed, in that the PC was able to make decisions on Kosovo, arms control, the Middle East, and counterterrorism policy, the last of which would become the driving force for the subsequent administration.

George W. Bush

President George W. Bush, like Clinton before him, came to the presidency from a governor's mansion and had little experience with or knowledge of foreign and security policy. President Bush's style was similar to Reagan's. Both presidents believed in setting an agenda, making decisions, and leaving the implementation to cabinet officials. Bush showed little inclination toward mastering the details of policy or revisiting decisions once made. Before the attacks of 9/11, Bush appeared to be searching for an overarching theme for his administration's foreign policies. Balancing against China and deploying missile defenses were topics frequently raised by administration officials. More generally, the Bush administration separated itself from the Clinton era by abolishing many Clinton administration policies, a pattern that was colloquially known as ABC, standing for "Anyway But Clinton." The ABC mantra was applied to everything from counterterrorism to North Korea, the Middle East peace process, and stability operations.[75] The 9/11 attacks gave the administration its missing theme. Preventing future terrorist attacks on the US homeland became the guiding principle for the administration.[76]

Condoleezza Rice became the NSA in Bush's first term. Bush had turned to her to guide him on international politics during the presidential campaign.[77] She grew to be closer to the president than perhaps any other advisor in the history of the NSC and was frequently referred to as an adopted member of the Bush family. She had total access to the president and was consulted on virtually every aspect of the administration's foreign policy and security agenda.[78] Given that close relationship, it is no surprise that Rice saw the NSA's primary role as providing staff for the president and ensuring that his priorities were disseminated across the government; managing the national security process was a secondary function. In her words,

I consider it my first responsibility to be staff and counsel to the president, because he doesn't have anywhere else to go for that. The second most important responsibility is to make sure that when he wants to move an agenda in a particular direction that you can get this huge ship of state turned around and moved in the direction he wants to go. . . . The third most important function is to coordinate the rest of the government.[79]

The NSC's *structure* did not change fundamentally under Rice's leadership from what had existed during the Clinton administration. The Bush administration kept the same basic PC and DC structure originated by Scowcroft in the first Bush administration and used by Clinton. As with many other administrations, the Bush team initially cut the size of the NSC staff, only to increase staff levels over time. They did away with a number of Clinton-era policy directorates, mainly dealing with Europe, international health, the environment, and legislative and media affairs.[80] But all told, the NSC structure remained relatively unchanged from what had existed in the previous two administrations.

A more fundamental structural change was the creation of the Homeland Security Council (HSC) in late October 2001. Homeland Security Presidential Directive 1 (HSPD-1) established a council that "shall ensure coordination of all homeland security-related activities among executive departments and agencies and promote the effective development and implementation of all homeland security purposes."[81] The HSC was structured like the NSC, with a PC, a DC, and policy coordinating committees. The membership was quite different, however, emphasizing domestically focused agencies, such as Treasury, Health and Human Services, Transportation, the Federal Bureau of Investigation (FBI), the Federal Emergency Management Agency (FEMA), and so on. HSPD-1 empowered the assistant to the president for homeland security (colloquially known as the homeland security advisor, or HSA) to call HSC PC meetings, to craft meeting agendas, and to prepare background papers for those meetings. In an effort to ensure coordination on counterterrorism issues between the HSC and NSC, the NSA and the HSA would share these tasks.

Two changes in NSC's *processes* during Bush's first term represented more fundamental differences from the Clinton administration. The first was the central and unprecedented role played by the vice president. Vice President Cheney was specifically empowered to attend any and all meetings of the NSC or HSC principals', deputies', or policy coordinating committees.[82] The vice president had his own fifteen-person NSC staff, parallel to the president's NSC staff, which dwarfed the three-person staff of Vice President Al Gore. Numerous Bush administration officials noted that Cheney's staff had real power. According to NSA Rice, "The vice president's staff actually sits in on the deputies meetings . . . his groups of deputies sit in with Steve [Hadley]'s deputies, so they're very well integrated into our process."[83] Richard Haass, director of the State Department's policy planning staff during the first term, noted, "The vice president's office has become the equivalent of a separate institution or bureaucracy. . . . The vice president has his own mini-NSC staff."[84] Some critics argued that agencies even reported directly to the vice president's staff, often without informing the regular NSC staff.[85] If true, this would seem to undermine the central role played by the NSC staff under most previous administrations.

The second procedural change in the Bush administration's NSC system related to the Defense Department. According to observers both within and outside the administration, Defense Department officials, up to and including Secretary of Defense Donald Rumsfeld, repeatedly undermined the formal NSC process. Defense officials would refuse to provide advance copies of decision papers or status reports ahead of scheduled meetings or leave copies of reports for further examination. No one except Secretary Rumsfeld was empowered to speak for or commit the Defense Department at PC, DC, or PCC meetings. And finally, Defense officials repeatedly failed to attend scheduled meetings. For whatever reason, Secretary Rumsfeld ignored demands from the NSC staff in general and Rice in particular.[86] According to one senior administration official, "I have never seen more high-level insubordination in the U.S. government in almost thirty years than I have seen in this administration."[87] Indeed, Rice was not perceived or treated as an equal by the secretary of defense, to say nothing of Vice President Dick Cheney, despite her bond with President Bush.[88]

A representative example comes from the early stages of the Iraq conflict. L. Paul "Jerry" Bremer was chosen by the Pentagon to head the Coalition Provisional Authority (CPA) in Iraq. He reported directly to Secretary Rumsfeld and the president. Though Defense Department civilians apparently approved Bremer's decision to disband the Iraqi army and remove Ba'athists from the Iraqi government in the summer of 2003, neither the president nor the NSC staff was provided with advance notice or the chance to review these decisions.[89] Certainly the intelligence community, which had warned of the adverse consequences of such actions in a prewar estimate, was not consulted by Bremer on the aforementioned decisions.[90] More generally, Bremer believed that Rumsfeld and his aides repeatedly withheld CPA reports from the NSC staff.[91]

Critics argued that the Bush NSC process during the first term suffered as a result of these factors.[92] Formal NSC meetings became meaningless exercises on many issues, with cabinet officials reading talking points but not engaging each other in any real sense.[93] According to published reports, real decisions were made during informal gatherings in the White House, at Camp David, or at Bush's ranch in Crawford, Texas. The problem was that these informal meetings often excluded Secretary of State Powell and CIA Director George Tenet, which meant that there was inadequate coordination across agencies when it came to Afghanistan and Iraq policies.[94] Moreover, Rice did not ensure that the NSC staff produced the background materials or asked the tough questions (i.e., questioning assumptions, examining consequences, assessing risks, and comparing policy options) during either these informal gatherings or formal NSC meetings.[95] In short, Rice and the NSC staff did not appear to be managing the interagency process in any real sense.[96]

The NSC process appeared to work more smoothly during the Bush administration's second term. Part of this can be attributed to personnel changes. Rice replaced Powell as secretary of state in 2005, and Robert Gates replaced Rumsfeld as secretary of defense in late 2006. Rice and Gates brought in their own senior staff and the combination of new cabinet members and senior staff improved the dynamic across all levels of the NSC structure. But as important, Hadley took on a more traditional broker role common to many previous NSAs. The two best examples of that came when the NSC coordinated the surge in Iraq in the winter and spring of 2007 and the broad review of Afghanistan policy at the end of the administration's tenure. But by then the administration had already made many of its major decisions, such as whether to invade Iraq, how to conduct post-conflict operations in Iraq, and how to treat detainees captured in Afghanistan, Iraq, and elsewhere.

THE NSC IN THE OBAMA ADMINISTRATION

This chapter began by noting patterns of continuity across NSC systems, particularly a White House–centered system with relatively strong NSAs, robust NSC staffs, and the use of advisory groups outside the NSC system. Evidence suggests that the Obama administration has acted consistently with expectations regarding continuity and change in the NSC system.

Presidential Policy Directive 1 (PPD-1) made clear that President Obama, his NSA, and by extension, the NSC staff were at the heart of the administration's national security system.[97] PPD-1 set out a broad NSC membership on par with that of the Clinton administration and far broader than the membership of the recent Bush NSC. Yet it firmly situated authority at lower levels in the NSC system, with each level run by the NSC staff. Specifically, the NSC was organized around the PC–DC–subordinate committee structure used by every administration since the first Bush presidency. In the Obama NSC, however, the NSA chaired PC meetings, called those meetings, set their agenda, and ensured that the appropriate supporting materials were prepared in advance and that decisions were communicated in a timely manner. In theory, this gave the NSA a tremendous amount of power and influence. The deputy NSA chaired DC meetings. Below these were interagency policy committees (IPCs), chaired by the appropriate NSC staff member. The Obama administration subsequently did away with a separate HSC, folding those tasks into functional directorates within the NSC staff system. That move essentially gave the NSA control over both staffs, which, in James Jones's words, would "allow the president to make better decisions even more rapidly."[98] In sum, PPD-1 structured the NSC in such a way that the NSC staff had firm control over the timing, agenda, preparation for, and dissemination of NSC products. And that, by extension, gave the White House control over the security policy process.[99]

In addition, the administration demonstrated an early preference for using special envoys that cut across traditional agency and departmental divisions. As a rule, special envoys answer directly to the president in most cases, which to some extent weakens the power of cabinet secretaries and bolsters White House control over major policy initiatives. Vice President Biden played that role in Pakistan, Latin America, the Balkans, and Iraq. Obama named Richard Holbrooke as his envoy for Pakistan and Afghanistan. George Mitchell was the special envoy for the Middle East. Dennis Ross was the special envoy for Southwest Asia before he moved to the NSC staff. Retired air force general Scott Gration was the special envoy for Sudan. Carol Browner was the special envoy for global warming. By one count the administration created almost fifty special envoy positions between 2009 and 2015.[100] According to one press report on these moves from the administration's first year, "Obama's moves formalize what White House veterans have always known—the Cabinet is close to a president, [but] his White House team [is] closer and more influential."[101]

In terms of process we would expect the NSC process to reflect the personalities of both the president and the NSA, as well as their reactions to past events. There is ample evidence that suggests that President Obama's temperament and operating style has played an important role in NSC procedures and that his operating style changed during his tenure in office. Consider the president's operating style in the first two years of the administration.[102] Obama's responses to the financial crisis and his health care rollout were more pragmatic than they were ideological, reflecting a desire to get things done rather than to make a political point. He seemed methodical, as witnessed by his Senate career, his presidential campaigns, and the length of time it took to decide on the Afghanistan surge in late 2009.[103] The president based decisions on copious information, according to confidants, rather than going with his instincts.[104] He made this clear in a December 2008 news conference:

> I think that's how the best decisions are made. One of the dangers in a White House, based on my reading of history, is that you get wrapped up in groupthink and every-

body agrees with everything and there's no discussion and there are no dissenting views. So I'm going to be welcoming a vigorous debate inside the White House. But understand, I will be setting policy as president. I will be responsible for the vision that this team carries out, and I expect them to implement that vision once decisions are made.[105]

Retired marine general James Jones, Obama's first NSA, took a low-profile approach to his job, similar to Scowcroft's or Lake's early behavior.[106] He was said to have a pragmatic, collegial style, well suited for the broker role he saw as his job.[107] In his words,

I want to make sure the right people are at the table and that they're able to say what they want—so that nobody walks away angry that their views weren't heard. So far at the principals' level it has been very collegial. Collegiality allows me not to have to be so much in the forefront. . . . This is what suits the president's comfort level, so he can go around the table and speak to every member of the NSC.[108]

In a March 18, 2009, memo to national security agencies titled "The 21st Century Interagency Process," Jones detailed how the NSC process would work on his watch. The memo's content seemed aimed at reversing many of the perceived shortcomings of the George W. Bush administration's NSC process. In an implicit criticism of Bush-era decisions on Iraq, Jones noted that he would ensure that a variety of opinions were heard during NSC meetings to "avoid the emergence of a premature policy consensus." In an implied criticism of Cheney, Jones noted that the NSC process would be transparent: "agencies have a right to be aware and participate," with the NSC staff "communicating information appropriately and comprehensively." In what could be a reaction to the rift between Powell and Rumsfeld regarding Phase IV in Iraq, Jones instructed NSC cabinet members to leave their bureaucratic interests behind and focus on advancing the administration's overall goals. Finally, in what seemed a critique of Rumsfeld's disdain for the NSC process, Jones noted, "The process—and the President—are not well served by interagency meetings that are held on short notice and defined by inadequate preparations . . . [including] when papers are circulated for approval at the last minute, when agencies fail to send appropriate level representatives to meetings, and when those who attend meetings are routinely unable to advocate on behalf of their 'Principals' when a decision is needed." To ensure that these mistakes did not occur, Jones then set out a series of requirements, including regular meeting schedules, an agreed-upon agenda, discussion papers circulated at least forty-eight hours before meetings, clear agreement on what was decided at each meeting, and mandatory attendance by two representatives from each agency who can speak for their agency. In short, Jones reinstituted a structured process to NSC deliberations centered on the NSC staff, consistent with the historic pattern of centralizing national security decisions in the White House.

Tom Donilon replaced General Jones in October 2010, after it had become apparent that Jones no longer had the trust of the NSC staff or the ear of the president. Donilon was a longstanding confidant of President Obama who had served as the deputy NSA under Jones and had previously worked on the Obama campaign. In that sense Donilon's selection supports the idea that proximate forces—namely, that individual NSAs ultimately rise or fall on the basis of their relationship with the president they serve—help shape the national security process.

Donilon's tenure also supports the underlying trends identified earlier in this chapter. The Obama NSC represents a culmination of greater and greater White House control over national security policy, and indeed all administration policy.[109] One indicator of this was the huge amount of data gathered by the NSC staff. Donilon adopted an NSC process that saw tremendous growth in the number of PCs, DCs, and lower level meetings, a much larger NSC staff, and a commensurate increase in staff papers and reports. Some figures are instructive. Under Donilon, the NSC Principals' and Deputies' Committees met frequently, sometimes two or three times a day.[110] And these meetings were chaired by Donilon or his deputy, Denis McDonough, which gave the NSC staff the ability to set agendas, control debate, and summarize results. Arguably these meetings allowed for a thorough airing of views across the national security enterprise on issues from China to Syria, trade to terrorism. Too often, according to critics, they were dominated by NSC staff and failed to produce decisions.[111] Agency officials below the secretary level grew frustrated, not least because the preparation required for those meetings left senior agency officials and the NSC staff constantly scrambling, with little time to reflect on broader US strategy, do their actual jobs, or engage in long-term planning.[112] So while the NSC staff grew to between 200 and 400 people under Donilon (depending on counting rules), the staff was run ragged by the crush of never-ending meetings, according to press reports.[113]

This large quantity of information, fed to a large NSC staff, enabled a close-knit circle of senior White House advisors to make decisions, rather than rely on a consensus among cabinet officials. Some of this centralization could be attributed to President Obama's frustration with being given binary choices by the federal bureaucracy, as well as his own comfort level with making decisions about national security issues.[114] According to close advisors, "the president has been relying more heavily on his own instincts and feeling less impelled to seek accord among advisors."[115] Others have argued that part of this stems from Donilon acting as a policy advocate rather than an honest broker in the Scowcroft mode.[116] Regardless of the cause, the result has been highly centralized decision making on important national security issues, consistent with trends that started with the creation of the formal NSC process.

Consider four examples. The May 2011 Osama bin Laden raid was kept to a very close circle and ultimately authorized over the objections of Vice President Biden and Defense Secretary Robert Gates.[117] On the drawdown of troops in Afghanistan, announced in June 2011, the president went against the advice of Gen. David Petraeus and other senior administration officials. The president decided on airstrikes in Libya after rejecting options initially given to him by the military. He instead solicited advice from relatively junior NSC staff and from his then–UN ambassador Susan Rice.[118] Finally, President Obama refused to intervene militarily in Syria or provide the Syrian rebels with lethal assistance in 2011–13 despite the advice to do so by the cabinet officials that make up the formal NSC.[119]

Whether these decisions advanced or undermined US interests will remain the subject of fierce debate. What is clear, however, is that the manner in which these decisions were made reinforces our earlier suppositions regarding the evolution of national security decisions. Such decisions are increasingly focused on White House staff rather than formal NSC processes.

President Obama's final NSA, Ambassador Susan Rice, assumed her duties in July 2013. Evidence suggests that she continued working in the same manner as did Donilon, if with less public visibility. According to agency and department critics, she, like Donilon, led a small circle of White House advisors who held the real decision-making authority in the administration. Most important, she self-identified as the president's policy advocate rather than as a broker, even when she disagreed with the president, as was reportedly the case with regard to military intervention in Syria.[120] In her words, "It is a very important part of my job, particularly at this stage in the president's tenure, to . . . make sure that the things he cares about—

his legacy interests, issues, accomplishments—are nurtured and carried into the end zone. We are trying to put points on the board."[121]

During Rice's tenure, the Obama White House faced growing criticism for using the NSC staff to run foreign policy initiatives. Critics include former Obama administration officials, particularly from the Defense Department, such as former secretaries of defense Robert Gates, Leon Panetta, and Chuck Hagel and Michelle Flournoy, the former under secretary of defense for policy.[122] In response, the administration announced in mid-2015 that it would shrink the NSC staff by roughly 10 percent. In the words of then–NSC chief of staff Suzy George, "To ensure the NSC staff is a lean, nimble, and policy-oriented organization, we are reversing the trend of growth." The cuts were "designed to result in fewer, more focused meetings, less paper to produce and consume, and more communication that yields better policymaking."[123] By some accounts, the administration had exceeded its goal by the end of Obama's second term, having cut the NSC staff by approximately 15 percent as of September 2016.[124]

These efforts were too little, too late in the eyes of many members of Congress. As early as January 2016, Representative Mac Thornberry (R-TX), chairman of the House Armed Services Committee, threatened to include language in the annual National Defense Authorization Act to limit the NSC staff to fifty people. The version of the defense bill that passed the House that May included a clause to impose a hundred-person limit on NSC staff or make the NSA subject to Senate confirmation. The Senate version of the bill, as passed by the Senate Armed Services Committee, included a proposal to cap the staff at no more than 150 people in NSC staff policy positions.[125] As of this writing, it is unclear what will be the final disposition of this language, but there is the growing awareness that the NSC staff has grown too big and that responsibility for policy development should be given back to national security agencies.[126]

CONCLUSIONS

The previous discussion intentionally begs the question as to which NSC system worked best, in large part because so many definitions of "best" have been applied to the NSC. Some have argued that a good NSC system is one in which the NSA plays the role of the honest broker within a well-articulated process, as exemplified by the tenure of Brent Scowcroft. Others, including some presidents (Johnson comes to mind), believe the NSC staff should act as the president's advocate in policy debates. A variant of that logic is that a good NSC system is one in which the president gets the policies that he wants, regardless of whether or not policy was made via the formal NSC process. Still others think that international outcomes, and whether those outcomes advance US interests, best reflect the success or failure of an NSC system. In the end then, it may be impossible to know which NSC system works best because such an assessment relies on an inherently subjective judgment.

What is certain is that the NSC system has exhibited both continuity and change over time. Since the 1947 National Security Act created the NSC system, presidents have operated in an era of expanded US international commitments, a huge national security bureaucracy, and tremendous public expectations. Presidents have responded by turning to a combination of NSC staff support and special envoys. Both are under direct presidential control and are not beholden to federal agencies or the legislative branch. The formal NSC system has suffered as a result. NSC meetings have been replaced by alternate forums that often do not have adequate staff support or exclude key foreign policy players.

Continuity, however, does not extend to the particular structures or organizational precepts of the NSC system itself. Nor does it hold for the role of specific NSAs. Change on these fronts seems to depend on the personalities and desires of each president and NSA and on the international and domestic contexts in which they find themselves. Consider the role of the NSA. For whatever reason, that role has fluctuated in a predictable manner across administrations. Eisenhower did not empower his advisors. Kennedy gave McGeorge Bundy significant authority. Johnson consciously took power away from his two advisors. Nixon empowered Kissinger. Ford had a caretaker in Scowcroft. Carter gave Brzezinski significant authority and influence. Reagan and his White House advisors demoted the NSA position significantly for most of the administration. George H. W. Bush empowered Scowcroft. Clinton did not cede as much power to Lake, though Berger appeared to wield more power and influence in the second term. George W. Bush certainly valued Rice's counsel but did not empower her vis-à-vis his cabinet secretaries or the vice president. Obama put Jones at the center of the national security debates but replaced him with Tom Donilon and then Susan Rice, two longtime presidential confidants, suggesting that the NSA will maintain a central role in policy. It seems likely, however, that future NSC systems will exhibit a combination of continuity and change that their predecessors would easily recognize.

NOTES

1. For a summary of the evidence linking various NSC decision processes and foreign policy behavior, see John Burke, "The Neutral/Honest Broker Role in Foreign Policy Decision Making: A Reassessment," *Presidential Studies Quarterly* 35, no. 2 (June 2005): 229–59.

2. See Pub. L. No. 80–235 and Pub. L. No. 81–216, respectively.

3. For recent NSC staff numbers, see Walter Pincus, "Daily Intelligence Briefings Yield Clues to a President's Approach on Foreign Policy," *Washington Post*, January 17, 2012, A11, which puts President Obama's NSC staff at around 200; and David Rothkopf, "Donilon's Legacy," *Foreign Policy*, June 5, 2013, which claims that the staff has grown to almost 400 people.

4. The main differences between the Eisenhower and Kennedy NSC structures included changes from an administrative to a policy formulation role; from a core of nonpartisan, professional staff to a set of political appointees; and from an NSA with subcabinet status to one with the equivalent of cabinet rank. See Andrew Preston, "The Little State Department: McGeorge Bundy and the National Security Council Staff, 1961–65," *Presidential Studies Quarterly* 31, no. 4 (December 2001): 635–60.

5. Amy Zegart, *Flawed by Design: The Evolution of the CIA, JCS, and NSC* (Stanford, CA: Stanford University Press, 1999), 85–87.

6. Ibid., 89.

7. One well-known exception is Richard Clarke, who served as a counterterrorism expert on the NSC staff throughout the Clinton administration and into the George W. Bush presidency.

8. Terry Moe, "The Politicized Presidency," in *The New Direction in American Politics*, ed. John Chubb and Paul Peterson (Washington, DC: Brookings Institution, 1985), 235–46.

9. Bert Rockman, "America's 'Departments' of State: Irregular and Regular Syndromes of Policy Making," *American Political Science Review* 75, no. 4 (December 1981): 911–27.

10. The exception was Richard Allen, Ronald Reagan's first NSA.

11. Stephen Hess, "Franklin Roosevelt: 1933–1945," in *Organizing the Presidency*, 2nd ed., ed. Stephen Hess (Washington, DC: Brookings Institution, 1988), 23–39.

12. Ferdinand Eberstadt, "Postwar Organization for National Security," in *Fateful Decisions: Inside the National Security Council*, ed. Karl Inderfurth and Loch Johnson (New York: Oxford University Press, 2004), 17–20.

13. For staff totals and trends, see Ivo Daalder and I. M. Destler, "Policy Brief No. 68: A NSC for a New Administration" (Washington, DC: Brookings Institution, November 2000).

14. See Ivo Daalder and I. M. Destler, *In the Shadow of the Oval Office* (New York: Simon & Schuster, 2009).

15. The exception was Kennedy's ExComm, which had as many as nine cabinet members in attendance, plus roughly a dozen other advisors as necessary. See Graham Allison and Phillip Zelikow, *Essence of Decision*, 2nd ed. (Reading, MA: Prentice Hall, 1999).

16. For a discussion of the Tuesday lunches, see John Prados, *Keeper of the Keys* (New York: William Morrow, 1991), 149–51. For Lyndon Johnson's operating style, see Chris Matthews, *Hardball* (New York: Free Press, 1999), 19, 25–34.

17. Burke, "Neutral/Honest Broker Role," 239.

18. Cecil Crabb and Kevin Mulcahy, "The Lessons of the Iran-Contra Affair for National Security Policy Making," in Inderfurth and Johnson, *Fateful Decisions*, 162–72.

19. Daalder and Destler, *In the Shadow of the Oval Office*; Matthew Shabat, *PNSR Chronology of National Security Structures*, Working Draft #10 (Washington, DC: Project on National Security Reform, July 23, 2007); Inderfurth and Johnson, *Fateful Decisions*; David Rothkopf, *Running the World* (New York: Public Affairs, 2004); Richard Best, *National Security Council: An Organizational Assessment* (New York: Novinka Press, 2001); Christopher Shoemaker, *The NSC Staff: Counseling the Council* (Boulder, CO: Westview Press, 1991); and Prados, *Keeper of the Keys*.

20. Cutler, "Development of the National Security Council," 442.

21. Quoted in Ivo Daalder and I. M. Destler, "The Role of the National Security Advisor" (Washington, DC: Brookings Institution, October 25, 1999), 52. For similar thoughts, see Colin Powell, "The NSC Advisor," *The Bureaucrat* (Summer 1989), reprinted in Inderfurth and Johnson, *Fateful Decisions*, 158–61.

22. This review does not include the relatively brief and largely caretaker Ford administration. President Ford essentially continued many of the Nixon administration's structures and procedures in place. For instance, Ford kept Henry Kissinger as NSA for the administration's first year, replacing him with Brent Scowcroft during the administration's final year. In addition to the following specific citations, this review draws extensively from Rothkopf, *Running the World*.

23. Rothkopf, *Running the World*, 65–72.

24. Cutler, "Development of the National Security Council," 442.

25. Ibid., 443.

26. Best, *National Security Council*, 55–57. For a discussion of this process, with particular emphasis on the role of the NSC Planning Board, see Andrew Krepinevich and Barry Watts, "Lost at the NSC," *National Interest*, January 6, 2009, www.nationalinterest.org/Article.aspx?id520498 (accessed on January 7, 2009).

27. Best, *National Security Council*, 57. For an organizational chart of the Eisenhower NSC staff structure, see Inderfurth and Johnson, *Fateful Decisions*, 30.

28. Preston, "Little State Department."

29. Henry Kissinger, "What Vietnam Teaches Us," *Newsweek*, November 3, 2008, 44.

30. Kai Bird, "McGeorge Bundy," in Inderfurth and Johnson, *Fateful Decisions*, 185.

31. Ibid., 186.

32. See Shabat, *PNSR Chronology of National Security Structures*, 15.

33. Preston, "Little State Department."

34. Quoted in Daalder and Destler, *In the Shadow of the Oval Office*, 33.

35. Best, *National Security Council*, 60–61.

36. Kevin Mulcahy, "Walt Rostow as National Security Advisor, 1966–1969," *Presidential Studies Quarterly* 25, no. 2 (Spring 1995): 223–36.

37. Ibid.

38. Best, *National Security Council*, 64.

39. Larry Berman, *Planning a Tragedy: The Americanization of the War in Vietnam* (New York: W. W. Norton, 1983).

40. For an organizational chart of the Nixon NSC staff structure, see Inderfurth and Johnson, *Fateful Decisions*, 69. See also Best, *National Security Council*, 19.

41. For a selection, see Robert Dallek, *Nixon and Kissinger: Partners in Power* (New York: Harper, 2007); Gary Wills, *Nixon Agonistes* (Boston: Houghton Mifflin, 2002); and Stephen Ambrose, *Nixon*, vol. 2, *The Triumph of a Politician* (New York: Simon & Schuster, 1989).

42. Daalder and Destler, *In the Shadow of the Oval Office*, 61, 69.

43. For a profile, see Marvin Kalb and Bernard Kalb, *Kissinger* (Boston: Little, Brown, 1974).

44. Daalder and Destler, *In the Shadow of the Oval Office*, 63, 92.

45. Shabat, *PNSR Chronology of National Security Structures*, 18.

46. Daalder and Destler, *In the Shadow of the Oval Office*, 94.

47. Dom Bonafede, "Zbigniew Brzezinski," in Inderfurth and Johnson, *Fateful Decisions*, 197.

48. For an organizational chart of the Carter NSC staff structure, see Inderfurth and Johnson, *Fateful Decisions*, 72. See also Best, *The National Security Council*, 23–24. For a discussion of the NSC staff's daily operations, see Bonafede, "Zbigniew Brzezinski," 200–202.

49. Best, *National Security Council*, 70.

50. Daalder and Destler, *In the Shadow of the Oval Office*, 119.

51. Some of the more well-known Reagan biographies include James Mann, *The Rebellion of Ronald Reagan: A History of the End of the Cold War* (New York: Viking, 2009); Haynes Johnson, *Sleepwalking through History: America in the Reagan Years* (New York: W. W. Norton, 2003); Peggy Noonan, *When Character Was King: A Story of Ronald Reagan* (New York: Penguin, 2002); and Lou Cannon, *President Reagan: The Role of a Lifetime* (New York: Public Affairs, 2000).

52. Daalder and Destler, *In the Shadow of the Oval Office*, 129, 137.

53. Ibid., 152.

54. Shabat, *PNSR Chronology of National Security Structures*, 21.

55. Daalder and Destler, *In the Shadow of the Oval Office*, 133, 146, 161; Best, *National Security Council*, 73.

56. Best, *National Security Council*, 73–74.

57. Daalder and Destler, *In the Shadow of the Oval Office*, 140.

58. The Tower Commission is the authoritative source on the scandal. See *Report of the President's Special Review Board* (Washington, DC: Government Printing Office, February 27, 1987).

59. Prados, *Keeper of the Keys*, 469, quotes Clark as having said to Haig in mid-June 1982, "You've won a lot of battles in this administration, Al, but you'd better understand that from now on it's going to be the *President's* foreign policy."

60. Prados, *Keeper of the Keys*, 482, 491.

61. Daalder and Destler, *In the Shadow of the Oval Office*, 154. See also Prados, *Keeper of the Keys*, 481.

62. For background on Carlucci, see Prados, *Keeper of the Keys*, 538–40.

63. See Frank Carlucci's comments at the "Forum on the Role of National Security Advisor, April 21, 2001," reprinted in Inderfurth and Johnson, *Fateful Decisions*, 145. Colin Powell did not have to deal with that rivalry when he became Reagan's sixth and last NSA, as Carlucci had replaced Weinberger at the Department of Defense.

64. Daalder and Destler, *In the Shadow of the Oval Office*, 172.

65. Ibid., 180. See also David Lauter, "The Man behind the President," *Los Angeles Times*, October 14, 1990, reprinted in Inderfurth and Johnson, *Fateful Decisions*, 203–7.

66. Lauter, "The Man Behind the President," 203.

67. Joe Klein, *The Natural: The Misunderstood Presidency of Bill Clinton* (New York: Doubleday, 2003); also Sidney Blumenthal, *The Clinton Wars* (New York: Farrar, Straus and Giroux, 2003); and David Gergen, *Eyewitness to Power* (New York: Simon & Schuster, 2000), 249–342.

68. Daalder and Destler, *In the Shadow of the Oval Office*, 235.

69. For an organizational chart of the Clinton NSC staff structure, see Inderfurth and Johnson, *Fateful Decisions*, 103.

70. Best, *National Security Council*, 78.

71. Daalder and Destler, *In the Shadow of the Oval Office*, 216, 227–29.

72. On NATO enlargement, see James M. Goldgeier, *Not Whether but When: The U.S. Decision to Enlarge NATO* (Washington, DC: Brookings Institution, 1999). On Lake's role in the Balkans, see David Auerswald, *Disarmed Democracies* (Ann Arbor, MI: University of Michigan Press, 2000).

73. R. W. Apple, "A Domestic Sort with Global Worries," *New York Times*, August 25, 1999, reprinted in Inderfurth and Johnson, *Fateful Decisions*, 208–12.

74. Ibid. Berger's perceptions of the role of the NSA are reprinted in "Forum on the Role of National Security Advisor, April 21, 2001," reprinted in Inderfurth and Johnson, *Fateful Decisions*, 141–57.

75. Rothkopf, *Running the World*, 403–4.

76. For reviews of the administration's mindsets immediately after the 9/11 attacks, see Bob Woodward, *Bush at War* (New York: Simon and Schuster, 2002); and Ron Suskind, *The One Percent Doctrine* (New York: Simon and Schuster, 2006).

77. For a profile, see Elaine Sciolino, "Compulsion to Achieve—Condoleezza Rice," *New York Times*, December 18, 2000, reprinted in Inderfurth and Johnson, *Fateful Decisions,* 213–15; also Rothkopf, *Running the World*, 394–95.

78. Rothkopf, *Running the World*, 393.

79. Quoted in Rothkopf, *Running the World*, 405. See also Daalder and Destler, *In the Shadow of the Oval Office*, 257, 260. Critics argued that she accomplished the first task but not the others, for reasons discussed later.

80. Rothkopf, *Running the World*, 405; and Daalder and Destler, *In the Shadow of the Oval Office*, 260.

81. For the text of HSPD-1, see www.fas.org/irp/offdocs/nspd/hspd-1.htm.

82. HSPD-1, for instance, ends with an assertion of vice presidential power: "The Vice President may attend any and all meetings of any entity established by or under this directive."

83. Quoted in Rothkopf, *Running the World*, 421.

84. Ibid., 407.

85. Daalder and Destler, *In the Shadow of the Oval Office*, 275.

86. See Rothkopf, *Running the World*, 418–19, for numerous examples.

87. Quoted in Rothkopf, *Running the World*, 414. See also Daalder and Destler, *In the Shadow of the Oval Office*, 273.

88. Daalder and Destler, *In the Shadow of the Oval Office*, 257, 273, 275, 281. Rothkopf, *Running the World*, 407, quotes a member of the DC making these exact arguments.

89. Bob Woodward, *State of Denial* (New York: Simon & Schuster, 2006), 197.

90. See Senate Select Committee on Intelligence, *S. Report 110–76: Report on Prewar Intelligence Assessments about Postwar Iraq* (Washington, DC: Government Printing Office, May 31, 2007).

91. Woodward, *State of Denial*, 236.

92. Numerous examples can be found in Rothkopf, *Running the World*, 406.

93. Woodward, *State of Denial*, 241.

94. Ibid., 230; Rothkopf, *Running the World*, 408; and Daalder and Destler, *In the Shadow of the Oval Office*, 277.

95. John Burke, "The Contemporary Presidency: Condoleezza Rice as NSC Advisor," *Presidential Studies Quarterly* 35, no. 3 (September 2005): 554–74; also Woodward, *State of Denial*, 241.

96. Glenn Kessler and Thomas Ricks, "Rice's Tenure Complicates New Post: Failure to Manage Agency Infighting Cited," *Washington Post*, November 16, 2004.

97. PPD-1 was signed on February 13, 2009.

98. Quoted in Helene Cooper, "In Security Shuffle, White House Merges Staffs," *New York Times*, May 26, 2009, A13.

99. Laura Rozen, "Obama's NSC Takes Power," *The Cable*, March 3, 2009, http://thecable.foreign policy.com/posts/2009/03/03/jones_s_nsc_moves_to_assert_greater_control_over_interagency_process.

100. American Foreign Service Association, "Special Envoys, Representatives and Coordinators," March 31, 2015, www.afsa.org/AboutAFSA/AFSAStatementonAmbassadors/SpecialEnvoysRepresen tativesandCoordinators.aspx.

101. Jonathan Martin, "West Wing on Steroids in Obama W.H.," *Politico*, January 25, 2009.

102. Fred Greenstein, "The Leadership Style of Barack Obama: An Early Assessment," *The Forum* 7, no. 1 (2009), article 6; and James Fallows, "Obama Explained," *Atlantic Monthly* 309, no. 2 (March 2012): 54–70.

103. In late 2009 President Obama took months to make a decision on US policy toward Afghanistan. See Joel Achenbach, "In His Slow Decision-Making, Obama Goes with His Head, Not Gut," *Washington Post*, November 25, 2009, A1.

104. Anne Kornblut and Michael Fetcher, "The Seeker as Problem-Solver," *Washington Post*, January 25, 2010, A1.

105. Quoted in Greenstein, "Leadership Style of Barack Obama," 8.

106. See Karen DeYoung, "In Frenetic White House, A Low Key 'Outsider,'" *Washington Post*, May 7, 2009; and Helene Cooper, "National Security Adviser Tries Quieter Approach," *New York Times*, May 7, 2009.

107. Secretary of Defense Robert Gates called Jones an "honest broker," noting, "I can trust Jim to represent my views on an issue to the president. . . . He is a facilitator, not an obstacle, and that hasn't always been true in that job." See David Ignatius, "Jim Jones's Team," *Washington Post*, June 7, 2009, A17.

108. David Ignatius, "National Security Facilitator," *Washington Post*, April 30, 2009.

109. Glenn Thrush, "Locked in the Cabinet," *Politico*, November 2013, www.politico.com/magazine/story/2013/11/locked-in-the-cabinet-99374.html.

110. This continued a trend begun by Donilon when he served as deputy NSA and chaired the DC. The DC sometimes met two or more times a day under Donilon. See James Mann, "Obama's Gray Man," *Foreign Policy*, May 28, 2013; and Rothkopf, "Donilon's Legacy."

111. For one take on this perspective, see David Rothkopf, "Managing the Oval Office," *New York Times*, January 20, 2013.

112. Background interviews with several senior Obama administration officials, 2013 and 2014. See also Mann, "Obama's Gray Man."

113. Defenders of the administration say that the tremendous growth in the Obama NSC comes from merging the NSC and Homeland Security Council, the addition of digital media staff, and growth in the number of personnel dealing with the Middle East. See Karen DeYoung, "White House Tries for a Leaner National Security Council," *Washington Post*, June 22, 2015, www.washingtonpost.com/world/national-security/white-house-tries-for-a-leaner-national-security-council/2015/06/22/22ef7e52-1909-11e5-93b7-5eddc056ad8a_story.html.

114. For President Obama's own words on this front, see Michael Lewis, "Obama's Way," *Vanity Fair*, October 2012.

115. Christi Parsons, "Obama Turns to His Instincts," *Los Angeles Times*, June 27, 2011, A1.

116. James Pfiffner, "Decision Making in the Obama White House," *Presidential Studies Quarterly* 41, no. 2 (June 2011): 244–62; see also Mann, "Obama's Gray Man."

117. See Mark Bowden, *The Finish: The Killing of Osama bin Laden* (New York: Atlantic Monthly Press, 2012); and Peter Bergen, *Manhunt* (New York: Broadway Books, 2013).

118. Lewis, "Obama's Way."

119. Dexter Filkins, "The Thin Red Line," *New Yorker*, May 13, 2013.

120. Administration critics, key among them David Rothkopf, also see her as the president's policy advocate. See Jeffrey Goldberg, "A Withering Critique of Obama's National Security Council," *Atlantic Monthly*, November 12, 2014. Rice was reportedly in favor of a military response to the Syrian crisis, but her views had not changed the president's overall policy direction through 2014. See Julie Pace, "Susan Rice Remains a Powerful Force as National Security Advisor," *Christian Science Monitor*, June 1, 2014.

121. Quoted in Pace, "Susan Rice Remains a Powerful Force."

122. Gordon Lubold, "White House's National Security Council Criticized as Bloated, Unfocused," *Washington Wire* (blog), March 24, 2016, http://blogs.wsj.com/washwire/2016/03/24/white-houses-national-security-council-criticized-as-bloated-unfocused/.

123. DeYoung, "Leaner National Security Council."

124. Jamie McIntyre, "House Republicans Push to Shrink Size of National Security Council," *Washington Examiner*, September 8, 2016, www.washingtonexaminer.com/house-republicans-push-to-shrink-size-of-national-security-council/article/2601281.

125. John Bennett, "Fight Looms over Size of White House National Security Staff," *Roll Call*, April 26, 2016, www.rollcall.com/news/policy/fight-looms-size-white-house-national-security-staff-2; Russell Berman, "Republicans Try to Rein in the National Security Council," *Atlantic Monthly*, May 20, 2016, www.theatlantic.com/politics/archive/2016/05/republicans-try-to-shrink-the-national-security-council/483596/; and US Senate Committee on Armed Services, "Senate Armed Services Committee Completes Markup of National Defense Authorization Act for Fiscal Year 2017," press release, May 12, 2016, www.armed-services.senate.gov/press-releases/senate-armed-services-committee-completes-markup-of-national-defense-authorization-act-for-fiscal-year-2017.

126. For an example, see Michael Goldfien, "How the NWC Hijacked U.S. Foreign Policy," *National Interest*, March 20, 2016, http://nationalinterest.org/feature/how-the-nsc-hijacked-us-foreign-policy-15625.

CHAPTER 3

The Office of Management and Budget

The President's Policy Tool

Gordon Adams, Rodney Bent, and Kathleen Peroff

> OMB is unexplainable to everyone who lives outside the Beltway and misunderstood by nearly everyone who lives inside the Beltway.
> —Paul O'Neill, former treasury secretary
> and former deputy director, OMB

In the federal government, as in real life, budgets are policy. In the area of national security, as with the federal budget as a whole, it is the president's annual budget request to Congress that is the opening stage of negotiations over resource levels to support policies.[1] Although presidents have had different preferences about the level of their involvement in budget planning, the preparation of the annual budget request is a responsibility they cannot ignore. This provides the president with the key opportunity to lay out a policy agenda and define his plans for implementing it in the executive branch. In the national security area, moreover, the executive must not only plan budgets for policy initiatives and priorities but also search for the flexibility he needs to react to events the administration does not fully control: humanitarian crises, international conflicts, terrorist attacks—all of which have resource implications. The national security agenda is rich and complex, and as a result, policy and budget planning are a year-round responsibility for the executive office of the president (EOP), with both routine and unforeseen elements.

The Office of Management and Budget (OMB) is at the heart of the EOP budgeting and resource planning process.[2] OMB is the central White House institution in executive branch budgeting and management decisions, for presidential approval of agency plans and programs, and for handling the relationship between the executive branch and Congress with respect to budgets and management.[3] It plays a key role in setting and implementing any administration's budgetary, management, legislative, and policy agenda. It serves as a technical and programmatic memory bank, handles implementation oversight for the White House, and is a "funnel" through which all executive branch operations and proposals move from the White House to Congress.[4]

OMB manages the executive branch budget process, integrates agency budgets, develops the budget dimensions of White House policy actions, adjudicates resource disputes between agencies and coordinates resource planning among the agencies, carries out oversight of agency budgeting and management, reviews all departmental regulations, approves all legislative proposals from the executive branch to Congress, and draws up the administration's most authoritative views on pending congressional legislation. With a staff of about 470, OMB is the largest permanent civil service organization for the EOP. The staff has detailed knowledge of executive branch operations, budgeting, and management that a president needs to shape and implement policy, ensure that resources support that policy, and control, to the extent possible, executive branch operations.

Created in the Budget and Accounting Act of 1921 as the Bureau of the Budget (BOB) in the Treasury Department, OMB has seen steady growth in its role as the budgeting process has become more complicated and as the federal budget itself has become a much larger element of the US economy. OMB's capabilities gradually grew, especially during the Roosevelt administration. Expanding budgets and the growing importance of federal spending in the Depression led to a decision to bring BOB directly under the president in 1939.[5] After World War II, BOB's responsibilities both for budget and management processes expanded further. Recognizing BOB's growing role in federal government management issues, the Nixon administration reorganized it in 1970 as the Office of Management and Budget and gave the restructured organization responsibility for administering the budget process, enforcing presidential priorities in that process, providing budgetary and management guidance to the agencies, and advocating for the budget after it was sent to Congress.

OMB's knowledge of the executive branch and congressional processes and its analytical capability are critical to a president. Each chief executive develops policies and initiatives he or she wants to implement. OMB plays a key role in shaping these initiatives, ensuring they are included in agency budgets, and overseeing their implementation once the funds have been provided by Congress. The strength of the organization lies in the permanence and capabilities of its civil service staff and its reputation as an impartial, neutral advisor, focusing on program knowledge and obtaining data to the extent available about program costs and outcomes. OMB is known for giving the best advice it can, regardless of the political stripe of the administration. The staff is renowned for its expertise on agency programs and operations and its willingness to provide unvarnished advice to the president.[6]

Over time, however, as OMB's functions have expanded to include shaping program, congressional, and public advocacy, these more politicized roles have conflicted with the agency's neutral and more technical image.[7] In the earlier budget deficit reduction debate, from 1981 through 2002, doubt was cast on OMB's economic and budgetary projections, which were described as a "rosy scenario," or "cooking the books."[8] As an entity within the EOP, OMB will often be criticized by members of Congress from the opposite party and other outsiders who assert that its work responds to the wishes of the party in power. Historically, however, the OMB staff has been and continues to be sensitive to this issue and to work hard to maintain analytic and professional neutrality. That culture, and the respect the president's political staff accord to that culture, has been critical to the long-term success of the institution in its service to different presidents.

OMB's budget and planning role has become even more complex in the post–Cold War era, as US national security policies, programs, and commitments have expanded to cover a widening agenda of global and regional issues. This expansion of the scope of national security is accompanied by an increasing amount of interagency activity at the White House level, activity that requires OMB involvement in the processes of other White House offices, particularly the National Security Council (NSC). Both NSC and OMB play growing roles in coordinating the interagency process for dealing with issues and programs that cut across agency lines.

OMB CULTURE: THE BUCK STOPS HERE

While OMB is essential to presidential authority over policy and resources, its role is not always well understood by other agencies, Congress, or the public. Inside any administration, staff and policymakers in other non–White House departments and agencies tend to feel ambivalent about OMB's central role and mission. Many agency staff would prefer not to have to deal with OMB, or do so warily, while others find OMB an instrumental partner as they seek to define programs and budgets and get presidential attention for their priorities. Outsiders in the media, the public, and even Congress do not understand OMB's role and wonder why the agency has a reputation for having such power.

And yet, as one former associate director of OMB put it, when senior OMB policy officials reflect on their work, they find, "You sit at the pure epicenter of policy. You're in a position to make a difference. And eventually, everything will come across your desk."[9] The centrality of OMB to executive branch decision making and the speed with which it must work for the White House, combined with a strong and very private professional ethos, shape the organizational culture of what is known as the president's budget office. Bluntly put, OMB is unique. Its organizational culture can be summed up as flat, swift, hardworking, loyal, trustworthy, professional, skeptical, and insular.

First, the organization has a very flat institutional structure and culture. With its wide array of responsibilities and only 470 employees (as of FY 2014), including a thinner layer of policy officials appointed by the president than many federal departments, the OMB culture cannot afford to stand on ceremony or spend lengthy amounts of time waiting for decisions to be processed through a hierarchy. When information, a briefing table, an options paper, or the budget cost ("pricing") of a presidential initiative is needed, there are only a few formal processes for working down into the organization for a response. The director and associate directors at the top can quickly reach to the examiner level for the answers. Typically, deputy associate directors (DADs), the senior level for career staff, will call branch chiefs and examiners together in a conference room for a quick review of papers, requests, or options, reaching a conclusion on the spot. Associate directors will frequently participate in these meetings, speeding the decision process. OMB directors' operating styles have varied, but in general they like to hear from the most knowledgeable person in the organization, no matter his or her rank. For example, when the director needs a brief on a particular topic, it can happen that an OMB budget examiner, management specialist, or regulatory analyst will participate in the meeting, as he or she may know more than policy officials about the substantive or technical aspects of the issue at hand. OMB career staffers sometimes worry about not being included in such meetings, as they bring history and expertise other participants sometimes lack; however, the practice of including OMB staffers in policy meetings can vary from administration to administration.

Second, the organization prides itself on its rapid responses to requests from White House policy officials. While staffers occasionally worry that short deadlines are sometimes more fictional than real, they are prepared to respond to requests within the same day given the intensity being felt in the White House (or federal agency) on a certain sensitive issue. A table on budget options for the defense "top-line" spending level may be needed in twenty-four hours. Analytical papers on options for defense procurement reform will be done in a matter of a few days. A detailed review, known in OMB terms as a "scrub," of a State Department emergency supplemental budget submission may take a day or two. An entire 200-page briefing book for an incoming policy official may even be ready ahead of time or produced virtually overnight.

OMB staffers are called on to price out policy options developed by the NSC, often when there is a national security crisis, such the bombing of an American embassy, an outbreak of Ebola, a tsunami, or renewed fighting in the Middle East, and decision-focused meetings that require OMB staff input have been scheduled quickly. OMB's input is particularly critical on cross-cutting issues that affect several agencies. It is the key organization in the executive branch of government that can pull together cross-cutting budget and cost information and analysis, working closely with relevant NSC and National Security Agency (NSA) staff. The disadvantage of this "quick-turnaround" culture, however, is that OMB staffers have a hard time doing longer-term, strategically driven analytical work.

Third, because OMB is small and expected to respond swiftly, the organizational culture is one of hard work. Although officials throughout the government are generally prepared to work hard, OMB's responsibilities mean little regard for weekends off or vacations for the staffers. Because the White House is a 24–7 operation, historically OMB has worked to the same calendar, though this culture has relaxed somewhat in recent years.

As this discussion suggests, OMB staff members also are extremely loyal, in the most professional sense of the term: they are committed to support the office of the presidency, regardless of the party of the incumbent. In the OMB case, this loyalty has particular features. Staffers are loyal to the organization and know they share in a high-intensity, high-demand work experience that is unusual in government. In addition, they are loyal to every president, his or her policies, preferences, and priorities. This has particular meaning, for presidents come and go but the presidency, EOP, and OMB are permanent. New presidents and their direct staffs sometimes come into office skeptical about OMB because it is a bureaucracy that served the previous administration well. There is often some initial doubt that the organization will be loyal to the policy priorities of the incoming chief executive team and be flexible enough to help carry them out.

It sometimes takes a year or more for those doubts to recede. Regardless of individual party registration of any given OMB staff member, the staff is willing to work with the policy priorities of any administration. The staff prides itself on this sense of loyalty, and it soon comes to be valued by a new White House. For example, when Vice President Al Gore came into office, he created an entirely separate vice presidential office, the National Performance Review (NPR), to carry out his responsibilities for reforming government management (the Reinvention in Government initiative). Initially, the vice president and the NPR staff were skeptical of the OMB commitment to such reform and saw the budget office as needing its own reform. After a year in office, however, the NPR office realized that OMB, through its budget and management knowledge and authorities, had the leverage to actually help implement NPR policies and goals, an authority that the Office of the Vice President lacked. OMB and NPR swiftly became partners in the NPR effort, overcoming the initial skepticism.

Overall, administration after administration has discovered the value of OMB as the most effective, flexible, loyal, and neutrally competent instrument the president has to shape policies, massage the budget to carry them out, and monitor the outcomes in the federal agencies. As one former associate director put it, "They are the only people I've ever met who work equally diligently on behalf of Democrats and Republicans." The OMB staff simply does not have a partisan agenda.

Working to execute the president's priorities, the OMB culture puts a priority on trust-worthiness. There is, perhaps, no more discreet institution in the White House or in the entire executive branch. Although various NSCs have been known to leak or be tight with information, there is no such variation with OMB. There is very little history of a porous OMB. The staff is known for its ability to hold information close. Being discreet is a key element of OMB training for new staff, one that is repeated over the years. Reporters repeat-edly express frustration at their inability to obtain access to key policy and budget details being developed at OMB. When budget details are sometimes revealed ahead of official release times, it is generally the result of a policy decision at the most senior level in the White House to obtain early or favorable coverage of their policies, not the result of a "leak" at lower levels in the organization. In the rare instance when an unauthorized disclo-sure has happened, the senior career and political leadership has taken appropriate actions to reprimand the offender.

In general, OMB staffers, particularly in the National Security Programs office, are party to a wide range of information that would produce headlines were it to become public. This virtually never happens. Discretion is a key element in the organizational culture, and the reason for this is relatively straightforward. If the organization came to be known as one that leaked information, the president or the agencies with which OMB must work would not trust OMB. That trust is the most critical commodity at OMB. If the president cannot trust that OMB will keep internal deliberations and information out of the public arena, he cannot rely on it to produce budgets and policy analysis he can use as part of his program. And if the agencies with which OMB works cannot trust OMB to safeguard the decision process and its contents, they will not trust it with the information OMB needs to do its job. Trustworthiness is built into the organizational responsibilities.

Many of these features of organizational culture can be grouped together in the word "professional." One of the distinguishing features of OMB professional culture, reflected on the budget side of the organization, is that the organizational positions are uniquely named: examiner, branch chief, deputy associate director. Even the policy positions have unusual names: program associate director (PAD), deputy director, director. While these titles have rough equivalents in standard executive branch agencies, their uniqueness says, "We are a bit different here."

Coming into the organization, OMB staff is highly educated (frequently from public policy schools, political science or economics departments but also, as needed, from the hard science and engineering fields). Most of the staffers "hit the ground running" at OMB and are handed responsibility for agency budgets and programs of which they have had little prior knowledge. Examiners pride themselves on getting up to speed quickly and even-tually knowing nearly as much about agency programs and processes as the agencies them-selves. As the examiners move up the institutional hierarchy, they acquire broader experience of agencies and programs. Branch chiefs and DADs are usually promoted to these senior executive service positions from the ranks of the OMB staff. Giving OMB staffers broader exposure through travel and training helps reduce their insularity (an occasional criticism of OMB made by officials in the federal departments OMB oversees) and increase their under-standing of what is really involved in implementing programs. While much of the training at OMB occurs on the job, there has been more effort recently to give staff significant outside experience, including temporary assignments to other federal agencies, to congressional offices, or even in the private sector.

Because a fair number of OMB staffers have, until recently, remained with the organization for a good part of their professional lives, they are highly experienced and have a strong network of sources inside the various government agencies. An incoming OMB policy official finds that he or she can rely on the staff to get answers quickly and produce top-quality work swiftly and reliably. OMB staffers' professional knowledge and experience make them precisely the kind of official that other executive branch agencies like to recruit. Lateral movement of OMB staffers to the budget and planning offices of other agencies is occurring more frequently, with two great advantages for the hiring agency: it is certain to be obtaining a skilled, experienced staffer, and as a bonus, it has a staffer who has access to OMB and knows its unique culture. As one former associate director put it, "Your single biggest asset is the OMB career staff. . . . [The DADs are] smart, experienced, accustomed to transition and ready to help you. Use them. You can trust them completely. The OMB staff is the most effective, analytic, pragmatic, and discreet group in government."[10]

The OMB organizational culture values evidence and analysis. No agency proposal or budget is taken on faith. No proposal is automatically accepted and approved. The staff is prepared to dig in hard, raise tough questions, and demand more information. The reality may often be that agencies have not done a rigorous analysis of their proposed programs and their impact or have not prepared sufficient justification for their budget proposals; in other cases, they are seeking more funding than they need or have not executed their programs effectively or efficiently. OMB examiners walk a careful line with the agencies. Good working relationships must be combined with a skeptical attitude. The better the relationship, the greater the likelihood that skilled agency staffers will share with OMB their private concerns and questions about proposals, enabling the OMB staff to focus on critical problems and issues. This balancing act can have positive results for the White House. If examiners fully understand an agency proposal or program, they can sometimes become an effective advocate in the White House for a good policy idea, helping anticipate issues or challenges. From an agency's point of view, however, the initial skepticism of OMB staffers to new proposals can lead them to see the organization as being habitually negative.

At the same time, OMB can be a critical tool in helping implement the president's initiative and goals. The downside of this role is the risk of friction between the White House and the agencies. OMB is often in a key position to mediate this friction. The best OMB staffers learn how to manage this duality both to understand and help develop agency programs and to encourage responsiveness to the White House agenda. The OMB staff and leadership also play a key role in helping federal agencies anticipate likely questions that will come from various congressional committees about their budget requests and new initiatives.

OMB staffers are in a unique position for civil servants. They work for the president, not a federal department. The OMB examiners, branch chiefs, and DADs participate in senior-level meetings in the Cabinet Room, the Situation Room, and interagency deliberations covering virtually every aspect of government operations. They become part of crisis management teams for situations in Iraq, Afghanistan, Pakistan, or the Middle East. They plan emergency budgets for major US foreign policy and national security operations. They have significant authority over agency planning and budgeting, with White House access and cachet. And at the same time, they are civil servants, career officials who have worked across several administrations. Few agency officials have this level of experience and access on a regular basis, which can lead to a certain amount of pride in the OMB staff.

OMB has a long-standing internal cultural tension that derives from its dual roles of budget and management oversight. While most of the staffers are immersed in the details of their programs and budget processes, they have not had the experience of actually managing or helping implement a program (a criticism that could be leveled against the staffs of many oversight entities). Specifically, while OMB has an important management oversight responsibility, it is also the case that OMB staffers can be promoted from a GS-9 all the way up to a GS-15 civil service level without having had any management responsibility, as promotions are tied to their analytic capabilities and contributions. Thus, some have rightfully criticized OMB for being deficient in management experience while at the same time telling agencies how to improve their own management. OMB has moved to address this issue through increased emphasis on training and through temporary assignments to other federal agencies and in the private sector, as mentioned previously. OMB has also moved to bring in staffers from other federal agencies with different experiences and backgrounds.

OMB is constrained to some extent by the structure of its budget offices. The OMB organizational architecture parallels the structure of both the executive branch and Congress—it is organized by agency. As a result, OMB (and Congress) struggles with issues that cut across agencies, as many foreign and national security issues do. This can be an organizational handicap when such problems as terrorism, proliferation, post-conflict reconstruction, or homeland security arise and require a cross-agency response and funding. OMB has found it difficult to carry out true cross-agency resource planning on a systematic basis because of this stovepiping. The organizational response is an interagency crosscut review. While these reviews can be helpful, they also consume valuable and scarce staff time and resources. Some have been very useful; others less so.

OMB AND NATIONAL SECURITY

In the area of foreign policy and national security, OMB's National Security Programs office (one of five resource management offices [RMOs] at OMB) has responsibility for diplomacy, foreign assistance, defense, nuclear weapon programs, intelligence, and veterans' affairs budgets and legislation. It is organized into two divisions: the International Affairs Division and the National Security Division. The International Affairs Division, in turn, has two branches: one for the State Department and one for economic affairs (including foreign assistance programs and operations). The National Security Division has four branches covering the following broad areas: command, control, communications, computers, and intelligence activities; operations, personnel, and support for the military; force structure, investment, and nuclear security; and veterans' affairs and defense health programs. The staffs of these branches have comprehensive responsibility for all program, management, legislative, and budget issues in these areas.

Homeland security programs and agencies are the responsibility of the separate General Government Programs RMO at OMB. The homeland security branch responsible for homeland security budgets and management issues is located in the Transportation, Homeland, Justice, and Services Division of that RMO. Because homeland security programs are found in most government agencies, other offices in OMB have oversight responsibility as well, but the homeland security branch coordinates with these other offices. (For an overview of the federal budget process, followed in particulars by the National Security Programs divisions, see box 3.1.)

BOX 3.1.
National Security Budget Process

The OMB process for planning national security budgets begins roughly eighteen months in advance of the start of the fiscal year for which the White House is requesting funds.

In the spring of any given year, OMB is dealing with three budgets simultaneously: the budget being implemented in that current fiscal year; the budget the president has already submitted to Congress for the next fiscal year; and the budget being planned for the following fiscal year. As a result, the planning of the third budget takes place in a context of uncertainty: How will funds be spent in the current fiscal year? How much funding will Congress provide for the coming fiscal year and for what programs?

The OMB resolves this uncertainty as best it can and provides guidance according to the out-year projections contained in previous budgets, new presidential priorities, deals cut with Congress, electoral considerations, and emerging economic and fiscal realities (growth of the economy, inflation, deficits, etc.). At times the fiscal guidance given the national security agencies is affected by broader fiscal, budgetary, policy, and political priorities that may have little to do with national security requirements. The budget caps on defense budgets created by the Budget Control Act of 2011 and subsequent cap adjustments in 2013, 2014, and 2015, for example, set limits on the extent to which the administration can request or expect increases in future defense budgets.

The OMB staff maintains a dialogue with agencies over the spring and summer, as the agencies carry out their own budget planning, in order to identify major budget issues and disagreements that could appear in OMB's fall budget process. Usually, by the middle of the summer, OMB delivers to agencies more formal budget planning instructions, which describe in detail the types of data and information agencies must provide in their budget submissions (called Circular A-11).[a]

A-11 provides OMB's expectations for the types of budget information each agency should provide and detailed schedules (formats) for reporting that data. It describes the materials agencies should provide to justify their budgets (justification requirements). A-11 also lays out expectations for agencies preparing emergency supplementary budget requests outside the normal budget process. These have been particularly important in the national security arena, as emergency supplemental requests for spending on operations in Iraq, in Afghanistan, and against terrorists grew in size and frequency after the 9/11 terrorist attacks. The submission of agency budgets, except for Defense, occurs in late September. Defense continues its dialogue with OMB until a final set of agreed data is supplied in December, before the release of the budget.

[a]Circulars are the OMB mechanism for providing guidance and instructions to executive branch agencies. A-11 is titled Preparation, Submission, and Execution of the Budget. Each year's version differs, following White House priorities and policies, and is generally available at the OMB website.

International Affairs (150 Account)

Given the range of issues on the international agenda—from international environmental issues and climate change, to the spread of communicable diseases, to protection against unfair child labor practices and human trafficking, to the promotion of American economic and political interests—almost every federal agency has a role in US foreign policy. The international affairs budget (sometimes referred to as Function 150 after its category in Congressional Budget Resolutions), however, refers to a subset of these activities: primarily spending by the Departments of State, Treasury, and Agriculture as well as a dozen independent and quasi-independent agencies, such the US Agency for International Development (USAID), the Millennium Challenge Corporation, and the Peace Corps. Most Americans assume that international assistance is foreign aid; they also assume foreign aid is somewhere between 10 and 20 percent of the budget. In fact, spending on international affairs averages less than 1 percent of the budget. (See chapter 5 on USAID for more details on budgets and policy.)

The process for developing and reviewing international affairs budgets has evolved since the end of World War II and the Marshall Plan through periodic reorganizations, such as creation of the Agency for International Assistance in 1961 and more recently the creation of the Millennium Challenge Corporation, with its own budget account, and the President's Emergency Plan for AIDS Relief (PEPFAR).

The preparation of annual budget submissions from the international affairs agencies to OMB varies owing to the multiplicity of the agencies and bureaus. Within the State Department, for example, two entirely separate bureaus prepare their respective portions of the department's budget request. One bureau, the Office of Foreign Assistance, known as "F" and reporting to the secretary of state, prepares the request for foreign assistance programs controlled by the State Department, such as Foreign Military Financing (FMF), International Military Education and Training (IMET), Economic Support Funds (ESF), counterterrorism, nonproliferation, counter-narcotics, and non-UN international organizations and peacekeeping activities. The other separate Bureau of Budget and Planning, reporting to the under secretary of state for management, prepares the budget for State Department operations, US assessed payments to the United Nations, and public diplomacy programs.

The assertion by the State Department of more central responsibility for foreign assistance programs has been a gradual process since the mid-1990s. As part of this trend, the State Department created the Office of Resources, Plans, and Policies (S/RPP), which reported to the secretary to coordinate budget planning for USAID and State and to hold budget hearings for other international affairs agencies to present their budget proposals to senior State Department officials. The government reform of 1998 that incorporated the Arms Control and Disarmament Agency and the US Information Agency into the State Department tightened the link between USAID and State as well. This trend accelerated during the Bush administration, when the State Department created the Bureau of Resource Management, headed by an assistant secretary, to increase budget planning coordination between State and USAID. This internal coordination grew even closer with the creation in 2005 of the Office of the Director of Foreign Assistance (F), which virtually integrated State and USAID budget planning. During the Obama administration the head of USAID was seen as essentially a third deputy secretary of state. OMB became increasingly involved in these more integrated internal budget discussions and hearings. The trend did not, however, extend to other international affairs agencies, such as Treasury or the Agriculture Department, and as a result, OMB, acting as the de facto integrator of the entire international affairs budget function, continues to deal separately with their budget submissions.

As the elements of the international affairs budget submissions are received at OMB, they are distributed to ten to fifteen budget examiners in the International Affairs Division, each of whom reviews a particular account or agency budget. The scrub includes hearings or meetings of an hour to a full day with State, USAID, and other international affairs program and budget personnel.

The hearings force agencies to explain budget requests for which there may not yet be adequate justification. The hearings also can provide an opportunity to make sure White House policy preferences are reflected in agency budgets. Without the hearings budget requests may reflect only the agency preferences and not White House priorities. The OMB hearings can begin a process of bargaining with agencies to ensure that White House policy goals are adequately funded.[11]

A director's review, based on these earlier hearings with the agencies, is conducted in November and early December to examine a budget options book prepared by the OMB staff. The review is a closed meeting between the career OMB staffers and senior OMB policy officials that generally does not include other White House or agency officials.[12] On the basis of this internal review, the OMB director sends a letter, known as the "pass back," to the international affairs agencies usually around Thanksgiving. State, USAID, and the other Function 150 agencies review the pass back and decide which decisions they will accept and which they wish to appeal.

Senior-level appeals meetings occur and often must be resolved by the OMB director, the president, or the latter's designee.[13] Many of these meetings involve only the president, the vice president, the White House senior staff, the OMB director, the PAD, and staffers. Some cabinet-level secretaries, however, seek a presidential meeting to clarify agency budget priorities directly, to appeal for a higher level of spending, or simply to have face time with the president. In the Bush administration Secretaries of State Colin Powell and Condoleezza Rice won significant budget increases through such meetings.[14] Not surprisingly, the budgetary endgame in the White House is an intense moment in the process.[15]

The final decisions from these meetings are put into OMB's overall budget database, which becomes the president's budget request. Once this request has been transmitted to Congress, OMB continues to play an important role. Typically, the president seeks more funding for the international affairs agencies than Congress is likely to approve. As a result, OMB staffers and policy leadership continue to play a role in coordinating the administration's response to congressional discussions, including participation in interagency meetings, organizing the White House response, and communicating with the key congressional committees.

National Defense (050 Account)

The national defense function in the federal budget (Function 050) includes funding for the Department of Defense (DOD), the National Nuclear Security Administration (NNSA) in the Department of Energy (DOE), and the intelligence community. At least 95 percent of national defense 050 budget resources go to DOD.

A key difference between the DOD budget and almost all other agencies is that DOD develops a resource and program plan for five years, referred to as the Future Years Defense Plan (FYDP). The FYDP displays total DOD resources, forces, and equipment associated with all DOD programs. The primary unit of data in the FYDP is called a "program element," of which there are more than 3,600. The second year of an FYDP, prepared as part of a budget request in a given year, becomes the starting point for the following year's budget. DOD uses its lengthy and elaborate budget and program review process, the Planning, Programming, Budgeting System (PPBS, created in 1961 by Secretary Robert McNamara), to allocate resource requests and plans across requirements and to adjust the existing, current FYDP.[16]

The interaction between OMB and DOD during the development of the president's budget for the DOD differs significantly from that for international affairs or other domestic agencies. This special relationship goes back to the creation of DOD in 1947. Historically, DOD has not submitted a complete budget request to OMB in the early fall (usually September), unlike other agencies. While the nature of the budgetary relationship between OMB and DOD has varied over time, since the 1970s OMB staffers have been integrated earlier and more deeply into the internal budget process at DOD, more so than at virtually any other federal agency.

In the first stage of defense budget development, OMB provides fiscal guidance for the overall defense budget amount in the framework of its broader fiscal guidance to agencies. This guidance can be critical if the top-line level is going to be lower than what the department had projected in its most recent FYDP. For example, in the early 2000s, the Bush administration wanted to add significant resources to DOD. The size of the increase was discussed early on among key White House policy officials and then communicated to DOD to help the department frame its base budget request. After the attacks of September 11, 2001, the White House, cabinet agency heads, and OMB agreed to additional increases, a "supplemental" budget request for what was called the Global War on Terror.

OMB's budgetary guidance may be given in writing or sometimes orally to DOD, given possible concern about leaks. To ensure that DOD's internal budget planning guidance to the military services is consistent with the overall White House and OMB budget frameworks, OMB reviews DOD's internal planning guidance to the military services.

The next stage is sometimes referred to as the "joint review" of the DOD budget, which is unique to the OMB–DOD process. OMB does not conduct such a formal joint review with any other department. This interaction generally starts in the summer, as issue groups begin to discuss major budget questions both within and across the services and to lay out decision priorities for the secretary of defense. OMB examiners usually participate in these issue teams, learning about service plans and making sure that issues of interest to the White House are addressed. They raise questions when proposed policy options are not consistent with OMB's budget scorekeeping rules or White House policy and management guidance.

In the fall the comptroller of the Defense Department and OMB staff hold joint hearings with the military departments and work on DOD program budget decision drafts that go to the deputy secretary or secretary for a final decision inside DOD. At the same time, OMB also holds an internal director's review on the defense budget, which leads to the previously mentioned pass-back letter, containing policy, budget, and management guidance, around Thanksgiving. This letter comes just as final budget decisions are being made in the department. Because of the joint review, OMB positions on many policy and programmatic issues are already known at this point, but they are reaffirmed officially in the pass back. The pass back also reaffirms overall DOD top-line fiscal guidance (see box 3.2). In some years this amount has been changed, although significant changes at this point are not the norm and cause disruption in DOD's internal budget processes.

Like the other federal agencies, DOD inevitably appeals some parts of the OMB pass-back decisions, usually in December. Discussions about these appeals can be intense, particularly those about the ultimate base budget top line and the overall size of overseas contingency operations (OCO) funding. Disagreements are negotiated first between OMB and DOD at lower levels and then, if necessary, at higher levels inside OMB. For major top-line and policy issues, it is not unusual for the president and national security advisor to become involved.

There has been much discussion over the years about the advisability of this joint review process, which goes from early summer through final budget submission. For OMB it has some distinct advantages. The defense budget is the largest and most complex on the discretionary side of federal spending. The timing of DOD's internal budget development processes means the department does not have a completed budget request to present to OMB in September for review, which is when most domestic agencies submit their requests. While there have been discussions between OMB and DOD about starting the internal DOD budget process earlier, DOD has argued strongly it is too difficult to move their process to earlier decisions.

BOX 3.2
Pass-Back Management

The pass-back decision's management guidance stems from congressional statutory requirements or the nonstatutory management initiatives of a particular administration. One example of a statutorily required management activity is the 1993 Government Performance and Results Act (GPRA), modified later in the 2010 GPRA Modernization Act. The GPRA Modernization Act focuses agencies, including DOD, on their highest priorities as well as key cross-agency goals, seeking to create a culture in which data and empirical evidence play a greater role in policy, budget, and management decisions. Implementing and achieving the GPRA goals is clearly a long-term effort.

Examples of administration-unique management efforts include the Bush administration's goal of evaluating every federal program using the Program Assessment Rating Tool (PART) and the Obama administration's initiative to have federal agencies identify ideas that save money and to give awards for the best ideas. DOD will often argue that some of the management initiatives from Congress or a particular administration are not helpful given the department's size and mission complexity. But in other cases, a DOD performance outcome or management process—for example, its PPBS—has been cited as a success that other agencies might follow.

The later DOD decisions are made, however, the harder it is for OMB to adjust. Given the budgetary time frame, waiting until final DOD decisions are made to present the budget to OMB in December, or even January in some cases, would put OMB in an infeasible place given the need to close a final president's budget and submit it by early February. OMB's defense staff is small—around forty people—making it difficult to scrutinize every part of DOD's budget request. Early identification of the key issues and early participation by OMB staff in the DOD process allow the White House to focus on priority programs and policies. The process makes it possible for the White House to insert key programs, views, and policies that DOD might not rank highly into the DOD budget process. And it gives the White House early access to the DOD process before internal negotiations have locked down decisions that are hard to reverse, although sometimes this happens.

The risk in the joint review is the potential for DOD to close off discussion on some issues with OMB prematurely, gaining approval of specific DOD programs and funding allocations ahead of the other agencies and before OMB has conducted its own hearings and director's review process. This can have the risk of limiting OMB's options at later stages in the budget process, especially with respect to specific programs.

There are advantages and disadvantages for DOD as well. The advantage is to expose OMB to DOD preferences early in the process and obtain White House agreement, rather than wait until late in the process, when negative OMB reactions could lead to chaos in internal DOD planning. For some at DOD, on the other hand, it is a disadvantage to have OMB staff sitting in on internal deliberations before final policy decisions are made. Sometimes, DOD staff will try to cut off OMB participation to avoid early knowledge outside DOD of planned decisions.

OMB IN THE ERA OF BUDGET CAPS

The Budget Control Act of 2011 (BCA) has added to the complexity of OMB's role. The act set caps on discretionary spending, one covering defense budgets and another covering non-defense budgets. If congressional action on the budget exceeded those caps, the law required a "sequester," or automatic reduction of the budget's level to lower the projected deficit, an event that actually occurred in fiscal year 2013.

OMB is responsible for managing all aspects of this sequester process; neither the Congressional Budget Office nor the congressional budget committees play a role. OMB produces the sequester report and defines the nature and details of the budget cuts required to meet the budgetary guidelines. In the case of defense, the BCA allows the president to exempt military personnel budgets from sequestration. This means that other budget accounts within DOD need to be cut proportionately more to ensure that the full sequester target is met. OMB is responsible for these calculations, setting the final amounts, an additional task beyond its normal role in the budget process. The organization's responsibilities under the BCA caps have added to the workload of an already heavily burdened office.

Budgeting for War

The budget cap requirements for OMB have become linked to the process of funding war costs. Since 2001 the defense and intelligence budgets have had two significant components and processes: the "base" defense budget and the OCO budget. Other agencies, such as State and Justice, have also had OCO budgets in many of these years. The DOD OCO request has been by far the largest, intended primarily to cover "temporary and extraordinary" incremental costs associated with military operations in Iraq and Afghanistan. The discretionary funding caps in the BCA do not apply to the OCO budget, however, which can create significant incentive in DOD budget planning to fund activities within the OCO that should be more properly funded in the base budget.

The OCO budget has served to some extent as a relief valve, reducing pressure for trade-offs within the base budget, which is constrained by the BCA given budgetary caps. OMB and DOD negotiated criteria for deciding what might be funded in the OCO budget and what belongs in the base budget, although exceptions to these criteria have been granted. Reaching an agreement each year on both how big the OCO request is and what is funded within it has involved considerable interaction between OMB and DOD since 2001. OMB examiners review each OCO line item and often negotiate directly with their Office of the Secretary of Defense counterparts. This process gives OMB visibility into the OCO budget at a detailed level. The goal of this OCO review has been to ensure that the military services have had adequate resources to carry out their missions. At the same time, OMB has also sought to prevent OCO from becoming, in effect, "free money" for uses that should otherwise be funded in the base budget.

As the wars in Iraq and Afghanistan wind down and counterterrorism struggles involve fewer US forces, the longevity and size of the OCO budget will become an increasingly controversial issue. It is possible that the OCO budget will remain and be funded in significant amounts. The United States is likely to retain a residual presence in Afghanistan and to operate smaller, but not insignificant, forces in Iraq. In addition, since the OCO budgets are not subject to the BCA caps, OCO has provided the Pentagon with considerable budgetary relief from those budgetary restraints.[17]

As a result, OCO could well be perpetuated as an indefinite, flexible funding source for ongoing and emerging global military operations, leading to a long-term, continuing negotiation between OMB and DOD about its size and contents. What the last several years seem to suggest is that the DOD base budget, as large as it is, either has not been big enough or has been structured in a way that accommodates the wide number of defense missions and combat activities, even if these missions are not on the scale of a major world war. Put another way, neither the executive branch nor Congress has been willing to make the trade-offs necessary to absorb the costs of war activities within the base budget, clearly a harbinger of the future.

Intelligence

OMB's intelligence branch, which is part of the National Security Division, oversees the National Intelligence Program (NIP) budget, which is implemented and funded across the seventeen agencies and organizations of what is called the intelligence community (IC). OMB works closely with the Office of the Director of National Intelligence (ODNI) in preparing this budget request. The ODNI was created by the Intelligence Reform and Terrorism Prevention Act of 2004 to coordinate and integrate policy and budget across the intelligence agencies. Using intelligence agency budget submissions, the ODNI is to "develop and determine an annual consolidated National Intelligence Program budget."[18] The ODNI's role in coordinating and integrating an IC-wide budget has made OMB's review of intelligence budgets easier than in prior eras. There have, however, been some bureaucratic conflicts between the ODNI and other agencies over who has ultimate control of agency requests for those NIP entities that are embedded in other departments, such as State, Treasury, and Justice, as well as the significant intelligence activities embedded in DOD (NSA, the National Geospatial-Intelligence Agency, the National Reconnaissance Organization, the Defense Intelligence Agency), reflecting unresolved issues in the 2004 act.

OMB's intelligence branch has a small number of staff members who are knowledgeable in the various intelligence disciplines. The examiners carry whatever security clearances are necessary for them to oversee all critical intelligence activities and participate with the NSC in interagency meetings concerning highly classified activities. Many of these examiners also have experience in prior intelligence or defense work and take the opportunity of getting into the field, mostly abroad, to learn firsthand about how these programs work.

Like the defense budget process, the intelligence budget development involves a joint review process whereby OMB examiners participate in internal discussions of the various intelligence agencies early on. Since 2001, as with the DOD budget, there have been annual base budget and OCO requests, given the IC's significant role in Iraq, Afghanistan, and other antiterrorism activities. OMB sends guidance, usually in the early fall, to both DOD and the ODNI on what their funding shares are within the part of the 050 budget that covers the DOD (where much of the intelligence budget is funded). IC funding for most of the intelligence agencies must fit within the overall BCA budget cap for Function 050, which could mean trade-offs between intelligence programs and DOD's military activities and programs. This guidance helps prevent confusion or conflict later on as DOD and the ODNI develop their respective budgets.

Over the last dozen or so years, OMB's National Security Division has made an effort to ensure that some of the administration's management priorities are applied to and implemented by the IC. Examples of such management priorities include obtaining clean financial audits, improving human capital management and acquisition of information technology (IT) infrastructure, and defining performance metrics—as challenging as the last can be in the classified world. Finally, OMB examiners participate in interagency meetings held by the NSC staff on intelligence-related policy issues, including discussions on covert action findings and operations. A key goal of this participation is to ensure that the nexus between policy priorities and resource allocation is in sync.

Most of OMB's role in the IC budget process is not public.[19] OMB's role is significant, however, in part because such programs do not get as much oversight as other programs because of their classification. ODNI has taken one initiative that has increased transparency slightly—the decision to make public the total amount of resources appropriated to the IC. Overall, however, the growth of intelligence budgets combined with the absence of growth in OMB staff makes review of this large account a challenge.

Department of Energy

National Nuclear Security Administration (NNSA) is an important entity within DOE with close ties to DOD and its nuclear missions. NNSA is primarily responsible for the safety, security, and reliability of the nation's nuclear deterrent. It also has important missions in preventing nuclear proliferation, designing and developing nuclear propulsion plants for the US Navy, and securing the nation against nuclear terrorism and responding to radiological or nuclear emergencies.

Funding for NNSA is part of the national defense budget function (050), meaning its funding must fit in the BCA caps for the defense budget, which can mean trade-offs between defense and NNSA budget requests. This budgetary relationship between DOD and DOE in recent years has been somewhat tense, which has amplified the role of OMB (along with NSC) in mediating interdepartmental conflict. The National Security Programs office of OMB took on oversight responsibility for NNSA in 2003.

Veterans' Affairs

Since 2001 OMB's National Security Programs RMO has overseen budgets for the Veterans Affairs Department (VA), which administers a sizable health-care system and the benefits provided to about 22 million military veterans and 35 million dependents and survivors. These benefits include disability payments, education assistance, housing loan guarantees, health services, and support (jointly with the Department of Housing and Urban Development) for homeless veterans. While funding for these programs falls under Function 700 (Veterans Benefits and Services) and is not part of the 050 budget function, resources committed to veterans' programs have increased significantly. OMB moved responsibility for oversight of veterans' programs to its National Security Division to improve coordination between VA and DOD health programs. The Obama administration highlighted the importance of helping veterans returning from Iraq and Afghanistan in terms of providing both more counseling to those suffering from post-traumatic stress disorder (PTSD) and more help in transitioning to the private sector through job counseling and working with the private sector to hire veterans. OMB played an important role in these initiatives, working hand in hand with the NSC and Domestic Policy Council staffs.

The VA budget process is similar to that for domestic agencies. The VA presents its official budget request to OMB for review in September, absent a joint review process. OMB reviews the request and, sometime in late November or early December, sends the VA a pass-back letter with its decisions on budget as well as other management and policy guidance. OMB's review cannot alter the benefits part of the VA budget (about half that budget), since the benefits are "mandatory" spending and not subject to congressional appropriation; any eligible veteran receives those benefits by law.

Homeland Security

The OMB's involvement with homeland security budgets is different, again, from the other two processes. Homeland security spending does not have a corresponding budget function. The Department of Homeland Security (DHS) does not have responsibility for *all* homeland security–related funding. Other agencies, such as DOD and Health and Human Services, carry out a number of homeland security programs and activities. In addition, nearly a quarter of the DHS budget is committed to programs that are not pure homeland security activities, such as Coast Guard rescue-at-sea responsibilities.[20]

These complexities have made OMB a key player in integrating the homeland security budgets because it is the only institution in the executive branch that has the cross-agency responsibilities that can pull all the elements together. The OMB played a key role in the creation of DHS in 2004, helping the small White House planning team identify which parts of federal spending might be considered part of the homeland security budget.

DHS prepares its agency budget request, which it submits to OMB in September; OMB and the NSC staff in the White House coordinate the related budget requests from other agencies in preparing the annual analysis. As a result, the OMB involvement in homeland security budgeting is neither as structured as its participation in the DOD process nor as traditional as its role in international affairs budgets.

The traditional OMB process does prevail with respect to DHS itself. Budget preparation is done inside the agency, with a budget delivered in September, followed by hearings with the department. The breadth of homeland security programs across departments, however, requires that the OMB hearings be coordinated by the homeland security branch of the Transportation, Homeland, Justice, and Services Division and cover other departmental budgets, including DOD, Justice and the Federal Bureau of Investigation, Health and Human Services, the Centers for Disease Control and Prevention, Agriculture, Labor, Interior, and the Environmental Protection Agency, among others. A pass back is sent to several agencies with respect to their parts of the homeland security budget.

Agency Crosscut Reviews

In addition to its focus on national security agency budgets, OMB also carries out budget reviews that cut across agency budgets, known as "crosscuts." In the security arena examples of such OMB crosscuts have included counterterrorism, cybersecurity, nuclear weapons activities, partnership capacity programs in developing countries, veterans' programs and benefits, and the "rebalance to Asia" of US national security strategy. The purpose of a crosscut is to gather data and program information on a policy area in which several agencies are involved. The goal is usually to identify the level of agency effort, gaps in program coverage, and duplications of activity, sometimes with the aim of proposing changes in the pass-back letter.

The OMB crosscut process can ask agencies to identify spending and programs in the policy area in question. Agencies sometimes resist such a data call, arguing that it is too difficult to separate out programs dedicated to the specific policy area from broader agency activity. A major reason for this resistance is because spending data is arranged by budget accounts that usually do not correlate well with a particular policy area. For example, an account like operations and maintenance in the DOD budget covers a wide range of activities from civilian pay to defense health to base operating support to training, among many other activities. Pulling out the data on activities within the account that apply specifically to a complex interagency issue like counterterrorism operations requires considerable effort. Even an apparently straightforward policy area like defense health is funded in several DOD accounts. In addition, one could argue that a comprehensive view of military health-care costs should also include spending by the VA, which could triple the overall amount of spending.

A second reason for agency resistance to a crosscut is that the definition of a policy may be open to debate, making budget coverage hard to pin down. Homeland security spending is a good example. Does most of the DOD budget contribute to homeland security, or is there a more narrow definition? It is equally difficult to determine which budget accounts at State or DOD contribute to the "rebalance to Asia." Resolving such challenges can be labor and time intensive, but the definition can have a significant impact on the ultimate estimate of spending. An additional challenge may arise if some programs in a policy crosscut, such as cybersecurity, are classified and the funding cannot be revealed in open documents. This can limit the usefulness of crosscuts if the goal of the exercise is to inform a wider public.

In spite of these challenges, crosscuts can still provide powerful tools to White House policymakers. They can help identify gaps and duplications in coverage and lead to reform proposals to be included in the president's budget. OMB often works closely on crosscuts with the NSC staff, which relies on OMB's ability to pull together and analyze budget and program information in a standardized format from multiple agencies for areas of significant policy interest. If the NSC staff is participating in a crosscut, it may send a strong signal to federal agencies about the priority the White House attaches to a particular area of policy.

OMB AND THE NATIONAL SECURITY COUNCIL

The NSC is the principal White House institution that advises on and coordinates national security strategy, working through the interagency process and responding as needed to national security crises.[21] (For the role of other White House offices, see box 3.3.) The NSC staff does not have a formal role in the OMB budget process, nor does it typically have expertise in resource planning. Most NSC staff are nonpermanent representatives from DOD, State, Homeland Security, and the IC, where they usually have policy- or program-focused positions and little budget background. Nevertheless, most decisions made in the NSC framework have resource implications, making regular OMB–NSC interaction necessary.

NSC views and interagency discussions in the NSC framework can have important implications for the contents of the president's budget. In return, budget decisions made in the OMB process can facilitate or limit NSC and interagency policy options.[22] NSC views on program priorities can sometimes differ from the programs and funding levels requested by national security agencies and departments. OMB, working with both the departments and NSC staff, often help resolve the conflict in these competing priorities.

The NSC process for articulating and communicating its views to OMB can differ from administration to administration and from year to year within an administration.[23] Sometimes, there is no internal coordination among NSC staffers, and budget views are simply expressed by the different NSC directorates, if they choose to do so. At other times, an NSC senior director may be tasked to gather budget recommendations from the other NSC regional or functional elements; this process can then lead to consultations with the deputy national security advisor for setting and communicating NSC priorities to OMB. These views are usually provided to the National Security Programs RMO at OMB. Some OMB directors might also invite affected NSC directors and senior directors to review meetings to express their views; however, others do not. For example, during the Bush administration when

---

BOX 3.3
Other White House Office Budget Players

While the president and the NSC play a central role in the White House budget process, other White House players sometimes are significant.

The president's personal staff can be involved, acting on the president's behalf. Leon Panetta, for example, who had been OMB director, continued to play a direct role in budget decisions as presidential chief of staff by holding regular budget decision meetings on key issues in his office and negotiating on budget bills with members of Congress.[a] Under President Clinton the National Economic Council (NEC) staff would regularly arrange three-way meetings between NEC, DOD, and OMB to argue for higher levels of funding for the Pentagon's Technology Reinvestment Program—which the president favored—than DOD wanted to request.[b] Many Bush White House staffers had a laser focus on the overseas wars, homeland security, and counterterrorism efforts and multiagency funding to support them. In the Obama administration a close partnership of the First Lady and Second Lady brought considerable attention to military family and veterans' issues, with their immediate staffs working closely with staffs from other White House policy councils, OMB, federal agencies, and outside stakeholders.

In recent decades the Vice President's Office has become more involved in budgets. Starting with Walter Mondale and George H. W. Bush, and increasingly with Al Gore, Dick Cheney, and Joe Biden, vice presidents have shown strong commitments to certain national security issues; for example, global climate change and Russia programs took precedence for Al Gore, national defense and counterterrorism for Dick Cheney, and strategic arms reduction and worldwide nonproliferation for Vice President Biden. Vice President Gore participated actively in virtually every appeals meeting held with the president. Vice President Cheney played an even broader role in the White House budget process, playing a central role in the overall budget process, particularly for national security, and chairing the agency budget appeals process that followed OMB pass back.[c] Vice President Biden was a key player in developing the Obama administration's nuclear posture review and obtaining additional funds for the modernization of the strategic stockpile.

Other EOP offices also intervene in the OMB process. The US Trade Representative, the trade agreement negotiating office in the White House, not only lobbies for its own operating budget but plays a key role in helping Treasury and OMB identify revenue options needed as offsets to compensate for the impact of trade agreements on projected federal receipts.[d] The White House Office of Science and Technology Policy frequently advocates higher levels of funding for research and development, including national security–related investments, than those requested by DOD, the National Aeronautics and Space Administration, the National Science Foundation, DOE, or other agencies with research and development investment programs.

[a]Observations from the author's direct involvement and experience.
[b]Ibid.
[c]Interviews with White House staff.
[d]These offsets were required between 1990 and 2002 as a result of the Budget Enforcement Act of 1990, which set out a number of deficit-reduction requirements, *including* the need to pay in budgetary terms for budget decisions on the mandatory side of the budget that would cause a loss of projected federal revenues (so-called Paygo). See Allen Schick, *The Federal Budget: Politics, Policy, Process*, 3rd ed. (Washington, DC: Brookings Institution Press, 2007), 162–90.

Joshua Bolten was the OMB director, key senior NSC staffers were invited and actively participated in the discussion of a wide range of policy-resource issues concerning both the war efforts and other defense base program issues.

For many years the NSC has run an organized interagency process, starting with interagency working groups and ending at the highest level of the Principals' Committee, which brings cabinet-level decision makers to the table. In recent years OMB has been increasingly involved in the NSC process at all levels, which has helped integrate policy and budget requirements more effectively than in the past. This closer cooperation has occurred because of the caps on defense spending legislated in the BCA, as modified in 2013. NSC priorities for spending must fit within those caps, making closer ties with OMB necessary.

OMB can often receive multiple, even conflicting budgetary recommendations from the NSC staff. This is especially true for international affairs budgets (Function 150). Responsibilities for foreign and national security issues are distributed widely across an increasingly large NSC staff. NSC regional desks will have views about priority programs and spending levels within their region. Functional offices may have differing priorities with respect to such cross-agency programs as counter-narcotics funding, democracy promotion, or post-conflict reconstruction and stabilization. During the Clinton administration, for example, the senior director for global affairs would regularly recommend a very high level of funding for counter-narcotics programs but more restricted support for democracy promotion. At the same time, the senior director for democracy might recommend a reverse priority.[24]

Nuclear weapons policy provides a good example of the role of OMB in coordinating with the NSC staff. Nuclear weapons funding is allocated to two different agencies: DOD and the NNSA at the DOE. Given the overall BCA cap for defense, which includes both agencies, it was critical that NSC and OMB be involved in setting spending priorities for the two agencies. OMB and NSC requested a major joint analytic review of requirements for the nuclear stockpile by both DOD and NNSA with recommended options. The conclusions and recommendations of this classified review were then briefed to OMB, NSC, DOD, and NNSA, with the final outcome reflected in the Obama administration's 2014 budget request.

The OMB–NSC relationship is not restricted to the preparation of the president's budget. NSC is the critical agency for crisis response and planning and for preparing the agenda for presidential travel and visitors. Both of these activities take place outside the budget cycle but can clearly have significant budget implications. As a result, the OMB–NSC relationship is continuous throughout the year.

An ability to work closely is especially critical when the administration is determining its response to international disasters or humanitarian crises. For example, OMB and NSC played complementary and critical roles in developing the administration's coordinated response to the earthquake in Haiti and the Japanese tsunami, earthquake, and nuclear disasters. OMB and NSC staffers interacted intensively with each other and with key agencies—State, DOD, as well as DOE and the Nuclear Regulatory Commission—during Japan's nuclear crisis. These conversations take place in an urgent time frame and require knowing or learning what authorities agencies have or would need to have to undertake certain responses and how resources can be brought to bear quickly. The ability of the OMB and NSC staffs to coordinate across multiple bureaucracies was key to moving quickly and effectively.

Occasionally, an NSC office might seek to coordinate program and budget planning on its own, separate from the normal OMB process, which can lead to conflicts. For example, in 1996 the NSC senior director for global affairs sought to coordinate a supplemental budget request for counterterrorism programs, outside normal OMB budget planning channels. Conversations at a senior level between OMB and NSC staffers reversed this course, making OMB the coordinator of the budget supplemental planning effort.[25]

The OMB–NSC relationship is critical to successfully planning the president's policy priorities and brokering conflict among agencies. That relationship has generally worked well in recent years, with OMB represented at NSC-coordinated interagency meetings on a wide variety of security issues. This means that OMB is at the table when key security policy decisions are being discussed and decided and can raise issues of cost and make sure that agency budgets reflect resource implications of these decisions. When the two organizations work in tandem, the White House can exercise considerable influence on national security. When they do not, budget decisions may not reflect presidential priorities or may actually frustrate the achievement of priorities.[26]

CONCLUSION

OMB works at the heart of the foreign policy and national security process. While it is not a foreign policy–making agency, its role in steering the budget process, coordinating presidential initiatives, and providing the resource input for crisis response and interagency planning in the NSC gives it a central, if less well-known role in US foreign and national security policy. As Bernard Brodie, a well-known strategic thinker in the nuclear age, put it in 1959, "Strategy wears a dollar sign."[27] If the resources cannot be mobilized, the strategy fails.

Presidents have needed their own capacity to coordinate the budget and to apply and distribute resources to foreign policy agencies. Inevitably, they have used the considerable OMB capacity to help set budget priorities and bring coordination and discipline to the budget process. In periods when there are constraints on budget resources, as was true in the 1990s and again after 2011, some central "steering" has been needed to establish priorities and make necessary budgetary trade-offs.

The OMB culture—private, professional, and neutral—serves the office of the president well, regardless of the incumbent. These responsibilities for disciplining agency planning and budgeting processes inevitably create friction if they are to ensure that presidential priorities receive the needed attention. At the same time, the process OMB runs provides an opportunity for agency planners to "get it right" and get their priorities and needs on the White House agenda. The OMB staff is small, resource challenged, and some might say, insular, but it is always hardworking and professional. If OMB did not exist, presidents and Congress would have to invent it.

NOTES

Some of the material in this chapter draws on Gordon Adams and Cindy Williams, *Buying National Security: How America Plans and Pays for Its Global Role and Safety at Home* (New York: Routledge, 2010).

As part of research for the book on which this chapter is based, one of the authors conducted a number of interviews with serving government officials who requested confidentiality. These are referenced as "confidential interviews" in the notes. In addition, some of the material was drawn directly from the authors' own experiences while serving as associate director for national security and international affairs at OMB, deputy director for international affairs, and deputy director for National Security Programs; this material is referenced as "authors' experience" in the notes.

1. Allen Schick, *The Federal Budget: Politics, Policy, Process*, 3rd ed. (Washington, DC: Brookings Institution Press, 2007), 17. The estimates were bound together but not analyzed or changed by the Treasury Department.

2. For a detailed discussion of the history of OMB, see Shelley Lynne Tomkin, *Inside OMB: Politics and Process in the President's Budget Office* (Armonk, NY: M. E. Sharpe, 1998), especially chap. 3.

3. The OMB's responsibility for defining and approving federal regulations, through the Office of Information and Regulatory Affairs (OIRA), is also an important function but is one that touches national security programs less, as those agencies engage in much less regulatory activity than domestic agencies. On OIRA's role, see Tomkin, *Inside OMB*, 203–16.

4. Tomkin, *Inside OMB*, 3, describes this function as an institutional memory. The memory bank function is critical for incoming administrations, especially if the new chief executive and his or her staff have little executive branch or Washington, DC, experience.

5. The OMB played an important role in World War II, assisting the White House with war mobilization programs and activities. See Tomkin, *Inside OMB*, 36–37, 191.

6. Paul O'Neill, once deputy director of OMB, described OMB's capabilities as "neutral brilliance." Quoted in Tomkin, *Inside OMB*, 3.

7. Schick, *Federal Budget*, 98.

8. Tomkin, *Inside OMB*, 94, 163–64, suggests this was a problem in the initial Reagan/Stockman forecasts and in the way a sequester under Gramm-Rudman-Hollings was avoided in the late 1980s.

9. Council for Excellence in Government, "Survey of Associate Directors," in *Prunes Online*, December 7, 2008, in the authors' possession.

10. Ibid.

11. See later discussion on agency crosscuts and the national implementation plan for counterterrorism.

12. Administrations differ in this regard. During the Clinton presidency, on occasion, NSC directors or senior directors would attend director's review sessions on national security agency budgets by invitation from OMB.

13. In the George W. Bush administration, Vice President Dick Cheney was frequently the ultimate decision maker on agency appeals.

14. Interviews with senior State Department budget officials, 2007–8.

15. Schick, *Federal Budget*, 96, notes, "Dozens of decisions are made in the home stretch, when all the numbers have been tallied and the deadline nears for sending the budget to the printer."

16. In 2003 PPBS was expanded to include review of the execution of DOD programs, which gave it a new acronym, PPBES.

17. See Susan B. Epstein and Lynn M. Williams, *Overseas Contingency Operations and Funding: Background and Status* (Washington, DC: Congressional Research Service, June 13, 2016), www.fas.org/sgp/crs/natsec/R44519.pdf.

18. *Intelligence Reform and Terrorism Prevention Act of 2004*, Pub. L. No. 108–458, sec. 102A.a.2.c.1.A and B; and Mark Lowenthal, *Intelligence: From Secrets to Policy*, 4th ed. (Washington, DC: Congressional Quarterly Press, 2009), 33.

19. For more detail on OMB's role in intelligence budgeting, see Adams and Williams, *Buying National Security*, 120–40.

20. See Cindy Williams, *Strengthening Homeland Security: Reforming Planning and Resource Allocation* (Washington, DC: IBM Center for the Business of Government, 2008).

21. On the structure, functioning, and evolution of the NSC, see Alan G. Whittaker, Frederick C. Smith, and Elizabeth McKune, *The National Security Policy Process: The National Security Council and Interagency System* (Washington, DC: National Defense University, ICAF, April 2007); Loch K. Johnson and Karl F. Inderfurth, *Fateful Decisions: Inside the National Security Council* (New York: Oxford University Press, 2004); David Rothkopf, *Running the World: The Inside Story of the National Security Council and the Architects of America's Power* (New York: Public Affairs, 2005); and Amy B. Zegart, *Flawed by Design: The Evolution of the CIA, JSC, and NSC* (Stanford, CA: Stanford University Press, 2000).

22. According to the National Security Act of 1947, the NSC "shall advise the President with respect to the integration of domestic, foreign, and military policies related to the national security . . . [and execute] other functions the President may direct for the purpose of more effectively coordinating the policies and functions of the departments and agencies of the government relating to the national security." The OMB, according to its Circular A-11, "evaluates the effectiveness of agency programs, policies, and procedures, assesses competing funding demands among agencies, and sets funding priorities."

23. At various times in the Clinton administration, the NSC would transmit a single document aggregating the views of the different offices, but generally without setting out clear priorities.

24. Authors' experience.

25. Ibid.

26. See, for example, a proposal made by President Bush in his State of the Union speech in January 2008 regarding a broadening of educational benefits for military families. The proposed policy was

not funded in the president's budget request transmitted to Congress in February 2008. It was apparently inserted in the speech without budgetary analysis in the Defense Department or any coordination with the OMB budget process. Michael Abramowitz and Robin Wright, "No Funds in Bush Budget for Troop-Benefits Plan," *Washington Post*, February 9, 2008; and Adams and Williams, *Buying National Security*, 245–54.

27. Bernard Brodie, *Strategy in the Missile Age* (Santa Monica, CA: RAND/Princeton University Press, 1959), 358.

PART II

Key Policy Players

CHAPTER 4

The State Department

Culture as Interagency Destiny?

Marc Grossman

> Without a doubt, the State Department has the most unique bureaucratic culture I've ever encountered.
> —James Baker, Former Secretary of State

There is no simple way to describe a culture as kaleidoscopic as the one at the State Department. This chapter argues that it is important first to understand the international culture of diplomacy and the way American diplomats place themselves both inside and outside this overarching culture. Recognizing the dangers of generalization, this chapter then makes some observations about the prevailing and evolving State Department culture. It has been on display since 9/11, both positively and negatively, as the United States has managed military operations and post-conflict challenges in Afghanistan and Iraq and entered an era of fighting terrorism and extremism, including the battle against Daesh.

Diplomats and the institutions that instruct and support them are as old as the earliest contact between groups of people who sought ways to communicate other than fighting.[1] Sophisticated systems of formal communication existed in the ancient Middle East and Anatolia, Persia, India, China, Greece, Rome, and Byzantium.[2] Scholars like Jean-Robert Leguey-Feilleux, Henry Kissinger, Paul Gordon Lauren, Gordon A. Craig, and Alexander L. George use diplomacy's past both to illuminate contemporary challenges and to make observations about the behavior of diplomats over the centuries and about their institutions and subcultures.[3]

Modern diplomacy began in Renaissance Italy.[4] Garrett Mattingly and others who write about this "revolution in diplomacy" showcase Bernard Du Rosier's "Short Treatise about Ambassadors," written in 1436, as a foundation for international diplomatic culture. Du Rosier wrote,

> Diplomats must be as clear as possible in exposition, but one need not say everything one has in mind at once before feeling out the opposite point of view. One must listen attentively and look especially for points of possible agreement; these it is usually desirable to settle first. One must adjust one's methods to circumstances, and be prepared to make all concessions consistent with the dignity and real interests of one's

principle and the clear tenor of one's instructions. One must press steadily and persistently but patiently toward an agreement. . . . One must remember that the diplomat's hope is in man's reason and good will.[5]

AMERICANS AS DIPLOMATS: A STATE DEPARTMENT CULTURE

American diplomats are part of the international diplomatic culture, but they simultaneously put themselves outside it because they represent a nation that embodies universal values and a belief that sustained effort can lead to progress. As Robert Kagan argued, "The Declaration of Independence is America's first foreign policy document."[6]

The State Department has developed an institutional culture that influences the way American diplomats both conceive of and carry out US foreign policy. Henry Kissinger astutely described the cultural anthropology of the State Department and the foreign service in *Years of Upheaval*, writing that he came to the State Department skeptical of the foreign service and left "a convert." He described foreign service officers (FSOs) as "competent, proud, clannish and dedicated." Kissinger recalled America's historic distrust of diplomacy by noting, "The conventional criticism, that they [diplomats] were a group of 'cookie pushers', contributed to a sense of beleaguered solidarity . . . long service abroad created greater sensitivity to the intangibles of foreign societies than to those of our own." Kissinger also made this crucial point: "The Foreign Service emphasizes negotiability—which is another way of saying consciousness of what the other side will accept. . . . Institutionally, the Foreign Service generates caution rather than risk taking; it is more comfortable with the mechanics of diplomacy than with its design, the tactics of a particular negotiation rather than an overall direction, the near-term problem rather than the longer term consequences."[7]

Secretary James Baker wrote in his 1995 memoir, "Most FSOs are talented and loyal public servants, and any Secretary would be foolish not to harness their strength. I did so, and was served very ably by many of them. But as with any large group, some of them tend to avoid risk taking or creative thinking."[8] Describing his work in the George W. Bush administration, Richard Haass wrote, "The State Department and those who worked there are by temperament and training inclined toward diplomacy and working with others. In this administration, those elsewhere were not."[9]

Of course, Kissinger, Baker, and Haass (and the many others who have commented on the State Department as an institution) do not define the outlook of every State Department employee. But the attitudes they portray are still foundations for an institutional culture that influences the way recommendations are shaped for the secretary of state (and for the president) and defines the way people at the State Department promote and defend their proposals and policies in the interagency arena, in foreign countries, and at international organizations. And while Kissinger and others focus on the foreign service, these traits define a larger State Department culture, including the members of the civil service, and affect the attitudes of the thousands of locally engaged staff at embassies around the world.

The institutional power of the State Department and a secretary of state's relationship to the foreign service and the civil service are separate issues. State's influence can increase even if a secretary of state uses the institution episodically. Conversely, the foreign service and civil service may occupy the commanding heights of the department, but without a strong connection to the White House, the department's influence over policy will recede. Baker's strong relationship with the president and his compelling ideas for foreign policy enhanced the clout of the institution even as Baker preferred to work closely with a small group of trusted advisors and assistants who were not FSOs.[10] Kissinger and George Shultz had close relationships with the White House, had important ideas about foreign policy, and made substantial use of the department. Secretary Colin Powell made many positive changes to the institution and was deeply admired by State's employees, but his belief in engagement was met with disdain at the White House and the Pentagon, and the department's influence waned. Serving in what has been described as a "Team of Rivals," Secretary Hillary Clinton was able, especially when aligned with Defense Secretaries Robert Gates and Leon Panetta, to keep the State Department engaged in the face of a White House committed to dominating both forming policy and forging the public message.[11] Secretary Kerry pursued a mix of approaches, leading the negotiating effort with Energy Secretary Ernest Moniz on the Iran nuclear deal, for example, while finding himself at odds with the White House on Syria.

SOURCES OF CULTURE

Six observations about the State Department culture and the system in which today's diplomats work are relevant to this examination of the American national security enterprise. First, the State Department (like other agencies) has a culture steeped in patriotism and service to the nation in a dangerous world. The commitment of State Department employees to their country allows the institution to function even when it is faced with internal tensions over policy, procedure, or external criticism. This is the lesson of a controversy in 2007 over whether Secretary Condoleezza Rice would need to force people to take assignments in Iraq and Afghanistan. After one or two officers made headlines by saying they would not serve because they disagreed with the policy, the reaction of the majority at State was to volunteer for vacancies in both war zones; no one had to be forcibly assigned.[12] That commitment has been maintained. Many FSOs and civil service employees have by now served multiple tours in Iraq and Afghanistan. The foreign service prides itself on supporting the president, regardless of party or individual policy preferences, and there are historically few resignations over policy differences.

Second, State has traditionally suffered from a lack of human and financial resources, especially when compared to spending on defense. As then–secretary of defense Gates noted in a speech at the Center for Strategic and International Studies (CSIS) in January 2008, the total foreign affairs request for FY 2008 was $36 billion, which is about what the Pentagon spent at the time on military health care.[13] The department has been better funded in recent years, thanks to the commitment of multiple secretaries of state, but the cultural norm is still to act as if the department is starved for resources. President George W. Bush's last budget and supplemental request and President Obama's first budget and supplemental requests produced real increases. Because of the automatic cuts that were a result of what was known as "sequestration," recent budgets have been more constrained. The administration's FY 2017 budget request for the State Department was $50.1 billion, down nearly $0.6 billion from the previous year's enacted level of $50.7 billion.[14] In June 2016 there were 8,196 FSOs (up from 6,347 in 2005), 5,752 foreign service specialists, and 11,037 civil service personnel working at State. By contrast, in mid-2016 there were over 1.3 million active-duty military personnel, 821,000 members of the Reserves and the National Guard, and 731,000 civilian employees in the Defense Department.[15] Sixty percent of the foreign service is always deployed overseas, compared to military forces, which have averaged between 22 and 31 percent since the 1950s.[16] The US Agency for International Development (USAID) currently has only around 2,600 personnel and relies heavily on contractors. Internal cultural challenges aside, this disparity between civilian and military spending distorts policymaking because, as many have noted, "money is policy."[17]

In his CSIS speech Gates also highlighted that "a certain percentage of [military] officers, even in time of war and when the force is stretched, is always enrolled in some kind of advance training and education in leadership, strategy or planning at the Staff or War Colleges and at graduate school. For many years, no such 'float' of personnel existed for the Foreign Service."[18] Secretary Powell sought to create such a float through the Diplomatic Readiness Initiative (DRI), but the new officers and staff were swallowed up by the personnel requirements in Iraq and Afghanistan. Both Secretary Rice and Secretary Clinton succeeded in obtaining additional new people for the State Department and for USAID, which made Powell's DRI a reality and then some. Maintaining the float remains a challenge, but the department's commitment to professional education is well entrenched.

Third, while the department has greatly benefited from changes in the way it recruits new foreign and civil service officers to enhance diversity, language skills, and technological capacity, more needs to be done, especially to attract a greater number of officers from the still underrepresented African-American and Hispanic communities. In 2016 around 40.2 percent of FSO positions were filled by women, 7.0 percent by Asian Americans, 5.3 percent by African Americans, and 5.7 percent by Hispanics.[19]

Today's new officers are marked by their skills in modern technology, their lack of patience for hierarchy, and their demand for both more professional education and a better balance between work and family. The enormous technological capacity that new officers have brought to the State Department has opened a cultural frontier: digital or "real-time" diplomacy. Diplomats at home and abroad now convey and debate America's message on Facebook, Twitter, and other new technologies. Before new media, public diplomacy, especially radio and television, was mainly about sending messages out. In the world in which today's diplomats operate, people talk back. *State Magazine*, the department's official publication, and the *Foreign Service Journal*, the publication of the American Foreign Service Association, have devoted many pages to articles about "Doing Diplomacy Online" or department offices at the forefront of digital diplomacy.[20] Digital transformation has also affected how the State Department manages its employees and organization; new media techniques have enhanced collaboration within the department and between headquarters and the field.

Social media has shown its power to organize protests and shed light on local or global problems, and so America's representatives must participate in the immediate, online conversations taking place around the world. But as they take advantage of the digital revolution and incorporate it into the department's diplomatic culture, US diplomats have also learned that despite the transformative possibilities of these new forms of global interaction, there are limits to the long-term commitments to action and enduring institutional connections that social media can make. The speed of the social media and digital world is another challenge to the diplomatic culture. As Philip Seib has written, "A fundamental incompatibility exists between speed and diplomacy. Effective diplomacy cannot be done on the fly; it requires back and forth among parties, ability to listen and to respond carefully." There are also two other key questions—about hierarchy and the enormous volume of information. What is the right balance between letting people tweet and hewing to the policies and messages set by the president and the secretary? How can senior officials manage and, more important, judge the importance or relevance of the tsunami of data, emails, cables, and other forms of modern communication? The aftermath of the tragedy in Benghazi is just one example of this new challenge.

However the department's culture evolves in the near term, today's diplomats are surely in what Anne-Marie Slaughter called a "networked world."[21] Cooper, Heine, and Thakur made the creative observation that there is a shift from "club" to "network diplomacy," writing, "The former is based on a small number of players, a highly hierarchical structure, based largely on written communication and on low transparency; the latter is based on a much larger number of players, a flatter structure, a more significant oral component and greater transparency."[22]

Fourth, the State Department simultaneously embraces and rebels against institutional hierarchy. Most State Department employees say they want clear direction from the top. But Kissinger described a well-known tactic: An assistant secretary who, "because he opposed the decision he feared I would make," used

> the splendid machinery so methodically to 'clear' a memorandum I had requested that it took weeks to reach me; when it arrived it was diluted of all sharpness and my own staff bounced it back again and again for greater precision—thereby serving the bureau chief's purposes better than my own. Alternatively, the machinery may permit a strategically placed official's hobby horse to gallop through, eliciting an innocent nod from a Secretary unfamiliar with all the code words and implications.[23]

An additional complication in managing hierarchy is the presence of noncareer (political) appointees in the department. The State Department benefits from first-rate outsiders who bring new energy, perspectives, and modern ways of doing business, and many outstanding noncareer appointees have served at home and abroad (and there have been poor career appointees as well). From the Kennedy administration to Bush 43, the percentage of career to noncareer appointees at embassies abroad has generally been two-thirds career and one-third political. The Obama administration raised this noncareer number to 35 percent.[24] A number of these nominees were campaign finance "bundlers" whose performance at confirmation hearings or at their posts once confirmed was cause for embarrassment. A report by the American Academy of Diplomacy repeats a call on presidents to meet the requirements of the Foreign Service Act of 1980 when making ambassadorial nominations and to cap the number of noncareer ambassadors at 10 percent.[25]

Fifth, the State Department, like other agencies in the government, has a mix of norms and organizational structures and behaviors, some still relevant, others legacies beyond their shelf life. As former ambassador Craig Johnstone has described one legacy habit, hundreds of people at State write "talking points" that move up the system as if the senior leadership of the department can solve foreign policy problems by reciting these lines in public or to foreign leaders. This might have been the right structure when the only conversation that mattered was between the secretary of state and the Soviet foreign minister. In today's world the major challenges cannot be solved by talking points. Fighting terrorism and extremism, combating cyber attacks, defeating narco-terrorism, preventing genocide, promoting sustainable development, stopping the trafficking in human beings, and combating outbreaks of disease are just a few examples that require frontline action by the State Department and other US government agencies. Since so many of the challenges involve a whole-of-government response, there is a premium on an efficient, strategically guided interagency process coordinated by the National Security Council (NSC) staff without its becoming a daily operator of the policy.

James Baker described the cultural legacy this way: "The State Department has the most unique bureaucratic culture I've ever encountered. . . . At State, the inanimate came alive. While to most people the State Department is just a rather ugly, monolithic post–World War II eight-story monstrosity overlooking the Mall in Foggy Bottom, to its inhabitants it's 'the building'—a living breathing being that has opinions and policies of its own."[26] The "building" can also produce action and information channels that promote the interests of some bureaus within the department over others. The result is often conflict instead of collaboration. For example, the unresolved tension between regional bureaus—which historically have the upper hand, as they have a major say in follow-on personnel assignments, especially to posts abroad—and functional bureaus is a significant impediment to collaboration. While regional bureaus can most quickly bring the art of what is possible to the table and galvanize embassy action, they also suffer the most "clientitis," the tendency to be overly concerned with another country's sensitivities. Regional bureaus have also historically resisted incorporating the new parts of the diplomatic agenda, such as human rights or environmental protection, into their work. This has resulted in a proliferation of functional bureaus, some demanded or established by Congress.

There also remains tension between the foreign service and civil service in the department. The department is strongest when both services are empowered to make their unique skills contributions. For example, functional bureaus have often struggled to recruit FSOs to serve in them; the fact that functional bureaus have more civil servants reinforces (wrongly) their second-class status in the institution. There are other cultural divisions as well: people at the department have developed and maintained an informal, internal cultural hierarchy based on functional cones and a "guild" system based on regional expertise, language training (which creates further subcultures of Arabists, Chinese language officers, Japanese language officers, etc.), and other skill-based subcultures, such as staff and special assistants.

One structure that stands the test of time is the country team, the organizing principle in American embassies abroad, which brings together under the ambassador's leadership the representatives of all of the federal agencies with personnel in that country. The CSIS study *Embassy of the Future* describes the interagency character of embassies: "The scope and scale of representation from other Federal agencies at Embassies have been growing steadily, with 27 agencies (and numerous sub-agencies) represented overseas. In some large Embassies, the proportion of State Department representation relative to other Federal agencies can be less than one-third of full-time U.S. personnel."[27] Defining the future of embassies and ambassadors is not just a question for American diplomatic culture, as former Indian diplomat Kishan Rana highlights in his book *The Contemporary Embassy*.[28]

An ambassador's ability to inspire all country team elements to pursue common objectives is validated by a letter from the president describing the ambassador's responsibility for all executive branch personnel assigned to his or her country with the exception of military units deployed under the command of a combatant commander (see box 4.1). The *Embassy of the Future* report notes that twenty-first-century challenges will require strengthening this presidential letter to increase ambassadorial authorities. As US diplomats become more dispersed geographically and even more interactions abroad involve law enforcement, the need for an in-country authority to ensure that US interests are being pursued increases.[29] The challenges of new media, reviewed earlier, will—perhaps paradoxically at first glance—require more on-the-scene judgment from ambassadors.

Sixth, despite recent efforts—including the 2010 and 2015 Quadrennial Diplomacy and Development Reviews (QDDRs)[30]—there is still an aversion at State to engaging in strategic

---

BOX 4.1
Sample Presidential Letter of Instruction to
Chiefs of Mission (Excerpts)

As Chief of Mission, you have full responsibility for the direction, coordination, and supervision of all U.S. Executive Branch employees in [country], regardless of their employment categories or location, except those under command of a U.S. area military commander or on the staff of an international organization. With these exceptions, you are in charge of all Executive Branch activities and operations in your Mission.

You have full responsibility for the direction, coordination, and supervision of all Department of Defense personnel on official duty in [country] except those under the command of a U.S. area military commander. You and the area military commander must keep each other currently and fully informed and cooperate on all matters of mutual interest. Any differences that cannot be resolved in the field will be reported to the Secretary of State and the Secretary of Defense.

I ask that you review programs, personnel, and funding levels regularly, and ensure that all agencies attached to your Mission do likewise. Rightsizing the United States government presence abroad is a continuing requirement. To better meet our foreign policy goals, the performance of priority Mission goals and objectives, I urge you to initiate staffing changes in accordance with established procedures.

Every Executive Branch agency under your authority must obtain your approval before changing the size, composition, or mandate of its staff.

Source: US Department of State

---

planning and to making the crucial operational link between policy and resources. This is not just to increase the resources available to the department but also to draw institutional interests within the department together simultaneously through joint planning and reviews. This is not a new observation. Writing in 1969, Andrew Scott noted that among the beliefs held by FSOs was that the

> skilled conduct of foreign affairs involved more of art than of science . . . one of the reasons that the conduct of foreign policy is art rather than of science is that each problem that confronts the Foreign Service Officer is unique. He must take up each problem as it presents itself . . . and deal with it as best he can. He must then pass on to the next problem, knowing that its solution will owe very little to the solutions found in earlier problems. Since this is the case . . . efforts at 'planning' can be of little use.[31]

It will be important that any updated QDDRs continue the effort to link policy and resources.

AFGHANISTAN AND IRAQ, 2001–3: CULTURE OPERATING IN THE INTERAGENCY

The international culture of diplomacy, American diplomacy's adaptation of that culture, and the lessons drawn from how the State Department behaves as an institution contribute to the way the department plays its role in the interagency process. The State Department's history and culture influenced the way America's diplomats reacted to the murderous attacks of September 11, 2001, and the way they then participated in the interagency debate about both pre- and post-conflict actions by the United States and its allies and partners in Afghanistan and Iraq, a debate that has continued into an era defined by the still vital global effort to defeat terrorism and extremism.

Post-9/11: Afghanistan

The State Department's immediate response to 9/11, diplomatically and in the interagency process, drew on the positive aspects of the diplomatic culture, seeking to create the widest coalition against terrorism. The North Atlantic Treaty Organization (NATO) declared the attacks of 9/11 an attack on all NATO members, invoking Article V of the NATO treaty for the first time in history. Even if for their own reasons, Russia and China supported an international effort against terrorism that translated (with the strong backing of and creative diplomacy from our traditional allies, especially the United Kingdom) into international obligations to fight terrorism, including cutting off terrorist financing.

Following work begun in the Clinton administration, State Department leaders had been focused since the Bush 43 inauguration on the overseas threat to US interests from the Taliban and al-Qaeda. Department managers were convinced that al-Qaeda would attack American interests outside the United States. Alert levels at diplomatic installations around the world in the spring and summer of 2001 were increased, and Washington directly warned the Taliban that if al-Qaeda attacked American interests anywhere in the world, they would be held responsible.

After President Bush's decision to invade Afghanistan, State worked closely with the Central Command (CENTCOM), taking the lead to gain the support of neighboring nations so that US forces could base and stage from these countries. Post-9/11 interagency groups included participants not previously considered part of the national security establishment, such as the Department of Health and Human Services and the Department of Transportation. September 11, 2001, highlighted another issue as well. Richard Haass noted, "In principle and design, the NSC ought to be neutral on policy or at least determined to make sure that its honest broker role enjoys pride of place before it assumes the stance of counselor." But it was "at least two and a half to one against State on almost every issue just by the time we sat down with our interagency peers."[32] Indeed, during this period there was conflict in the interagency system, especially between the Department of Defense (DOD) and State. The conflict was often based on personality clashes at all levels; however, at root the struggle had organizational cultural and ideological foundations.

There was profound disagreement, for example, about whether the United States should engage in nation building, a policy President Bush had campaigned against in 2000. State Department professionals were generally proud of the effort the United States had made in nation building and in peacekeeping: for example, supporting the deployment of US military forces to participate in the Multinational Force and Observers (MFO) in the Sinai, which DOD was determined to end; peacekeeping and nation-building activities in East Timor, Haiti, and the Balkans, including strong continuing support for the Dayton Accords; and the restoration of civil society after NATO military action in Serbia and Kosovo. Most department officials believed nation building, properly funded and done right, could be an effective long-term foreign policy tool of the United States.

The aftermath of 9/11 and the war in Afghanistan put stress on some of State's cultural traits. For example, by joining the US government consensus to reject NATO's immediate offer of military assistance in Afghanistan, the department jettisoned too much of its cultural instinct for allies and engagement.[33] The department too quickly accepted the notion that a formal NATO role in support of US forces would provoke a clash of civilizations. The DOD opposed NATO's involvement because it felt the alliance would constrain US military operations. The interagency was thus united in opposition to NATO participation for different (and both wrong) reasons. Many allied and friendly forces eventually operated in Afghanistan with great valor and effect, but an approach that had initially embraced a NATO role would have better served the larger cause.

Collaboration, competition, or misunderstanding between agencies is not, of course, limited to interactions between DOD and the State Department. Thirty years ago, the State Department's relationship with elements of the intelligence community was often contentious. These relationships have over time become more routine and collaborative. As law enforcement took an increasingly important role in American foreign policy after the mid-1980s, the department struggled to establish an understanding with the Department of Justice and its elements deployed overseas, such as the Federal Bureau of Investigation (FBI). As counterterrorism became a priority for the US government, agencies fought over turf, information, and credit, frighteningly well described by Lawrence Wright in *The Looming Tower*.[34] The creation of the Department of Homeland Security (DHS) after the attacks of September 11, 2001, also required adjustment on the part of the State Department and other players in the interagency arena, especially as DHS deployed officers abroad and began to adjudicate visa questions.

Iraq

While State Department leaders were reluctant to invade Iraq in spring 2003, most did not rule out the use of force against Saddam Hussein forever; the department sought instead to use the year to try to re-create the successful Gulf War coalition of President George H. W. Bush, an outcome more consistent with State Department culture. The department argued that the United States and its allies might compel Saddam to submit through a show of force in early 2003 or, if this failed, might move forward with a sustained diplomatic effort to create a broad coalition to use force in the fall of 2003. This possibility lost all relevance on January 20, 2003, when the French government announced Paris would never support a second UN Security Council resolution (the first resolution was seen as a success for American diplomacy) to authorize the use of force in Iraq.

The department's cultural preference for negotiation did not serve as a good guide to institutional behavior for most of the senior State people who participated in the interagency debate leading to the invasion of Iraq. Senior department officers participated in planning for the conflict and its aftermath assuming—or, perhaps better put, hoping—that events either at home or abroad would turn preparations for conflict into successful coercive diplomacy rather than the military action that took place in the spring of 2003. Then–State Department director of policy planning Richard Haass observed that while he was "60–40 against going to war" (he was assuming that Iraq had weapons of mass destruction [WMDs]; if he had known they did not, he would have been 90–10 against the war), "no organization could function if people left every time they lost out on a 60–40 decision."[35]

While one intensive diplomatic effort ended, another began in earnest. From January 20, 2003, on, the State Department supported CENTCOM commander Gen. Tommy Franks in order to make the war as short and successful as possible to limit American, allied, and Iraqi civilian casualties. Just as in the run-up to the invasion of Afghanistan, the department worked with military commanders to seek access to facilities for US forces and to participate in the public diplomacy effort to gain as much support as possible for the armed liberation of Iraq from Saddam Hussein. Ironically, there was substantial State–DOD collaboration on the effort to persuade Turkey to allow the Fourth Infantry Division to transit that country to create a northern front in the battle against Saddam's forces. Although the department had serious reservations about the size of DOD's request to Ankara, State worked with both civilian and military authorities at the Pentagon to try to meet the need that had been identified by the chairman of the Joint Chiefs of Staff. Unfortunately, this joint DOD–State diplomacy could not overcome a negative vote in the Turkish Parliament.

Looking back on the Afghanistan and Iraq episodes, the State Department's response to these post-conflict challenges displayed both the pluses and minuses of the department's culture and the influence of resource restraints under which US foreign policy operates. The political effort to create a new Afghan government, which began in 2001, drew on the strengths of the department—for example, the capacity to forge consensus among disparate interests, including working with Iran—and is well described in Ambassador James Dobbins's book *After the Taliban*.[36] Although the State Department participated in planning for post-conflict Iraq, the department did not have the capacity to take responsibility for the immediate post-conflict administration.[37] While it might have made more sense to have State in charge, the department leadership, faced with the lack of State resources, agreed to the executive order creating the post-conflict Iraq structure that reported to the secretary of defense. On July 1, 2004, the State Department did open (on time and on budget) an embassy in Baghdad that allowed an expansion of diplomacy in Iraq and more effective senior civilian cooperation with US military forces.[38]

SOME LESSONS LEARNED: THE 2011–12 DIPLOMATIC CAMPAIGN IN AFGHANISTAN AND PAKISTAN

The decade of war in Afghanistan and Iraq has changed the way the State Department and the US government more generally have conceived and carried out their strategies. Drawing on successful examples of a whole-of-government approach to multifaceted challenges—such as Plan Colombia, the Proliferation Security Initiative, the Millennium Challenge Corporation, or the historic response to AIDS—the Obama administration looked for a new way to proceed in Afghanistan and Pakistan that tried to more holistically orchestrate the diplomatic, development, and defense instruments of national power.

This effort began when President Barack Obama and Secretary Clinton announced Richard Holbrooke's appointment as the US special representative for Afghanistan and Pakistan (SRAP) in January 2009. The message was that the whole-of-government philosophy—employing expertise and resources from all relevant parts of government—was required to address the nation's most important challenges. This is, in fact, the right model for twenty-first-century diplomacy and reflects a further evolution in the State Department culture. The author fully embraced this philosophy, having both advocated and practiced it during his career. After Holbrooke's death in December 2010, some asked if that effort would continue. Secretary Clinton promised that it would, and starting in February 2011, when the author was appointed to succeed Holbrooke, he continued the approach.[39]

President Obama laid the foundations for the 2011–12 diplomatic effort in Afghanistan and Pakistan in the first two years of his administration. Secretary Clinton launched the effort in a speech at the Asia Society in New York on February 18, 2011.[40] In her remarks she made clear that the military surge then underway in Afghanistan was a vital part of American strategy. Without the heroic effort of US forces, joined by many allies, friends, and partners, there was no chance of pursuing a diplomatic end to thirty years of conflict. But Clinton also reminded her audience of the civilian surge underway in Afghanistan, which had brought thousands of courageous, non-DOD Americans from many US government agencies, as well as international and Afghan civilians, to promote economic development, good governance, the power of civil society, and the advancement of women within their society.

In her speech Secretary Clinton called for a "diplomatic surge" to match the military and civilian efforts to try to catalyze and shape a political end to the war. This goal required orchestrating, with SRAP in the lead, all of our diplomatic resources to engage the countries in the region to support Afghanistan. It also meant, she said, trying to sustain a dialogue with the Taliban to see if its leaders were ready to talk to the Afghan government about the future.

The SRAP team rebranded this diplomatic surge, calling it a "diplomatic campaign," to emphasize that this would not be a series of ad hoc engagements, but rather an effort that followed a comprehensive plan. The campaign would require simultaneous, coordinated action by the SRAP team to connect the military effort with the instruments of nonmilitary power in South and Central Asia, including official development assistance, involvement of the private sector, support for civil society, and the use of both bilateral and multilateral diplomacy. The SRAP team devised, along with our Afghan partners, a road map designed to shape, direct, and leverage the international agenda on Afghanistan, which was punctuated by four international meetings already set for 2011–12.

The other key component of the diplomatic campaign's regional strategy was based on the recognition that no regional structure in support of Afghanistan would succeed without a strong economic component, including a key role for the private sector. (Getting the private sector more involved is yet another necessary part of the cultural evolution of American diplomacy.) Secretary Clinton announced the US vision—a "New Silk Road"—at a speech in Chennai, India, in July 2011.[41] The American objective was to connect the vibrant economies in Central Asia with India's economic success, with Afghanistan and Pakistan in the center so they could both benefit. In his book *Monsoon*, Robert Kaplan provided a view of the larger connections: "Stabilizing Afghanistan is about more than just the anti-terror war against al-Qaida and the Taliban; it is about securing the future prosperity of the whole of southern Eurasia."[42] The Chinese government has expanded this vision into a comprehensive infrastructure and development project they call One Belt, One Road.

The future of both Afghanistan and Pakistan remains a key issue for today's diplomats. Elections brought new governments to both countries, although the two main Afghan leaders have yet to consolidate a working relationship, and the military in Pakistan retains a major say in government policies. The United States, supported by NATO and other nations, has decided to maintain a modest troop presence in Afghanistan to train and support Afghan forces who have shown a willingness to fight in the face of Taliban efforts to control territory, strike coalition forces, and launch brutal terrorist attacks. At a meeting in Brussels in October 2016, the international community committed to continuing significant funding levels of assistance for Afghanistan through 2020.

As SRAP, the author found the Obama interagency process to be positive, especially compared to some of its predecessors. The president, Secretary Clinton, the NSC, the principals and deputies, as well as special groups formed to support the diplomatic campaign in 2011–12, including the conversation we attempted to have with the Taliban, gave support and guidance. There were occasions when some colleagues tried to micromanage the conversation with the Taliban in ways designed to make it impossible to continue, but the need to keep interagency representatives engaged and as supportive as possible overrode the periodic frustrations.[43] The chairman and vice chairman of the Joint Chiefs of Staff, along with Gen. James Mattis, Gen. David Petraeus, and Gen. John Allen, military leaders of US CENTCOM and the International Security and Assistance Force (ISAF), were always ready to consult on ways the diplomatic campaign could support the military strategy in Afghanistan and the region and vice versa. SRAP also worked closely with the intelligence community.

It is worth stepping back from this discussion of SRAP to consider the larger question of special envoys. Secretary Powell made a point of abolishing those that existed at the start of his tenure, but even he had to allow a few into the department over his four years as secretary. President Obama and Secretary Clinton posed a considerable test to the department's culture by appointing of a large number of special envoys, many noncareer. This trend has continued under Secretary Kerry, who has, for example, appointed special envoys or representatives to the peace talk in Colombia, to organize the fight against Daesh, to focus on issues in Africa, and to promote the human rights of LGBT people. Reaction to the envoys in the department is always mixed, reflecting ambivalence to those outside the institutional structure taking roles that appear to diminish the primacy of the traditional leadership in the regional bureaus and country teams. Some regional bureaus have embraced the special envoy and have tried to use her or his presence to enhance the department's role in diplomacy. Other parts of the bureaucracy hope that the permanent institutions of the department will overwhelm the newcomers. The author sought to manage these natural challenges as a special envoy (SRAP) by promoting the whole-of-government logic for the position while forging a productive relationship with the Bureau of South and Central Asian Affairs (SCA) and other department relevant offices.

Special envoys and representatives will be a part of American diplomacy for the foreseeable future, and the department culture will need to adapt to that reality. A 2014 report on special envoys by the US Institute for Peace made a series of practical suggestions worth noting, including the need for clear "objectives and scope determined carefully at the outset, examined regularly in light of the situation, adapted to reflect changing US priorities, and reassessed when they seem to be losing credibility." The report concluded that special envoys and representatives need to be directly engaged with the president or secretary of state and they "must have earned and must continue to display the skills of building consensus and trust" among various stakeholders.[44]

GLOBAL CHALLENGES TODAY:
TRANSFORMING THE STATE DEPARTMENT

The wars in Afghanistan and Iraq have changed the State Department. Beyond the policy and interagency challenges, they produced new structures and experiences for State Department employees, especially the provincial reconstruction teams (PRTs), which require close interaction with US military forces at a more junior level than has been the norm since Vietnam. These conflicts also produced broader and deeper expertise in directing programs for State Department officers and employees. Tours of duty in these war zones and other conflict areas are also influencing promotions and assignment. Service in Iraq, Afghanistan, and Pakistan will be a key factor for future advancement. The promotion of those who have gained experience in conflict zones will bring whole-of-government practices and experiences further into the department's mainstream culture.

Happily, war was not the only catalyst for change at State. Reform of America's diplomatic infrastructure has accelerated since the late 1990s.[45] Secretary of State Madeleine Albright supported major changes in the way the department recruits and retains its personnel. New functional bureaus have been added to the organization to reflect new missions, including post-conflict stabilization and combatting human trafficking. As noted earlier, Secretary Powell launched the DRI, hiring almost 1,200 new State Department employees during his tenure and emphasizing leadership and accountability by senior managers. Secretary Rice continued to highlight the need for diplomatic transformation and increased the department's resources, including personnel.[46] Secretary Clinton took advantage of the tipping point that had been reached in favor of increasing civilian capacity. However, shrinking federal budgets will pose challenges to Secretary Kerry and his successors; this continuing challenge is another reason for the department to take its QDDR process seriously.

Future leaders of the department will continue to confront cultural challenges as they press for an ever more modern American diplomacy; the international culture of diplomacy is attractive, and bureaucratic interests are strong. Some will argue that it is not State's job to try to close the gap Kissinger identified so many years ago: that State can be an institution more interested in the mechanics of diplomacy and negotiation than in the creation of policy. And as the CSIS report *Embassy of the Future* made clear, more people and more money are only part of the answer: better training, better technology, and a continued evolution in the department's attitude to allow a move from strict force protection to risk management are required so that, for example, ambassadors can make risk-based judgments about security in the service of the mission and not fear that any security incident at their posts will result in questions about their capacity to carry out their mission.[47] The events in Benghazi in 2012 and the subsequent furor over exactly these difficult trade-offs will likely prompt an unwelcome return to a strict definition of force protection as the default position.

There are other challenges to transforming American diplomacy. The American public is impatient; diplomacy requires a long-term perspective. There will always be a strain in American thinking that equates diplomacy with weakness.[48] Others argue State can never meet its twenty-first-century obligations without a wholesale renovation.[49] It is also crucial to recognize that diplomacy is not the answer to every question; maintaining a strong defense and demonstrating the willingness to use force (preferably with others in coalitions, but alone if necessary) are essential to successful diplomacy.

We are entering a new era when the role of diplomacy will be both more important and more challenging. Will the American public be prepared to continue to shoulder global responsibility? As Robert Kagan has written, "American foreign policy may be moving away from the sense of global responsibility that equated American interests with the interests of many others around the world and back to a defense of narrower, more parochial interests."[50] This at a time when there are, as Henry Kissinger wrote in his 2014 book, *World Order*, serious challenges to the legitimacy of an international system that has by and large promoted US goals and interests, ranging from Vladimir Putin's attack on Europe's post–Cold War borders to the Daesh's effort to remake the Middle East.[51]

America's diplomatic culture is rooted in the optimistic and pragmatic nature of the American people, who believe that problems can be solved, crises avoided or mitigated, wars avoided, and peace made. Harry Kopp and the late Charles Gillespie started their book *Career Diplomacy* by describing a conversation between a businessperson and a former FSO. The businessperson wants to know why we needed diplomats in the twenty-first century. It seemed to him we could get all the information we needed from the news. Kopp and Gillespie wrote, "We need to make sense of the world, and we need to make sure the world makes sense of us. We need to understand, protect, and promote our own interests. Whenever and wherever we can, we need to shape events to our advantage."[52] These objectives are principles worth recalling as future presidents, future secretaries of state, and the people of the State Department work to further change the culture of American diplomacy so that it can live up to its calling as America's first line of defense.

NOTES

The author wishes to reiterate his appreciation to all those cited in the first edition for their support. The revised edition benefitted again from the support of the Cohen Group: Jenny McFarland, Seth Gainer, Hannah Hudson, Destin Moag, and Thomas Cohen all made crucial contributions. Mildred Patterson again made the text better in every way. All errors remain, of course, the author's responsibility.

1. Paul Gordon Lauren, Gordon A. Craig, and Alexander L. George, *Force and Statecraft: Diplomatic Challenges of Our Time*, 4th ed. (London: Oxford University Press, 2007).

2. Jean-Robert Leguey-Feilleux, *The Dynamics of Diplomacy* (Boulder, CO: Lynne Rienner, 2009), 23–36.

3. Lauren, Craig, and George, *Force and Statecraft*; Leguey-Feilleux, *Dynamics of Diplomacy*; and Henry Kissinger, *Diplomacy* (New York: Simon & Schuster, 1994).

4. Garrett Mattingly, *Renaissance Diplomacy* (New York: Courier Dove, 1988).

5. Mattingly, *Renaissance Diplomacy*, 35.

6. Robert Kagan, *Dangerous Nation* (New York: Knopf, 2006), 41. There is, of course, plenty of ambivalence in America about America's proper role in the world. See Henry Kissinger, *World Order* (New York: Penguin, 2014).

7. Henry Kissinger, *Years of Upheaval* (London: Little, Brown, 1982), 442–45. For an excellent review of many non-American diplomatic cultures, see Kishan Rana, *21st Century Diplomacy* (New York: Continuum International, 2011).

8. James A. Baker III, *The Politics of Diplomacy* (New York: G. P. Putnam's Sons, 1995), 31.

9. Richard Haass, *War of Necessity, War of Choice* (New York: Simon & Schuster, 2009), 182.

10. Baker, *Politics of Diplomacy*, 31.

11. Hillary Rodham Clinton, *Hard Choices* (New York: Simon & Schuster, 2014).

12. Helene Cooper, "Foreign Service Officers Resist Mandatory Iraq Postings?" *New York Times*, November 1, 2003.

13. Robert Gates, speech at CSIS, Washington, DC, January 26, 2008.

14. US State Department and USAID Fact Sheets, Bureau of Public Affairs, March 4, 2014, www.state.gov/documents/organization/252179.pdf. CBO Estimate of Discretionary Appropriations for Fiscal Year 2014, Including HR 3547, the Consolidated Appropriations Act, 2014, as posted on the website of the House Committee on Rules on January 13, 2014, https://cbo.gov/sites/default/files/cbofiles/attachments/hr3547.pdf.

15. Bureau of Human Resources, Department of State, "HR Fact Sheet," June 30, 2016, http://afsa.org/sites/default/files/0616_state_dept_hr_factsheet.pdf; and Defense Manpower Data Center, "Military and Civilian Personnel by Service/Agency by State/Country (Updated Quarterly)," June 2016, www.dmdc.osd.mil/appj/dwp/dwp_reports.jsp.

16. J. Anthony Holmes, "Where Are the Civilians? How to Reveal the US Foreign Service," *Foreign Affairs* 88, no. 1 (January/February 2009): 151; and Tim Kane, *Global U.S. Troop Deployment, 1950–2005* (Washington, DC: Heritage Foundation, May 24, 2006), http://www.heritage.org/research/reports/2006/05/global-us-troop-deployment-1950-2005.

17. Gordon Adams and Cindy Williams, *Buying National Security* (New York: Routledge, 2010), 1; and Alison Stanger, *One Nation under Contract* (New Haven: Yale University Press, 2009), 34–83.

18. Gates, speech at CSIS.

19. Department of State, "Diversity Statistics Full-time Permanent Employees," September 30, 2016, www.state.gov/documents/organization/254216.pdf.

20. See, for example, *Foreign Service Journal*, January/February 2014, and *State Magazine*, December 2009.

21. There is already considerable interesting reading on this subject, including Eric Schmidt and Jared Cohen, *The New Digital Age* (New York: Alfred Knopf, 2013); Philip Seib, *Real Time Diplomacy*

(New York: Palgrave Macmillan, 2012); *Foreign Service Journal*, January/February 2014; Malcolm Gladwell, "Small Change," *New Yorker*, October 4, 2010, 42–49; Thomas L. Friedman, "Facebook Meets Brick and Mortar Politics," *New York Times*, June 9, 2012; "The Internet: For Better or for Worse," *New York Review of Books*, April 7, 2011, 20–24; "ISIS Displaying a Deft Command of Varied Media," *New York Times*, August 31, 2014; and Anne-Marie Slaughter, "America's Edge," *Foreign Affairs*, January/February 2009.

22. Andrew F. Cooper, Jorge Heine, and Ramesh Thakur, eds., *The Oxford Handbook of Modern Diplomacy* (Oxford: Oxford University Press), 22.

23. Kissinger, *Years of Upheaval*, 440.

24. American Foreign Service Association, List of Ambassadorial Appointments, January 15, 2015, http://www.afsa.org/ambassadorlist.aspx.

25. American Academy of Diplomacy, *American Diplomacy at Risk* (Washington, DC, April 2015), 61, www.academyofdiplomacy.org/wp-content/uploads/2016/01/ADAR_Full_Report_4.1.15 .pdf.

26. Baker, *Politics of Diplomacy*, 28. Secretary Clinton also refers in *Hard Choices* to hearing "the building" referred to as if it were a living object.

27. George L. Argyros, Marc Grossman, and Felix G. Rohatyn, *Embassy of the Future* (Washington, DC: Center for Strategic and International Studies, 2007), 47.

28. Kishan Rana, *The Contemporary Embassy: Paths to Diplomatic Excellence* (New York: Palgrave Macmillan, 2013).

29. Argyros, Grossman, and Rohatyn, *Embassy of the Future*, 48.

30. US Department of State, *Leading through Civilian Power: The First Quadrennial Diplomacy and Development Review* (Washington, DC, 2010); and US Department of State, *Enduring Leadership in a Dynamic World* (Washington, DC, 2015).

31. Andrew M. Scott, "The Department of State: Formal Organization and Information Culture," *International Studies Quarterly* 13, no. 1 (March 1969): 3.

32. Haass, *War of Necessity*, 184.

33. State Department employees were affected by the 9/11 attacks, not just as professionals (State Department officers had been the victims of terrorism for thirty years) but as citizens; they, too, were surprised and shocked. Many officers in the State Department building look out across the Potomac to the Pentagon, and so hundreds, if not thousands, of State Department employees watched the smoke rise as DOD colleagues, friends, and family perished, were injured, or fought the flames. *Washington Post* columnist David Ignatius has said that the surprise and violence of the 9/11 attacks knocked America's individual and national gyroscopes off center. State Department employees (I certainly include myself) suffered from this gyroscopic imbalance. One example of this loss of balance is that our post-9/11 foreign policy became militarized. This seemed required at the time. It was not. The imbalance between civilian and military capabilities in our government is a continuing national challenge.

34. Lawrence Wright, *The Looming Tower: Al-Qaida and the Road to 9/11* (New York: Vintage Books, 2007).

35. Haass, *War of Necessity*, 247. Haass's book contains other examples of the cultural clash between the State and Defense Departments over Iraq. A more recent view of the trade-offs at the highest levels is in the December 22–29, 2014, edition of the *New Yorker*, in a profile of US United Nations ambassador Samantha Power by Evan Osnos, 90–107.

36. James Dobbins, *After the Taliban* (Washington, DC: Potomac Books, 2008).

37. James Dobbins, *America's Role in Nation Building: From Germany to Iraq* (Santa Monica, CA: Rand, 2003).

38. Much of the NSC-led postwar planning was detailed but focused on lessons learned from the first Gulf War. There were elaborate plans to forestall another Kurdish refugee crisis and plans that would, no doubt, have successfully stopped starvation. The department's Future of Iraq: Project, while important, would not have solved Iraq's postwar problems.

39. I have previously discussed this diplomatic campaign. "Seven Cities in Two Years: The Diplomatic Campaign in Afghanistan and Pakistan," *Yale Journal of International Affairs* 8, no. 2 (Summer 2013): 65–75.

40. Hillary Clinton, "Remarks at the Launch of the Asia Society's Series of Richard C. Holbrook Memorial Addresses" (speech given at the Asia Society, New York, February 11, 2011).

41. Hillary Clinton, "Remarks on India and the United States: A Vision for the 21st Century" (speech given Anna Centenary Library, Shehnai, India, July 20, 2011).

42. Robert D. Kaplan, *Monsoon* (New York: Random House, 2011), 14.

43. Clinton, *Hard Choices*, 163. I have dealt at more length with the attempt to talk to the Taliban in *PRISM* 4, no. 4 (2014): 21–37.

44. US Institute for Peace, *Using Special Envoys in High Stakes Conflict Diplomacy* (Washington, DC, October 2014), 3–7.

45. Marc Grossman, "An American Diplomacy for the 21st Century" (speech given at Foreign Affairs Day, Washington, DC, September 10, 2001).

46. Secretary Rice's speeches at Georgetown University, January 18, 2006, and February 12, 2008.

47. Argyros, Grossman, and Rohatyn, *Embassy of the Future*.

48. Angelo M. Codevilla, *Advice to War Presidents* (New York: Basic Books, 2009), 75–109.

49. Kori N. Schake, *State of Disrepair* (Stanford: Hoover Institution Press, 2012).

50. Robert Kagan, "Superpowers Don't Get to Retire," *New Republic*, May 26, 2014.

51. Kissinger, *World Order*.

52. Kopp and Gillespie, *Career Diplomacy*, 3.

CHAPTER 5

The US Agency for International Development

More Operator than Policymaker

Desaix Myers

> Fundamentally, AID's purpose is National Security. By national security, we also mean a world of independent nations capable of making economic and social progress through free institutions.
> —David Bell, second USAID administrator (1962–66)

There are a number of reasons why the US Agency for International Development (USAID), the lead US government agency for development assistance, has been an inconsistent player in the national security enterprise for much of its more-than-fifty-year history. It is a field agency established to produce transformational change through development assistance, and its culture and structure bend it toward field operations and policy implementation overseas rather than policy analysis and advocacy at home. The gap between the time required to achieve the change sought by development programs and the urgency of national security demands creates a natural tension between USAID and the national security community. Many in USAID have been ambivalent about their role in national security while members of the national security community, interested in the resources represented in development assistance, have been disappointed that USAID can't produce results more quickly.

There have been times, during the Cold War and particularly in Vietnam, when USAID has been seen as integral to national security strategy. Called on to help defeat an enemy—communism—it worked with the government and civil society organizations to address root causes with programs to boost jobs, health, and education and to combat poverty and bad government. More recently, with the wars in Iraq and Afghanistan, the White House has described development as "a strategic economic and moral imperative" and called it one of the three pillars (the Three Ds) of national security, equal to defense and diplomacy in advancing US interests abroad.[1]

But the institutional change sought by development programs takes time, and those looking to USAID to reconstruct government capacity in Vietnam, Iraq, Afghanistan, or other unstable environments have been disappointed. They have seen USAID as falling short. But in fact, their expectations have been unrealistic. They have seen USAID's successful work in emergency response and so frequently look to the agency to respond to international crises with national security dimensions—Yazidis trapped on Mt. Sinjar; Syrian refugees in Jordan,

Lebanon, and Turkey; a tsunami in the Philippines; Boko Haram in Nigeria; Ebola in West Africa. Increasingly, USAID has been called on, in the words of one ambassador, to be "an operational arm of diplomacy,"[2] to advance short-term political objectives in national security hotspots like Ukraine, Yemen, or Central America.

The tension between short-term and long-term objectives has contributed to USAID's inconsistent role in national security. So too has debate over USAID's authorities and responsibilities. There is general agreement on the importance of foreign aid, described by political scientist Hans Morgenthau as one of the "real innovations which the modern age has introduced into the practice of foreign policy."[3] But questions remain about exactly what it is, how it should be used, how much it is worth, and who should be responsible for it.

Part of this confusion stems from a common conflation of terms; "foreign aid" and "development assistance" are easily confused. Foreign aid is broader and can be used for a variety of policy objectives—humanitarian, political, commercial, tactical—including development itself. Development assistance, one form of foreign aid, is aimed at producing transformational change, economic and social progress, and the betterment of the human condition.[4] It contributes to national security in the long term by working with governments and civil society to address underlying issues like poverty, weak institutions, and bad policy. It builds resilience and the capacity to respond to national security threats—demographic or environmental changes, resource shortages, infectious disease, violent extremism, and cross-border crime.

With their focus on development, USAID's staffers have had mixed feelings about the demands from the national security community for short-term results. This ambivalence has been reinforced by the agency's structure and culture. The agency is structured to support field operations rather than make national security policy. The culture is dominated by a foreign service whose members spend most of their time overseas rather than in Washington and have limited experience in the interagency policy community. Historically, many have avoided linking themselves too closely with security programs or the intelligence community for fear of jeopardizing local working relationships. Except for those who served in Vietnam or Bosnia/Kosovo, few had experience with the military. All that changed with September 11, 2001.

This chapter explores the nature of this change and what it might mean for USAID's role in the national security enterprise. It begins by reviewing USAID's history. It then looks at USAID's structure and the way the environment for development has evolved since USAID's creation. It concludes with discussion of USAID's response to its new environment and offers suggestions as to how USAID's role in the national security enterprise might be more effective.

HOW DID WE GET HERE?

Policymakers have often viewed development resources as a "means" to a foreign policy objective rather than development as an "end" in itself. They have repeatedly redefined USAID's objectives. Originally created with a focus on economic growth, USAID's mission has grown to include short-term crisis response, humanitarian assistance after disasters, post-conflict stabilization, long-term help to build institutional and human capacity, and support for political or diplomatic objectives. Its programs have been used to project values, demonstrate good will, or buy behavior change. It has developed projects to improve governance, create jobs, educate, fight infectious disease, improve maternal and child health, get cooperation on environmental issues and climate change, and counter extremism.

As its responsibilities have increased, the agency has grown, in the words of one senior USAID official, "to combine skills from all the elements of government, from Departments of

Treasury and Justice to Health and Education, in one place."[5] To strengthen institutions and systems around the world, it has become an agency doing everything from delivering food and medical supplies to advising on central banking, agricultural price policy, and fuel subsidies. How did this happen?

Origins and Principles

What may have been the earliest aid effort came as a projection of democratic values—Thomas Jefferson's advice to the Marquis de Lafayette in 1789 on the Declaration of the Rights of Man. Shortly thereafter, as a complement to the Monroe Doctrine, James Monroe introduced humanitarian assistance, sending four ships of flour to feed Venezuelan earthquake victims in 1812.[6] Aid to the Russians and Eastern Europeans after World War I, led by Herbert Hoover, combined humanitarian objectives with an effort to project values. Modern foreign assistance as we know it, tied directly to national security, really began with George Marshall's 1947 speech at Harvard calling for aid to help "the return of normal economic health of the world."[7]

President John Kennedy picked up this theme. In a speech to the United Nations, he called on the world to produce a "decade of development" in which "an enlarged community of free, stable and self-reliant nations can reduce world tensions and insecurity."[8] It was the height of the Cold War. Colonial empires were collapsing. New states were emerging. The connection between foreign assistance and national security was clear, and the United States needed foreign assistance to combat communism. The country had moral, economic, and political obligations to meet, Kennedy said, and without the capacity to meet them, "our own security would be endangered and our prosperity imperiled." In 1961 he asked Congress to create a new agency to join our "separate and often confusing aid programs into a single administration . . . so that foreign aid can more effectively play its part as an effective instrument of our over-all efforts for world peace and security."[9] USAID would become the lead agency on development and incorporate existing programs being run by other agencies and departments.[10]

USAID as an Agent of National Security

USAID's role in national security has depended in large part on the president's perspective. When presidents, most notably Presidents John Kennedy and Lyndon Johnson, have seen development as important to strategy, they have fought for resources and made USAID an integral part of the national security team.[11] Other presidents—Bill Clinton, George W. Bush, and Barack Obama—while recognizing development as one of the Three Ds, have emphasized USAID's operational capacity rather than its policy role. Development has been more a tool than a national security objective, subservient to policy and not key to its formulation. When USAID is invited to interagency meetings, its job has been to describe the situation on the ground and say what might be possible given the means at its disposal.[12]

Exactly how involved the new agency would be in national security policymaking was not clear when President Kennedy called for its creation. In 1962, when he named David Bell, then head of the Bureau of the Budget, USAID's administrator, the intention became clearer.[13] "Both Kennedy and he [Bell] decided that it was more important to run AID than it was to run the Bureau of the Budget, which gives you some idea of the sense of priority that the foreign aid program had at the time," an early USAID official noted.[14] After Kennedy had recruited leaders for the new agency from the ranks of businesses across the country in what became known as Operation Tycoon,[15] he invited USAID's first mission directors and deputies to the White House just before they left for their posts overseas. He emphasized the link between their work and national security: "The job that you are engaged in as important as any work that is being done by anyone in this country at this time to protect the security of the country."[16]

The agency was structured with limited independence. According to Bell, "there was strong feeling . . . that aid decisions had been improperly subordinated in the previous arrangement to the views and judgments of the State Department's Assistant Secretaries and office chiefs."[17] Nevertheless, although President Kennedy would include Bell in meetings of the Special Group (Counter Insurgency), the task force he set up and chaired after the Bay of Pigs, he still had the administrator report to the secretary of state, whom he made responsible for coordinating civilian and military aid programs.

With the growing US involvement in Vietnam, Lyndon Johnson took personal interest in development as a tool of policy. He called his interim national security advisor, Bob Komer, into the Oval Office to tell him personally that he was to lead "the other war" in Vietnam for the hearts and minds of the people.[18] As John Norris writes in a history of USAID, "Over the protests of the USAID mission director who argued that a lighter footprint actually made for more effective counterinsurgency efforts, Johnson pushed USAID resources and personnel into Vietnam, forward deploying aid workers in a massive hearts and minds campaign. By 1968 there were some 2,300 American USAID personnel in Vietnam, the single-largest deployment of USAID staff in history."[19]

President Johnson's efforts to use aid as a policy tool were not limited to Vietnam. He called USAID's then administrator, William Gaud, to his ranch in Texas to design programs to counter a famine in South Asia, laying the groundwork for what became the "Green Revolution."[20] Johnson argued for family-planning programs in response to national security concerns about overpopulation. He intervened directly on food shipments to India, halting supplies until India made the policy changes he sought.[21]

Few presidents have been as hands-on as Johnson in their use of foreign assistance, and the experience in Vietnam brought a backlash. By 1971, despite significant USAID achievements in Korea, Taiwan, India, and Indonesia, congressional support for USAID's work on economic policy, long-term institution building, and infrastructure was waning. Weary with war and frustrated that development programs had not captured hearts and minds, Congress defeated the administration's foreign assistance bill and replaced it with "New Directions" legislation that focused on "rural development, small farmers, rural-urban linkages, and small business." New Directions later expanded to "Basic Human Needs" to include health and education, aimed at "the poorest of the poor,"[22] and under President Jimmy Carter, to a greater concern for human rights and the projection of American values as a national security objective.

Mission Creep

The resources for development assistance have been too attractive for policymakers to resist. They became a natural source of support for policy objectives. President Carter encouraged peace in the Middle East with generous assistance after the Camp David accords; aid to Israel and Egypt—close to $2 billion—represented about a quarter of the total foreign USAID assistance budget for years.[23] President Reagan used aid to fight insurgencies in Central

America; the fall of the Soviet Union brought new opportunities for programs in support of democratic and economic transitions. Wars in Bosnia and Kosovo and financial collapse in Asia brought new demands. The attacks of September 11, 2001, ushered in a raft of issues, particularly terrorism, identified with fragile states. The wars in Iraq and Afghanistan pushed USAID to address immediate crises of stabilization, reconstruction, governance, and public service delivery.[24] By 2014 the agency's inspector general was describing USAID's "lack of focus" as one of its most serious challenges: "The Agency's many initiatives and priorities, coupled with external mandates, divert missions' attention from core responsibilities and long-term vision."[25] It was hard to maintain a focus on long-term development.

USAID'S STAFFING AND STRUCTURE CREATE A FIELD-BASED CULTURE

Despite many distractions, throughout the agency's history USAID's mandate has remained the design and implementation of development programs in the field. The agency's primary attention is directed toward its eighty field missions operating some 2,000 projects in more than a hundred countries. Decision making has been largely delegated to field missions, and the vast majority of USAID's $20 billion annual budget goes to their programs.[26] The missions are responsible for building relationships with host governments, identifying needs, drawing up strategies, and designing projects to meet long-term development objectives. Their emphasis on field programs is reflected in both USAID's staffing and its culture.

The Job Is in the Field

More than two-thirds of USAID's nearly 10,000 employees work overseas: 1,702 foreign service officers (FSOs) spend most of their careers in field missions; 4,560 foreign service nationals (FSNs) come from the countries in which USAID operates; 1,660 civil service employees work primarily in Washington, complemented by nearly 1,000 private contractors, transfers from other US government agencies, or fellows from universities.[27]

To develop their programs, missions draw up individual multiyear strategic plans (Country Development Cooperation Strategies) for each country, based on an assessment of needs, past evaluations, and discussions with country officials and civil society representatives. The strategy reflects the country's conditions and needs and US priorities, objectives, and resources. Washington approves it and sets the budget levels reflecting congressional and administration priorities. Missions develop projects to implement the strategy: help for health systems in Ethiopia, for example, and refugees in Jordan; advice to Burmese officials on economic policy and to Ukrainian activists on civil society organization; expertise to Laos on trade and investment. Washington provides technical oversight and support and joins in monitoring and evaluation. Regular reviews test assumptions and allow modifications as part of an ongoing process.

Because USAID's focus is in the field, FSOs play a dominant role in defining the agency's culture. Many have come from the Peace Corps; historically, nearly a third has been former volunteers. The tradition continues. Of thirty-six officers recently joining USAID, for example, fourteen were former Peace Corps volunteers.[28] They joined for the fieldwork. They describe themselves as purpose driven, field oriented, operational, and practical. Employees have specific skills in health, agriculture, economics, business, or governance, or increasingly, as the agency struggles to meet compliance requirements, they are lawyers and procurement

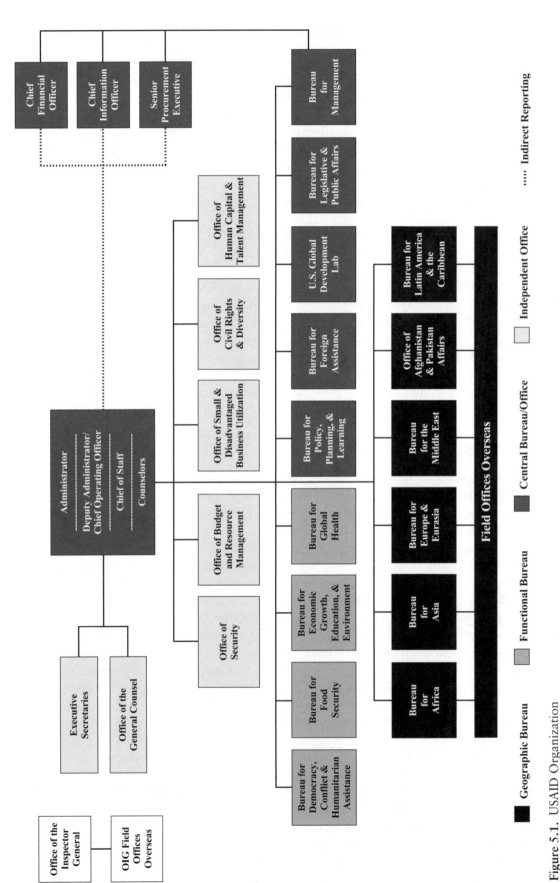

Figure 5.1. USAID Organization
Source: USAID, "Organization," March 12, 2015, www.usaid.gov/who-we-are/organization.

specialists. Most have graduate degrees.[29] They develop strategic planning skills, given their mandate to develop sustained programs as part of long-term strategies.

By choice FSOs spend the bulk of their careers in field missions, outside Washington. Overseas tours normally run at least two years; most FSOs stay for two tours, and some extend for as many as five or six years. Some return for follow-on assignments. They build long-standing relationships, and as their counterparts rise through the ranks, they become valuable partners in host governments and civil society.

But FSO focus abroad carries costs at home. Because so much of their time is spent in the field, FSOs may not develop the Washington interagency skills and personal networks that would maximize their effectiveness in the interagency when they do take Washington assignments. They are ambivalent about being tied too closely to national security or short-term political objectives. As a senior FSO said in 2014, "Basically we are blue-collar workers. Give us a problem and we want to solve it. Leave the guys in Washington to debate national interests; we just want to get the budget, roll up our sleeves, and get the job done in the field."[30]

FSNs, making up close to two-thirds of mission staff, strengthen field perspective. Drawn from the communities in which USAID operates, they provide local knowledge, perspective, and continuity in addition to their management and technical expertise. A third to a half are professionals—PhDs, lawyers, doctors, engineers, comptrollers, or other technical specialists—bringing a lifetime of understanding and contacts in the host country. Their networks can support not just USAID activities but those of other agencies in the embassy as well. They have the health contacts, for example, for the Centers for Disease Control; they know the agriculture minister and can support USDA initiatives; they can help the US Forest Service or the Environmental Protection Agency with meetings with their counterparts on issues of common concern. In countries where security is an issue, like Yemen, Pakistan, or Nigeria, their role becomes even more important—they may be able to travel to project areas where their American colleagues are unable to go.

Operational Support for National Security, Limited Influence on Strategy

The Washington structure supports the agency's field orientation. Geographic or regional bureaus (for Africa, Europe and Eurasia, the Middle East, Afghanistan and Pakistan, Asia, and Latin America) link directly to the field missions. They represent their interests in the interagency, coordinate with Congress and the White House, mesh field strategies with Washington's strategies, political priorities, and budget realities. Technical or functional bureaus in areas such as health, economic growth, education, environment, democracy, and humanitarian affairs offer expertise to the field, funding, and support for research and pilot projects.[31] They coordinate programs across the interagency with the Department of Health and Human Services in the case of health or with the Department of Treasury or Commerce for economic policy. One bureau, for Democracy, Conflict, and Humanitarian Assistance (DCHA), has ten quite different offices and hundreds of technical experts, mostly contractors, and is responsible for emergency assistance, stabilization, post-conflict crisis response, and human rights. It maintains close contact (and some overlap) with offices in State and Defense. (See box 5.1 for details.)

USAID's Culture

Creating a coherent culture is complicated by the agency's diversity. Each group—civil service, foreign service, political appointees, contractors, other agency personnel, interns and fellows,

---

BOX 5.1
USAID's Interagency 911 Teams

Bureau for Democracy, Conflict, and Humanitarian Assistance (DCHA): With a staff of 400 and annual budget levels depending on the year's crises, this bureau is the most likely to be called in case of emergency. Three of its offices in particular—foreign disaster assistance, transition initiatives, and civilian-military affairs—are crisis related. They are staffed with contractors, have years of experience with the interagency during crises, and maintain close relationships with counterparts within the State and Defense Departments.

Office of Foreign Disaster Response (OFDA): OFDA fulfills the Foreign Assistance Act of 1961 mandate that USAID's administrator act as the government's special coordinator for international disaster response. Nearly seventy foreign disasters occur every year, ranging from tsunamis in Southeast Asia to earthquakes in Haiti. OFDA has special authorities to hire experts and borrow technical staff from other agencies. Its network ranges from the Department of Defense and the Centers for Disease Control to the search and rescue services for Los Angeles and Fairfax Counties. When a call comes, OFDA forms a disaster assistance response team (DART) to contact local authorities, assess damage, determine needs, and manage the response. It has stockpiled commodities in locations around the world and maintains a strong planning and operating relationship with DOD.

Office of Transition Response (OTI): Set up in 1994 as countries in the former Soviet Union faced difficult political and economic transitions, OTI provides the same kind of quick response to political crises that OFDA does for humanitarian ones. Operating under special authorities from Congress focusing on "fast, flexible, short-term assistance for key political and stabilization needs," it draws on a "bull pen" of experts for short-term projects, generally less than two years (although missions may stretch the time frame on occasion). After 9/11 OTI's stabilization work in Afghanistan, Pakistan, Iraq, and other post-conflict situations increased markedly. With a budget of close to $50 million a year, OTI now has programs in more than fourteen countries.

Office of Civilian-Military Cooperation (CMC): Formed in 2005, at the height of the wars in Iraq and Afghanistan, CMC coordinates USAID's efforts in stabilization, reconstruction, and recovery of fragile or failed states with the military. It hosts military officers on detail from the Navy, Army Corps of Engineers, and Marines and has senior development advisors in the six combatant commands and with the Joint Staff at the Pentagon to coordinate planning, training, and preparing for joint operations.

---

local hires—comes to the agency with a different background. Each works with different systems of incentives, evaluation, and promotion. Some, like those handling crises and disaster assistance, for example, develop their own subculture—practical, action oriented, and more tolerant of risk.[32]

Further challenging creation of a common culture has been a rapid increase in hiring and the generational change as millennials take over from those who joined in the shadow of Vietnam. From a high of 4,000 during the Vietnam War, the number of FSOs had been allowed to drop to fewer than 1,000 in 2005.[33] Recognizing that close to 100 percent of USAID's senior officers were eligible for retirement within three years, the George W. Bush administration committed to doubling those officers. By 2014 USAID had run close to seven years of increased recruiting, outstripping attrition and adding nearly 800 FSOs.[34] Today more than 60 percent of its employees have fewer than five years of experience.

Recognizing the challenge, the agency launched an extended effort in 2013 to unite the workforce around a new mission statement: "We partner to end extreme poverty and to promote resilient, democratic societies, while advancing our security and prosperity."[35] The process helped solidify a common vision. Many took pride in working on long-term development issues while also being the go-to organization for crisis response. They shared a sense of purpose. USAID officers estimated that more than 75 percent saw their work as an opportunity to change the world. Far fewer, less than 20 percent, saw it as directly tied to national security.[36]

Growing Influence of Political Appointees

Political appointees have always been influential in shaping the agency's role in the national security community, and that influence is growing. The number of political hires doubled between 2004 and 2012, from 52 to 110, and the number in the office of the administrator tripled to 22.[37] To the agency's benefit, these appointees often bring relationships and political contacts, new ideas and perspectives. When the administrator has been close to the president or when the president has seen development as key to national security, USAID's role has been enhanced. David Bell regularly sat in sessions chaired by President Kennedy.[38] Peter McPherson, formerly a lawyer for Ronald Reagan, attended cabinet meetings. On the negative side, appointees' incentives, goals, and objectives do not always mesh neatly with those of the career development staff. Appointees may feel pressure to act on short-term political demands that career staff see as distracting from long-term objectives. And they may lack experience in development or in the Washington interagency.

The administrator, appointed by the president, confirmed by the Senate, and reporting to the secretary of state, sets the tone for the agency. Party affiliation has been less important to an administrator's effectiveness than experience, personal contacts across the interagency, and personality. Some administrators have come with a development background: Peter McPherson (1981–87) was a former Peace Corps volunteer in Peru with White House experience; Brian Atwood (1993–99), a former State Department officer with experience in Ivory Coast, came to USAID after serving as president of the National Democratic Institute, a key partner in elections work; Andrew Natsios (2003–7) was the former head of the USAID's Office of Foreign Disaster Assistance and senior officer at World Vision, one of the largest development and humanitarian assistance organizations in the world; Raj Shah (2009–15), a medical doctor, came from the Gates Foundation; and Gayle Smith, appointed in December 2015, served on both the Obama and Clinton NSCs, as senior director for development and democracy and senior director for Africa, respectively, after a career as a journalist in Africa, work with international nongovernmental organizations (NGOs), and time with a Washington think tank.[39] The most successful have combined an understanding of development with an ability to manage a complex bureaucracy and complicated constituency of NGOs, contractors, universities, religious groups, and various members of the national security enterprise, including the White House and Congress.

Senior appointees, including deputy and assistant administrator, have worked on Capitol Hill, in think tanks, and in technical fields relating to development. As with the administrator's contacts, their connections with other political appointees across the administration have enhanced coordination and USAID participation in the interagency. Lower level appointees often come from presidential campaign staff and can provide interagency links. Their effectiveness depends less on party than on experience and, as so often is the case, personality. Party ties may affect policy emphasis. "Republicans have generally been stronger advocates of free market approaches . . . and more prone to 'securitize assistance.' Democrats have tended to have more of a people focus, have stressed human rights to a greater degree, been more willing to work with multilaterals, and [been] stronger supporters of family planning and environmental protection."[40]

Engaging the Interagency

USAID is not structured for interoperability with its other national security agencies. Its bureaus do not align with those of the Departments of State and Defense. Its bottom-up approach to strategic planning conflicts with that of State and Defense. Its roles and responsibilities, particularly in areas relating to conflict, stabilization, and democracy, overlap. There are even logistical challenges. Senior USAID officials (with the exception of a few of the most senior, like the administrator) lack easy access to classified communications equipment or offices set up for classified briefings, either in Washington or in the field, a critical obstacle to USAID participation in national security discussions.

The field focus of so much of the agency's top talent, however, increases its effectiveness abroad on the embassy country team. USAID often has its greatest influence on the interagency process through the mission director's role on the country team. Mission directors may be among the most senior officers at post. They serve as senior development advisors to the ambassador and may act in the ambassador's stead when he or she and the deputy chief of mission are away.

But strength in the field does not necessarily translate into effectiveness in Washington. USAID's greatest assets—its field presence, knowledge, and experience—give the agency the potential to offer a development perspective in interagency discussions, but senior officers are not consistently available. There's a shortage of senior leadership overall and a paucity of FSOs in Washington. Traditionally, USAID has had few officers serving on staff in Congress or on the National Security Council (NSC), although this may be changing. Since 2001 USAID has detailed more than forty civil service, foreign service, and contract employees to the NSC.[41] Recognizing the need for more senior foreign service representation in Washington, the agency began to enforce a rule limiting consecutive time overseas to twelve years, after which officers must return to Washington—an order long on the books but often resisted. Nevertheless, for the foreseeable future, USAID's representation on the NSC and in high-level interagency discussions will continue to be led predominantly by political appointees and long-term civil service employees.

DEALING WITH CHANGING TIMES

Today the agency is operating in an environment totally different from that at its creation. Institutions, politics, and technology have changed. Countries like India and Brazil are launching development assistance programs. Funding by private foundations has grown dramatically. Internet connections have created channels for individuals to contribute directly to local organizations. Foreign direct investment by private companies and pressure for corporate social responsibility offer opportunities for public–private partnerships. Diaspora interest groups provide generous flows of remittances to their home countries. Universities have started development labs researching innovative approaches to age-old problems like malaria, inadequate sanitation, and energy shortages. Silicon Valley is offering ideas and capital. Technology has created a revolution in communications. Perhaps most important, problems in fragile states—refugees, infectious disease, climate change, instability, and conflict—

have gone global, and USAID is increasingly being called to mount programs in insecure environments.

More Players in Development Assistance

One of most significant changes in the aid environment has been its remarkable democratization. When USAID was established in 1961, capital flow from developed to underdeveloped countries was dominated by governments; USAID was the biggest game in town. Today everybody, from business associations to rock stars and individual donors, has become actively involved. By 2014, as shown in table 5.1, more than 90 percent of transfers were coming from private sources. As the Hudson Institute noted in a 2013 report, "Government aid . . . is now a minority shareholder, the opposite of 40 years ago."[42] For example, in 2014 remittances outpaced official development assistance: US workers abroad sent abroad more than $108 billion; official US development assistance was $33.1 billion. Private philanthropy from US foundations, corporations, voluntary organizations, churches, and private individuals provided nearly $44 billion.[43] Between 2006 and 2010, the Bill and Melinda Gates Foundation gave more funding for global health than any country in the world except for the United States.[44]

There has also been a great increase in the number of institutions, private companies, and NGOs interested in developing countries. Originally, USAID depended on in-house expertise, hiring trained agriculturalists, economists, public health specialists, and engineers for its own staff. Large international NGOs and private international development companies can now provide surge capacity to complement the agency's own shrinking staff.[45]

Table 5.1. US Total Net Economic Engagement with Developing Countries, 2013–14

Flow	Amount Given (in billions of $)	Percent of Total
Official development assistance	33.1	9
US private philanthropy	43.9	12
Foundations	*4.7*	*11*
Corporations	*11.3*	*26*
Private and voluntary organizations	*15.4*	*35*
Volunteerism	*4.3*	*10*
Universities and colleges	*2.2*	*5*
Religious organizations	*6.0*	*14*
Remittances	108.7	30
Private capital flows	179.3	49
Total economic engagement	**365.0**	**100[a]**

Source: Center for Global Prosperity at Hudson Institute, Table 1, in *The Index of Global Philanthropy and Remittances 2016* (Washington, DC: Hudson Institute, 2016), 9. Used by permission.
[a] Variation due to rounding.

A third change has been the challenge to USAID's mandate as lead agency on development assistance. In 2003 President George W. Bush launched the President's Emergency Plan for AIDS Relief (PEPFAR) to provide billions of dollars to fight HIV and AIDS. The administration assigned responsibility for coordinating the effort to a new office in the State Department. The next year, it established the Millennium Challenge Corporation (MCC) as an independent agency to test a new model of development assistance, basing country eligibility on government effectiveness and providing close to a billion dollars annually.

Challenges to USAID were not limited to MCC and PEPFAR. With the end of the Soviet Union, a flood of agencies had become interested in overseas programs. From the Departments of Treasury, Labor, Energy, and Health and Human Services to the US Forest Service and Environmental Protection Agency, all had projects in former Soviet states. The dramatic increase in funding for civilian assistance in Iraq and Afghanistan encouraged this interest. By 2011 more than twenty-seven US government agencies were running development projects.[46] Both the Department of State and the Department of Defense (DOD) developed new units to deal with issues relating to stabilization and fragile states.[47] In 2006, for a limited period, DOD was responsible for about a quarter of US official development assistance.[48]

The proliferation of development activities and players raised concerns about coordination. Although successive administrations, beginning with President Kennedy, have expected USAID to lead, they stopped short of making USAID's administrator a cabinet officer or giving USAID authority for coordination. In an attempt to impose greater discipline, in 2006 the George W. Bush administration created a new position of director of foreign assistance in the State Department to serve concurrently as administrator of USAID and to coordinate foreign assistance strategy. It shifted USAID's Office of Budget and Planning to the State Department and moved toward a closer integration of assistance under the State Department. For regions of particularly high political interest and correspondingly large budgets, like Iraq, Afghanistan, Pakistan, and the Middle East, USAID programs have operated under State Department coordinators or special representatives charged with overseeing all assistance activities.

It's All about Politics

The push to integrate USAID into the State Department reflected USAID's continuing challenges with Congress. Winning support for foreign assistance has never been easy. Public skepticism of government aid reflects a long-standing American concern about big government and welfare on an international scale. Natural skepticism is compounded by a misunderstanding of just how much of the US budget goes to foreign assistance. A 2013 Henry J. Kaiser Family Foundation survey found Americans on average thought 28 percent of the budget went to foreign aid.[49] In fact, as noted in chapter 3 on the Office of Management and Budget, foreign assistance has been less than 1 percent of the national budget for years.

Supporters have always had to fight for foreign aid, given its lack of constituency. George Marshall spent months traveling the country campaigning for his plan, visiting schools, Boy Scout gatherings, and town meetings to make the case. To sell aid programs to voters, presidents and lawmakers have talked about its importance to US trade and investment, employment, and American values. They have often turned to earmarks, initiatives, and directives.[50] Members (or staffers) have used earmarks to tilt support to favorite projects, foundations, institutes, or individuals. They have divided foreign assistance up into functional accounts with separate line items and assigned categories, essentially determining exactly how much can be used for what purposes.[51] The 1961 Foreign Assistance Act, under which USAID continues to function, now includes 140 broad priorities and 400 directives on how USAID should pursue them.[52]

Initiatives and functional accounts cut two ways. They rally public interest and congressional support, creating specific pools of funds that can be tapped for field programs, but they are not strategic and cut into discretionary funds. In Nigeria, for example, the bulk of aid funds are slated for HIV/AIDS, not particularly useful for a strategic effort to promote jobs and undercut popular unrest in the country's northeast.[53] Mission directors complain that virtually all of their budget is now tied up in initiatives, directives, or earmarks with little

Table 5.2. Aid Recipients by Country

FY 2014 Estimate		FY 2015 Original Request	
Country	Aid (in millions of USD)	Country	Aid (in millions of USD)
1. Israel	3,100	1. Israel	3,100
2. Egypt	1,508	2. Afghanistan	1,595
3. Afghanistan	1,123	3. Egypt	1,506
4. Jordan	1,011	4. Pakistan	882
5. Pakistan	933	5. Nigeria	721
6. Nigeria	703	6. Jordan	671
7. Tanzania	588	7. Tanzania	590
8. Kenya	560	8. Kenya	553
9. South Africa	490	9. Ethiopia	483
10. Uganda	490	10. Uganda	465
11. Ethiopia	479	11. West Bank / Gaza	441
12. Zambia	406	12. South Africa	438
13. Mozambique	406	13. Mozambique	390
14. Iraq	373	14. Zambia	381
15. West Bank / Gaza	334	15. South Sudan	331

Source: Susan B. Epstein, Alex Tiersky, Marian Lawson, *State, Foreign Operations, and Related Programs: FY 2015 Budget and Appropriations* (Washington, DC: Congressional Research Service, December 8, 2014), 19, http://fas.org/sgp/crs/row/R43569.pdf. Country allocation table provided to CRS by the State Department in late March 2014.

Note: The FY 2015 figures do not reflect amendments to the request, for which country-level allocation data are not currently available but which would likely boost funding levels in some of the countries listed in the table. As in FY 2014 and recent years, the top recipient list for FY 2015 includes long-standing strategic partners such as Israel, Egypt, and Jordan; frontline states in the war against terrorism, such as Pakistan; and global health focus countries.

One notable change under the original request is the ranking of Iraq, which has been a top recipient since the 2003 US invasion but would fall just under the top fifteen in FY 2015 with the requested allocation of $309 million. However, the request was made before the security situation in Iraq deteriorated in the midst of a Daesh insurgency, and a large portion of the additional funds requested for activities to fight Daesh would likely support activities in Iraq. Similarly, the amended request for increased funds to fight Ebola may move some of the countries hardest hit by the virus onto the top recipients list.

money available for discretionary activities in economic growth or democracy, for example.[54] The political nature of the assistance budget (and its link to national security objectives) is apparent in country allocation totals, as seen in table 5.2. Of $20 billion requested for foreign aid in 2015, more than a third was targeted to four countries—Israel, Egypt, Pakistan, and Afghanistan.[55] As one mission director commented, "Congress doesn't give a billion dollars for development but for politics. We at USAID have to understand that there are bigger issues at play."[56]

Technology Opens Doors but Tightens Controls

The revolution in communications has created new opportunities but challenged field authority. It has increased private fund-raising by highlighting needs—streaming pictures showing the vivid human costs of conflict or natural disasters—and making giving only a click away. Technology has also encouraged creative problem solving. Venture capitalists in California, students in university development laboratories, individuals in their garages are seeking innovative approaches to everything from malaria prevention to micro-banking. And it has brought innovations from health (cell-phone diagnosis) to conflict management (reporting and responding) and finance (banking and microfinance).

At the same time, new technologies have encouraged centralized decision making. Coming as concerns about aid effectiveness were growing, new communications tools have enabled greater Washington oversight and encouraged policymakers to believe that aid management could be done better with Washington help—fine-tuning with the "ten thousand mile screwdriver." USAID in Washington has reduced field authorities. Policymakers have launched initiatives designed in Washington and increased reporting requirements. They have pushed for more scientific metrics, monitoring, and evaluation. Tensions between those in Washington wanting greater accountability and those in the field looking for flexibility have grown, pitting those concerned with "compliance" against those focused on "program."

USAID's leadership saw the drive to make development assistance more measurable and accountable as necessary to improve programs and reassure Congress. Reports of problems in managing the huge budgets for Afghanistan and Iraq had threatened USAID's reputation and future funding.[57] At the same time, increased reporting requirements and data-driven programs threatened to create what Andrew Natsios calls a "counter-bureaucracy," distorting USAID's programs by tilting them toward those activities that are "measurable" rather than "transformational" and forcing field managers to spend more time in monitoring than in designing and implementing programs.[58]

USAID Plays Catch-Up

Responding to these changes early his term as administrator, Raj Shah announced, "USAID Forward . . . an effort to strengthen the Agency by embracing new partnerships, investing in the catalytic role of innovations and demanding a relentless focus on results."[59] He developed new initiatives on agriculture and food security, health, and climate change and a set of new programs aimed at Africa.[60] In 2014 he launched the Global Development Laboratory, a metaphor for the new USAID. The goal was to draw in the best ideas from the private sector, universities, and foundations and use USAID's field infrastructure to test them, measure the results closely, find what works, and scale it up. With success in food security, health, and education, the agency would showcase its strength as a convener of the new players in development, a partner with the private sector, an innovator and catalyzer of great ideas. It would make the most of its budget, frugally leveraging the funding of others while creating a new image for itself as innovative and cutting-edge.

These efforts to reform and modernize the agency won support from Congress and the administration. They demoralized staffers who felt that field prerogatives were being replaced by Washington's top-down decision making and development objectives were being super-seded by political goals.[61] Although the reform initiatives had managed to maintain support for USAID's budget, they left unanswered questions about USAID's mission, purpose, and authorities and the balance between work on long-term transformational change and human and institutional capacity building on one hand and short-term, post-conflict stabilization programs on the other. The answers to these questions, including USAID's role in national security, hinge on USAID's relationship with the State Department.

SIBLING RIVALRY

For much of its life, USAID has had a contested relationship with its larger and more power-ful sibling, the Department of State (see chapter 4). In part the tension results from the gravitational pull of their respective cultures, reinforced by the respective centers of gravity—the State Department's in Washington and USAID's in the field.[62] But it also grows out of differences in mission. The State Department is responsible for making policy. It is natural that it has a predominant capability in the national security enterprise. USAID's mandate is operations, although it aspires to shaping policy to reflect development objectives and impact.

Differences in mission affect the way the two agencies view the resources embodied in development assistance. For the State Department diplomacy is government-to-government engagement to reach an accommodation; assistance is often a useful inducement to that accommodation. State likes having USAID's resources at its disposal. On the other hand, USAID views development as a discipline, requiring relationship building with counterparts, careful analysis of problems, application of theories, development of strategies, and design and implementation of programs for transformational change. USAID professionals resent being pushed to use resources for short-term political objectives, particularly at the expense of long-term development.[63] The agency has chaffed under the State Department's efforts to control budget or programs and has longed for independence as a cabinet-level agency with an institutional seat on the NSC.

In the run-up to the 2008 US elections, with USAID's growing role in Afghanistan and Iraq, supporters of foreign assistance embraced hopes not only that development would become one of the Three Ds but that USAID might become a cabinet agency.[64] As a cabinet member, USAID's administrator would be able to offer perspective on the development con-sequences of policies being espoused by departments like State, Treasury, and Commerce and to resist efforts by other agencies to take on development programs in its purview.

While that hope was never realized, USAID's boosters were encouraged when President Obama issued the first-ever Presidential Directive on Global Development. The directive described development as "indispensable in the forward defense of America's interests" and "essential to advancing our national security objectives." It pledged to make development "a central pillar of national security policy, equal to diplomacy and defense" and to rebuild USAID "as our lead development agency—and as the world's premier development agency."[65] It restored USAID's capacity for strategic analysis and oversight—lost to the State Depart-ment in 2006—by authorizing the new Bureau of Planning, Programs, and Learning.

The directive seemed to portend greater influence for USAID. This interpretation was encouraged by statements by the secretaries of defense and state promoting development as one of the Three Ds. But the concept of the Three Ds proved unrealistic. Resources never matched rhetoric, and the asymmetry in political support for each pillar has proved too great for them to be seen as carrying even proximate importance. Today USAID's budget remains one-thirtieth that of defense; its staff numbers are smaller than those in military bands.[66]

Moreover, a close reading of the directive itself makes clear the limits of USAID's role. The directive stipulates, "The Administrator of USAID will be included in the meetings of the National Security Council, as appropriate." In other words, when invited. The position reports to the secretary of state, "who will ensure that development and diplomacy are effectively coordinated and mutually reinforcing." USAID may help draft a US global development strategy every four years; the NSC will lead the Interagency Policy Committee on Global Development.[67]

The directive also called for the Quadrennial Diplomacy and Development Review (QDDR), modeled on the Defense Department's review. Completed in 2012, the first QDDR proposed a "lead agency approach" with the State Department responsible for responding to "political and security crises" and USAID responsible for responding to "humanitarian crises resulting from large-scale natural or industrial disasters, famines, disease outbreaks and other natural phenomena."[68] The QDDR put in writing what had transpired in practice over years. USAID would lead—except where it wouldn't, and the State Department would decide.[69]

Senior USAID officials describe the QDDR process "as more of a treaty negotiation than an exercise in coordination and collaboration."[70] It left the State Department and USAID sharing overlapping authorities and areas of responsibility. Displaced people, for example, are USAID's responsibility; the State Department helps refugees. Both give grants for work on democracy and human rights—sometimes to the same organization. Both fund groups promoting human rights, free elections, legislative capacity building, open media, and an independent judiciary. In interviews with USAID's inspector general, USAID officers expressed frustration and talked about the need for clearer guidance. They reported that confusion about interagency roles and responsibilities "clouds USAID's identity and mission."[71]

Competition over responsibilities spills into decisions as small as who will attend which NSC meetings. Although USAID has been invited to participate in an increasing number of meetings of the NSC in recent years,[72] senior officers report that State Department officials have counseled NSC staff that USAID need not be invited to some meetings—State can represent both—or have intervened to disinvite USAID after invitations have already been issued. USAID officers say these slights are not new.[73]

A DECADE OF WAR: IMPACT ON USAID'S MISSION AND CULTURE

More than a decade of war has taken a toll on USAID's staffing and focus and continues to shape its culture in ways that affect its role in national security. With the programs in Iraq and Afghanistan, USAID's budgets soared to levels unseen since the war in Vietnam. Not surprisingly, expectations skyrocketed, and the demand for staff to serve on provincial reconstruction teams (PRTs) and at embassies in Baghdad and Kabul grew exponentially. At the same time, the agency was supposed to shift its ways of operating—away from using private contractors and grantees to implement its projects. It was to run up to 50 percent of its budget directly through the Afghan government, a government not known for its financial management systems.

The demand that USAID's development programs support military and political objectives in Afghanistan and Iraq raised unachievable expectations and pushed the agency beyond its capacity. By some metrics—numbers of girls in school, maternal and child health programs, life expectancy, and roads built—USAID succeeded remarkably well in its development objectives. However, in terms of security produced, effective government, and efficient contracting and monitoring of dollars spent, the agency fell short. Hopes that USAID could step into insecure environments and produce a government in a box or forge partnerships with local organizations to deliver public services overnight were clearly unrealistic. The agency could not build resilient states in insecure environments. It was hard-pressed to field staff. Civilian agencies like the State Department and USAID have no surge capacity. They do not have swing staff, and they aren't trained to deploy rapidly; indeed, they do not have the mechanisms to support employees in conflict situations.

To be sure, some parts of the agency working on conflict and post-conflict problems adjusted reasonably well. For example, the Office of Transition Initiatives (OTI) and the Office of Foreign Disaster Assistance adapted quickly and were credited with major contributions to handling refugees, stabilization, and reconstruction. However, these two units, with fewer than 400 employees, represented a relatively small part of the total agency, which was, after all, set up to work primarily on long-term development rather than short-term crises.

The rest of the agency did what it could. USAID began recruiting a new category of employee specifically designated for "crisis, stabilization and governance" and contributed to the newly established Civilian Response Corps. It began to assign staff to combatant commands and PRTs. It expanded OTI and shifted the agency's entire personnel placement system to free staff for critical priority countries (CPCs) like Iraq, Afghanistan, Pakistan, and Sudan. It encouraged FSOs to apply by offering one-year tours with extra time off, incentive pay, priority consideration on next assignments, and promotions. But the recruiting also set up a cultural clash between those taking CPC assignments and development purists who saw the work as outside the USAID mainstream, "a sabbatical to work on political foreign aid" rather than development.[74]

The result was a constant turnover of employees worldwide as USAID's staff scrambled to meet the demands. When then–special representative Richard Holbrooke called for a civilian surge to match the military in Afghanistan, USAID was expected to add a hundred FSOs—10 percent of the total worldwide pool. So many were moving in and out of Kabul, when it came time to evaluate staff, the mission was unsure how many people it actually had.[75] Around the world FSOs cut their tours short to serve in CPCs, causing a ripple effect and leaving some missions short of leadership. Office chiefs were turning over every year, undercutting USAID's key strengths—local knowledge, experience, and long-term in-country relationships.

At the same time, the dramatic budget increase brought greater scrutiny. In Afghanistan, for example, five oversight agencies—auditors and inspectors general—worked in the same compound as USAID.[76] This kind of oversight encouraged the counter-bureaucracy to demand more data and reporting; it increased concerns that risk taking and creativity would be sacrificed for measurement. It also forced USAID to add regulatory people—contract officers and lawyers—rather than anthropologists, economists, and program designers and managers.[77]

It also brought more USAID staff directly into the national security enterprise at a tactical level. By 2014 nearly half of USAID's FSOs had worked in CPCs, many on PRTs. They had developed a far deeper understanding of stability operations, the military, and the role of security, and the agency had strengthened its commitment to closer collaboration with DOD. In 2015 it issued the new Policy on Cooperation with the Department of Defense, aimed at better aligning policies, plans, and operations,[78] and in 2016 its Office of Civilian–Military Cooperation had forty-nine positions, including fourteen military officers deputed from their respective services. Of thirty-five USAID officers, fourteen were posted to geographic combatant commands, Special Operations Command, and the Pentagon.

Greater collaboration will be important in the future. USAID is now operating 550 programs in thirty-five nonpermissive environments,[79] countries with severe security restrictions. The demand for assistance programs in fragile states is unlikely to go away and raises critical issues relating to management of personnel and resources, which are only beginning to be addressed.[80]

THE WAY AHEAD

Inevitably, foreign aid will be a part of future national security strategies, but questions introduced in this chapter remain. What will be the trade-offs between development resources for short-term versus long-term objectives? Who will decide? Who will be responsible for which programs, from humanitarian assistance and disaster response to stabilization, reconstruction, transition, and development? Can one agency do it all, and should USAID be that agency? How will changes in USAID's structure and culture affect its role in the national security enterprise? While those questions are debated and until they are resolved, USAID's effectiveness in the national security enterprise will be limited by continuing tensions over roles and authorities. Resolving these tensions will require clear vision and concerted effort by administration and congressional leadership.[81] Among the items to be considered:

- Clarified roles, responsibilities, and authorities for coordination and management of development assistance. The State Department and USAID could combine efforts on stabilization and disaster response, refugees and displaced, democracy, human rights, and rule of law, giving greater coherence to their work. Whether lodged in the State Department or USAID may be less important than simply getting them together under the same roof.
- Strategic use of USAID's unique field capacity. USAID could be playing a much larger role in supporting and coordinating departments and agencies like Treasury, Justice, or Agriculture in their international programs. Field missions and local staff are well positioned to provide the context and logistics for agencies lacking permanent field presence but interested in development programs. They can also do more to inform interagency discussion in Washington with a field perspective.
- Greater flexibility over funding. For decades employees have been told to do more with less. Congress has not matched USAID's operating expense (OE) budget—7.3 percent of its program budget—to ever-expanding responsibilities. For example, it provided USAID $2.8 billion to work on Ebola but only $63 million in OE to manage the expanded program. Congress should allow USAID to use program funding for operations to improve oversight and management.
- Increased staff and FSOs in Washington. USAID has a vision to grow the foreign service from 1,800 to 2,250 over the next five years. If successful, it would be better

positioned to rotate officers into the NSC; spend more time on training, planning, and strategy; and participate more effectively in the national security enterprise.[82]

- An institutional seat at the table. The competition between diplomacy and development, policy and operations, the Department of State and USAID, is unlikely to be resolved in the near future. Providing USAID an institutional seat on the NSC and ensuring invitations to the interagency depend in large part on the personal clout of senior USAID officials and their political connections. As long as the State Department speaks for USAID, the national security enterprise will lose the development perspective and field context USAID can provide.

- Risk management. Negotiations with the State Department's Office of Diplomatic Security, Congress, and various auditors are needed to develop risk management strategies for operations in insecure environments. Operations in unstable environments require greater flexibility and tolerance of failure. Setting realistic expectations would be particularly helpful; strategies for personnel protection, procurement, and oversight need to balance security and accountability requirements against development objectives and outcomes.

As the United States faces new threats from fragile states and violent extremism, transnational crime, changes in climate, demography, income inequality, and resource competition, taking full advantage of USAID's assets becomes all the more urgent. While USAID's participation in the national security enterprise may be increasing, its role is not what it could be. Political will and strong interagency leadership could produce the structural and cultural changes required to make USAID more effective. Until they do, USAID's contribution to national security strategy will be limited largely to its accomplishments in the field, not in the power centers in Washington. The agency will remain central on issues relating to humanitarian aid and development assistance but less engaged in other areas of national security, even when a development perspective could be important.

NOTES

The epigraph is from Eric Pace's "David. E. Bell, Budget Director for Kennedy, Is Dead at 81," *New York Times*, September 12, 2000, at www.nytimes.com/2000/09/12/us/david-e-bell-budget -director-for-kennedy-is-dead-at-81.html. For an excellent review of USAID's history through its administrators, see John Norris, "Kennedy, Johnson and the Early Years," USAID: A History of US Foreign Aid, pt. 1, *Inside Development*, July 23, 2014, www.devex.com/news/kennedy-johnson-and-the-early-years-83339.

1. White House, *National Security Strategy* (Washington, DC, May 2010), 15, www.whitehouse .gov/sites/default/files/rss_viewer/national_security_strategy.pdf.

2. William Wood, former ambassador to Afghanistan and Colombia, discussion with the author, December 2014.

3. Carol Lancaster, *Foreign Aid* (Chicago: University of Chicago Press, 2007), 1.

4. Ibid, 10. Lancaster defines development as "economic or social progress in poor countries, sustained by economic growth, and leading eventually to a reduction in poverty."

5. Senior USAID retiree, talk to USAID senior executive and FSOs (USAID Headquarters, Washington, DC, January 2015).

6. John Sanbrailo, "Extending the American Revolution Overseas: Little Known Origins of U.S. Foreign Assistance and Lessons for Today" (presentation at USAID Alumni Meeting, Center on Global Development, Washington, DC, January 30, 2014).

7. George C. Marshall, "The Marshall Plan Speech" (Harvard University, June 1947), http:// marshallfoundation.org/marshall/the-marshall-plan/marshall-plan-speech/.

8. John F. Kennedy, "Special Message to the Congress on Foreign Aid," March 22, 1961, in *The American Presidency Project*, ed. Gerhard Peters and John T. Woolley, www.presidency.ucsb.edu/ws/?pid=8545.

9. Ibid.

10. Among these programs were the International Cooperation Agency, the Development Loan Fund, the Food for Peace Program, and aid programs within the State Department and Export Import Bank.

11. Norris, "Early Years."

12. Senior USAID officials, conversations with the author, 2014.

13. The Bureau of the Budget was the predecessor agency to the Office of Management and Budget (OMB).

14. Norris, "Early Years."

15. William Gaud Oral History Interview, JFK#1, February 12, 1966, 11, John F. Kennedy Presidential Library and Museum, Boston, MA.

16. USAID, "50th Anniversary: President Kennedy Addresses USAID Mission Directors," *Impact Blog*, June 8, 1962, http://blog.usaid.gov/2011/08/50th-anniversary-president-kennedy-addresses-usaid-mission-directors/.

17. "The President was aware in 1961 . . . of the importance of having an aid agency which could . . . be in a position to establish . . . central policy in the aid field for the United States. He wanted the aid program more centralized . . . and he wanted it elevated so that the AID Administrator would report directly to the Secretary of State and the President rather than through an Under Secretary [and] . . . permitted . . . safeguards against short-range political pressures." David Bell Oral History Interview, JFK#2, January 2, 1965, 130, John F. Kennedy Presidential Library and Museum, Boston, MA.

18. Frank L. Jones, "Blowtorch: Robert Komer and the Making of Vietnam Pacification Policy," *Parameters*, August 2005, 104.

19. Norris, "Early Years."

20. Gaud Oral History Interview.

21. Norris, "Early Years."

22. Ibid.

23. Lancaster, *Foreign Aid*, 79.

24. Nathaniel Myers, "How USAID's Growing Relevance Could Destroy It," *National Interest*, December 12, 2014.

25. Michael Carroll, "Most Serious Management and Performance Challenges," memorandum, USAID, Washington, DC, October 15, 2014, 5, https://oig.usaid.gov/sites/default/files/other-reports/USAID_Management_Challenges_2014_0.pdf.

26. USAID's actual budget—the budget that it manages directly—may be well below $20 billion. USAID describes its budget ambiguously: "In total, funding for accounts from which USAID administers assistance is $22.7 billion, of which $11 billion is in core USAID-managed accounts." USAID, "FY 2017 Development and Humanitarian Assistance Budget," fact sheet, n.d., www.usaid.gov/sites/default/files/documents/9276/FY2017_USAIDBudgetRequestFactSheet.pdf.

27. All employee numbers are from author interviews with USAID's Office of Human Resources staff. The numbers are under constant revision and represent a snapshot as of February 2015.

28. USAID's Development Leadership Initiative Class 22, USAID's Office of Human Resources, December 2014.

29. A USAID survey in 2014 showed 80 percent with master's degrees or PhDs.

30. Retired minister counselor, USAID Senior FSO, interview by the author, November 2014.

31. The technical and functional bureaus include Economic Growth, Education and Environment, Food Security, Global Health, and Democracy, Conflict, and Humanitarian Assistance.

32. There are twenty-three different mechanisms for hiring new employees, including agreements with other agencies, contracts with private companies, positions for fellows from universities or think tanks, or interns.

33. USAID Office of Human Resources staff interviews.

34. Ibid.

35. Lancaster, *Foreign Aid*, 10.

36. Retired USAID minister counselor interview, May 2014.

37. House Committee on Government Reform, *US Government Policy and Supporting Positions* (*Plum Book*) (Washington, DC: US Government Printing Office, 2004), 202, www.gpo.gov/fdsys/pkg/GPO-PLUMBOOK-2004/pdf/GPO-PLUMBOOK-2004.pdf; and House Committee on Oversight and Government Reform, *US Government Policy and Supporting Positions* (*Plum Book*) (Washington, DC: US Government Printing Office, 2012), 187, www.gpo.gov/fdsys/pkg/GPO-PLUMBOOK-2012/content-detail.html.

38. Bell Oral History Interview, 130.

39. Norris, "Early Years."

40. John Norris, "Lesson for the Future," USAID: A History of US Foreign Aid, pt. 5, Inside Development, July 23, 2014, https://www.devex.com/news/lessons-for-the-future-83343.

41. Senior USAID official, private email to the author, October 3, 2016. The State Department may have as many as twenty fellows on the Hill and thirty in the NSC, according to one State Department official. USAID had one on Capitol Hill and six in the NSC in 2015 (the number had doubled during the past five years).

42. Hudson Institute, *The Index of Global Philanthropy and Remittances 2013* (Washington, DC, November 15, 2013), 5.

43. Ibid., 12, 33–35.

44. Rifk Ebeid, "Five Global Health Giving Trends," Borgen Project *The Blog*, November 15, 2013, http://borgenproject.org/five-global-health-giving-trends/.

45. Tony Barclay, *50 Years in Development: How Private Companies Adapt and Deliver* (Washington, DC: Council of International Development Companies, 2013).

46. Organisation for Economic Cooperation and Development (OECD), *The United States: Development Assistance Committee (DAC) Peer Review 2011* (Geneva, 2011), 29.

47. The State Department established the Office of the Coordinator for Reconstruction and Stabilization in 2004 "to lead, coordinate, and institutionalize US government civilian capacity to prevent or prepare for post-conflict situations and to help stabilize and reconstruct societies in transition from conflict or civil strife." In 2005 the Department of Defense issued its own directive outlining "Military Support for Stability, Security, Transition and Reconstruction," making stabilization a core Defense objective. Department of Defense, Directive 3000.5 (Washington, DC: Undersecretary of Defense [Policy], November 28, 2005).

48. Amy B. Frumin, *Equipping USAID for Success: A Field Perspective* (Washington, DC: Center for Strategic and International Studies, July 2009), 9. (Most of DOD assistance was going to Iraq and Afghanistan.)

49. "2013 Survey of Americans on the U.S. Role in Global Health," Henry J. Kaiser Family Foundation, November 7, 2013, http://kff.org/global-health-policy/poll-finding/2013-survey-of-americans-on-the-u-s-role-in-global-health/.

50. Earmarks are provisions in legislation directing spending to specific projects.

51. The functional accounts include Global Health, Development Assistance, International Disaster Assistance, Transition Initiatives, Complex Crises, Economic Support Fund, Development Credit Authority, and Migration and Refugees.

52. OECD, *United States*, 29.

53. In 2013 USAID's budget for Nigeria totaled $303.5 million: $600,000 was for peacekeeping, conflict mitigation, and reconciliation; $2.2 million was for civil society; $246 million supported health, $180 million of which was for HIV/AIDS and malaria. No funding was available for rule-of-law activities. USAID, "Dollars to Results: Nigeria," January 26, 2015, https://results.usaid.gov/nigeria#fy2015.

54. Senior USAID officials, discussions with the author, April 2016.

55. Susan B. Epstein, Alex Tiersky, and Marian Lawson, *State, Foreign Operations, and Related Programs: FY 2015 Budget and Appropriations* (Washington, DC: Congressional Research Service, December 8, 2014), 19, http://fas.org/sgp/crs/row/R43569.pdf.

56. Mission director, e-mail to the author, February 5, 2015.

57. See the reports published by the special inspector general for Iraq reconstruction (SIGIR), http://cybercemetery.unt.edu/archive/sigir/20131001084741/http://www.sigir.mil/publications/index.html; and Joel Brinkley, "Money Pit: The Monstrous Failure of US Aid to Afghanistan," *World Affairs*, January/February 2013, www.worldaffairsjournal.org/article/money-pit-monstrous-failure-us-aid-afghanistan.

58. Andrew Natsios, *The Clash of the Counter-bureaucracy and Development* (Washington, DC: Center for Global Development, July 2010), www.cgdev.org/sites/default/files/1424271_file_Natsios _Counterbureaucracy.pdf.

59. USAID Forward, www.usaid.gov/usaidforward.

60. The new initiatives include Feed the Future, focusing on agriculture and food security; the Global Health Initiative on maternal and child health, infectious disease, and neglected tropical diseases; and Global Climate Change. The set of Africa programs included Power Africa, the Young African Leaders Initiative, and the African Global Competitiveness Initiative.

61. Michel Igoe, "Rajiv Shah's USAID Legacy," *Inside Development*, February 12, 2015, www .devex.com/news/rajiv-shah-s-usaid-legacy-85239.

62. Ambassadors with close White House connections may be able to take on the secretary of state or combatant commanders on key policy issues, but power in the State Department normally tilts to the seventh floor; in USAID power has, historically, laid with the mission directors in the field. Communications technologies, particularly e-mail, may be blurring the lines, clipping the independence of the field but also complicating coordination of messages.

63. The conflict between aid for short-term political objectives and development for long-term transformational change is not new. William Gaud commented in 1966: "It seems to us that the State Department is primarily interested in the immediate, short-term objectives, keeping the other country happy. . . . We are much more interested in the long-term objective, in having the country take the steps which, over the long run, will mean that it has a sounder economic base, that it will make better use of its own resources and better use of the resources we are putting into it. The State Department is interested in what they call impact programs, programs that will be flashy and have an immediate effect. . . . We say, by and large, sure, you may need impact programs, occasionally, but as a general proposition, to hell with impact programs. We're working with a long-term objective in view." Gaud Oral History Interview.

64. Sheila Herrling and Steven Radelet, "Modernizing US Foreign Assistance for the Twenty-First Century," Center for Global Development, policy brief, 2008, www.cgdev.org/files/16559_file_Foreign _Assistance_web.pdf.

65. White House, "U.S. Global Development Policy," Presidential Policy Directive 6, September 22, 2010, 11, 12, http://fas.org/irp/offdocs/ppd/ppd-6.pdf.

66. Walter Pincus, "Defense Department Uses Thousands of Musicians, Spends Many Millions to Strike Up the Bands," *Washington Post*, September 7, 2010, www.washingtonpost.com/wp-dyn/content/ story/2010/09/06/ST2010090603042.html?sid=ST2010090603042.

67. White House, "U.S. Global Development Policy," 13, 14.

68. US Department of States and USAID, *Leading through Civilian Power: The First Quadrennial Diplomacy and Development Review* (Washington, DC, 2010), 124, 133–43, http://pdf.usaid.gov/ pdf_docs/PDACQ604.pdf.

69. The State Department's "F" Bureau retained overall authority for coordinating all foreign assistance budgets; it now has separate offices coordinating assistance for HIV/AIDs (PEPFAR), the Middle East, and Eastern Europe and a Bureau for Conflict and Stabilization Operations.

70. Senior USAID FSO, interview by the author, August 2014.

71. Carroll, "Management and Performance Challenges," 5.

72. In December 2014 a senior USAID manager reported that the agency had been invited to 263 NSC meetings in 2014.

73. "I found that while . . . deputy administrator . . . it was often difficult for USAID to get an invitation to high-level interagency policy discussions—even when development related issues were on the agenda. Cutting agencies out of senior meetings is a venerable bureaucratic tactic in Washington, one that is a lot easier to pull off where the agency in question is a subcabinet one." Lancaster, *Foreign Aid*, 101. Andrew Natsios argued that in 2008 USAID had lost its seat at the national security table because "the State Department claimed it would represent the Agency." A recent memo from a deputy assistant secretary, seen by several USAID staff, reportedly argues that USAID's development perspective does not align with the State Department's objectives in the region and therefore USAID need not participate in strategy discussions.

74. USAID officer, e-mail to the author, February 11, 2015.

75. USAID officials in Afghanistan, discussions with the author, April 2012.

76. The five oversight authorities were two inspectors general (State Department and USAID), the US General Accounting Office, the War Time Contracting Commission, and the SIGAR.

77. This distortion has been reflected in overall hiring. Classes recruited the last few years showed an increase in lawyers, contract specialists, and budget comptrollers. In one recent class of thirty-six, three were slated to work on stabilization whereas ten were destined for contracting assignments. (Author's review of records of the USAID Office of Human Resources, Development Leadership Initiative, 2014. The office is now called the Office of Human Capital and Talent Management.)

78. USAID, *USAID Policy on Cooperation with the Department of Defense* (Washington, DC, June 2015), www.usaid.gov/policy/dod-cooperation.

79. Ericka Clesceri and Emily Kunen, *Planning and Monitoring Environmental Compliance in Non-Permissive Environments* (Washington, DC: USAID, DCHA, 2014), 5; and Office of Afghanistan and Pakistan Affairs, *Non-permissive Environments* (Washington, DC: USAID, May 14, 2014), 2.

80. Post-Benghazi security and political considerations have made the Department of State's Bureau of Diplomatic Security more conservative. Increasingly, in places like Lebanon and Yemen, USAID must rely on contractors, often local, who do not operate under the same security requirements as diplomatic passport holders and are often willing to work in insecure environments for extended periods. They are able to develop contacts, language skills, and regional expertise. Driving in beat-up Toyotas instead of armored SUVs, the contractors do site monitoring that FSOs would do under other circumstances. Although there is political reluctance to delegate program implementation to contractors, there may be little choice.

81. Still operating under the 1961 Foreign Assistance Act.

82. USAID could detail more FSOs to the NSC even without an increase in personnel. By one estimate, only three FSOs (two currently) had served on the NSC in the last fifteen years. Private e-mail to the author, February 11, 2015.

CHAPTER 6

The Office of the Secretary of Defense

Joseph McMillan and Franklin C. Miller

> This office will probably be the biggest cemetery for dead cats in history.
> —James V. Forrestal, 1947

A familiar aphorism says that mighty oaks from little acorns grow. Nothing could be a more apt description of the role of the Office of the Secretary of Defense (OSD) in influencing national security policy over the past several decades. Few of those present at the creation of the Department of Defense (DOD) would recognize the powerful organization into which the Pentagon has evolved, let alone the clout that the secretary of defense has come to wield both in the internal processes of running the US armed forces and in formulating and implementing national security policies.

As originally created, the post of secretary of defense was practically powerless. The National Security Act of 1947 allowed the secretaries of the military departments to keep their traditional cabinet status as well as to retain "all powers and duties relating to [their] departments not specifically conferred upon the Secretary of Defense by this Act." The staff of the new secretary was as limited as his authorities. The law allowed him only three "special assistants," of lower rank than the under secretaries and assistant secretaries of the military departments. These special assistants were assigned portfolios covering legal and legislative, budgetary, and international issues. The first secretary of defense, James V. Forrestal, initially brought only forty-five employees from the Navy Department, mostly low-level administrative staff, to run the new National Military Establishment, as it was called. He believed that large staffs "begin to gather the attribute of God to themselves very fast."[1]

Forrestal soon realized, however, that without directive authority over the services, he could not function as the central decision maker. He had hoped to exercise authority by coordination rather than command but discovered that he had misjudged the magnitude of the challenges.[2] Apart from flaws in the statutory distribution of duties among "the respective Secretaries," the lack of a proper staff was perhaps the new organization's most serious deficiency.[3] Forrestal and his successors thus worked not only to increase the power and authority of the secretary of defense over the department but also to expand and strengthen his supporting civilian staff.

A succession of legislative reforms and internal reorganizations has transformed the relatively weak post created in 1947 into one of the most powerful offices in the United States. Unlike Forrestal, today's secretary possesses not only administrative control over the department but actual military control over operational units; he is now second only to the president in command of the world's preeminent military force. He directs the budgeting and expenditure of more than a half-trillion dollars a year, oversees the work of 3 million military and civilian personnel at hundreds of installations, and directs the distribution and employment of US forces worldwide. DOD is truly the "800-pound gorilla" of the US national security enterprise: big, strong, and (some have argued) uncontrollable. The history of OSD is largely about learning how to control the gorilla.

EVOLUTION OF OSD

Since 1947 OSD has grown from Forrestal's few dozen people into a large multifunctional organization. It has grown in stature as well as size, both within the department and in the interagency policy arena. As the Cold War deepened and US defenses and alliances grew in the 1950s, so did the complexity of DOD operations, making necessary a staff that could help the secretary of defense manage the huge military–civilian complex. Amendments to the National Security Act in 1949, 1953, and 1958 substantially increased the secretary's authority. The 1949 revision brought some of the most important changes: converting the National Military Establishment into the Department of Defense, stripping the service secretaries of cabinet rank, and stipulating that "no function [of the military departments or other DOD components] should be performed independent of the direction, authority and control of the Secretary of Defense." The secretary was given a deputy secretary, while the three special assistant positions were converted into assistant secretaries, appointed by the president and confirmed by the Senate. In 1953 the number of assistant secretaries was increased to nine. These were the first of many steps to enhance the secretary's ability to control and direct the national defense effort.

When Robert McNamara took office in 1961, he introduced a further series of organizational changes to give him additional leverage over the services and rationalize the department's procurement, budgeting, and evaluation processes. Among the most important were the creation of an independent program evaluation office and a separate defense intelligence agency.[4] These steps made McNamara and future secretaries less dependent on the potentially self-serving assessments and judgments of the uniformed services, especially on programmatic issues. Needless to say, uniformed military leaders did not welcome these innovations. Welcome or not, McNamara's reforms took hold and have shaped the way DOD operates to this day.

Beyond the Pentagon McNamara was one of the most powerful figures in the Kennedy administration. He persuaded the president to let him select his own subordinates, a privilege rarely allowed to cabinet secretaries. As Vietnam came to dominate the national security agenda, having a senior staff that was beholden to him and not the White House gave McNamara a major advantage in his efforts to control the interagency process guiding the administration's Southeast Asia policy.[5]

Ever since the McNamara era, OSD has been a powerful bureaucratic player both within DOD and with the other agencies involved in national security policy. It now comprises some 2,000 civilian and military personnel organized into five major sections, each headed by an under secretary: Acquisition, Technology, and Logistics (AT&L); Policy; Personnel and Readiness (P&R); Comptroller; and Intelligence.[6] The staffs of the five under secretaries, subdivided into units headed by assistant secretaries or the equivalent, develop policies, budget recommendations, and supporting analyses and generally run the day-to-day operations of the department within their respective areas of responsibility (see figure 6.1). These functions are performed both independently and in coordination with the Joint Staff, the combatant commands, and the military departments.

Externally, OSD represents the department in the complex government-wide national security policy process. The OSD staff must articulate and, wherever possible, secure interagency consensus for the secretary's top priorities and equities, not only on military issues but also, given the secretary's role as a statutory member of the National Security Council (NSC), on national security and foreign policy in general. Although most of the department's interagency work is done by the Office of the Under Secretary for Policy (known as OSD Policy), other OSD elements also engage with outside agencies depending on the particular issue. For example, the under secretary for intelligence (USD[I]) is the secretary's representative in the intelligence community and the key interlocutor with the director of national intelligence (DNI) on the budgets and operations of the various intelligence organizations under DOD control. Another example is the role of the comptroller and staff in working with the Office of Management and Budget (OMB) on the DOD budget, both its formulation and the process of gaining congressional approval. The role of OSD Policy in the interagency national security process will be considered in more depth later.

Within the Pentagon, OSD works with the Joint Staff, the combatant commands, and the military departments in an atmosphere that can be both adversarial and cooperative at the same time. This intradepartmental bargaining often focuses on the development of long-term guidance and strategy documents such as the National Defense Strategy, Defense Planning Guidance (DPG), and Guidance for Employment of the Force (GEF), among others. These documents must take into account the combined views of civilian and military leaderships, accord with the secretary's own preferences, and be consistent with the president's overall national strategy. Equally challenging is forming a common Pentagon position on a myriad of weapons development and procurement decisions. Naturally, the civilian OSD leadership and the services often disagree on these issues, leaving the secretary to make controversial decisions and creating a strong temptation (not always resisted) for the services to make end-run appeals to their allies in the White House, OMB, or Congress or to re-litigate matters in the media. A big part of OSD's role is to enforce discipline in the process, to equip the secretary with fair and accurate analysis on which to base decisions, and finally, to ensure, through a combination of persuasion with the Hill and dissuasion with the military departments, that the final budget and procurement program reflect those decisions.

It is important to understand that OSD interacts with but does not direct the Joint Staff, combatant commanders' staffs, and individual service staffs (see chapter 7 on the military services).[7] To the extent that OSD, as a staff, leads the department, it does so "horizontally," by a combination of reasoned argument, compromise, and superior access to upper-level decision makers. Even at best, however, and although intensive efforts are made to reach consensus among the key players on most issues, crystallizing only the most important disagreements for the secretary's attention, it is entirely possible for the secretary of defense to receive widely differing or even opposing recommendations from the OSD staff, the chairman of the Joint Chiefs of Staff (JCS), and the military departments. The extent to which the

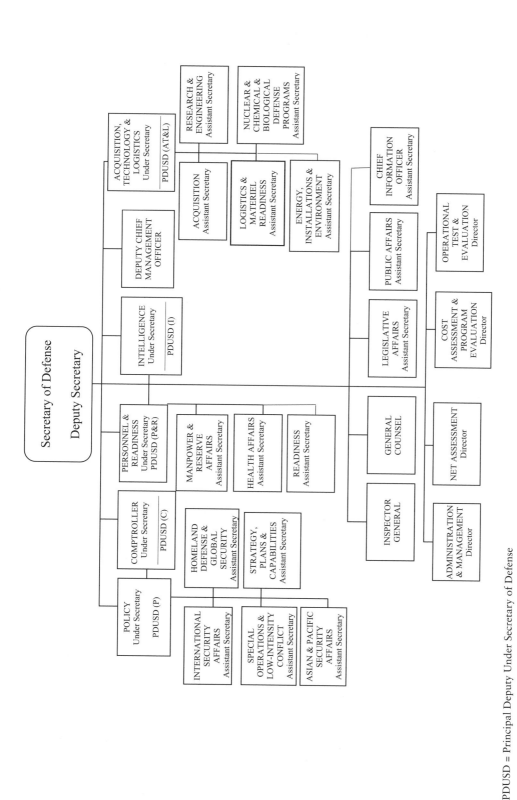

PDUSD = Principal Deputy Under Secretary of Defense

Figure 6.1. Office of the Secretary of Defense, 2016

various players present consensus or competing views depends to some degree on the personality and management style of the secretary of defense.

SECRETARIES OF DEFENSE:
MANAGERS OF THE DEFENSE ENTERPRISE

I have no patience with the myth that the Defense Department could not be managed.

—Robert S. McNamara, 1995

There is no single model of how to be a secretary of defense. No two secretaries have run the department exactly the same way, but each can be characterized by how much or how little autonomy he allowed the military departments to run their respective domains, how deeply he personally got involved in setting the agenda and framing and analyzing options, and how much deference he accorded to military judgments in various aspects of the department's business.

Centralization versus Decentralization

The archetypal centralizing secretary was undoubtedly Robert McNamara, but such diverse figures as Harold Brown, Donald Rumsfeld, and Robert Gates also fall into this category. There is often a correlation between centralization or decentralization and budget trends. Caspar Weinberger, for example, was charged by President Reagan with strengthening American military capabilities and was given a substantially increased budget to do it. He believed the most expeditious way to accomplish his task was to give the military departments relatively free rein. When budgets are constrained, on the other hand, allowing the services to operate as separate fiefdoms makes it difficult to make coherent choices between winners and losers in a zero-sum resource game. But the correlation does not always hold true. During his second stint as secretary in 2001–6, Rumsfeld presided over a period of rapid budget growth but gave the services little latitude on key issues, particularly those related to his sweeping force transformation agenda.

Gates also took a centralized approach to control over the services, although for him this was less a matter of asserting his personal standing as the man in charge (as often seemed to be the case with Rumsfeld) than of keeping the department focused on the objective of "winning the wars we are in." Gates's emphasis on ongoing wartime operations drove his FY 2010 budget decisions moving investment away from future-oriented programs favored by the services to those that would directly benefit the war efforts in Iraq and Afghanistan, as well as his dismissal of Secretary of the Army Francis Harvey in 2007 over poor conditions at Walter Reed Army Medical Center.[8] Although less dramatic, similarly clear central direction from Gates's successor, Leon Panetta, and strong management of the process by the OSD staff were critical in the major strategic reorientation contained in the January 2012 defense strategic guidance.

Personal Involvement

Nearly a half century after he left office, Robert McNamara is remembered largely for his role in the Vietnam War, but at the time he was revered or reviled by his subordinates and colleagues primarily for the active personal role he took in running the department, providing "aggressive leadership, questioning, suggesting alternatives, proposing objectives, and stimulating progress,"[9] to a far greater extent than his predecessors had done. More recently, Robert Gates explained his approach to running the department in much the same terms that historians use to describe McNamara's:

> If a secretary actually intends to run the Pentagon—and make real changes—as opposed to presiding over it, he must be selective in identifying his agenda and both realistic and single-minded in developing strategies for achieving each specific goal. . . . Very specific objectives, with tight deadlines and regular in person reports to the secretary himself, provide the only way to get people focused and to ensure that they are performing. The organization must understand that the secretary is personally invested in these issues and determined to drive the process to specific outcomes.[10]

In relatively steady-state periods, the Pentagon staff can run the department successfully with a hands-off secretary who sets the general course but leaves details and implementation to subordinates. As Gates observes, however, major redirection can only be achieved by an activist secretary who is prepared to force the generation of genuine, out-of-the-box options that hierarchical, risk-averse organizations will seldom put forward on their own. Even when a secretary is working in a fundamentally status quo environment, the heavy reliance that modern US military doctrine places on relatively scarce "enabling" assets (e.g., theater missile defense; intelligence, surveillance, and reconnaissance [ISR]; armed drones) makes it necessary to adjudicate competing demands for these capabilities in plans developed by the various combatant commands. Only the secretary of defense can fill this role.

Civil–Military Relationship

It is a common misconception that a clear line can be drawn between the roles of civilian leaders and soldiers in defense policy, particularly the conduct of wars, a view often expressed as "give the military the mission, stand out of the way, and let them do their jobs."[11] In reality there is a wide and ineradicable area of overlap between civilian and military responsibilities and competencies in both peacetime and war. The challenge presented by this overlap is magnified in wartime by the fact that the civilian secretary of defense is in the military chain of command—and thus accountable for the outcome of US combat operations—while the uniformed chairman and other members of the JCS are not. It is the secretary who signs the orders putting US forces in harm's way and commencing hostilities; the chairman merely transmits them. Balancing between too much deference to military judgment and too much micromanagement of execution is one of the trickiest tasks any secretary of defense must face.

On the one hand, military expertise is indispensable not only in executing a mission established by the political leadership but in formulating the objectives, assessing risks, and determining force and resource requirements beforehand. At the same time, a secretary who is reluctant to challenge and sometimes override the recommendations of his military commanders and advisors is likely to find his decision space—and by extension the president's—limited to a small number of all-or-nothing options derived from the services' established doctrinal repertoire.[12] The military's habit of producing such canned courses of action has frustrated policymakers from Eisenhower to Obama. At worst it can create a sense in the White House that the military is trying to box the president in or impose its own agenda on him and that the secretary has become irrelevant. For this reason, among others, the secretary and his OSD civilian staff frequently serve as a buffer between military commanders and a

West Wing populated by people who often do not understand military culture and may instinctively distrust the armed forces as an institution.

The tension inherent in this process can be either creative or destructive, depending on how the secretary manages it. This is not merely a function of strength or weakness. A strong secretary may, through his style of leadership, aggravate fissures within the department and thus undermine the implementation of his own initiatives. Donald Rumsfeld, for example, came into office with his own agenda for transforming the army and dismissed without a hearing any thinking the army itself had been doing on the subject. The presumption of service recalcitrance—underlined by constant reminders to military commanders about who was giving the orders—turned out to be a self-fulfilling prophecy. By contrast a strong secretary who is willing to engage, discuss, and explain can push through initiatives to which the military leadership actually is averse, as was the case with Gates's handling of repeal of the "don't ask, don't tell" policy on homosexuals in the military. Panetta's style of engagement with the senior military leadership was more intuitive and less analytical than Gates's,[13] but Panetta was equally successful in securing military support for other sensitive social policy initiatives, including opening up combat assignments to women and confronting the problem of sexual assault.

Balancing this civil–military tension is easier if the secretary enjoys a relationship of mutual trust and confidence with the chairman of the JCS (as Dick Cheney had with Gen. Colin Powell, Robert Gates with Adm. Michael Mullen, and Leon Panetta with Gen. Martin Dempsey), but that alone is not enough. A sound civil–military relationship must go beyond the personal; it must be mirrored in the institutions under the secretary's control, particularly OSD and the Joint Staff. Above all the secretary must remain a commander and not a friend, making clear his expectation that orders will be carried out but not stifling the willingness of subordinates to give advice he may not want to hear and to express disagreement with decisions behind closed doors.

SECRETARIES OF DEFENSE:
SHAPERS OF THE INTERAGENCY PROCESS

While the National Security Act assures the secretary of defense a seat on the NSC, the department's role and influence in the interagency formulation of strategy and policy, like OSD's role in the management of the department itself, depends at least as much on the incumbent secretary's personality, background, and attitudes as on the formal language of the statutes. It also depends on the secretary's relationship with the president and his or her team—the other senior officials at the White House (notably the chief of staff, the national security advisor, and the director of OMB) and the heads of other key departments and agencies. As Gates observes, the part the secretary "chooses to play on that team can have a big impact on the nation's, and a president's, success."[14]

The Rejectionists

Some secretaries have viewed interagency cooperation as useful and necessary to the effective operation of the US government. Others, seeing the State Department and the White House staff as interlopers in DOD's business, have been inclined at best to accept interagency cooperation grudgingly as a necessary evil, at worst to resist and reject it altogether. There is no particular connection between a secretary's approach to internal management of the department and cooperation with outside agencies. Rejectionist secretaries have included such otherwise diverse figures as McNamara, Weinberger, and Rumsfeld. Despite differences in managerial approach, all three believed their department should have a self-contained role in developing and implementing US defense strategy and decisions without the meddling of other agencies or outsiders, including Congress. All relied on personal closeness to their respective presidents, strong convictions, and enormous self-confidence to weather the consequent bureaucratic bloodletting.

McNamara was determined to dominate US strategy on Vietnam, and he did. He fought strenuously and for a long time successfully to prevent the State Department and others from providing independent assessments of US efforts to carry out what is now called nation building in South Vietnam. The Pentagon's tight control over Vietnam policy included pressuring intelligence agencies to alter bleak assessments or self-censor themselves to "keep with the policy." At the same time, the steps taken by McNamara in the opening years of the Kennedy administration to enhance OSD's clout within the department also made that civilian staff a powerful tool for helping him and his successors dominate the interagency process—for better or worse—when they chose to do so.

Although his approach toward internal management was quite different, Caspar Weinberger's attitude toward interagency cooperation closely resembled McNamara's. Given his priority on restoring US military power at all costs,[15] Weinberger inevitably found himself at odds with successive secretaries of state on arms control and Soviet policy. Rather than having to work out mutually acceptable compromises with his colleagues, Weinberger was able to leverage his close relationship with President Reagan to win most of his interagency battles. Meanwhile, Reagan's decision to reduce the role of the national security advisor (of which he went through six in eight years), made the NSC staff largely irrelevant and gave freer rein to Weinberger and other cabinet secretaries within their respective domains and sometimes beyond.[16]

Donald Rumsfeld, during his 2001–6 tenure under the second President Bush, did not merely disdain the interagency process; he actively encouraged his staff to obstruct and hamper interagency cooperation as much as possible. Just as he insisted on personal authority and control within his department, Rumsfeld constantly reiterated DOD's right to exclusive direction of military operations and anything connected with them. As one senior aide recounts, Rumsfeld told the commander of US Central Command in the run-up to the Iraq War, "It's clear to you and everyone that DOD is in charge of the war. You're in charge and I'm in charge and other departments put in ideas, but we make the decisions, right?"[17] This uncooperative approach reflected the belief, openly expressed by Rumsfeld, his under secretary for policy, and his assistant secretary for international security affairs, that the interagency system was not only broken but irrelevant to twenty-first-century warfare and therefore not worth trying to repair.[18]

Nowhere was the impact of this hostility to the interagency process felt more strongly than in the case of Iraq. Both before the invasion and for the first several years of the operation, OSD took little active interest in interagency work to prepare for combat operations and even less in postwar reconstruction and stabilization. Its participation in the Executive Steering Group (ESG) created by the NSC staff in early 2003 to manage the panoply of interagency tasks necessary to support the anticipated combat operations was grudging and desultory at best. Once combat operations commenced, OSD promptly made clear that any further outside assistance with stabilization and reconstruction was unnecessary and unwelcome.

National Security Presidential Directive 24 (NSPD-24), issued by the president in January at Secretary Rumsfeld's urging, had assigned primary responsibility for postwar Iraq to DOD, and OSD interpreted that as a license to go it alone. This same rejectionist approach continued even after it became clear over the summer of 2003 that the situation in Iraq was going badly, and even though many of the problems on the ground fell well outside DOD's expertise and competence. As a direct result of OSD's unwillingness to play in this most important of the Bush administration's national security priorities, US policy and strategy were in disarray, reconstruction and security efforts were floundering, and American soldiers were dying.

The Participants

Most other secretaries of defense have been inclined to work cooperatively with their cabinet colleagues, whether because they had confidence in the national security advisors who ran the process, because they worked for presidents who demanded a collegial approach, or because they simply saw interagency cooperation as yielding better policy outcomes. Those who have participated in the process most effectively often had close personal connections with the president and other key members of the national security team.[19] This was the case with Dick Cheney, who, as secretary of defense from 1989 to 1993, was an effective participant in the interagency process, thanks in large measure to his long-standing friendships with Secretary of State James Baker and National Security Advisor Brent Scowcroft. The positive relationships among the three were mirrored among the second-tier political appointees in their organizations, just as Rumsfeld's dysfunctional relations with his counterparts would later be mirrored by his subordinates under George W. Bush.

A secretary who is not personally close to the president or his inner circle may nevertheless establish himself as a vital, trusted member of the interagency team by bringing to the table a reputation for effective management of his own department, a strategic vision held in common with his most important colleagues, or political skills (particularly in dealing with Congress). This was clearly the situation when Robert Gates was asked to remain as secretary in an Obama administration in which he had no personal connections with either the president or anyone else in the White House inner circle. It was also true to a lesser but still substantial degree with both William J. Perry and Leon Panetta, who, while no strangers to their colleagues, had nothing like the close personal ties to the Clinton and Obama inner circles respectively that Cheney had enjoyed vis-à-vis his counterparts.[20] Even Gates himself, although very close to the elder President Bush and his team, did not have the same kind of relationship with the younger Bush and those surrounding him at the time he was appointed secretary in 2006. All three, however, were very highly regarded by their colleagues for the knowledge and skills they brought to their jobs and came to be among the most effective members of their respective presidents' cabinets. By contrast, Chuck Hagel, another outsider, was never able to establish himself as a vital part of Obama's team. The result was an abbreviated tenure as secretary of defense.

Willingness to be part of the interagency team does not necessarily mean that a secretary will be equally effective with all his or her colleagues. Harold Brown, for example, worked extremely well with President Carter's national security advisor, Zbigniew Brzezinski, largely because they took the same basic approach to the national security process, held the same views on the most salient policy issues (especially skepticism about Soviet intentions), and had similar work habits. But neither of them was as influential with Secretary of State Cyrus

Vance or, for that matter, the president himself. It was only after the Soviet invasion of Afghanistan in late 1979 that Brzezinski and Brown were able to impress their strategic perspective on national policy.

GOLDWATER–NICHOLS ACT

Other than the sometimes dramatic changes in secretarial personalities every few years, nothing has transformed the internal dynamics of the Pentagon and the way it operates with other agencies so much as the Goldwater–Nichols Department of Defense Reorganization Act of 1986. Much has been written about how this major reform affected the way the military services, combatant commanders, and JCS relate to each other, strengthening the role of the chairman of the JCS vis-à-vis the service chiefs and shifting considerable power from the services to the unified combatant commands, even on budget issues. Less has been said about its impact on the civilian side of the Pentagon and OSD's relationship with the uniformed military.

Among the notable changes, the act assigned the under secretary for policy (USD[P]) statutory responsibility for assisting the secretary "in preparing written policy guidance for the preparation and review of contingency plans; and in reviewing such plans."[21] Initially, only the under secretary personally was permitted to review these contingency plans,[22] but additional members of the Policy staff were eventually given access to support the USD(P) in carrying out this role. A more fully developed review process was introduced in the early 2000s in response to Secretary Rumsfeld's dissatisfaction with the initial plans for the invasion of Iraq. Supporting the secretary in the plans development, review, and approval process is now one of the most important functions of the USD(P) and the OSD Policy staff, carried out in close cooperation with the Joint Staff and the combatant command responsible for the plan.

Goldwater–Nichols also had a positive effect on the quality of military personnel assigned to joint service organizations, including OSD. Previously, the services had filled positions in these organizations only grudgingly, retaining most of their best people on their own staffs. Because promotion boards discounted the value of time away from the mother service, officers tended to shun joint assignments whenever they could. As a result of the Goldwater–Nichols requirement making joint service a prerequisite for promotion to flag rank, however, field grade officers began to seek these assignments avidly rather than avoiding them as career killers. OSD Policy proved to be a particularly attractive destination for ambitious and highly qualified officers.

The act also had unintended negative consequences, however, particularly on how DOD functions in the interagency process. Before 1986 OSD and the JCS / Joint Staff would collaborate to develop a consolidated DOD position on a given issue and submit a single DOD paper to the NSC staff. OSD would take the lead in the interagency meetings. Presenting a united front often gave Defense the upper hand with other agencies, especially the Department of State, which frequently came to meetings still trying to sort out differences among its regional and functional bureaus. After 1986 the Joint Staff interpreted Goldwater–Nichols as giving it an autonomous seat at the table and began to insist on the right to make its own inputs to the NSC process independent of OSD. Although the separate Pentagon positions generally did not differ widely, other agencies (especially the NSC staff) learned to exploit variations in nuance to DOD's disadvantage. This problem can be mitigated by good coordination, which obviously depends in large measure on the tone the secretary and chairman set for the civilian–military relationship within the Pentagon. Under Rumsfeld divergences between OSD and the Joint Staff were a constant impediment to DOD's effectiveness within the interagency process; under his successors a more positive civil–military atmosphere has made the challenge easier to manage.

UNDER SECRETARY FOR POLICY AND STAFF

As noted previously, all five under secretaries of defense and their teams play a part in the development and implementation of US national security policy, but of them all it is USD(P) and the OSD Policy organization who work most continuously and closely with non-DOD elements of the national security establishment, particularly the NSC staff and the State Department.

In historical terms USD(P)'s organization grew out of the small cadre assigned to the secretary's special assistant for foreign military issues in 1947. Two years later, this official was redesignated the assistant to the secretary of defense for foreign military affairs and military assistance, supported by a staff of about seventy.[23] As it became clear that the department's international responsibilities went far beyond foreign assistance, Secretary George C. Marshall expanded the office in 1951 to about 200 people and gave it a new name, International Security Affairs (ISA). The head of the renamed office was given a broadened mandate to serve as the secretary's principal advisor on all defense policy and international security issues, including DOD interaction with the NSC, and his strengthened staff became "a full-fledged clearinghouse for politico-military affairs" throughout DOD.[24] Reflecting the office's new stature within and beyond the department, ISA's chief was upgraded in 1953 to the level of assistant secretary of defense (ASD).

For the next three decades, ISA was *the* policy organization. Often known as the Pentagon's "Little State Department," ISA was a relatively small organization—about the same size in the late 1970s as in the early 1950s[25]—with vast responsibilities. It was composed of a mix of career civil servants and active-duty military officers, with the upper echelons occupied mainly by political appointees with a sprinkling of flag officers and senior foreign service officers (FSOs) on loan from the State Department. Five deputy assistant secretaries of defense (DASDs) had regional responsibilities while a sixth was in charge of policy planning. Because their areas of responsibility aligned with those of the State Department's regional bureaus, ISA's geographic DASDs punched above their weight in the interagency process, operating as the de facto counterparts of assistant secretaries of state and senior directors on the NSC staff.

In 1977 Congress created the post of USD(P). At first the under secretary simply sat between the ASD (ISA) and the secretary with nothing more than a small personal staff, but in 1979 parts of ISA were stripped out to become direct reports to the under secretary. In 1981 a new ASD for international security policy (ISP) was created. The new position was given responsibility for issues concerning the North Atlantic Treaty Organization (NATO) and Europe (including the Soviet Union), nuclear forces, arms control, and technology export control policy, with ISA retaining responsibility for the rest of the world and conventional forces policy.[26] In 1982 Congress mandated the establishment of an additional ASD for special operations and low-intensity conflict (SO/LIC) and another in 2002 for homeland defense. After numerous shifts in alignment,[27] Policy took its current form in 2014 with assistant secretaries for (1) ISA; (2) Asian and Pacific security affairs; (3) SO/LIC; (4) homeland defense and global security; and (5) strategy, plans, and capabilities, as illustrated in figure 6.2.

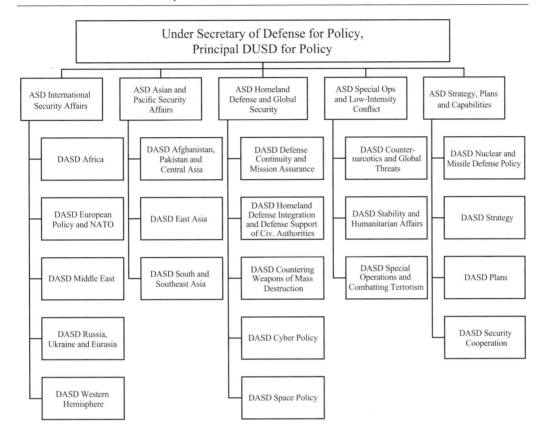

ASD = assistant secretary of defense

DASD = deputy assistant secretary of defense

DUSD = deputy under secretary of defense

Figure 6.2. Office of the Under Secretary of Defense for Policy, 2016

OSD Policy and the Interagency Process

OSD Policy's central place in DOD interaction with other elements of the national security apparatus can be traced to Secretary Marshall's decision, when he established ISA in the early 1950s, to designate it as the central office for all dealings with the Department of State on foreign affairs issues. While State initially objected to the implicit limitation on its contacts with other Pentagon officials, Marshall's action has proved indispensable not only to DOD but to the orderly operation of the interagency process itself.[28]

To the public the most visible manifestation of the interagency national security policy process is the congressionally mandated National Security Strategy (NSS), but this is perhaps its least important aspect from a DOD perspective, given that the document seldom addresses the ways and means by which the broad goals it sets forth are to be achieved. It is thus of limited utility as practical guidance.[29] Of much greater consequence are the interagency studies, led by the NSC staff, conducted to obtain presidential guidance on a particular aspect of national security policy. After interagency review up to cabinet level, the decisions coming out of these studies are embodied in directives from the president, binding on all agencies.[30] OSD Policy represents the secretary in this process, ensuring through coordination with other elements of OSD and the Joint Staff that all the department's equities are taken into account. The same is true of DOD's participation in day-to-day interagency interaction on a host of issues, from ongoing military operations to long-term diplomatic initiatives to management of breaking crises.

A major proportion of OSD Policy's work is devoted to the department's participation in the various tiers of interagency committees, supporting the secretary in the NSC itself and the Principals' Committee and representing him in the Deputies' Committee and lower-level bodies (see chapter 2 on the NSC). DOD's success or failure in maneuvering through this interagency process rests in large measure on the working-level Policy action officer handling a particular country or issue. To a surprising degree, relatively junior officers can drive national policy by persuading their bosses that a particular issue needs attention and giving them workable solutions to push through the process. For example, it was the initiative of ISA's Iran team in late 2009 that led Secretary Gates to call his colleagues' attention to the potential for an unexpected and unwanted conflict with that country.[31] Even when the initiative comes from elsewhere in the government or is driven by external events, Policy action officers work with their counterparts in the NSC staff, State Department, and other agencies—and even more closely with their Joint Staff colleagues—to share analysis, identify areas of agreement and disagreement, and harmonize positions when possible. They then prepare briefing materials to support senior officials in the interagency meeting, coordinating fully with the Joint Staff officers who are doing the same for their superiors. Finally, Policy action officers are responsible for obtaining a readout from each meeting and ensuring the completion of any necessary follow-up.

An OSD representative who can speak with certainty for the secretary on a given issue is in a much stronger position than one who is merely guessing or who has to take everything back to the Pentagon for approval. This is a particular advantage when, as is often the case, the State Department comes to the table with the representatives of multiple bureaus expressing diverse positions rather than a consolidated position endorsed by the department's top leadership.

OSD Policy Inside the Pentagon

> An effective secretary is not a congenial chairman of the Board.
> —Robert Gates, 2014

During the first three decades of its existence, ISA enjoyed a degree of clout inside the Pentagon by virtue of its authority to oversee and coordinate the department's overseas activities, but its influence over what the rest of the building saw as DOD's core business—budgeting, weapons acquisition, and force structure—was almost negligible. This situation has been transformed beyond recognition since the establishment of USD(P).

The empowerment of OSD Policy in these areas began under Caspar Weinberger, who, despite early deference to the military leadership, soon became a believer in the value of the OSD staff and pioneered the idea of giving it increased responsibilities in the direction and implementation of the war-planning processes. Specifically, he tasked Policy's civilian staff rather than the Joint Staff with leading the overhaul of strategic (nuclear) war planning and preparing the contingency planning guidance for conventional forces.[32] This start was built on in 1992, when Under Secretary Paul Wolfowitz issued the first defense planning guidance, by which OSD provides strategic policy direction to the services for programming and budgeting. A year later, in 1993, Secretary Les Aspin initiated the Bottom-Up Review (BUR), based on work he had begun as chairman of the House Armed Services Committee (HASC) on the changes necessary to reorient the US military for the post–Cold War era. In organizational terms the BUR was significant because it was led not by the Joint Staff, as it would have been in the past, but by a newly created ASD for strategy and resources, part of OSD Policy. This can be said to mark the shift of the lead for long-term strategic thinking in DOD from military to civilian hands.

OSD Policy's responsibility for the closely associated areas of strategy and planning has inexorably given the organization a major role in shaping the future of US military capability. By law the secretary is required to publish a Quadrennial Defense Review (QDR) every four years, an exercise that, when it functions as intended, has a major impact on future force development. This massive effort is led and managed by Policy. Policy has the pen on the secretary's National Defense Strategy and, through the DPG, establishes the planning framework within which the department's programming and budgeting will take place. It is also responsible for a series of other guidance documents, such as the GEF, introduced under Donald Rumsfeld to address more specific aspects of force employment. In 2009 DOD faced the daunting task of conducting major congressionally mandated reviews of nuclear posture, space, and ballistic missile defense simultaneously with the QDR. All were led by Policy, as was the quick turnaround Defense Strategic Guidance, a sort of mini-QDR, conducted in the final months of 2011.

Managing OSD Policy: Political Appointees and Civil Servants

One of the most distinctive aspects of OSD—especially the Policy organization—compared to other parts of the interagency national security community is the extent to which it is dominated by political appointees. The entire intelligence community has only a handful of political appointees, the top two or three officials each in the Office of the DNI and in the Central Intelligence Agency (CIA). The Joint Staff has none. At the State Department more than 75 percent of the deputy assistant secretaries and about half the assistant secretaries are FSOs or civil servants. By contrast, until 2008 no DOD civil servant had ever been nominated for a post requiring Senate confirmation (assistant secretary or above).[33]

The large political presence in OSD Policy has both pros and cons and affects not only the internal management of the staff but also the way it interacts with other organizations. On the positive side it brings in fresh thinking, offsetting the tendency of any large organization to become mired in potentially outdated approaches to problems. Political appointees also tend to have connections, either political or personal, with appointees elsewhere in government, which can be leveraged to good effect. On the negative side, the en masse turnover of Policy's top three management layers every four or eight years not only decapitates the organization for many months at the beginning of each new administration but also undercuts continuity and forces the career staff to expend enormous amounts of time and effort bringing new appointees up to speed. Organizational effectiveness during transitions is also hampered by the culture clash between civil servants and new political appointees, especially those from congressional staffs who are serving in the executive branch for the first time. Brought up in a culture of partisanship, personal loyalties, and strong patron–client networks, former Hill staffers often have difficulty understanding that civil servants' loyalty is more institutional than personal, that the career staff feels no sense of residual obligation to the former bosses. Appointees usually come to recognize the value and loyalty of the career staff within a few months, but even afterward the relatively short tenure of most political appointees—typically two or three years—causes the constant repetition of periods of friction, albeit less intense than at a change of administration.

When political personnel persist in their distrust and disdain for the career staff, the damage can be severe and long lasting. Many of the highly ideological appointees who came to Policy with Rumsfeld's USD(P), Douglas Feith, allowed their contempt for President Clinton to spill over onto anyone who had worked in his administration. The atmosphere was particularly poisonous for many of the more experienced career action officers, who found any professional judgment that did not coincide with the ideological disposition of the political leadership treated as presumptively disloyal and even threatening to their boss's sense of authority. As a direct consequence many of Policy's most capable professionals departed for other government departments or the private sector in the early 2000s.

How political appointments are made also matters. As noted previously, it is unusual for a cabinet officer to have a free hand in choosing his or her own subordinates, but the degree to which the White House overrides secretaries' preferences varies from one administration to another. As Gates demonstrated on several occasions, the ability of the DOD leadership to enforce accountability is directly correlated with the plausible threat that those who occupy senior positions can be removed. Conversely, when a deputy assistant secretary owes his or her job to someone in the White House rather than the Pentagon, the implied immunity can make him or her difficult to control. The negative impact of conflicting guidance from different echelons of leadership should not be underestimated.

Finally, we must consider the impact a large political presence has on career management for the civil service cadre. With so many senior slots set aside for political appointees, career civil servants face stiffer odds against reaching high rank than their military, intelligence, and foreign service counterparts. Combined with a broader societal trend of rapid mobility from one job to another, this structural obstacle to advancement makes it harder to retain Policy's most talented young members.

An effort by Under Secretary Walter Slocombe in the mid-1990s to redress this political–career imbalance in Policy's senior ranks initially yielded remarkable results, increasing the number of career DASDs and principal DASDs from four to ten (out of a total of sixteen) between 1995 and 2000. It was probably inevitable that these advances would not be sustained following the 2000 election, given any new administration's desire to place its own people in key jobs. What was not foreseen, however, was that the new team would push aside not just some of the senior careerists they inherited but virtually all of them. Only one career DASD was kept in place. The others retained their Senior Executive Service (SES) rank but, apparently considered unreliable for having been promoted under Clinton, were relegated to positions outside the Policy mainstream. Even some posts below DASD level that had been continuously held by careerists since the creation of ISA in the 1950s were converted to political under the Rumsfeld regime.

By the end of the Bush administration in 2009, the share of DASD and principal DASD positions held by DOD civil servants had decreased to only two out of what was then a total of twenty-two such posts. In the early years of the Obama administration, the distribution returned to roughly the pre-1995 norm, with about a fifth of the DASD and principal DASD slots held by civil servants. Since then the proportion has climbed to about a third. Several more such positions have gone to candidates who gave up civil service status, either in DOD or another agency, to take them on a political basis.

Striking the right balance between political and career staffing of OSD Policy's critical senior positions is likely to remain a key challenge in ensuring the organization's long-term effectiveness. While the benefits of a substantial admixture of political appointees are indisputable, so are those to be gained from the continuity afforded by a well-qualified senior career cadre. For example, political appointees often (although not always) bring substantial subject matter expertise to DASD positions, but their skills in handling the internal and external bureaucratic politics that come with the job rarely equal those of an experienced senior civil servant. Moreover, with a few outstanding exceptions, political appointees who expect to be in their jobs only a few years seldom give serious attention to the nurturing and management of the working-level staff, an essential aspect of leadership in any organization.

It is unrealistic to expect Policy to reserve 75 percent of DASD positions for careerists, as is the case at the State Department, but half would not be an unreasonable target. Included within this 50 percent should be all five of the principal DASDs. In addition, the recent practice of placing political appointees in supervisory positions below the DASD level should be abolished.[34] Taken together, such steps would go a long way toward ensuring that Policy can develop and retain a capable, experienced, trustworthy, apolitical career cadre, ready and able to support the secretary regardless of political vicissitudes.

Trends in Policy Staffing since 9/11

In the composition of its staff, as in so many other ways, Policy today is a very different organization from the one the USD(P) first took over from ISA in 1977. Many of the changes came about in response to 9/11 and the ensuing wars in Afghanistan and Iraq; others were the result of trends that were already well established several years before.

The most obvious impact of 9/11 was a rapid and substantial growth in personnel numbers, reaching a peak of around 500, including temporary overstrength hires and "technical" contractors, in the 2008–9 time frame. A portion of the enlargement can be attributed to the establishment of the new ASD-ship for homeland defense, which brought together a number of people working elsewhere in the department under the Policy umbrella. But OSD Policy offices grew across the board, both by increasing the size of many existing organizations—most notably, but not exclusively, the offices handling Middle Eastern and South Asian issues—and creating new offices to focus on specific issues that were considered especially salient by successive administrations over the course of 2001 to 2011. As one extreme example, before 9/11 Policy had two people handling the entire Indian subcontinent, including Afghanistan. As of early 2015 there are well over twenty. Meanwhile, the new offices established for cyber and space policy during the Obama administration have about twenty members apiece.

To some degree, as Forrestal would have predicted, these expanded staffs have "gather[ed] the attribute of God to themselves," particularly the attribute of omniscience. Unfortunately, at the strategic level at which OSD Policy is supposed to function, it is not particularly useful to be mindful of the fall of every sparrow or the number of hairs on everyone's head.[35] Any tendency toward divine omnipotence, however, has been sharply limited by the equally predictable increase of bureaucratic layering that accompanied the organization's growth in numbers.

Another consequence of the post-9/11 environment has been a decline in the number of military personnel assigned to OSD Policy, both as a proportion of the total workforce and in absolute terms. This decline began even before 2001, with the expansion of the unified command staffs in the 1990s, but it has been accelerated by the demand for officers for combat duty since 2001. In sharp contrast to the early 1980s, when military officers accounted for about half of Policy's working-level professional staff, they now make up barely a fifth. Whether this trend will be reversed as post-9/11 operations draw to an end remains to be seen.

A third trend, only partly related to the aftermath of 9/11, has been a downward shift in the median age, experience level, and bureaucratic seniority of Policy's career civilian cadre. As with the drop in the military presence in the organization, this pattern originates from decisions made in the 1990s. Besides placing more civil servants in senior leadership positions, Under Secretary Slocombe introduced the opportunity (and for a brief period the requirement) for careerists to rotate from one job to another across the Policy organization as a way to broaden their expertise and make them more competitive for higher-level positions, both within Policy and across the broader national security establishment. To make the rotation system work, however, it was necessary to fill vacancies from within the existing staff whenever possible. As a result, Policy's intake of experienced career professionals from elsewhere in OSD or the department more broadly dried to a trickle. The Presidential Management Fellows (PMF) program became the principal—and at times the only—source of outside hiring.[36] Where employees retiring in their sixties would once have been succeeded by personnel in their thirties or early forties, usually with at least ten to fifteen years of government service under their belts, they were now replaced by former PMFs in their mid-to-late twenties with only the two-year fellowship behind them. The youth trend was accelerated by the exodus of experienced personnel in reaction to the hostile work environment of the Rumsfeld years and then magnified in the early 2010s by the conversion to career status of a large number of junior personnel brought in as temporary hires after 9/11.

Finally, the organization's well-intentioned emphasis on service in a variety of offices as a criterion for advancement has created a tendency for employees to jump frequently from job to job, often without regard to whether the succession of assignments helps them develop a meaningful body of expertise. In combination with the way Rumsfeld's short-lived National Security Personnel System (NSPS) was implemented within Policy, action officers below grade GS-15 (or, while NSPS was in place, pay band 3) have a strong incentive to move as often as every eighteen to twenty-four months to position themselves for promotion consideration as soon as they become eligible.

All these changes present challenges to Policy's ability to sustain the competitive advantage it has historically enjoyed in the interagency process and within the department.

- Traditionally, the Policy action officer on a particular subject was supposed to bring a strategic perspective that could pull together all DOD's activities in that area. That unifying vision is difficult to sustain when a given issue set is being handled by four or five people, let alone twenty.
- The increased number of bureaucratic layers tends to be detrimental to two long-standing Policy strengths: quick responsiveness to taskings and external events and easy access to senior leaders.
- Before the introduction of the rotational system, Policy civil servants were typically hired to handle a particular portfolio and expected to remain in that assignment indefinitely. The depth of expertise created by this continuity gave DOD a strong advantage in the working-level interagency process, enabled quick and accurate reaction to events, and generally made senior officials comfortable with allowing action

officers a fair degree of autonomy in day-to-day business. It is unusual for anyone to develop a comparable depth of expertise in a two-year rotation.

- The sharp reduction in hiring from elsewhere in DOD means that the typical career civilian in Policy has little if any direct familiarity with such core aspects of DOD operations as logistics, programming and budgeting, contracting, or systems development. This reduces Policy's credibility as a knowledgeable and impartial representative of competing intra-DOD interests and concerns.
- The fact that most OSD Policy desk officers are now junior in rank, less experienced, and considerably younger than their counterparts in other agencies, the Joint Staff, and the services and commands sharply reduces their ability to "lead horizontally."

An interesting and unprecedented response to the issues just described has emerged in the last ten years or so. This is the substantial number of officials at the DASD-level and above—including the previous USD(P), a recent principal deputy USD(P), one ASD, and several DASDs—who worked in Policy as civil servants for a number of years, left for the private sector or Washington's think tank community during the early 2000s, and then came back to Policy as political appointees in either the Bush or Obama administration. There are substantial advantages to this development, not the least of which is that political officials who have served in the Policy trenches do not face the same cultural adjustment to life in the Pentagon as those without that background. Given the enduring reality that working up the ranks of the civil service is not the most promising way to reach the top levels of the Policy organization, many of today's most capable and ambitious action officers seem likely to emulate this new hybrid career path in the future.

IS THERE AN OSD POLICY CULTURE?

Given the constant changes in its upper leadership, the large number of senior officials who serve in the organization for only a few years, and the personnel trends just described, one may wonder whether it is possible to speak of a characteristic OSD Policy culture. Yet people from other parts of the national security establishment actually do perceive a distinctive OSD approach to things—an organizational culture—that differs significantly from their own agencies'.

Much of what sets OSD Policy apart from other participants in the interagency arena reflects a broader DOD culture. For example, those in DOD commonly observe that the State Department does not do planning; conversely, DOD often seems to outsiders to be obsessed with planning. This is partly a function of the vast number of moving parts that have to be synchronized in any military operation and partly a function of the long lead times necessary in the hardware acquisition process, neither of which is a significant element of the work of other elements of the national security structure. Aware of the need to think through these issues, OSD Policy is frequently frustrated by politically driven prohibitions on planning for one contingency or another. From a White House perspective, thinking about what to do if something the president has declared unacceptable actually happens shows a lack of confidence. From the Pentagon, it looks more like a lack of seriousness. Former USD(P) Michèle Flournoy's mandate to her staff that *nothing* is too sensitive to plan for would undoubtedly horrify many in the West Wing, but it aptly sums up the Policy culture on the subject.

Closely related to the disposition for planning is DOD's acute consciousness of the time factor in decision making. Unlike the State Department, where a diplomatic initiative can be conceived today, dispatched by an instruction cable tonight, and presented by the embassy in a foreign capital tomorrow morning, almost everything DOD does requires lead time, whether the procurement of matériel, the mobilization and marshaling of units, or the transportation of troops and equipment. As a result, OSD Policy and the Joint Staff invariably find themselves pressing for clear decisions before other departments and agencies—let alone the president—are ready to make them and reminding their colleagues that delaying in the name of keeping options open actually has the effect of taking some of those options off the table. For the same reason DOD tends to see a decision as something to be implemented, not as the starting point for the next debate.

One consequence of the multiyear nature of DOD's acquisition and budgeting processes is a departmental disposition to "give the future a seat at the table." In contrast to other agencies, which are more often oriented to the immediate term, the challenge in DOD is making sure that the present has a seat. In this respect Policy differs somewhat from other parts of OSD, particularly AT&L and the comptroller. While Policy certainly does its share of long-term strategic planning, the fact that so much of its day-to-day work involves managing crises and ongoing operations makes it more focused on immediate challenges than the rest of OSD. It also means that in contrast to both the other parts of OSD and the State Department's regional and functional bureaus, OSD Policy sees the provision of advice and support to the secretary as its most important function. Accordingly, under most secretaries of defense, members of the Policy staff have far more personal contact with their secretary—even despite the recent trend toward increased bureaucratic layering—than their counterparts elsewhere.[37] As a result, the organization tends to identify its interests with those of its principal to a greater degree than any other part of the interagency except the NSC staff.

Perhaps the most important impact of DOD culture on Policy's interaction with non-DOD agencies is the gloves-off nature of the department's internal deliberations and debate. When Robert Gates was nominated as secretary of defense in 2006, former deputy secretary John Hamre gave him a brief education on decision making in DOD, comparing it to "the old Roman arena—gladiators come before the emperor to battle and you [the secretary] decide who is the winner."[38] In contrast to matters decided by the secretary of state, most matters coming before the secretary of defense have resource implications—money, people, and equipment are all finite, and committing them to one program or mission means taking them away from another. Thus, whereas FSOs are conditioned to look for win–win outcomes, DOD careerists are more likely to see interagency disputes as zero-sum games. This clash of styles often plays out to DOD's advantage, although not always the nation's.

OSD officials, particularly careerists, also tend to be more conservative in their approach to international issues, focusing on adversary capabilities rather than intentions and viewing the commitments and promises of friends and even close allies with a dose of skepticism. Understanding that their military colleagues will have to face the consequences of diplomatic failure, OSD Policy staff members generally try to reach and maintain a common position with the Joint Staff in interagency deliberations, which can reinforce the tendency to see challenges as risks rather than opportunities. This is the case even though, in the department's internal deliberations on the same issue, OSD may take an adversarial, even confrontational, approach with military colleagues, especially those it sees as less than forthcoming with information.

CONCLUDING THOUGHTS

The evolution of OSD has led it to become in some respects the most powerful player in the interagency process. Given its formidable capabilities, DOD has come to be seen as the first responder for almost every urgent problem facing the US national security enterprise. This tendency has been reinforced by Donald Rumsfeld's success in obtaining for DOD the legal authorities and money to conduct a host of international activities traditionally under the purview of the Department of State. Since 2006 successive secretaries of defense have advocated shifting some of this responsibility and funding back to civilian agencies with the expertise for such tasks, most notably in Robert Gates's November 2007 speech calling for substantial increases in funding for State and USAID. We may yet see some rebalancing, but Congress's chronically parsimonious attitude toward the foreign affairs budget is unlikely to change substantially. Even if it does, however, that would not significantly alter the important role played by DOD in all aspects of national security policy.

The inherent power of DOD and the bureaucratic clout of its Policy shop are such that a secretary of defense can dominate or destroy the interagency process, but doing so is hardly in the best interest of the nation, the president, or even DOD itself. As experience in our post-2001 conflicts has demonstrated, no single agency is capable by itself of handling the array of military, social, political, economic, and cultural challenges that such complex operations require. Secretary Rumsfeld may have believed that twenty-first-century challenges, such as transnational terrorism and proliferation, have made the interagency process irrelevant, but going it alone has clearly proved to be no solution. It may indeed be necessary to reinvent how the interagency process is organized and controlled, but if so, the reinvention must be more than yet another violent swing between DOD obstructionism and White House micromanagement.

As we have seen, how OSD Policy is managed internally has a direct bearing on its ability to provide the secretary of defense the advice and support necessary to function effectively. We have offered several recommendations in this area; future administrations will doubtless have ideas of their own. One area to be wary of, however, is yet another drastic reorganization of the kind indulged in by every administration since Clinton's. The shuffling of existing bureaucratic boxes almost never yields real benefits, certainly not enough to offset the enormous inefficiencies created by the organizational turbulence involved. Moreover, the urge to show seriousness about some issue or other by creating a new ASD or DASD should generally be resisted. Such measures just create additional overhead and requirements for coordination and sometimes lead to the devaluation of entire echelons of the organization. There are many examples, one of which is the substantial decline in the stature of Policy DASDs in the interagency process. As noted previously, when Policy's regional offices aligned geographically with the regional bureaus of the Department of State, DASDs operated on par with nominally more senior officials in other agencies, effectively enhancing not only their own clout but that of their ASDs as well. Unfortunately, decisions made during the early 2000s to align Policy geographically with the combatant commands and more recently to demonstrate greater attention to Asia by giving it its own ASD have altered this arrangement dramatically. Where there were once five geographic DASDs, there are now eight, four of which cover significantly different territories than the State bureaus with which they work,[39] with predictable bureaucratic consequences.

In conclusion, as the United States enters an era of reduced budgets but not reduced security challenges, the analysis and advice provided by all elements of OSD to support the secretary and the president in guiding the development and employment of the US armed forces will become ever more critical. Experience shows that both a smoothly functioning interface between civilian and military leadership and close collaboration among the defense, diplomatic, development, and intelligence arms of the government are essential to our success as a nation. OSD is and will remain at the center of these processes.

NOTES

1. Steve Vogel, *The Pentagon: A History: The Untold Story of the Wartime Race to Build the Pentagon—And to Restore It Sixty Years Later* (New York: Random House, 2007), 345.

2. Steve L. Rearden, *History of the Office of the Secretary of Defense* (Washington, DC: US Government Printing Office, 1984), 1:24. (Hereafter cited as *History of OSD.*)

3. Samuel P. Huntington, *The Soldier and the State: The Theory and Politics of Civil–Military Relations* (Cambridge, MA: Belknap Press, 2000), 449.

4. The program evaluation office was originally designated the Office of Systems Analysis. It was later known as Program Analysis and Evaluation (PA&E) and is now Cost Analysis and Program Evaluation (CAPE).

5. Rearden, *History of OSD*, 5:36–37.

6. What counts as part of OSD is a matter of ongoing debate. The 2,000 figure reflects the department's position that various field activities, agencies, and support functions that were formerly performed within OSD should be omitted. It also excludes the DOD Inspector General's Office, which is part of OSD by statute but does not carry out the staff functions typical of OSD proper. If all these other offices are included, the total comes to something over 4,000.

7. The deputy secretary and under and assistant secretaries are empowered to give direction to the services and other DOD components only if explicitly authorized by the secretary to do so.

8. Robert M. Gates, *Duty: Memoirs of a Secretary at War* (New York: Knopf, 2014), 109–14. The subsequent firing of Air Force Secretary Michael Wynne and Chief of Staff Gen. T. Michael Moseley can also be attributed to failure to give sufficient attention to an ongoing mission, although in this case, according to Gates, the distraction was not the future force but the air force leadership's emphasis on other mission areas. Gates, *Duty*, 239–45.

9. Roger B. Trask and Alfred Goldberg, *The Department of Defense, 1947–1997: Organization and Leaders* (Washington, DC: Historical Office, Office of the Secretary of Defense, 1997), 78.

10. Gates, *Duty*, 377–78.

11. Paul Ryan, *Fox & Friends*, Fox News, October 1, 2014, www.facebook.com/video.php?v=10152541853431336 (accessed January 22, 2015), addressing operations against the Islamic State in Iraq and the Levant (ISIL).

12. Janine Davidson examines this problem in "Civil–Military Friction and Presidential Decision Making: Explaining the Broken Dialogue," *Presidential Studies Quarterly* 43, no. 1 (March 2013): 129–45.

13. Leon Panetta, *Worthy Fights: A Memoir of Leadership in War and Peace* (New York: Penguin Press, 2014), 349.

14. Gates, *Duty*, 83.

15. Charles F. Stevenson, *SECDEF: The Nearly Impossible Job of Secretary of Defense* (Washington, DC: Potomac Books, 2006).

16. See Peter Rodman, *Presidential Command: Power and Leadership and the Making of Foreign Policy from Richard Nixon to George W. Bush* (New York: Alfred Knopf, 2009); and Douglas Feith, *War and Decision: Inside the Pentagon at the Dawn of the War on Terrorism* (New York: HarperCollins, 2008).

17. Feith, *War and Decision*, 106.

18. Bob Woodward, *State of Denial: Bush at War Part III* (New York: Simon & Schuster, 2006), 379.

19. As shown by the cases of Robert McNamara and Caspar Weinberger, however, enjoying the president's personal confidence can also be used to facilitate rejection of the interagency system.

20. Panetta, *Worthy Fights*, 190–93.

21. 10 U.S.C. §134(b)(2).

22. The Single Integrated Operational Plan (SIOP) for strategic nuclear forces was reviewed through a different process in which OSD Policy career civil servants already played the key role.

23. Joel C. Christenson, *ISA: A Brief History* (Washington, DC: Historical Office, Office of the Secretary of Defense, 2014), 2.

24. Ibid., 3.

25. I. M. Destler, *Presidents, Bureaucrats, and Foreign Policy: The Politics of Organizational Reform* (Princeton, NJ: Princeton University Press, 1974), 229.

26. This division of responsibility reflected the personal interests of the nominees for the ISA and ISP posts rather than any grand strategic policy design.

27. Over the last two decades, Policy has undergone a substantial reorganization at the ASD level more than once every three years on average.

28. Rearden, *History of OSD*, 1:127–28.

29. Former secretary Robert Gates wrote, "The practical effect of the contents of these documents is limited at the most senior levels of government." Gates, *Duty*, 44.

30. The designation of such documents varies from president to president—"National Security Decision Directive," "Presidential Decision Directive," etc. The term used in the Obama administration is "Presidential Policy Directive" (PPD).

31. Gates, *Duty*, 391–92.

32. The latter role was put on a statutory footing by Goldwater–Nichols in 1986, as previously noted.

33. Even then, the individual concerned was required to give up his or her career status to take the position, unlike FSOs appointed to such positions at State or, for that matter, the four serving FSOs who have been appointed to under secretary and assistant secretary posts in OSD Policy itself.

34. Four of OSD Policy's eighteen principal directors—essentially each DASD's second in command—were political appointees at the time of writing.

35. Matthew 10:29–30.

36. PMFs were previously known as Presidential Management Interns (PMIs).

37. As long as four decades ago, frequent access to the secretary was recognized as an important factor in ISA's effectiveness. Destler, *Presidents, Bureaucrats*, 235, 241.

38. Gates, *Duty*, 21.

39. The European bureau with three deputy assistant secretaries; the Near East, South and Central Asia, and East Asia bureaus with two each.

CHAPTER 7

The Military

Forging a Joint Warrior Culture

Michael J. Meese and Isaiah Wilson III

> Many feel that the Pentagon is like a giant log floating slowly down a turbulent river. The log has lots of ants running around on top who stick their legs into the water on occasion to try to steer the log in some direction or the other. Some of these ants have somewhat longer legs than others, some seem to avoid ever sticking their legs in the water, while some others fall or are pushed off the log. Most seem to be in a great hurry as they run from one side of the log to the other.
> —Perry Smith, *Assignment Pentagon: How to Excel in a Bureaucracy*

The US Department of Defense (DOD) spends $560 billion annually and commands global forces that are unprecedented in their relative size compared with other forces throughout the world.[1] It is the ultimate expression of the military might of America as a superpower and undergirds much of US influence in the world. Simultaneously, DOD has the greatest personnel system, budgetary process, bureaucracy, and government building in the world: the Pentagon. The "greatness" of the DOD gives it extraordinary resources that can achieve unequalled accomplishments but also can have significant drawbacks. First, the sheer size and power of the military—occasionally referred to as the 800-pound gorilla—can have extraordinary power in both national and international policy environments.[2] Second, multiple competing organizational structures and bureaucratic cultures can make change within DOD problematic. Finally, DOD requires management structures to ensure that greatness does not mask inefficiency. Understanding both the positive and negative aspects of DOD is essential to navigating the national security enterprise.

This chapter builds on the previous one by expanding the discussion beyond the Office of the Secretary of Defense (OSD) to the overall structure of DOD to include the Joint Chiefs of Staff (JCS), military departments and services, the combatant commands, and the defense agencies. This chapter will first provide a general explanation of DOD itself, the way it is organized, and the brief history of its evolution. Next, it will explain significant cultural and organizational influences on DOD, specifically the role of the military as a profession and the cultures of the several military services and the Joint Staff that affect DOD. Finally, it will illustrate the effect of organizational culture on policy by examining different case studies of DOD decision making and then draw conclusions concerning the future of the military establishment.

THE MILITARY ESTABLISHMENT AS AN INSTITUTION

The story of the establishment of DOD is one of independent services chafing at the loss of institutional identities amid continued efforts toward unification to improve the coordination, efficiency, and effectiveness of the US military forces as a whole. Before 1947 the War Department included the army and later the Army Air Corps, and the Department of the Navy included the navy, with its associated marine corps. Consequently, there was limited interservice rivalry because the services were in different cabinet departments and received legislative approvals from separate congressional committees.[3] During both world wars, the need for centralized coordination forced the development of ad hoc arrangements: President Wilson established the Council on National Defense during World War I, and President Roosevelt established the State–War–Navy Coordinating Committee during World War II.[4] In the aftermath of World War II, the National Security Act of 1947 was the first attempt to unify formally the military services in peacetime.[5] Notably, the structure in Congress also changed, with the Military Affairs Committee and the Naval Affairs Committee being combined into a single Armed Services Committee to provide unified oversight over a newly unified National Military Establishment.

While the 1947 act was the most significant step toward unification, it was still a compromise document that required additional modifications. The first three amendments to the National Security Act, in 1949, 1953, and 1958, "were major landmarks . . . aimed primarily at strengthening the centralized entities on the civilian side of the Pentagon."[6] The Goldwater–Nichols Act of 1986 is the most recent piece of major legislation affecting the Pentagon organization. The Goldwater–Nichols Act generally defines the structure of DOD as it exists today with several major components: the management structure of DOD and the Joint Staff, the military departments and services, the combatant commands, and the defense agencies.[7]

DOD MANAGEMENT: OSD, JCS, AND THE JOINT STAFF

As described in chapter 6, the management of DOD is accomplished by the secretary of defense with the assistance of the deputy secretary, five under secretaries, several assistant secretaries, and other staff members. Although there are some military assistants to these officials, all of the ultimate management decisions are made by civilian leaders appointed by the president and, in many cases, confirmed by the Senate. This reinforces the historical importance of civilian control of the military, which will be discussed in more detail later.

The JCS includes the chairman, vice chairman, and the chiefs of each of the military services: army, navy, air force, and marine corps. As specified in the 1986 Goldwater–Nichols Act, the chairman is the principal military advisor to the president, the National Security Council (NSC), and the secretary of defense and is the senior officer in the US military. The chairman's term begins on October 1 of odd-numbered years, which is designed to limit the influence of election cycles on the selection of senior military leaders. The vice chairman must be from a service other than that of the chairman and is the second-highest-ranking military officer. The other four members of the JCS are also advisors to the president, NSC, and secretary of defense in addition to their roles as chiefs of their own services.[8]

The Joint Staff consists of approximately 1,500 military personnel, equally selected from all military services, who assist the chairman and other members of the JCS in the performance of their duties.[9] They interact with the OSD staff, the services, and the combatant commands, as well as the other agencies of government, to assist in providing strategic advice on planning, preparedness, requirements, programs, and budgets, as well as joint doctrine, training, and education. Neither the chairman individually nor the JCS collectively is in the chain of command. Direction flows directly from the president to the secretary of defense to combatant commanders. The JCS and Joint Staff facilitate coordination and communication but "shall not operate or be organized as an overall Armed Forces General Staff and shall have no executive authority."[10] This prohibition of command by the Joint Staff reflects the concern for a powerful military staff that might undermine civilian control of the military or the role of individual military services.[11]

Taken together, OSD, the JCS, and the Joint Staff provide the strategic direction and management of DOD. They engage with other agencies of government, Congress, the public, and other national and international actors on behalf of the National Military Establishment as a whole. However, they rely on the two other components of DOD—the services and the combatant commands—to actually execute tasks.

THE MILITARY SERVICES AND DEPARTMENTS

The US armed forces consist of the four military services: the army, the air force, the navy, and the marine corps. The US Coast Guard is part of the Department of Homeland Security, but elements of it can be placed under operational control of the navy in time of war or when directed by the president.[12] The services are organized within military departments with their own civilian service secretaries, which are vestiges of the pre–World War II independent services; however, service secretaries no longer hold cabinet rank and are subordinate to the secretary of defense.

The primary purposes of the Department of the Army, the Department of the Air Force, and the Department of the Navy (which controls both the navy and the marine corps) are to recruit, organize, train, and equip their military forces so that they can be provided to combatant commands for employment. This includes all of the nonoperational and administrative functions that are necessary to prepare a soldier, airman, sailor, or marine as part of a unit before their engagement in a military mission:

- personnel functions (recruiting, education, leader development promotions, punishments, retirements, housing, finance, health care);
- material functions (research and development, procurement, fielding, sustainment, disposal);
- operations functions (doctrine, organization, training, evaluation, readiness); and
- support functions (budgeting, base operation, communications, transportation, life support).

These tasks are detailed in Title 10 of the US Code and are often referred to as Title 10 functions. Because each service has the authority to execute them separately—not under the direction of the Joint Staff, for example—they can tailor their functions to their specific service, which can both account for and accentuate service-specific differences.

The chief of staff of the army, chief of staff of the air force, chief of naval operations (CNO), and commandant of the marine corps are the senior military officers in their services. They both direct the functions of their service and participate as members of the JCS. They do not employ any of their forces but prepare forces for operational employment in their service chief role and advise for (or against) employment of forces in their JCS role. Similar to the OSD staff, each military department has a staff of civilians and under- and assistant secretaries that assist the service secretary in fulfilling his or her role. Each service chief has a military staff that works with the Joint Staff and the civilian leaders in his or her own service to develop and execute policy to accomplish Title 10 functions. The vice chief of staff, vice CNO, or assistant commandant, in each service, normally runs the day-to-day operations of the staff.

THE COMBATANT COMMANDS

With OSD, the JCS, and Joint Staff providing management, and the services providing the forces, the nine combatant commands are the organizations that actually employ military forces on operational missions. Six of the combatant commands are geographically organized, as indicated in figure 7.1, with each part of the globe assigned to the responsibility of a four-star general or admiral. The US Northern Command (NORTHCOM) is responsible for Canada, the United States, and Mexico. The US Southern Command (SOUTHCOM) is responsible for Central and South America. The US European Command (EUCOM) is responsible for

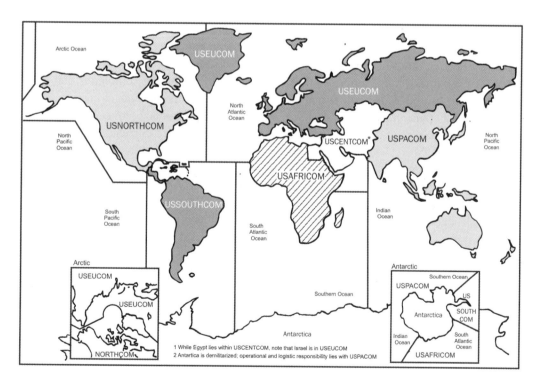

Figure 7.1. US Military Geographical Combatant Commands, 2016. (The boundaries of the combatant commands are under review and may change in future years.) © Jeffrey Murer

Europe, to include Russia to the east and Israel to the south. The US Africa Command (AFRICOM) is responsible for most of Africa, except Egypt. The US Central Command (CENTCOM) is responsible for most nations in the Middle East and Central Asia from Egypt in the west to Pakistan in the east. Finally, the US Pacific Command (PACOM) is responsible for India to the west and all nations bordering the eastern Pacific Ocean (except Russia).

Additionally, there are three functional commands that have global responsibility. The US Strategic Command (STRATCOM) is responsible for strategic deterrence, which includes command and control of US nuclear weapons and global missile defense, as well as military operations in space and cyberspace. The US Special Operations Command (SOCOM) is responsible for the training, equipping, and employment of US Special Operations units and has been given the additional mission of synchronizing global planning against terrorism. The US Transportation Command (TRANSCOM) is responsible for global military deployment and distribution systems. In 2010 US Cyber Command (USCYBERCOM) was established as a sub-unified command, which reports to STRATCOM. Because of its unique capability and the growing importance of cyber warfare, USCYBERCOM will likely become an additional combatant command in the future.[13]

The Goldwater–Nichols Act substantially strengthened the power of the combatant commanders, and today they operate with significant power, access, and authority in their regions. Some have described them as "the modern-day equivalent of the Roman Empire's proconsuls—well-funded, semi-autonomous, unconventional centers of US foreign policy," with disproportionate power within their region that sometimes can dwarf the power and influence of ambassadors or other interagency players in the same region.[14] Not only do combatant commanders wield significant authority in their regions and in the interagency, but they have increasing influence within DOD itself. Combatant commanders have direct access to the president and the secretary of defense, and they represent the demand side for military forces. The services are the supply side of military forces and, in spite of the unprecedented size of the US military, must apportion those forces among combatant commands that seemingly have an insatiable demand for military forces in their areas. Budget stringency has exacerbated this tension as service chiefs endeavor to rebuild units, recover lost readiness, and invest in modernization, while combatant commanders have current real-world warfighting demands. Moreover, many combatant commanders have become well-known (e.g., Generals Austin, Abizaid, Clark, Franks, Jones, Mattis, Petraeus, Schwarzkopf, and Zinni, and as well as Admirals Blair and Fallon) whereas most service chiefs are generally unknown outside their service. While any four-star position is certainly important, as a significant cultural shift from decades ago, when the pinnacle of any military career would have been to be the chief of one's own service, increasingly the more powerful and prestigious jobs are perceived to be those of combatant commanders, who are *executing* US national security policy throughout the world.

ORGANIZATIONAL CULTURE WITHIN DOD

Merely understanding the components of DOD provides a necessary but not sufficient knowledge of the way that DOD functions. While entire books have been written on DOD organizational culture, this section describes the most important features and sometimes least understood aspects of that organizational culture.[15] These include the military *as a profession*, the civilian control of the military, and the cultural perspectives of each of the services.

The Military as a Profession

On an organization chart DOD appears to be analogous to, albeit bigger than, the other large bureaucratic cabinet departments that exist to carry out policies established by Congress and the president in accordance with appropriate laws, regulations, and policies. However, there are two critical distinctions in DOD, both of which significantly affect organizational culture.

First, while there are certainly many aspects of a bureaucracy involved in the day-to-day management of processes, in accomplishing the essential mission of DOD—defending the nation and fighting and winning the nation's wars—the military is entrusted with significant discretion. As professionals, military leaders must develop specialized expertise in the conduct of warfare so that they can effectively make judgments in the face of substantial uncertainty. No policymaker could ever imagine all of the circumstances in combat and specify bureaucratic responses to each, which is why the conduct of warfare is entrusted to the professional judgment of military leaders. As Don Snider observes with regard to the army in particular, "The Army must be a vocational profession—a calling—rather than just a big government bureaucracy, and it must be recognized as such by its client, the American people."[16] In a bureaucracy the primary method of interacting with individuals is through rules and incentives that are developed to maximize the efficiency of the organization. In a profession society delegates to the profession responsibilities to develop a specialized expertise and negotiate professional jurisdictions on behalf of the client—in this case, the nation.

Part of the challenge, however, is that the military will always have some of the features of a bureaucracy. Don Snider further explains the tension and the resulting problem:

> Maintaining an appropriate balance between the Army's two natures is thus ever elusive; at any time, bureaucracy can come to predominate over profession. The result is an Army whose leaders, self-concepts, decisions, and organizational climate for soldiers reflect a high degree of bureaucracy and efficiency rather than military professionalism and effectiveness. In the bureaucratic mode, the self-concept of the Army's members is likely to become one of "employee," while in the mode of a calling their self-concept is one of professional. . . . Historically, militaries that do not resolve this tension in favor of their professional identity can experience the "death" of their professional character. As their bureaucratic nature comes to dominate, they cease to be a profession and become little more than an obedient military bureaucracy, treating their officers and soldiers as bureaucrats. One need only look to the current armies of western European nations, with one or two exceptions, for examples of this phenomenon.[17]

To effectively address the myriad uncertainties involved in the complexity of battle, military leaders must develop professional trust with their superiors and with the American people so that they can be given the appropriate discretion to employ the nation's violent force on behalf of the American people. Officers within each service are responsible for particular specialized expertise in their areas—land warfare, air warfare, or sea warfare—and they are expected to develop that expertise, convey that knowledge to civilian decision makers, and then execute the decisions of civilian leaders who represent the profession's client—the American people.

Second, in addition to being a profession, the military is generally a closed labor force that recruits individuals at roughly the time that they enter the workforce and then develops, trains, educates, promotes, and selectively retains them.[18] There is limited lateral entry into the military so that, for all intents and purposes, the workers that the military recruits this year will be the base from which it selects its middle-grade managers in twelve to eighteen years and its senior leaders in twenty-five to thirty-five years. While some have proposed increasing lateral entry into the military, most military officers and noncommissioned officers have spent their entire adult lives in their chosen service.[19] Consequently, they are collectively both benefactors and prisoners of an entire career comprising similar experiences. On a positive note this provides a unique opportunity to use the military personnel system to educate, train, and develop officers in a particular way. For example, when Congress wanted to emphasize jointness in 1986, the Goldwater–Nichols Act provided incentives for officers to have education and assignments in joint specialties. Over the next twenty-five years, nearly all officers increasingly developed joint backgrounds until joint operations became second nature. On a negative note a lack of lateral entry can lead to generational groupthink. For example, when the Cold War ended and the generation of officers whose primary concept of war had been the defeat of the Soviet army confronted situations in places such as Somalia, Haiti, Bosnia, Kosovo, and Afghanistan, the army's official term for those operations became "operations other than war." The Cold War officers emphasized that these operations, while important, were distinctly subordinate to "real war," which many believed should be the primary, if not sole, focus of the army. It was only after challenges in Iraq that the army reexamined its preconceived notions of warfare expressed in doctrine and concluded that "stability operations . . . are now given the same weight as offensive operations and defensive combat operations and are considered a critical part of US military operations."[20] Recognizing the implications of generational learning within the military's closed labor force is important to understanding the military's organizational culture and effectiveness.

The implication of the military as a profession with limited lateral entry is that more than in any other element of the US government, education and training are significant and integral parts of DOD. By the time generals or admirals are advising policymakers in Washington, it is not uncommon for them to have spent up to ten years of their military career in various types of schools, including undergraduate education at service academies (four years), junior officer training (six months to two years), graduate education (two years), intermediate staff colleges (one year), and senior service college (one year). In addition to educating officers, these schools develop and codify the specialized expertise of war fighting in military doctrine. During periods of budget stringency, such as the 1930s, 1950s, 1970s, 1990s, and today, sustaining relatively modest funding for professional development schools has been particularly important to develop the leaders, doctrine, and specialized expertise that are critical for future war.[21] What officers see, hear, and do at these schools really matters because the experience affects their self-concept and the way that they provide professional military advice.

Subordination to Civilian Control

If the military constituted only a power-seeking element within the DOD bureaucracy, then it might use its specialized expertise to dominate policy debates with a concurrent diminution of the authority of civilian leaders who are nominally superior to military officers. However, one of the integral components of the military, as a servant of society, is that it is both nonpartisan and subordinate to civilian control. That subordination to civilian control within the American military dates back to George Washington, who not only put down the Newburgh conspiracy in 1783 but also resigned his commission before becoming president and in so doing preserved the important separation between civilian and military leadership in the United States.[22] Today, that subordination of civilian control of the military is codified in law. Two examples are the prohibition of the Joint Staff acting as a general staff and the fact that no military officer can serve as secretary of defense or as a service secretary until he or she has been retired from the military for at least ten years or five years, respectively.[23]

In 2003 some pointed to Army Chief of Staff Eric Shinseki's response to a congressional question in which he disagreed with the Bush administration's estimate of troops needed in Iraq as insubordination. General Shinseki addressed the importance of civilian control directly when he said,

> So when some suggest that we, in the Army, don't understand the importance of civil-ian control of the military—well, that's just not helpful—and it isn't true. The Army has always understood the primacy of civilian control—we reinforce that principle to those with whom we train all around the world. So to muddy the waters when import-ant issues are at stake, issues of life and death, is a disservice to all of those in and out of uniform who serve and lead so well.[24]

In 2010 Gen. Stanley McChrystal, commander of US and NATO forces in Afghanistan, resigned after derogatory comments from him and his staff about civilian leaders involved in Afghanistan policy were published in a *Rolling Stone* magazine article.[25] Although General McChrystal fully supported the president's strategy, he offered his resignation and by doing so reinforced the importance of professional military conduct and subordination to civilian con-trol. McChrystal said, "Throughout my career, I have lived by the principles of personal honor and professional integrity. What is reflected in this article falls far short of that standard."[26] Recognizing the standards of conduct is essential to the effectiveness of the military as a pro-fession. This concept of civilian control of the military is of significant importance to military professionals and is reinforced through education and training throughout their careers.

An integral part of civilian control of the military is that any advice is based only on pro-fessional military judgment backed up by specialized expertise, education, and doctrine and is not influenced by the particular political party that happens to be in power. This historic nonpartisanship has even led some officers to believe that they should abstain from voting in national elections.[27] Whereas military officers have been steeped in the tradition of nonparti-san subordination to civilian leadership, some civilian leaders fail to recognize the importance of the proper civil–military relationship. For example, chief of staff of the army during World War II, Gen. George Marshall, had to insist on his own nonpartisan independence from President Roosevelt: "Marshall did not visit Roosevelt's estate, Hyde Park. He made a point not to laugh at his jokes. When, on one occasion, Roosevelt called him George, Marshall said that he was George only to his wife. He insisted that the President call him General Marshall. Roosevelt was famed for his charm and powers of manipulation. Marshall felt it essential for the prosecution of the task ahead [World War II] that he maintain his full independence."[28]

American political leaders undermine this independence when they leverage close associa-tion with military leaders for political purposes. For example, President George W. Bush made a point of using General Petraeus's first name, David, when referring to military advice from Iraq several times in press conferences. Shortly after he did that, senior advisors explained the importance of an independent military, and after July 2007, President Bush virtually always referred to the Iraq commander as "General Petraeus," and never "David" again.[29] A recent comprehensive historical review of US command during war, *Presidents and Their*

Generals, finds that presidents who select generals because of a perceived allegiance to administration priorities often suffer from poorly conceived policy and badly executed strategy.[30] An independent, nonpartisan, subordinate, professional military that is believed by the American public to be independent, nonpartisan, and subordinate to civilian control is integral to DOD's organizational culture and success in war.

SERVICE CULTURES: DOMINATED BY THE MEDIUM IN WHICH THEY FIGHT

Aside from the concept of the profession and the subordination of the military to civilian control, which are common to all services, the significant service-specific education and closed labor force develops and perpetuates distinct organizational cultures that dominate each military service. These organizational cultures are a function of the services' individual histories, which are largely driven by the warfare in which they have been engaged. While any generalization is made with great trepidation because there are certainly many exceptions, the following is a broad attempt to depict the general culture of each military service.

The Army: Obedient Servant Emphasizing People

Carl Builder described the army as "first and foremost, the Nation's obedient and loyal military servant."[31] The army focuses on the readiness and preparation of its personnel and emphasizes that its boots on the ground in an area are the ultimate expression of American national will and power. At the US Military Academy at West Point, cadets spend four years walking past statues of Washington, MacArthur, Eisenhower, Patton, and other leaders, reinforcing the criticality of the human dimension of leadership. The army hallways of the Pentagon are adorned with division and regimental flags, pictures of battles, and tributes to individuals from the army's history. The army emphasizes cooperation and coordination both within and between services because success in battle requires the effective coordination of all arms and services. Although officers from maneuver branches—infantry and armor—still tend to dominate leadership positions, no battle can be won without sea and air transport, fires from artillery, transport and fires from aviation, data from intelligence sources, communications from signal units, mobility from engineers, security from military police, sustainment from logisticians, and myriad other functions. This need for the complex coordination and independent synchronization of all units leads to a great emphasis on fairness, inclusiveness, and to the extent possible, decentralization among all branches and units in the army.

Even as it is difficult to make generalizations about a service culture, it is even more difficult to generalize about intellectual progenitors of any organization's doctrine or thinking. And it is equally difficult to summarize a comprehensive body of thoughts about military power into a few sentences. However, making such generalizations is important because it provides a window through which the specialized expertise of a service can be understood. For the army, if one were to ask senior leaders to identify an intellectual godfather, many would name Carl von Clausewitz and his writings from the eighteenth century in *On War*.[32] Clausewitz's dictum that "war is an extension of politics by other means" resonates well with the army as the obedient and loyal military servant of political masters. His emphasis on the "fog and friction in war" reinforces the need for military judgment, indeed what Clausewitz calls "military genius." Army leaders are comfortable with Clausewitz's emphasis on the human dimension of warfare and the need for consistent linkages between political leadership and military decision making. They strive to develop the specialized expertise in land warfare that supports effectiveness in battle.

The Air Force: Victory through Technology

As the youngest service, spun off from the army in 1947, the air force sees itself as the service that best embodies the modern American way of war—use of decisive technological superiority to overwhelm and defeat any potential foe while avoiding risk of American casualties. From Gen. Billy Mitchell's use of airpower to sink battleships in 1921 and the World War II air raids over Europe to the nuclear bombs dropped in Japan and the shock and awe at the opening of the Iraq War, the air force emphasized the use of high technology to deliver decisive military victory. At the Air Force Academy, cadets hold formation in a quadrangle surrounded by airplanes on pedestals and gaze at the academy chapel's cold-metal roof that sweeps up to the heavens. The air force halls in the Pentagon, like most air force headquarters and the newly dedicated air force monument, emphasize sleek, functional, modern designs, much as one would see in the corporate offices of a high-technology firm. In contrast to the army's general equanimity with regard to all branches, the air force prioritizes the pilot as the focus of their human capital strategy because the pilot commands the sophisticated and expensive technology and renders the decisive power in combat.

Air force proponents will often point to several strategists who have recognized the decisive nature of airpower in warfare, including Guiluo Dohet, Billy Mitchell, Hap Arnold, and Curtis LeMay. Recently, John Warden has been an influential strategist as he helped design and implement the use of airpower in Desert Storm. Expanded information technology has enhanced centralization and prioritization of precision technology so that the air force can provide more effectively and efficiently decisive effects on targets anywhere in the world. This centralized control is embodied in two mainstays of air force operations—the Single Integrated Operational Plan (SIOP) for nuclear weapons and the Air Tasking Order (ATO) for conventional engagements. Both plans are developed by dynamically assimilating all possible intelligence and environmental information and then precisely allocating virtually every weapon of each plane or each warhead of each missile against an optimal target. With its penchant for precision application of technology, the air force has also pushed for leadership in the development of cyber warfare capabilities as well. With increasingly sophisticated intelligence and network connectivity, airpower can become an even more decisive element of modern warfare.

The Navy: Independent Exercise of Sovereignty

The navy is "the supranational institution that has inherited the British navy's throne to naval supremacy. . . . Sea power [is] the most important and flexible kind of military power for America as a maritime Nation."[33] In spite of the 9/11 attacks on the US homeland, the navy is quick to point out, "70 percent of the earth is covered by water, 80 percent of the world's population lives in close proximity to the coast, and 90 percent of the world's international commerce is transported via the sea."[34] The navy can exert American sovereignty throughout the globe and literally show the flag without the inconvenience of placing US soldiers in harm's way on another nation's soil. Moreover, the navy is its own complete joint force with airpower through navy aviation, land power through the marines, and navy SEAL teams providing special operations. At the Naval Academy the midshipmen's lives are dominated by

Bancroft Hall—a single imposing dormitory that houses all midshipmen. Like a large ship, it subordinates the accomplishments of any single individual to the success of the institution as a whole. In the Pentagon the navy hallways exude tradition and imposing dignity with dark wooden walls, brass door hardware, and impressive model ships that reflect the extension of naval influence throughout the globe. In spite of modern communications that can impede the previously cherished independent sea operations, there is still great autonomy that is ascribed to a ship's captain or a navy admiral. Being accustomed to giving orders that cause a ship full of sailors and marines to change course, navy leaders are more deferential toward senior-ranking officers, who, in turn, are more likely to act autonomously and be somewhat less concerned with inclusiveness of all components in their decision making.

Most navy leaders would point to Alfred Thayer Mahan as the grand theoretician that underpins the navy's view toward global warfare. Mahan's belief that a state's power and sovereignty were inextricably linked to its sea power reinforces the navy's self-image and importance.[35] This view is consistent with that of the American founding fathers, who specified in the Constitution that "Congress shall have the power . . . to provide and maintain a navy" but only to "raise and support armies." These directives reflect the intended permanence of the naval service for the United States as a maritime power.[36] Currently, the navy, like the air force, has leveraged information technology to exploit network-centric warfare and increased the effectiveness of its ships, while reducing the force's overall size.

The Marine Corps: The Nation's Force of Choice

The marine corps organizational culture is summed up in their recruiting motto: "The few. The proud. The Marines." Completely dependent on the navy for budgetary, administrative, and logistics support and competing with the army for many land power missions, the marine corps is the only military service that the nation could potentially choose to do without. Although the marines will never be disbanded, marine leaders act as if it could happen any day if they fail to forcefully and publicly demonstrate their continuous relevance to US national security. That is why marine documents advertise themselves as "the nation's 911 force" or "the expeditionary force of choice" and endeavor to be recognized as the lead force in nearly any global engagement. And the corps makes every individual marine believe that the fate of the service (and the nation) is in his or her hands and he or she must make the corps proud. Every marine is first a rifleman and will endure any burden and suffer any sacrifice, "to do what must be done 'in any clime and place' and under any conditions . . . to respond quickly and win."[37] The marines do not have their own academy but derive many of their traditions from the navy and are always careful to never bite the navy hand that feeds, budgets, and equips them. In the Pentagon the marines have a relatively smaller presence, preferring to have most of their headquarters in nearby Henderson Hall. But any time there is a marine near any headquarters, just like the marine guards at every US embassy, they are highly visible and exemplify spit-and-polish standards that are second to none.

The marine stereotype might imply that they have little or no intellectual godfather, but actually nearly all senior marine leaders are extremely well read and borrow extensively from both army and navy strategic thought to develop their own professional identity and specialized expertise. If pressed to name an individual that drives their thought, marines might identify the persona of heroic individuals such as Lt. Gen. Lewis "Chesty" Puller, whose five Navy Crosses for heroism epitomize the marine's can-do attitude.[38] It is more likely, however, that they would identify the current or a recent commandant of the marine corps as the source of their intellectual thought. In contrast to the other services, which frequently have from eight to eleven four-star generals or admirals each, the marine corps is much smaller and typically has only three or four four-star generals. Consequently, the commandant is truly king within the marine corps, and when he issues directives, there is little pushback because, other than the assistant commandant, there is no other four-star general within the service proper.[39] In the most recent commandant's initial planning guidance for the marine corps, for example, General Dunford reified the importance of his position by citing no outside authorities, other than five quotes from four previous commandants.[40] The ability to carefully craft and then focus the marine corps on a single, compelling, and consistent message is important to the marine corps' organizational culture.

The Joint Staff: A "Purple" Profession in the Making?

With over sixty years since the unification of the DOD and thirty years since the passage of the Goldwater–Nichols Act, one might ask whether a "joint profession" with a "purple" identity independent of the services is emerging.[41] There are several significant steps toward cooperation among the services that reflect integration. First, the planning and execution of wars in Iraq, Afghanistan, and elsewhere are fully developed by joint staffs with officers generally being strong advocates of their organizational perspectives much more than any particular service perspective. Correspondingly, the prevalence and prestige of joint assignments has increased, which coincides with the increased relevance and influence of combatant commanders. Second, several of the defense agencies and organizations have developed their own organizational cultures that supersede those of the services from which they draw their people. For example, personnel spending most assignments with SOCOM, the Defense Logistics Agency, or the National Security Agency soon develop their primary personal identity as members of the special operations, logistics, or intelligence communities, respectively, and only secondarily identify with the culture of their parent service. Third, as DOD increasingly engages with other agencies, the cooperation among military services in the Joint Staff is critical. This joint coordination facilitates the military providing a unified, powerful position as it engages with the Departments of State, Treasury, Justice, and Homeland Security, the Office of Management and Budget, and other elements of government. So while interservice rivalries still exist, especially with regard to roles, missions, and resource allocation, there is unquestionably a more unified approach among the military services.

On the other hand, the military is still a long way from developing a joint profession. Bureaucratic unification around issues is extremely slow to create long-term change in the overall DOD. Properly understanding the perspectives of individuals in the Joint Staff is vital to implementing any fundamental, lasting change in DOD. One of the reasons that Secretary of Defense Donald Rumsfeld's priority on defense transformation met with limited success, for example, is that he focused on technology and equipment and not people: "Rightly understood, military transformation is less about emerging technologies, hardware, and software and more about the mindset of military and civilian professionals, including the vision and commitment they carry into their future professional service in behalf of the American people. . . . *Military institutions do not transform, people do; and in so doing they transform the institution.*"[42]

The Rumsfeld transformation planning guidance only briefly mentioned the human aspects of military transformation and never led to any long-term changes. To make fundamental changes within DOD, it is important to recognize and provide incentives for coordinated, joint approaches to defense challenges. While the Joint Staff has increasing influence in the national security enterprise, there is still a long way for it to develop so that it becomes as influential as any particular service.

CASES OF ORGANIZATIONAL CULTURE AFFECTING POLICYMAKING

Although some examples were provided earlier, the following three short case studies illustrate the impact of bureaucratic structure and organizational culture on security policy.

Prewar Planning for Postwar Iraq, 2003

The failure to effectively plan for the postwar occupation of Iraq has many explanations, including the impact of organizational culture and bureaucratic structures throughout the various levels of DOD. The CENTCOM staff was significantly under-resourced for the coordination and execution of wars in two different theaters and had difficulty gaining additional support from the services. CENTCOM had asked for a planning headquarters for postwar planning, but the Joint Forces Command (JFCOM) failed to create one because it did not want to degrade its overall mission of force experimentation and integration.[43] The army staff under General Shinseki had researched and identified the likely needs in postwar Iraq, but planning for postwar operations in Iraq was not within the army's Title 10 responsibilities, so the army's studies of the cost of occupation were viewed as interesting at best and a nuisance at worse.[44] The senior civilian leadership in the Pentagon (Secretary Donald Rumsfeld, Deputy Secretary Paul Wolfowitz, and Under Secretary [Policy] Douglas Feith) had articulated that there would be little need for postwar planning, and as noted in chapter 6, they used National Security Presidential Directive 24 (NSPD-24) as a "license to go it alone." The chairman of the Joint Chiefs of Staff decided to provide his advice through the secretary of defense and deferred to his civilian supervisor.[45]

Ultimately, when a semipermanent postwar headquarters—first the Office of Humanitarian and Reconstruction Affairs (ORHA) under Lt. Gen. (ret.) Jay Garner and then the Coalition Provisional Authority (CPA) under Ambassador Paul Bremer—was established, these offices reported directly to the OSD staff, not to the combatant command (CENTCOM). In contrast to combatant commands and services that are staffed for and used to executing policy, OSD, as discussed previously, is a management headquarters, which is not properly staffed to supervise operations in a combat theater. In spite of the best military judgment to the contrary, the historical subordination of military input to civilian control led to a combatant command that was overworked, a service that was ignored, and a management structure that leveraged its control over the military to hamper any effective opposition to administration beliefs about the needs in postwar Iraq.

Had the civilian leadership recognized that they needed to be more receptive to military objections, which are historically, legally, and culturally muted; had CENTCOM been resourced from either the services or JFCOM with an adequate planning staff; had the army had a role to play other than merely being the loyal, obedient servant complying as a force provider, then the outcome of the immediate postwar crisis in Iraq might have been different.

Approaching Irregular Warfare, 2004–7

Another way of highlighting the differences among organizational cultures within DOD is to examine their responses when new challenges emerge. One such challenge was the situation the United States confronted after the major combat operations in Afghanistan and Iraq: bands of guerrillas, insurgents, and terrorists. These groups challenged the strength of the US military not in force-on-force battles but in what is termed "irregular warfare," which the US military conducts as part of "stability, security, transition, and reconstruction" operations. The DOD management (OSD and the JCS) responded by issuing a directive, DOD Directive 3000.05, which established the following policy: "Stability operations are a core US military mission that the DOD shall be prepared to conduct and support. They shall be given priority comparable to combat operations. . . . US military forces shall be prepared to perform all tasks necessary to establish or maintain order when civilians cannot do so."[46] Simultaneously, the army had recognized the challenge and turned back to its home of doctrine and specialized expertise—Fort Leavenworth, Kansas—and developed an entirely new manual for counterinsurgency operations, FM 3–24, to confront irregular warfare. True to its organizational culture, the army did not necessarily resolve the issue and refocus efforts on counterinsurgency by issuing a manual. The army did not emphasize counterinsurgency to the exclusion of any individual or branches whose engagement in other types of future warfare might prove critical. Consequently, a robust debate has ensued in the army among professionals who vehemently and publicly disagree on the merits of counterinsurgency as a primary task for the US Army.[47]

The marines, on the other hand, had no such debate. They fully participated with the army's counterinsurgency manual development (incorporating concepts from the marine corps' 1940 Small War Manual) and simultaneously issued the new manual as Marine Corps Warfighting Publication No. 3–33.5.[48] The marines rapidly adapted their approach to focus on the pressing needs, stating, "Our unique role as the Nation's force in readiness . . . will ensure that we remain highly responsive to the needs of combatant commanders in an uncertain environment against irregular threats."[49] As soon as the nation identified the need to fight irregular warfare, the marines were ready to fight it—and would figure out how to do so as rapidly as they could.

The air force, on the other hand, while assisting the army in irregular warfare wherever it could, culturally viewed this messy, complex, and long-lasting form of war as antithetical to the American public's preference for conflict that is quick, leverages American technology, and minimizes casualties. Air Force major general Charles Dunlap decried the "boots-on-the-ground-zealots," explaining, "As television screens fill with heartbreaking stories of dead and wounded soldiers and their families, such images over time often create political limitations as to how long a democratic society will sustain an operation like that in Iraq." He explained that the solution is airpower:

> Air power is America's asymmetric advantage. . . . For example, huge US transports dropping relief supplies or landing on dirt strips in some area of humanitarian crisis get help to people on a timeline that can make a real difference. Air power . . . can apply combat power from afar and do so in a way that puts few of our forces at risk. If America maintains its aeronautical superiority, the enemy will not be able to kill 2,200 US aviators and wound another 15,000, as the ragtag Iraqi terrorists have

managed to do to our land forces. . . . The nature of the air weapon is such that an Abu Ghraib or Hadithah simply cannot occur. The relative sterility of air power—which the boots-on-the-ground types oddly find distressing as somehow unmartial—nevertheless provides greater opportunity for the discreet application of force largely under the control of well-educated, commissioned officer combatants. . . . The precision revolution has made it possible for air power to put a bomb within feet of any point on earth. . . . Eventually any insurgency must reveal itself if it is to assume power, and this inevitably provides the opportunity for air power to pick off individuals or entire capabilities that threaten US interests. The real advantage—for the moment anyway—is that air power can do it with impunity and at little risk to Americans. The advances in American air power technology in recent years make US dominance in the air intimidating like no other aspect of combat power for any nation in history.[50]

From the perspective of the air force organizational culture, concentrating warfare into the identification of discrete targets that can be engaged with precision weapons will ensure that American military force is used most efficiently.

Interestingly, the navy's organizational culture, steeped in tradition, has not taken a strong position on irregular warfare, although the (re)emerging threat of piracy has provided an opportunity for the navy to engage irregular threats directly. While never forsaking the need for global maritime presence, without another blue-water navy to compete with, the navy stresses the adaptation of navy units to support the fight on shore. The navy's posture statement, organizational documents, and professional writings emphasize its contribution, with many sailors being nominated by their service to serve as members of provincial reconstruction teams, explosive ordinance detachments, construction battalions, and other units that contribute to the current fight, even on shore.

Postwar Planning for the Next War in Iraq, 2015

The United States now finds itself caught between Iraq and a harder place: Syria. Many of the organizational perspectives that affected planning in the 2003 case continue to influence policy today. The trans-regional threat of Daesh exemplifies emergent "new wars" that demand greater jointness, interagency, intergovernmental, and multinational approaches.[51] Designing the regional coalition campaign plan to degrade and ultimately defeat Daesh illuminates both the strides made in improving jointness and the organizational and bureaucratic legacies that hinder the US national security enterprise. In the broadest sense, the challenge today is building new houses on old foundations as wholly new purpose-driven campaigns are designed by defense institutions that have not been significantly changed since the Goldwater–Nichols Act in 1986.

When an effective status-of-forces agreement could not be achieved between Iraq and the United States in 2011, nearly all military personnel departed, and responsibility for US coordination in Iraq was given to the State Department. The roughly 300 military personnel who remained in Iraq were under "Chief of Mission" authority—reporting to the US ambassador. (See chapter 4 for a discussion of chief of mission responsibilities.) Although Iraq was still in CENTCOM's area of responsibility, there was less US government focus on the Iraqi military situation and less ability to influence regional security. As a result, in spite of the presence of the largest US embassy in the world in Baghdad, the deterioration of the Iraqi Security Forces and the spread of Daesh in Iraq was generally a surprise to US policymakers when Mosul (the second-largest city in Iraq) was taken by Daesh in June 2014.

When the United States intervened in August 2014, the debate about airpower versus the need for boots on the ground reemerged. Air and navy proponents quickly highlighted airpower's role—not just bombing but providing operationally significant supplies, such as those that helped save the Yezidi minority trapped on Mount Sinjar.[52] On the other hand, army and marine proponents argued for ground forces to bolster Iraqi forces.[53] Chairman of the Joint Chiefs of Staff Gen. Martin Dempsey, in testimony to Congress, reinforced both the civilian control of the military and his requirement to provide his best professional military advice based on his specialized expertise. General Dempsey said, "At this point [the president's] stated policy is that we will not have US ground forces in direct combat. . . . But he has told me as well to come back to him on a case by case basis. . . . If we reach the point where I believe our advisors should accompany Iraqi troops on attacks against specific Daesh targets, I'll recommend that to the President."[54] Organizational perspectives and the role of candid professional advice continue to dominate defense policymaking.

In contrast to the 2003 example, in which OSD made an effort to manage military operations, there was no such concentration of power within DOD in 2015. As noted in chapter 6, there has been no close relationship between President Obama and any of his four secretaries of defense, and with four different people serving as the under secretary for policy, none had the tenure or the desire to direct policy from the Pentagon. Gen. Lloyd Austin, the CENTCOM commander, is appropriately empowered to plan and execute the coalition military campaign against Daesh. However, that does not mean that others in Washington, with their own perspectives, won't "help" him with the strategy for his mission. For example, retired general John Allen was appointed as the president's special representative (envoy) for countering Daesh, with former senior NSC staff member Brett McGurk as deputy envoy. Additionally, the training of Syrian rebels to help the United States fight Daesh has been publicly assigned to Maj. Gen. Michael Nagata, who is part of SOCOM and assigned to lead SOCOM forces in CENTCOM on behalf of the SOCOM commander, Gen. Joe Votel.[55]

Within Iraq itself, military leaders struggled to adapt traditional command and control structures that were designed to command standing conventional combat units. Initially, Maj. Gen. Dana Pittard, the deputy commander for the Third US Army in Kuwait (CENTCOM), was designated to oversee 300 US troops in the advise-and-assist mission in Iraq. As that mission expanded, Maj. Gen. Paul Funk, commander of the First Infantry Division, and elements of his headquarters deployed to head the joint operations center in Iraq.[56] Eventually, Lt. Gen. James Terry was named as the commander of Operation Inherent Resolve with the mission of overall command of a forty-nation combined joint task force to counter Daesh.[57] With all of these potentially disparate headquarters involved in a critical, nonstandard mission, it is not surprising that in his first week in office, Secretary of Defense Ashton Carter convened a meeting in Kuwait with everyone involved in countering Daesh. His meeting included most of those named previously and was "an unorthodox gathering meant to sidestep government protocol and encourage candid discussion."[58] Although defense organizational structures are not inherently well suited to coordinate US special operators and high-tech precision fires supporting local forces, nearly everyone in the room with Secretary Carter had a decade of professional experience to prepare them to counter Daesh. Not only did they have success in adapting US military structures on other battlefields, but also most had close, productive personal relationships forged through military professional development experiences with each other.

There is little experience or doctrine to support the US military "leading from behind," with special operations, precision fires, advisors, and trainers working to enable indigenous forces to conduct combat operations to secure military objectives that are critical to their nation's and US policy. Although the counter-Daesh campaign is certainly ripe for a perfect storm of organizational culture battling in the years ahead, it provides a great case to judge whether unifying forces within DOD can transcend some of the traditional organizational perspectives that dominate defense policymaking.

CONCLUSION

After fourteen years of warfare, Perry Smith would find "more ants on a bigger log floating down a faster and more turbulent river." The challenges of complex, diverse, hybrid threats require DOD to adapt its institutions and to better leverage joint, interagency, intergovernmental, and multinational relationships. Adaptation requires national security decision makers to understand the culture within DOD and each of its parts: the civilian leadership, the Joint Staff, the combatant commands, and the services. This is particularly important today as DOD is faced with significant budget stringency. As the 2014 Quadrennial Defense Review observed, "The Department of Defense is also facing a changing and equally uncertain fiscal environment. . . . The Department is committed to finding creative, effective, and efficient ways to achieve our goals and in making hard strategic choices. . . . Innovation is paramount given the increasingly complex warfighting environment we expect to encounter."[59] Rather than being a catalyst for innovation and hard choices, budget stringency is more likely to cause military leaders to focus on preserving their traditional interests, which are rooted in their distinct organizational cultures.

Recalling three of the most substantial changes in DOD since the Vietnam War—the implementation of the all-volunteer force in 1973, the Goldwater–Nichols Act of 1986, and the repeal of the "Don't Ask, Don't Tell" policy in 2011—provides insights into the interplay of organizational culture and bureaucratic decision making. In all three cases most uniformed leaders in all the services opposed the changes on the grounds that they would erode the effectiveness of their force. The president, secretary of defense, and Congress, in each case, understood the organizational cultures involved, considered the professional military advice, made decisions that incorporated those cultures and advice, and then oversaw the implementation of those decisions. As a result, with the benefit of hindsight, most observers have praised all three changes as essential to the current success of the US military.

As the nation confronts the challenges of developing a military structure that is capable of both providing security in the near term and adapting to emerging threats, it must recognize the organizational dynamics that affect defense decision making. Organizational culture matters because, like institutions, cultures persist and they can impede needed change. Organizational dynamics will influence both what change is implemented and how long it will take to implement changes within DOD.

NOTES

The views expressed in this chapter reflect the opinions of the authors and are not the positions of the American Armed Forces Mutual Aid Association (AAFMAA), the US military, or any other agency.

1. The $560 billion budget is the enacted for FY 2015. See Office of the Under Secretary of Defense (Comptroller), *DOD Fiscal Year 2016 Budget Request* (Washington, DC, February 2015), 1–2.

2. DOD is often called the 800-pound gorilla in reference to the joke: "Question: Where does an 800-pound gorilla sit? Answer: Anywhere it wants." See, for example, Lock K. Johnson, "The DCI vs. the Eight-Hundred-Pound Gorilla," *International Journal of Intelligence and Counterintelligence* 13 (January 2000): 35–48.

3. Allan R. Millett and Peter Maslowski, *For the Common Defense: A Military History of the United States of America* (New York: Free Press, 1984), 369.

4. Vincent Davis, "The Evolution of Central U.S. Defense Management," in *Reorganizing America's Defense: Leadership in War and Peace*, ed. Robert J. Art, Vincent Davis, and Samuel P. Huntington (New York: Pergamon-Brassey's, 1985), 149–67.

5. Reference the 1947 National Security Act. See Charles A. Stevenson, "Underlying Assumptions of the National Security Act of 1947," *Joint Forces Quarterly* 48 (1st Quarter, 2008): 129–33.

6. Davis, "Evolution of Central U.S. Defense Management," 153.

7. Goldwater-Nichols Department of Defense Reorganization Act of 1986, Pub. L. No. 93–433 (1986).

8. The role of the JCS and Joint Staff are specified in 10 U.S.C. § 5, www.law.cornell.edu/uscode/10/ (accessed on February 1, 2015).

9. The size of the Joint Staff estimated at 1,500 is from Perry M. Smith, *Assignment Pentagon: How to Excel in a Bureaucracy* (Washington, DC: Brassey's, Inc., 2002), 128.

10. 10 U.S.C. § 155(e).

11. Chris Gibson proposes further increasing the unity of planning and execution by replacing the chairman of the JCS with a commanding general of the armed forces. See Christopher P. Gibson, *Securing the State: Reforming the National Security Decisionmaking Process at the Civil–Military Nexus* (Stanford, CA: Hoover Institution, 2008).

12. Institute of Land Warfare, *Profile of the U.S. Army 2014/2015* (Arlington, VA: Association of the US Army, 2014), 10.

13. The creation of Cyber Command is discussed in Robert M. Gates, *Duty: Memoirs of a Secretary at War* (New York: Knopf, 2014), 449–51. See also Shawn M. Dawley, "A Case for a Cyberspace Combatant Command," *Air and Space Power Journal*, January–February 2013, 130–42.

14. Dana Priest, "A Four-Star Foreign Policy," *Washington Post*, September 28, 2001. See also Dana Priest, *The Mission: Waging War and Keeping the Peace with America's Military* (New York: Norton, 2003).

15. See, among others, Smith, *Assignment Pentagon*; Sam C. Sarkesian, John Allen Williams, and Stephen J. Cimbala, *U.S. National Security: Policymakers, Processes, and Politics* (Boulder, CO: Lynne Rienner, 2008); Carl H. Builder, *The Masks of War: American Military Styles in Strategy and Analysis* (Baltimore: Johns Hopkins University Press, 1989); and James M. Smith, "Service Cultures, Joint Cultures, and the US Military," *Airman-Scholar*, Winter 1998, 3–17.

16. Don M. Snider, "The U.S. Army as Profession," in *The Future of the Army Profession*, 2nd ed., ed. Don M. Snider and Lloyd J. Matthews (New York: McGraw-Hill, 2005), 4.

17. Ibid., 15.

18. The evolution of the army's management system since Vietnam is explained in Michael Meese and Samuel Calkins, "Back to the Future: Transforming the Army Officer Development System," *The Forum* 4, no. 1 (2006), www.bepress.com/forum/vol4/iss1/art3/.

19. Dina Levy et al., *Expanded Enlisted Lateral Entry: Options and Feasibility* (Santa Monica, CA: RAND National Defense Research Institute, 2004), xvi.

20. Institute of Land Warfare, *The U.S. Army's Role in Stability Operations* (Arlington, VA: Association of the US Army, October 2006), 3.

21. For a discussion of the importance of education during stringency, see Michael J. Meese, "The Army in Times of Austerity," chap. 10 in *American Grand Strategy and the Future of U.S. Landpower*, ed. Joseph DeSilva, Hugh Liebert, and Isaiah Wilson III (Carlisle Barracks, PA: US Army War College Press, 2014), 204–5.

22. In March 1783, when the Continental Army was encamped at Newburgh, New York, some officers, believing that Congress had not supported the army sufficiently, threatened to disband the army and ignore the authority of Congress. Washington appealed to the nascent concept of the American military profession and put down the revolt: "How inconsistent with the rules of propriety!—how unmilitary!—and how subversive of all order and discipline." See David Ramsey, *The Life of George*

Washington (New York, 1807), www.earlyamerica.com/earlyamerica/milestones/newburgh/text.html (accessed June 1, 2009).

23. See 10 U.S.C. §§ 113(a), 3013(a)2, 5013(a)2, 8013(a)2.

24. Eric K. Shinseki, "Retirement Ceremony Remarks," June 11, 2003, www.army.mil/features/ ShinsekiFarewell/farewellremarks.htm (accessed June 1, 2009).

25. Michael Hastings, "Runaway General," *Rolling Stone*, June 25, 2010.

26. Gen. Stanley McChrystal, as quoted in Peter Spiegel, "McChrystal on Defensive for Remarks," *Washington Wire* (blog), June 21, 2010, http://blogs.wsj.com/washwire/2010/06/21/mcchrystals-next -offensive/ (accessed on July 3, 2010).

27. Gen. David Petraeus has publicly said that he has refrained from voting since his promotion to the rank of major general. See Andrew Bacevich, "Petraeus Opts Out of Politics—or Does He?" *Huffing- tonPost*,November22,2008,www.huffingtonpost.com/andrew-bacevich/petraeus-opts-out-of-poli_b_13 6891.html (accessed on June 1, 2009).

28. Greg Behrman, *The Most Noble Adventure: The Marshall Plan and the Time When America Helped Save Europe* (New York: Free Press, 2007), 11.

29. Awkwardly, President Bush followed the appropriate independent respect for General Petraeus but often continued to refer to the US ambassador by his first name without a title. See, for example, President Bush's remarks when he says, "General Petraeus and Ryan Crocker know the troops are necessary . . ." in "President Bush and Prime Minister Brown Remark on Iraq and Terrorism," *Washing- ton Post*, April 17, 2008.

30. Matthew Moten, *Presidents and Their Generals: An American History of Command in War* (Cambridge, MA: Belknap Press, 2014).

31. Builder, *Masks of War*, 33.

32. Carl von Clausewitz, *On War*, ed. and trans. Michael Howard and Peter Paret (Princeton, NJ: Princeton University Press, 1976).

33. Builder, *Masks of War*, 32.

34. Donald C. Winter, *Posture Statement of the U.S. Navy, 2008* (Washington, DC: Department of the Navy, 2008), 3.

35. Philip A. Crowl, "Alfred Thayer Mahan: The Naval Historian," in *Makers of Modern Strategy: From Machiavelli to the Nuclear Age*, ed. Peter Paret (Princeton, NJ: Princeton University Press, 1986), 444–77.

36. U.S. Const., art. I, § 8.

37. Joseph F. Dunford Jr., *36th Commandant's Planning Guidance* (Washington, DC: US Marine Corps, 2015), 4. An excellent history of the development of marine corps organizational culture is Aaron B. O'Connell, *Underdogs: The Making of the Modern Marine Corps* (Cambridge, MA: Harvard University Press, 2012).

38. Jon T. Hoffman, *Chesty: The Story of Lieutenant General Lewis B. Puller, USMC* (New York: Random House, 2002).

39. Other marine four-star generals may command combatant commands or serve as chairman or vice chairman of the JCS.

40. Dunford, *36th Commandant's Planning Guidance*, 1–12.

41. The term "purple" is used in the Defense Department to describe joint issues and is reflected in the color of the joint publications. It started in the 1960s, when briefings were done with view graph slides. At that time the backgrounds of many army slides were usually green, navy slides dark blue, air force slides lighter blue, and marine slides red. When the slides were stacked on top of each other and shown on an overhead projector, the color resembled purple (and, perhaps fittingly, none of the content was intelligible). An officer who reflected no particular service bias was known as a "purple-suiter." See "Defense News Policy Passes on Unmourned," *Los Angeles Times*, July 16, 1967.

42. Don M. Snider and Jeffrey Peterson, "Opportunities for the Army: Defense Transformation and a New Joint Military Profession," in Snider and Matthews, *Future of the Army Profession*, 238–39. Italics in the original.

43. After the Millennium Challenge exercise in fall 2002, a standing joint task force (JTF) was requested from JFCOM for postwar planning. Because the standing JTF was a secretary of defense priority, JFCOM did not want to commit the single standing JTF that was trained. Instead, a "pickup

team" of individual augmentees formed the nucleus of JTF-4, which did not have the capacity to adequately plan for postwar Iraq.

44. Conrad C. Crane and W. Andrew Terrill, *Reconstructing Iraq: Insights, Challenges, and Missions for Military Forces in a Post-Conflict Scenario* (Carlisle, PA: US Army War College, February 1, 2003).

45. With regard to General Myers's relationship with Secretary Rumsfeld, see, among other reports, John Hendren, "General Ranked on Rumsfeld Campaign," *Los Angeles Times*, May 9, 2005.

46. Department of Defense, "Military Support for Stability, Security, Transition, and Reconstruction (SSTR)," Directive 3000.05 (Washington, DC: Under Secretary of Defense [Policy], November 28, 2005), 2.

47. See John Nagl, "Let's Win the Wars We're In," and Gian Gentile, "Let's Build an Army to Win All Wars," *Joint Forces Quarterly* 52 (1st Quarter, 2009): 20–33. Also see Isaiah Wilson, "Beyond COIN," *American Interest*, Autumn 2013.

48. US Marine Corps, *Small Wars Manual* (Washington, DC: US Government Printing Office, 1940).

49. James T. Conway, *Marine Corps Vision and Strategy, 2025* (Washington, DC: US Marine Corps, 2008), 5.

50. Charles J. Dunlap Jr., "America's Asymmetric Advantage," *Armed Forces Journal*, September 2006.

51. The term "new wars" in this context refers to the prescient book by Mary Kaldor and Basker Vashee, eds., *New Wars* (London: Pinter, 1997).

52. Wanda Carruthers, "Air Force Secretary: Humanitarian Aid Making Headway in Iraq," *Newsmax*, August 14, 2014.

53. Dan Lamothe, "Gen. James Mattis on Iraq: 'You Just Don't Take Anything off the Table Up Front,'" *Washington Post*, September 18, 2014.

54. Raf Sanchez and Richard Spencer, "US Ground Troops May Need Return to Iraq to Fight ISIL, Top General Warns," *Telegraph* (UK), September 16, 2014.

55. Josh Rogin, "Obama Taps Star General to Build Syrian Rebel Army to Fight ISIS," *Daily Beast*, September 21, 2014, www.thedailybeast.com/articles/2014/09/21/obama-taps-star-general-to-build-syrian-rebel-army-to-fight-isis.html.

56. Dan Lamothe, "Army Maj. Gen. Dana Pittard to Lead U.S. Operations in Iraq," *Washington Post*, June 17, 2014.

57. Michelle Tan, "Big Red One Boss Outlines New Iraq Missions," *Army Times*, October 9, 2014; and Department of Defense, "Press Briefing by Lt. Gen. Terry," December 18, 2014.

58. Dion Nissenbaum, "Ash Carter Meets with U.S. Officials Overseeing Fight against Islamic State," *Wall Street Journal*, February 23, 2015.

59. Department of Defense, *Quadrennial Defense Review 2014* (Washington, DC, March 4, 2014), 22.

CHAPTER 8

The Department of the Treasury

Brogues on the Ground

Dina Temple-Raston and Harvey Rishikof

The [1947 National Security] act and the organizations it created performed well during the cold war, the post-cold-war decade and the period after 9/11. But they need to be updated to recognize the close connection between security and economic issues as we look forward from the global financial crisis of the last few years. . . . The growth areas in national security policy are economic and financial.
—Robert Kimmitt, former Deputy Secretary of the Treasury, 2012

Treasury is at the table and has been at the table for addressing some of our most important security issues, national security issues—whether it be the terrorist threat, or it be the North Korea challenge, or the non-proliferation challenge in Iran.[1]
—Thomas Donilon, former National Security Advisor, 2015

In the fall of 2012, Iran's economy was in free fall. The country's currency, the rial, had lost half its value in just two weeks. In Ferdowski Square, where the majority of Tehran's foreign exchange shops operated, uniformed antiriot forces fanned out to drive customers away. Across the country, televisions were turned to an unusual press conference. The Iranian president, Mahmoud Ahmadinejad, was taking questions from reporters, and he seemed intent on steering the conversation around to a repeated and simple refrain: the economic troubles roiling Iranian markets were not his doing, he said. Instead, the blame should fall squarely on the shoulders of the United States.

"While the bulk of Iran's foreign exchange revenues come from selling oil," he told the assembled reporters and the television audience in Iran, "the enemy has banned Iran's oil sales and banking transactions, so Iran is not able to transfer or spend money—even if it sells oil. . . . The enemy has mobilized all its forces to enforce its decision," he emphasized. "A hidden war is underway on a very far-reaching global scale."[2]

The "hidden war" had been actually been going on for more than six years by the time the Iranian president made his remarks. US-led sanctions had slashed Iran's oil sales, banned its bank transfers, and forced Tehran to dip into its foreign currency reserves at an alarming rate.

As a consequence, all over Tehran, Iranian citizens began converting their savings in underground currency exchange shops to try to insulate themselves from further declines in the rial. The Iranian leader begged Iranian citizens to stop their black market dealing. "I ask you, dear people, do not change your money into foreign currency," he said at the press conference, accusing those who did so of aiding the enemy.[3] What he didn't mention was that the Iranian economy had been brought to its knees by something he hadn't anticipated: a new set of financial weapons developed after the 9/11 attacks.

PRE-9/11 TREASURY ROLE: BIT ACTOR

For much of the American government's history, the Treasury had a minimal role in national security issues. To be sure, Alexander Hamilton argued for a strong national bank and a department of the treasury to ensure the US financial system was a strong competitor to its larger and more established European counterparts. The full faith and credit of the US Treasury was an important instrument of national power, on which US presidents depended as America became a global player at the turn of the nineteenth century. Much of the Treasury's involvement in international affairs focused on its role in representing the US position on important international debt problems. After World War I, the Treasury negotiated much softer terms (the so-called Dawes Plan) for Germany's repayment of debts to the Allied Powers; likewise, Treasury officials like Harry Dexter White briefly became central players in the fashioning of the post-1945 "Bretton Woods" international monetary system. The resulting system of World Bank and International Monetary Fund (IMF) institutions, with their rigorous lending practices, gave the United States a commanding position to shape the Free World economic system and a not too subtle instrument of power to display when needed.

Occasionally, the United States would call on the Treasury to exercise this economic muscle in the service of its national interests. In the 1956 Suez Crisis, an irate President Eisenhower directed the Treasury Department to cast its votes against new IMF loans to Britain, thereby forcing a close ally to halt its operations against Egyptian president Gamal Abdel Nasser. Decisions regarding US approval of international loans or other monetary benefits often were guided by the National Security Council (NSC) on national security grounds rather than overarching economic and monetary principles. The Treasury Department's episodic representation at national security discussions reflected its less than full status within the national security enterprise. The Treasury, much like the US Agency for International Development (USAID), often saw its own priorities and policies set aside for national security reasons.

In the main Treasury officials were left to shape G-7 summits, provide bailouts to countries whose stability was important to the United States, and represent America at the world's international financial institutions or at global economic summits. To be sure, these were not unimportant duties. The 1994 bailout of Mexico during the Clinton administration rescued a key neighbor whose financial decline would have had profound impact on the US economy and might well have hobbled the negotiations of the North American Free Trade Agreement (NAFTA). Likewise, the 1993 American-led effort to fashion a "stabilization" package for Russia was seen as critical to bolstering a teetering Yeltsin government. At the time Secretary of State James Baker promised President Boris Yeltsin that the United States would support the World Bank, IMF, and other G-7 partners to develop credits and loans in exchange for Moscow's efforts to cut spending, privatize state enterprises, and tighten credit.[4] A former secretary of the treasury himself, Baker found the department too slow to act, as its "green eyeshade" culture wanted to weigh the financial risks of undertaking such an ambitious program, assigning less weight to the national security aspects of the effort.

The Treasury's role in representing the United States at G-7 and G-20 meetings was, at first blush, its most obvious and routine assignment. But often the issues that dominated G-7 and G-20 meetings revolved around the *crise du jour* rather than more traditional international monetary issues. The Treasury's involvement remained marginal, unless the central topic was debt relief for developing states or a failing state's fiscal needs. This relatively modest role was reflected by the fact that the Treasury was not a statutory member of the NSC and was invited to participate only when international economic issues were on the agenda.

POST-9/11 TREASURY ROLE: ON CENTER STAGE

That changed under George W. Bush, who, as matter of policy, included the Treasury in NSC meetings with his National Security Presidential Directive 1 (NSPD-1) memo, which laid out a new vision for the NSC. Almost immediately after 9/11, the Treasury stepped up its role in combatting terrorism with the initiation of the Terrorist Finance Tracking Program (TFTP), whereby the Treasury asked the Society for Worldwide Interbank Financial Telecommunications (SWIFT) for help in terrorism investigations. Following the money, in addition to analyzing the new data, would prove to be a game changer. By 2010 the Treasury had entered into an agreement with the European Union to modify and safeguard the process and data under the auspices of the TFTP.

Over the next decade, the new post-9/11 Treasury with its new NSC role was critical in the policymaking process, whether it was reaching out to China under its Strategic Economic Dialogue forum, later renamed the Strategic and Economic Dialogue (with State as cochair), or helping Pakistan avoid a balance of payments collapse in 2008, or finally, elevating the G-20 deliberations from financial matters to what is now considered the premier global leaders' forum.

The United Nations Security Council set the stage for this profound change in the Treasury's role. Resolution 1540 in 2004 declared weapon of mass destruction (WMD) proliferation to be a threat to world peace under Chapter VII of the UN Charter; it mandated legal frameworks for prosecutions for both non-state and state actors. A quick review of Security Council resolutions related to US sanctions programs on the Treasury's home page listed Iran, Somalia, North Korea, Congo, Sudan, Syria, and Iraq. It also included nonproliferation and counterterrorism resolutions. Together, these resolutions provided a foundation for the Treasury's evolving role in the national security enterprise. The UN support helped globalize pressure and defuse tensions with allies so that US sanctions appeared to be part of a broader consensus rather than unilateral action.

The new financial sanctions leveled against Iran after 9/11, for example, were not of the traditional variety, specifically targeting individuals or goods. Instead, the Treasury embarked on something more subtle: reputational suasion to change behavior and disrupt illicit conduct. The idea behind it was simple: If someone wanted to use dollar-denominated assets at some point, they would need US banks to clear the transactions. That meant that just threatening to exclude these assets from US markets could send a frisson through a financial institution. These "U-turn transactions"—the name emerged because a foreign company routed monies through a US bank in order to convert them into dollars[5]—came to fundamentally change the role of the Treasury Department in national security. This power allowed men in shiny brogues and pinstripe suits to become operational, and eventually, the new sanctions became extremely effective, even more effective, in some cases, than traditional kinetic force. Reputational suasion was not only changing the culture at the Treasury but transforming its officials—they were becoming key players on the national security stage.

THE TREASURY'S LAW ENFORCEMENT HISTORY

Alexander Hamilton, the first secretary of the treasury, was sworn in on September 11, 1789, exactly 212 years before the 9/11 attacks. As Congress envisioned it, the Treasury's job was to focus on the sale of lands belonging to the United States and "perform all such services relative to the finances" of the country. Bestowing law enforcement powers on the department seemed not only unnecessary but beside the point.[6] The original culture was focused on finance. While the Treasury would eventually have a hand in sanctions and embargoes, it was never envisioned as a principal national security player. The Justice Department and the Federal Bureau of Investigation (FBI) had the guns and the badges. Treasury agents had contented themselves with small walk-on parts and cameo roles; the crime fighting was left to the others. That began to change with President Abraham Lincoln.

On April 14, 1865, Lincoln signed legislation to create a division in the department called the US Secret Service. He created the Secret Service so there would be a law enforcement arm to curb the scourge of the day: the rampant counterfeiting of US dollars and Treasury bonds during the American Civil War. By the mid-1800s roughly a third of the nation's currency was thought to be fake. The Treasury secretary at the time, Hugh McCulloch, had the same inclination that Washington does today. When the president asked him to look at how to stop the rampant counterfeiting, McCulloch assembled a commission to study the issue. The group decided that the president needed to form a federal law enforcement division to concentrate on the problem.[7]

President Lincoln signed the law to create the division just hours before John Wilkes Booth shot him at Ford's Theater—an ironic moment, given that the Secret Service would in 1894, during Grover Cleveland's administration, eventually become in charge of presidential security. After the 9/11 attacks the Secret Service was moved out from under the Treasury's umbrella to that of the Department of Homeland Security (DHS), where it remains today (see chapter 12).

THE CONTROL

The officials who eventually wielded the Treasury's financial weapons were part of a little-known agency called the Office of Foreign Funds Control (FFC). Internally, the office was known simply as "the Control." A quiet behind-the-scenes player during World War II, FFC was in charge of programs aimed at preventing the Nazis from using occupied countries' financial holdings for their own ends.

The US government had first considered the use of such economic weapons in 1937, after the Japanese bombed and sank an American gunboat, the *Panay*, in Chinese waters. Herman Oliphant, the Treasury Department's general counsel at the time, told Treasury Secretary Henry Morgenthau that one way to starve the Japanese war machine of cash was to institute foreign exchange controls and a system of licenses for financial transactions.

When tensions with Japan subsequently eased, Oliphant's suggestion was shelved. Then, in 1938, after Germany annexed the Sudetenland, reports circulated that the Germans were forcing Czechs to turn over all the assets they held in the United States. That, and Germany's quick march across Czechoslovakia, prompted the Treasury to revisit Oliphant's proposals, though there was some concern about whether such controls could be imposed in the absence of a formally declared state of war. The United States didn't respond to Germany's actions in 1938 and 1939, but by April 1940 the Treasury had begun to act: freezing assets, country by country, across the European continent almost as quickly as the Nazis overran their neighbors.

The Treasury's actions at the time—and later as well—did not please everyone. The State Department objected, as might be expected because of its mission, out of concern that freezing assets would somehow threaten America's neutrality. Assistant Secretary of State for Economic Affairs Dean Acheson noted, "From top to bottom our [State] Department, except for our corner of it, was against Henry Morgenthau's campaign to apply freezing controls to Axis countries and their victims."[8]

The broadening of the war eventually rendered Acheson's objections moot. On June 14, 1941, through Executive Order (EO) 8785, the United States extended freezing controls to cover all of continental Europe, including "aggressor" nations and annexed or invaded territories as well as neutral nations, small principalities, and countries from Spain to Liechtenstein that had not previously been included. Turkish assets never fell under the regime, and Soviet assets were only blocked for a relatively short time because when Germany invaded Russia in June 1941, the Treasury lifted the freeze. As the United States moved from neutrality to belligerency, the role of FFC, a solely administrative agency within the Treasury Department, grew in importance.

The Control eventually became the Office of Foreign Assets Control (OFAC). Shortly after China entered into the Korean War, in December 1950, President Truman declared a national emergency and blocked all Chinese and North Korean assets subject to US jurisdiction. OFAC was the instrument that made sure it happened.

THE POWER OF OFAC

Today, OFAC is headquartered in a building across the street from the White House that used to house the Freedman's Bank, the financial institution that had helped emancipated slaves. The 200 or so people who work at OFAC almost all carry sensitive compartmented information (SCI) clearances so they can access and use decrypted signals intelligence and classified analysis. Many of the officials are former federal prosecutors.

It was not until 1986 that the Treasury began using what would eventually become one of its most effective weapons: the naming and shaming of individuals and organizations that appeared to be laundering money or flouting US laws. Officials created a public list, called Specially Designated Nationals (SDNs), and used the leverage that came from making it public. Assets of SDNs could be seized, and doing business with them became illegal for US interests and risky for all others. Naming individuals specifically and openly made it difficult for banks and businesspeople overseas to claim they did not know a particular person or institution was targeted. Banks in Latin America, for their part, used the list as part of an effort to identify drug cartels. It was so effective in identifying bad actors it was often referred to in Spanish as "la lista Clinton" because of its prominence during the Clinton administration.

Before they are named, SDNs are subject to a robust, deliberative, and evidenced-based review. OFAC then sends letters to Federal Reserve Banks across the country telling them which bad actors have been added to the list; overnight, the SDNs become pariahs. The department creates an administrative record that combines classified and unclassified materials into a package for review by the secretary to ensure that file meets the standards established by EO 13224. Both the civil division and National Security Divisions of DOJ are also included in the process, to ensure their equities are taken into consideration.[9] Roughly 5,500 people, organizations, and businesses are listed on the OFAC website as SDNs today, and not only are they cut off from any contact with the US financial system, but banks that deal with them may face a similar exclusion. "We want people to be worried that they might be having lunch with an SDN or might be accidentally doing business with an SDN so they stop doing it," said Juan Zarate, one of the first officials working on terrorist financing and author of the authoritative *Treasury's War: The Unleashing of a New Era of Financial Warfare.*[10]

Originally, SDNs were not formally advised of their status. Instead, they often learned of their designation when a US bank declined an ATM transaction. Then their names would appear on the OFAC website. Finding out precisely why a person or business was listed used to be difficult, since OFAC is under no obligation to give anything but a vague explanation to Americans and need not give any explanation at all to foreigners. But more recently, when the Treasury adds a name to the list, it will issue a press statement with declassified information about why the SDN was designated.

The SDN system doesn't always work. The first transnational criminal with a link to al-Qaeda designated as an SDN was a man named Dawood Ibrahim, a notorious Indian crime lord. Ibrahim had shown a willingness to help al-Qaeda and supported Lashkar-e-Taiba, the Pakistan-based terrorist organization probably best known for the 2008 attack on Mumbai. He helped finance the narcotics trade in Afghanistan and allowed Osama bin Laden and al-Qaeda to use his smuggling routes.[11] The Treasury designated Ibrahim in October 2003 and asked banks and finance ministers around the world to freeze his assets. Ibrahim was financially isolated, but the Pakistani government allowed him to live fairly unhindered in Karachi, and he continues to do so today. As is often the case in policy matters, sometimes other interests or equities prefer different results and exert their power to make them happen.

In 2014 President Obama used the Treasury's SDN designations to target Russian financial, energy, and defense industries in retaliation for Moscow's intervention in Ukraine. Several dozen Russian individuals and key Russian operations like the energy companies Rosneft and Gazprombank suddenly had only restricted access to American capital markets. The jury is out on whether these kinds of designations will work to change Russian behavior or bring them to the table on a number of pressing foreign policy concerns—the sanctions have been in place a relatively short time. But it is clear that they are having some impact on the Russian economy—particularly as oil prices have fallen—and Russian president Vladimir Putin wants them removed.

Because generating the list is considered an administrative matter, the Treasury needs specific facts to conclude people or businesses are acting illegally to level the SDN designation. There is a long back-and-forth during which the new SDNs need to list assets and business activities and answer a roster of questions from the Treasury. The process is laborious so individuals, companies, and banks will go to great lengths to avoid the designation in the first place. Similarly, getting removed from the list is quite onerous.

Technically, of course, the US government's authority stops at the water's edge, but because everyone wants (and needs) access to the US financial system, OFAC's designation has a ripple effect—it brings with it secondary sanctions and reputational risk. Global banks have to monitor the OFAC lists to ensure they don't run afoul of the regulations and can keep working with US banks. (Again, the key is that any US dollar–denominated transaction—from oil sales to business contracts—eventually has to pass through dollar-clearing accounts, and access to the US market is denied to those who defy OFAC.)

As mentioned previously, the techniques the Treasury is using today originated in the 1980s, when US administrations sought to break the Latin American drug cartels with an array of "targeted" sanction programs focusing on the cartels and narcotics traffickers. The reasoning behind the initial effort was that to operate on a global scale, kingpins required an extensive financial support network. To disguise their profits, cartels purchased, and continue to purchase, legitimate businesses to launder their money.

President Clinton signed EO 12978 in October 1995 to target narcotics traffickers in Colombia, and although no more than two dozen people were working the issue in the Treasury, the sanction program was tremendously effective. The big idea was to call out the cartels publicly so financial institutions lost any fig leaf of deniability. "If the US started talking about cartels publicly, the international banks couldn't turn a blind eye because they knew their access to the US banking system was at risk so they did a lot of their own actions to clean up," said Zarate.[12]

The action against the cartels informed the Treasury's later action against al-Qaeda because it established the notion that ownership and control were sanctionable under OFAC. Eventually, network analysis allowed the Treasury to think about these connections more creatively, Zarate explained. "And then when we got more information to play with; that changed the game entirely."[13] Information, big data, and networks became the critical factors in boosting the program's effectiveness.

OFFICE OF INTELLIGENCE AND ANALYSIS

In 2004, in an effort to consolidate information and resources, a number of new Treasury offices were created, including the Office of Intelligence and Analysis (OIA, to analyze financial institutions), the Office of Terrorism and Financial Intelligence (TFI, which uses intelligence and enforcement to protect the financial system and track the movements of rogue nations, WMD proliferators, and other national security threats), the Financial Crimes Enforcement Network (FinCen, to enforce the Bank Secrecy Act), OFAC (to enforce sanctions), the Treasury Executive Office for Asset Forfeiture (TEOAF, to administer forfeited funds), and the Office of Terrorism and Financial Crimes (TFFC, to build international coalitions). All were placed under the control of a new under secretary of the treasury.[14]

The Treasury maintains and has access to unique financial data about flows of funds within the international financial and commercial system—from tax information to currency transactions. Right after the 9/11 attacks, the Treasury depended on the intelligence community for the information it needed to make its SDN designations. But as time went on, officials in the Treasury decided they had a genuine need to manage and develop their own intelligence products; thus, OIA is now seen as critical to identifying illicit financial networks. The idea behind OIA was to use the Treasury's information, authorities, and relationships around the world to focus completely on financial crimes and illicit networks. Formally establishing this office would cement the Treasury's role in the national security enterprise. Congress agreed with the Treasury's proposal and created OIA in December 2004 as part of the Intelligence Authorization Act (Pub. L. No. 108-177).

To run the operation, the Treasury was looking for someone who could integrate the department's information with the broader intelligence community. OIA's first leader, Janice Gardner, came from within the department. A Japanese American who had been a CIA analyst and then had come to the Treasury as Secretary John Snow's intelligence briefer and liaison with the agency, Gardner had two key skill sets: she knew what the Treasury needed, and she understood how to work with officials in the intelligence community. The goal for OIA was not just to pull together raw data but instead to provide an intelligence community's perspective on financial information—something that had never been done formally before. Eventually, the office's responsibilities were threefold: help with the designation of those who were a threat to national security, perform intelligence functions and integrate the Treasury into the larger intelligence community, and designate a jurisdiction, financial institution, class of transactions, or type of account that was, in the words of the USA PATRIOT Act, issued right after the 9/11 attacks, a "primary money laundering concern."[15]

The Treasury became the first finance ministry in the world to have its own intelligence arm. It would take six more years before OIA would produce original intelligence reports and analysis and apply that to national security.[16]

THE BAD BANK INITIATIVE

The Treasury's intelligence function armed it with a new ability to build cases against banks suspected of being bad actors. Riggs Bank, which for years had billed itself as the "the most important bank in the most important city in the world," was a case in point. The Senate's Permanent Subcommittee on Investigations concluded in July 2004 that Riggs had failed to monitor suspicious transactions that involved hundreds of millions of dollars. Riggs had long been suspected as working with bad actors on the margins of US banking laws.

In 1994, for example, Riggs officials offered Augusto Pinochet, the former dictator of Chile, an account at their bank even though the United States had ordered his assets frozen. The Senate investigation found that Riggs executives helped Pinochet hide millions of dollars from federal regulators and illegally allowed him access to his accounts. But Pinochet was hardly the only problem. The investigation also uncovered other worrisome irregularities: account holders based at Equatorial Guinea's embassy in the United States, for example, were permitted to make enormous withdrawals without properly notifying federal authorities. There were also questions about Saudi embassy accounts that might have been linked to the 9/11 attacks, although spokespeople for all the embassies denied any wrongdoing.

Under US law banks are required to vet their customers' backgrounds and report large movements of cash or other suspicious activities. The Office of the Comptroller of the Currency and the Financial Crimes Enforcement Network fined Riggs $25 million in May 2004 because the bank failed to comply with this law.[17] The move rocked the Washington banking establishment. Riggs had been serving a long list of distinguished clients, including foreign diplomats and embassies in Washington. Now that its operation was tainted, some countries, including Saudi Arabia, were having trouble finding banks willing to take their business. Embassies cried foul, arguing that what the Treasury had done was illegal; under the Vienna Convention for Consular Affairs, the United States was required to provide financial services to all embassies. The Riggs Bank case had indirectly made that difficult to do. The State Department was taking the brunt of international ire.

Embassies argued that the Treasury, to be in compliance with the Vienna Convention, had to demand that banks open accounts for them. But it wasn't that simple: the banks wanted some sort of guarantee from the Treasury that if they took on the new business, they wouldn't find themselves targeted for helping former Riggs customers. The Treasury couldn't make that promise. Eventually, the State Department and Treasury Secretary John Snow called CEOs at Citibank, J.P. Morgan Chase, and other big banks and asked them to assist. The banks took on the business but at a premium, charging some of the shadier customers more.

Eventually, PNC Bank from Pittsburgh swooped in and bought Riggs Bank. The Riggs name disappeared, actually chiseled off storefronts in some cases. The lesson was clear, however: a venerated Washington bank had been destroyed because of its lax regulatory controls—and when it came to terrorist financing and the national security enterprise, the Treasury had emerged a major player.[18]

EO 13224

Less than two weeks after al-Qaeda sent planes crashing into the Twin Towers, the Pentagon, and a field in Pennsylvania, President George W. Bush appeared in the Rose Garden with an announcement. "At 12:01 this morning a major thrust of our war on terrorism began with the stroke of a pen," he told the assembled reporters on September 24, 2001. "Today, we have launched a strike on the financial foundation of the global terror network. . . . We will starve the terrorists of funding, turn them against each other, and rout them out of their safe hiding places and bring them to justice."[19]

The president explained that his new EO would put banks and financial institutions around the world on notice. "If you do business with terrorists," he said, "if you support or sponsor them, you will not do business with the United States of America."[20] EO 13224 granted the Treasury new powers, such as managing the Specially Designated Global Terrorist (SDGT) list, which allows OFAC to name individuals or entities that have committed acts of terrorism or pose significant risk of committing or supporting terrorism (see box 8.1).

In the days after the 9/11 attacks, Treasury officials rifled through reams of data on al-Qaeda's financial network and made some surprising discoveries. Government officials had thought that Osama bin Laden's inheritance was about $300 million. It turned out to be more in the neighborhood of $25 million. Rather than use bin Laden as the moneyman, al-Qaeda was financing itself through a network of private enterprises, corporations, and charities, not unlike organized crime syndicates. Treasury officials, with the help of the EO, began sitting down with governments in the Middle East and Europe and confronting international charities it believed were sending money to al-Qaeda. "Jump teams" of forensic accountants and lawyers arrived in foreign countries with the express mission of ferreting out suspected al-Qaeda connections and ending them.[21]

Court records from the 1998 East Africa embassy bombings trial in Manhattan, for example, established conclusively that bin Laden had formed a company called Wadi al-Aqiq in Sudan. The company managed the investments of at least nine businesses in which bin Laden was listed as chairman. At first blush the businesses seemed banal; among them were a furniture store and a cattle-breeding operation. But officials, after having working on the embassy bombings case, tracked money flows that made it clear that the Khartoum-based concern was a front and was focused on raising money to fund al-Qaeda attacks. Wadi al-Aqiq landed in the center of the new EO's crosshairs.[22]

In December 2001 the Treasury blocked the accounts of a Mogadishu-based financial network called al-Barakaat, which was an umbrella company for a roster of *hawalas*, informal remittance systems that move money around the world. Treasury officials discovered that some hawalas associated with al-Barakaat would commingle legitimate remittances with illicit proceeds. The money would be transferred to accounts in Dubai, where terrorist organizations would then skim off a portion for al-Qaeda. Some hawalas charged a 5 percent fee on the transfers and a piece of that would find its way to al-Qaeda's coffers. The belief at the time was that hawalas left no paper trail. In fact, Treasury officials who visited the hawala

---

BOX 8.1

Executive Order 13224: Blocking Property and Prohibiting Transactions with Persons Who Commit, Threaten to Commit, or Support Terrorism (Excerpts)

I hereby order:

Section 1. . . . All property and interests in property of the following persons that are in the United States or that hereafter come within the United States, or that hereafter come within the possession or control of United States persons are blocked:

(a) foreign persons listed in the Annex to this order;

(b) foreign persons determined . . . to have committed, or to pose a significant risk of committing, acts of terrorism that threaten the security of U.S. nationals or the national security, foreign policy, or economy of the United States;

(c) persons determined . . . to be owned or controlled by, or to act for or on behalf of those persons listed in the Annex to this order or those persons determined to be subject to subsection 1(b), 1(c), or 1(d)(i) of this order . . .

Sec. 2. . . .

(a) any transaction or dealing by United States persons or within the United States in property or interests in property blocked pursuant to this order is prohibited, including but not limited to the making or receiving of any contribution of funds, goods, or services to or for the benefit of those persons listed in the Annex to this order or determined to be subject to this order;

(b) any transaction by any United States person or within the United States that evades or avoids, or has the purpose of evading or avoiding, or attempts to violate, any of the prohibitions set forth in this order is prohibited . . .

Sec. 5. . . . The Secretary of the Treasury, in the exercise of his discretion and in consultation with the Secretary of State and the Attorney General, may take such other actions than the complete blocking of property or interests in property as the President is authorized to take . . . if the Secretary of the Treasury, in consultation with the Secretary of State and the Attorney General, deems such other actions to be consistent with the national interests of the United States.

Sec. 7. The Secretary of the Treasury, in consultation with the Secretary of State and the Attorney General, is hereby authorized to take such actions, including the promulgation of rules and regulations, and to employ all powers granted to the President . . . to carry out the purposes of this order. . . .

Issued by the White House, September 23, 2001.

---

exchanges found that since the system is based on trust, the moneylenders kept meticulous track of the cash that exchanged hands within a penny's certainty.[23]

In the years after the embassy bombings and the USS *Cole* attack in Yemen, terrorist-financing information was tracked and analyzed but in a piecemeal fashion, activated when terrorism prosecutions required a money trail to link defendants to a specific attack. The information, as a general matter, wasn't widely distributed to other agencies that might benefit from the additional intelligence. The Bush administration, after 9/11, sought to change that by creating a policy coordinating committee to regulate interagency equities for designation with officials from Treasury, State, Justice, Defense, the NSC, the FBI, and the Central Intelligence Agency (CIA). The committee sought to make the money trail an integral part of intelligence and investigation from the start of an inquiry. Until that time, although the Treasury would occasionally announce an enforcement action against a group of companies or individuals or charities, most of that work was done in secret. Post-9/11 the Treasury found partners more willing to give and take intelligence information.

For example, the Bahamas, which had strict bank-secrecy laws, had a change of heart after the attacks. It quietly allowed Americans to look through the records of a shuttered financial institution that appeared to have a terrorist connection, Al-Taqwa Bank. The bank was suspected of funneling money to al-Qaeda, and the Bahamian records helped lead investigators to other connected organizations. The details not only helped build criminal cases but shed light on how funds flowed to terrorist organizations and allowed Treasury officials to determine which assets could be blocked without tipping off al-Qaeda financiers.

Treasury officials note that although EO 13224 went through a number of iterations before its announcement in the weeks after the attacks, no one envisioned such an entirely new role for the Treasury emerging as a result. "The executive order served as a catalyst for this kind of campaign," said Zarate. "No one realized everything that would follow."[24] The EO paved the way for the Treasury Department to methodically reshape the financial regulatory environment into a new kind of weapon. In the past freezing assets had been a process requiring hard evidence connecting individuals and accounts to specific illegal activity. Institutions or individuals needed to be tied to terrorists rather directly. The EO changed that by stipulating that under the new standard, the department needed only a reasonable suspicion to freeze the assets of individuals and other entities believed to be supporting terrorism. The onus to prove their actions were legal shifted to the targeted individuals or institutions. President Bush had fired the first salvo in this new era of financial warfare.

That morning, the president froze the financial assets of and prohibited transactions with twenty-seven different entities suspected of terrorist ties; he established a tracking center at the Treasury that would follow terrorist money flows. The goal was to disrupt terrorist networks by choking off their funding, and the best way to do that was to follow the money. As always there was a tension between whether to disrupt or follow the trail.

It may seem obvious now, but at the time unleashing bankers in pinstripe suits and brogues into the field was revolutionary. Instead of traditional sanctions that might make it hard for particular goods to be exported or imported to a rogue nation, the new regime used international financial institutions to make the very act of raising money more difficult, costly, and risky for a terrorist. "If you do that, you end up changing their behavior," said Zarate. "Without money, spectacular international attacks become more difficult to do and less attractive to try and that was one of the things we wanted to do."[25]

Another innovation in financial sanctions came after it became clear that not all the people who were helping terrorists were necessarily motivated by conviction. Often, legitimate businesspeople help launder terrorist funds on the side out of some misplaced sense of religious duty. Once the Bush administration understood this dynamic, it put another financial weapon in its quiver: the once-obscure Section 311 provision in the Patriot Act. When combined with the new EO 13224, it proved extremely effective.

Under Section 311 the Treasury could threaten a bank or a businessperson's legitimate interests if they were designated as involved in "primary money laundering concerns." Section 311 was traditionally a defensive tool to protect the financial system from abuse and worked under the umbrella of a concept a bit ephemeral but critical in finance: reputational cost. Under US law American banks aren't allowed to do business with rogue actors; thus, if an international bank or individual is working with those kinds of groups, it can't use the US financial system. Section 311 codified this belief and turned it into a financial scarlet letter of sorts. Even if a small fraction of someone's transactions was going to terrorists, the taint was enough to stain a legitimate business. The idea was to use Section 311 designations to make it difficult for someone to do business anywhere, even if he or she had only a gossamer tie to terrorism.

Zarate, one of the early architects and champions of the program, contended Section 311's power was in not being presented to other nations as a designation that was solely in America's interest. Instead, Treasury officials couched it as a way to protect the integrity of the international financial system and emphasized the responsibilities of everyone—not just the United States—in protecting that system. According to Zarate,

> If you think about it the government, as a general matter, has to take bank shots to change behavior. They have regulations or control how someone has access to the commercial world, but banks and shippers and insurers are much more direct—they control access. They can stop doing business with someone just by making a decision. If the government tries to close an account, it takes a long time. If a bank says, "Sorry, we don't want your business anymore because it causes us too many headaches," it is done. It can happen overnight. The beauty of this is that the market is doing the work.[26]

Markets are nothing if not efficient. Rogue states would soon find out.

North Korea's Hidden Talents

North Korea had been hobbled with classic trade sanctions since the Korean War, and as a result, little trade or commercial activity existed between Pyongyang and the rest of the world. To keep itself afloat and circumvent those sanctions, North Korea had built an effective criminal enterprise operation. It smuggled. It made counterfeit goods. And it used its embassies and missions around the world to keep that illicit activity humming.

What is less known is that North Korea was a first-class counterfeiter of US one-hundred-dollar bills. The Treasury considered the North Korean bills the highest quality counterfeit in the world. The Secret Service referred to them as the "supernotes." The ink, the paper, and the printing made the fake bills almost identical to the real ones. North Korean agents and front companies sold the notes at a discount to foreign buyers, and the buyers got full value of the currency in return. "Under international law, counterfeiting the currency of a country qualifies as a proxy attack on its national integrity and sovereignty," said Zarate. "So the way we saw it, North Korea was engaged in financial warfare by undermining the integrity of the one-hundred-dollar bill."[27]

In September 2005 a Macao bank, Banco Delta Asia (BDA), was found to be "a willing pawn for the North Korean government to engage in corrupt financial activities." The Treasury alleged that for twenty years BDA had been providing "financial services," including circulating counterfeit money and laundering cash for North Korean firms. BDA called the accusations "totally unfounded," but that didn't stop depositors from lining up outside the bank's offices to demand their money back.[28] The bank was excluded from the US financial system, other banks that wanted access to the US system would not do business with BDA, and depositors understood this.

The chairman of the bank, Stanley Au, told newspapers at the time that the authorities in Macao and Hong Kong had known about the bank's relationship with North Korea for years. But, he added quickly, if this caused a problem with the United States, he would suspend business with North Korean firms right away. And he did. The looking the other way came to an end.

"Macao was a perfect test case for what we were trying to do," said Zarate. "It was important enough to North Korea to have an impact, and the bank was demonstrably bad enough that it was relatively easy for us to make the case. The beauty of it was that it wasn't so big that we'd be on the receiving end of massive retaliation. We spent a lot of time worrying about the impact, and we were able to contain it."[29] The Macao case proved the rule for the Treasury. Senior officials soon discovered that most banks need not be bullied. Reputational persuasion sufficed. The banks, motivated by the need not to be tarred with the same brush, moved on their own against shady accounts and bad actors. The Treasury operated as the head of an exclusive club of the world's financiers, so it had a series of conversations to convince bankers and businesspeople to act honestly; these were frank conversations about the Treasury's concerns and the consequences of not acting properly.

What Treasury officials would soon realize, however, is that while designating a country under Section 311 seemed like a precision strike, the United States had no control over market reaction. After authorities had cut off BDA from the US financial system, all North Korean assets at the bank were frozen out of the US banking system—about $25 million. While that total was not much, it sparked a much bigger chain reaction. As previously mentioned, depositors who worried that they might be caught up in the enforcement action made a run on the bank. Lines formed outside its branches as soon as the Treasury designation became public. Depositors understood the consequences; international financial transactions ended.

Traders, trying to gauge the fallout, began speculating that the Bank of China, Seng Heng Bank, and other local financial institutions might be caught up in similar investigations if they left any assets with BDA, so the other banks took their money out too. BDA required help from the government of Macao to cover the withdrawals. By September 30, 2006, a spokesman from BDA had announced publicly that any accounts the bank held for North Korean depositors had been closed.

The effect spread to Europe. Within days Austria shuttered the only North Korean bank operating in Europe, Golden Star Bank. About a month later the North Koreans called the State Department through their United Nations office in New York, saying they needed to talk. To some, in retrospect, the campaign might have worked too well.

The Interagency Locks Horns

Not everyone in the interagency process was supportive of the Treasury's newfound arsenal or the way officials decided to wield it. Particularly ruffled were officials at the State Department who, Zarate realized, were already skeptical about the program. State saw the Treasury's financial suasion campaign as at times competing with the State Department's diplomacy.[30]

Daniel Glaser, a deputy assistant secretary for terrorist financing and financial crimes, was dispatched to Beijing in March 2006 to try to sit down with the North Koreans and hammer out a solution to the BDA crisis. Pyongyang used the biggest brickbat it had to ease the pressure the Section 311 had put on its financial system. It refused to return to the six-party talks on its nuclear program unless the assets the Treasury froze—some $25 million—were released.

To the State Department and Chinese officials supporting Pyongyang's position, the solution seemed simple. The Treasury just needed to unfreeze North Korea's assets. What both the US and Chinese diplomats failed to understand was that in the world of finance that was not so easy. The Treasury hadn't really frozen anything in the traditional sense. It had simply sanctioned North Korea's illicit activity at BDA, and the market and the secondary consequences did the rest. It was out of the Treasury's hands.

Diplomats didn't understand and wanted the Treasury to make an about-turn to fix it. But the only way to cause a reversal was to have the North Koreans themselves change their behavior—to stop their illicit activity—and convince the market they had done so. North Korea had a different strategy: It launched a Taepo Dong ballistic missile capable of targeting the US West Coast. Next, it conducted its first nuclear test. Then, it would sit down with Glaser to work on the Section 311 designation. State and the Treasury appeared at cross-purposes, and the question became, which equity was more critical to the national security enterprise?

The State Department's top diplomat working the issue, Chris Hill, just wanted the Treasury to release the money and remove any designation leveled at the North Koreans. But it wasn't so simple. For one thing the accounts being scrutinized for illicit activity at BDA were not all officially held by the North Korean government, so each account had to be unwound separately.

What's more, the North Koreans clearly had no intention of cleaning up their illicit practices; they just needed to find a way to look like they had. Essentially, they needed to convince world markets that all was fine now. North Korea demanded that the $25 million be returned to Pyongyang via international banks to demonstrate they were no longer toxic. That was what the North Koreans viewed as a resolution. They would not talk about counterfeiting US currency or smuggling or the host of other charges the Treasury had leveled against the Koreans.

The State Department found its own solution. The Chinese agreed to transfer the $25 million back to North Korea through a Chinese bank, and that would take care of the problem and pave the way for the six-party talks to begin anew. Glaser was confused. Everything he had heard from his Chinese counterparts indicated that they rejected being in the middle of the transaction and feared being sullied by the North Korean's illicit activity. But here was the State Department contending a deal would be done with Chinese support and announcing such at a press conference the next day.

When Glaser pushed back, tensions ignited. Bitter words were exchanged between US officials in a Beijing conference room, and motivations were questioned before the State Department press conference. In the end the State Department spent weeks trying to find a bank that would help transfer North Korea's tainted assets—just as State had in the Riggs Bank case. Eventually, the North Korean funds were transferred between central banks and a bank in Vladivostok under the condition that the Russian bank wouldn't be sanctioned or targeted for its participation.[31]

SEPARATING MONEY FROM ITS INTENT

To understand terrorist financing, one might think about it as a type of reverse money laundering. Instead of trying to make illegitimate funding look legitimate, terrorists often get money from legitimate-looking sources—such as charities or businesses. The inherent problem is separating the money from its intent.

One example of the strategy is Hezbollah, the Lebanese-based terrorist group and political party. In addition to receiving hundreds of millions of dollars from Iran each year, the group used social and charitable networks and business operations—often unlikely operations, like used-car businesses—to make additional millions. In 2012 thirty used-car dealerships in the United States were investigated for their part in an international money-laundering scheme that sent roughly $300 million to Hezbollah.[32]

According to a Justice Department lawsuit filed in a Manhattan court, Lebanese money was funneled through North American financial institutions before it was used to purchase used cars in the United States. The cars were then shipped to West Africa and sold, so the profits could be smuggled back to Lebanon.[33] George Baaklini, the owner of a used-car dealership who allegedly made $1.4 million from the scheme, claimed innocence. His lawyer argued he was a victim, unaware of what his customers did with the cars or where the money came from. Hezbollah denied the connection too.

The Treasury argued that drug traffickers and launderers were wiring suspicious amounts of money to US used-car dealerships and were buying hundreds of used cars and transporting them to West Africa. The drug money was then laundered through used-car sales, and the used cars themselves became literal money-laundering vehicles.[34]

Similarly, al-Qaeda's arm in Somalia, al-Shabab, created one of the most modern diversified funding operations—from taxes to extortion to diaspora remittances with US domestic implications. Amina Farah Ali and Hawo Mohamed Hassan of Rochester, Minnesota, were arrested in August 2010 for providing material support to al-Shabab. The women, both US citizens from Somalia, raised money by soliciting funds door to door in Somali communities in Minneapolis, Minnesota; Rochester, New York; and other locations in the United States and Canada. They also held teleconferences that featured speakers who encouraged people on the calls to support the group. Ali told potential donors that the money was for the poor and needy. She and others transferred the raised money to al-Shabab though a *hawala*. Many mothers who gave thought they were helping Somali refugees; instead, they were unwittingly helping to send their own sons to the battlefield.[35]

In the case of al-Qaeda, while the group still had some die-hard donors for a while, most of its traditional support dried up. The loss of funds made it difficult to run a terrorist organization but also dramatically affected the choices al-Qaeda leaders made. Because they had only limited funds for an attack, they couldn't attempt something spectacular. Instead, for example, al-Qaeda's arm in Yemen, known as al-Qaeda in the Arabian Peninsula (AQAP), placed explosives in the underwear of a young Nigerian named Umar Farouk Abdulmutallab, traveling on Northwest Flight 253, bound for Detroit. AQAP hoped—for a small investment of $5,000 (the price of an airline ticket and the explosives)—to bring down a US plane.

"It is hard to stop attacks altogether," Zarate commented in an interview, "but we know our efforts to cut off their funding had a dramatic effect on their plans."[36] The financial approach disrupted the planning process with different degrees of success but made the logistical process harder and by extension changed behavior.

IRAN SANCTIONS

The effectiveness of sanctions brings us back to Iran and Ahmadinejad. In addition to isolating Iran from the world through sanctions, the modern Treasury could also target specific Iranian financial and commercial activity. Treasury officials visited foreign capitals to present dignitaries with a choice between Tehran and Washington. It began as a whisper campaign. Treasury officials arrived in the carpeted executive suites of the world's financial leaders with a pragmatic message: the international financial system needed to be kept healthy, officials explained, so the United States was going to target suspect Iranian financial and commercial activity. "We thought we would present the argument directly to banks and companies around the world," explained Zarate, who was one of the architects of the plan.[37]

> We'd talk about reputational risk and warn, "Are you willing to risk everything you have built by doing business, even inadvertently, with the Islamic Revolutionary Guard Corps or the Qods Force? Are your compliance officers one hundred percent

certain who they were doing business with? Is doing business with Iran worth risking access to American banks and markets?" Then we'd leave and inevitably they came to their own conclusion: doing business with Iran wasn't worth risking it all. It proved to be very effective.[38]

Initially, the Treasury was focused on whether its actions could slow the nuclear program. The question that worried Treasury officials was whether making it harder for Iran to acquire what it needed for its program would end up making their efforts more secretive and harder to detect. Noted Zarate,

> Eventually, the thinking was that if they needed to go through more steps to buy something while that might not stop the program, it would put sand in the gears. It was all part of a discovery process. We'd respond to how they react and how markets reacted. By the time we got to including banks and insurance and transport in the mix, we had a real sense that it was working. It became a virtuous cycle, they had to parry our moves and every parry made them look more suspicious. Part of that was intentional.[39]

What was unclear was whether that would bring the Iranians to the table in any meaningful way. Zarate reasoned it would be wrong to place too much emphasis on the Treasury's program alone. The Permanent 5 was already talking to the Iranians; Ambassador Nick Burns had secretly met with their negotiators toward the end of the Bush administration. To many, the sanctions regime was seen as a catalyst that helped move all the other pieces along.

TARGETING DAESH

The military has also come to exploit the Treasury's terrorist financing program. Central Command worked effectively with the Treasury in Iraq to recover documents and gather financial intelligence that would reveal funding flows and members of the insurgency there.[40] The Treasury and Defense Departments in 2005 established in Baghdad an interagency intelligence unit, the Iraq Threat Finance Cell (ITFC), to enhance collection, analysis, and timely dissemination of relevant financial intelligence to combat the insurgency. The commanders began to rely on the cell's strategic and tactical analysis to fight the Iraqi insurgency and disrupt terrorist, insurgent, and militia financial networks.[41] Similarly, the Afghan Threat Finance Cell (ATFC), which the Treasury co-leads with the Drug Enforcement Administration (DEA), has embedded sixty personnel across the Afghan command to focus on the insurgent financial structure and has raided *hawalas* suspected of illicit activities involving insurgent finance and narcotics trafficking.[42]

Eventually, Gen. David Petraeus, Gen. Stanley McChrystal, and Adm. Eric T. Olson devoted a growing number of resources to efforts to disrupt financial flows in and out of war zones. "Threat finance" is now part of the US national security lexicon. But the program is not equally successful everywhere. Consider Daesh, which has presented the Treasury with a unique set of challenges. Daesh is the first terrorist organization to have the ability to draw funding from its own territory independently. Some terrorist organizations control territory—Hamas in Gaza and al-Shabab, to a certain extent, in Somalia—but none have the resources Daesh has been able to control. That's why one of the cornerstones of the US policy against Daesh is to deny the group territory.

The most important source of revenue for Daesh by the summer of 2015, after oil and the extortion of the local population, was the money in bank vaults it found when it seized control of territory. The Central Bank of Iraq in Mosul and ninety other bank branches in Daesh territory were raided, and by the Treasury's calculations, the deposits alone came to some $500 million to $1 billion. The good news, officials noted, was that Daesh could rob a bank only once—the resource was not renewable—so once the organization burned through that money, it was gone. Daesh had clearly anticipated that there would be efforts to cut off its funding, so it established renewable sources of wealth, the most important of which are extortion and taxation. By the Treasury's estimation, extortion brings hundreds of millions of dollars into Daesh coffers every year.

While the territory Daesh controls changes with each passing month, so far the group has maintained a firm grip on oil fields, which are a huge source of the group's wealth. The numbers are soft, but the Treasury estimates Daesh makes about $40 million a month on the sale of oil. Other sources of wealth—kidnapping, donations from the region—pale in comparison. Thus, Treasury officials have a limited number of options if they want to squeeze the group's funding. Some Treasury officials fear that Daesh, given its sophistication, might begin using digital currency, or Bitcoin, to mask the movement of funds and make it harder to track the flows and patterns.[43]

According to Daniel Glaser, who was appointed assistant secretary for terrorist financing in 2011, the Treasury's strategy for Daesh has three parts. First, to the extent Daesh gets money from foreign donors, the Treasury has tried to identify who those donors are and to discourage them from continuing to give. Second, the Treasury is trying to make the ability to transfer funds to Daesh through the traditional banking system more difficult. Contended Glaser,

> The irony here is we're using some of the same tools we use when we apply pressure on foreign countries. We're working closely with the Iraqi government to work with authorities to make sure banks in Iraq can't be used by ISIL. To work with them to make sure exchange houses aren't available to ISIL. We can make money much less valuable to them if they can't spend it and can't circulate it. If all they can do is circulate it in their own territory it loses value.[44]

And finally, the Treasury is working with other countries in the region to stop smuggling along the borders that Daesh controls so that it has to use internal resources and deplete them.

The Treasury is also trying to understand the group's internal financial structure. The hope is that the Treasury can identify and target Daesh's internal financiers and then squeeze their external networks. Daesh may not use the international banking system, but the thinking goes, maybe some of its partners do.

Daesh has plenty of money. But its expenses are substantial. To pay 30,000 fighters $1,000 each a month is $360 million a year—just in salaries. That would presumably be Daesh's major expense. The organization can cover that cost. The challenge and the goal are to disrupt the financing and bring the revenue down to make it harder for Daesh to meet its costs.[45]

Documents captured in 2016 show there have been financial pressures on Daesh : an estimated two-thirds of Daesh expenditures are on military upkeep; there were salary cuts of up to 50 percent for all fighters in the Raqqa Province in November–December 2015; the circulation of the US dollar has increased because of the diminishing value of the Syrian pound; and significantly, since August 2015, the Iraq government has ceased to pay salaries of government workers living inside Daesh territory to stop Daesh taxation.[46] According to Glaser,

The message that I have is that we are going to succeed in applying economic and financial pressure on ISIL and we are going to succeed in depriving them to use their resources. I have been at the Treasury for over 15 years and I've spent that entire time listening to people explain to me that financial measures don't work and can't work. I was there in 2006 at the very beginning when we first started to devise our Iran sanctions strategy and the one thing that everyone agreed on at the time was that Iran sanctions can't work and now the one thing—the only thing—that everyone agrees on is that what brought them around to the table was the economic and financial pressure. We can do this, we know how to do this and we will succeed in depriving them of their ability to use their resources.[47]

Time and environment folded the intelligence community into the Treasury mission. Zarate recalled that there were enormous battles in the intelligence community both before and after the 9/11 attacks because the Treasury was building a sensitive compartmentalized information facility (SCIF). "There was a lot of angst around that," remembered Zarate. "Security people were concerned about it, because we weren't an intelligence agency."

When the Treasury became more of a part of the intelligence community after 9/11, OFAC was a small but important part of the department. OFAC was a subculture that mixed finance with intelligence but was, in many ways, hived off from the traditional Treasury mission. The Treasury's overall financial ethos had not changed, but a complementary, if subordinate, intelligence culture grew up inside the building in the wake of the 9/11 attacks.

CONCLUSION AND ASSESSMENT

For policymakers the question is, How effective is this new financial tool, when should it be employed, and under what conditions will it be successful? Consider Syria by the end of 2016. Employing sanctions to stop the atrocities and remove strongman Bashir al-Assad has proved problematic, partly because of the backing of Syria's traditional supporters. Undercutting the regime's business relationships at the time of a civil war, with a terrorist organization moving into the vacuum, has made it difficult to form a policy. Sanctions are most effective against deep pockets or commercial enterprises that use a legitimate financing system, but al-Shabab, Boko Haram, and Daesh exploit third parties and the Dark Net, complicating the financial ramifications.

Financial and economic sanctions must be viewed as only one tool that can be used to institute the democratization of authoritarian or rogue regimes. Other agencies and allies are critical, and all must follow an orchestrated plan with clear objectives. Over the years authoritarian regimes have proved to be quite resilient. Some of the variables that will influence success with sanctions include how comprehensive the sanctions are, how dense the ties of the target nation are to the international system, how vulnerable the nation is given its military and economic strength and its use of repression, and how the state has established its domestic legitimacy.[48]

A test for the Treasury's sanctions is the EO President Barack Obama issued in April 2015 on cyber activities. Titled "Blocking the Property of Certain Persons Engaging in Significant Malicious Cyber-Enabled Activities," the object of the EO was to give the president, in the wake of the North Korean attacks on Sony Pictures and the alleged Chinese attack on the Office of Personnel Management, new tools to combat cyber intrusions that go beyond mere verbal condemnation but stop short of declaring war. The order authorizes the Treasury to impose sanctions on individuals and entities that are determined to be responsible for or complicit in malicious cyber-enabled activities that "are reasonably likely to result in, or have materially contributed to, a significant threat to the national security, foreign policy, economic health, or financial stability of the United States."

As of this writing, the tool has yet to be wielded, so it is unclear how effective the threats will be in deterring cyber attacks from nation-states, criminal gangs, and "hacktivists." The attempt to hold entities responsible is encouraging given that, up to now, attacks in cyberspace have been more or less penalty free. This new cyber domain in the Treasury's war will be a test: Will officials at the Treasury craft a series of sanctions that will quietly change behavior, as it did in Iran, or will the cyber realm present the same sort of difficulties the United States has faced in Syria and Iraq?

Congress's approval of the Iran nuclear agreement, the Joint Comprehensive Plan of Action, has once again brought Treasury into the spotlight. Many believe the original Treasury sanctions were critical to bringing the Iranians to the bargaining table because they were designed to hit specific individuals and companies and were enforced globally to cripple the Iranian economy. The new nuclear agreement grants Iranian access to the international banking system by lifting sanctions on approximately 690 companies and individuals.

The expectation is that if Iran chooses to cheat on the agreement, it will likely happen through a host of front companies that Treasury officials will have to identify.[49] Similarly, the Treasury and US allies will play a key role in enforcing any decision to "snap back" sanctions if it is determined that Iran has broken its end of the bargain. One interim solution that has been suggested: designate the Revolutionary Guard as a terrorist organization and use the Treasury to block all its transactions. Again, the Treasury, not the US military, will be on the front lines of this battle.

As this chapter has laid out, the Treasury is a new and key player at the heart of the national security enterprise decision-making process. It is part of the administration's "all tools" approach in projecting foreign policy. It is not just engaging financial members and central bankers but also talking with diplomats and working with warriors and spies to safeguard American national security interests. The Treasury has evolved to fill a gap in the national security enterprise and, in so doing, is no longer a department in which officials are wondering why a SCIF is necessary. Treasury now, in combination with the Department of Justice (DOJ) and DOJ's tools under the material support and terrorist financing statutes (18 U.S.C. §§ 2339A–2339D), the International Emergency Economic Powers Act (IEEPA) (50 U.S.C. §§ 1701–5), and international money laundering powers (18 U.S.C. § 1956[a] [2][A]), established a powerful legal framework to combat financial terrorism activities.[50] The Obama administration's under secretary for terrorism and financial intelligence at the Treasury summed it up this way after he had gone to Israel to discuss Hezbollah's terrorist financing in 2015: "There is whole lot we need to be doing jointly to target Hezbollah's lines of support, the Quds Forces' lines of support—how they are procuring parts for the U.A.V.s, how are they funneling money from their diaspora communities. We have the tools."[51]

These tools have proved, since the 9/11 attacks, to have a significant impact on the global economic system and the behavior of bad actors. Sanctions have critical short- and long-term consequences, and they must be implemented in a transparent manner and approached as an international mechanism with appropriate world support.[52] As cautioned by the 2015 National Security Strategy, the economic world is deeply connected, and international affairs, as a result, is more complex:

Power among the states is more dynamic. The increasing use of the G-20 on global economic matters reflects an evolution in economic power, as does the rise of Asia, Latin America and Africa. As the balance of economic power changes, so do the expectations about influences over international affairs. Shifting power dynamics create both opportunities and risks for cooperation, as some states have been more willing than others to assume responsibilities commensurate with their greater economic capacity.[53]

Treasury officials are moving to use the department's new power in a dynamic economic world.

NOTES

The authors would like to express special thanks to Juan Zarate for his help with this chapter. We also found his book *Treasury's War: The Unleashing of a New Era of Financial Warfare* (New York: Public Affairs Books, 2014) to be an invaluable resource.

1. Hagar Chemali, "Treasury's Role in Advancing U.S. National Security," *Treasury Notes* (blog), June 4, 2014, www.treasury.gov/connect/blog/Pages/TFI-10-Wrap-Up.aspx.

2. "Ahmadinejad: Hidden War on a Global Scale Waged against Iran's Oil Sector," *Iran Daily Brief*, October 8, 2012.

3. Ibid.

4. James Baker, *The Politics of Diplomacy: Revolution, War & Peace, 1989–92*, with Thomas DeFrank (New York: Putnam, 1995), 654–56.

5. Michael R. Gordon, "After Victory for Nuclear Agreement, a Battle over Iran Sanctions," *New York Times*, September 12, 2015.

6. Department of the Treasury, "History of the Treasury," December 1, 2010, www.treasury.gov/about/history/pages/edu_history_brochure.aspx.

7. Zarate, *Treasury's War*, 4.

8. Presidential Advisory Commission on Holocaust Assets in the United States, *Plunder and Restitution: Findings and Recommendations of the Presidential Advisory Commission on Holocaust Assets in the United States* (Washington, DC, December 2000), SK-44.

9. See Jeff Breinholt, "Parallel Criminal and Civil/Administrative Investigations in Terrorist Financing Cases," *U.S. Attorney's Bulletin* 62, no. 5 (September 2014): 36–37.

10. Juan Zarate, interview with the author, March 2015.

11. Zarate, *Treasury's War*, 115–17.

12. Juan Zarate, interview with the author, April 2015.

13. Ibid.

14. Government Accountability Office, *Combatting Illicit Financing: Treasury's Office of Terrorism and Financial Intelligence Could Manage More Effectively to Achieve Its Mission*, GAO Report 09–794 (Washington, DC, September 2009).

15. USA PATRIOT Act, Pub. L. No. 107–56, 115 Stat. 298, www.fincen.gov/statutes_regs/patriot/index.html?r=1&id=311#311.

16. Patrick O'Brien, remarks at the Washington Institute for Near East Policy, Washington, DC, February 2008; and Zarate, *Treasury's War*, 47.

17. Timothy O'Brien, "At Riggs Bank, A Tangled Path Led to Scandal," *New York Times*, July 19, 2004.

18. Zarate, *Treasury's War*, 148–50.

19. White House, "President Freezes Terrorists' Assets," September 24, 2001, https://georgewbush-whitehouse.archives.gov/news/releases/2001/09/20010924-4.html.

20. David Sanger and Joseph Kahn, "Bush Freezes Assets Linked to Terror Network," *New York Times*, September 25, 2001.

21. Kurt Eichenwald, "A Nation Challenged, Terror Money Hard to Block, Officials Find," *New York Times*, December 10, 2001.

22. United States v. bin Laden, Atef el_hage, Fazul Mohammed, Odeh, and al-Owhali indictment, US Department of Justice, November 4, 1998.

23. Zarate, *Treasury's War*, 99–100.

24. Zarate interview, March 2015.

25. Ibid.

26. Ibid.

27. Ibid.

28. David Lague and Donald Greenlees, "Squeeze on Banco Delta Asia Hits North Korea Where It Hurts," *International Herald Tribune*, January 18, 2007.

29. Zarate interview, March 2015.

30. Zarate, *Treasury's War*, 259–63.

31. Ibid., 263.

32. "Thirty U.S. Car Dealers Caught in Hezbollah Terror Financing Scheme," Homeland Security News Wire, January 4, 2012.

33. Ibid.

34. Department of the Treasury, "Treasury Targets Major Money Laundering Network Linked to Drug Trafficker Ayman Joumaa and a Key Hizbollah Supporter in South America," press release, June 27, 2012.

35. Zarate interview, April 2015.

36. Ibid.

37. Dina Temple-Raston, "14 Charged with Supporting Somali Terrorist Group," *All Things Considered*, NPR, August 5, 2010.

38. Zarate interview, March 2015.

39. Ibid.

40. See Aymenn Al-Tamimi, "A Caliphate under Strain: The Documentary Evidence," *CTC Sentinel* 9, no. 4 (April 2016): 1–8.

41. See Stuart Levey, testimony before the Senate Committee on Finance, 110th Cong. (2008).

42. Department of the Treasury, "Combating the Financing of Terrorism, Disrupting Terrorism at Its Core," fact sheet, September 8, 2011.

43. See Sue Halpern, "In the Depths of the Net," *New York Review of Books* 62, no. 15 (October 8, 2015): 56.

44. Daniel Glaser, discussion at the Aspen Security Forum, Aspen, CO, July 23, 2015.

45. Dina Temple-Raston, "How Much Does It Cost to Run a Caliphate," *All Things Considered*, NPR, October 30, 2014.

46. See Al-Tamimi, "Caliphate under Strain," 2–3.

47. Glaser, discussion at the Aspen Security Forum.

48. See Julia Grauvogel and Christian von Soset, *Claims to Legitimacy Matter: Why Sanctions Fail to Instigate Democratization in Authoritarian Regimes*, GIGA Working Papers No. 235 (Hamburg: German Institute of Global and Area Studies, October 2014).

49. Gordon, "After Victory for Nuclear Agreement."

50. See Michael Taxay, ed., "Parallel Criminal and Civil/Administrative Investigations in Terrorist Financing Cases," *U.S. Attorney's Bulletin* 62, no. 5 (September 2014).

51. Gordon, "After Victory for Nuclear Agreement."

52. Richard Nephew, *The Future of Economic Sanctions in a Global Economy* (New York: Columbia Center on Global Energy Policy, May 2015).

53. White House, *2015 National Security Strategy* (Washington, DC, February 2015), 10.

PART III

Intelligence and Law Enforcement

CHAPTER 9

Office of the Director of National Intelligence

From Pariah and Piñata to Managing Partner

Thomas Fingar

> The new intelligence law makes the Director of National Intelligence (DNI) responsible for integrating the 15 independent members of the Intelligence Community. But it gives him powers that are only relatively broader than before. The DNI cannot make this work unless he takes his legal authorities over budget, programs, personnel, and priorities to the limit. It won't be easy to provide this leadership to the intelligence components of the Defense Department, or to the CIA. They are some of the government's most headstrong agencies. Sooner or later, they will try to run around—or over—the DNI.
>
> —Transmittal letter to the *Report to the President of the United States*

> Congress' failure to reform itself is especially jarring in light of the massive changes it has mandated in the executive branch. The director of national intelligence and a National Counterterrorism Center, two reforms recommended by the commission, are ensuring that intelligence agencies work together, instead of hoarding information and feuding over turf as they did before 9/11. That is real progress.
>
> —Tom Kean and Lee Hamilton on the tenth anniversary of the 9/11 Commission Report

In less than a decade, the Office of the Director of National Intelligence (ODNI) has evolved from unwanted stepchild of intelligence reform to managing partner of the intelligence community (IC). It did so more quickly and with less disruption than anyone had anticipated and many had feared. The IC is better integrated and performs a broader range of missions more effectively than ever before. The ODNI deserves much of the credit for achieving fundamental transformation of the intelligence component of the national security enterprise (NSE) without "breaking" anything. This chapter examines the transformation and notable successes of the ODNI.

Proposals to create a director of national intelligence (DNI) whose primary responsibility would be to integrate and optimize the performance of IC component agencies had been advanced, without effect, for decades.[1] The rationale for creating the position was clear but not sufficiently compelling to overcome vested interests and concerns that attempting significant change to improve performance that was generally satisfactory would jeopardize the IC's ability to meet current and anticipated national security requirements. That changed dramatically on September 11, 2001. Although postmortems revealed that what happened was the result of inadequacies in many parts of the NSE, publication of a badly flawed national intelligence estimate (NIE) on Iraq's weapons of mass destruction (WMDs) narrowed the search for scapegoats and the scope of reforms intended to fix the broader problem by fixing the IC.[2] The establishment of the ODNI was the centerpiece of the reform legislation signed in December 2004, but the office's formative years were characterized by ambiguity, ambivalence, and animosity. At the beginning, and to some extent still, the ODNI manifests fissures and flaws of the agencies from which it was created. But after a decade of experimentation and accommodation, it has gained traction and proved to be more than "just another layer of bureaucracy."[3] The ODNI is making a positive difference and has the potential to do more, but even if all components of the intelligence enterprise pull in the same direction, that accomplishment will not cure all the ills of the NSE.[4]

When President George W. Bush signed the Intelligence Reform and Terrorism Prevention Act (hereafter referred to as the Intelligence Reform Act) on December 17, 2004, he described the legislation as "the most dramatic reform of our nation's intelligence capabilities since President Harry S. Truman signed the National Security Act of 1947."[5] That may prove to be the case, and indications are that it will, but even after a decade, the reforms of 2004 remain a work in progress, demonstrating once again that institutional and attitudinal changes are difficult to achieve.[6] Inevitable start-up problems frustrated those with unrealistic expectations about how easily or quickly existing national security institutions could be transformed, but persistence, patience, and pragmatism have produced greater coherence, efficiency, and effectiveness within the intelligence components of the NSE.[7] Realizing the full potential of the 2004 reforms will require equally significant changes in the nonintelligence elements of the national security apparatus.[8]

GENESIS OF THE ODNI

As the chapters in this book make clear, the NSE is less efficient and effective than it should be because of institutional rivalries, overlapping authorities, and a host of other deficiencies that are easier to describe than to correct. The performance of the enterprise as a whole is constrained by shortcomings in its constituent elements and shaped by structural and serendipitous imbalances in the relative clout of individual agencies and the leaders who head them. Rifts and rivalries within the IC were—and in some respects remain—as problematic as they are in other parts of the NSE. This is widely recognized, but Washington is a political town with strongly entrenched interests determined to limit the impact of any change to the status quo. Moreover, all attempts to improve the performance of the NSE, including the creation of the ODNI, have been shaped and constrained by persistent beliefs and behaviors.

One such belief undergirds the pretense that even the most complex problem can be solved with an organizational solution. A corollary belief is that if mandated organizational changes do not achieve promised results immediately, it is because those responsible for implementation have deliberately or incompetently failed to overcome bureaucratic pathologies. Among other consequences, this gives individuals and institutions unhappy with some aspect of the mandated change an incentive to frustrate implementation in hope of rolling back or revising organizational changes they do not like. As predicted by the Commission on the Intelligence

Capabilities of the United States Regarding Weapons of Mass Destruction (hereafter referred to as the WMD Commission) in its letter of transmittal, the Department of Defense and the Central Intelligence Agency (CIA) at times attempted to thwart or distort reform initiatives.[9] The Federal Bureau of Investigation (FBI) also resisted efforts to reduce the scope of its autonomy, albeit on different issues, and every constituent agency was wary of new structures, authorities, and guidelines.

A second recurring practice is to explain or excuse policy failures by citing inadequacies in the IC. A perennial joke—and for many IC professionals a deeply held conviction—is that in Washington, there are only two possibilities: policy success and intelligence failure. In other words, if a policy proves ineffective—or misguided—the knee-jerk explanation is that the IC failed to provide accurate information, timely warning, or expertise-based insight. Such judgments are sometimes warranted, but during roughly the same period that the ODNI has existed, scapegoating the IC appears to have diminished. The reason may be, in part, that IC performance has improved. Performance has improved, and the ODNI deserves substantial credit for the improvement, but a more important reason, in the view of this author, is that national security issues and decisions have become grist for partisan politics to an unprecedented degree. In the somewhat imaginary days of yore when partisan politics stopped at the water's edge, defective but often bipartisan policies were blamed on intelligence shortcomings. Now, however, responsibility for real or imagined policy defects is more often attributed to the White House, Congress, or the "other party."

For a time the creation of the ODNI was viewed by some as a silver bullet solution that would fix all shortcomings of the NSE without requiring change in the non-intelligence components. Such a view was never realistic, but a decade after the 9/11 Commission called for wide-ranging changes to meet new security challenges, the commission's cochairs lament, with reason, that few such changes have been initiated.[10] In other words, the IC may be less often in the crosshairs because the big guns of the blame game are focused elsewhere. Recognizing that this is the case is important if the IC is to avoid excessively positive assessments of what has been achieved and underestimation of what remains to be done.

Rivalries within the IC were and are a problem, but they were not the most important defect identified by those eager to correct deficiencies identified by the 9/11 Commission, the WMD Commission, and virtually every other examination of impediments to achieving better integration of and improved performance by the IC and other components of the NSE. Every postmortem assessment of what went wrong cited inadequate information sharing across institutional boundaries and impediments to cooperation between the realms of foreign intelligence and domestic law enforcement as reasons for the failure to discover and disrupt preparations for the attacks on September 11, 2001.[11]

The case for breaking down barriers and making the IC function as an integrated enterprise rather than a collection of special-purpose agencies was convincing, but it probably would not have been compelling without the shock caused by the 9/11 attacks and the political firestorm triggered by the war in Iraq and the flawed 2002 NIE on Iraq's WMDs.[12] The findings and recommendations of the 9/11 Commission were supplemented and reinforced by the Senate Select Committee on Intelligence's narrowly focused critique of the 2002 NIE and the preliminary conclusions of the WMD Commission.[13] The specific deficiencies identified by commission members surprised no one familiar with the workings of the intelligence and law enforcement communities, but their enumeration in yet another set of reports would not by itself have been sufficient to persuade Congress to create the ODNI. What made the situation different than when previous commission reports were issued was the combination of shock and chagrin caused by the 9/11 attacks, dismay and ire triggered by the flawed performance of the IC with respect to Iraq's WMDs, and politically charged assertions about the role of intelligence in the decision to overthrow Saddam Hussein's regime. Together, two high-profile events characterized as intelligence failures created a sense that it was necessary—or politically expedient—to fix the NSE by correcting deficiencies in the IC.

Even the conjunction of obvious need for reform and imperatives to punish poor performance probably would not have overcome inertia, vested interests, and administration disinterest in undertaking another bureaucratic reorganization as big and complex as the creation of the Department of Homeland Security while waging wars in Afghanistan and Iraq were it not for the political skill of 9/11 Commission members in making their proposals for intelligence reform the centerpiece of what became an unstoppable, and very rushed, congressional effort to fix intelligence.[14] The 9/11 Commission Report was released on July 22, 2004, and both houses had passed competing bills before the November election. When Congress and the executive branch refocused on these bills after the election, it quickly became apparent that many senior administration and IC officials wanted to preserve as much of the status quo as possible and that members of Congress had very different visions of what was desirable. What emerged from the legislative process was ambiguous and left wide latitude for continuing the struggle during implementation.[15]

REASSIGNING ROLES AND RESPONSIBILITIES

Members of Congress, the IC, and the punditocracy disagreed on precisely what the Intelligence Reform Act and the ODNI were supposed to accomplish. Differences in perception and prescription fueled debate over authorities, expectations, and performance.[16] A more serious consequence was the need for and difficulty of achieving substantive revisions to the executive order that clarified DNI authorities on issues critical to the director's ability to lead and transform the IC.[17]

Many ambiguities remain unresolved, but consensus has emerged with regard to most of the higher-order objectives of the Intelligence Reform Act and the recommendations that helped shape the legislation. Those objectives, and provisions incorporated into the reform legislation, define the formal roles and responsibilities of the ODNI. The principal responsibilities assigned to the DNI are

1. serve as head of the IC;
2. act as the principal intelligence advisor to the president, the National Security Council (NSC), and the Homeland Security Council (HSC) for intelligence matters related to the national security;[18] and
3. consistent with section 1018 of the National Security Intelligence Reform Act of 2004, oversee and direct the implementation of the National Intelligence Program (NIP; i.e., the IC budget).[19]

Before examining how these and other enumerated responsibilities affect the NSE, it will be useful to provide a brief summary of their genesis and additional detail on the problems the Intelligence Reform Act was intended to solve.

Although it sometimes muddied the water in doing so, the Intelligence Reform Act responded to oft-repeated arguments that the dual responsibilities of the director of central intelligence (DCI)—who was both head of the IC and head of the CIA—effectively forced a choice between managing a very large agency and leading a collection of highly disparate organizations. History had shown that every DCI gave priority to managing the CIA. That was understandable, and perhaps inevitable, because the DCI had clear and extensive authorities with respect to the CIA but little authority to lead other elements of the IC, all of which reported to the secretary of defense or other cabinet secretaries.[20] As a result, IC integration was more nominal than real, rivalries impeded cooperation, and opportunities for comparative advantage and synergy were lost. In essence the Intelligence Reform Act divided the DCI's portfolio, assigning primary responsibility for oversight and integration of the IC as a whole to the DNI and reducing the mandate of the position now designated as the director of the Central Intelligence Agency (DCIA).

Dividing the portfolio made it possible—and a priority—for the DNI to focus on integrating and improving the performance of the IC as a whole, but that step alone did not solve the problem of competing authorities or the DCI's (now DNI's) limited ability to influence the work of IC components that reported to another cabinet-level official. Indeed, Adm. (ret.) Mike McConnell, who served as DNI from 2007 to 2009, frequently characterized his position as "coordinator of national intelligence" because of his limited ability to direct the activities of IC agencies other than the CIA.[21] Members of Congress recognized the need to give the DNI more power over IC component agencies than had been vested in the DCI, but Secretary of Defense Donald Rumsfeld waged a successful campaign within the executive branch and with key members of Congress to preserve his (and other cabinet members') authorities. As a result, the Intelligence Reform Act gave the DNI the ability to effect change through his or her authority for the NIP budget but constrained his or her ability to act by specifying in Section 1018 that authorities granted to the DNI must respect and not abrogate the statutory responsibilities of the heads of departments.[22] The net effect was to give the DNI more power than had been accorded the DCI but less than was needed for uncontested leadership of the IC. In part because of the way the legislation was written, but also because Washington is a political town, the ability of successive DNIs to lead and manage the IC has been determined more by the personality and skills of the incumbent and the incumbent's relationship with the president than by statutory authorities.[23]

To address deficiencies identified by the studies that examined IC performance related to the 9/11 attacks and the decision to invade Iraq, the Intelligence Reform Act and a subsequent decision by the president to endorse most of the recommendations made by the WMD Commission assigned a number of specific tasks to the DNI.[24] The assigned tasks, individually and collectively, were designed to enhance the quality of intelligence support to the NSE and to restore confidence in the accuracy, reliability, and objectivity of information and assessments prepared by the IC. Fixing the IC was an instrumental goal; the ultimate objective was to enhance the performance of the NSE by improving the quality of intelligence support provided to all members of the national security team so that they might better protect our nation and advance its interests. The ODNI-led efforts to accomplish the mandated tasks and to achieve other integration and quality-enhancing goals have been beneficial to the NSE, but their impact has been limited primarily to the performance of the IC per se. They have had—and could have had—virtually no impact on the procedures and performance of other components of the NSE. Indeed, it can be argued—and this observer believes—that there has been a de facto diminution of the roles played by other NSE components caused by partisan politics, lack of consensus about priorities, and abandonment of grand strategy in favor of ad hoc reaction to specific developments. The effect of these developments has been to increase the real and perceived importance of IC activities.

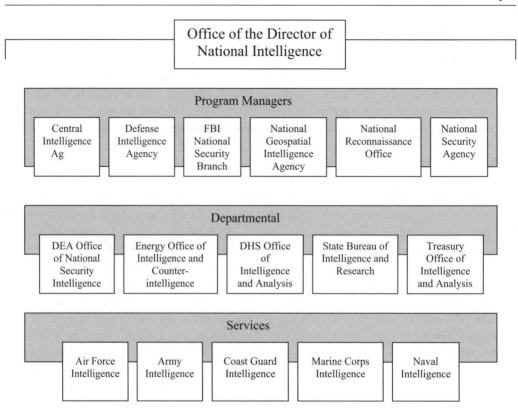

Figure 9.1. US Intelligence Community

BETTER INFORMATION SHARING

Space restrictions preclude a comprehensive review of mandated and self-initiated reforms designed to improve intelligence support to the NSE, but a few key examples will suffice to illustrate what is desired, what has been accomplished, and what remains to be achieved.[25] Perhaps the most important cluster of tasks, accomplishments, and impediments is that subsumed under the heading of information sharing. Reduced to its essence, one of the key conclusions of the 9/11 Commission Report was that the failure to share information among agencies and across the once-sacrosanct barrier between intelligence and law enforcement had severely limited our ability to detect terrorist preparations to attack the United States.[26] The remedy was obvious and easy to assert: Reduce or eliminate impediments to information sharing. Actually doing so proved to be difficult and contentious.

The Intelligence Reform Act specified, "The Director of National Intelligence shall have principal authority to ensure maximum availability of and access to intelligence information within the IC consistent with national security requirements."[27] Although efforts focused initially on the sharing of terrorism-related information, it quickly became apparent that the need to share transcended terrorism. It also became apparent that Intelligence Reform Act ambiguities, previously concluded agreements with foreign governments restricting the sharing of their information even within the US IC, proclaimed special sensitivities of many kinds, incompatible systems and software, and myriad other obstacles made the task far more difficult than most had anticipated. Resolution of some issues required revision of Executive Order 12333 governing intelligence activities and had to overcome protracted debate and bureaucratic maneuver. Others required changes to internal policies and operating directives, and still others required development of new software, risk management strategies, and metadata standards.[28]

The premise underlying all of these enabling measures was a simple one: the best way to ensure that nothing is missed, that collection resources are not squandered by seeking what we already know, that alternative explanations are examined, and that the expertise and experience of analysts across the IC can be brought to bear on any problem is to share information across bureaucratic boundaries within the IC. This will improve our understanding of difficult puzzles and enhance support to all IC customers. Nearly four years were required to put key prerequisites in place, but the IC has made significant progress toward full implementation of DNI McConnell's mandate to change the paradigm from need to know to responsibility to provide.[29] Further progress, and maintaining what has been achieved, will not be easy.

Despite the obvious advantages of information sharing, it was always controversial because greater sharing increased the risk of unauthorized disclosure. Many of the restrictions on sharing information had been put in place because of legitimate—if sometimes exaggerated—counterintelligence concerns. In the post-9/11 atmosphere the ODNI and other IC officials accepted somewhat greater counterintelligence risk in order to reduce the risk that threats would be missed or misinterpreted. Wider and easier sharing of information brought immediate benefits to IC analysts, but the theft and release of thousands of US government documents to WikiLeaks in 2010 rekindled controversy over how much material should be shared within the NSE.[30] Assessments by some that information overload caused by the sharing of "too much" information had impeded the ability of analysts to detect the radicalization of army major Nidal Hasan before he killed thirteen and injured thirty in a shooting rampage at Fort Hood in 2009 and the extreme damage to the US national security caused by the revelations of Edward Snowden in 2013 reignited debate on information sharing, albeit for different reasons.[31] These developments are noteworthy here for two ODNI-related reasons.

One reason is that the DNI was not made the scapegoat for any of these developments—as he was, for example, in the case of Umar Farouk Abdulmutallab, the so-called underwear bomber who attempted to detonate a bomb on a flight from Amsterdam to Detroit in December 2009.[32] A second is that by the time these events had occurred, the ODNI had become sufficiently established and accepted that it was entrusted with responsibility to work the problem and institute necessary changes. The shift from treating the DNI as a bureaucratic piñata to be whacked by any and all critics of IC performance to regarding the DNI as the official best able to manage intelligence problems is notable, good for the NSE, and a testament to the skill of DNI James Clapper (discussed later).

IMPROVED ANALYSIS

The second cluster of tasks and accomplishments is designed to enhance the accuracy, completeness, objectivity, and utility of analytic products. An equally important objective is to restore customer confidence in the quality of the assessments and judgments provided by IC analysts and to build confidence in the quality of work done by colleagues across the IC in order to facilitate divisions of labor and reduce unnecessary duplication of effort. The ultimate objective, however, is to improve national security decisions by improving the quality and reliability of analytic support to the agencies and individuals that together constitute the NSE.[33] Progress on all dimensions of this cluster has been quite good (e.g., mandatory analytic tradecraft standards for the entire IC were promulgated in June 2007, mandatory sourcing standards were issued in October 2007, and the Intelligence Reform Act–required ombudsman for analytic integrity was appointed in 2005).[34]

The net effect of these and other ODNI initiatives, such as the institution of a common course in basic analytic tradecraft (Analysis 101) for analysts from across the IC, and the demonstration and pull effect of applying higher standards to the preparation of NIEs and articles for the President's Daily Brief (PDB), is improved analytic performance in every analytic component and across the IC as a whole.[35] Better analytic tradecraft and improved analytic products do not in and of themselves ensure better national security decisions or more effective policy, but they do address key deficiencies identified by the WMD Commission. The measures and their results have enhanced confidence in the IC's analytic judgments, promoted dialogue between policymakers and analysts with the potential to deepen and better focus analytic work in support of national security decision making, and facilitated trust-based divisions of labor and greater ability to engage experts from across the IC to address difficult issues.[36]

Improved information sharing, better analytic products, more effective use of experts from outside the IC, greater use of open-source (i.e., unclassified) information, strengthened capabilities to analyze scientific and technical issues, enhanced integration of and cooperation between law enforcement agencies and the IC, and other objectives codified in the Intelligence Reform Act and the WMD Commission recommendations endorsed by President George W. Bush have been routinized but require continuous effort for improvement and reinforcement to prevent backsliding. Improving the quality of IC analysis is and always will be a work in progress. The ODNI has done more to achieve and sustain better analytic performance across the IC than was attempted in the pre-ODNI era, and the results have been welcomed by NSE customers.[37] Senior officials in the IC have embraced the goals—some more enthusiastically than others—and further progress is likely, unless there is another failure-driven or politically motivated crusade to improve national security by fixing the IC. The picture is not entirely positive, however. Outreach to non-IC and non–US government experts remains far less than it should be and was rolled back by agencies and the ODNI in response to the unauthorized disclosures of information by IC insiders or contractors.[38]

PRINCIPAL INTELLIGENCE ADVISOR . . .
IF THE PRESIDENT SO WISHES

The discussion thus far has focused on new requirements assigned to the DNI, but the ODNI also has important formal and informal roles in the NSE resulting from the transfer of responsibilities from the DCI to the DNI. First and foremost is the DNI's role as "the principal intelligence advisor to the President, the National Security Council, and the Homeland Security Council for intelligence matters related to the national security." The transferred responsibilities include representing the IC in the NSC process.[39] In addition to these participatory duties, the DNI inherited the responsibility to inform—and ability to influence—national security decision making through other means, including the presentation of information and analysis through the PDB.

As inheritor of DCI responsibilities to support the NSC process, the DNI now attends NSC and Principals' Committee (PC) meetings as the senior representative of the IC. However, he frequently is not the only senior IC official at the meetings. The fact that the ODNI was created midway through the two-term Bush administration precluded a clean break with the past. Given the importance and complexity of the issues confronting the NSC, most of which antedated the appointment of the first DNI and were therefore more familiar to the newly renamed DCIA, it was both natural and prudent that the DCIA continue to attend meetings during a period of transition. The same is true with respect to dual participation by ODNI and CIA senior officials in lower-level NSC meetings. This arrangement was continued during the Obama administration, presumably because of subject matter expertise and operational responsibilities, but possibly also because of the personal relationship between the president and former deputy national security advisor (and later DCIA) John Brennan.[40]

The DNI's formal role in the NSC process entails four core responsibilities:

1. ensuring that he is up to speed on developments and intelligence information germane to the subjects to be discussed at each meeting and that he or his "plus one" is prepared to provide an update briefing or answer questions about new developments or new intelligence;[41]
2. receiving and shaping intelligence-related requirements generated during the meeting and assigning tasks to appropriate collection or analytical components of the IC;
3. providing appropriate feedback on the discussion to elements of the IC working on the issues discussed or providing intelligence support to the other senior officials attending the meeting (the purpose of this feedback is to enable collectors and analysts to know what is already well understood, what officials said they needed, and what information and insights the senior intelligence professional thought would assist the deliberations even though no one else had requested it);[42]
4. contributing to the decision-making process by commenting on proposed options and offering proposals of his own.

The fourth responsibility is the most ambiguous and trickiest because the DNI must maintain—and be seen to maintain—objectivity when presenting assessments and updates germane to the discussion while contributing his own insights and ideas as a responsible member of the group entrusted to make national security decisions. Other senior attendees could legitimately present the policy preferences of their agencies, but the IC as such is supposed to be objective and policy neutral.[43]

DNI MECHANISMS: NATIONAL INTELLIGENCE OFFICERS, NATIONAL INTELLIGENCE MANAGERS, AND THE JOINT INTELLIGENCE COMMUNITY COUNCIL

The ODNI is represented at virtually all meetings convened by the NSC process (e.g., meetings of the PC, chaired by the national security advisor; the Deputies' Committee (DC), chaired by the deputy national security advisor; and interagency meetings of subordinate officials chaired by appropriate NSC senior directors), but only the DNI has the authority and responsibility to offer or comment on policy recommendations. All other IC representatives attending such meetings are required to eschew policy advice in order to maintain objectivity.[44]

When the DNI succeeded the DCI as the senior IC participant in the NSC process, the first DNI, John Negroponte, decided to make a symbolic break with the past that had substantive consequences. Previously, analysts in the CIA's Directorate of Analysis (DA) who had ready access to colleagues in the Directorate of Operations routinely monitored developments and intelligence in order to prepare the DCI for participation in NSC meetings. DNI Negroponte reassigned this responsibility to the National Intelligence Council (NIC), which the Intelligence Reform Act had transferred from the DCI to the ODNI.[45]

The assignment of this new responsibility had profound consequences for the NIC and, subsequently, for efforts to integrate and improve the performance of IC analysts and analytic components. One consequence was that national intelligence officers (NIOs) had to assume greater responsibility for, and spend more time on, current policy issues. This eventually enhanced the utility and policy relevance of NIC products, including NIEs, but in the short term it both compelled and enabled the NIOs to engage analysts from across the IC. The DA had been able to handle this task internally. The NIC, which is roughly one-thirtieth the size of the DA, did not have that option.

As a practical matter, NIOs frequently turned to CIA analysts for help in preparing briefing materials for NSC, PC, and DC meetings because they were located in the same building and had been doing this before the ODNI existed. But the NIOs were encouraged and empowered (by Intelligence Community Directives [ICDs] 200 and 207) to elicit written and verbal input from the most knowledgeable analysts in the IC, regardless of their bureaucratic home. The process was cumbersome and onerous at the beginning but eventually became routinized and effective in identifying analytical differences and ensuring that the DNI or other ODNI officials attending a national security meeting understood why analysts with access to the same information had reached different conclusions. In addition, participation by analysts from multiple agencies in premeeting briefings of the DNI or other ODNI participants gave the analysts better understanding of the specific issues under discussion, the principal's thought process, and the way their own work fit into the larger process. It also enabled them to provide better-informed support to other NSC officials (e.g., the secretary of state and the secretary of the treasury). In the pre-DNI era access to such important insights was limited almost exclusively to the CIA.

The roles of the NIC and NIOs continued to evolve as the NIC became the go-to place for an increasing number of analytic products and as DNI Clapper redefined the responsibilities of NIOs and national intelligence managers (NIMs). Before 2010 NIOs functioned as both senior subject matter experts in their respective areas of responsibility and quasi-official coordinators of requests for additional collection and other intelligence tasks. It was logical and convenient to vest "all" facets of intelligence related to a particular subject in a single individual, but it became increasingly impractical to do so as NIC responsibilities increased and the IC became better integrated.

To ensure that all dimensions of an NIO's expanded portfolio of responsibilities received the attention they required, Clapper reconceived the role of national intelligence managers (previously called mission managers), a position recommended by the WMD Commission.[46] Instead of using the NIMs for only a limited number of high-profile intelligence targets, Clapper put one in charge of each of the NIO accounts. Predictably, some NIOs felt that their status and authority had been degraded, and others welcomed the ability to focus on a smaller number of tasks. Rather quickly, however, the new arrangement took hold, demonstrated its value, and won acceptance.[47]

One additional formal DNI role in the NSC process warrants brief attention even though it is qualitatively different from those discussed previously, namely, the role as chair of the Joint Intelligence Community Council (JICC). Membership of the JICC includes the statutory members of the NSC plus the secretary of energy, the secretary of homeland security, and the attorney general.[48] The function of the JICC is to assist the DNI to develop and implement a joint, unified national intelligence effort to protect national security. As a practical matter this involves few meetings or JICC-specific interactions, largely because the DNI sees all of the members frequently in other venues. But it does provide a vehicle for periodic discussions to ensure that key national security policymakers understand DNI goals and priorities and that these priorities are consistent with and support the intelligence needs of the members and their agencies. The intelligence requirements and priorities of JICC principals are codified in the National Intelligence Priorities Framework (NIPF), which is updated semiannually.[49] The JICC has not played a central role in linking the IC to other elements of the NSE, however. The far more important links between policymakers and IC professionals are through regular and trusted interaction between policymakers and the analysts who support them.[50]

THE PDB PROCESS AS SOURCE OF INFORMATION AND INFLUENCE

Since the inception of the ODNI, the DNI or the principal deputy has participated in intelligence briefings of the president. Each president decides how, and how frequently, he or she wants to be briefed, but the process and its key vehicle are referred to as the President's Daily Brief (PDB). The process has existed since the Truman administration, but DCI participation in the daily briefing was episodic, and generally infrequent, before the administration of George W. Bush. This gave the DCI, and subsequently the DNI, sustained time with the president, vice president, and national security advisor. Designated sessions also include other members of the NSC. The subjects covered in these briefings are informed by the NSC agenda, but they also help shape that agenda. The timing and focus of items prepared for the PDB often reflect IC knowledge of the issues being considered by NSC principals and are written to inform their deliberations. The converse is also true; decisions to add or defer discussion of specific subjects are sometimes influenced by developments reported in the PDB. Whether the resultant situation is an integral and beneficial part of the NSC process or a perversion of that process giving intelligence a larger role in the making of national security decisions than it should have can be argued both ways.

On the positive side of the ledger, this engagement provides information and analytic judgments that give the president an independent base for assessing the appropriateness and practicality of policy recommendations brought to him or her through the NSC process. The same is true, mutatis mutandis, of the briefings and written assessments provided by the IC to other NSC principals. When the system works properly, which it usually does, subordinate officials in each of the national security agencies receive essentially the same intelligence-based information as do their superiors. Subordinates also receive additional intelligence keyed to their specific responsibilities. Providing the information directly to superiors enables them to judge whether proposals developed by subordinates make sense in light of available intelligence and, if they seem inconsistent, to find out why. Intelligence should not automatically trump policymaker judgments, but it should be a visible part of the decision-making process at every stage.

Whether, or the extent to which, the DNI's (and therefore the IC's) potentially daily access to the president has a detrimental impact on the NSE is probably a function more of personalities and interpersonal relationships than of structure. An attempt to preclude the possibility of adverse influence by eliminating the president's daily intelligence briefing or precluding, except in unusual circumstances, regular DNI participation in the briefing would be unwise, but it is appropriate for every DNI (and the presidents they serve) to consider carefully the opportunity costs of daily participation in the briefing session, especially the consequences of having less time for leadership of the IC.[51]

The PDB process also manifests other important elements of continuity and change. Perhaps the most notable continuity is the systematized effort to provide the same information to all NSC principals. Information provided through the PDB process certainly is not the only intelligence the principals receive (e.g., the secretary of state also receives intelligence-based analytic products from the State Department's Bureau of Intelligence and Research and the CIA), but the process does ensure that all have access to the same core body of information. In addition, as a result of changes introduced by the ODNI, all are also made aware of the existence of, and reasons for, analytic disagreements.[52]

FORGING AN ODNI ORGANIZATIONAL CULTURE

As a new organization the ODNI had no hoary traditions, limited staff loyalty, and few routinized procedures. It exists because of dissatisfaction with the performance and procedures of the DCI-led structure and was intended to remedy a number of real and imputed maladies, but it did not emerge from the Congress like some latter-day Athena sprung from the head of Zeus. There were almost as many different visions of what the ODNI should be as there were people with opinions on the subject. This was almost as true within the ODNI as without because, in many ways, the ODNI was, and in some respects still is, a microcosm of the IC. With limited and partial exceptions, such as the requirement that the ODNI not be collocated with any component of the IC (a provision clearly intended to prevent the ODNI from becoming a captive of the CIA), both the legislation and the Bush administration refrained from telling the DNI how to organize and run the new cabinet-level agency.[53]

For practical reasons the ODNI took then-existing Director of Central Intelligence Directives (DCIDs) and CIA policies and procedures governing personnel, access to computer systems, etc., as its starting point. Disengaging from and replacing these legacy guidelines and requirements was difficult and time consuming, in part because of ambiguities in the legislation, disagreement over precisely what the ODNI should be and do, and the palpable desire of some to ensure that the new structure ended in failure. Moreover, as staffers joined the ODNI from roughly two dozen organizations inside and outside the IC, they brought with them the cultures of their previous institutional homes. This bureaucratic baggage included both practices that were considered valuable and worth preserving, and behaviors and attitudes that were incompatible with the objectives of the Intelligence Reform Act. Inevitably, people did not agree on what should be retained and what should be jettisoned. The challenge of forging a new organizational culture was further complicated by the fact that most of the new staffers were seconded from other elements of the IC and expected to return eventually to their home agencies.

The net result of these factors was that the ODNI lacked a distinct culture of its own, was populated by well-intentioned individuals who did what came naturally and resisted efforts to adopt new procedures or inculcate new values out of concern that following them might jeopardize return to their home agencies. In addition, most attached higher priority to mission (i.e., providing the best possible intelligence support to policymakers, military commanders, and those responsible for homeland security) than to institution building. The demands of two shooting wars, the war on terror, preparation of budgets, congressional requirements, and myriad other imperatives effectively precluded a sustained effort to create and inculcate a new organizational culture. This was further compounded by the decision, which the author believes to have been the right one, to limit the proportion of ODNI permanent cadre to roughly 50 percent of its staff. The inevitable result was the absence of a coherent organizational ethos with shared norms, values, and expectations.

The inability of persons inside and outside the ODNI to articulate a clear vision of what the office is, what it does, and what it stands for impeded progress and contributed to the view of critics that it was little more than another layer of bureaucracy. That was a problem for the new organization, but it was also a problem for the IC as a whole and the efforts of successive DNIs to integrate the IC by instilling norms and values conducive to collaboration across institutional boundaries. This was not a trivial problem because the ODNI was created to integrate the IC so that it can function as a single enterprise with specialized, mission-specific components, effective divisions of labor, and sufficient redundancy to avoid single points of failure or unchallenged analytic judgments.

In the absence of an established organizational culture and with multiple contending approaches to what the culture of the new organization should be, the personalities and operational styles of key leaders, especially successive DNIs, played a larger role than in established organizations with the capacity to "capture" the people appointed to lead or transform them. That appears to have happened in the case of the ODNI, albeit not until James Clapper had served in the position of DNI long enough to put his personal stamp on the organization. One could speculate about how the culture of the ODNI might have evolved if one of Clapper's four predecessors (three confirmed and one acting) had remained in the position for longer than he did, but rapid turnover produced a level of instability that impeded crystallization of a new organizational culture until procedures and attitudes had been in place long enough to be perceived as permanent. This development was important for the success of the ODNI and its ability to integrate and improve IC support to the NSE.

THE ODNI AT TWELVE: AN APPRAISAL

More than a decade ago, many would have bet against the survival of the ODNI. Some would have been motivated by animosity and wishful thinking, others by judgments that it would prove unnecessary or ineffective. Few regarded it as a panacea for IC shortcomings, but a sufficient number of people in key positions were determined to seize the opportunity provided by the Intelligence Reform Act to enhance IC performance and adapt to new intelligence challenges. Some wanted to give the new organization a fighting chance because they believed better integration was essential. Others simply wanted to ensure that it did not diminish the ability of the IC to perform its diverse and critical missions. Despite, and perhaps because of, this mixed bag of motivations and expectations, the ODNI has made the transition from pariah and piñata to institutionalized and (largely) accepted leader of the IC.

Relative success in achieving the goals of intelligence reform is probably the most important reason the ODNI continues to exist and now seems destined to be a permanent part of the bureaucratic landscape, but it is not the only one. Even if it had been less successful in accomplishing the goals discussed later, the paralysis caused by partisan politics and the need to focus on other national problems, such as the great recession and budget-related issues, precluded a serious or sustained effort to redo or replace the intelligence reforms mandated in 2004. In other words, the ODNI benefitted from inertia and paralysis in the political system. Senior officials in the IC and the NSE more broadly recognized that and saw the opportunity or necessity to make the ODNI work because it was not going to go away.

The survival and increasing effectiveness of the ODNI was also facilitated by the increasingly important role assigned to the IC as a key component of the NSE. Policymaker preoccupation with immediate challenges put a premium on information and insights from the IC, and few were willing to risk impeding IC performance by adopting another wave of potentially disruptive reform. In other words, the ODNI benefitted from reform fatigue and fear of "breaking" what had become a, if not the, most important component of the NSE. This provided an opportunity as well as an incentive for the IC as a whole to work with the DNI to sustain and improve performance, especially as it entered a period of increasing responsibilities and shrinking budgets.

Personalities and relationships also played a role. Rapid turnover in the top position—there were four confirmed and one acting DNI during the first five years—fueled uncertainty about the future of the organization and impeded acceptance of the ODNI. But each of the successive DNI's built on what he inherited and eschewed calls to adopt radically different approaches. All took a lot of flak from critics who opposed creation of the ODNI, complained that the DNI did not conform to their idea of what it should be, or demanded immediately flawless performance on every dimension of reform. Progress was slow, as it always is when making fundamental changes while maintaining high levels of performance in all mission areas, but it was steady and cumulative. That the process took time should surprise no one; that it succeeded as fast as it did testifies to the vision and skill of those who led the effort and the commitment to mission of professionals across the IC.[54]

The pace of transformation and acceptance accelerated in the ODNI's second half decade because of the foundation that had been laid earlier and because of the focus, skill, and approach of DNI James Clapper. His focus on integration in order to perform assigned missions rather than on integration per se and single-minded pursuit of ways to meet everescalating demands and expectations for intelligence support to the NSE achieved results and demonstrated that the community performed better when it functioned as a team. Clapper built support for the ODNI by assisting agency heads to achieve their goals more efficiently. Under his leadership the ODNI began to be perceived as a partner that helped get the job done rather than as a nuisance that made it harder to perform mission.

Integration of the IC, like improvement of collection, analysis, and acquisition procedures, is a never-ending process that will never be fully satisfactory but is clearly more extensive and more effective than it was in the pre-ODNI era or the first years of DNI leadership. Agency heads and managers across the community now have a much better understanding of what counterparts are doing, where centers of excellence are located, how to tap expertise and other capabilities across the entire enterprise, and how to reduce unnecessary duplication. These and many other forms of integration are valuable because they enhance performance by helping to ensure continuous optimization of effort to meet the needs of the IC's myriad customers. They are invaluable in times of shrinking budgets, escalating demands, and de facto transfers of responsibility from other parts of the NSE to the IC. In contrast to the situation a decade ago, the community now looks to the ODNI to help work through planned budget cuts in ways that will maximize capacity and minimize losses of capability.

One can still find faults to criticize, but this author's bottom-line assessment of the ODNI at ten is that it has played a critical role in achieving greater integration of the IC, more extensive and effective sharing of information, more efficient collection and processing of intelligence, less duplicative and better quality analytic products, and significant progress toward espousal of a common culture in all components of the community. Many of these gains were difficult to achieve, but all are now taken for granted by IC professionals and the policymakers they support. There is no way to ensure that there will be no "failures" in the future, but changes adopted and accepted during the ODNI era have improved the quality of day in and day out support to the large and diverse mix of national security customers, missions, and challenges.

NOTES

1. Michael Warner and J. Kenneth McDonald examine fourteen studies of the IC, the reasons they were undertaken, and the recommendations they proposed in *US Intelligence Community Reform Studies since 1947* (Washington, DC: Strategic Management Issues Office, Center for the Study of Intelligence, Central Intelligence Agency, April 2005).

2. The most detailed and influential postmortem was the National Commission on Terrorist Attacks upon the United States, *The 9/11 Commission Report* (Washington, DC: Government Printing Office, 2004) (hereafter cited as *9/11 Commission Report*). See also Charles Perrow, "A Symposium on *The 9/11 Commission Report*," *Contemporary Sociology* 34, no. 2 (March 2005): 99–107; and Richard A. Falkenrath, "The 9/11 Commission Report," *International Security* 29, no. 3 (Winter 2004/5): 170–90. The flawed estimate was *Iraq's Continuing Programs for Weapons of Mass Destruction*, October 2002. Declassified key judgments released on July 18, 2003, are available at www.fas.org/irp/cia/product/iraq-wmd.html. The legislative fix is the Intelligence Reform and Terrorism Prevention Act of 2004, Pub. L. No. 108-458, § 102(b) (2004), www.gpo.gov/fdsys/pkg/PLAW-108publ458/pdf/PLAW-108publ458.pdf (hereafter cited as Intelligence Reform Act).

3. For examples criticizing the ODNI as an extra layer of bureaucracy, see Peter Hoekstra, remarks at "Intelligence Reform and Oversight: The View from Congress," CFR Events, June 26, 2008, www.cfr.org/intelligence/intelligence-reform-oversight-view-congress-rush-transcript-federal-news-agency/p16663; and Aki J. Peritz and Eric Rosenbach, "Intelligence Reform," memorandum, Belfer Center for Science and International Affairs, July 2009, http://belfercenter.ksg.harvard.edu/publication/19154/intelligence_reform.html.

4. Brief descriptions of the roles and missions of the institutional members of the IC can be found on the ODNI website, www.dni.gov/index.php/intelligence-community/members-of-the-ic. These materials list sixteen constituent agencies, one more than the fifteen referenced in the quotation from the WMD Commission letter of transmittal cited in the chapter epigraph. The reason for the difference is the addition of the Drug Enforcement Administration's Office of National Security Intelligence in 2005. For more on problems in other parts of the NSE, see, for example, Project on National Security Reform, *Forging a New Shield* (Arlington, VA, November 2008), http://0183896.netsolhost.com/site/wp-content/uploads/2011/12/pnsr_forging_a_new_shield_report.pdf.

5. White House, "President Signs Intelligence Reform and Terrorism Prevention Act," press release, December 17, 2004, http://georgewbush-whitehouse.archives.gov/news/releases/2004/12/20041217-1.html.

6. Much has been written on the challenges of organizational change. See, for example, Charles Perrow, *Complex Organizations: A Critical Essay*, 3rd ed. (New York: McGraw-Hill, 1986).

7. In certain respects the start-up of the ODNI and the challenges inherent in the attempt to reduce the independence of the sixteen constituent elements of the IC in order to achieve a more integrated and effective intelligence enterprise are similar to those attending the creation of the Office of the Secretary of Defense in 1949. It took more than a decade—and the strong-willed personality of Robert McNamara and strong backing of President Kennedy—for the secretary of defense to gain primacy over the military services. See, for example, Lawrence S. Kaplan, Ronald D. Landa, and Edward J. Drea, *History of the Office of the Secretary of Defense*, vol. 5, *The McNamara Ascendancy* (Washington, DC: Historical Office, Office of the Secretary of Defense, 2006).

8. The *9/11 Commission Report*, for example, called for major transformation of congressional oversight of intelligence and homeland security (sec. 13.4, 419–23). See also Project on National Security Reform, *Forging a New Shield*; and Michèle A. Flournoy, "Reforming an Outmoded Federal

Government," *Washington Post*, August 22, 2012, www.washingtonpost.com/opinions/reforming-an-outmoded-federal-government/2012/08/22/311c039c-ebe4-11e1-9ddc-340d5efb1e9c_story.html.

9. Illustrative examples of resistance to ODNI-initiated changes include the CIA's opposition to and efforts to severely limit contact between IC analysts and nongovernmental experts and Defense efforts to frustrate attempts to reform the acquisition process for systems used by the IC and the military.

10. See, for example, Thomas Kean and Lee Hamilton, "Column: 9/11 Commission Holes Yet to Be Filled," *USA Today*, September 7, 2011, http://usatoday30.usatoday.com/news/opinion/forum/story/2011-09-07/Column-911-Commission-holes-yet-to-be-filled/50301014/1.

11. *9/11 Commission Report*. See also Senate Select Committee on Intelligence and US House Permanent Select Committee on Intelligence, *Joint Inquiry into Intelligence Community Activities before and after the Terrorist Attacks of September 11, 2001*, S. Rep. No. 107–351, H. R. Rep. No. 107–792 (2002).

12. See Select Committee on Intelligence, *Postwar Findings about Iraq's WMD Programs and Links to Terrorism and How They Compare with Prewar Assessments Together with Additional Views*, S. Rep. 109–331 (2006) (hereafter cited as *WMD Findings*). See also Richard A. Best Jr., *U.S. Intelligence and Policymaking: The Iraq Experience* (Washington, DC: Congressional Research Service, December 2, 2005), www.fas.org/spg/crs/intel/RS21696.pdf; and Select Committee on Intelligence, *Report on Whether Public Statements Regarding Iraq by U.S. Government Officials Were Substantiated by Intelligence Information Together with Additional and Minority Views*, S. Rep. 110–345 (2008).

13. See *WMD Findings*. The final report of the WMD Commission was not published until March 2005, but many of its key findings were known when Congress and the administration were deliberating and debating what became the Intelligence Reform Act. See Commission on the Intelligence Capabilities of the United States Regarding Weapons of Mass Destruction, *Report to the President of the United States* (Washington, DC: Government Printing Office, 2005) (hereafter cited as *WMD Commission Report*).

14. Members of the 9/11 Commission aggressively and effectively lobbied the executive branch, Congress, and the public to ensure that their report and recommendations did not suffer the fate of most such reports. In important respects they drove the process that produced the Intelligence Reform Act. See, for example, Philip Shenon, "Sept. 11 Commission Plans a Lobbying Campaign to Push Its Recommendations," *New York Times*, July 19, 2004, www.nytimes.com/2004/07/19/us/sept-11-commission-plans-a-lobbying-campaign-to-push-its-recommendations.html.

15. Congress played an active role in drafting the Intelligence Reform Act and, ultimately, had more impact than did the specific recommendations of the 9/11 and WMD Commissions. See Michael Allen, *Blinking Red: Crisis and Compromise in American Intelligence after 9/11* (Washington, DC: Potomac Books, 2013); and Laurie West Van Hook, *Reforming Intelligence: The Passage of the Intelligence Reform and Terrorism Prevention Act* (Washington, DC: ODNI, National Intelligence University, n.d.).

16. See, for example, Peter Spiegel and Doyle McManus, "Spy Czar, Rumsfeld in a Turf War," *Los Angeles Times*, May 6, 2006; Greg Miller, "Intelligence Office Has Swollen, House Panel Says," *Los Angeles Times*, March 31, 2006; Richard A. Posner, *Uncertain Shield: The U.S. Intelligence System in the Throes of Reform* (Lanham, MD: Rowman & Littlefield, 2006); House Permanent Select Committee on Intelligence, Subcommittee on Oversight, *Initial Assessment on the Implementation of the Intelligence Reform and Terrorism Prevention Act of 2004*, July 27, 2006, www.fas.org/irp/congress/2006_rpt/hpsci072706.pdf.

17. See Executive Order 12333, "United States Intelligence Activities" (as amended by Executive Orders 13284 [2003], 13355 [2004], and 13470 [2008]), https://fas.org/irp/offdocs/eo/eo-12333-2008.pdf. For media commentary on the debate over how to revise the 1981 executive order signed by President Reagan, see, for example, Scott Shane, "Bush Issues Order Seeking to Unite the Efforts of U.S. Spy Agencies," *New York Times*, August 1, 2008; and Pamela Hess, "Agencies Fight for Spy Control," *USA Today*, May 28, 2008.

18. President Obama abolished the HSC and reassigned its responsibilities to the NSC on May 26, 2009. See Helene Cooper, "In Security Shuffle, White House Merges Staffs," *New York Times*, May 26, 2009, www.nytimes.com/2009/05/27/us/27homeland.html?_r=1&ref=us.

19. Intelligence Reform Act.

20. IC agencies reporting to cabinet secretaries other than the secretary of defense are the Office of Intelligence and Counterintelligence (secretary of energy), Office of Intelligence and Analysis (secretary of homeland security), Bureau of Intelligence and Research (secretary of state), Office of Intelligence and Analysis (secretary of the treasury), Office of National Security Intelligence of the Drug Enforcement Administration (attorney general), National Security Branch of the FBI (attorney general); and Intelligence Component of the US Coast Guard (secretary of homeland security). Agencies reporting to the secretary of defense are the Defense Intelligence Agency, National Geospatial Intelligence Agency, National Security Agency, National Reconnaissance Office, and intelligence components of the air force, army, navy, and marine corps.

21. See, for example, J. Michael McConnell, "DNI Addresses the Richard W. Riley Institute of Furman University," March 28, 2008, www.dni.gov/files/documents/Newsroom/Speeches%20and%20 Interviews/20080328_speech.pdf.

22. Intelligence Reform Act, § 1018, "Presidential Guidelines on Implementation and Preservation of Authorities."

23. For general analysis of the importance of personality and leadership, see, for example, Bernard M. Bass and Bruce J. Avolio, "Transformational Leadership and Organizational Culture," *Public Administration Quarterly* 17, no. 1 (Spring 1993): 112–21.

24. See White House, "President Bush Administration Actions to Implement WMD Commission Recommendations," press release, June 29, 2005, http://georgewbush-whitehouse.archives.gov/news/releases/2005/06/20050629-5.html.

25. This chapter focuses on analysis-related missions of the ODNI, in part because space limitations preclude even cursory discussion of ODNI responsibilities and innovations with respect to intelligence collection, personnel policy, acquisition, and other mission areas.

26. See, for example, Barbara A. Grewe, "Legal Barriers to Information Sharing: The Erection of a Wall between Intelligence and Law Enforcement," declassified staff monograph prepared for the Commission on Terrorist Attacks upon the United States, August 20, 2004, http://fas.org/irp/eprint/wall.pdf.

27. Intelligence Reform Act, § 102 (g), "Intelligence Information Sharing."

28. For a partial list of steps taken to improve access to information and information sharing, see Office of the Director of National Intelligence, *Discovery and Dissemination or Retrieval of Information with the Intelligence Community*, ICD No. 501, January 21, 2009, www.dni.gov/files/documents/ICD/ICD_501.pdf; Tim Starks, "Intelligence Chief Says New Policy Will Dramatically Boost Information Sharing," *CQ Today Online News*, January 16, 2009; and Ben Bain, "A-Space Set to Launch This Month," *Federal Computer Week*, September 3, 2008.

29. See, for example, Mike McConnell, remarks at the Project on National Security Reform Conference, Washington, DC, July 26, 2007, www.dni.gov/files/documents/Newsroom/Speeches%20and%20Interviews/20070726_speech.pdf; and Mike McConnell, "Preparing Intelligence to Meet the Intelligence Community's 'Responsibility to Provide,'" Intelligence Community Policy Memorandum 2007–200–2, December 11, 2007, www.dni.gov/files/documents/IC%20Policy%20Memos/ICPM%20 2007-200-2%20Responsibility%20to%20Provide.pdf.

30. Articles describing the release of thousands of US government documents to WikiLeaks can be found at http://topics.nytimes.com/top/reference/timestopics/organizations/w/wikileaks/index.html.

31. For details on information sharing and the case of Nidal Hasan and the Fort Hood shootings, see Joseph I. Lieberman and Susan M. Collins, "A Ticking Time Bomb: Counterterrorism Lessons from the U.S. Government's Failure to Prevent the Fort Hood Attack," Senate Comm. on Homeland Security and Governmental Affairs, February 3, 2011, http://msnbcmedia.msn.com/i/MSNBC/Sections/NEWS/A_Politics/__Politics_Today_Stories_Teases/forthoodexecsummary.pdf. For information on the release of classified documents by Edward Snowden, see, for example, Barton Gellman, Aaron Blake, and Greg Miller, "Edward Snowden Comes Forward as Source of NSA Leaks," *Washington Post*, June 9, 2013, www.washingtonpost.com/politics/intelligence-leaders-push-back-on-leakers-media/2013/06/09/fff80160-d122-11e2-a73e-826d299ff459_story.html.

32. For coverage of Umar Farouk Abdulmutallab and the failed attempt to blow up an airliner on Christmas Day 2009, see coverage by *New York Times*, http://topics.nytimes.com/top/reference/timestopics/people/a/umar_farouk_abdulmutallab/index.html.

33. See Thomas Fingar, *Reducing Uncertainty: Intelligence Analysis and National Security* (Stanford, CA: Stanford University Press, 2011).

34. Relevant IC policy documents can be found at www.dni.gov/index.php/intelligence-community/ic-policies-reports. See particularly "Analytic Standards," ICD No. 203; "Sourcing Requirements for Disseminated Analytic Products," ICD No. 206; "Write for Maximum Utility," ICD No. 208; and "Role of the Office of the Director of National Intelligence Analytic Ombudsman," Intelligence Community Policy Memorandum 2006–202–2.

35. The ODNI is required to report to Congress annually on the performance of the analytic community as measured against Intelligence Reform Act standards and the additional standards adopted in ICD No. 203. These reports are classified, but they document the improvement noted in the text. The requirement to provide this report to Congress can be found in Intelligence Reform Act, § 1019. See also Richard Immerman, "Transforming Analysis: The Intelligence Community's Best Kept Secret," *Intelligence and National Security* 26, no. 2–3 (2011): 159–81.

36. See also Thomas Fingar, "Building a Community of Analysts," *Analyzing Intelligence: National Security Practitioners' Perspectives*, 2nd ed., ed. Roger Z. George and James B. Bruce (Washington, DC: Georgetown University Press, 2014), 287–301. Other ODNI initiatives to ensure that IC materials prepared for national security decision makers are informed by insights and information from experts who are not in the IC include "Analytic Outreach," ICD No. 205; and consolidation and expansion of mechanisms to tap outside expertise through the IC affiliates program that the State Department's Bureau of Intelligence and Research manages for the IC.

37. Christopher Kojm, "Change in Response to the Times: The National Intelligence Council, 2009–2014," *Studies in Intelligence* 59, no. 2 (June 2015).

38. See, for example, "Media Contacts," ICD No. 119, March 20, 2014, www.dni.gov/files/documents/ICD/ICD%20119.pdf.

39. The "NSC process," as that term is used here, subsumes meetings and deliberations of the NSC chaired by the president as well as the cascade of Principals' Committee, Deputies' Committee, and other subordinate arenas. This chapter treats the HSC as part of the NSC process, but it is important to note that the existence of two structures with overlapping missions further complicated the ability of the ODNI, and the IC more generally, to support the policymaking process.

40. See, for example, Peter Baker and Mark Mazetti, "Brennan Draws on Bond with Obama in Backing CIA," *New York Times*, December 14, 2014, www.nytimes.com/2014/12/15/us/politics/cia-chief-and-president-walk-fine-line-.html?_r=0.

41. "Plus one" is the NSC term for the person who accompanies the principal. A senior analyst, usually an NIO or deputy NIO, normally accompanied the DNI, but when appropriate to the agenda, the plus one would come from the National Clandestine Service or another element of the collection community.

42. Before creation of the DNI, the DCI provided feedback only to the CIA. Other agencies resented this, and more important, it impeded the ability of analysts in other agencies to tailor their own work to the needs and time lines of the officials they supported.

43. On the importance of objectivity and policy neutrality, see Thomas Fingar, "Its Complicated," *American Interest*, May/June 2013, 31–35.

44. An example of DNI input into the policymaking process is the role played by DNI Mike McConnell in decisions affecting cybersecurity. His knowledge and experience as former director of the National Security Agency, in the private sector, and as DNI made him well qualified to comment on and recommend policies to address the security challenges that he presented to decision makers as the senior representative of the IC. The participation of the DCIA (or his representative) at most meetings of senior policymakers and the important operational role played by the CIA in the war on terror and ongoing military conflicts makes it likely that he, too, sometimes acts as a policymaker as well as the conveyor of IC judgments.

45. Kojm, "Change in Response to the Times." For additional information on the NIC, see the descriptive materials at www.dni.gov/nic/NIC_home.html.

46. See *WMD Commission Report*, "Overview."

47. Kojm, "Change in Response to the Times."

48. Intelligence Reform Act, § 1031.

49. For additional information on the national intelligence priorities framework process, see "Roles and Responsibilities for the National Intelligence Priorities Framework," ICD No. 204, January 2, 2015,

www.dni.gov/files/documents/ICD/ICD%20204%20National%20Intelligence%20Priorities%20 Framework.pdf.

50. See Thomas Fingar, "Analysis in the US Intelligence Community: Missions, Masters, and Methods," in *Intelligence Analysis: Behavioral and Social Scientific Foundations*, ed. Baruch Fischhof and Cherie Chauvin (Washington, DC: National Academies Press, 2011), 3–27.

51. How much time the DNI devotes to directly supporting the president has been a recurring topic of debate. See, for example, Edward Maguire, *Critical Intelligence Community Management Challenges* (Washington, DC: Office of the Director of National Intelligence, Office of the Inspector General, November 12, 2008), www.globalsecurity.org/intell/library/reports/2008/081112-oig-intel -report.pdf; and Mark Mazzetti, "Report Faults U.S. Spy Agencies," *New York Times*, April 2, 2009.

52. Fingar, *Reducing Uncertainty*.

53. The proscription on collocation is in Intelligence Reform Act, § 103(e).

54. The ODNI gained traction and acceptance much faster than did the Office of the Secretary of Defense or the reforms mandated by the Goldwater–Nichols Department of Defense Reorganization Act of 1986, for example.

CHAPTER 10

Central Intelligence Agency

The President's Own

Roger Z. George

> The sole element of the intelligence community independent from a cabinet agency is the CIA. As an independent agency it collects, analyzes, and disseminates intelligence from all sources. The CIA's number one customer is the president of the United States, who also has the authority to direct it to conduct covert operations.
>
> —9/11 Commission Report

The Central Intelligence Agency (CIA) is a major player in the national security enterprise, witnessed by the frequency with which it has become embroiled in controversy surrounding its covert operations in war zones, its collection methods, and its analysis on major foreign policy issues. This chapter will examine how the CIA's role and cultures have been adapting to the changes resulting from the end of the Cold War and the onset of a post-9/11 world.

Although intelligence is now a central feature of the national security enterprise, it was not always so. Indeed, until 1947 American intelligence was a marginal player in the formation of national security policy and was dominated by the military departments that focused on wartime needs. The drafting of the 1947 National Security Act challenged this bureaucratic tradition of departmentally focused wartime intelligence. The military services and the Federal Bureau of Investigation (FBI)—which had domestic and foreign counterintelligence authorities at the time—remained critical of the proposed new national security framework. The strong biases of the nation's diplomats, warriors, and law enforcement officials drove them to see no need for a new intelligence organization.[1]

Yet the failings of intelligence at Pearl Harbor and the onset of the Cold War overrode those interests, propelling the president and Congress to agree—reluctantly at first—that a more coherent intelligence function was important if future failures were to be averted. Between 1947 and 1951, the makings of the new CIA were evident. First, its director became the president's senior intelligence advisor. Second, the CIA was given the role of coordinating and bringing together the information available to various parts of the US government for the National Security Council (NSC). Third, its intelligence collection function—carried over from the earlier Office of Strategic Services (OSS)—was reaffirmed by virtue of the growing need for information on the Soviet Union's political, economic, military, and scientific developments. And fourth, the CIA's covert action (CA) responsibilities (termed "special activities" in the 1947 NSC directives that laid the groundwork for such duties) also grew in response to the spreading communist challenges faced in Europe, Asia, and other parts of the world.[2]

The 1947 National Security Act dictated a much more formal interagency process, which would require a more ambitious intelligence role than departmental intelligence units could provide. The original and core mission of this new "central" intelligence agency was to inform the national security decision-making process and bring together all the available intelligence found throughout the US government. Operations—either to collect secret information or to conduct CA in support of a president's policies—were not mentioned in the National Security Act of 1947. Some scholars believe their absence in the legislation was to avoid details and possibly congressional delays in approving the legislation's principal purpose: unifying the military and establishing a national security–making process. In addition, playing down CIA operations would not highlight US actions vis-à-vis its adversaries as well as its friends.

There would be lively debate over which function—analysis, collection, or CA—was now the core mission of the CIA. Regardless, a unique feature of the CIA—unlike other parts of the intelligence community (IC)—has been to provide *independent* and *nondepartmental* finished intelligence analysis that the president and senior advisors need. That mission remains the one that dominates the CIA's role in the interagency process.

As the core missions of the CIA grew, so too did the development of a new set of bureaucratic players: the analysts and the operators with their own unique cultures. Not surprisingly, then, the CIA began to emerge with interests and behaviors that were distinct from those of the other national security organizations. Two noticeable fault lines became evident—the internal one of analysts versus operators and an external one of intelligence versus policy. It is the interaction of these two sets of fault lines that characterizes much of the CIA's operation in the interagency process.

THE INTERNAL FAULT LINE: CULTURES OF THE CIA

As former CIA director Richard Helms remarked, "There is a CIA culture. Any circumscribed group of people engaged in a demanding, isolated and occasionally dangerous activity is likely in time to develop a culture."[3] Providing objective, accurate, and timely intelligence to every president since 1947 has shaped that culture for nearly seventy years. Yet the reality is more complex. The CIA contains subcultures reflecting its separate but intertwined analytic and operational missions. More important, these subcultures also reflect differing priorities, norms, and operational styles for the CIA's role within the national security enterprise.

Analysts and the Culture of Objectivity

From its early beginnings, CIA officials faced a challenge in providing objective intelligence to an inherently political policy process. By its very nature, policymaking is a battleground of ideas in which strong-willed players in the different departments compete for the president's attention and support. In such a politically charged and personality-driven atmosphere, could independent and objective information and analysis actually make a difference? According to Sherman Kent, a Yale historian, OSS veteran, and early director of the CIA's Office of National Estimates, the proper role of intelligence was to raise the level of the policy debate, not take sides. Kent's 1949 book, *Strategic Intelligence for an American World Policy*, became the touchstone for how intelligence officers view their craft and its relationship to the policy process: "Intelligence is not the formulator of objectives . . . drafter of policy . . . maker of plans . . . carrier out of operations. Intelligence is ancillary to these: . . . it performs a service function. Its job is to see that the doers are generally well informed . . . call their attention to the stubborn fact they may be neglecting, and—at their request—to analyze alternative courses without indicating choice."[4] In Kent's view intelligence must be close enough to policy to give guidance and support but not so close as to lose its objectivity and analytic integrity.

The CIA's Directorate of Analysis (DA) contains the largest number of all-source intelligence analysts serving the president, key advisors, and increasingly, Congress.* The analysts came to see themselves as uniquely placed to provide objective and unbiased information from which policymakers could draw insight and wisdom. During the 1960s the CIA left the crowded spaces of its wartime offices in downtown Washington, DC, to take up permanent residence in the suburbs of Langley, Virginia. Situated on a sprawling campus-like compound more than a twenty-minute drive from the White House, the CIA symbolically remained apart from the world of departmental politics and White House intrigues.

The evolution of the DA over nearly seventy years has seen numerous organizational changes to reflect the expanding list of intelligence priorities far beyond the Soviet threat. University-trained social scientists, economists, and military historians initially staffed the CIA, to be joined over time by scientists, engineers, and other technical disciplines.[5] The DA now represents a more diverse workforce focused on the special political, economic, scientific, and military interests of US government officials. Additionally, in-house training focuses on how to task secret collection systems, effectively write for and brief the busy policymaker, and apply analytic rigor to challenge one's own thinking process.[6] Training and mentoring emphasize the analyst's responsibility for producing objective (free of any political agenda) analysis. This notion of objectivity and analytical integrity has become the sine qua non for a fully professional analyst.

Since 9/11 there has been a steady generational shift in the analytic cadre. The founding generations focused on the Soviet threat are almost entirely gone, steadily being replaced by a large number of millennial and Gen-X analysts. This gradual shift has broadened the gender diversity, witnessed by the numerous senior women occupying deputy director positions throughout the agency. The new generations bring with them strong views regarding work–life balance, comfort in using social media technologies, and an eagerness for broadening experiences and greater responsibilities than their predecessors. These analysts now have opportunities for cross-directorate and overseas assignments to provide more analytic support to counterterrorism and counter-proliferation operations. The huge post-9/11 influx of analysts—roughly a 50 percent increase—now confronts the agency with the challenge of accommodating these aspirations as it enters an era of relative budget austerity.

The all-source analyst's performance is measured by his or her file of analytic production, ability to brief senior officials, and flexibility to cover suddenly emerging intelligence priorities. CIA analysts also tend to profile clandestine human intelligence (HUMINT) and signals intelligence (SIGINT) reporting more in their analysis; this results in CIA analysts producing more highly classified—therefore, more restrictively controlled—analysis than other intelligence agencies produce. The 24–7 world of today has put an even higher premium on producing analysis that is both timely and concise. As one analyst admitted in an insightful study

---

*Until 2015 the analytical directorate was called the Directorate of Intelligence (DI). The recent modernization plan has adopted the Directorate of Analysis, which will be used throughout this chapter.

of the analytical culture, he had not joined a university as much as a government-run news-paper business.[7] The rush to produce analysis carries with it the nagging analytic concern about correctly capturing "what we know and don't know." In a word, analysis is an error-prone business in which uncertainty is as high as the risks of being wrong. Intelligence failures come with the turf.

Clandestine Service and the Operational World

The creators of the 1947 National Security Act probably did not anticipate how the CIA's role would change so quickly to encompass other critical missions beyond those specified in the vague legislation that established the agency. Although the CIA's collection of intelligence was not mentioned in the 1947 National Security Act, it was not long before espionage was added to the CIA's growing list of responsibilities. And it was the growth in the CIA's collection operations and CA mission that gave rise to the agency's dominant culture found in the Directorate of Operations (DO).[†] What now most distinguishes the CIA from other intelligence agencies is its cadre of HUMINT collectors (often called case officers) who recruit agents, steal secrets, and mount CA operations at the direction of the president. This unique function has given the CIA a character and ethos all its own and strongly shapes the way the CIA operates in the policy process—even when it is primarily the DA that is engaged with Washington policymakers.

By virtue of its authorities to operate overseas and to recruit foreign spies, the DO values secrecy more than almost any other organization in the US government. As the first career analyst to become a director of the CIA, Robert Gates was uniquely situated to observe the operators' different culture: "Secrecy is not a convenience or a bureaucratic matter, but the essential tool of their craft—without it, sources are executed, operations fail, case officers' careers are cut short, and sometimes they and their agents die. . . . [DO] ran the Agency bureaucratically and dominated it psychologically. And few questioned the rightness of that."[8] To be accurate, however, outside critics have questioned this culture of secrecy, which they often complain is used by the agency to hide its failures and escape proper oversight.[9]

The selection and training of clandestine officers also tends to reinforce a feeling of uniqueness that binds clandestine officers together into a guild-like organization. Unlike the DA, which finds its workforce largely in American universities, the DO has recruited heavily from the military and the business world. It sees its origins in the wartime OSS, which had its own military traditions and operated (as one veteran described it) as an "extremely hierarchical organization."[10] The DO cultivates the image of a can-do culture, not unlike the marine corps or an enterprising multinational corporation. Stationing many of its officers in overseas locations conveys a sense of independence from the Washington policy world as well as encourages a sense of self-reliance on each other. Specialized training, kept secret to protect the case officer's tradecraft from adversaries, builds this operator's code of behavior. Armed with countersurveillance and recruitment skills, these officers are rewarded for running agents, filing reports that gain the attention of senior policymakers, and handling difficult situations without causing publicity or blowback. Working overseas, with various kinds of cover arrangements, the DO works with a range of other agencies, most especially with the military and diplomatic missions (see box 10.1).

---

†From 2005 until recently, the DO was called the National Clandestine Service, but it reverted back to the DO under the 2014 Brennan modernization plan.

BOX 10.1
CIA Abroad

The CIA's global intelligence and operational capabilities and responsibilities are significantly greater than those of virtually every other US intelligence agency. As a result, historically, the senior officer serving overseas has been from the CIA, most often from the DO. The chief of station (COS), as the senior intelligence officer representing the US intelligence community, is triple-hatted, reporting to the ambassador, to CIA Headquarters, and to the director of national intelligence. A COS's success often depends on the relationship with the chief of mission. If that relationship is neglected or deteriorates, or if a serious intelligence flap occurs, a COS can find him- or herself on an airplane home.

The COS and station team work closely with other US intelligence representatives, particularly defense attachés (DATT) who represent the Defense Intelligence Agency and the FBI's legal attachés (LEGAT). Just as important are the CIA's responsibilities to liaise with the host government's internal security and foreign intelligence services. These ties enable cooperation on activities of mutual interest and allow the agency a measure of latitude for DO operations officers to selectively conduct independent operations. In the post-9/11 era collaboration with foreign services has become increasingly important to effective counterterrorism operations.

The president and the ambassador expect the COS to be the leader of the intelligence program, and the CIA jealously guards its power to select the COS. It bases this practice on the CIA being "central" to the national intelligence mission. The CIA is an integrated microcosm of core US intelligence capabilities. It has the primary role in HUMINT and counterintelligence operations abroad, has primacy in liaison relations with foreign counterparts, and is a recipient of all-source raw intelligence to enable all-source analysis. Sustaining control over COS selection is one barometer of whether the CIA remains primus inter pares in relation to the sixteen other US intelligence organizations.

The decade of war in Iraq and Afghanistan dramatically expanded the CIA's overseas war-zone presence and representation in the military headquarters of Central Command (CENTCOM) and Special Operations Command (SOCOM), as well as in Baghdad and Kabul. Among many other intelligence specialists, analysts seek these forward deployments out of a sense of duty and for their expertise-building opportunities, not to mention the excitement and promotion potential.

Clandestine operators' quest for secrecy extends even to other parts of the agency. Indeed, for the first several decades, physical barriers separated the DO from the analysts; what contact existed was only at the very senior levels. Jack Smith, one of the early Directorate of Analysis (DA) senior managers, admitted, "Most of us on the analytic side had little or no knowledge of the techniques of clandestine work and were prone to scoff at the excessively tight security about operations and to sneer at the bumbling of the 'spooks.'"[11] Conversely, Smith and others in the analytic ranks were well aware of the operational side's subtle disdain for their thinking profession. Analysts were sometimes viewed as security risks to highly sensitive operations, which were not shared with those not having a genuine need to know. Analysts routinely complained that they did not know enough about the clandestine sources—whose identities were well protected—to evaluate how credible they were.

This legacy of separation and secrecy has diminished over time. Increasingly, more operators and analysts find themselves working together in fusion centers like the CIA's Counterterrorism Center and the DNI's National Counterterrorism Center. Some CIA analytical units have also been collocated with their clandestine service counterparts in the main headquarters building, just as analysts are now deployed overseas to work closely with case officers on many difficult intelligence topics. Analysts working closely with the DO are also permitted more information regarding sources than they would have been only a few years ago. The Iraq and Afghanistan Wars have also thrust hundreds of analysts to the front lines, shoulder-to-shoulder with their case officer colleagues, further increasing these subcultures' understanding of each other and fostering greater trust and cooperation. The mere fact that

> **BOX 10.2**
> **Agency Blueprint for the Future**
>
> In 2014 CIA Director Brennan established a study group of officers from across the CIA to examine its organization—its people, processes, and structure—and recommend how to operate in the future given the challenge of a changed security landscape that is more complex, dynamic, and driven by rapid technological developments. The study group recommended major organizational changes that would fuse elements of operations and analysis into a set of mission centers. This would permit the CIA to continue to attract the best employees, leverage the digital revolution, and construct an organizational structure and business model that would support the fast-paced decision-making process.
>
> Of the major changes announced by the director in March 2015, the following are the most significant:
>
> - New *mission centers* will bring the full range of operational, analytic, support, technical, and digital personnel and capabilities to bear on critical security issues. New assistant directors of regional or functional areas will be responsible for the mission centers' integration and interoperability with other parts of the agency.
> - The directorate heads will continue to be responsible for developing officers in their respective occupations and skills. The NCS will again be named the *Directorate of Operations*, and the Directorate of Intelligence will be renamed the *Directorate of Analysis*.
> - A new *Directorate for Digital Innovation* will be responsible for accelerating the integration of digital and cyber capabilities across the new mission areas. It will manage the careers of digital experts and establish a digital tradecraft.
> - A new *Talent Development Center for Excellence* will be responsible for recruiting, managing, and training a more diverse workforce and for promoting leaders who can function in more integrated mission environments.
>
> *Source:* John Brennan, Message to the Workforce, March 6, 2015.

the DA has established a "targeting" analyst category suggests that there can be a more symbiotic relationship between analyst and collector than ever before. As of this writing, the CIA is undergoing a major reorganization that could integrate operations and analysis functions into more "centers"—a move that could have a major impact on the morale and self-identities of the DO and the DA.[12]

That said, differences remain at least on an interpersonal, if not institutional, basis. As recently as 2003 a senior operations officer in Afghanistan could openly dismiss the idea of having analysts in the field to lead operations.[13] A common perception was that CIA directors—either because they came from within the ranks of the clandestine service or because as outsiders they quickly appreciated the power and risks of the larger operational side—tended to favor operators over analysts. Many directors, including retired general Michael Hayden, have made it a priority to develop a one-agency concept. Yet many officers recognize that "despite all the 'bonding' and cross-fertilization that has taken place between the DA and the DO over the past decade, with symbolic and real successes, the fact remains that the two cultures are very different."[14] The 2015 announcement by CIA Director John Brennan regarding the new agency blueprint seems designed to overcome his continuing separation while safeguarding the unique and valuable features of the separate cultures (see box 10.2).

One reason for the DO's exclusivity, of course, is the risky nature of the operations business. An enduring feature of the DO culture is its long-standing history of doing a president's bidding and suffering the consequences of programs gone awry. Every president since Harry

Truman has relied on the CIA to conduct clandestine operations. Many have also had reasons to distance themselves from those operations when they proved embarrassing or questionable, legally or ethically.[15] Since the Church Committee Senate hearings in the 1970s (during which then–CIA director William Colby revealed a long list of illegal activities), senior DO officers have felt a sense of dread when they have been asked to conduct risky activities to support a president.

Other practitioners have echoed the sentiment that too often zealous policymakers place too much weight on CA. Former CA planners dispute the image of the rogue elephant and cowboys given to the clandestine service. In fact, "officers . . . who manage the covert action programs have always shied away from this side of the business as quickly as a pony shies from a rattlesnake." CA tends not to be career enhancing, and only a few officers warm to the thrill and risk of such operations.[16] The 9/11 Commission Report similarly concluded that the DO was largely unenthusiastic about CA as its leaders thought that it had gotten them in trouble in the past. What critics call risk aversion professionals call common sense or good political judgment.[17] The fact remains that overseas operations are the stock-in-trade by which the DO is measured, whereas the DA's mission as well as its hazards exist largely inside the Washington Beltway.

The Afghan and Iraq operations underline how quickly the CIA's operational role took on a prominent place in the overall US strategy, with all the controversies that sensitive covert collection and paramilitary operations bring with them. Just as Harry Truman found CA an attractive option, so too has President Barack Obama relied heavily on drone attacks in his counterterrorism and counterinsurgency policies. Current CIA director John Brennan, who previously ran these policies from the White House as a deputy national security advisor, reportedly wanted to rein in these programs. Senior DO officers at the time recognized the risks of failure or success such expanded operations carried for those officers conducting them. Hank Crumpton, a former senior DO manager and counterterrorism coordinator, lamented, "If we lose, we're blamed for everything. They hang us. If we win, everybody in the building hates us, and we're finished. . . . Some already hate us because we have resources and the authority."[18]

The 2014 controversy surrounding the release of the Senate Intelligence Committee's critique of CIA-run detention and interrogation programs merely highlights the risks the agency can sometimes undertake to satisfy presidential requests. White House support and congressional oversight committees' initial acquiescence reportedly encouraged the clandestine service to take on an operation for which it was not prepared and to use methods that were judged legal if not necessarily effective.[19] The clash between the legislative and executive branches over the report's findings will probably cause the agency to be more risk averse for the time being.

EXTERNAL FAULT LINE: INTELLIGENCE VERSUS POLICY

How the CIA's cultures and practices interact with the policy world has shifted over the years to reflect a changing view of what intelligence can bring to the national security–making process. In principle the CIA was always there to serve the president. The DO understood this by virtue of having to conduct CAs at the president's behest. However, the DA for many years felt it had to remain more aloof from the policy arena. To be sure, even Sherman Kent appreciated that analysts needed to be cognizant of the policymakers' needs, but he and others cautioned not to get so close as to become advocates of the policy. Over time a gulf developed that undermined the CIA's credibility. As a young analyst in the late 1970s, the author recalls senior analysts proudly saying, "It does not matter whether CIA papers are read downtown, this is what we believe." Yet the national intelligence estimates (NIEs), considered the most authoritative published intelligence, were often ignored or seen merely as the CIA's biased views on what policy ought to be. Policymakers always wanted the facts, but seldom the CIA's opinions.

An intelligence analyst who had the good fortune to work in several presidents' NSCs early in his career, Robert Gates observed this steady decline in intelligence's role. As Gates ascended the career ladder at the CIA to become director of intelligence (the senior-most analytic position), deputy director of the CIA, and ultimately, director of the CIA (DCIA), he steadily spread the message that relevance had to trump independence. Writing about his revelations in the White House, Gates noted,

> CIA knew how foreign policy was made in every country in the world except one—our own. Analysts and their supervisors were oblivious to how information reached the president. They had no idea of the sequence of events preceding a visit by a foreign leader or a presidential trip abroad, or even the agenda of issues the president and his senior advisors would be working during a given week. In short, the distance from CIA's headquarters to the White House was vastly greater than the drive down the George Washington Parkway.[20]

The First Customer: The President

Gates's insights and impact were both profound and far-reaching. By the 1980s the CIA was more focused than ever on providing tailored intelligence that focused explicitly on the president's agenda. The President's Daily Brief (PDB) became the coin of the realm, more so than the NIEs, which still seemed time-consuming to draft, ponderous to read, and prone to miss the mark for many policymakers. Primary attention was paid to what current intelligence was needed to inform the Oval Office and those closest to the president. Senior agency officials established an elaborate process for preparing, reviewing, and briefing the most highly prized—and usually highly classified—intelligence items in the daily meetings with the president and the few other senior cabinet officials designated to receive the PDB. Even after 2005, when the PDB became an IC product run under the auspices of the DNI, this attitude persisted. The CIA proudly noted that as the largest all-source analysis organization, it still provided most of the staffing of the PDB process and produced over 80 percent of the PDB items. One clear advantage of this first-customer approach was that it provided the CIA much more impact and input to senior-level thinking. As the PDB was tightly controlled and therefore not widely read in the US government, leaks also were seldom if ever a problem.[21]

Owing to the agency's unique mission of providing the president with the best intelligence, the CIA's relationship to the NSC has been especially close as well. CIA operators and analysts have served within the NSC regional directorates (e.g., Europe and Russia, the Middle East, or Asia) and its functional directorates responsible for counterterrorism and defense; in a few cases, they have worked directly in the president's and vice president's personal offices. The NSC senior director for intelligence is typically a CIA officer who is the White House focal point for overseeing all intelligence programs and for preparing presidential findings for CA. Most recently, John Brennan, a career analyst before he became DCIA, served as deputy national security advisor for homeland security and had broad responsibilities for counterterrorism policies in the Obama administration. Many senior CIA leaders have spent time in such jobs to gain a presidential perspective on intelligence's role as well as future clout with the White House. Numerous junior CIA officers also have staffed the White House Situation Room, where raw intelligence and diplomatic reporting is received and disseminated throughout the NSC and White House.

Because of its small size, the NSC staff tends to use the CIA as a ready research service. It is not uncommon for NSC directors to commission analyses that can be used in developing internal working papers or briefing memos to the president and national security advisor. Nor is it unusual for NSC directors to arrange for regular weekly briefings or regular phone calls with their counterparts in the CIA and the National Intelligence Council. Such close cooperation between the CIA and the NSC has reinforced a feeling on the part of the CIA that it works primarily for the president. This special relationship has reinforced the CIA officer's self-image of providing national, not departmental, intelligence.

One by-product of closeness to the policy arena was the ever-present—if not blatant—danger of politicization. Like art, politicization is hard to define, but people claim to know it when they see it. Efforts to slant intelligence to please policymakers—either by analysts themselves or through policy-driven pressures or preferences—challenged the analytic culture to its core. Hence, as the CIA moved away from Kent's model of an arm's-length distance from the policy world and into the Gatesian world of policy relevance, the opportunities for politicization seemed to rise accordingly. Indeed, Robert Gates became the target of politicization charges during his 1991 confirmation hearings for CIA director, when he was charged with altering analytic judgments and pressuring analysts to develop an analytic line closer to the Reagan administration's views of the Soviet Union.[22] More recently, former national intelligence officer for the Middle East Paul Pillar has charged that the Bush administration subjected CIA intelligence analysis on Iraq to persistent, if subtle, forms of politicization.[23]

Presidents and the CIA

Despite the CIA's efforts to support the president, few officeholders have been entirely satisfied with the agency's performance. Historically, some presidents enter office distrusting the CIA bureaucracy, either for its analytic views or for its operational methods. President Nixon is said to have blamed the CIA and its analysis for undermining his campaign in 1960. Jimmy Carter—on the heels of the Church investigations and the Watergate scandals—wanted little to do with the agency; he allowed his national security advisor to screen intelligence provided to him, thereby preventing much direct contact with senior agency officers. On the latter point, CIA careerists have preferred to provide intelligence directly to a president. However, strong national security advisors—perhaps best typified by Henry Kissinger—have chosen to preview CIA analysis and select what a president should see. Tony Lake as national security advisor galvanized the DA into reengineering the PDB to be more relevant to the White House agenda; President George W. Bush took it a step further in admonishing CIA officials to bring him "actionable" intelligence.[24] President Obama has continued the daily briefing routine with more of a penchant for reading his briefs on a classified notebook computer. Regardless of the pattern selected, each White House and NSC has pressed the CIA and now the DNI to adapt intelligence support and priorities to match the president's style and interests.

CIA directors have tried to forge close relationships with their first customer to help educate and support the president. John F. Kennedy initially was impressed by Allen Dulles and the CIA's abilities, but the Bay of Pigs incident caused him to find another director and to assign his brother Robert to watch over the CIA and its CA plans thereafter. CIA Director Helms professed never to have developed a close relationship to Presidents Nixon or Johnson, nor was he accorded regular access to either. More recently, directors of central intelligence (DCIs) have found that their clout in the interagency process partly flowed from their closeness to the president and their ability to deliver actionable intelligence. One can contrast the short tenure of James Woolsey—who failed to develop a close relationship with President Clinton—with the nearly seven years that George Tenet served under Presidents Clinton and George W. Bush. Director Tenet's remarkably long tenure was the result of good chemistry between himself and the president, as well as his conscious effort to focus the CIA's analytic skills and CA capabilities to satisfy President Bush's desire for actionable intelligence.

With the creation of the DNI in 2005, the CIA director's relationship with the president has seemingly changed. The relationship between the DCIA and DNI was initially very tense. In May 2006 CIA Director Porter Goss resigned under pressure after continual struggles with the newly appointed DNI, John Negroponte; the CIA's morale was judged to be at a low point by well-informed outsiders, requiring a change at the top.[25] With Goss's departure, Gen. Michael Hayden—formerly the director of the National Security Agency and John Negroponte's deputy DNI—took the reins at the CIA with the goal of restoring the agency's clout and removing this public dissention.

Under President Obama the tables were turned. Obama found himself firing his first DNI, Dennis Blair, after Blair's repeated struggles with CIA Director Leon Panetta. Blair's failure to connect with Obama and his efforts to exert too much operational control over the CIA no doubt contributed to his downfall.[26] The DNI's public comments also revealed, in the minds of many observers, Blair's skepticism regarding the administration's possible overuse of CA in what he believed to be a new era: "When it comes to the activities in which the hand of the U.S. government must be hidden, we must acknowledge that context—the whole surrounding conditions for this activity—have changed in fundamental ways. There are many more overt tools of national power available to attack problems in areas of the world that were previously the place where only covert action could be applicable."[27]

Since then CIA Directors Leon Panetta and John Brennan have further reestablished the agency's clout with the White House and worked out a much better working relationship with the current DNI, James Clapper. No small part of this reconciliation has to do with DNI Clapper's different approach. A career intelligence officer who had previously led both the Defense Intelligence Agency (DIA) and the National Geospatial Intelligence Agency, Clapper prefers to coordinate with the CIA rather than attempt to direct it. This approach, in which the DNI has clear authority over the presentation of intelligence analysis through the PDB while the DCIA has authority over collection and CA programs, seems to be working. Clapper has used his excellent working relationships throughout the IC to reduce tensions with the CIA, but of course, any successor will have to prove him- or herself to the CIA, which often "gets what it wants."[28]

LESSONS FROM A DECADE OF WARS IN AFGHANISTAN AND IRAQ

No single episode can capture the full range of CIA involvement in the interagency process. However, a brief review of what is publicly known about CIA actions in Afghanistan and Iraq can at least illustrate some of the internal and external fault lines at work. From this brief narrative, one can draw some lessons regarding the CIA's relationship to the interagency process.

Into Afghanistan: Are Operations Policy?

Following 9/11 the CIA was tapped to lead the United States into Afghanistan because of its knowledge of the country's tribes and its understanding of Osama bin Laden. More than any other agency, the CIA had been following bin Laden and al-Qaeda and warning of the organization's growing influence and intentions. President Bush gave the CIA unprecedented authority to fight and kill terrorists in not only Afghanistan but also globally, which permitted CIA covert operators more freedom of action than the typical case officer would have. According to Bob Woodward's account, the presidential instructions authorized the CIA to disrupt the al-Qaeda network and other global terrorist networks on a worldwide scale, using lethal CA to keep the US role hidden. Bush also instructed the CIA to operate in Afghanistan with its own paramilitary teams, case officers, and the newly armed Predator drone.[29]

These presidential instructions thrust the CIA into the middle of the War Cabinet and made it not just an observer of policy but also a major operational partner and somewhat independent player alongside the Department of Defense (DOD), the State Department, and the NSC. Inevitably, when the DCIA and his deputy sat at the Principals' Committee and Deputies' Committee meetings, they now held both analytic and operational responsibilities. In his own memoir, CIA Director George Tenet acknowledges that the CIA was built to gather intelligence, not conduct wars. However, now it had a leading role in defeating al-Qaeda, requiring that it devote far more resources and take more risks than the agency had for some time.[30] Despite the president's decision to send the CIA in first, Tenet also claims that "there was a lot of bureaucratic tension" with senior Pentagon officials about who would be in charge. Tenet tried to solve this by signing a memorandum of understanding with Central Command (CENTCOM) that would protect CIA prerogatives.[31] Echoing Tenet's own recollections, former under secretary for policy in the Pentagon Douglas Feith recalled that the CIA's Afghan experts often clashed with the Pentagon's Afghanistan strategy.[32]

When all is said and done, however, the Afghan operations amounted to an unprecedented collaboration between the CIA and the DOD. CIA teams operated more or less independently under an agreement between Secretary Donald Rumsfeld, CENTCOM commanding general Tommy Franks, and CIA Director Tenet but supplied CENTCOM with information on the military tactics, locations, and intentions of Northern Alliance fighters as well as the Taliban. The CIA teams worked closely with Special Forces teams to designate targets. The CIA also operated the armed Predator unmanned aerial vehicles (UAVs) in conjunction with the US Air Force and CENTCOM to target key leaders. The lengthy process by which the CIA and the military reached an accommodation on the Predator's use in Afghanistan is itself a study in bureaucratic politics.[33] Even with this unprecedented degree of cooperation, the military at least concluded that better interagency cooperation—including understanding different agency cultures and capabilities—in post-conflict circumstances still need to be fostered in order to achieve "unity of effort" at the beginning of complex operations.

Iraq: The Intelligence–Policy Fault Line

Iraq is likely to take a special place in the CIA's history, but not simply to highlight failures in assessing Iraq's weapons of mass destruction (WMDs) program. Rather, the CIA's support to policy beginning with the first Gulf War in 1990 through the 2003 invasion and post-conflict environment shows a mixed record of successes and failures—both in its forecasts but also in its ability to support and influence the policymaking process. The tension between policy and intelligence was evident in the 1990 Gulf War but also later in the 2002–3 prewar invasion and post-invasion operations. These episodes exposed the external fault line in a way that is likely to have a lasting impact on how the CIA operates in the interagency in the future.

In August 1990, when Saddam Hussein invaded Kuwait, CIA analysts were surprised, as were many in the first Bush administration. Most accounts have credited the CIA for being on top of the steady buildup of forces on the Iraq–Kuwait border, but only a few CIA officials interpreted Saddam's military movements as actual preparation for war. An ominous memo warning of war was issued late on July 25, 1990. One week later, a full-scale invasion began, far exceeding what most CIA and other US analysts believed Saddam was contemplating. Bush administration advisors, although surprised by this move and the CIA's slowness in warning about it, took seriously the agency's subsequent intelligence reporting and assessments. These reports contributed to a US decision to move forces to Saudi Arabia and prepare Operation Desert Storm to expel Saddam from Kuwait. More significant, CIA analysis of the Iraqi military capabilities—describing its army as battle tested and the fourth largest in the world—proved wrong but influential in debates over a congressional resolution endorsing the plans.[34]

After the war congressional hearings and after-action assessments dissected the CIA's role in preparing the battlefield and in supporting policymakers' decisions. Battlefield commanders complained most about the lack of intelligence sharing by the CIA and other national intelligence agencies, leading to major reforms to push more intelligence to the field. Senior officials, such as Defense Secretary Dick Cheney and Under Secretary Paul Wolfowitz, would continue to harbor the views that they could not rely on the CIA to fully understand a devious enemy.[35] They would become key skeptics of the CIA and major players in the 2003 Iraq War.

Iraq 2003: How Relevant Was Intelligence?

CIA involvement in the Iraq policy process during 2002–3 was dramatically different from its role in 1990. For much of the later period, the CIA stood on the sidelines of the policy process and only in the final phases played any role in the decision to invade. As participants in that policy process tell it, there was little formal discussion of the Iraq problem within the interagency. There were no NSC meetings at which the question of war or peace was formally addressed. Nonetheless, Secretary of Defense Rumsfeld had asked CENTCOM commander Tommy Franks to review his war plan for dealing with Iraq, and the Joint Staff and CENTCOM planners were revising these plans and getting major inputs from the secretary himself in early 2002.

Until summer 2002, however, senior CIA officials felt in the dark about the extent to which serious war planning had begun. Paul Pillar, national intelligence officer for the Middle East at the time, recalled that until August 2002, when Vice President Cheney addressed the Veterans of Foreign Wars and pronounced Iraq to be a serious threat, he was unaware of how actively the White House had been working to prepare for an Iraq operation. That speech caught George Tenet off guard as well. The speech touched on intelligence but had not been shared with CIA officials for clearance; moreover, it went "well beyond what our [CIA] analysis could support."[36] In Tenet's view the military had become convinced by early spring that war was inevitable, while most intelligence analysts came to this conclusion much later. Tenet seems to conclude that by summer 2002 war became inevitable, although the rationale for it was still being fashioned and would ultimately involve the IC's own flawed assessments of Iraq's WMD capabilities.

After CIA Director Tenet and his analysts had become convinced the United States was headed for war, serious analytical work on Iraq—including assessments regarding the regional and domestic consequences of removing Saddam—began. Even then Pillar felt he needed to justify such analysis by first getting a senior State Department official—in this case Richard Haass at Policy Planning—to request these assessments. It would have been difficult to justify any self-initiated studies by the IC, given the sensitivity of the White House and the Pentagon to the CIA, a non-policy agency, questioning the correctness of the emerging Iraq policy. Tenet notes that a prescient CIA paper produced in late August for a national security team meeting in September 2002 was titled "The Perfect Storm: Planning for Negative Consequences of Invading Iraq." By then the battle lines seemed well formed, with Secretary Powell favoring more diplomacy through the UN and other advisors convinced that diplomacy was a road to nowhere. A subsequent Deputies' Committee meeting the following week focused on developing the arguments for "Why Iraq?"

On the CIA's operations side, the unease with the sudden decision for war was also noticeable. During the Clinton administration Iraq had taken a backseat to other higher priority collection concerns like Iran and North Korea. The US reliance on UN inspections—aided by some tip-offs provided by US intelligence—was deemed sufficient to monitor Iraq's disarmament. Containment, the stated US policy, had effectively taken Saddam off the radar. Yet when Saddam kicked out the UN inspectors in 1998, the CIA found itself without major sources. Now, in late 2001 and early 2002, there was an urgent need to know as much about Iraq as possible. Many accounts of the later Iraq WMD intelligence failure recount the absence of good HUMINT in reaching judgments on Saddam's WMD program. But the CIA's Iraq Operations Group (IOG) suddenly ramped up to develop whatever sources it could on Saddam's WMD program.[37]

Perhaps the most important intelligence and policy dispute had nothing to do with WMD but rather focused on the alleged links between al-Qaeda and Iraq. Ever since the 9/11 attacks, there had been rumored reports of senior al-Qaeda connections to Iraq's security services. CIA analysts doubted such connections existed, and CIA Director Tenet himself said, "CIA found absolutely no linkage between Saddam and 9/11."[38] Over the course of 2002, the CIA produced a series of papers to assess how close a connection there was or was not.[39]

Civilian defense officials firmly believed that the CIA had dismissed important information and had interpreted the data incorrectly. Then–under secretary Feith led the charge in challenging the agency's judgments regarding the al-Qaeda–Iraq links. To bolster his case, he had intelligence professionals on his policy staff critique CIA analysis; the Pentagon believed the CIA was filtering out data that did not support a benign view of Iraq. Tenet found this accusation "entirely inappropriate" and cautioned senior defense officials that this issue needed to be handled by professional analysts in intelligence channels rather than by policy officials with agendas. This was perhaps the most blatant case of "politicization," but it was driven more by policymakers than by biased analysts.

Wartime Intelligence: Impact on Organizational Culture

The decade of war in Afghanistan and Iraq calls for some assessment of how it has altered the CIA's operations and analysis. One way of thinking about this is to acknowledge that the CIA's original mission was to provide strategic warning and analysis, based on the collection and analysis of all-source intelligence. The CIA was never intended to become like other departmental intelligence agencies, which were tasked to support specific diplomatic or military operations in the way the State Department's Bureau of Intelligence and Research (INR) or the DIA did. And yet the twenty-first-century wars have transformed the CIA's mission to become both a war-fighting and counterterrorism support organization. The combination of 9/11 and the Iraq and Afghanistan conflicts propelled CIA operators to be hunters and killers of terrorists and insurgency groups. CA has expanded as a principal mission, in some ways supplanting the collection of foreign intelligence as the DO's key mission. The Special Activities Division, where CA is planned and executed, has assumed a much larger role in the DO organization. One sign of this is the reported development of a major "lessons learned" study of CA programs, suggesting this is likely to be a major ongoing activity for which best practices should be developed and implemented.[40]

Likewise, the DA culture is shifting from its traditional focus on strategic warning of broader trends to more tactical support to military and counterterrorism operations. Over the past decade many analysts have been encouraged to take rotational assignments to the DO-led centers focused on counterterrorism and counter-proliferation. There, they work hand in glove with operators to target, disrupt, or defeat terrorist or WMD networks. The "targeting" analysis discipline has now entered the lexicon of the analytic profession, and analysts are promoted as much for bringing down a terrorist group as for alerting policymakers to an emerging threat or potential surprise. Analysts, to be sure, find this type of work more rewarding, as the feedback is immediate and usually positive, compared with the often dismissive or challenging reaction of policymakers to analysis that potentially complicates their policy agenda.

The question is how far should the CIA allow itself to be drawn into the policy realm through its expanded CA responsibilities and its ongoing tactical support to operations, as opposed to conducting more strategic and forward-looking analysis? Several past instances of intelligence failure suggest that too much focus on operational matters can blind analysts to important strategic threats. The investigation that followed the 9/11 attacks found that the Counterterrorism Center had failed to conduct any strategic analysis of al-Qaeda after 1997, even though the center had taken over that responsibility from the National Intelligence Council; the center's focus on continuous operations was in part responsible for inadequate attention to the "strategic threat" that should have been conveyed to the White House. More recently, the CIA and other agencies have been faulted for not understanding the rampant spread of unrest in the Arab world—that is, Arab Spring revolutions in Tunisia, Libya, Egypt, and Syria, among others. One explanation provided by a few policymakers is that so much attention has been placed on counterterrorism operations in those countries that there was less emphasis on intelligence collection and analysis regarding the socioeconomic trends that led to the unrest in 2011. Similar complaints have been made by senior military commanders in Afghanistan who believed that analysts and collectors were too focused on terrorists and insurgents to understand the deeper sociocultural context that was producing those threats.[41]

LESSONS LEARNED: INTELLIGENCE MATTERS, BUT NOT ALWAYS

The CIA's performance over the past decade of war provides a number of useful lessons about the relationship between intelligence and policy. Among the most important is the difficulty in drawing a line between what constitutes objective intelligence and policy advocacy. When vital issues of war and peace are at stake, strong-minded policymakers will view CIA analysis influencing the debate and becoming either a useful weapon or a major complication. The CIA's involvement in the policy process, then, requires that intelligence officials acknowledge the inherently political nature of their work. To be naive about how intelligence is likely to be used can allow the CIA to become a victim of the contending forces on both sides of a disputed policy.

A second lesson is that the CIA will periodically be at the interagency table not solely as an intelligence advisor but also as a policy player. Having its own programs—covert to be sure—to manage, fund, and implement gives it a voice alongside the State and Defense Departments, although this is not sufficiently appreciated. The CIA, not surprisingly, is a bureaucracy with its own priorities, missions, and jurisdictions. So when conflicts or controversy over programs such as detainee interrogations arise within the interagency process, it can be expected to defend its views no less firmly than the Pentagon, the services, or the State Department defend theirs.

In an era when CA is seen as an important instrument for a president, the CIA becomes the executive agent for parts of a presidential decision and will have to assume a policy-implementing role. Legitimately, it will at times question whether other policymakers are relying too much on this instrument—when other parts of the policy might not be working—and worry that it will be instructed to conduct operations that will eventually come back to haunt the agency. Other policymakers naturally may find the CIA less eager to step forward to implement risky policies for which it is responsible, which is no different from the Pentagon's or the State Department's reactions to presidential initiatives for which they are going to be held responsible. In the wake of the controversies surrounding the CIA's detention and interrogation programs, there will no doubt be a greater reluctance to take risks in the absence of a clear and present danger.

Third, whenever the CIA is actively supporting presidential policies with major operations as well as with analytic analysis, it will be a challenge to distinguish when senior CIA officials are speaking as policy advocates or as analysts. Particularly for other policy agencies, as seen in the case of Afghanistan, this becomes a murky area. Non-intelligence participants in the interagency process may resent this infringement on their turf and not see such fine distinctions being made by intelligence officials. They particularly resent former intelligence officials or their surrogates using the media to argue their case. Periodically, DCIAs have found themselves becoming policy advocates, like John McCone's advocacy during Kennedy's Executive Committee deliberations over the Cuban Missile Crisis, or William Casey's strong policy views on Central America and the Soviet Union. Former CIA directors Panetta and Petraeus reportedly supported early intervention into Syria, which demonstrates how the line between intelligence and policy gets blurred at the most senior levels.[42]

Fourth, formal intelligence is not necessarily the most important information in forming a policy. Administrations and presidents rely on a range of opinions and information channels to reach important decisions. In many cases the CIA's analytic views will not count or be as instrumental as others' views in the policy community. Often policymakers come into government with strongly held opinions; they know what they think, and they cannot be persuaded by CIA analysis. Indeed, as other chapters in this book make clear, information flowing from a variety of think tanks and advocacy groups can be just as influential as anything the CIA might produce. Of course, policymakers have every right to accept or reject CIA analysis. Indeed, policymakers also have a right to challenge CIA analysis. There is a fine line between a decision maker's pressing analysts to explain and justify their conclusions and forcing changes in those judgments.

Fifth, in the real world intelligence is never perfect, but it is seldom an entire failure. Intelligence can count on having both successes and failures on whatever issue the inter-agency is focused. Having provided strategic warning but no tactical warning of the 9/11 attacks, the CIA restored its reputation in the rapid implementation of a CA plan to bring down the Taliban, disrupt al-Qaeda's worldwide operations, and ultimately bring bin Laden to justice. Policy agencies, not to mention Congress, the media, and the public, will tend to focus more on what the agency got wrong than on what it got right.

Finally, the CIA and the IC more generally cannot provide good intelligence support if the interagency process is not operating in a transparent and open fashion. Having regular inter-agency discussion of policy options, during which issues are debated, allows CIA analysts to perform their role of producing analysis on those issues. When that interagency process is more informal, kept within a small circle, or entirely hidden, the CIA is unable to understand what policy options are being considered and cannot produce timely and relevant intelligence. Analysts are not prone to guessing about whether policy options are under consideration and are reluctant to rely on media stories to explain where US policy stands at any given moment. When operating in a vacuum, they cannot, in Kent's words, raise the level of policy discourse. Hence, the CIA's unique role of serving the president rests on the national security system operating in a transparent fashion. As the national security enterprise evolves, efforts to ensure a healthy exchange of diverse opinions within the interagency process is one guarantee that the agency will play a positive role in formulating successful foreign policies.

NOTES

1. Amy Zegart, *Flawed by Design: The Evolution of CIA, JCS and NSC* (Stanford, CA: Stanford University Press, 1999).

2. NSC Directive 4/A (December 14, 1947) established the CIA's CA responsibilities with political guidance from the State Department. Secretary George Marshall did not wish the State Department to be running these operations, nor did the military see it as its mission. Michael Warner's review of the origins of the CIA's authorities discusses the changing focus and continuing ambiguity of the CIA director's responsibilities. See Michael Warner, "Central Intelligence: Origins and Reforms," in *Intelligence and the National Security Strategist*, ed. Roger Z. George and Robert D. Kline (Lanham, MD: Rowman & Littlefield, 2006), 47–56.

3. Richard Helms, *A Look over My Shoulder: A Life in the Central Intelligence Agency* (New York: Random House, 2003), vii.

4. Cited in Jack Davis, "The Kent-Kendall Debate of 1949," *Studies in Intelligence* 36, no. 5 (1992): 91–103.

5. See John Hedley, "The Evolution of Intelligence Analysis," in *Analyzing Intelligence: Origins, Obstacles, and Innovations*, ed. Roger Z. George and James B. Bruce (Washington, DC: Georgetown University Press, 2008), 19–34.

6. The creation in 2000 of a Sherman Kent School for Intelligence Analysis was recognition of the need for a specialized set of training courses for analysts to improve their analytic methods. The school would also instill the sense of analytical integrity and transparency in the workforce that would protect the reputation of the CIA as providing independent and objective assessments to presidents and their advisors. The school was named after Sherman Kent, symbolizing the importance attached by the DA culture to Kent's legacy of objectivity and professionalism.

7. Rob Johnston, *Analytic Culture in the U.S. Intelligence Community: An Ethnographic Study* (Washington, DC: Center for the Study of Intelligence, 2005), 27.

8. Robert Gates, *From the Shadows: The Ultimate Insider's Story of Five Presidents and How They Won the Cold War* (New York: Simon & Schuster, 1996), 33.

9. Tim Weiner's *Legacy of Ashes: The History of the CIA* (London: Penguin, 2011) argues that secrecy is used to hide agency failures and to avoid accountability.

10. Charles G. Cogan, "The In-Culture of the DO," in George and Kline, *Intelligence and the National Security Strategist*, 213. The DO logo is a spear that the OSS had adopted as its logo from its military roots to reflect the martial nature of its work; its meaning was that intelligence must be the first line of defense and the leading edge of any military operation.

11. Russell Jack Smith, *The Unknown CIA: My Three Decades with the Agency* (Washington, DC: Pergamon-Brassey's, 1989), 140. Smith boasted that Dick Helms occasionally told outsiders that the clandestine service actually had a supporting, not primary, role, describing his DI as having the primary role of informing the president. Even so, the clandestine service maintained far larger budgets and personnel and considered itself the muscle of the CIA. Smith also recounts that analysts characterized "the 'spooks' as reckless blunderers who were paranoid about secrecy, especially as it pertained to their reports, which, in the view of the analysts were often trivial and second- or third-rate compared to State Department reporting or intercepted communications of the National Security Agency" (p. 9).

12. Greg Miller, "CIA Director John Brennan Considering Sweeping Reorganization," *Washington Post*, November 20, 2014, www.washingtonpost.com/world/national-security/cia-director-john-brennan -considering-sweeping-organizational-changes/2014/11/19/fa85b320–6ffb-11e4-ad12–3734c461eab6 _story.html.

13. Gary Berntsen, *Jawbreaker: The Attack on Bin Ladin and Al Qaeda* (New York: Crown, 2005), 9. The same complaint was made by longtime case officer Robert Baer when a senior DA manager was selected to become the head of the DO (itself a deviation from the usual practice). "He knew nothing about operations . . . never met or recruited an agent" and, more important, handed out overseas jobs to people (analysts) whose primary qualifications were being briefers, working at the NSC, or being close to the DCI. See Robert Baer, *See No Evil* (New York: Crown, 2001), 233. Likewise, another senior DO officer has written similarly dismissive comments about the DA's importance: "Without [the DO] the analysts would have nothing out of the ordinary to analyze, the technical experts would have no one to invent for, and human resources would be twiddling their thumbs with no double agents to unearth and fewer eccentric individuals to manage." See Tyler Drumheller, *On the Brink: An Insider's Account of How the White House Compromised American Intelligence* (New York: Carroll & Graf, 2006), 138.

14. Cogan, "In-Culture of the DO," 214.

15. William Daugherty, a former CA operator, has written the definitive look at the presidential role in mounting covert operations. See William J. Daugherty, *Executive Secrets: Covert Action and the Presidency* (Lexington: University of Kentucky Press, 2004). He asserts that even Presidents Carter and Clinton, who openly distrusted the CIA and the use of covert operations, ultimately relied on them when other overt methods proved insufficient.

16. Ibid., 4. Gary Schroen, in his own book on the Afghan War, also describes himself as one of the few who thrived on these sorts of operations, which did not necessarily earn him promotions within the agency. See Gary Schroen, *First In: An Insider's Account of How the CIA Spearheaded the War on Terror in Afghanistan* (New York: Ballantine, 2005).

17. 9/11 Commission, *Final Report of the National Commission on Terrorist Attacks upon the United States* (New York: W.W. Norton, 2003), 351.

18. Henry R. Crumpton, *The Art of Intelligence: Lessons from a Life in the CIA's Clandestine Service* (New York: Penguin Press, 2012), 186. Crumpton, a career DO officer, also recounts in this book the internal CIA and interagency battles over whether to take the risk of leading the counterterrorism effort in Afghanistan, supporting other presidentially approved CA programs, including arming the Predator drones and operating the detention and interrogation program; he laments that what one president approves the next might condemn, which in fact happened.

19. Scott Shane, "Report Portrays a Broken CIA Devoted to a Failed Approach," *New York Times*, December 9, 2014, www.nytimes.com/2014/12/10/world/senate-torture-report-shows-cia-infighting-over -interrogation-program.html.

20. Gates, *From the Shadows*, 56.

21. As the PDB is for the president, it is regarded as having the protections of executive privilege. As of this writing only two PDBs—heavily sanitized—have been revealed as part of the 9/11 Commission investigations. Even commissioners had to fight to gain limited access to the PDBs written during the period under scrutiny.

22. Following his confirmation hearings, Gates addressed the workforce to acknowledge the dangers of politicization, and he set up a task force to investigate what could be done about the problem.

He further created an independent ombudsman for politicization, a position held by a retired senior officer who would conduct annual surveys of politicization and be available to any officer who felt he or she was coming under management or policy pressure to alter an analytic line. This position is still operating and was active during and after the Iraq War controversies.

23. Paul Pillar, *Intelligence and U.S. Foreign Policy: Iraq, 9/11, and Misguided Reform* (New York: Columbia University Press, 2011), 163–67.

24. "Actionable" in this context refers to intelligence related to a presidential interest or policy that would permit the president to reach a decision regarding a policy or take some action in support of it. A perennial problem has been intelligence reporting that suggests an event or trend is occurring, which presidents view as inevitable or for which there is no obvious US response.

25. David Ignatius, "The CIA at Rock Bottom," *Washington Post*, May 7, 2006.

26. Max Fisher, "Why Director of National Intelligence Resigned," *AtlanticWire*, May 21, 2010, www.theatlanticwire.com/opinions/view/opinion/Why-Director-of-National-Intelligence-Blair-Resigned-3690.

27. Dennis C. Blair, remarks at the State of Intelligence Reform Conference, Bipartisan Policy Center, Washington, DC, April 6, 2010, www.dni.gov/files/documents/Newsroom/Speeches%20and%20Interviews/20100406_5_speech.pdf.

28. Ibid.

29. Bob Woodward, *Bush at War* (New York: Simon & Schuster, 2002), 101.

30. George Tenet, *At the Center of the Storm: My Years at the CIA* (New York: Harper Collins, 2007), 213.

31. Ibid.

32. Douglas Feith, *War and Decision: Inside the Pentagon at the Dawn of the War on Terror* (New York: Harper, 2008), 78.

33. Numerous accounts by both CIA and NSC officials recount the interagency disputes over how to develop, fund, and operate the unmanned drone programs designed to track and eventually kill terrorists. George Tenet's testimony to the 9/11 Commission acknowledged that the US Air Force and the CIA have to negotiate the cost-sharing arrangements of damaged or lost Predators. Richard Clarke separately claims this dispute delayed deployment to the field. Other NSC counterterrorism staff claim the CIA was also worried that running the Predator program would endanger CIA operatives on the ground. Finally, when "arming" the Predator arose after 9/11, there were arguments both within the DO and with the Joint Staff over the pros and cons of allowing the CIA to operate a "kinetic" system. See George Tenet's *Written Statement for the Record of the Director of Central Intelligence Before the National Commission on Terrorist Attacks upon the United States*, March 24, 2004, 15; Daniel Benjamin and Steven Simon, *The Age of Sacred Terror* (New York: Random House, 2002), 321–22; and Crumpton, *Art of Intelligence*, 156–57.

34. According to several eyewitnesses to this episode on both the congressional and executive branch sides, the most alarming briefings came from the DIA, which implied huge casualties would result. Nonetheless, when the invasion proved to be successful, congressional accounts recorded senior senators as most upset by the CIA's analysis, and few criticized the DIA for its alarmist analysis of Iraq's conventional capabilities. CIA briefings, along with many others provided by the DIA, to congressional intelligence committees convinced some key Democratic leaders, like Senators David Boren and Sam Nunn, not to support the administration's request for a resolution backing the use of military force to oust Saddam from Kuwait.

35. John Diamond, *CIA and the Culture of Failure* (Stanford, CA: Stanford University Press, 2008), 180.

36. CIA Director Tenet claims there was never a single meeting at which the central questions were discussed. But Pentagon officials have since argued that the president already knew the minds of his key advisors and didn't need such a meeting. Under Secretary of Defense Douglas Feith also explains that disagreements between Defense, on the one hand, and the CIA and State, on the other, led National Security Advisor Condoleezza Rice to avoid the debate rather than resolve it; hence, Feith concluded that this allowed the "bureaucracy's innate bias in favor of inaction."

37. James Risen, *State of War: The Secret History of the CIA and the Bush Administration* (New York: Free Press, 2006), 76–83. Elsewhere, Risen recounts a senior-level meeting in November 2002, when the CIA's IOG representatives met with the agency's senior operators in Europe. There was clearly

tension between those in the field and the headquarters, where the sense of urgency was far higher. At this meeting IOG stressed that field officers needed to "drop their reluctance to engage on Iraq. War was just a few months away."

38. Tenet, *At the Center of the Storm*, 341.

39. One June 2002 paper, titled "Iraq and Al Qaeda: Interpreting a Murky Relationship," purposely took a devil's-advocate position in trying to find connections; it provoked such divisions among the CIA's regional and terrorism analysts that some complained to the CIA's ombudsman for analytical integrity. Two later papers issued in September received similar testy reactions from policymakers, according to George Tenet. Other participants in those DOD–CIA meetings confirm that contentious but cordial differences arose. They also highlight that the CIA's terrorism analysts were more comfortable reaching forward-leaning judgments as they seldom get corroboration for some sensational reports; the CIA's regional analysts typically take a skeptical view of single reports and demand more independent corroboration. Hence, these different analytical styles set up internal CIA tensions quite apart from the policy–intelligence frictions that existed at the time.

40. Mark Mazetti, "CIA Study of Covert Aid Fueled Skepticism about Helping Syrian Rebels," *New York Times*, October 14, 2014.

41. CIA director and later defense secretary Leon Panetta and International Security and Assistance Force (ISAF) intelligence chief Maj. Gen. Michael Flynn have made these points. See Leon Panetta, *Worthy Fights: A Memoir of Leadership in War and Peace* (New York: Penguin Random House, 2014); and Michael Flynn, Matt Pottinger, and Paul D. Batchelor, *Fixing Intel: A Blueprint for Making Intelligence Relevant in Afghanistan* (Washington, DC: Center for a New American Strategy, January 2010).

42. Adam Entous, "Obama Blocked Rebel Arms," *Wall Street Journal*, February 12, 2013, www.wsj.com/articles/SB10001424127887324906004578290060794022912.

CHAPTER 11

The Evolving FBI

Becoming a New National Security Enterprise Asset

Harvey Rishikof and Brittany Albaugh

Meeting the strategic goals requires that the FBI supplement its reactive
capability with bold and innovative proactive efforts designed to deter
and prevent—to the maximum extent feasible—criminal activities that
threaten vital American interests.
—Draft FBI Strategic Plan, 1998

The Bureau is designed, and has always operated, as law enforcement and
as an intelligence agency. . . . History has shown that we are most effective
in protecting the U.S. when we perform these two missions in tandem.
—FBI Response to "A Review of the FBI's Handling of Intelligence
Information Prior to the September 11, 2001 Attacks"
Special Report, November 2004

We remain focused on defending the United States against terrorism, foreign
intelligence, and cyber threats; upholding and enforcing the criminal laws of
the United States; protecting civil rights and civil liberties, and providing
leadership and criminal justice to federal, state, municipal and international
agencies and partners.
—Director James Comey's statement before
the House Appropriations Committee, 2014

The Federal Bureau of Investigation (FBI) plays a unique role in the national security enterprise. It is the domestic intelligence agency that has primary responsibility for counterintelligence, counterterrorism, and espionage. Created in the early twentieth century, it has been the envy of many law enforcement agencies owing to its reputation and élan; however, to its critics it has at times stepped outside its boundaries, and it has been obstinate in how it shares information in the interagency process because of its criminal law enforcement mission. To others it is too constrained in the manner it carries out its missions owing to its commitment to "American legal ethics."[1]

In this new era of threats, the FBI has been challenged to adapt its law enforcement organization and culture of the past hundred-plus years to address new transnational issues that are both domestic and foreign. In 2014 the bureau's fact sheet cited its "primary function" had changed from "law enforcement" to "national security."[2] This has not been an easy transformation for a number of reasons, among them historic legal restrictions, policy guidance, and organizational culture. While the bureau addressed issues of foreign intelligence and the war on terror, it still placed the most emphasis on domestic security. To many observers the question of whether a domestic intelligence organization might be needed to replace the FBI turns on whether the FBI's culture proves to be too resistant to change.

New missions have created new challenges. The challenges presented in the world of cybersecurity are the most significant faced since the 1920s, when the automobile was introduced, giving criminals the ability to travel across the country easily.[3] Cyber presents not only a new mission but also a new battlefield. At risk are Americans' personal information, trade secrets, and critical infrastructure, which could be attacked by other nation-states, terrorist organizations, or hackers. In 2008 a presidential directive established the National Cyber Investigative Joint Task Force (NCIJTF). The NCIJTF is administered by the FBI but comprises nearly two-dozen federal intelligence, military, and law enforcement agencies.[4] The task force is able to combine all of the agencies' resources to broaden the scope to the entire cyber landscape instead of relying on individual investigations. In 2014 FBI and Department of Justice (DOJ) investigations led to the indictment of five Chinese military hackers,[5] disruption of the Game-Over Zeus Botnet,[6] and the public accusation of North Korea for hacking Sony.[7] Most recently, FBI has taken a leading role in investigating the Russian hacking of the Democratic National Committee and state electoral systems.

To understand the FBI's role in the national security enterprise, this chapter will trace the historic origins and development of the pre-9/11 FBI culture and the challenges 9/11 presented. In the process the chapter will assess how successful the reforms of its culture have been and suggest recommendations for additional reforms. To some experts the recent reforms still remain incomplete and insufficient and may prove to be unworkable, requiring even more institutional rearrangement. As the cliché goes, the FBI remains a work in progress—but a major attack on the United States, either kinetic or cyber, would renew the debate over whether an independent, dedicated domestic intelligence agency is required.[8]

THE FBI CULTURE: SIZE, STRUCTURE, AND ETHOS

The bureau's history, organizational culture, and capabilities have left legacies of views and behaviors that make FBI agents stand out in the law enforcement community. They are professional, competent, and desirous of being in charge of investigations. Furthermore, unlike the CIA, the FBI can arrest suspects or targets and testify in court. These capabilities have reinforced a tough, court-oriented approach to evidence and prosecutions among agents. This institutional characteristic has both enhanced and hindered an integrated approach to national security.

Origins: The Need for a Federal Law Enforcement Agency

In the beginning of the twentieth century, there was no systematic way to enforce federal law across the nation.[9] Few federal criminal laws existed, and the few federal law enforcement agencies, such as the Secret Service, were limited in resources. The advent of the Model-T automobile created a cross-state gateway that handicapped local police, who had no authority outside their states. Meanwhile, the growth of a small anarchist movement that assassinated President William McKinley finally pushed the government to create a federal law enforcement agency.

At its origin the FBI would borrow agents from the Secret Service for investigations, until Congress banned this practice in 1908. Attorney General George W. Wickersham named the unit—the Bureau of Investigation. The agents were "special" because Congress, in its legislation, had created a subcategory for "special federal crimes." For its first fifteen years, the FBI focused on white-collar crime, civil rights, antitrust, and fraud cases. In 1910, with the passage of the Mann Act, a law to halt interstate prostitution and human trafficking, the FBI became the lead agency and gained resources. With World War I came the passage of the Espionage Act and the Sabotage Act, and the FBI took primary jurisdiction for these federal crimes. To tackle its new missions, the FBI grew to 360 agents and support staff.

The continuing riddle for the FBI over the years has been how to balance its multiple missions while protecting and respecting the right of privacy and constitutional norms. This challenge arose following World War I, when domestic terrorism rocked the postwar celebrations and tranquility. Anarchists' bombs in front of Attorney General A. Mitchell Palmer's home and on Wall Street resulted in the infamous "Palmer Raids," whereby over a few years thousands were arrested without warrants in a preventive action. Other bombs were planted that same day in eight other cities, and over the next few months, bombs were intercepted in the mail.[10] Massive arrests followed the bombings and attempted bombings, and both President Herbert Hoover and young FBI agent J. Edgar Hoover, who was in charge of the investigations, were widely criticized for civil rights violations given who had been targeted. During the next few decades, a wave of professional criminals courtesy of Prohibition and the emergence of the Ku Klux Klan (KKK) generated more work for the FBI.

During the Teapot Dome scandal in the 1920s, it was discovered that the FBI had spied on members of Congress, and calls for reform again were made. The attorney general was fired, and the new attorney general, Harlan Fiske Stone, promoted twenty-nine-year-old J. Edgar Hoover to lead the reform. With Hoover at the helm as the new director, a series of reforms were put into place to "modernize" the FBI. Agents were fired. A strict code of conduct was instituted with background checks for hires. Prospective agents had to be between the ages of twenty-five and thirty-five and had to be physically fit (lawyers and accountants were preferred). Within five years Hoover had shrunk the agency from 650 agents to 441. But the legend of a tightly organized, professional, scientific, and special police force was forged.

With World War II President Franklin D. Roosevelt expanded the primarily domestic intelligence–focused agency to handle overseas intelligence matters. Since there was no CIA and the Office of Strategic Services did not come into existence until 1942, the FBI created its Special Intelligence Service. During the next few war years, over 340 undercover personnel were sent to Central and South America. By 1946 the FBI had assembled an impressive list of achievements: it had identified 887 Axis spies, 281 propaganda agents, 222 agents smuggling strategic war matériel, 30 saboteurs, and 24 secret Axis radio stations.[11] After the war the FBI continued its domestic focus in its anticommunism investigations, such as the Rosenberg spy case in the 1950s, and in the KKK cases in the 1960s.

The advent of left-wing movements such as the civil rights movement, the Weathermen, the Black Panthers, women's liberation, and the anti–Vietnam War protests coalesced into a broad counterculture threat for the FBI. Without any guidelines for national security investigations, the FBI launched the Counterintelligence Program (Cointelpro). The National Security Council had approved the Cointelpro in 1956 to oppose the Communist Party. The program was slowly expanded to include the Socialist Party, the KKK, the Black Panthers, and eventually "leftist" groups.[12] The use of infiltration techniques against and the discrediting of left-wing protests such as Dr. Martin Luther King Jr.'s civil rights demonstrations, however, were a clear abuse of investigative power. Although these techniques had been sanctioned by the attorney general and were legitimate when used against communists and the KKK, they violated constitutional norms of the First Amendment when focused on protest groups. The 1970s congressional investigations of the FBI and CIA by Senator Frank Church and Representative Otis Pike produced a new attorney general, Edward Levi, who issued clear guidelines for domestic security investigations. Only protesting groups breaking the law or clearly engaging in violent activity were to be investigated. With the new guidelines the number of domestic security investigations fell dramatically from 21,000 in 1973 to 626 in 1976.[13] In addition, in 1978 the Foreign Intelligence Surveillance Act (FISA), establishing a special court to hear requests for warrants and helping to establish the new rules for domestic foreign surveillance, was passed.

The history of FBI overreaction and congressional reprimand, particularly in the 1970s, made the FBI "more cautious and more willing to strictly delineate between national security and criminal investigations."[14] Commingling investigative techniques used against both foreign threats and domestic protest movements had resulted in severe rebukes and a national loss of public reputation. It led to the so-called wall between law enforcement activities and foreign intelligence operations. Ironically, this structure of controlling excessive domestic investigative aggressiveness proved to be a political disaster post 9/11, as the FBI was subsequently attacked for not having more fully integrated its foreign national security and criminal investigations (see box 11.1).

FBI Culture—Becoming the Special Agent

To appreciate the culture of the FBI, it is necessary to understand the incentive system of promotion and status for special agents. The goal of most agents is to become a special agent

---

BOX 11.1
Recent Record on Counterintelligence

The FBI's hardworking agents have occasionally strayed over the line in the name of protecting the public and have had "chalk on their cleats." The FBI has been rightly praised for prosecuting high-profile espionage cases—against John Walker, Jonathan Jay Pollard, Larry Wu-tai Chin, Ronald William Pelton, Aldrich Ames, Harold Nicholson, and Ana Belen Montes. In the domestic terrorism arena, the capture of Eric Rudolph (the abortion clinic bomber), Theodore Kaczynski (the Unabomber), and Timothy McVeigh (the Oklahoma bomber) demonstrated a commitment to marshal resources over a long period. The Anthrax attack in early 2001 killing five Americans resulted in an investigation over seven years ending with the suicide of the major suspect, Dr. Bruce Ivins, and the dropping of the investigation against all other subjects.

In contrast is the list of celebrated cases involving missteps: the laboratory investigation over whistle-blower Frederic Whitehurst's allegations of "cops in lab coats"; the shootings at Ruby Ridge; the Waco, Texas, assault; the Centennial Olympic Park bombing and the false Richard Jewel accusation; the botched investigation of Wen Ho Lee as a spy stealing nuclear secrets; and finally, the discovery of FBI agent Robert Hanssen as a double-agent working for the Russians.[a] This medley of errors has conspired to create a negative image of the bureau as an effective counterintelligence agency; moreover, the more recent Bradley/Chelsea Manning and Edward Snowden leaks have intensified attention on insider threat programs.

[a]It is instructive to remember that many of these individuals operated undetected for years: Walker over seventeen years, Ames over seven years, Hanssen over twenty-one years, and Montes over fifteen years. See Michelle Van Cleave, "The NCIX and the National Counterintelligence Mission: What Has Worked, What Has Not, and Why" (Washington, DC: Project on National Security Reform, 2007), www.pnsr.org/wp-content/uploads/2007/12/michelle.pdf.

in charge (SAC), head of a field office (FO), or "captain of one's own ship." The journey begins at the FBI Training Academy at Quantico, where the recruits are given a twenty-week course of instruction. The overall training at the academy is over 800 hours, including classes in four concentrations: academics, case exercises, firearms training, and operational skills.[15] Following the initial training, agents are assigned to one of six career paths: intelligence, counterintelligence, counterterrorism, criminal, cyber, or specialty.[16]

A typical FBI career includes tours as an agent, desk officer, unit chief, section chief, and assistant division director, with multiple tours at headquarters (HQ) in Washington, DC, along with as many as five different FO assignments. Agents usually will spend only two to three years in one FO, and then they will move to a new city. The intent is to prevent agents from becoming too close to local officials so that they retain their distance in public corruption cases. For many years only agents had blue badges; the rest of the support staff was white so agents could pick each other out quickly in a meeting. Support staff, analysts, and so on felt like second-class citizens.[17] Although the badges have been changed in recent years, SACs still have a gold badge. A SAC is the equivalent of a general officer in the army or an admiral in the navy, and the gold badge reflects a senior position. To become a SAC, an agent has climbed up through the ranks.

Toughness is part of the FBI image and culture. At Quantico the recruits are given boxing gloves, headgear, and mouth guards and arranged in circles in the gym, according to weight, to fight each other.[18] For many this is the first time they have been in a physical fight. Firearms training includes using a pistol, a carbine, and a shotgun; trainees fire approximately 5,000 rounds of ammunition during their training.[19] They must pass a firearms qualification test and will carry a .40-caliber Glock 22, a 9mm Smith & Wesson, or a 9mm SIG Sauer. The bureau's operational style remains hierarchical and quasi-military-like. As one recruit recently noted about Quantico, "Until you get there, it's hard to explain. . . . It was the demands, the pressure, the lifestyle. It's much more of a military-type organization than I expected. A lot of the agents are police or military. I wasn't used to calling people 'sir' and 'ma'am.'"[20]

Trainees also receive seventy hours of instruction on a critical FBI skill: interviewing and interrogation. Over the course of their careers, they will probably conduct thousands of interviews and interrogations, honing their skills as questioners. The FBI inculcated the ethos of a law enforcement agency; the fact that it is an agency that makes arrests is enshrined as part of the early training. The object of the interrogation is to preserve evidence and admissions for an eventual trial. For many years the key to success in the FBI was a criminal-focused career path in the Criminal Division based on significant cases and successful trials. The counterintelligence or counterespionage jobs, although somewhat glamorous, did not have the status or resources of the criminal components. Agents made names for themselves by making cases, making arrests, and demonstrating ability to "get things done" in the field leading to criminal convictions.

Beyond the Special Agent

The 9/11 Commission Report found that the FBI had not shifted enough human resources to counterterrorism (twice as many agents remained devoted to drug enforcement); the new division of analysis had "faltered" (lacking appropriate education and expertise); and FBI intelligence collection was weak (insufficient translators or appropriate tracking of source reporting).[21] With the shift of priorities from criminal investigation to national security, the FBI has increased the number of positions beyond the special agent. Hiring talented people to be intelligence analysts is even more important as analysts are the front line in protecting America's security. Since 9/11 the FBI has more than tripled the number of intelligence analysts. While a significant number of staffers still comes from military or law enforcement backgrounds, increasingly recruits come from other intellectual disciplines—the sciences, computer technology, accounting, or intelligence. Increased hiring of information technology professionals and experts in applied science, engineering, and technology is intended to support FBI investigations, provide state-of-the-art identification and information services, and allow work with the most advanced technologies. In addition to hiring the people behind the technology, the FBI has also acquired better hardware and software.[22]

Capabilities—Small but Focused

The FBI comprises FBI HQ and a network of FOs. FBI HQ, located in Washington, DC, provides centralized operational, policy, and administrative support to FBI investigations conducted throughout the United States and in foreign countries.[23]

The FBI operates fifty-six FOs in major cities and 381 resident agencies (RAs) throughout the country. These RAs are satellite offices that support the larger FOs and allow the FBI to maintain a presence in and serve communities that are distant from main FOs. FBI employees assigned to FOs and RAs perform the majority of the investigative and intelligence work of the FBI. The FBI also operates seventy-eight legal attaché (LEGAT) offices and sub-offices in foreign countries around the world.[24]

In comparison to the Department of Defense (DOD) or Central Intelligence Agency (CIA), the FBI budget and agent power are quite modest.[25] In fact, the New York Police Department (NYPD) has a larger police force than the FBI does.[26] But the FBI has always been able to project a Wizard of Oz effect of being all-powerful and effective. The FY 2015 FBI budget request proposed a total of $8.34 billion in direct budget authority, including 34,970 permanent positions (13,050 special agents, 3,048 intelligence analysts, and 18,872 professional staff).[27] That budget request of $8.34 billion as stipulated by the Senate Appropriations Committee was "for [the] detection, investigation, and prosecution of crimes against the United States." Of the total, $3.36 billion was requested for the counterterrorism and counterintelligence unit, and $1.65 billion was requested for the intelligence unit.[28]

THE WALL: PRE-9/11 ATTEMPTS AT REFORM

For historic reasons the United States had established a legal regime that clearly distinguished between criminal law enforcement and national security.[29] This paradigm was established primarily to keep in check the broad investigative powers of the FBI separate from the roles and missions of the CIA. This framework was established in 1946, and over the years the two agencies have enjoyed periods of cooperation and of intense competition. The two agencies have struggled for control over issues of domestic espionage, counterterrorism, counterintelligence, and national security.[30] Yet by the end of the Cold War, the increase of transnational crimes—narcotics, terrorism, money laundering, economic espionage, and weapons of mass destruction trafficking—increasingly created challenges for the old paradigm. The 9/11 attacks finally shattered it.[31]

Two critical documents created a framework that shaped the FBI's mission and roles in the area of national security: the 1978 FISA and the 1981 Executive Order (EO) 12333. This framework, reinforced with court decisions, established a "bright line" between the domestic and international arenas. Under FISA records could be sought only "for purposes of conducting foreign intelligence" when the target was "linked to foreign espionage" and an "agent of a foreign power."[32] Surveillance of "agents of a foreign power" was appropriate so long as the "primary purpose" was to obtain foreign intelligence information. Procedures were established to ensure that FISA warrants would not be issued as a way to overcome weak "probable cause" warrants on the criminal side of the FBI house.[33]

A regime of court rules and internal DOJ procedures developed that barred FBI agents and other intelligence community personnel working intelligence cases that employed the FISA tool from coordinating and swapping leads with agents working criminal cases. As a result of this legal wall, intelligence agents and criminal agents working on a terrorist target had to proceed without knowing what the other might be doing against that same target. The wall theory gained prominence as an explanation of constrained performance during the 9/11 Commission hearings.[34] From this perspective the FBI was fighting international terrorism with one arm tied behind its back. Ironically, FISA had been passed to stop previous perceived abuses of power by the executive branch and the FBI.

The wall made sense if one held that the FBI should remain principally a law enforcement agency that investigates crimes and gathers evidence for criminal trial prosecutions. Prevention had never been a priority, nor had national security been the fast track for a career at the FBI. The fear was that different standards in the intelligence area would be used to avoid the criminal requirements of "probable causes." Although there have been some celebrated national security cases, this was not the focus of the organizational mission. During the late 1980s and 1990s, limited reforms and innovations took place to integrate the FBI and CIA communities and make intelligence and counterterrorism higher FBI priorities.[35] Successes such as the investigation and prosecution of double agents like Aldrich Ames and Katrina Leung did not convince policymakers that the FBI was up to the task.

The FBI continued to be viewed in the interagency process as having the dominant culture of an elite national police force that did not share its information and expertise easily with local law enforcement or other agencies. Agents continued to be drawn primarily from police, military, and legal backgrounds with little representation from other intellectual disciplines such anthropology, mathematics, logic, or philosophy. Senior FBI appointments of "outsiders," or non–law enforcement experts, were usually restricted to the director's or deputy director's staffs. (Only recently have significant numbers of assistant directors been chosen from outside the ranks of the FBI.)

Before September 11, 2001, the bureau had no truly centralized structure for the national management of its Counterterrorism Program, and terrorism cases were routinely managed out of individual FOs.[36] An al-Qaeda case, for example, might have been run out of the New York Field Office; the Washington Field Office might have managed a Hamas case. This arrangement functioned for years, and though it produced a number of impressive prosecutions, it did not reflect an integrated effort. Director Robert S. Mueller III concluded that as counterterrorism emerged, the FO focus had a number of failings:

> It 1) "stove-piped" investigative intelligence information among field offices; 2) diffused responsibility and accountability between counterterrorism officials at FBI Headquarters and the lead Special Agents in Charge who had primary responsibility for the individual terrorism investigations; 3) allowed field offices to assign inconsistent priorities and resource levels to terrorist groups and threats; 4) impeded effective oversight by FBI leadership, and 5) complicated coordination with other federal agencies and entities

involved in the war against terrorism. For all these reasons, it became apparent that the Counterterrorism Program needed centralized leadership.[37]

1998 STRATEGIC PLAN: TOO LITTLE

The first major systematic attempt to turn the FBI into a national security asset began with the Strategic Plan of 1998.[38] The plan was radical in a number of ways. First, it placed terrorism, espionage, and other national security threats in tier one, the top priority, whereas more traditional domestic crimes were given lower tiers of significance. Second, the plan called for more resources and improvements in the intelligence collection and analysis capabilities. Third, the plan identified the crucial need for improvements of the information and technology systems.

The Strategic Plan was to supplement and build on the LEGAT program, whereby the FBI stationed agents in embassies abroad to facilitate "law enforcement to law enforcement" cooperation and to create ties to an international network.[39] In the 1990s, recognizing that global crime and terrorism were on the rise, the FBI had made it a priority to open new LEGAT offices. In 1993 the bureau had twenty-one offices in embassies worldwide (mostly in Europe and Japan); within eight years that number had doubled. Offices were opened, for example, in such tactical locations as Pakistan, Egypt, Israel, Jordan, Turkey, South Korea, and Saudi Arabia.[40]

The stated goal of the Strategic Plan was to transform the bureau from being a reactive criminal prosecutorial law enforcement agency into a proactive intelligence-processing national security asset that made counterintelligence and counterterrorism the focus. But the careerists resisted the Strategic Plan. The 9/11 Commission Report recognized the attempt to reform but concluded that a number of forces undermined its success: lack of human resources and its notorious and woefully inadequate information technology system. In sum the Maximum Capacity program—the attempt to bring the FBI FOs to "maximum feasible capacity" in counterterrorism—was undermined by the FOs' lack of analysts, linguists, or technically trained experts.[41]

In the end the FBI leadership was unsuccessful in changing the cultural mindset of the institution, and there was no similar change at either the DOJ or the US Attorney's Office. Congress in its oversight capacity lacked the fortitude to oversee the reform as it focused on one cause célèbre after another. In 2004 a released bureau document revealed that it was still largely measuring its performance by the number of criminals it arrested—a standard too restrictive when applied to counterterrorism or counterintelligence, for which preemptive actions are required.[42] Sadly, the forces of reform retired or moved on, and a new director was appointed. The criminal culture mindset was reinforced with statutes and legal opinions that made resistance to change all the more effective. It would take 9/11 to usher in real reform.

POST-9/11 REFORM: THE FALL OF THE WALL

Only a week in office before the 9/11 attacks, Director Robert Mueller acted quickly to work with the new administration, law enforcement officials, other intelligence agencies, and foreign allies in the investigation process. In addition, the creation of the Department of Homeland Security (DHS), the director of national intelligence (DNI), the National Counterintelligence

Executive (NCIX), and the National Counterterrorism Center and a new amended EO 12333 reinforced the ongoing process to integrate law enforcement and national security equities. The national security enterprise had created more institutions, more silos, and more integration mechanisms.

The congressional enactment of the USA PATRIOT Act in 2001 fundamentally changed the EO 12333/FISA paradigm that had shaped the FBI's culture.[43] Over the years judicial rules and DOJ internal procedures had prohibited FBI counterterrorism agents working intelligence cases from coordinating and sharing information with criminal agents who often were working investigations against the same targets.[44] As then–Democratic senator Joe Biden explained during the Senate floor debate about the USA PATRIOT Act, "The FBI could get a wiretap to investigate the mafia, but they could not get one to investigate terrorists. To put it bluntly, that was crazy! What's good for the mob should be good for terrorists."[45] The difference was that the Fourth Amendment applied to criminal investigations, but after 1978 and the introduction of FISA, a different standard of review was required for a FISA investigation.

By definition the FBI now understood that investigations of international terrorism were both "intelligence" and "criminal" investigations. They are intelligence investigations because their objective, pursuant to EO 12333, is "the detection and countering of international terrorist activities." Therefore, agents may employ the authorities and investigative tools—such as FISA warrants—that are designed for the intelligence mission of protecting the United States against attack or other harm by foreign entities. But on the other hand, these cases are criminal investigations since international terrorism against the United States constitutes a violation of the federal criminal code.

In essence, the USA PATRIOT Act eliminated the wall, and the FBI subsequently believed it was now authorized to coordinate among agents working criminal matters and those working intelligence investigations. On March 6, 2002, the attorney general issued new Intelligence Sharing Procedures for Foreign Intelligence and Foreign Counterintelligence Investigations Conducted by the FBI to capitalize on this legislative change.[46] These new procedures specifically authorized FBI agents working intelligence cases to disseminate to criminal prosecutors and investigators all relevant foreign intelligence information, including information obtained from FISA. Likewise, the new procedures authorized prosecutors and criminal law enforcement agents to advise FBI agents working intelligence cases on all aspects of foreign intelligence investigations, including the use of FISA.

With the dismantling of the legal wall under Section 218 of the PATRIOT Act and the integration of criminal and intelligence personnel and operations, the FBI believed it would have the latitude to coordinate intelligence and criminal investigations and to use the full range of investigative tools against a suspected terrorist. On the intelligence side the FBI could conduct surveillance on the suspected terrorists to learn about their movements and identify possible confederates; it could obtain FISA authority to monitor their conversations or approach and attempt to cultivate them as sources or operational assets. On the criminal side the bureau now had the option of incapacitating the target through arrest, detention, and prosecution. It could decide among these options by continuously balancing the opportunity to develop intelligence against the need to apprehend the suspects and prevent them from carrying out their terrorist plans. For the FBI this integrated approach has guided its operations, successfully foiled terrorist-related operations, and disrupted cells from Seattle, Washington, to Detroit, Michigan, to Lackawanna, New York.

One measure of the FBI's new aggressiveness was the extent to which FISA coverage increased significantly post 9/11, reflecting an increased focus on counterterrorism and counterintelligence investigations. The inspector general (IG) reported that the number of FISA applications filed each year from 2001 to 2003 increased by 85 percent.[47] The number of applications has fluctuated up and down, reaching its peak at 2,371 in 2007, and was down to 1,588 in 2013.[48] Although touted as a success by the administration, to the critics of the FBI the dip in applications was seen as the FBI's failing to use FISA tools properly by shortcutting the procedures. Soon the FBI was embroiled in a scandal on the improper use of national security letters (NSLs).[49] As critics noted in 2001, the USA PATRIOT Act significantly expanded this authority in several ways.[50]

Challenges to these expanded activities were sure to reach the courts. In 2013 the US District Court judge in Northern California found that the gag order placed on providers when they receive an NSL was an unconstitutional impingement on free speech. The judge ordered that the FBI stop sending out NSLs entirely but placed a stay on the order pending the government's appeal in the Ninth Circuit Court of Appeals. The court heard appeals in October 2014, in which the plaintiff argued that the FBI is allowed to "directly impose content-based prior restraints on speech and then insulates that Executive action from any kind of meaningful judicial review,"[51] but the government continued to argue that NSLs are "an extremely useful tool to use."[52] The 2014 report of the Office of the Inspector General (OIG) found that the FBI had implemented thirty-one of forty-one recommendations and included ten new recommendations to improve the use and oversight of NSLs.[53]

Most believe that this case will not be settled until it reaches the US Supreme Court. In anticipation of this FBI Director Comey has already spoken out against increased judicial oversight, stating that it would "actually make it harder to conduct a security investigation than a bank fraud investigation."[54]

RENEWED FBI REFORMS AND RESTRUCTURING

In view of the decade-long battle against terrorism, the FBI leadership has continued to restructure the organization. In October 2002 Mueller initiated programs to modify FBI structure and operations to focus on the prevention of potential attacks, to counter foreign intelligence operations against the United States, and to begin to assess the impact of cybercrime-based attacks and other high-technology crimes.[55] In reorganizing the Counterterrorism Division, the bureau created a position for an assistant director with oversight authority. The division recognized that counterterrorism had national and international dimensions that went beyond traditional local FO jurisdiction. Centralized coordination was required to ensure that individual pieces of an investigation could be compiled into a single and coherent picture. Before this new system was put in place, there had been little accountability because responsibility had been diffused.[56] The assistant director for counterterrorism, however, was now accountable for taking all steps necessary to develop the bureau's counterterrorism capacity. Mueller also pledged that the FBI would continue to enhance its analytical, information-sharing, and technology departments to meet the demands of global counterterrorism efforts.

When Director Mueller came before Congress in 2004 to discuss new transitions in FBI culture, he noted the need to adapt constantly to face diverse crimes such as terrorism, corporate fraud, identity theft, human trafficking, illegal weapons trade, and money laundering. Mueller believed that the bureau had to be "flexible, agile, and mobile in the face of these new threats."[57] This meant making the following changes to strengthen flexibility and accountability:

- refocusing the FBI's mission and revising its priorities;
- realigning its workforce to address these priorities;
- shifting its management and operational environment to strengthen flexibility, agility, and accountability;
- restructuring FBI HQ; and
- undertaking dozens of projects aimed at reengineering internal business practices and processes.[58]

In addition, Mueller discussed how the bureau would implement these new goals by building a more diverse and capable workforce. It would do this by

- expanding the FBI's applicant base for critical skills and diversity;
- updating new agent training to reflect revised priorities;
- establishing new career tracks for counterterrorism, counterintelligence, cyber, security, and analysis; and
- improving management and leadership development.[59]

Equally important to its internal reforms, the bureau also increased its efforts to expand communication between itself and other "federal partners" at the local, state, federal, and international level. By 2006 the FBI had finished most of its transitional development programs and presented its new look: the deputy director would focus on operational matters, a new associate deputy director (ADD) would focus on information management, and five new branches (including the National Security Branch [NSB], which would have four components—the Counterterrorism Division, Counterintelligence Division, Directorate of Intelligence, and Directorate of Weapons of Mass Destruction). (See box 11.2.) Because of these new structural changes, the position of executive assistant director for law enforcement services became obsolete. The ADD now had a more streamlined oversight of the Human Resources Branch, Office of the Chief Information Officer (OCIO), Inspection Division, Facilities and Logistics Services Division, Finance Division, Records Management Division, and Security Division.

The creation of the NSB at the FBI paralleled the creation of the National Security Division (NSD) at the DOJ. The NSD merges the primary national security elements—the Counterterrorism and Counterespionage Sections, the Office of Intelligence, the new Law and Policy Office, and the Office of Justice for Victims of Overseas Terrorism. The NSD is also currently making the same shift toward cyber as the NSB is. Working closely with DHS, the FBI, Commerce, DOD, and other law enforcement agencies, the NSD has brought over a hundred cases since 2007.[60]

The structural changes continued with the change in leadership. In 2014 Director Comey moved the Directorate of Intelligence from the NSB to its own Intelligence Branch. The new branch is hoped to solidify the integration of intelligence across all components while bringing the head of intelligence into daily briefings with the director.

BOX 11.2
Reorganizational Reforms Post 9/11

The *deputy director (DD)* continues to oversee the National Security Branch; the Criminal, Cyber, Response, and Services Branch; and the Science and Technology Branch. Also reporting to the deputy director are the assistant directors in charge and special agents in charge of FBI field offices, the Office of Public Affairs, the Office of Congressional Affairs, the Office of the General Counsel, the Office of Equal Employment Opportunity, the Office of Professional Responsibility, and the Office of the Ombudsman.

The new *associate deputy director (ADD)* oversees the management of the FBI's Human Resources Branch and the Office of the Chief Information Officer through the respective executive assistant directors (EADs) and directly oversees the Inspection Division, the Facilities and Logistics Services Division (FLSD), the Finance Division (FD), the Records Management Division (RMD), the Security Division (SecD), and the Resource Planning Office (RPO)—or personnel, budget, administration, and infrastructure—to ensure that these areas are aligned with the bureau's mission. This allows the director and deputy director to focus on operations, intelligence, and liaison. New executive management policies and a larger focus on long-term strategic efforts were needed to adapt to the growth of the bureau's workforce and budget. The office of the ADD, therefore, meets these new sorts of demands.

The *six new branches*, each headed by an EAD, are the National Security Branch; the Criminal, Cyber, Response, and Services Branch; Investigations Branch; the Human Resources Branch; the Science and Technology Branch; and the Office of the Chief Information Officer.

Reporting to the DD

The *National Security Branch (NSB)* is composed of the Counterterrorism Division, Counterintelligence Division, and Directorate of Intelligence. In 2006 the NSB added a new Weapons of Mass Destruction (WMD) Directorate, which merged WMD and counter-proliferation initiatives. This new directorate studies the consequences of a WMD attack, increases the bureau's level of preparedness, and coordinates the federal government's response in the event that the United States is attacked with a WMD.

The *Criminal, Cyber, Response, and Services Branch (CIB)* encompasses the Criminal Investigative Division, the Cyber Division, the Critical Incident Response Group, the Office of International Operations, and the Office of Law Enforcement Coordination. This directorate is accountable for criminal and cyber investigations, coordination with law enforcement, international operations, and crisis response. Giving one individual complete responsibility over this directorate ensures that criminal programs receive strategic guidance and support and that the FBI maintains its unparalleled level of excellence in criminal investigations.

The *Science and Technology Branch (S&T)* combined the Criminal Justice Information Services Division, the Laboratory, the Operational Technology Division, and the Special Technologies and Applications Section (formerly part of the Cyber Division). "The S&T Branch will ensure that the FBI continues to provide exceptional service to the law enforcement community and stays on top of technical innovation and developments in the sciences to support investigative and intelligence-gathering activities."

Reporting to the ADD

The *Human Resources Branch (HR)* combined the Human Resources Division and the Training and Development Division (TDD). This merger restructured the bureau's human capital program in order to allow the FBI to focus on its most crucial assets: its people. HR demonstrates that the bureau is committed to recruiting, training, developing, and retaining people who will further its reputation for excellence.

The composition of the *Office of the Chief Information Officer (OCIO)*, when created, was not changed but was reformed to be more aligned with the components handling strategic planning, finance, security, and facilities. Because information technology in the FBI's restructuring plan is important, this new alignment was critical.

THE CURRENT ERA

The FBI today is far different than it was only a decade ago. Today, more than half of the bureau's agents are working on national security issues. Before he became director, James Comey admitted, he did not fully understand the terrorism threat currently posed to the United States by the affiliates and offshoots of al-Qaeda. However, seeing the brutality of the "foreign fighters" of Daesh—some of whom are "homegrown" extremists—appears to have convinced Comey to maintain the FBI priority on national security and combating terrorism.[61]

That being said, the FBI must also be flexible enough to adapt to an evolving threat picture, one that increasingly will include cyber. During a conversation with Comey, outgoing director Mueller stressed that he thought cyber issues would dominate the new director's tenure, as his tenure had been dominated by counterterrorism.[62] The 9/11 Commission also recognized that not realizing the gravity of a threat until it is too late can be devastating, and cyber may be that next big threat.[63] The FBI's Next Generation Cyber Initiative, which was launched in 2012, established a Cyber Task Force in every FO, hired more computer scientists, and expanded participation with the NCIJTF.

In January 2015 Director Comey addressed the International Conference on Cyber Security, sharing the five-point strategy devised by the FBI to handle the cyber threat.[64] The strategy includes focusing efforts on those that can do the most harm and deploying resources in the most efficient way. The next steps are to "shrink the world" by forward-deploying more cyber agents and to divide resources more effectively within the government. The third element of the strategy is to increase the cost of cybercrimes by indicting and penalizing those who break the law, the way the Treasury Department placed sanctions on North Korea after the Sony attack. The last two points are about cooperation—cooperation between state and local law enforcement and partnerships with the private sector.

One example of the FBI's successful team efforts using private–public partnerships is Operation Clean Slate, a mission to eliminate the most significant botnets and to increase the cost of botnets by increasing the practical consequences.[65] This mission helped to disrupt the Gameover ZeuS botnet, the most sophisticated botnet the FBI has every gone up against. While the FBI has been able to eliminate some cyber threats, cybersecurity is still at the top of the DNI's list of global threats.[66] In 2015 the president announced a new cyber information integration center to be housed under the DNI. The FBI has been working with DHS to protect critical infrastructure under its mandate. The FBI has assisted DHS in attending meetings with national gas pipeline sector companies to deploy onsite assistance and brief personnel on how to best protect energy assets against cyber intrusions.[67] More than 170,000 Internet Protocol addresses of computers the FBI and DHS believe to be infected with malware have been released.[68]

In addition to adversary nation-states, terrorist groups, and talented individuals, the FBI is battling companies in America that are launching efforts "to go dark," as the law has not kept up with technology. Google and Apple have announced plans to make their devices encrypted by default, meaning that the companies themselves will not be able to unlock the device if given a court order. Comey has been outspoken about the negative effects this encryption will have on the FBI's ability to get information from terrorists' and criminals' smart phones and tablets, and he has called on Congress to pass new legislation to stop unlockable encryption. The technology companies have responded that encryption is necessary to protect users' personal information.[69] This struggle between privacy advocates and the state, which needs to be able to conduct effective investigations, will ultimately define how we understand privacy in the next few decades.

HAS THE CULTURE AND ORGANIZATION BEEN TRANSFORMED ENOUGH?

Will changing attorney general guidelines, new legal rules, and the recent organizational restructuring solve the perceived problem of the FBI culture?[70] Change is taking place, but is it fast enough and thorough enough? Was the FBI truly hamstrung in its efforts to combat domestic terrorism before 9/11? Most people in the bureau believe that before 9/11 there were restrictions to the FBI doing its job. One former FBI official was quoted as saying, "You have to wait until you have blood on the street before the Bureau can act."[71] So, has the FBI been successful in changing the culture? In March 2015 the FBI 9/11 Review Commission, which was established by congressional mandate to examine the bureau's implementation of the 9/11 Commission's recommendations, released a report titled *The FBI: Protecting the Homeland in the 21st Century*. The commissioners concluded, "Over the past decade, the Bureau has made measurable progress building a threat-based, intelligence-driven national security organization. In the same period, however, global threats to the US Homeland have become more complex, challenging the FBI's traditional orientation as the primary federal law enforcement organization, its change-resistant culture, and its core capabilities in criminal investigation, counterintelligence, intelligence collection and analysis, and technology."[72] The commission reviewed the FBI in the following categories: understanding the threat, intelligence analysis and collection, leadership, integration in the community, information sharing, the LEGAT program, countering violent extremism (CVE), science and technology, cybersecurity, strategic planning, and the continued investigation of the 9/11 attacks. After their rather extensive study, the commissioners made twelve recommendations to change FBI culture, shown in figure 11.1.

To some the FBI's inability to change may necessitate more structural changes in the national security enterprise. A nation can take different approaches to pursue national security, maintain privacy, and have a domestic intelligence agency lawfully perform its mission. One of our closest allies, Great Britain, has divided domestic intelligence, international intelligence, and law enforcement among three agencies: MI5, MI6, and Scotland Yard. The FBI has always been a combination of MI5 and Scotland Yard, MI6 being equivalent to the CIA. Resistance to creating a stand-alone domestic intelligence service in the United States has always been based on the fact that the FBI has the tradition, training, and discipline to perform the domestic mission within the boundaries of our constitutional framework of the First and Fourth Amendments.

In early 2003 debate began to find an alternative solution to the FBI, an American version of British MI5. Creating such an agency would entail restructuring the FBI, DHS, and the Department of Treasury by hiving off the national security, counterterrorism, and counterintelligence analysis functions in order to combine the relevant analysts into one agency, as is currently the practice in Great Britain. MI5, like the CIA, has no arrest powers and specializes in analysis. After the restructuring, the FBI would function more like Scotland Yard and concentrate on traditional national crimes and organized crime violations. Presumably, the new entity would also work closely with DOD assets to act as a clearinghouse for all the relevant information from the fifteen major intelligence-gathering agencies.[73] Needless to say the resistance to the creation of an American MI5 comes not only from a philosophical aversion to the

#1 The FBI director and leadership need to speed up the reforms and efforts to transform the culture.	#2 A top priority of the FBI should be to enhance the analyst career service.	#3 The director, with the help of Congress and the Office of Personnel Management, should focus on retaining senior leaders.
#4 The director, in collaboration with the DNI and US intelligence community, should increase interagency relationships by supporting rotational training assignments.	#5 The FBI needs to reinforce and strengthen its communication, collaboration, and information sharing with federal, state, and local partners.	#6 Efforts to counter violent extremism should be moved to DHS or distributed among other agencies.
#7 The FBI should provide the LEGAT program with the resources it needs, including adequate funding and improved analytic capabilities.	#8 The S&T needs to keep tempo with the global technological transformation and fund selective research and development.	#9 The FBI needs work faster to address the cyber threat. This includes accomplishing technology, procurement, and personnel goals and working in collaboration with the entire government.
#10 Congress should provide the FBI with the authorities, technology, and tools it needs to address threats.	#11 The FBI should develop a five-year, implementable, metric-based strategic plan.	#12 When it has finished investigating and prosecuting the 9/11 attacks, the FBI should summarize the lessons learned for the director and congressional committees.

Figure 11.1. Recommendations of the FBI 9/11 Review Commission, March 2015

Source: Bruce Hoffman, Ed Meese III, Tim J. Roemer, *The FBI: Protecting the Homeland in the 21st Century* (Washington, DC: FBI, March 2015).

notion of a "domestic spy agency" but also from all the existing intelligence bureaucracies that oppose the concept of losing assets. The creation of a DHS without significant intelligence powers reflects this reservoir of resistance to an American MI5 (see chapter 12 on DHS).

Given these constraints, a group of experienced former government officials suggested an interim MI5 approach that would prove to be more bureaucratically acceptable to the intelligence community.[74] Arguing for more information on domestic terrorist cells and the need to integrate counterintelligence with counterterrorism beyond a "case-file mentality," the group called for the creation of a new and accountable organization within the FBI. Using the National Security Agency and the National Reconnaissance Office as models, it envisioned the new organization embedded within the FBI with its director not from law enforcement but appointed by the president, responsible to the DNI and the director of the CIA. The organization would be governed by attorney general guidelines, have its own independent personnel system for hiring, and be subject to direct oversight by the FISA Court and Congress. The ultimate outcome of the debate was the creation of the National Security Branch in the FBI—the bureau within the bureau. The FBI resisted the more radical aspects of the proposed reform by requiring the head of the branch to report to the director of the FBI.

As one can readily deduce from any proposed solution, one of the continuing questions is, Who is in charge of integrating domestic law enforcement intelligence from the approximately 650,000 police officers, from domestic federal agencies, and from foreign national intelligence? Although the new DNI is the titular head of the intelligence community, he or she has no control of approximately 80 percent of the intelligence budget, which is under the authority of the secretary of defense. As a matter of law, neither the DNI nor the CIA director can operate domestically without severe legal constraint.

All the proposals for reform agree that one problem with the FBI, and for that matter with the intelligence community, is that the current institutional configuration was not established to counter the threat posed by domestic terrorism with international links. Fighting terrorism requires the gathering of both domestic and international intelligence to prevent attacks and provide national security. The elaborate and enviable legal and bureaucratic structures that were created to protect and guarantee our privacy can prove to be impediments to prosecuting and preventing terrorist acts, as the Fort Hood shooting revealed.[75] Empowering the agencies while protecting privacy and avoiding abuse of power is the critical issue. Since 9/11 new legislation has been passed to address the problems. The debate has rightly focused on how to reengineer this framework while sufficiently protecting our domestic liberties. Questions of cybersecurity and technology have only exacerbated the problem as we have seen with the revelations of Wikileaks and Edward Snowden and with questions about the FISA Court and smart phone encryption.

REMAINING QUESTIONS

Analysis of the FBI reforms in the post-9/11 world raised criticisms that continue to be debated today. First, according to its historic critics, the FBI was still focused on making cases for criminal investigations. All incentives for agents reinforced the view that they were encouraged to be "reactive, case-driven, and conviction-oriented." In 2011 the bureau made a "strategic shift," including changing its mission from law enforcement to national security and law enforcement, changing its focus from case-driven to intelligence-driven and threat-focused, and changing its measurement of success from activity-based to impact-bound.[76] Comey has worked to implement this strategy with the creation of the Intelligence Branch and his commitment to keep half of the FBI's agents working on national security issues. But the bureau did not abandon its criminal investigation roots, and the number of criminal fraud cases investigated by the FBI has increased by 65 percent since 2008.[77]

The second major debate focused on the FBI's timidity to pursue investigations in the counterterrorism, counterintelligence, and national security arenas owing to a reluctance to reignite the Church Committee criticism that the bureau, in the name of security and domestic intelligence, had violated certain First Amendment and Fourth Amendment rights. Of course, it could be argued that the FBI has gone in the opposite direction. It has increased the number and scope of NSLs, increased data collection, and is becoming much more aggressive in combating cybercrimes, including cyberterrorism.

The third criticism of the FBI was that it lacked a talented, effectively trained, cyber-savvy special agent cadre as well as a modern computerized record-keeping system to help analyze information in a coherent and timely manner. Recently, the FBI released a statement saying, "Today, however, the most sought-after candidates possess a uniquely 21st century quality: cyber expertise."[78] The bureau wants to hire 1,000 agents and 1,000 analysts in the upcoming months.[79] A press release, however, does not solve the problem; the bureau must still compete with the private sector in hiring those with cyber expertise.[80]

A new computer system, Sentinel, launched in July 2012 over budget and years late, did replace the antiquated one that had relied heavily on paper files. Sentinel was created to make entering and sharing information between HQ and the FOs more efficient and to allow agents to search that information. The solicitor general audited this program and found that a majority of those surveyed found that Sentinel helped them better carry out the mission while increasing their efficiency; however, users also had problems with the search function and the indexing function.[81] It is clear from all the reports that the bureau still has a long way to go in updating its computer systems.

The fourth criticism was that too much poor and unverified information was still being collected in an uncoordinated manner. This added to the difficulty of sharing the information with the domestic law enforcement and intelligence communities. The FBI was criticized for this problem in the investigation of the Boston Marathon bombing. The IG found that the bureau failed to follow up on significant information about the suspects.[82] The FBI has made changes to improve its information sharing with state and local partners as well as other federal agencies, but the OIG still contends there is room for improvement.

RECOMMENDATIONS FOR REFORM

Clearly, further reforms are still needed. Among other things, the authors suggest that the FBI hire more senior executive service specialists from outside the bureau, create an FBI IG, and revamp the Training Division. Of these three recommendations Director Comey has so far only reformed the Training Division and the FBI Academy. He has chosen a training director who has implemented Comey's vision to integrate the education of new agents and new analysts and to add new classes in both curriculums. The assistant director of training used the old adage "Train how you fight and you'll fight like you train" to describe the importance of teamwork throughout the organization and the way it will help as the FBI's role as a national security asset expands. Also, those agents who only have experience in national security are being given criminal investigative experience.[83]

A New Talent Base

Both Directors Mueller and Comey have broadened the spectrum of those hired as agents and increased the number of intelligence analysts to partner with them in the field. Where change has significantly faltered is putting those with experience beyond the FBI in leadership positions. The director needs outside assistance to evaluate both plans for change and new personnel. Relying solely on inside knowledge and FBI careerists makes a new director too captive to insider views. The overwhelming majority of executive assistant directors appointed by Comey have been SACs, and all of them have spent most of their careers in the FBI. The leadership of the Intelligence Branch should include career intelligence analysts or those with careers in intelligence.

Most important, the members of the FBI need to be trained to be cyber capable. The DOD is beginning to envision soldiers who fight in a cyber battlefield, and the FBI must consider changing its view of a cyber FBI agent. In this battlefield physical endurance and gun skills are not as important understanding botnets, malware, and metadata and connecting dots.

An Inspector General for the FBI

Although the IG for the DOJ has traditionally done an excellent job, the FBI should have an internal IG. As the FBI expanded its powers, the IG could ensure clear and transparent accountability. The director should create an IG for the FBI who reports to both the director and the attorney general. The IG would have broad powers to ensure that investigations followed constitutional limits and privacy restrictions. The historic turnaround of the FBI Laboratory in the mid-1990s and the role played by an independent IG in the process are proof of how effectively an IG can work. But the OIG must be large enough to ensure its success. The current Office of Professional Responsibility, although staffed with agents of integrity and energy, is too small, with too limited powers. The reports of the DOJ IG have helped correct past abuses of the DOJ and FBI in the fight against terrorism in a number of cases. This type of transparency builds legitimacy in the long run. As the general counsel for the FBI noted when he explained the revised attorney general rules for investigation in 2009, "Those who say the FBI should not collect information on a person or group unless there is a specific reason to suspect that the target is up to no good seriously miss the mark. The FBI has been told to determine who poses a threat to the national security—not simply to investigate persons who have come onto our radar screens."[84] With expanded power must come expanded accountability—and an institutional office that guarantees impartial review.

Finally, the key to solving the threat posed by cyber attacks is sharing private and public information. The majority of networks and infrastructure is privately held. Currently, the FBI, along with a number of agencies and departments—the NSC, DHS, DOD, the National Security Agency, Cyber Command, the CIA, Treasury, the DNI—has a variety of authorities and capabilities. Cyber governmental organization structure to this point has not been well coordinated and structured. Although not an FBI problem alone, serious reform is required in this arena, and this reform may require congressional legislation on the issues of encryption and immunity when information is shared.

THE NEXT CROSSROADS

One should not believe that even if all of these reforms were made, or even if an American MI5 were established, then there would not be any more acts of terrorism in the United States. Israel, a much smaller country with infinitely more experience in fighting terrorism and without our evolved sense of private liberties, still has not been able to stop suicide bombers on the West Bank and in Gaza. Moreover, given our vulnerabilities to cyber attacks, lone gunmen, and Internet radicalized terrorists, we cannot be 100 percent successful. The amount of the vulnerable infrastructure controlled by the private sector makes government–private market cooperation vital, but these partnerships are deeply complex. Many industries, such as the financial sector, have a structural disincentive to making known their computer vulnerabilities: fear of financial penalty. Our ports are so open that even the positioning of agents in foreign ports of origin will not secure the commercial traffic.

In the film *Minority Report*, a top detective in an experimental "pre-crime" unit wires the brains of genetically altered "precogs" (short for "precognition") to computers that display their glimpses of the future. The super sleuth stands before the display as if he is conducting a symphony and directs the images so that he can find the perpetrators before they kill. There is no way to know if everyone arrested under this program would in fact have become a murderer, but in the film, since the program has been in place, there has not been a single murder in the city.[85] Unlike in the film *Minority Report*, the FBI, CIA, or Office of the DNI probably will never have a set of precogs that can predict when an act of violence will take place, days before it happens. Our only hope is the corrective measures the government can take to stymie violent events. In reality we will have to infiltrate terror cells at home and abroad, use spy satellites to track movements, trace deposits with money-laundering specialists, increase eavesdropping, deploy code breakers, and then piece it all together.[86]

As the FBI 9/11 Review Commission noted in its report,

> The FBI has made strides in the past decade but needs to accelerate its implementation of reforms to complete its transformation into a threat-based, intelligence-driven organization. The increasingly complex and dangerous threat environment it faces will require no less. The Review Commission believes that the FBI's vision of the future should be one in which criminal investigation, counterintelligence, intelligence collection and analysis, and S&T applications are seen as complementary core competencies of a global intelligence and investigative agency.

> - The Bureau must work toward a culture that integrates its best efforts into both criminal and national security missions; where its highly skilled people intersect synergistically in mission support; but where its core competencies still are nurtured by distinct professional disciplines requiring their own investment strategies, specialized training, and discipline-managed career services.
> - The FBI will fulfill its domestic intelligence role when its analysts and collectors, like its special agents, are grounded in criminal investigation; have ready access to state-of-the-art technology; continuously exploit the systems, tools, and relationships of the national intelligence agencies; and both cultivate and benefit from robust CONUS [continental United States] and OCONUS [outside of continental United States] collaborative relationships that widen the Bureau's access to investigative leads and reportable intelligence.
> - Achieving these ambitious goals should not be a zero-sum game between intelligence and law enforcement. It should mean a continued FBI commitment to a growing criminal investigation mission, to a tighter and smoother integration of intelligence analysts and collectors into the USIC [US intelligence community], to a more strategic approach to its growing international footprint, and to greater investment in closer collaborative relationships with US and foreign partners. Accomplishing all this will be hard in any case, but impossible without a firm commitment from FBI leadership and support from the DNI and Congress to accelerate reform.[87]

We seem ever at a crossroads on the issue of law enforcement and the national security enterprise; the integration of the two is a critical function. The attacks in Paris and Berlin have intensified the debate on surveillance and the need for a forward-leaning security apparatus. The national security enterprise at its worst is a process of overcoming turf battles, poor leadership, bureaucratic intransigency, incompetence, and limited budgets with misaligned priorities. But in the end terrorism is a political act. Although there may be a small number of self-destructive nihilists for whom violence is in itself the goal, the response to reorganize the state is being made with political terrorism as the object. If in the desire to fight terrorism we create an intrusive state that erodes the right of privacy—without effective checks and accountability on government officials to avoid abuses—the irony will be that in the attempt to fight terrorism we will have delegitimized the very institutions created to protect ourselves. We will have lost being a beacon for ourselves as well as others.

Whatever the new reforms, as we expand the FBI detention, questioning, and surveillance functions; as local police use new electronic identification profiling; as we wrestle over encryption and computer security; as we experiment with rules of evidence for military tribunals and federal courts; as we increase the use of the death penalty; as we use more special forces, targeted killing, and covert operations; as we institutionalize preemption doctrines; and as we continue to blur the line between domestic and international and citizen and noncitizen, it becomes even more imperative that we increase institutional accountability. For in the war of ideas, we will have defeated ourselves if accountability is not maintained, enforced, and privileged.

The emerging national security enterprise may not exhibit as much patience as the previous Cold War national security state if it appears the FBI organization has failed to reform its culture and itself. A new domestic intelligence institution may be no guarantor of success, but such repeated perceived institutional failures tend to lead to new organizations—it is the way of the national security enterprise and Washington political culture.

NOTES

The authors would particularly like to thank Trudi Rishikof and Roger George for their invaluable suggestions and assistance in writing this chapter.

1. Reuel Marc Gerecht, "Major Hasan and the Holy War," *Wall Street Journal*, November 23, 2009; and Harvey Rishikof, "Economic and Industrial Espionage," in *Vaults, Mirrors, and Masks: Rediscovering U.S. Counterintelligence*, ed. Jennifer E. Sims and Burton Gerber (Washington, DC: Georgetown University Press, 2009).

2. John Hudson, "FBI Drops Law Enforcement as 'Primary' Mission," *Foreign Policy*, January 5, 2014, http://foreignpolicy.com/2014/01/05/fbi-drops-law-enforcement-as-primary-mission/.

3. FBI, "Addressing the Cyber Security Threat," *News* (blog), January 7, 2015, www.fbi.gov/news/news_blog/addressing-the-cyber-security-threat.

4. FBI, "Cyber Security: Task Force Takes 'Whole Government' Approach," *News* (blog), October 20, 2014, www.fbi.gov/news/stories/2014/october/cyber-task-force-takes-whole-government-approach.

5. Department of Justice Office of Public Affairs, "U.S. Charges Five Chinese Military Hackers for Cyber Espionage against U.S. Corporations and a Labor Organization for Commercial Advantage," press release, May 19, 2014, www.justice.gov/opa/pr/us-charges-five-chinese-military-hackers-cyber-espionage-against-us-corporations-and-labor.

6. FBI, "GameOver Zeus Botnet Disrupted: Collaborative Effort among International Partners," *News* (blog), June 2, 2014, www.fbi.gov/news/stories/2014/june/gameover-zeus-botnet-disrupted.

7. FBI, "Addressing the Cyber Security Threat."

8. Gregory F. Treverton, *Reorganizing U.S. Domestic Intelligence: Assessing the Options* (Santa Monica, CA: Rand, 2008).

9. See also, for history, ibid.

10. See David Cole, *Enemy Aliens* (New York: New Press, 2003), 116–28.

11. Department of Justice, *The FBI: A Centennial History, 1908–2008* (Washington, DC: Government Printing Office, 2008), 35.

12. Ibid., 57.

13. Ibid., 70.

14. Ibid.

15. FBI, "New Agent Training," www.fbi.gov/about-us/training/sat.

16. FBI, *Today's FBI—Fact and Figures 2013–2014* (Washington, DC: Department of Justice, n.d.), www.fbi.gov/stats-services/publications/todays-fbi-facts-figures/facts-and-figures-031413.pdf/view.

17. This culture of special agents being superior still exists today. When Director Comey named a new executive assistant director for intelligence, he chose a former special agent and not an intelligence officer. Dan Verton, "Reinventing the FBI: The Comey Vision," *Fedscoop*, September 21, 2014, http://fedscoop.com/comey-reignites-fbi-reform-efforts.

18. See Sari Horwitz, "Over 18 Weeks, an Arduous Path to the Badge," *Washington Post*, August 17, 2006.

19. FBI, "New Agent Training."

20. See Horwitz, "Over 18 Weeks."

21. 9/11 Commission, *Final Report of the National Commission on Terrorist Attacks upon the United States* (New York: W.W. Norton, 2003).

22. Ibid.

23. Major FBI facilities include the FBI Academy; the Engineering Research Facility; the FBI Laboratory at Quantico, Virginia; a large complex in Clarksburg, West Virginia, for fingerprint identification and other services; information technology centers in Pocatello, Idaho, Fort Arsenal, Alabama, and Monmouth, New Jersey; operational support centers in Butte, Montana, and Savannah, Georgia; and the Hazardous Devices [Bomb] School at Redstone Army Base at Huntsville, Alabama.

24. FBI, *Today's FBI*.

25. Office of the Undersecretary of Defense (Comptroller) / Chief Financial Officer, *United States Department of Defense Fiscal Year 2015 Budget Request: Overview* (Washington, DC, March 2014), http://comptroller.defense.gov/Portals/45/Documents/defbudget/fy2015/fy2015_Budget_Request _Overview_Book.pdf; and Office of the Director of National Intelligence, "DNI Releases Updates Budget Figure for FY 2015 Appropriations Requested for the National Intelligence Program," press release, November 21, 2014, www.dni.gov/index.php/newsroom/press-releases/198-press-releases-2014/1141 -dni-releases-updated-budget-figure-for-fy-2015-appropriations-requested-for-the-national-intelligence -program-14.

26. The NYPD FY 2015 executive budget allocates $47.2 million to counterterrorism security and counterterrorism grants. Council of the City of New York, *Report on the Fiscal Year 2015 Executive Budget for the Police Department*, May 20, 2014, http://council.nyc.gov/downloads/pdf/budget/2015/15/ eb/police.pdf.

27. The 2015 FBI budget request represented an increase of 3,630 new positions, including 825 special agents, 401 intelligence analysts, and 2,404 professional support since 2009.

28. FBI, *FY 2015 Authorization and Budget Request to Congress* (Washington, DC: Department of Justice, March 2014), www.justice.gov/sites/default/files/jmd/legacy/2013/10/03/fbi-justification.pdf.

29. This section and the conclusion are drawn from a recent op-ed. See Harvey Rishikof, Op-Ed in the *Providence Journal Online* at www.projo.com/opinion/contributors/content/projo_20020727 _ctrish27.721d2.htm.

30. See Mark Riebling, *Wedge: From Pearl Harbor to 9/11: How the Secret War between the FBI and CIA Has Endangered National Security* (New York: Simon & Schuster, 2002). For the lack of cooperation between the agencies during the early stages of the investigation of Aldrich Ames, see Michael R. Bromwich, "Review of the FBI's Performance in the Uncovering of the Espionage Activities of Aldrich Hazen Ames," in *Intelligence and the National Security Strategist*, ed. Roger Z. George and Robert D. Kline (New York: Rowman & Littlefield, 2004).

31. Richard A. Best Jr., *Intelligence and Law Enforcement: Countering Transnational Threats to the U.S.* (Washington, DC: Congressional Research Service, December 3, 2001).

32. Dahlia Lithwick and Julia Turner, "A Guide to the Patriot Act, Part I: Should You Be Scared of the Patriot Act?" *Slate*, September 8, 2003.

33. See Michael J. Woods, *Foreign Intelligence Surveillance Act Procedures to Ensure Accuracy* (Washington, DC: FBI, April 5, 2001), www.fas.org/irp/agency/doj/fisa/woods.pdf.

34. 9/11 Commission, *Final Report*, 78–80.

35. The creation of the Counterterrorism Center (1986); the National Drug Intelligence Center (1992); Intelligence–Law Enforcement Policy Board and Joint Intelligence–Law Enforcement Working Group (1994); National Counterintelligence Center (1994); and the Antiterrorism and Effective Death Penalty Act of 1996.

36. See the FBI Response to "A Review of the FBI's Handling of Intelligence Information Prior to the September 11 Attacks" Special Report, November 2004 (released publicly June 2005), www.usdoj .gov/oig/special/0506/app3.htm.

37. Ibid.

38. Description of the plan from Amy B. Zegart, *Spying Blind: The CIA, the FBI, and the Origins of 9/11* (Princeton, NJ: Princeton Press, 2007), 130–34.

39. The LEGAT program stemmed from World War II, when agents had been dispatched to South and Latin America to combat Nazi spying operations, before the creation of the CIA. The number of

LEGATs operating from the 1950s through the 1980s fluctuated owing to crime trends and budget allowances with offices opening, closing, and reopening at various times.

40. FBI, "International Operations: Leadership and Structure," www.fbi.gov/about/leadership-and -structure/international-operations. It is interesting to note that this program continues today, and the bureau has more than 200 special agents and support professionals in more than sixty overseas offices, pursuing terrorist, intelligence, and criminal threats with international dimensions in every part of the world. As part of the modern global outreach, the FBI also takes part in all manner of global and regional crime-fighting initiatives, including Interpol and Europol, the Budapest Project, and Resolution 6, which co-locates FBI agents in Drug Enforcement Administration offices worldwide to combat drugs.

41. 9/11 Commission, *Final Report*, 76–78.

42. See Office of the Inspector General, *A Review of the FBI's Use of National Security Letters: Assessment of Corrective Actions and Examination of NSL Usage in 2006* (Washington, DC: Department of Justice, March 2008), https://oig.justice.gov/special/s0803b/final.pdf.

43. *Uniting and Strengthening America by Providing Appropriate Tools Required to Intercept and Obstruct Terror* (USA PATRIOT Act), Pub. L. No. 107–56 (2001). For a quick summary of how the USA PATRIOT Act changed the legal framework—for example, by introducing the "roving" wiretap— see Department of Justice, "The USA PATRIOT Act: Preserving Life and Liberty," www.justice.gov/ archive/ll/highlights.htm.

44. The following section is drawn from the FBI Response to "A Review of the FBI's Handling of Intelligence."

45. See Cong. Rec., 10/25/01, quoted at Department of Justice, "USA PATRIOT Act."

46. Office of the Attorney General, "Procedures for the Dissemination by NSA to Foreign Governments of Information from FISA Electronic Surveillance or Physical Search Conducted by the FBI," August 20, 2002, https://s3.amazonaws.com/s3.documentcloud.org/documents/1061347/ashcroft -new-dissemination-procedures.pdf.

47. FBI Response to "A Review of the FBI's Handling of Intelligence," Appendix 3.

48. Electronic Privacy Information Center, "Foreign Intelligence Surveillance Act Court Orders 1979–2014," https://epic.org/privacy/wiretap/stats/fisa_stats.html.

49. An NSL is a letter request for information from a third party that is issued by the FBI or by other government agencies with authority to conduct national security investigations. NSL authority is provided by five provisions of law. Robert S. Mueller III, Testimony Before the Senate Committee on the Judiciary, "The FBI's Use of National Security Letters," Washington, DC, March 23, 2004, https:// archives.fbi.gov/archives/news/testimony/the-fbis-use-of-national-security-letters-2.

50. See Electronic Privacy Information Center, "EPIC Letter on National Security Letters," March 21, 2007, http://epic.org/privacy/pdf/nsl_letter.pdf.

51. Under Seal v. Holder, Appellant Under Seal's Opening Brief.

52. Jim Carlton and Zusha Elison, "U.S. Asks Court to Overturn National Security Letters Ruling," *Wall Street Journal*, October 8, 2014, www.wsj.com/articles/appeals-court-asked-to-overturn-nsl -ruling-1412803781.

53. "The review found that five recommendations from our prior NSL reports require additional information or attention to address the accuracy of information entered into the FBI's web based NSL workflow and database (the 'NSL subsystem') and improve the FBI's record keeping practices. . . . In addition, during our compliance review, the OIG identified compliance challenges in certain areas with regard to NSLs issued in 2007 through 2009, including FBI personnel's identification of information the FBI is not authorized to receive in response to an NSL, documentation of the justification for an NSL request, and adherence to the FBI's record keeping policies." Office of the Inspector General, "Summary of Findings: A Review of the FBI's Use of National Security Letters: Assessment of Progress in Implementing Recommendations and Examination of Use in 2007 through 2009," Department of Justice, August 2014, https://oig.justice.gov/reports/2014/s1408-summary.pdf.

54. Peter Baker and Chalrie Savage, "Obama Seeks Balance in Plan for Spy Crimes," *New York Times*, January 9, 2014, www.nytimes.com/2014/01/10/us/obama-seeks-balance-in-plan-for-spy -programs.html.

55. Robert S. Mueller III, Testimony Before the Senate Select Committee on Intelligence and the House Permanent Select Committee on Intelligence, Washington, DC, October 17, 2002, www.fbi.gov/ news/testimony/joint-intelligence-committee-inquiry.

56. Ibid.

57. Robert S. Mueller III, Testimony Before the Senate Appropriations Committee, Subcommittee on the Departments of Commerce, Justice, and State, the Judiciary, and Related Agencies, Washington, DC, March 23, 2004, www.fbi.gov/news/testimony/information-technology-management-and-training.

58. Ibid.

59. Ibid.

60. See Department of Justice, "Fact Sheet: Major US Export Enforcement Prosecutions (2007 to the present)," press release, March 2010, http://usarecht.de/wpcontent/uploads/sites/2/2010/04/summary-eaca.pdf.

61. "The agency he inherited had roughly half of its 16,000 agents and analysts working on national security issues, and Mr. Comey made it clear that he would not be changing those priorities." Michael S. Schmidt, "At F.B.I., Change in Leaders Didn't Change Focus on Terror," *New York Times*, May 18, 2014.

62. James Comey, "The FBI and the Private Sector: Closing the Gap in Cyber Security" (speech at the RSA Cyber Security Conference, San Francisco, CA, February 26, 2014), www.fbi.gov/news/speeches/the-fbi-and-the-private-sector-closing-the-gap-in-cyber-security.

63. 9/11 Commission, *Final Report*.

64. "The notion of space and time and venue doesn't make sense in the context of a sophisticated cyber threat." FBI, "Addressing the Cyber Security Threat."

65. A "botnet" is "a network of computers created by malware and controlled remotely, without the knowledge of the users of those computers." *Dictionary.com*, s.v. "botnet," http://dictionary.reference.com/browse/botnet. As of November 2013 it is estimated that Operation Clean Slate has freed more than 2.1 million robot computers from this malicious network. James B. Comey, "Homeland Threats and the FBI's Response," FBI News, November 14, 2013, www.fbi.gov/news/testimony/homeland-threats-and-the-fbis-response.

66. James Comey, "FBI Budget Request for Fiscal Year 2015," Statement Before the House Appropriations Committee, Subcommittee on Commerce, Justice, Science and Related Agencies, May 26, 2014, www.fbi.gov/news/testimony/fbi-budget-request-for-fiscal-year-2015.

67. James B. Comey, "Oversight of the Federal Bureau of Investigation," FBI News, May 21, 2014, www.fbi.gov/news/testimony/oversight-of-the-federal-bureau-of-investigation-5.

68. Robert Anderson Jr., "Cyber Security, Terrorism, and Beyond: Addressing Evolving Threats to the Homeland," FBI News, September 10, 2014, www.fbi.gov/news/testimony/cyber-security-terrorism-and-beyond-addressing-evolving-threats-to-the-homeland.

69. Nancy Scola, "FBI Director Comey Calls on Congress to Stop Unlockable Encryption: Good Luck with That," *The Switch* (blog), October 17, 2014, www.washingtonpost.com/blogs/the-switch/wp/2014/10/17/fbi-director-comey-calls-on-congress-to-stop-unlockable-encryption-good-luck-with-that/.

70. Note the following paragraphs on attorney general guidelines and the FBI's pre-9/11 investigations are quoted from the Center for National Security Studies—The FBI Domestic Counterterrorism Program material at Gelman Library, April 26, 1995, https://cdt.org/files/security/usapatriot/19950426cnss-fbi-analysis.html.

71. Neil Lewis, "Terror in Oklahoma: Legislation; Clinton Plan Would Broaden F.B.I. Powers," *New York Times*, April 25, 1995.

72. Bruce Hoffman, Ed Meese III, Tim J. Roemer, *The FBI: Protecting the Homeland in the 21st Century* (Washington, DC: FBI, March 2015).

73. John Edwards, Homeland Security Address, Brookings Institute, Washington, DC, December 18, 2002.

74. Robert Bryant, John Hamre, John Lawn, John MacGaffin, Howard Shapiro, and Jeffrey Smith, "America Needs More Spies," *The Economist*, July 12–18, 2003.

75. Department of Defense, "Army Releases Report on Fort Hood Shooting Investigation," January 23, 2015, http://archive.defense.gov/news/newsarticle.aspx?id=128024.

76. FBI, *FY 2015 Authorization and Budget Request*.

77. James Comey, "Confronting Corporate Crime" (speech given at New York City Bar Third Annual White-Collar Crime Institute, New York, May 29, 2014), www.fbi.gov/news/speeches/confronting-corporate-crime.

78. FBI, "Most Wanted Talent: Seeking Tech Experts to Become Cyber Special Agents," December 29, 2014, www.fbi.gov/news/stories/2014/december/fbi-seeking-tech-experts-to-become-cyber-special-agents/fbi-seeking-tech-experts-to-become-cyber-special-agents.

79. Dune Lawrence, "The U.S. Government Wants 6,000 New 'Cyberwarriors' by 2016," *Bloomberg*, April 15, 2015, www.bloomberg.com/bw/articles/2014–04–15/uncle-sam-wants-cyber-warriors-but-can-he-compete.

80. Ellen Nakashima, "Federal Agencies, Private Firms Fiercely Compete in Hiring Cyber Experts," *Washington Post*, November 13, 2012, www.washingtonpost.com/world/national-security/federal-agencies-private-firms-fiercely-compete-in-hiring-cyber-experts/2012/11/12/a1fb1806–2504–11e2-ba29-238a6ac36a08_story.html.

81. Office of the Inspector General, *Sentinel Audit V: Status of the Federal Bureau of Investigation's Case Management System* (Washington, DC: Departmentof Justice, November 2009), https://oig.justice.gov/reports/FBI/a1003_redacted.pdf.

82. Because the lead from the FSB included information about Zubeidat Tsarnaeva, the DOJ OIG believes that the counterterrorism supervisor and counterterrorism agent should have given greater consideration to opening an assessment on her. However, given that the bulk of the derogatory information in the lead arguably focused on Tamerlan Tsarnaev, the DOJ OIG concluded that it was within its discretion not to open an assessment on Zubeidat Tsarnaeva and instead to conduct limited database queries using her name and other relevant identifiers.

83. Schmidt, "Change in Leaders."

84. Charlie Savage, "Wider Authority for FBI Agents Stirs Concern," *New York Times*, October 29, 2009.

85. IMDB, *Minority Report* Plot Summary, www.imdb.com/title/tt0181689/plotsummary.

86. Eric Lichtblau, "Connecting the Dots," *New York Review of Books*, March 16, 2003.

87. Hoffman, Meese, and Roemer, *FBI*.

CHAPTER 12

The Department of Homeland Security

Civil Protection and Resilience

Susan Ginsburg

> Our *National Strategy for Homeland Security* recognizes that while we must continue to focus on the persistent and evolving terrorist threat, we also must address the full range of potential catastrophic events, including man-made and natural disasters, due to their implications for homeland security.
>
> —2007 National Strategy for Homeland Security

> Modern society runs on complex critical infrastructure systems that did not exist prior to the last century. Fragility—the opposite of resilience—is a symptom of complexity.
>
> —Ted G. Lewis

The national security enterprise (NSE) entered a new phase after September 11, 2001, when the Bush administration introduced the most dramatic expansion and reform of the national security structure since 1947. The Department of Homeland Security (DHS) was the first new department created explicitly for national security reasons. Legislated in 2002, established in March 2003, and completed along with the other new government agencies in 2004, it became the third largest department behind the Department of Defense (DOD) and the Department of Veterans Affairs. Its 2015 budget of $61 billion employed over 240,000 people and nearly as many contract employees.

Despite anticipation of the need for such an organization before 9/11, DHS was hastily formed and was as much the product of political, ideological, and strategic conflict as emotional consensus. Its organizational culture is new, still developing, and challenged by internal and external factors. Indeed, DHS hit a low point in early 2015, when Congress nearly defunded the department altogether over a policy dispute with the president concerning immigration.

The need felt by both the White House and Congress to create a new organization to respond to an altered security environment is understandable. Nevertheless, this urgency did not produce a clear strategic logic for DHS, ensure its effectiveness, or guarantee its long-term future. However, if the problems that gave rise to DHS are ongoing or deepening, then it or some alternative government organization is essential. As its near defunding illustrates, DHS does not enjoy anything like the consensus about its mission and criticality that DOD does.

Whether DHS consolidates its place in the national security framework will depend on how well it meets four significant challenges. First, this chapter will examine DHS's creation and Congress's difficulty establishing a coherent mission. Second, it will describe the challenges of structuring twenty-two diverse organizations making up the new department and creating a unified culture. Third, the chapter will tackle this new department's tricky constitutional pathway. Lastly, it will assess DHS's management and performance. In the course of exploring these challenges, this chapter will describe the agencies and functions that make up DHS and leadership decisions and significant events that have shaped its activities. It will also sketch the homeland or civil security culture that DHS is engendering, criticism that it is encountering, and some possible directions DHS may take in the future.

MISSION DEFINITION: FLAWED AT BIRTH

The most important challenge for DHS is resolving its unsettled role in the counterterrorism field. Congress joined with a reluctant White House to establish DHS as the department responsible for preventing terrorism. But political leaders placed DHS into an NSE already endowed with significant responsibilities for counterterrorism assigned to the established intelligence, law enforcement, and military agencies. How the weighty imperative of terrorism prevention and the circumscribed counterterrorism role for DHS would be reconciled was unclear and has remained problematic. Moreover, DHS's enabling statute dictated considerably wider responsibilities than terrorism prevention. In the years since DHS's establishment, these statutory authorities and compelling events have combined to broaden the scope of DHS's missions. Congressional and public expectations for civil security surpass terrorism to encompass natural disasters, high-impact industrial accidents and infrastructure failures, and cybersecurity.

This gradual expansion of actual and accepted mission scope has followed the course of destructive events—the 9/11 attacks, Hurricane Katrina in 2005, the Deepwater Horizon oil spill in 2010, and the intensification of cyberattacks, among other significant incidents and trends. Pandemics and climate change, and other global, potentially catastrophic risks, also engage the department. But DHS does not benefit from a central strategic rationale or an updated legislative authorization that sets out an overarching purpose encompassing its protective and resilience activities.[1] As will be discussed later, DHS's mandate is complicated by the fact that numerous other federal departments and agencies, from DOD to the Federal Trade Commission, have some responsibilities in these areas. Lack of clarity—and shared conviction—about its mission has placed DHS on the defensive. DHS's situation in this regard reflects ambivalence among many about the concept and nomenclature of homeland security in relation to US national security, rendering DHS's strategic foundations unclear.

The Hart–Rudman Commission

DHS's conceptual roots lie in the US Commission on National Security / 21st Century better known as the Hart–Rudman Commission.[2] Assessing dangers arising with the end of the Cold War and intensifying globalization and drawing on ideas current in the White House, the commission foresaw the growth of terrorism as an asymmetric tactic that could use weapons of mass destruction (WMDs) to strike the US population and critical infrastructure. In its final report in January 2001—just nine months before the attacks of September 11, 2001—it recommended the establishment of a new National Homeland Security Agency (NHSA). But as conceived of by the Hart–Rudman Commission, the new department was not intended to engage in traditional counterterrorism. Instead, it was to combine existing border security organizations with the Federal Emergency Management Agency (FEMA) and create new cyber and infrastructure protection capabilities. As envisioned by the commission, NHSA was to plan, coordinate, and integrate border and immigration security activities, critical infrastructure protection, and emergency preparedness and response to natural and human-instigated disasters. A science and technology office would support these functions, and a national crisis center would monitor emergencies and coordinate federal support to state and local governments and the private sector. At about the same time, a separate commission, led by former Virginia governor Jim Gilmore, issued a series of reports emphasizing, among other issues, the need to boost public health resources and augment state and local governments' participation in the new security.[3]

These two commission reports remain the most coherent blueprint for DHS's organization and homeland security priorities. The central point of the recommendations was that even strengthened law enforcement and foreign intelligence organizations were radically insufficient to cope with twenty-first-century terrorism. The proposed homeland security agency was not to supplant existing law enforcement and intelligence functions but instead to augment their impact with new capabilities relating to the domestic context. It would have its own analytic intelligence capabilities intended to connect with the existing, reformed counterterrorism agencies, primarily to support infrastructure protection.[4]

The White House's first National Strategy for Homeland Security (2002), however, combined existing and new counterterrorism functions under one definition.[5] The strategy's singular focus was terrorist attacks: to prevent terrorist attacks within the United States, reduce America's vulnerability to terrorism, and minimize the damage and recover from attacks that do occur. It laid out six mission areas and called all of them homeland security: intelligence and warning, border and transportation security, domestic counterterrorism, critical infrastructure and key asset protection, defense against catastrophic threats, and emergency preparedness and response.

Homeland security as a concept thus became more than shorthand for the add-ons to counterterrorism enumerated by the Hart–Rudman Commission. It became a new branch of national security incorporating the previously configured domestic counterterrorism mission and these augmentations. When Congress adopted this strategic formulation wholesale in the Homeland Security Act of 2002 (HSA), which established DHS, the department nominally became responsible for homeland security writ large, including established counterterrorism in the domestic environment.[6] The many implications were not examined. Most important, the HSA placed singular focus on DHS's terrorist-preventing mission although the law incorporated agencies having little to do with standard terrorism; rather, their primary authorities lay in migration and border security, cyber and infrastructure protection, and disaster preparedness and response, arenas relevant to but transcending terrorism.

Intelligence and Law Enforcement Reforms

During the same period a parallel discussion was taking place about post-9/11 reform in the intelligence, law enforcement, and military communities to deal with more potent terrorism, building on the work of prior administrations. Prominent advisors and commissions pushed for a wave of renovations of existing institutions, especially in the intelligence and law enforcement communities.[7] Of these commissions only the Hart–Rudman and Gilmore Commissions paid close attention to border and mobility protection, cyber and infrastructure protection, special weapons defense and public health, and disaster preparedness and response. The Gilmore Commission focused on the population's defense against biothreats and WMDs and also recommended that there be a new stand-alone agency equivalent to the United Kingdom's MI5 to conduct domestic intelligence to supplement the law enforcement role of the Federal Bureau of Investigation (FBI) and the foreign intelligence role of the Central Intelligence Agency (CIA).[8] Advocates for this proposal did not prevail. President George W. Bush famously told his attorney general, John Ashcroft, never to let this happen again, thus charging the Department of Justice (DOJ) with preventing terrorist acts rather than relying on the deterrent of prosecutions after the fact. But the issuance of a homeland security strategy centered on counterterrorism left a question mark hanging over DHS—what would be its role in the domestic intelligence arena?

A drawn-out conflict ensued over reorientation in the intelligence community and the counterterrorism effort generally. One battle involved DHS. Congress in the HSA specifies nineteen responsibilities for DHS's information analysis function that would make it pivotal to the national counterterrorism effort and to upgrading and consolidating the US domestic intelligence effort. Congress assigned DHS with three main responsibilities: (1) receive and analyze intelligence and law enforcement information to understand the nature and scope of a terrorist threat; (2) conduct comprehensive assessments on the vulnerability of critical infrastructure and key resources; and (3) consult with the director of central intelligence and other appropriate intelligence and law enforcement to establish collection priorities and strategies for information. The bridge between new generation homeland security, in particular its intelligence functions, and existing counterterrorism organizations was never fully conceptualized, designed, resourced, or built. Thus, no MI5 equivalent ever emerged. The White House chose not to fully develop these ideas but instead to allow existing agencies to enhance their counterterrorism roles.

President Bush further circumscribed the authority of DHS with respect to counterterrorism with his surprise announcement creating the Terrorist Threat Integration Center (TTIC) in his State of the Union address on January 28, 2003. TTIC reduced the fledgling DHS from a leading player in terrorism prevention to the weakest member of a multiple-agency NSE comprising the intelligence community, FBI, DOJ, and DOD; all of it reporting to the director of central intelligence (and later the director of national intelligence [DNI]). Even before they could be exercised, DHS's legal authorities were coopted by other agencies. The most visible impact was on personnel. The intelligence community agencies that had committed to sending personnel to DHS now had to send them to TTIC. DHS was severely disadvantaged in competing for people, leaving it to rely excessively on contractors.

Subsequently, the 9/11 Commission in 2004 and the WMD Commission in 2005 made recommendations that left the FBI and CIA primarily responsible for terrorism prevention. Congress in December 2004 replaced TTIC with the National Counterterrorism Center (NCTC), reporting to the DNI and to the president, granting it strategic operational planning authority for counterterrorism. The DNI stood up a new intelligence community structure that gave minimal attention to DHS. Intelligence community leaders saw to it that DHS would not have the authority to collect intelligence and would receive only what the CIA gave it. The FBI threw itself into boosting domestic intelligence capacity, establishing multiple programs and significantly boosting the function and number of joint terrorism task forces

(JTTFs) across the country. The FBI overpowered DHS in the bureaucratic competition surrounding investigations relating to terrorism and usually declined to share information. If there was ever to be an MI5-type agency—and the question still lingers—it would not be part of DHS.

Searching for Its Place

The gap between its statutory mandate of terrorism prevention and actual powers has challenged DHS leadership to redefine the department's overall purpose. While reiterating that DHS's primary statutory mission is to prevent terrorism, the secretaries of DHS have struggled to explain how counterterrorism conventionally understood is functionally primary at DHS and to retain its place in the NSE. DHS's first secretary, Tom Ridge, mindful that local authorities would have to make potentially costly decisions on the basis of federal statements, insisted that DHS independently evaluate and communicate intelligence about terrorist threats to state and local officials, rather than simply disseminate information provided by the FBI, the CIA, or other agencies. But he bowed to FBI control over terrorism "watchlists" and accepted the number-two position for DHS in the management of the Terrorism Screening Center (TSC); taking a backseat to the FBI despite the terrorist lists' integral role in DHS's core functions of screening travelers and immigrants symbolized DHS's weak bureaucratic prowess. DHS similarly relinquished the leadership of the Human Smuggling and Trafficking Center, intended to integrate investigative and open-source information and intelligence about human smuggling and trafficking and terrorist travel.[9]

DHS efforts to define itself as the interface with the public on terrorism have been equally compromised. The first generation DHS terrorism warning system based on color alerts had to be scrapped as too simplistic. Now DHS's role in the National Terrorism Advisory System is classified. DHS has a few original domestic counterterrorism programs. These include state-level fusion centers as nodes for information sharing, which DHS instigated and supports but which operate under state and local law. There are also homeland security grants distributed to state and local authorities and programs aimed at bolstering community partnerships to counter violent extremism. Perhaps the most noticeable program, the If You See Something, Say Something campaign, was launched by Secretary Janet Napolitano. Compared with DHS's overall activities, these are small programs, several of which are equally attributable to cyber and infrastructure protection. DHS's Office of Intelligence and Analysis, established in 2007, remains fragmented and weak, which the intelligence community prefers. To date, primary counterterrorism resources and functions as defined by the National Counterterrorism Strategy continue to belong to other departments and agencies.

Despite DHS's limited intelligence function, it makes critical contributions to the national counterterrorism effort through its border and mobility security protection programs. The ability to detect a terrorist, track illicit articles and funds, disrupt human traffickers and smugglers, and seize evidence is no small matter.[10] DHS's role in managing lawful immigration and confronting illicit mass migration is equally significant. Its three other arenas—cyber and infrastructure protection, defense against biothreats and WMDs generally, and disaster preparedness and response—are also vital to countering twenty-first-century terror in all its forms. However, neither Congress nor any of the DHS secretaries has articulated an overarching DHS mission that would resolve the counterterrorism conundrum and definitively characterize DHS's missions.

While presidents have directed DHS secretaries to take the lead on immigration, DHS secretaries otherwise have tended to be event driven. After Hurricane Katrina in 2005, the dizzying series of crises through which Secretary Napolitano led DHS is illustrative:

- in 2009 the H1N1 flu pandemic originating in Mexico and the failed Christmas Day attempt by a passenger to ignite a bomb hidden in his underwear on board a flight from Amsterdam to Detroit;
- in 2010 bombs hidden inside printer cartridges departing on flights to the United States from Yemen and the Deepwater Horizon oil spill;
- in 2012 Super Storm Sandy, which flooded Long Island, coastal New Jersey, and Lower Manhattan; and
- in 2013 the Boston Marathon bombing.[11]

Cabinet officers who surmount such tumultuous events with their reputations intact offer profiles in resilience, a key goal of homeland security. It may well be asked whether more is possible, such as a leader with a defining intellectual vision, an ability to forge a congressional consensus, and an intradepartmental management structure to carry it out.

STRUCTURING THE CIVIL SECURITY MISSION

The second and related challenge is to rationalize DHS's structure and knit together the disparate cultures that the department's twenty-two agencies reflect. Resolving which components and functions belong in DHS, improving its internal organization, elevating its external networks of collaborative relationships, and streamlining its framework for political oversight by Congress and the White House are huge, ongoing tasks. A number of hurdles remain on all these fronts.

Congress fused nearly two dozen agencies from other departments in whole or in part to form DHS, an unprecedented and ambitious amalgamation. Unity of effort has been wanting. The central problem is that DHS cannot be organized only around its declared statutory mission of preventing terrorism because, as discussed earlier, counterterrorism assets in a traditional sense largely reside elsewhere. Moreover, DHS's mission is also much broader than counterterrorism as typically understood. Primary responsibilities are border and mobility protection—encompassing DHS's duties concerning borders and coastlines, transportation, travel and shipping, and immigration and migration—cyber and infrastructure protection, and disaster preparedness and response. In addition, DHS has domestic responsibilities for defense against chemical, biological, radiological, nuclear, and explosive (CBRNE) threats, historically dispersed among multiple departments. Lack of a well-articulated, unified purpose that encompasses and makes all its missions transparent renders DHS susceptible to the view that its collection of agencies and functions may be somewhat arbitrary and subject to either being returned to their former agency homes or eliminated altogether.

Since its formation it has been clear that DHS cannot achieve its goals without an array of critical partnerships: with other federal departments and agencies; with state, local, tribal, and territorial authorities; with private and nonprofit sectors; and with foreign governments and international entities. All NSE components deal with foreign relationships to an increasing degree, but for DHS international partnerships, those with domestic government and nongovernment organizations, and those with the private sector are uniquely central. At each stage on the spectrum of homeland or civil security, from risk analysis and prevention through incident response, new strategic needs require new legal and organizational structures to incorporate actors previously not present in the center of security practice. In effect, key DHS activities are taking place on multiple levels simultaneously: (1) at the intersection of the public and private sectors (its cyber and infrastructure security roles); (2) at the intersection of the domestic and international (border protection and traveler screening with foreign partners); and (3) where whole-of-government coordination and community collaboration occurs (its cyber and infrastructure protection and incident-response roles). The redesign of these non-regulatory relationships is emerging incrementally but is radical in nature; establishing the right organizational constructs has been a particularly important challenge. There are as yet few widely accepted best practices, and the relationships are not yet generally recognized as established governance channels. Thus, DHS initiatives in these areas are susceptible to being dismissed as overreach or simply discounted.

While Congress established two new authorizing committees to oversee homeland security, it left jurisdiction over many component DHS agencies in the committees that had historically overseen them. DHS jurisdiction is consequently diffused among some ninety committees and subcommittees and thirty other congressional groups.[12] This has compounded DHS's internal structural problems. Each congressional entity seeks to drive its legacy element of the department, making it difficult to rationalize and unify the department. Congress's failure to completely adapt its own committee structure to help unify the new department's oversight reinforces the centrifugal forces inherent in an aggregation of multiple preexisting agencies. Congress and the White House have partially adapted the National Security Council (NSC) structure to the formation of DHS. But multiple overlapping working groups make it difficult to reach decisions efficiently or to be confident that critical perspectives have been incorporated in major decisions.

Organizing the Agencies

The list of the twenty-two agencies Congress combined to create DHS speaks plainly to the obstacles to uniting behind a straightforward counterterrorism mission and achieving managerial or cultural cohesion. (See table 12.1.) The core of the new civil security missions are border and mobility protection, cyber and infrastructure protection, and disaster preparedness and response, as well as DHS's pandemic and CBRNE programs. How these diverse functions and cultures can be unified remains a major DHS hurdle.

Border and Mobility Protection

Border and mobility protection is a newly important mission, first, in the context of terrorism, nonproliferation, and international criminal activity. Second, the immigration policy agenda has been elevated by increased global mobility, legal and illegal, for work and personal reasons. Finally, migration has also become strategically important owing to large-scale movements of people caused by war, political chaos, extreme poverty, and environmental events. Congress combined three major services with venerable histories to form the core of what has become DHS's border and mobility protection function and to these added one new agency. The US Customs Service was established in 1789, and its collection of duties served as the principal source of revenues for the new republic. Congress decided to move it from the Treasury Department to DHS and broke it up in the process. Few realize the Customs Service is the largest agency incorporated in DHS, with extensive commercial responsibilities

Table 12.1. Legacy Agencies in the Department of Homeland Security

General Function	Legacy Agency	Original Department	New Agency / Office
Border and Mobility Protection	Immigration and Naturalization Service	Justice	US Customs and Border Protection US Immigration and Customs Enforcement US Citizenship and Immigration Services
	US Customs Service	Treasury	US Customs and Border Protection US Immigration and Customs Enforcement
	Animal and Plant Health Inspection Service (part)	Agriculture	US Customs and Boarder Protection
	US Coast Guard	Transportation	US Coast Guard
	Transportation Security Administration	Transportation	Transportation Security Administration
	Federal Law Enforcement Training Center	Treasury	Federal Law Enforcement Training Center
	Federal Protective Service	General Services Administration	US Immigration and Customs Enforcement
Cyber and Infrastructure Protection	US Secret Service	Treasury	US Secret Service
	National Communications System	Defense	Office of Cybersecurity and Communications National Protection and Programs Directorate
	Federal Computer Incident Response Center	General Services Administration	US-CERT, Office of Cybersecurity and Communications National Protection and Programs Directorate
	Energy Security and Assurance Program	Energy	Office of Infrastructure Protection
	National Infrastructure Protection Center	FBI	Office of Operations Coordination Office of Infrastructure Protection
Preparedness and Response	Federal Emergency Management Agency	none	Federal Emergency Management Agency
	Office for Domestic Preparedness	Justice	Responsibilities distributed within FEMA
	Domestic Emergency Support Teams	Justice	Responsibilities distributed within FEMA
	National Domestic Preparedness Office	FBI	Responsibilities distributed within FEMA
	Nuclear Incident Response Team	Energy	Responsibilities distributed within FEMA
	Strategic National Stockpile National Disaster Medical System	Health and Human Services	Returned to HHS, July 2004
Pandemic and CBRNE Defense Countermeasures	CBRN Countermeasures Programs	Energy	Science & Technology Directorate
	Environmental Measurements Laboratory	Energy	Science & Technology Directorate
	National Biological Warfare Defense Analysis Center	Defense	Science & Technology Directorate
	Plum Island Animal Disease Center	Agriculture	Science & Technology Directorate

Source: Department of Homeland Security, "Who Joined DHS," 2003, www.dhs.gov/who-joined-dhs#.

as well as inspection and investigation skills. Its traveler, shipper, and criminal databases are a key tool in border security and a focus for debates about privacy and civil liberties.

The US Coast Guard also has its origins in the Revenue Marine, created by Congress in 1790 to collect customs duties. A military service linked to the Navy, originally housed in the Treasury Department and later in the Department of Transportation, it operates under civilian leadership during peacetime and may be merged with defense forces during wartime. It has a hybrid set of safety, security, and stewardship missions, as well as regulatory, law enforcement, intelligence, and search and rescue–emergency management authorities. These well-practiced functions, along with its close ties to DOD, have enabled the Coast Guard to provide models, lessons, and leadership for DHS.

The federal government began regulating immigration in 1890 through a series of departments culminating in the formation of the Immigration and Naturalization Service in DOJ in 1933. Broken up and restructured within DHS, it brought to DHS its contributing roles in managing American pluralism, adjusting the American labor supply, integrating immigrants, preventing and responding to humanitarian and migration crises, and securing US borders. Its supercharged strategic, policy, and policing role became the hottest political flashpoint for DHS.

This can be seen in the political battles relating to the three newly constructed agencies, Customs and Border Protection (CBP) and its Border Patrol, Immigration and Customs Enforcement (ICE) and its Homeland Security Investigations unit (HSI), and Citizenship and Immigration Services (CIS). The Transportation Security Administration (TSA), created in November 2001 in the Department of Transportation and moved to DHS at its inception, covers security for aviation, highways, railroads, buses, mass transit systems, pipelines, and ports. To millions of passengers who encounter its airport screeners, TSA represents DHS's public face.

DHS's border and mobility protection role is its most well-known and accepted mission. A proposal to unify the immigration and customs agencies to achieve better synergy in border security and management had been developed during the 1990s and was picked up and acted on after 9/11 in the formation of DHS. The integration of transportation security has been more controversial; there are sporadic calls to return TSA to the Department of Transportation. Achieving closer coordination among border and mobility agencies, internally and globally, remains a challenge. For instance, the system failed dramatically when in 2009 the Christmas bomber, Umar Farouk Abdulmutallab, traveled from Amsterdam to Detroit. The terrorist was able to board a plane after the Department of State had issued him a visa, despite simultaneously alerting the NCTC to concerns about him and precluding future visas. CBP did not have the analytic resources to probe the visa adjudication, and there were no provisions for US or coordinated international inspection on the ground in Amsterdam. More ability to know about him—Abdulmutallab previously had been denied a visa to the UK— and what he was carrying, rather than less, at more stages of travel, would have been useful.

Notwithstanding the flawed process surrounding Abdulmutallab, one of DHS's greatest successes is in building bridges across borders. The first four DHS secretaries have each contributed to expanding counterterrorism and counter-crime partnerships to secure and facilitate the movement of people and goods between the United States and other countries, not always with the support of the State Department.[13] Collaborative efforts to manage the borders with Canada and Mexico have deepened since 9/11, preclearance programs currently exist in six countries, partnerships with the business community have expanded, the visa waiver program engages partners in intelligence sharing, and in-country refugee processing is in use in Central America.[14] The EU, after fifteen years of opposition, has adopted DHS's model of airline–government passenger name record sharing.

Domestic politics surrounding illegal immigration is another matter. Although apprehensions on the southwest border are nearly as low as they have been since 1972, public attention to CBP's and ICE's activities is unavoidably subject to sudden national level flare-ups relating to immigration politics, as well as ongoing state- and local-level tensions; immigration as an issue divides citizens and the numbers of people, families, communities, and countries affected by it are enormous. The goal of comprehensive immigration reform, incorporating alliances with sending and transit countries, that would achieve a national political equilibrium remains elusive. TSA is also subject to political attack that reflects policy disagreements. Its reassuring airport screening presence brought air travelers back to flying in the months after 9/11 but is pilloried by commentators as security theater.[15] Even TSA leadership has called for more flexibility from Congress in managing risk.[16] Such tactical questions won't be resolved outside larger strategic discussions about terrorism prevention and how much security investment makes sense given the inability to prevent all attacks—for example, as in the Brussels Airport in 2016, where terrorists targeted visitors dropping off passengers or in a ticketing line, well outside airport screening locations.

Cyber and Infrastructure Protection

In contrast to border and mobility protection, cyber and infrastructure protection is a fundamentally new security mission for the United States. The Internet was only made publicly available and commercialized in 1991. Both the dependence on infrastructure and its complexity have been increasing, subjecting the population and economy to more risk of major disruption by attack, natural disaster, or technological breakdown.[17] In the context of any of these scenarios, infrastructure protection represents a necessary, defensive strategy.[18] Resilient infrastructure and communities and effective response practices enable society and constitutional government to withstand and recover from extraordinary and exceptionally destructive events for which traditional national security means are neither effective nor affordable.

President Bill Clinton's Commission on Critical Infrastructure Protection first foresaw the need for this new dimension of security. It defined national infrastructure as "a network of independent, mostly privately-owned, man-made systems that function collaboratively and synergistically to produce and distribute a continuous flow of essential goods and services" and critical infrastructure as "an infrastructure so vital that its incapacity or destruction would have a debilitating impact on our defense and national security."[19] The commission warned that terrorism with WMDs could threaten critical infrastructure and that computerization of critical infrastructure systems, and their linkage through the Internet, would create cyber vulnerabilities. The Hart–Rudman Commission agreed. Congress transferred four existing offices from different departments to DHS to form the core of a new infrastructure security function: the National Communications System, the Federal Computer Incident Response Center, the Energy Security and Assurance Program, and the National Infrastructure Protection Center. With these offices came the seeds of a new critical infrastructure culture: computer science, mathematical risk analysis, and sectoral expertise, none of which had been developed for these purposes.

Notwithstanding this initiative, the question has persisted whether a new civilian agency can properly provide cyber leadership or whether DOD should be front and center.[20] Congress has affirmed that DHS is responsible for cybersecurity in the ".gov" and ".com" environments, while DOD protects the ".mil" environment.[21] But DHS's cybersecurity effort is relatively small and weak compared with the department's long-standing border security and disaster response services, and it has suffered from comparison with the National Security Agency (NSA), the vast signals intelligence agency housed in DOD.[22] The FY 2016 DOD budget requested $5.5 billion for cyberspace activities, while Congress only appropriated $819 million for DHS cybersecurity programs.[23] The public's attention has been drawn to cybersecurity mainly through high-profile attacks on businesses and other nongovernmental institutions.[24] For DHS's cybersecurity units, the alleged Chinese hack of the Office of Personnel Management (OPM) in 2015 was the equivalent of 9/11 for the counterterrorism community or Hurricane Katrina for disaster management—a signal of strategic shift, in this case requiring that formerly humdrum government systems be treated as major security assets.[25]

Because Congress has not granted DHS conventional regulatory authority over cyber systems, the public has little sense of what DHS does. DHS is consolidating its cybersecurity activities under the National Cybersecurity and Communication Integration Center (NCCIC). NCCIC's primary focus is on incident response, including providing analysis of threat data and an institutional framework for information sharing. NCCIC is the hub for sharing information because Congress authorized DHS to grant liability protection to participating companies.[26] The National Protection and Programs Directorate (NPPD) provides guidance on voluntary vulnerability and risk assessments; however, strategic thinking concerning cybersecurity with significant involvement of the private sector is only beginning.[27] Cybersecurity research and development is sponsored both by NPPD and by DHS's Science and Technology Directorate.[28] DHS is transforming the current NPPD into the Cyber and Infrastructure Protection Agency, intended to be an operational unit comparable to FEMA and the border and mobility protection services.[29]

With respect to infrastructure protection beyond cybersecurity, DHS has responsibilities for both government and private sector infrastructure.[30] The Federal Protective Service handles physical security for nonmilitary government installations.[31] DHS has regulatory authority over the chemical industry to guard against chemical releases but no comparable authority in other sectors.[32] Instead, as with cybersecurity, it is institutionalizing new forms of partnerships. It employs protective security advisors (PSAs) who conduct site visits, coordinate the vulnerability risk assessments, and plan outreach activities with federal, state, local, and private owners and operators. Information sharing and analysis centers (ISACs) and their statutory successors, information sharing and analysis organizations (ISAOs), were an early construct to share cyber and other information that is still evolving.[33] Government coordinating councils (GCCs) and counterpart private sector coordinating councils (SCCs), also established by executive order, are policy-oriented structures through which DHS and other departments consult and coordinate with the private sector on civil security matters.[34] DHS has the lead for most such coordination, as shown in table 12.2; however, other departments are involved, and even regulatory agencies are increasingly addressing cybersecurity.[35] DHS has been short on sectoral expertise, and the entire field has lacked organizing theoretical insight and robust funding. However, DHS is developing new risk assessment practices.[36]

One of the key problems for DHS in aligning the department's diverse agencies around its central missions has been Congress's insistence on internal autonomy and independent direct reporting to the secretary for particular components. The US Secret Service (USSS) came to DHS from the Treasury Department, where it originated with a mission to safeguard the US currency against counterfeiting. It acquired the duty of presidential protection after the 1901 assassination of President William McKinley and also protects foreign heads of state. Its primary strategic role is to support continuity of the presidency, a government continuity mission similar to other sector-specific security missions. A secondary priority is investigating financial and computer crimes, also congruent with DHS's cyber and infrastructure security mission. Notwithstanding its fit within DHS's cyber and infrastructure protection unit, Congress permits the USSS to operate relatively independently within DHS. This and having the

Table 12.2. Critical Infrastructure and Key Assets

Sector	Sector-Specific Agency
Chemical	Department of Homeland Security
Commercial facilities	Department of Homeland Security
Communications	Department of Homeland Security
Critical manufacturing	Department of Homeland Security
Dams	Department of Homeland Security
Emergency services	Department of Homeland Security
Information technology	Department of Homeland Security
Nuclear reactors, materials, and waste	Department of Homeland Security
Government facilities	Department of Homeland Security / General Services Administration
Transportation systems	Department of Homeland Security / Department of Transportation
Defense industrial base	Department of Defense
Energy	Department of Energy
Financial services	Department of the Treasury
Food and agriculture	Department of Agriculture / Department of Health and Human Services
Health care and public health	Department of Health and Human Services
Water and wastewater systems	Environmental Protection Agency

Source: Presidential Policy Directive 21, 2013.
Note: "The term 'Sector-Specific Agency' indicates the federal department or agency responsible for providing institutional knowledge and specialized expertise as well as leading, facilitating, or supporting the security and resilience programs and associated activities of its designated critical infrastructure sector in the all-hazards environment" (Presidential Policy Directive 21, 2013).

ear of the president has made the USSS resistant to cabinet direction and a management headache associated with recurring scandals.[37]

Defense against Pandemics and Special Substance Incidents

DHS's efforts in the arena of pandemics and CBRNE weapons make up its one major mission (or missions) that defies summary in plain language. Aum Shinrikyo's release of sarin gas, a toxin, in a Tokyo subway and al-Qaeda's video of its animal experiments with chemical dispersants were among the incidents that set the stage for concern, which reached a fever pitch with anthrax attacks—and deaths—in Florida and Washington, DC, in late 2001.[38] The 2002 Homeland Security Strategy called for defense against catastrophic threats, referring to "chemical, biological, radiological, nuclear and explosive." CBRNE is generally used to describe agents relating to one of those categories. With the increasing commoditization of weaponry and Internet-accessible scientific information, it made sense to elevate the problem of attacks on the population with special weapons to a higher level of strategic concern.[39] But definitional problems persist. In the National Strategy for CBRNE Standards, CBRNE "incidents" are only used to describe incidents in which one or more of these agents are weaponized, not to describe a naturally occurring incident.[40] According to DHS, biological threats are defined as biological agents (bacteria, viruses, or toxins) that can kill or incapacitate people, livestock, and crops.[41] A biological attack is defined as "the deliberate release of germs or other biological substances that can make you sick."[42] The consequences of a human-instigated biothreat and one caused by zoonotic disease may be indistinguishable, both resulting in massive loss of life, pressure on the nation's health resources, and cascading consequences across the economy and communities. Thus, the recent Blue Ribbon Study Panel on Biodefense combined biological warfare, bioterrorism, and infectious disease within the term biological threat.[43]

Congress made an incomplete effort toward establishing a CBRNE defense function within DHS by transferring four centers for research relating to animal disease and chemical, biological, nuclear, and radiological weapons from the Departments of Agriculture, Defense, and Energy to DHS's S&T. DHS also established the Domestic Nuclear Detection Office (DNDO) in 2005 at the instigation of the Office of the Vice President to enhance and coordinate federal, state, and local efforts to combat nuclear smuggling domestically and overseas.[44] DNDO is the primary entity responsible for domestic nuclear detection, for coordinating response to radiological and nuclear threats, and for integrating federal nuclear forensics programs. Lastly, DHS, on its own initiative in 2007, established the Office of Health Affairs to carry out its responsibilities with regard to pandemics. Under the 2006 Strategy for Pandemic Influenza, DHS supports communities and businesses to develop and execute pandemic contingency plans and preparedness actions.

During a possible pandemic response, the DHS secretary coordinates nonmedical support and response actions and supports the health and human services secretary's coordination of public health and medical emergency response efforts. DHS coordinates federal operations and resources, establishes reporting requirements, and maintains ongoing communications with federal, state, local, and tribal governments, the private sector, and nongovernmental organizations pursuant to the National Response Plan (NRP). Other federal agencies, notably DOD, the Department of Health and Human Services (HHS), and the Department of Energy (DOE), all have jurisdiction over aspects of special substance threats and pandemics. For pandemics an order of responsibility is relatively discernable. For CBRNE matters there is no centralized leadership and splintered responsibilities. DOD's accidental shipment of live anthrax to nearly 200 laboratories over a dozen years through 2015 signals the disarray and complacency.[45] DHS in 2015 proposed merging its CBRNE-related organizational components into one unit to begin to build critical mass based on a strategic mission.

Disaster Preparedness and Response

Like border and mobility protection, disaster preparedness and response is a known mission with a storied history but with new salience and demands placed on it in the twenty-first century. It is integrally connected with cyber and infrastructure protection. Both missions contribute to achieving continuity and resilience in the society and state. Both assume an ongoing level of threat and vulnerability, with an active potential for disastrous or even catastrophic consequences. But simply stated, infrastructure protection in theory aims to diminish vulnerability and increase resilience, while emergency preparedness and response specializes in crisis assistance. The two overlap conceptually and practically when they focus on mitigation, resilience, and continuity, especially in relation to contemporary cyber and other technological infrastructure risks. For example, DHS's cybersecurity role includes an incident response function for system operators that dovetails with FEMA's for a potentially affected population should the crisis more widely compromise vital infrastructure systems.

President Jimmy Carter created FEMA after the Three Mile Island nuclear accident in 1979. FEMA is widely known for its support to first responders and federal aid in disasters that overwhelm state and local governments. It administers a flood insurance program that attempts to reconcile flood zone resident wishes with economic and environmental realities, seemingly a doomed proposition. FEMA also has one foot in the world of wartime civil defense and national security preparedness.[46] President Carter gave FEMA the authority to coordinate mobilization planning. President Reagan redirected the agency toward mobilization of local partnerships to respond to catastrophic natural disasters. Five civil defense offices transferred to DHS from the Departments of Justice, Energy, and Health and Human Services also are now housed in FEMA. With these transfers came responsibility for planning for evacuations, continuity of government, establishment of local emergency operations centers, and the emergency broadcast system. DOD also has authority to mobilize resources from the private sector in emergencies, under the 1950 Defense Production Act, bringing DHS and DOD into an undefined partnership for such circumstances as pandemic response. Practiced in dealing with seasonally and geographically predictable weather disasters, FEMA must grapple with unfamiliar technology-oriented crises associated with fragile cyber, electrical, and other infrastructure systems and slow-moving global climate change. In these arenas the risks are differently distributed geographically; forecasting tools and solutions are undeveloped or new and sophisticated, and not integrated into FEMA; and political pressure is intense.

Hurricane Katrina in 2005 had almost as much impact on the current DHS as 9/11. It affected over half a million people across three states, caused the deaths of over 1,600 people, and destroyed large parts of New Orleans. The grossly mismanaged White House and FEMA response to Hurricane Katrina in August 2005 caused Congress to rewrite FEMA's governing authority and the Bush administration to make its own significant changes.[47] Congress not only altered FEMA's operating authorities, but it also elevated FEMA within DHS's structure by placing the FEMA administrator at the deputy secretary level. This increased the scope of that officer's responsibilities, mandating direct reporting to the secretary and giving the position a statutory advisory relationship to the president, the Homeland Security Council (HSC), and the secretary, particularly during disasters.[48] The post-Katrina reforms represent a de facto recognition that terrorist attacks are not the singular source of terror potentially resulting in massive loss of life, public disorder, and domestic crises and that such risks require comparable attention.[49] Despite its far-reaching and important legal improvements to FEMA, Congress left untouched DHS's primary mission as preventing terrorism.[50] And although Congress recently considered the prospect of a major, enduring electricity blackout, DHS's mandate does not address the equivalent of a 9/11 or a Hurricane Katrina in the infrastructure domain.

DHS'S CONSTITUTIONAL CHALLENGES

The third challenge is to uphold a high standard of constitutionalism—adherence to constitutional principles—while responding to altered national security realities. All departments must operate in accordance with the Constitution. But most tread well-understood legal paths, whereas DHS acts in a theater of constitutional conflict. DHS's fundamental mission is to preclude terrorism in order to sustain Americans' constitutional rights, including, in addition to life, both civil liberties—such as freedom of speech and other rights of personal autonomy—and democratic rights associated with American federalism.[51] The methods needed to address the security problems with which DHS deals strain both these constitutional axes. US national security strategy has traditionally been constrained by international law and the law of war. However, DHS's missions intersect with US domestic law enforcement, border policing, and new domestic intelligence issues. As DHS must—unlike most other NSE members—operate substantially in relation to US citizens, the obligation to be both effective and constitutionally correct makes for an especially challenging objective. If DHS programs are found to violate the Constitution or other laws, the department loses legitimacy and public support, as did the NSA in connection with its telephone metadata collection program. But failure to be effective would also likely lead to more authority being granted to military and police forces. As discussed later, DHS has received its share of criticism with respect both to its approach to civil liberties and to state and local jurisdictions; it must overcome both to be sustainable as a department.

Congress emphasized the importance of civil liberties for DHS by establishing an internal privacy office, a first for the US government. Little known to most citizens, this is designed to keep DHS in compliance with US privacy laws, to address Freedom of Information Act (FOIA) requests made to DHS, and to address departmental privacy issues. This unique role has been influential government-wide even if not always praised.[52]

DHS participates in the effort to reconcile the different rules for law enforcement and for intelligence operations in their application to domestic counterterrorism. When its intelligence unit issued a report for local law enforcement in 2009 suggesting that extremists in the United States could recruit veterans to commit violence, DHS ran into a political firestorm.[53] Although its speculation proved correct—a number of veterans did later engage in the foreseen forms of violence—the backlash led the department to reduce domestic terrorism analysis for a time.[54] While not primarily responsible for the developing laws governing electronic and drone surveillance, DHS is involved through its own investigations and its assistance grants to State and other authorities. Like the FBI and NSA, it has been accused of excessive intrusiveness.[55]

DHS's border and mobility security mission also has given rise to a significant set of constitutional issues centering on freedom of movement internally and internationally. The courts and executive branch are struggling to delineate the rules governing: (1) the rights of an individual to contest being barred from flying or other travel and a citizen's right to movement, including returning to the United States;[56] (2) the power of DHS to search citizens, including their laptops, at borders;[57] (3) the extension of searches beyond the border itself;[58] and (4) DHS's use of personal information, or failure to use that information, including social media, to screen non-US persons.[59]

The biggest flashpoint with the US public has been TSA's deployment of an intrusive body-screening technology. An outcry caused DHS to withdraw the technology and to reconfigure another body scanner to minimize the visualization of the naked body, but litigation is ongoing.[60] CBP's migrant detention practices, especially in relation to the treatment of family units, children, and the sick, have been another focus of persistent criticism.[61] Border agencies' excessive use of force in the tense and sometimes violent border environment—in the past thirteen years thirty-three DHS personnel have been killed in the line of duty, four of them murdered—is a problem that DHS has struggled to overcome.[62] Both through its own enforcement programs and its grant programs, DHS has been implicated in the excessive use and transfer of military special operations equipment.[63] Because DHS is a federal government agency with national power, perceived excesses contribute to a local backlash against federal overreach.

When terrorism occurs domestically, it affects civil life and infrastructure involving local government, business, and community organizations. This domestic environment is predominantly the constitutional purview of states and municipalities. Citizens, localities, states, tribal authorities, and businesses traditionally have provided for their own policing, safety rules, and emergency management, with federal involvement only in extreme circumstances. While businesses have been subject to economic regulation, their duties in the new security environment are uncertain. By charging DHS with safeguarding the population and critical infrastructure against or in the event of catastrophic occurrences, Congress has required DHS to navigate a new federal security role in relation to states, local governments, tribal and territorial governments, and the private sector.

FEMA's preparedness and response role and DHS's cyber and infrastructure protection responsibilities place the department at the center of a debate over federalism. Insufficient preparedness capability in DHS could lead to loss of life and, in the most catastrophic of scenarios, descent into martial law and constitutional collapse. But an excessively centralized FEMA without the right state and municipal participation may undermine citizen and business capacity to cope with disasters and larger catastrophes, as well as tread on state and local constitutional authority, causing political friction and unduly burdening the federal budget.[64] An instance of such backlash occurred during response to the massive Deepwater Horizon oil spill in 2010, when "much of the external political pressure exerted on the response organization was the direct result of not engaging local officials prior to and during the spill response."[65] These issues have yet to be given the attention they merit at senior levels of government and business, to be fully engaged with by risk and resilience experts or resolved by the American people.

CONTINUING PERFORMANCE CRITICISM

The final challenge is that of management, performance, and results. The fundamental question is whether DHS's personnel and functions provide a force structure and a set of methods that adequately address the range of problems it confronts. As the previous discussion illustrates, measuring DHS's performance is not simply a matter of counting the number of domestic terrorist events uncovered, prevented, or managed. It is far more complex, having to do as well with the four main types of missions conducted by a dozen or so substantial agencies under the relatively loose control of the DHS secretary. Being recognized for results is particularly important for DHS because of lingering skepticism about the value of the department. If an FBI operation goes awry, commentators and Congress do not suggest that the FBI should be removed from DOJ or abolished altogether, but rather they specify and fund necessary improvements. Weaknesses in DHS performance are more likely to trigger commentary that the entity or activity may not belong in DHS or that DHS may itself have no valuable role since its supervision was inadequate.

DHS's reputation is so weak, and the morale of its personnel so poor, that it indeed can seem that Congress and the White House either erred in establishing DHS or botched its implementation. This section takes a closer look at its performance strengths and weaknesses—in its emerging civil security culture, its unity of effort, employee morale and capacities, and political oversight.

Culture

Especially as regards its legacy elements, DHS could easily be viewed as a culture of incongruent and competing agencies, still smarting from their reconfigurations within DHS. They are diverse and deeply anchored in rich histories of American immigration, trade, land and maritime borders, the presidency, and famous natural disasters. The Coast Guard flag has a meaning to its service that DHS's seal cannot replace; similar internal loyalty binds the Border Patrol and Secret Service. Each agency draws its own constituencies—boat owners, shippers, refugees and families of immigrants, agribusiness, natural disaster zone residents, and so on. But this image is simplistic. In fact, DHS's amalgamation process has been transformative. Two large cultural blocks emerged: law enforcement with its border security missions and federal primacy and emergency management with its first responders and state and local ties. A law enforcement culture has forced a tough approach to borders and immigration. An emergency management culture has promoted a concept of homeland security as a spectrum of domestic preparedness, protection, response, and recovery, which subsumes border security, critical infrastructure protection, and disaster management within an emergency management mindset. Both communities value loyalty and produce heroic figures willing to take extraordinary risks for others; paradoxically, this commonality has imprinted DHS with a culture of intense dedication. DHS personnel unhesitatingly rack up long hours during crises. A new department-wide volunteer force stands ready to deploy during disasters.[66]

The law enforcement–emergency management duopoly also has had costs. Both forces have played down emerging constitutional concerns. Competition between the two camps accentuates the seams within the department and between DHS and intelligence, military, and other organizations. Most important, by elevating operations, the duopoly crowds out the development of broader strategy and policy formulation. Both cultures want to take on the development of new expertise needed for cyber and critical infrastructure protection, but their operational bias stands in the way of a more strategic and unified approach. DHS's almost theory-free operational culture contrasts sharply with the military culture, which elevates strategy, and an intelligence culture that relies on comprehensive analysis and autonomous judgment. National energy, transportation, and health care policy also display more of the creative tension between strategists and implementing structures that fosters innovation if not always success.

DHS's lack of a guiding policy organization has its roots in ambivalence surrounding its establishment. Immediately following 9/11 the White House believed that locating the Office of Homeland Security in the executive office of the president (EOP) would be sufficient to develop and oversee implementation of strategy; it feared that establishing a new department would expand the federal government and budget. Senator Joseph Lieberman and a bipartisan group of members of Congress disagreed and sought the creation of a new department.[67] The president and Congress negotiated the creation of DHS after the White House staff drew up its own legislative proposal in response. Its initial organization featured a version of four of the five Hart–Rudman components: border and transportation security; infrastructure protection, combined with information analysis; emergency preparedness and response; and science and technology. (See figure 12.1.) But seeking to maintain its own dominance over DHS, contain its budget, and constrain its lateral and vertical reach among other government authorities, Congress declined to give DHS leadership a central policy office or establish a national operations center to better organize incident response. No fewer than twenty other

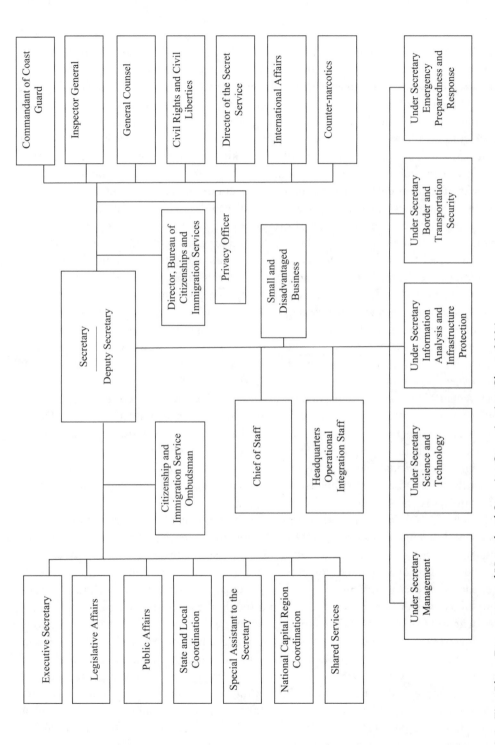

Figure 12.1. First Phase Department of Homeland Security Organization Chart, 2004

Source: Department of Homeland Security, *Brief Documentary History of the Department of Homeland Security* (Washington, DC, 2008).

functions dot DHS's first phase organization chart, reflecting conceptual confusion, political compromises, and constituency pressures.

Weak political and budgetary support have been most problematic for DHS's new missions of cyber and other infrastructure security and defense against biothreats and other special substances, both of which draw on education, mindsets, expertise, and experience that differ profoundly from law enforcement or emergency management cultures. DHS's challenge with respect to the growth and influence of its cyber and infrastructure protection and CBRNE mission and personnel is a work in progress that in some respects is analogous to DOD's burgeoning Special Operations and Cyber Commands in relation to its three primary services.

Unity of Effort

Unity of effort is continually cited as a prime challenge for DHS. Cultural integration is challenging because, as mentioned, DHS aggregates entities with inherited and new missions that are not only diverse but also not entirely consistent with its overriding terrorism-prevention mandate. A lack of initial budget support for their integration made molding new agencies and missions from parts of the older, established agencies even more difficult. Separate administrative and information systems and agency locations have complicated efficient consolidation. In the absence of a unifying strategic understanding, the weak culture that has emerged so far prizes operations. The domination by law enforcement officials, on the one hand, and emergency manager cadres, on the other, each supported by national networks of colleagues in their respective fields, militates against organizational efficiencies and unity of effort. Both the cultures have their own authorities, norms, operational routines, and hierarchies and compete for preeminence. Add to this cultural clash the fact that DHS's new mission of cyber and infrastructure protection is developing cadres that rely on entirely new practices of risk and resilience assessment and countermeasures. These focus on new relationships with business and technology personnel for which long-standing law enforcement and emergency management training does not provide preparation.

Although Congress failed to give DHS the tools, it set high expectations for departmental unity operationally and culturally. Secretary Ridge experimented with generating that unity by assigning a pilot Miami-based intradepartmental task force to carry out a hybrid security mission—to protect safety of life at sea and to deter mass migration from the Caribbean. A reorganization under Secretary Michael Chertoff approached unity through centralization at the top in 2005. It abandoned DHS's organization into the major divisions suggested by Hart–Rudman and created seven separate operational components, resulting in an unwieldy twenty-six direct reporting lines to the secretary.[68] (See figure 12.2.) The idea was to unburden components of bureaucratic layers and reinforce a field-based operational culture, analogous to the separate armed forces within DOD. But DHS personnel lack what the military services have in the way of unity of command, which is reinforced by a statutorily imposed central command structure and a promotion system that rewards officers who execute the commander's intent.[69]

Because this reorganization failed to institute a centripetal, strategically driven leadership structure and culture, it significantly set back DHS's ability to integrate and evolve. Reconfigured agencies, especially CBP and ICE, still struggle to function effectively. Secretary Jeh Johnson has made unity of effort a major theme and directed intradepartmental planning for southwest border security and cybersecurity, empowering the DHS policy office as the chief

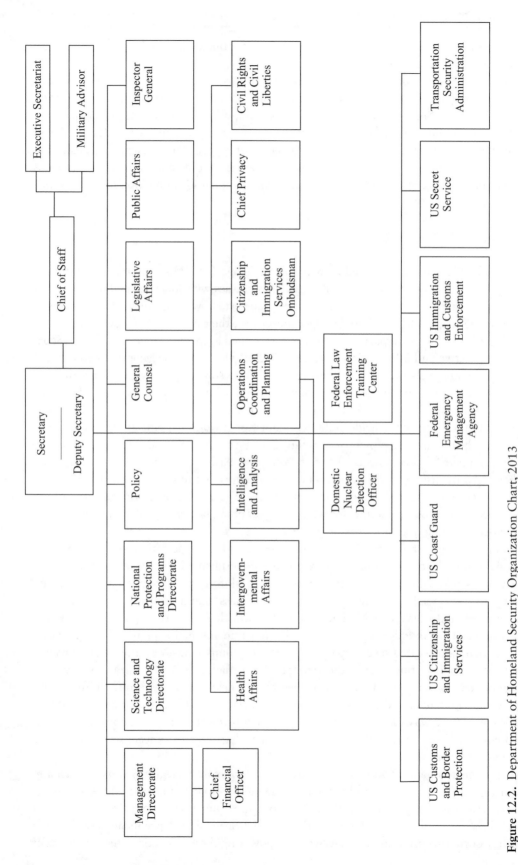

Figure 12.2. Department of Homeland Security Organization Chart, 2013

Source: Department of Homeland Security, "Department Org Chart," August 2016, www.dhs.gov/sites/default/files/publications/Department%20Org%20Chart.pdf.

strategist. He is also tying acquisitions to departmental missions, a basic but bureaucratically demanding step. These efforts have elicited praise from Congress.

External Coordination

The phrase "unity of effort" has an old-fashioned ring as applied to DHS, which has coordinating roles across the federal government, throughout the nation with public and private entities, and around the world. These demands reflect the breakdown of traditional divisions among government agencies, between public and private sectors, and between the domestic and the international. DHS secretaries have fought hard to gain coordinating authority for federal response to disasters. Congress and the White House reluctantly acquiesced to a more authoritative role for FEMA within the federal government only after Hurricane Katrina in 2005 revealed failures of leadership and federal process. FEMA's response in Super Storm Sandy in 2012 was met with far less criticism.[70] These improvements are likely only the beginning of the process of tightening internal federal collaboration and strengthening relationships with DOD.

DHS secretaries' most complex challenge has been leveraging the federal system within the United States. Former governors Ridge and Napolitano especially appreciated and embraced the critical roles of other levels of government—state, local, tribal, and territorial governments (SLTT in DHS parlance)—and of the business sector, voluntary organizations, and citizens. Secretary Ridge sought unsuccessfully to devolve FEMA's authority to its ten regions, and regionalism remains a topic of discussion. DHS leadership wrestles with Congress and interest groups to steer assistance grant programs using a meaningful risk calculus—an elusive holy grail of homeland security research and development—rather than the congressional "pie-sharing" arrangement that distributes grants more uniformly to local communities regardless of strategic value.

Employee Morale and Talent Acquisition

DHS has rock-bottom employee ratings recorded in surveys conducted by OPM.[71] This puts the department in the US government cellar on talent management, leadership and knowledge management, job satisfaction, and achievement of a results-oriented performance culture. The scores reflect a dismal view of the department's leadership and management at every level. The human resources weaknesses have undermined the substance of DHS's performance as well. Relying excessively on intelligence community and military detailees and contractors for their skills meant that those with DOD experience pushed DHS toward a culture of in-depth planning, not necessarily transferable from military to civil catastrophe orientation.[72] Fourteen years after the department's formation, it is not possible to argue that time alone will right the ship.

Without excusing this performance, two factors may be relevant. First, it is hard to achieve satisfaction on the job when the overall mission stated does not match what one is actually doing. Preventing terrorism, DHS's primary responsibility, simply does not capture what most employees do. This is true whether an employee is involved in border and mobility protection, immigration and migration management, cyber and infrastructure protection, pandemic and WMD defense, or disaster preparedness and response. No matter how skilled DHS leaders are, they will not be able to meet employee needs until they can fully acknowledge, budget, and plan around and recognize their actual activities. Second, many of the organizational problems that burden DHS, including in the human resources arena, are pervasive throughout all federal agencies, but they affect DHS disproportionately. A critical example is the inability to hire cybersecurity personnel.[73] The prescriptions from the 2003 Report of the National Commission on the Public Service sound as if they were based on an analysis of DHS. Among its recommendations the commission called for "immediate changes in the entry process for top leaders and the long-term development of a highly skilled federal management corps," as well as a "significant increase in executive salaries to ensure a reasonable relationship to other professional opportunities." To improve operational effectiveness in government, the commission stated, "the federal workforce must be reshaped, and the systems that support it must be rooted in new personnel management principles that ensure much higher levels of government performance."[74]

When grading DHS, one must also take into account that some problems cannot be solved entirely of the department's own accord. Certain criticisms of DHS's personnel reflect convictions about government as a whole rather than DHS in particular. Perhaps the most tenacious argument is over whether TSA's airport screeners should be privatized.[75] Although reasonable arguments exist on both sides, privatization would be unlikely to be acceptable to the public without government standard setting and enforcement authority and would probably force the government to insure airport authorities to cover liability costs in the event of major attacks, with the prospect of government personnel being reinstated.

Political Oversight

DHS does not benefit from well-designed channels to the White House nor effective oversight from Congress. Both disabilities contribute to a fragmented department that has no real backing for fundamental reforms to deal with the aforementioned challenges. President Bush saw homeland security as a discrete function, different from national security. Accordingly, his HSC and NSC were two separate organizations. In 2009 President Barack Obama merged the HSC staff into the NSC staff without eliminating the HSC. Two major homeland security offices, the Transborder Directorate and the Resilience Directorate, answer to the president's homeland security advisor, who is a deputy national security advisor. Functionally, these directorates mirror DHS's border and mobility protection function and FEMA. In practice, the Transborder Directorate has functioned well in shaping and coordinating strategy and policy because it reports directly to the corresponding deputy national security advisor. In contrast, the Resilience Directorate has sought to use FEMA and a concept of preparedness to guide all DHS approaches to risk, including for cyber and infrastructure protection. However, DHS responsibilities for cyber and infrastructure protection and defense against WMDs are dealt with as part of four different NSC staff directorates—counterterrorism, cybersecurity, intelligence, and nonproliferation; importantly, they report to the principal deputy national security advisor. Thus, discussions of joint foreign policy and of homeland security challenges still occur in separate groups. More important than the inevitable overlapping jurisdictions and rivalries among agencies arising from this framework is the signal that the NSC still sees strategy dominantly in foreign policy terms without comparable focus on reducing risk and increasing resilience in the susceptible infrastructure networks on which the population and government depend.[76]

Fragmented congressional oversight of DHS creates centrifugal pressures that undermine departmental unity around its central missions. In addition to each DHS secretary, a chorus of commentators have pilloried this disjointed congressional process.[77] Since DHS's founding in 2004, Congress has not written a dedicated authorization law for the department, signaling a lack of commitment to the department. Indeed, the political environment for DHS is especially difficult. Initial White House reluctance to form a new department has been compounded by civil libertarian concerns and exploited by rival departments. DHS's confusing mandate and congressional criticism has engendered an aura of second-rate status for DHS. This makes it less likely that the department's problems, beginning with the statement of its fundamental mission, will receive first-rate, policy-based attention, enhancing its vulnerability to political vagaries.

THE FUTURE OF DHS

Despite its flawed birth and persistent problems, DHS remains a significant new player in the NSE. Most important, since 9/11 new risks to the homeland have come to be regarded as strategically significant because they may cause massive loss of life, economic crisis, terror, and civil breakdown.[78] These include the growing zoonotic pandemic threat, technological disruptions to complex systems, and enhanced risk from environmental events. Citizens' expectations for safety, economic continuity, freedom, and individual dignity raise the bar on government's ability to achieve effective protection. Events that in previous eras would have been regarded as unimaginable now are viewed as foreseeable.

To protect the population, the government must expand its understanding of the NSE and enlist new participants in security in new ways. DHS is essential to identifying and implementing some of these new responses. Its accomplishments are too often minimized, given the complexity of the challenges. They should give more confidence than has been evident. Still, it will take a strong, combined effort by the White House and Congress to empower DHS to fulfill its responsibilities and to build civil security across government. A number of reforms might be worth considering.

Mandate for Civil Security

DHS's statutory mandate, and to some extent its name, remains a congenital defect for DHS. Analysts describe it, leaders decry it, and commentators can barely bring themselves to even use the term "homeland security."[79] DHS has looked for a solution, declaring in 2014 that homeland security is "multi-threat and all-hazard."[80] Indications of congressional recognition that DHS's mandate to prevent terrorist attacks was overstated suggest a future opening for legislative modification.[81] First, this rethinking has to highlight the profound strategic importance of its four purposes (shown in table 12.3): border and mobility protection, cyber and infrastructure protection, bio-threat and WMD security, and disaster preparedness and response. Most of these implicate protection from terrorist attacks, but they also constitute fundamental responsibilities in their own right. Second, Congress must acknowledge the mission is not only the preservation of human life but also our constitutional way of life. A term that would encompass both the distinctive twenty-first-century risks and what is at stake in defeating them is civil security or civil protection, terminology that is fully consistent with preventing terrorism.[82] One suggestion is to rename DHS the Department of Civil Security. Such "rebranding" would give the department a fresh start in explaining the broader scope of its activities.

Table 12.3. DHS Distribution of Resources by Agency

General Function	Agency	Number of Full-Time Employees	Percent of Total Full-Time Employees	Budget Request ($)	Percent of Total Budget Authority
Analysis and operations	Analysis and Operations[a]	850	0.4	302,268,000	0.5
Border and mobility protection	US Citizenship and Immigration Services	13,196	5.5	3,259,885,000	5
	US Customs and Border Protection	62,552	26	13,096,590,000	21
	US Immigration and Customs Enforcement	19,374	8	5,359,065,000	9
	US Coast Guard	49,547	20.6	9,796,995,000	16
	Transportation Security Administration	53,670	22.4	7,305,098,000	12
	Federal Law Enforcement Training Centers	1,092	0.5	259,595,000	<1
	Total	200,281	83.4	39,379,496,000	Approx. 64
Cyber and infrastructure protection	US Secret Service	6,572	2.7	1,895,905,000	3
	National Protection and Programs Directorate	3,463	1.4	2,857,666	5
	Total	10,035	4.1	1,898,726,666	Approx. 8
Disaster preparedness and response	Federal Emergency Management Agency	12,134	5	14,721,986	24
	Total	12,261	5.05	319,144,986	24.5
Science and technology	Science and Technology	467	0.2	1,071,818,000	2
Pandemics and CBRNE	Office of Health Affairs	99	0.04	125,767,000	<1
	Domestic Nuclear Detection Office	127	0.05	304,423,000	.5
	Total	226	0.09	430, 190, 000	Approx. .5
Office of the Inspector General	Office of the Inspector General	725	0.3	145,457,000	<1

Source: Department of Homeland Security, *Budget in Brief* (Washington, DC, 2015).
[a] The Analysis and Operations appropriation provides resources for the support of the Office of Intelligence and Analysis (I&A) and the Office of Operations Coordination and Planning (OPS).

Restructuring by Function

Structural clarity would reinforce this rebranding, and it would also assist the department in its interactions with the NSC and Congress. It is not unusual for major departments to be reorganized repeatedly and significantly, as has been the case with DOD at least five times over the past fifty or so years.[83] A major "modernization" is also underway at the CIA, reflecting a belief that new challenges require new forms of organizational behavior as well as structure. But there needs to be a strong strategic impetus. In DHS's case it should be to consolidate, direct, and oversee its four major functions—border and mobility security, cyber and infrastructure protection, disaster preparedness and response, and defense against bio-threats and WMDs generally. Progress toward such mission solidification can be seen by recalling alternatives that were rejected after 9/11. One option was to create a freestanding border and mobility protection agency; the Gilmore Commission argued for an MI5-type organization. Expanding DOD's role to take on cyber and infrastructure protection for the public and commercial sectors as well as for the military had been rejected; so ultimately was leaving FEMA as a stand-alone response agency statutorily supported by DOD's defense to civil authorities. Consolidating defense against CBRNE events was not discussed. Some of these and other alternatives still have advantages and disadvantages worth considering.

In particular, a question remains whether the current allocation of authority and resources among DOD, DHS, and other agencies concerning cyber and infrastructure protection is workable, whether DHS's resources should be expanded, whether DOD's role should evolve to provide the principal operational response to cyber attacks, or whether these risks should be addressed through a new hybrid civilian organization that draws on military culture and its massive resources where needed and on the private sector and academia. Congress has decided to stand by DHS as the key civilian institution to steward the ".com" and ".gov" environments and develop infrastructure security with the private sector with the passage of the Cybersecurity Act of 2015. Properly supporting and resourcing DHS to lead and partner with DOD, the intelligence community, the broader research and development community, and other agencies in cyber and infrastructure protection remains a work in progress.

Focus on Resilience

A number of developments suggests there is need for more focus on resilience as a key defensive dimension of civil security. First, the conception of FEMA as nearly a stand-alone agency, with some arguing for its full independence, needs to change. It is important for both FEMA and the cyber and infrastructure protection agency to be located within DHS (or the Department of Civil Security), and preferably co-located and working closely together, for the foreseeable future. FEMA's and DHS's cyber and infrastructure protection units theoretically focus on different phases in the continuum of achieving resilience. They need to work together and with all levels of government, private interests, and academia to develop the science of risk and resilience, as well as to create and make available new methods of mitigation, response, and recovery. Only such institutionalized collaboration can provide a basis for successfully confronting this era's concatenating risks, whether related to the Internet or other infrastructure and to human or nonhuman causes. Second, DHS efforts to consolidate its own CBRNE functions make sense,[84] but the challenge extends across a patchwork of federal efforts.[85] These problems suggest that there is a need for a deputy secretary for resilience who can elevate, direct or coordinate, and conduct departmental outreach involving programs in which resilience is the objective, including cyber and infrastructure protection, pandemics and special substances defense, and disaster preparedness and response. A second deputy secretary could oversee border and mobility protection.

In sum, a renewed mandate and invigorated civil security culture, with structured consolidation, would permit DHS to manage its numerous units more effectively. It would also have a better chance to develop its core missions and become a transformative player in the NSE. Such measures may well have to be part of a broader reengineering of government for the twenty-first century.

NOTES

With thanks and appreciation to my editors, Roger George and Harvey Rishikof, for their advice in shaping the chapter; to those who commented so helpfully—Chris Bellavita, Joel Brenner, Chris Bronk, Alan Cohn, Bob Deitz, Ted Lewis, Philip Palin, Paul Rosenzweig, and two anonymous reviewers—and to our copy editor, Brittany Albaugh. Special thanks to Ann Daniels for her impeccable research and to Holly McMahon for her support. Errors and omissions are mine.

1. What exactly the concept of homeland security signifies is the subject of ongoing debate. William L. Painter and Shawn Reese, *Selected Issues in Homeland Security Policy for the 114th Congress* (Washington, DC: Congressional Research Service, 2015), 2–4; Christopher Bellavita, "Waiting for Homeland Security Theory," *Homeland Security Affairs* 8 (August 2012), www.hsaj.org/articles/231; Christopher Bellavita, "Changing Homeland Security: What Is Homeland Security?" *Homeland Security Affairs* 4 (June 2008), www.hsaj.org/articles/118; Jeffrey Rosen, "Man-Made Disaster," *New Republic*, December 24, 2008, https://newrepublic.com/article/64075/man-made-disaster.

2. US Commission on National Security / 21st Century (Hart–Rudman Commission), *Road Map for National Security: Imperative for Change* (Washington, DC, 2001), vi.

3. The Advisory Panel to Assess Domestic Response Capabilities for Terrorism Involving Weapons of Mass Destruction (Gilmore Commission), created in 1999, issued five annual reports ending in December 2003: *Assessing the Threat* (1999), *Toward a National Strategy for Countering Terrorism* (2000), *For Ray Downey* (2001), *Implementing a National Strategy* (2002), *Forging America's New Normalcy: Securing Our Homeland, Protecting Our Liberty* (2003). A third commission provided additional recommendations: National Commission on Terrorism (Bremer Commission), *Countering the Changing Threat of International Terrorism* (Washington, DC, 2000).

4. Hart–Rudman Commission, *Road Map for National Security*, 18. "It [NHSA] will need also to create and maintain strong mechanisms for the sharing of information and intelligence with US domestic and international intelligence entities. We suggest that NHSA have liaison officers in the counter-terrorism centers of both the FBI and the CIA."

5. Office of Homeland Security, *National Strategy for Homeland Security* (Washington, DC: Executive Office of the President, 2002).

6. *Homeland Security Act of 2002*, Pub. L. No. 107–296, 116 Stat. 2135 (2002).

7. President Bush in 2001 directed a study of intelligence in National Security Policy Directive 5 and assigned Brent Scowcroft to lead it. See also Aspin–Brown Commission, *Preparing for the 21st Century: An Appraisal for U.S. Intelligence* (Washington, DC, 1996); White House Commission of Aviation Safety and Security, *Final Report to President Clinton* (Washington, DC, 1997); Gilmore Commission (Washington, DC, 1999, 2000, 2001, 2002, 2003); USS *Cole* Commission, *USS* Cole *Commission Report* (Washington, DC: Department of Defense, 2001); and Bremer Commission, *Countering the Changing Threat of International Terrorism*.

8. Gilmore Commission, *The Fifth Annual Report: Forging America's New Normalcy: Securing Our Homeland, Preserving Our Liberty* (Washington, DC, 2003), 30–31.

9. *Intelligence Reform and Terrorism Prevention Act of 2004*, §§1001–1095, Pub. L. No. 108–458, 118 Stat. 3638, 3643–99 (2004). The Human Smuggling and Trafficking Center is now operated by the US Department of State. See Department of State, "Human Trafficking Center," www.state.gov/m/ds/hstcenter/.

10. See Susan Ginsburg, *Securing Human Mobility in the Age of Risk: New Challenges for Travel, Migration, and Borders* (Washington, DC: Migration Policy Institute, 2010); Susan Ginsburg, *Countering Terrorist Mobility: Shaping an Operational Strategy* (Washington, DC: Migration Policy Institute, 2006); and National Commission on Terrorist Attacks upon the United States, *9/11 and Terrorist Travel* (Franklin, TN: Providence Publishing, 2004).

11. Janet Napolitano, remarks at the National Press Club, Washington, DC, August 27, 2013; Janet Napolitano and Kathleen Sebelius, Statements on World Health Organization Decision to Declare Novel H1N1 Virus Outbreak a Pandemic (Washington, DC, June 11, 2009). See also Janet Napolitano, Statement on Increased Security Measures (Washington, DC, November 8, 2010); US Coast Guard, *BP Deepwater Horizon Oil Spill: Incident Specific Preparedness Review (ISPR)* (Washington, DC, January 2011); and Offices of the Inspector General of the Department of Justice, Department of Homeland Security, Central Intelligence Agency, and the Intelligence Community, *Unclassified Summary of Infor-*

mation Handling and Sharing Prior to the April 15, 2013 Boston Marathon Bombing (Washington, DC, April 10, 2014).

12. Tom Coburn, *A Review of the Department of Homeland Security's Missions and Performance* (Washington, DC: Senate Committee on Homeland Security and Governmental Affairs, 2015), 150, n. 705.

13. Napolitano, remarks at the National Press Club; Stewart Baker, *Skating on Stilts* (Stanford, CA: Hoover Institution Press, 2010); Michael Chertoff, *Homeland Security, Assessing the First Five Years* (Philadelphia: University of Pennsylvania Press, 2009), 153–59; and Tom Ridge, *The Test of Our Times: America Under Siege . . . And How We Can Be Safe Again* (New York: St. Martin's Griffin, 2010), 185–95.

14. US Customs and Border Protection, "Preclearance Locations," www.cbp.gov/border-security/ports-entry/operations/preclearance; Lisa Seghetti, *Border Security: Immigration Inspections at Ports of Entry* (Washington, DC: Congressional Research Service, 2015), 11–12; Jeh Johnson, Statement on the Safety and Security of the Homeland, and How Congress Can Help (Washington, DC, November 23, 2015); Carl Ek and Ian F. Fergusson, *U.S.-Canada Relations* (Washington, DC: Congressional Research Service, 2014), 28–34; Clare Ribando Seelke, *Mexico: Background and U.S. Relations* (Washington, DC: Congressional Research Service, 2016), 20–24; and Alison Siskin, *Visa Waiver Program* (Washington, DC: Congressional Research Service, 2015).

15. Rosen, "Man Made Disaster." "He [Tom Ridge] was assailed by the DHS inspector general, Clark Ervin, for showy but ineffective transportation security measures."

16. Kip Hawley, "Why Airport Security Is Broken and How to Fix It," *Wall Street Journal*, April 15, 2012, www.wsj.com/articles/SB10001424052702303815404577335783535660546.

17. See Ted G. Lewis, *Book of Extremes: Why the 21st Century Isn't Like the 20th Century* (New York: Springer, 2014). See also Nassim Nicholas Taleb, *The Black Swan: The Impact of the Highly Improbable* (New York: Random House, 2010).

18. Philip Bobbitt, *Terror and Consent: The Wars for the Twenty-First Century* (New York: Alfred A. Knopf, 2008), 403.

19. US President's Commission on Critical Infrastructure Protection (Marsh Commission), *Critical Foundations, Protecting America's Infrastructure* (Washington, DC, October 1997).

20. William Jackson, "McCain Slams DHS, Wants DOD to Defend Cyberspace," *GCN*, March 27, 2012, https://gcn.com/Articles/2012/03/27/Cyber-defense-hearing-McCain-slams-DHS-favors-DOD.aspx.

21. *Cybersecurity Act of 2015*, Div. N., Pub. L. No. 114–113 (2015). See also Executive Office of the President, National Security Presidential Directive 54 (NSPD-54) / Homeland Security Presidential Directive 23 (HSPD-23) (Redacted) (Washington, DC, 2008); and Stratfor, "The Pentagon Defines Its Role in Cybersecurity," June 3, 2015, www.stratfor.com/analysis/pentagon-defines-its-role-cybersecurity.

22. Chris Bronk, *Cyber Threat: The Rise of Information Geopolitics in U.S. National Security* (Santa Barbara, CA: Praeger Security International, 2016), chap. 3.

23. William Painter et al., *DHS Appropriations FY2016: Protection, Preparedness, Response, and Recovery* (Washington, DC: Congressional Research Service, 2016); Aliya Sternstein, "The Military's Cybersecurity Budget in 4 Charts," *Defense One*, March 16, 2015, www.defenseone.com/management/2015/03/militarys-cybersecurity-budget-4-charts/107679/; and Cory Bennett, "Cyber Gets $1B Boost in White House Budget," *The Hill*, February 2, 2015, http://thehill.com/policy/cybersecurity/231449-cyber-gets-1-billion-boost-in-white-house-budget.

24. Federal Bureau of Investigation, "Update on Sony Investigation," news release, December 19, 2014, www.fbi.gov/news/pressrel/press-releases/update-on-sony-investigation; Miles Parks, "Target Offers $10 Million Settlement in Data Breach Lawsuit," *The Two-Way*, NPR, March 19, 2015, www.npr.org/sections/thetwo-way/2015/03/19/394039055/target-offers-10-million-settlement-in-data-breach-lawsuit; and Robin Sidel, "Home Depot's 56 Million Card Breach Bigger than Targets," *Wall Street Journal*, September 18, 2014, www.wsj.com/articles/home-depot-breach-bigger-than-targets-1411073571.

25. Ellen Nakashima, "Chinese Breach Data of 4 Million Federal Workers," *Washington Post*, June 4, 2015, www.washingtonpost.com/world/national-security/chinese-hackers-breach-federal-governments-personnel-office/2015/06/04/889c0e52-0af7-11e5-95fd-d580f1c5d44e_story.html. See also Ellen Nakashima, "Security of Critical Phone Database Called into Question," *Washington Post*, April 28, 2016, www.washingtonpost.com/world/national-security/security-of-critical-phone-database-called-into-question/2016/04/28/11c23b10-0c8d-11e6-a6b6-2e6de3695b0e_story.html.

26. *National Cybersecurity Protection Act of 2014*, Pub. L. No. 113–282, 128 Stat. 3066 (2014).

27. Katie Bo Williams, "MasterCard CEO, Former NSA Head Tapped to Lead WH Cyber Commission," *The Hill*, April 16, 2016, http://thehill.com/policy/cybersecurity/276279-white-house-names-mastercard-ceo-former-nsa-head-to-cyber-commission. See also Joel Brenner, "How Obama Fell Short on Cybersecurity," *Politico*, January 21, 2015, www.politico.com/magazine/story/2015/01/state-of-the-union-cybersecurity-obama-114411_full.html?print#.VcOSaHhRfdk.

28. Jennifer C. Ricklin and Robert Hummel, "Science and Technology for Homeland Security: How Is It Going with the DHS S&T Directorate?" preprint, submitted to Homeland Security Affairs, September 2, 2016.

29. See, generally, Department of Homeland Security, *Cyber and Infrastructure Protection Transition Way Ahead: Fiscal Year 2016 Report to Congress* (Washington, DC, March 17, 2016).

30. Executive Office of the President, "Critical Infrastructure Protection," Presidential Decision Directive 63 (PDD-63) (Washington, DC, 1998). See also *Homeland Security Act of 2002*.

31. See Shawn Reese, *The Federal Protective Service and Contract Security Guards: A Statutory History and Current Status* (Washington, DC: Congressional Research Service, 2009).

32. Dana A. Shea, *Chemical Facility Security: Issues and Options for the 113th Congress* (Washington, DC: Congressional Research Service, 2014). See also Executive Office of the President, "Critical Infrastructure Protection."

33. Executive Office of the President, "Promoting Private Sector Cybersecurity Information Sharing," Executive Order 13, 691 (Washington, DC, 2015).

34. Executive Office of the President, Homeland Security Presidential Directive 7 (HSPD-7).

35. See, e.g., Federal Trade Commission v. Wyndham Worldwide Corporation, No. 14–3514 (3rd Cir. 2015); Securities and Exchange Commission, "SEC Charges Investment Adviser with Failing to Adopt Proper Cybersecurity Policies and Procedures Prior to Breach," press release, September 22, 2015, www.sec.gov/news/pressrelease/2015-202.html.

36. See Todd Masse, *The Department of Homeland Security's Risk Assessment Methodology: Evolution, Issues, and Options for Congress* (Washington, DC: Congressional Research Service, 2007); and *Review of the Department of Homeland Security's Approach to Risk Analysis* (Washington, DC: National Academies Press, 2010).

37. House Homeland Security Committee, *Ongoing Challenges at the U.S. Secret Service and Their Government-Wide Implications*, 114th Cong. (2015); Kevin Liptak, "Gate-Crashing Agents Make 4 Secret Service Scandals in 3 Years," CNN, March 13, 2015, www.cnn.com/2015/03/12/politics/secrect-service-scandals-gate-crasher-dui/index.html; Office of Inspector General, *Adequacy of USSS Efforts to Identify, Mitigate, and Address Instances of Misconduct and Inappropriate Behavior*, OIG 14–20 (Washington, DC: Department of Homeland Security, December 2013); and Office of Inspector General, *Adequacy of USSS' Internal Investigation of Alleged Misconduct in Cartagena, Colombia*, OIG 13–24 (Washington, DC: Department of Homeland Security, January 2013).

38. Richard Danzig et al., *Aum Shinrikyo Insights into How Terrorists Develop Biological and Chemical Weapons* (Washington, DC: Center for a New American Security, July 2011); Judith Miller, "Qaeda Videos Seem to Show Chemical Tests," *New York Times*, August 19, 2002, www.nytimes.com/2002/08/19/world/qaeda-videos-seem-to-show-chemical-tests.html; "Anthrax Diagnosed in Two More People," CNN, October 15, 2001, www.cnn.com/2001/HEALTH/conditions/10/15/anthrax; and Joby Warrick, "FBI Investigation of 2001 Anthrax Attacks Concluded; U.S. Releases Details," *Washington Post*, February 20, 2010, www.washingtonpost.com/wp-dyn/content/article/2010/02/19/AR2010021902369.html.

39. David Albright, *Peddling Peril: How the Secret Nuclear Trade Arms America's Enemies* (New York: Free Press, 2010).

40. Executive Office of the President, *A National Strategy for CBRNE Standards* (Washington, DC, May 2011).

41. Ready, "Biological Threats," www.ready.gov/biological-threats.

42. Ibid.

43. Blue Ribbon Study Panel on Biodefense, *A National Blueprint for Biodefense: Leadership and Major Reform Needed to Optimize Efforts* (Washington, DC, October 2015).

44. DNDO was codified by the *Security and Accountability for Every Port Act of 2006* (SAFE Port Act), §§ 501–2, Pub. L. No. 109–347, 120 Stat. 1884, 1932–36 (2006). See Government Accountability

Office, *Domestic Nuclear Detection Office Should Improve Planning to Better Address Gaps and Vulnerabilities*, GAO 09–257 (Washington, DC, January 2009).

45. Alison Young and Tom Vanden Brook, "Egregious Safety Failures at Army Lab Led to Anthrax Mistakes," *USA Today*, January 15, 2016, www.usatoday.com/story/news/nation/2016/01/15/military -bioterrorism-lab-safety/78752876/. See US Army, *AR 15–6 Investigation Report—Individual and Institutional Liability for the Shipment of Viable Bacillus Anthracis from Dugway Proving Ground* (Unclassified) (December 17, 2015).

46. John Fass Morton, *Next Generation Homeland Security: Network Federalism and the Course to National Preparedness* (Annapolis, MD: Naval Institute Press, 2012), 26–31.

47. *Post-Katrina Emergency Management Reform Act of 2006*, Pub. L. No. 109–295, 120 Stat. 1355 (2006). See White House, *The Federal Response to Hurricane Katrina: Lessons Learned* (Washington, DC, February 2006); *A Failure of Initiative: The Final Report of the Select Bipartisan Committee to Investigate the Preparation for and Response to Hurricane Katrina*, H. R. Rep. No. 109–377 (2006); Office of Inspector General, *A Performance Review of FEMA's Disaster Management Activities in Response to Hurricane Katrina*, OIG 06–32 (Washington, DC: Department of Homeland Security, March 2006); and American Bar Association, *Hurricane Katrina Task Force Subcommittee Report* (Washington, DC, February 2006).

48. Keith Bea, *Federal Emergency Management Policy Changes after Hurricane Katrina: A Summary of Statutory Provisions* (Washington, DC: Congressional Research Service, 2007). See also Government Accountability Office, *National Preparedness: Actions Taken by FEMA to Implement Select Provisions of the Post-Katrina Emergency Management Reform Act of 2006*, GAO 14–99R (Washington, DC, November 26, 2013).

49. Richard A Posner, *Catastrophe: Risk and Response* (Oxford, UK: Oxford University Press, 2004); Cass R. Sunstein, *Worst-Case Scenarios* (Cambridge, MA: Harvard University Press, 2007); Charles Perrow, *The Next Catastrophe: Reducing Our Vulnerabilities to Natural, Industrial, and Terrorist Disasters* (Princeton, NJ: Princeton University Press, 2011); and Bernice Lee et al., *Preparing for High-Impact, Low-Probability Events: Lessons from Eyjafjallajökull* (London: Chatham House, January 2012).

50. The Post-Katrina Emergency Management Reform Act of 2006 defined FEMA's mission as "to reduce the loss of life and property and protect the Nation from all hazards, including natural disasters, acts of terrorism, and other man-made disasters, by leading and supporting the Nation in a risk-based, comprehensive emergency management system of preparedness, protection, response, recovery, and mitigation." The language is slightly different than FEMA's mission in the *Homeland Security Act of 2002*, Pub. L. No. 107–295 (2002), in that the new mission specifically emphasizes "natural disasters, acts of terrorism, and man-made disasters" as well as focuses on the five focuses of emergency management: "preparedness, protection, response, recovery, and mitigation."

51. Bobbitt, *Terror and Consent*, 254.

52. Government Accountability Office, *DHS Privacy Office: Progress Made but Challenges Remain in Notifying and Reporting to the Public*, GAO 07–522 (Washington, DC, April 2007).

53. Department of Homeland Security, *Rightwing Extremism: Current Economic and Political Climate Fueling Resurgence in Radicalization and Recruitment* (Washington, DC, April 7, 2009); and Janet Napolitano, Statement on the Threat of Right-Wing Extremism (Washington, DC, April 15, 2009).

54. See instances of right-wing terrorism in 2009 and after: Robbie Brown, "Georgia Soldiers Face Death Penalty in Killings," *New York Times*, August 30, 2012, www.nytimes.com/2012/08/31/us/ 3-georgia-soldiers-face-death-penalty-in-killings.html; Federal Bureau of Investigation, "Washington Man Sentenced to 32 Years for Attempted Bombing of Martin Luther King Unity March," news release, December 20, 2011, www.fbi.gov/seattle/press-releases/2011/washington-man-sentenced-to-32-years -for-attempted-bombing-of-martin-luther-king-unity-march; Erica Goode, "Wisconsin Killer Fed and Was Driven by Hate-Driven Music," *New York Times*, August 6, 2012, www.nytimes.com/2012/08/07/ us/army-veteran-identified-as-suspect-in-wisconsin-shooting.html; and "Kansas City Area Jewish Center Shootings Suspect Frazier Glenn Miller; Who Is the Man with 2 Names?" CBS News, April 14, 2014, www.cbsnews.com/news/kansas-city-jewish-center-shootings-suspect-frazier-glenn-miller-cross/. See also Jeffrey Smith, "Homeland Security Department Curtails Home-grown Terror Analysis," *Washington Post*, June 2, 2011, www.washingtonpost.com/politics/homeland-security-department-curtails-home -grown-terror-analysis/2011/06/02/AGQEaDLH_story.html; Kellan Howell, "DHS Report Warns of Domestic Right-Wing Terror Threat," *Washington Times*, February 21, 2015, www.washingtontimes

.com/news/2015/feb/21/dhs-intelligence-report-warns-of-domestic-right-wi/; and Evan Perez and Wes Bruer, "DHS Intelligence Report Warns of Domestic Right-Wing Terror Threat," CNN, February 20, 2015, www.cnn.com/2015/02/19/politics/terror-threat-homeland-security/index.html.

55. Ellen Nakashima, "ICE Twice Breached Privacy Policy with License Plate Index," *Washington Post*, October 30, 2014, www.washingtonpost.com/world/national-security/ice-twice-breached-privacy-policy-with-license-plate-database/2014/10/29/df3a8e6c-5096-11e4-8c24-487e92bc997b_story.html; Peter Robison, "Homeland Security Arms Local Cops with Super Spy Bug," *Bloomberg Businessweek*, August 27, 2014, www.bloomberg.com/news/articles/2014-08-27/homeland-security-arms-local-cops-with-super-cell-phone-spy-bug; Josh Hicks, "Homeland Security Wants National Database Using License Plate Scanners," *Washington Post*, February 18, 2014, www.washingtonpost.com/news/federal-eye/wp/2014/02/18/homeland-security-wants-to-build-national-database-using-license-plate-scanners/; and Robert Beckhausen, "5 Homeland Security 'Bots Coming to Spy on You (If They Aren't Already)," *Wired*, February 2, 2013, www.wired.com/2013/02/dhs-drones/.

56. Jared Cole, *Terrorist Databases and the No Fly List: Procedural Due Process and Hurdles to Litigation* (Washington, DC: Congressional Research Service, 2015); and Jeffrey Kahn, *Mrs. Shipley's Ghost: The Right to Travel and Terrorist Watchlists* (Ann Arbor: University of Michigan Press, 2013). See for database of recent court case activity, Watchlist Law website, www.watchlistlaw.com.

57. Yule Kim, *Border Searches of Laptop Computers and Other Electronic Storage Devices* (Washington, DC: Congressional Research Service, November 16, 2009).

58. Ron Nixon, "T.S.A. Expands Duties Beyond Airport Security," *New York Times*, August 6, 2013, www.nytimes.com/2013/08/06/us/tsa-expands-duties-beyond-airport-security.html?pagewanted=1; and "ACLU Sues for Record on Border Patrol's 'Roving' Agents," *NBC San Diego*, February 11, 2015, www.nbcsandiego.com/news/local/ACLU-sues-for-record-on-Border-Patrols-roving-agents-291521651.html.

59. Brian Ross, "Secret US Policy Blocks Agents from Looking at Social Media of Visa Applicants, Former Official Says," *ABC News*, December 14, 2015, http://abcnews.go.com/US/secret-us-policy-blocks-agents-social-media-visa/story?id=35749325; Ron Nixon, "U.S. to Further Scour Social Media Use of Visa and Asylum Seekers," *New York Times*, February 23, 2016, www.nytimes.com/2016/02/24/us/politics/homeland-security-social-media-refugees.html?_r=0; and cf. Government Accountability Office, *Secure Flight: TSA Should Take Additional Steps to Determine Program Effectiveness*, GAO 14–531 (Washington, DC, September 2014).

60. Ashley Halsey III, "Lawsuit Challenges TSA's Use of Full-Body Scanners in Airports," *Washington Post*, May 2, 2016, www.washingtonpost.com/local/trafficandcommuting/lawsuit-challenges-tsas-use-of-full-body-scanners-in-airports/2016/05/02/a0006b44-1099-11e6-8967-7ac733c56f12_story.html?wpmm=1; and Steve Fries, "TSA Scanners That Saw You Naked Can Be Tricked to Miss Guns, Bombs," *Bloomberg Businessweek*, August 20, 2014, www.bloomberg.com/news/articles/2014-08-20/tsa-scanners-that-see-you-nude-can-miss-guns-bombs.

61. Jerry Markon, "Judge: Lawsuit Saying Central American Migrants Are Held in Filthy, Inhumane Conditions Can Go Forward," *Washington Post*, January 14, 2016, www.washingtonpost.com/news/federal-eye/wp/2016/01/14/judge-lawsuit-saying-central-american-migrants-are-held-in-filthy-inhumane-conditions-can-go-forward/; and Kristian Hernandez, "Cold and Overcrowded: Immigration Advocates Report Deplorable Conditions at CBP Holding Centers," *The Monitor*, December 21, 2015, www.themonitor.com/news/local/immigration-advocates-report-deplorable-conditions-at-cbp-holding-centers/article_7a1262fa-a859-11e5-b736-af813e928dd1.html.

62. US Customs and Border Protection, "In Memoriam to Those Who Died in the Line of Duty," www.cbp.gov/about/in-memoriam/memoriam-those-who-died-line-duty; Jason Ryan et al., "Slain Border Agent Identified, Drug Traffickers Suspected," ABC News, October 2, 2012, http://abcnews.go.com/US/slain-border-agent-identified-nicholas-ivie-drug-traffickers/story?id=17376159; Devin Dwyer, "Agent Brian Terry Shot in Back with AK-47 During Gunfight, Family Says," ABC News, December 15, 2010, http://abcnews.go.com/US/border-patrol-agent-shot-killed-us-mexico-border/story?id=12401948; Federal Bureau of Investigation, "Defendant Pleads Guilty to Murder Charge for the Death of US Customs and Border Protection Border Patrol Agent Robert W. Rosas, Jr.," press release, November 20, 2009, www.fbi.gov/sandiego/press-releases/2009/sd112009.htm; Federal Bureau of Investigation, "Man Convicted in the Death of U.S. Customs and Border Protection Border Patrol Agent Luis Aguilar Receives Life Sentence in Federal Prison," press release, July 1, 2011, www.fbi.gov/sandiego/press

-releases/2011man-convicted-in-the-death-of-u.s.-customs-and-border-protection-border-patrol-agent
-luis-aguilar-receives-life-sentence-in-federal-prison; Office of Inspector General, *CBP Use of Force
Training and Actions to Address Use of Force Incidents* (Redacted), OIG 13-114 (Washington, DC:
Department of Homeland Security, September 2013); and Department of Homeland Security, "DHS,
CBP, ICE Release Use of Force Policies," press release, March 11, 2014, www.dhs.gov/news/2014/03/07/
dhs-cbp-ice-release-use-force-policies.

63. Bob Ortega, "Border Killings: 46 People Killed, No Agents Disciplined," *Arizona Central*, September 14, 2014, www.azcentral.com/story/news/arizona/investigations/2014/09/14/border-deaths-agents
-transparency-secrecy/15616933/; Emily Von Hoffman, "Does ICE Pressure Schools for Student Info?"
The Atlantic, April 11, 2016, www.theatlantic.com/education/archive/2016/04/does-ice-pressure-schools
-for-student-info/477600/; Matt Vasilogambros, "ICE Raids Reopen Old Wounds for Families in This
Small Town," *The Atlantic*, January 25, 2016, www.theatlantic.com/politics/archive/2016/01/ice-raids
-reopen-old-wounds-for-families-in-this-small-town/458868/; "The Flow of Money and Equipment to
Local Police," *New York Times*, December 1, 2014, www.nytimes.com/interactive/2014/08/23/us/flow
-of-money-and-equipment-to-local-police.html; Mark Landler, "Obama Offers New Standards on Police
Gear in Wake of Ferguson Protests," *New York Times*, December 1, 2014, www.nytimes.com/2014/12/02/
us/politics/obama-to-toughen-standards-on-police-use-of-military-gear.html; and Max Ehrenfreund, "How
the Obama Administration Gives Away Military-Grade Weapons to Local Police," *Washington Post*, November 25, 2014, www.washingtonpost.com/news/wonk/wp/2014/11/25/how-the-obama-administration
-gives-away-military-grade-weapons-to-local-police/.

64. See Matt A. Mayer, *Homeland Security and Federalism: Protecting American from Outside the
Beltway* (Santa Barbara, CA: Praeger Security International, 2009). See also Chris Edwards, *The Federal Emergency Management Agency: Floods, Failures, and Federalism* (Washington, DC: CATO Institute, 2014).

65. US Coast Guard, *ISPR*, 4.

66. Department of Homeland Security, "Surge Capacity Force," www.dhs.gov/topic/surge-capacity
-force.

67. Representative Mac Thornberry (R-TX) in March 2001 proposed the National Homeland
Security Agency Defense Act, H. R. 1158 (107th Cong.), which would have implemented the Hart–
Rudman recommendations. The House instead adopted a bill agreed on with the Bush administration.

68. Harold C. Relyea and Henry B. Hogue, *Department of Homeland Security Reorganization:
The 2SR Initiative* (Washington, DC: Congressional Research Service, 2005).

69. See, generally, *Goldwater-Nichols Department of Defense Reorganization Act of 1986*, Pub. L.
No. 99–433, 100 Stat. 922 (1986).

70. Brian Naylor, "Lessons from Katrina Boost FEMA's Sandy Response," *Weekend Edition Saturday*, NPR, November 3, 2012, www.npr.org/2012/11/03/164224394/lessons-from-katrina-boost-femas
-sandy-response.

71. Partnership for Public Service, "Best Places to Work Agency Index Scores," 2014, http://best
placestowork.org/BPTW/rankings/overall/large; and Jerry Markon et al., "Top Level Turnover Makes
It Harder for DHS to Stay on Top of Evolving Threats," *Washington Post*, September 21, 2014, www
.washingtonpost.com/politics/top-level-turnover-makes-it-harder-for-dhs-to-stay-on-top-of-evolving
-threats/2014/09/21/ca7919a6-39d7-11e4-9c9f-ebb47272e40e_story.html.

72. Philip J. Palin, *Considering Catastrophe: Regional Catastrophic Preparedness Planning Grant*
(report prepared for Grants Programs Directorate, FEMA, 2014).

73. "We are competing in a tough marketplace against the private sector, that is in a position to
offer a lot more money. . . . We need more cyber talent without a doubt in DHS, in the federal government, and we are not where we should be right now, that is without a doubt." Senate Homeland Security
and Governmental Affairs Committee, *The Homeland Security Department's Budget Submission for
Fiscal Year 2017*, 114th Cong. (2016) (testimony by Jeh Johnson, Secretary of Homeland Security).

74. The National Commission on Public Service (Volcker Commission), *Urgent Business for
America: Revitalizing the Federal Government for the 21st Century* (Washington, DC, January 2003),
x–xi.

75. David Rittgers, *Policy Analysis: Abolish the Department of Homeland Security* (Washington,
DC: CATO Institute, September 11, 2011); and Chris Edwards, *Policy Analysis: Privatizing the Transportation Security Administration* (Washington, DC: CATO Institute, November 19, 2013).

76. For example, China's cyber intrusions are separately discussed in two groups, for China–Asia and cyber matters, and neither answers to the homeland security advisor although cybersecurity is a defining DHS responsibility.

77. See, e.g., 9/11 Commission, *Final Report of the National Commission of Terrorist Attacks upon the United States* (New York: W. W. Norton, 2004), 421.

78. Bobbitt, *Terror and Consent.*

79. Painter and Reese, *Selected Issues in Homeland Security Policy*, 1–4; Ridge, *Test of Our Times*, 191 ("If we were ever going to rename the agency, we might call it the Department of Worldwide Security and Prosperity"); Coburn, *Review of the Department of Homeland Security's Missions*, 152.

80. Department of Homeland Security, *Homeland Security Quadrennial Review* (Washington, DC, 2014), 30.

81. Coburn, *Review of the Department of Homeland Security's Missions*, 152–53. "In fact, the Department appears to do little of this work, with other agencies taking lead responsibility for terrorism prevention."

82. Ginsburg, *Securing Human Mobility*, 35–36; James Fallows, "Year End Pensees: More on Security," *The Atlantic*, January 15, 2009, www.theatlantic.com/technology/archive/2009/01/year-end -pensees-more-on-security/9354/ (citing a quote on "civil security" by David McIntyre, director of the Integrative Center for Homeland Security, Texas A&M University).

83. House Committee on Governmental Reform, Subcommittee on Civil Service, Census and Agency Organization, *Assessing the Proposed Department of Homeland Security*, 107th Cong. (2002) (testimony of Paul C. Light).

84. Chertoff, *Homeland Security*, 136–43.

85. Steven Brill, "15 Years after 9/11, Is America Any Safer?" *The Atlantic*, September 2016, www .theatlantic.com/magazine/archive/2016/09/are-we-any-safer/492761/.

PART IV

The President's Partners and Rivals

CHAPTER 13

Congress

The Other Branch

David P. Auerswald and Colton C. Campbell

> The legislator is an indispensable guardian of our freedom. The great executives have given inspiration and push to the advancement of human society, but it is the legislator who has given stability and continuity to that slow and painful progress.
>
> —J. William Fulbright

> Sustained consultation between the president and Congress is the most important mechanism for fostering an effective foreign policy with broad support at home and respect and punch overseas.
>
> —Lee Hamilton

Congress's authority to legislate national security issues is clear. It has the constitutional power to declare war, regulate the nation's armed forces, restrict war aims or military regulations, procure weapons systems, and alter the end strength and responsibilities of the different services. Congress authorizes federal policies, creates new programs vital to national security matters, and determines the scope of national security agency actions and portfolios. The United States is only able to form alliances, agree to strategic arms control accords, or enter into trade agreements with the explicit approval of Capitol Hill. But while its ability to establish or change national security policy is indisputable, that is no guarantee that Congress will choose to do so. Whether or not Congress acts often depends on the issue at stake and the incentives facing individual members related to that issue.

In this chapter we begin by examining the traditions, structures, and procedures of each legislative chamber. As one student of the first branch aptly notes, Congress does not exist so much as an institution, but rather as two separate chambers that operate in "different atmospheres."[1] The unmistakably majoritarian House can act quickly, decisively, and predictably, whereas the Senate often needs a supermajority to pass even mildly controversial measures. So while Congress has a variety of legislative tools at its disposal to affect the national security enterprise—such as appropriations, legislation, hearings, and individual members' actions—differences across the two chambers make using some congressional tools more difficult.

In the following section we explore the congressional ability to affect national security in more detail. Here we draw on the distinctions among crisis, strategic, and structural policies to argue that Congress's ability to shape security policy depends on the issue area in question. Some congressional tools, like altering budgets or legislation, require time to use and are thus more applicable for strategic and structural policies. Other tools, such as hearings, press statements, and nonbinding measures, remain useful during crises. The message from this section is that Congress has the powers and prerogatives to remain an active player across the national security enterprise if it chooses.

Whether Congress chooses to act is another question altogether, however. In the third section we discuss Congress's will to influence the national security enterprise. That will is often shaped by the electoral payoffs (or costs) associated with taking action, partisan relationships between members of Congress and the president, and the partisan composition within each congressional chamber. The willingness of any one member of Congress to become involved in national security decisions depends on how that official balances local, partisan, and national interests within the context of the campaign pressure cooker.

In the final section we apply these lessons to congressional oversight of the national security enterprise. Here we argue that Congress has developed sophisticated oversight tools and reporting requirements levied on the executive branch, all in an effort to keep appraised of executive actions on national security. We conclude with thoughts on the future congressional role in the national security enterprise.

LEGISLATIVE PROCEDURES

Any discussion of Congress's influence over national security policy must begin by reviewing various features of the legislative process, the most powerful tool in the congressional toolkit. It may seem basic, but people often overlook how different the procedures used in each chamber are and how those procedures affect each chamber's way of doing business. One key to understanding Congress is to remember that the majority party rules the House of Representatives because of the chamber's historical notion that the majority should rule. Conversely, the Senate has protected the privileges of the minority, particularly the rights to debate and to offer amendments.

The House is an institution in which the majority dominates because the governing rules are tilted in favor of what the majority party's leadership wants. With authorizing measures, leadership uses the chamber's internal rules to set agendas and secure the adoption of policy proposals by determining which bills to bring to the floor and the terms and conditions for their consideration. Even with appropriations bills, which, under the long-standing custom of the House, are usually debated on the floor under an open rule—a state that allows a member to offer an amendment to the bill during debate—leadership shapes the agenda by blessing which amendments are considered by voice votes rather than recorded votes or by offering several amendments en bloc—as a group—after obtaining unanimous consent. In recent Congresses leadership has negotiated and moved spending bills without ever consulting rank-and-file members. So when House members tried to bypass the Republican leadership's support for North Atlantic Treaty Organization (NATO) surveillance and backdoor access to encrypted communications, for example, backbench members used open-rule defense appropriations bills in 2014 and 2015 rather trying to insert their amendments in an authorization bill. Despite passing the House, these legislative changes were stripped from the House–Senate conference committee.[2]

These powers enhance the majority party leadership's ability to depart from the regular order of business and schedule legislation according to its priorities. As former House Speaker Denny Hastert (R-IL), said, the job of Speaker is not to move legislation that runs counter to the wishes of the majority of his or her party. This unmistakable feature of the House helps to explain why it can act quickly, decisively, and (usually) predictably on controversial matters.

Thus, an important key to advancing just about any piece of legislation in the House of Representatives is the majority party leadership and its skillful management of the Rules Committee—long considered an arm of the leadership regardless of which party controls the House. While the leadership schedules which bills are brought to the floor and in what order, the Rules Committee sets the terms and conditions for how those measures are considered— the length of the floor debate, the division of time in the debate, the number and type of amendments that will be considered, the order in which they will be addressed, as well as whether to waive any points of orders against consideration of a bill. In short, by controlling the terms of debate, the majority party leadership can in most circumstances determine the legislative outcome.

The Senate is a fundamentally different body. By contrast with the impersonal, hierarchical, and disciplined House, the Senate has long tolerated and even promoted individualism, reciprocity, and mutual accommodation. For instance, unlike the representatives, where members must respect time limits on the floor and in committee, senators are accorded all the time necessary to speak. This allows every senator a platform from which to persuade colleagues or voice a contrarian point of view. Even the physical structure of the chamber encourages individualism. Senators choose their seats at the start of a new Congress according to seniority and traditionally inscribe their names in the drawers of their desk. By contrast, members of the House sit in less formal, bench-like seats. While an increasing number of decisions are crafted with partisan purpose, many are still made with attention to historical precedent, which the upper body so carefully relies on to clarify and preserve its legislative practices.

There is unlimited debate on the Senate floor absent concerted action by a supermajority of senators. In the Senate much of the floor debate is conducted by unanimous consent (UC) agreements negotiated by the leadership of both parties. They are applicable to Senate consideration of legislation, nominations, treaties, and even movement from one agenda item to another. Important to remember is that any senator can object to a UC agreement, thus bringing a swift halt to the legislative process. Essentially, the Senate cannot do anything without having unanimous consent from all senators. The objections of one can halt all progress of the many. In the 111th Congress (2009–11), for instance, Senator Richard Shelby (R-AL) held up seventy-plus nominations made by President Barack Obama, to include officials from the Pentagon and State Department, because of unaddressed national security concerns.[3] Specifically, Senator Shelby placed his holds over concerns about a proposed contract involving an air force tanker and over financing he sought for building a counterterrorism center in Alabama. Senator Rand Paul (R-KY) filibustered the 2015 USA Freedom Act for ten and a half hours over concerns about domestic surveillance and to further his national visibility.[4]

In terms of legislation, UC agreements set out the terms of Senate floor debate—how many amendments will be considered, the time allotted to debate each amendment, the order of consideration, and so on—akin to a House special rule. Absent a UC agreement, there is unlimited debate on the Senate floor, which equates to no action on the bill in question unless sixty senators agree to invoke "cloture" to limit debate. Even then, cloture allows for up to thirty hours of debate, and getting to a vote on the underlying legislation may require multiple cloture votes. That means that a single senator can stymy legislation (or a nomination or a treaty), and it takes sixty senators to overcome that objection. In short, minorities rule in the Senate.

National Security Committees

Complicating this picture is the role of the four major national security committees and four national security appropriations subcommittees that control most foreign policy legislation. Woodrow Wilson observed over a century ago that the committee system is the very heart of the legislative process.[5] This maxim continues to account for much of Congress's business today. Committees write legislation that goes before the full chambers, oversee the implementation of legislation, and educate members. Indeed, the traditional model of congressional power has been one in which committees exercise major influence in shaping the work of the House and Senate, and each committee generally has the right to proceed at its own pace and with relative autonomy over its own agenda. Committees begin the calendar year with weeks of hearings on the administration's budget request and on oversight activities. Witnesses include executive branch officials, nongovernmental experts, and other interested parties. Subcommittees draft and vote on functional sections of each bill. Then the full committee amends and votes on the overall bill.

The legislative process in committees is fraught with tension. There are inevitably differences between the majority and minority parties on each committee, to say nothing of the often-heated negotiations that are held with the administration. Perhaps equally important, there are tensions across the eight aforementioned committees and subcommittees, which are led by sixteen key chairs and ranking minority members. The relationships among these individuals are extraordinarily complex. There are jurisdictional disputes between the authorizing and appropriating committees. The Defense Subcommittee of the Appropriations Committees, for example, may disagree with the policy priorities included in the Defense Authorization Bill written by the Armed Services Committees. Foreign Relations / Foreign Affairs and the Armed Services Committees have overlapping responsibilities that can lead to friction, particularly during military conflicts or with regard to treaty advice and consent. And these are just the core national security committees. Add to them the Homeland Security Committees in each chamber, the Select Committees on Intelligence and the Committees on Agriculture, Energy and Commerce, Governmental Affairs, and the Judiciary. Each has some foreign policy jurisdiction, which makes forging consensus even more difficult when it comes to the national security enterprise. For example, the House and Senate Intelligence Committees share oversight of the intelligence community with the House and Senate Armed Services Committees because many of the intelligence agencies are funded through the defense budget.

A bill that makes it out of committee is often subjected to the same intense scrutiny on the floor of the Senate or House. There, the bill is only as successful as its committee of origin is disciplined and deliberate. Without the proper leadership and anticipation of issues, bills become lightning rods for controversial amendments on the floor. It is critical, therefore, that committees thoroughly investigate their issues and prepare themselves to defend their conclusions. There is nothing more embarrassing to a committee chair or ranking minority member than to have a "runaway" bill—one over which he or she has lost control and that must be either pulled from consideration or go down to defeat—on the floor.

Legislative Tools

These are important inter- and intra-chamber factors when we consider the tools available to Congress to influence the national security enterprise. Certain tools require the support of both congressional chambers and particular committees in each chamber. Other tools can be used by sub-portions of Congress or even by individual members of Congress. The hurdle for action on the former is significantly higher than is that for the latter. And when you add in partisan differences, as we will discuss later, some tools become almost unusable to change security policy.

There are several primary tools Congress can use to affect the national security enterprise. These include, but are not necessarily limited to, spending legislation (to include appropriations restrictions), stand-alone legislation, "sense of the Congress" resolutions, supplemental appropriations, hearings and briefings, press conferences and interviews, and committee report language. The first four tools are derived from Article I of the Constitution, as listed in table 13.1 below. Legislation is required to regulate commerce; establish tariffs; raise, support, and regulate the armed forces; and make laws to implement Article I powers. As the preceding discussion implies, however, legislation or concurrent resolutions require a majority of the House and a supermajority in the Senate. These are high bars for action, made even higher, in the case of legislation, if the president exercises his veto power. Stopping a treaty or presidential appointment, on the other hand, requires no actual action from Congress. Senate inaction will essentially kill either initiative. In between these extremes are the congressional tools that are derived from practice, not the Constitution. These include holding hearings, coordinating executive branch briefings for members of Congress or their staff, and interacting with the press. All of these latter actions only require the initiative of a single member of Congress.

Differences between the majority and minority parties on major security issues, to say nothing of the often-heated negotiations between the two congressional chambers, influence Congress's ability and will to influence the national security enterprise. Within each chamber, there are jurisdictional disputes between the authorizing and appropriating committees and between different authorizing committees. Moreover, a large number of committees are involved in complex issues like national and homeland security, requiring consensus from each

Table 13.1. Actions Required to Use Article I Powers

Powers	Actions
Regulate commerce with foreign nations, establish tariffs	Legislation to authorize negotiations and approve presidential trade agreements
Establish court systems below the Supreme Court	Legislation
Declare war and authorize the use of military force	Legislation
Raise, support, and regulate the armed forces	Legislation (annual authorization or appropriations bills)
Advise and approve treaties and presidential appointees (Senate)	Stopping a presidential appointee or treaty requires no action. Senate supermajority to affirm treaties; Senate majority to confirm appointees
Make laws to implement these powers	Legislation
Use the power of the purse	Annual authorization and appropriations or supplemental appropriations

committee before legislation can be sent to the president. And initiatives challenging presidential priorities are subject to vetoes that then require two-thirds majorities to overturn, which raises the bar to effective action even higher.

CAN CONGRESS INFLUENCE THE NATIONAL SECURITY ENTERPRISE?

Many scholars argue that Congress lacks the means or ability to constrain presidents. Presidents are able to drive the country's foreign policy agenda owing to their constitutional powers and the accrued prerogatives of their office while Congress must often pass veto-proof legislation to constrain them. The executive branch, speaking with one voice, can articulate unified positions while Congress speaks with a chorus of voices, making agreement on executive constraints unlikely. The executive can respond to international conflicts in a timely manner, but Congress often takes months or longer to respond to presidential initiatives.[6] Congress is better suited to indirectly affect presidential behavior by manipulating public opinion, but even that gives Congress relatively little influence during military conflicts owing to the rally-around-the-flag phenomenon or the president's ability to take his or her case to the people directly.[7] From a structural perspective then, US presidents retain substantial autonomy from legislative control in the realm of international decision making, at least according to some scholars of American foreign policy.[8]

Critics also contend that Congress is too slow to change and is poorly organized to deal with the security needs of the twenty-first century. By most accounts the intent to involve Congress in the most extreme matters of national security, such as making war, was a calculated attempt by the Founding Fathers to slow the process down.[9] A large deliberative body like Congress naturally moves slowly. When faced with problems of monumental dimensions, Congress often approaches solutions in small discrete steps, building agreement from the bottom up, reflecting the institution's decentralized structure. Even following the terrorist attacks of September 11, 2001, the Senate's unabashed historian, the late Senator Robert C. Byrd (D-WV), cautioned against the president's excessive authority and use of force. "But in the heat of the moment, in the crush of recent events, I fear we may be losing sight of the larger obligations of the Senate," he said. "Our responsibility as Senators is to carefully consider and fully debate major policy matters, to air all sides of a given issue, and to act after full deliberation. Yes, we want to respond quickly to urgent needs, but a speedy response should not be used as an excuse to trample full and free debate."[10] Congress, in Byrd's view, is an institution rooted in history, embracing many vestiges from bygone eras. But some question whether the legislative branch can adequately manage today's national security concerns, especially at a time when new and delicate challenges minimize the margin of error.

The reality is more nuanced than this black-and-white picture implies. To better understand congressional capabilities, it helps to disaggregate national security policy into the issue area in question.[11] Samuel P. Huntington provides useful distinctions among crisis, strategic, and structural policies.[12] Structural policy includes issues that deal with money and the structure of the national security enterprise. Here we are talking about things like budgets, procurement and acquisition decisions, the organization of government departments, personnel policies, and military basing and force structure. In normal times structural policies do not have an immediate time requirement for their enactment. Once decided, they tend to endure for some time. Strategic policies deal with general foreign policy, such as diplomatic relations, treaties, and agreements. Strategic policy shapes broad foreign policy behavior and, while important, does not normally need to be decided on immediately. Crisis policy involves responses to dire national threats that have at least a reasonable probability of escalating in intensity, even to the point of using force. Crisis policy involves high stakes, quick decisions on issues, and an immediate time horizon.

As we will see, Congress has the ability to influence each type of policy. The usefulness of particular congressional tools, however, will vary depending on the issue being considered. Table 13.2 summarizes the relationship between issue type and congressional tools.

Table 13.2. Congressional Tools Most Applicable for Each Policy Type

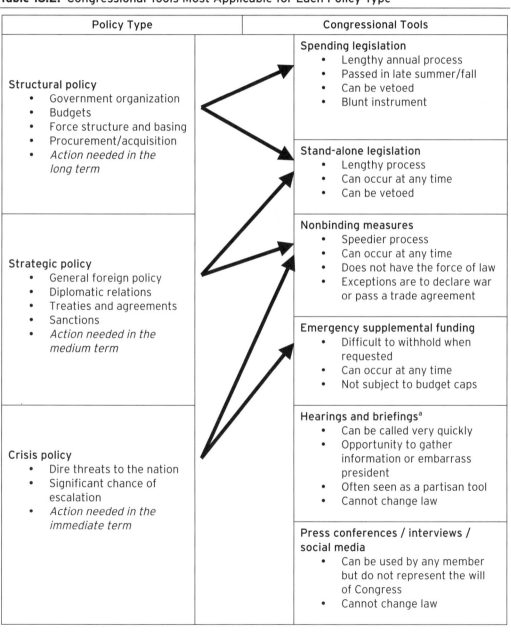

Policy Type	Congressional Tools
Structural policy • Government organization • Budgets • Force structure and basing • Procurement/acquisition • *Action needed in the long term*	**Spending legislation** • Lengthy annual process • Passed in late summer/fall • Can be vetoed • Blunt instrument
	Stand-alone legislation • Lengthy process • Can occur at any time • Can be vetoed
Strategic policy • General foreign policy • Diplomatic relations • Treaties and agreements • Sanctions • *Action needed in the medium term*	**Nonbinding measures** • Speedier process • Can occur at any time • Does not have the force of law • Exceptions are to declare war or pass a trade agreement
	Emergency supplemental funding • Difficult to withhold when requested • Can occur at any time • Not subject to budget caps
Crisis policy • Dire threats to the nation • Significant chance of escalation • *Action needed in the immediate term*	**Hearings and briefings**[a] • Can be called very quickly • Opportunity to gather information or embarrass president • Often seen as a partisan tool • Cannot change law
	Press conferences / interviews / social media • Can be used by any member but do not represent the will of Congress • Cannot change law

[a] All members of Congress can use hearings, briefings, press conferences, interviews, and social media for all policy types.

Structural Policy

As noted previously, structural policy deals with large government muscle movements—for example, the organization of government departments and agencies, changes to military force structure and portfolios, and government procurement and acquisition. The creation of the Department of Homeland Security (DHS), the 1986 Goldwater–Nichols Act, and the 1947 National Security Act are all extreme examples of structural policy. Each was a major initiative that took significant time to complete. The defense and foreign assistance budgets are also examples of structural policy. The commonality across structural policies is that they require the use of either stand-alone or spending legislation. In many cases structural policy requires both.

This has advantages and disadvantages from the congressional perspective. On the positive side, spending legislation is an annual requirement for the continued operation of government. For that reason attaching policy initiatives to authorization or appropriations bills is an attractive means of changing US policy. Spending bills and freestanding legislation also are squarely within Congress's Article I powers; Section 9 of Article I declares, "No money shall be drawn from the treasury, but in consequence of appropriations made by law." And the president cannot selectively enforce legislation, at least without a court battle.[13] On the negative side the legislative process is a slow process. Legislation has to work its way through both congressional chambers, differences between the chambers have to be reconciled, and the president has to sign the resulting bill or Congress has to get even larger majorities to override his veto. But those obstacles can be overcome in due time by a determined Congress. Congress thus has significant influence over structural policy because such policy plays to Congress's strengths: lengthy deliberation that results in a take-it-or-leave-it proposal for the president, often tied to must-have budgets.

Strategic Policy

Strategic policy deals with more amorphous policy initiatives—for example, broad foreign policy behavior, diplomatic relations, sanctions, and treaties and international trade agreements. The NATO alliance, passage of trade promotion authority to facilitate the negotiation of trade agreements, or the imposition of sanctions against a country could all be considered examples of strategic policy. As is the case with structural policy, there are advantages and disadvantages to congressional attempts to influence strategic policy. Direct methods, such as stand-alone legislation, can take a long time to enact—because winning coalitions must be built—and can require significant compromises to get to final passage. Less direct methods, such as when Congress wants to send a message or state an opinion, can take less time to pass and can even influence strategic policy but are nonbinding and carry no force of law. Often in the form of a "sense of the Congress" resolution, these resolutions are frequently used as a way for individual members to go on the record as supporting or opposing a particular policy, as an attempt to get the president to take or not take some specific action, or as a means to express the opinion of Congress to the government of a foreign nation.

Crisis Policy

Congress has the least direct influence over crisis policy, in large part for two reasons. First, crises empower presidents through Article II, section 2 of the Constitution, which states that the president is the commander in chief of the armed forces, appoints US ambassadors, receives foreign ambassadors, and commissions all officers of the United States. Presidents thus hold most of the useful levers in crises: direction of the military, choice of US diplomatic envoys, and choice of who to treat with internationally. The president is essentially at the zenith of his or her authority during international crises. Congress has far fewer weapons at its disposal during crises or war. Congress cannot directly instruct the military except through legislation, legislation that can be vetoed by the president. Use of the budget power is a blunt instrument, may not advance US interests during crises, and carries with it considerable political risks. Cutting off money for the military, for example, risks deployed troops in harm's way. Cutting off money for the State Department could mean closing one or more embassies, essentially shutting off diplomatic exchanges at the time they are most needed.

Second, legislation, and by extension budgets, is not a useful tool during crises because legislation often takes a long time to enact. Remember that legislation is usually generated in committees, must pass muster in each full legislative chamber, and then have differences reconciled between House and Senate versions, to say nothing of being signed by the president or having a supermajority to override a presidential veto. All this takes time. Congress rarely acts quickly enough given the time pressures involved in crises. Spending legislation is particularly ill-suited for crises. Crises can happen at any time. The budget process happens once a year (in theory) and spending bills are often not passed until late in the calendar year, which may not correspond to an international crisis.

Congress has episodically used other mechanisms to influence crisis policy, mechanisms that play to the legislature's strengths. One is to use legislation to proactively prohibit the use of force in particular regions or circumstances. The 1957 Middle East Resolution was an attempt at constraining President Eisenhower's use of force in the region, prohibiting interventions unless they were in response to communist aggression. Another mechanism is to place constraints on the long-term presidential use of force unless and until Congress authorizes said use. The 1973 War Powers Resolution attempted to do just that by putting a sixty-to-ninety-day limit on the use of force unless the president had authorization from Congress.

These attempts have not yielded the results hoped for by their sponsors. Eisenhower circumvented the Middle East Resolution by calling his 1958 Lebanon intervention an action against communists. And while presidents have engaged in less frequent long-term, unauthorized military interventions since the War Powers Resolution, Congress has rarely asserted itself during war powers debates, at least during crises.[14] That Congress refused to act on President Obama's 2015 request to authorize the use of force against Daesh, despite calls from individual members for the president to "do something," proves the rule.[15] The consensus view on crises is that Congress "cannot compel [the president] to follow any of the advice that members might care to offer."[16] Analysts of US foreign policy conclude that the president's foreign policy tools and motivations simply overwhelm the efforts of Congress to control security policy during crises.[17]

OTHER CONGRESSIONAL TOOLS

Two other tools listed in table 13.2 deserve mention but are not limited to a specific type of policy. These are hearings and briefings and interactions with the media via press conferences, interviews, and social media. These resources allow today's legislative branch to actively engage in national security matters, if not directly control security outcomes. The proliferation of congressional support staff, traditional media outlets, and online social media have facilitated congressional activism and provided individual members an incentive to be involved in major national security debates. That is a dramatic change from fifty to sixty years ago. In the 1950s national security decisions essentially were made by a handful of powerful committee chairmen. In the late 1960s and early 1970s, in reaction to Vietnam and Watergate and the growth and complexity of the federal government, Congress increased the number of congressional oversight subcommittees and their associated staffs and created various legislative branch research entities.[18] These resources gave members of Congress the means to become assertive on security issues.

At the same time, the proliferation of media outlets and the explosion of interest groups gave members of Congress an incentive to speak out. Today's members are adept at harnessing television coverage and interacting with interest groups to get their points across. Former chairman Darrell Issa (R-CA) of the House Committee on Oversight and Government Reform adroitly used the media to advance his committee's investigations of the Obama administration. Another example is the March 2015 "open" letter to Iran's leadership from forty-seven Senate Republicans, warning Iran that any agreement it negotiated with the Obama administration would not constrain future administrations absent Senate advice and consent. The letter had no force of law, but its distribution through the media served as an international and domestic signal of Republican discontent with the negotiations. In short, individual members now have both the means and an incentive to challenge the president's security priorities. Indeed, virtually every member of Congress can now become involved to some degree in national security debates. That said, Congress as an institution is better equipped to affect security policy when it has time to react to international events, typified by structural policy, compared to fast-paced crisis policy.

CONGRESSIONAL WILL

Scholars often argue that Congress lacks the will to challenge presidential control of the national security enterprise. Presidents have powerful incentives to take charge of security policy, incentives that Congress does not share.[19] Congress has at times even empowered the president, as occurred in the immediate post-9/11 world.[20] As late as 2006 the prevailing post-9/11 threat perception and Republican control of the legislative and executive branches reinforced historical congressional deference to the president on national security.[21] Republican-controlled Congresses gave only a cursory examination to the Bush administration's creation of Northern Command, a significant change to US security policy. Similarly, these Congresses argued over the distribution of the foreign aid budget for Afghanistan and Iraq rather than the need for a whole-sale review of America's new nation-building missions and capability.

Yet this pattern started to change in the 110th Congress (2007–9), when Democratic majorities in each chamber became more assertive on Iraq and Afghanistan, military tribunals, detainee policy, extraordinary rendition, and electronic surveillance of American citizens.[22] To explain why, we next discuss several factors that can affect the willingness of individual members to become involved in national security debates.

Electoral Incentives

"All politics is local," goes the long-held adage of the late Speaker of the House, Thomas P. "Tip" O'Neil (D-MA). Members of Congress face electoral incentives to focus on their constituents' priorities rather than the national interest. Indeed, one of the great forces in representative government is the relationship between the legislator and his or her constituency.[23] Although individual legislators do not necessarily mirror their constituents in terms of demographic characteristics, the recruitment process yields many who favor local views and priorities. Contacts with voters throughout the campaign process and while in office reinforce this convergence of views, as do representational norms adopted by most members. Indeed, members' electoral fortunes depend less on what Congress produces as an institution than on the support and goodwill of constituents who vote for them and contribute to their campaigns. Often these local interests conflict in ways that make compromise difficult—across party lines and between chambers. When this happens, it is important to know that members inevitably have reelection on their minds. Lawmakers also serve the nation, of course, and are expected to keep the national interest in mind when legislating. Yet they frequently are influenced by local attitudes even when those attitudes conflict with the national interest. The result is a constant tension between the demands of representation and those of legislating. The former requires advocacy, the latter requires accommodation of differing views and interests.

Members tend to focus their energies on policies that directly affect their districts. That preoccupation with domestic issues, especially constituency concerns and business, has traditionally been the cause for selective congressional intervention in foreign policy debates, often precipitated by crises abroad or by a widely publicized foreign policy debacle.[24] In those instances Congress usually engages in symbolic criticism of the president's leadership without making a concerted effort to change national security policy. Most lawmakers then move on to the next issue, reinforcing the impression that the typical congressional attention span for national security is episodic and lacks an overall strategy.[25]

Members of Congress who become more deeply involved in national security matters do so for one of the following reasons. Taking positions on security budgets or military procurement, or during foreign policy crises or military conflicts, may help the electorate distinguish between political parties, and partisan identification is a strong determinant of voting behavior.[26] Members may also care about the national interest irrespective of electoral gains, particularly when there is a significant threat to the nation. National security in general, and military conflicts in particular, are also important issues for a broad range of constituencies, such as friends or family of the military, military contractors, industries affected by the outcome of international crises, those concerned with human rights, and "ethnic" lobbies, just to name a few. These involved constituencies may demand a legislator's participation in security debates to help protect their threatened interests. In sum, legislators participate in security policy if some portion of their core reelection constituency is concerned with the policy outcome.[27]

Involvement is not without its risks, particularly if the national security policy is placed under the umbrella of a consensus issue. Such instances create electoral disincentives for congressional engagement. Past presidents, for example, often labeled a military conflict as consistent with US containment policies or the Monroe Doctrine as a way to ensure congressional support during the Cold War. Speaking out against consensus goals risked electoral punishment. Being labeled as soft on communism for taking a position contrary to containment was something most elected officials avoided during the Cold War. Being labeled soft on terrorists has the same resonance today. That reluctance has often extended to the means used by the president to reach a consensus goal, at least if critiquing the means used could be equated with having dissimilar policy goals. For example, speaking out against military intervention in the early years of Iraq or Afghanistan might have led to being labeled as soft on terrorism.

Finally, the duration of a military conflict or national security concern may also affect levels of congressional opposition. Congressional inaction during short-term crises, for instance, holds few electoral risks or rewards. Should the crisis end badly, members of Congress can always blame the president and avoid the blame themselves. Success, on the other hand, rarely reflects on Congress. Instead, either the military or the president receives all the praise. Inactivity during longer crises poses more significant electoral risks. Congress may suffer an electoral backlash for taking no action should the crisis result in defeat. Congress can justify taking action during long-term initiatives as reining in a reckless president or avoiding another Vietnam.

Interbranch Partisanship

Shared partisanship with the president is a second reason for congressional inactivity. The greater the number of presidential partisans in Congress, the less likely that Congress will act collectively to halt a presidential initiative. Those lawmakers might share the president's goals and see no need to speak out. Or they might fear to challenge their president because confronting a president of their own party might decrease their chances of reelection in a number of ways. First, helping overturn the security policies of one's own president cannot but hurt that president's chances for reelection. By extension, losing the presidency hurts a member's chances of riding the president's coattails into office. Second, overturning one's own president weakens the party image in the minds of the voters, either in terms of its unity or its record of accomplishments. Third, challenging one's own president in all likelihood means an end to party leaders helping the member of Congress with fund-raising and campaigning. Fourth and related, the insurgent member might face sanctions from party leadership in Congress, ranging from losing a committee chairmanship to being excluded from party log rolls on appropriation bills.

At the end of the World War II, for example, Congress was wary of making an open-ended military commitment to the United Nations. Congressional members of the American delegation to the UN Charter negotiations ensured that participation in UN military operations would be in accordance with each member nation's constitutional processes. The 1945 UN Participation Act codified that sentiment into law, stipulating that the president could not commit substantial US forces to UN missions without expressed congressional consent. Five years later, President Harry Truman ignored both the letter and the spirit of the law when deploying US forces to the Korean peninsula.[28] Truman disregarded the *ex-ante* constraint because he faced little chance of domestic penalties from a Congress controlled by his own party.[29]

Intra-branch Partisanship

Congress's willingness and ability to influence national security policy intersect when we consider partisan divides in each chamber. The politics of national security are no more immune to the increasing partisan atmosphere in Washington than any other area of public policy.[30] Some members, particularly those departing the institution and reflecting on their congressional careers, readily comment about the steady march by both parties toward ever more partisan and personal attacks. Partisanship has worn away the comity that normally encourages the flow of legislation, as negotiating with those on the opposite side of a debate, according to Senator Susan Collins (R-ME) is "vilified by the hard-liners on both sides of the aisle."[31] Moreover, such partisanship has "infused the rhetoric surrounding national security discussions" and obstructed Congress's critical role of oversight.[32]

For many congressional observers of the political strife on Capitol Hill—from committee turf battles over jurisdiction within a congressional chamber to conference committee tug-of-war struggles between members of the House and Senate—the real conflict stems from the distinctly partisan alignment between Democrats and Republicans and their subsequent struggle for majority status. The two parties have become increasingly polarized over time,[33] often finding that partisan politics wins elections, despite the costs to governing.[34] Congressional parties have allowed their extreme wings to dominate decision making at the expense of the middle and, for some, have "broken" Congress as a branch of government.[35]

Partisanship has entered the legislative arena from the electoral process. Constituency changes have led to the election of representatives and senators who are more ideologically compatible with their party colleagues than with the rest of the country.[36] This has been especially evident in the Senate, an institution long steeped in the tradition of individualism. By contrast with the impersonal, hierarchical, and disciplined House, the Senate long tolerated and even promoted reciprocity and mutual accommodation. For the past several decades, however, rising partisanship has worked to reverse these senatorial traditions, as more and more members of the House of Representatives are elected to the Senate. More than half of the Senate in the 114th Congress (2015–17), for instance, consists of members who were first elected to the hyperpolarized House.

Heightened partisan polarization has decreased legislative productivity, especially in the Senate. In the last fifty years, the percentage of major legislation before the Senate that has encountered problems related to extended debate has risen from 8 percent to 70 percent.[37] When in the minority, senators of both parties increasingly exploit dilatory devices, such as the filibuster and secret "holds," to bring the chamber to a standstill. Defenders say this protects minority rights, permits thorough consideration of bills, and dramatizes contentious issues. Critics contend that filibusters and holds enable minorities to extort unwanted concessions and has caused the Senate to descend into complete dysfunction.[38] In response to such increased minority obstructionism, the majority party leadership or rank-and-file members routinely file cloture motions rather than agreeing to allow amendments to be debated or employ other procedural tactics, such as "filling up the amendment tree" to prevent consideration of alternative amendments by minority members.[39]

The hyper-partisanship that characterizes the current climate on Capitol Hill, for instance, has made congressional parties much more active in agenda formation, elevated interparty tensions,[40] and affected the working relationship in Congress.[41] Partisan divides have muddied the classic adage articulated by Senator Arthur H. Vandenberg (R-MI), a longtime chairman of the Foreign Relations Committee, that "politics stops at the water's edge" with regard to national security issues. That is, members of Congress and other elected officials are no longer apt to set aside their partisan differences in the interest of common defense.

This was readily apparent in the congressional reaction to the aforementioned negotiations with Iran, as well as to the 2012 attacks against the US embassy building in Benghazi, Libya. Congressional partisans engaged in a series of highly polarized investigations seemingly aimed at discrediting the Obama administration rather than fixing the problems associated with embassy security in unstable parts of the world. Democratic members of the House Select Committee on Benghazi sent multiple letters to the panel's chairman complaining about the partisan proceedings of the select committee and accusing Republicans of excluding them by holding secret meetings with witnesses and withholding information.

"Members of this Committee began our work with a pledge to pursue the truth and reform in a bipartisan manner that honored the lives of those that passed away in this tragedy," charged Representative Tammy Duckworth (D-IL). "Unfortunately, the majority is again pursuing a partisan investigation that has yet to define its scope or goals."[42] Ranking Member Elijah Cummings (D-MD) added, "This one-sided process—in which you selectively inform Democrats only after-the-fact and when you deem appropriate—impairs the efforts of Committee Members who are seeking the truth."[43]

CONGRESSIONAL OVERSIGHT

Congressional oversight underpins any attempt by Congress to direct the national security enterprise. Ideally, Congress will gather information before taking action, whether that action takes the form of legislation, budgetary changes, "sense of the Congress" resolutions, and so on. The difficulty confronting the Hill, as one might imagine, is that many national security programs are highly classified, making oversight difficult.

It is just not easy to gather information on classified programs, to say nothing of discussing those programs in public forums, with constituents, or with the press. Consider three examples. First, oversight of the military is not easy given the security surrounding military doctrine, capabilities, and operations and the varying levels of military expertise possessed by congresspersons or their staffs. Second, congressional fragmentation of homeland security oversight is unparalleled in other executive departments; more than ninety committees and subcommittees reach into DHS, nearly three times the number that oversee the Department of Defense.[44] This undermines the overall clarity and coherence of homeland security policy and has presented the DHS leadership with a significant opportunity cost. Third, how does one do effective oversight of the sixteen federal intelligence agencies that make up America's intelligence community? Efforts by Congress to maintain accountability over the intelligence agencies have been uneven, with some lawmakers displaying a strong interest in carrying out "oversight" but most engaging in overlook.

The first way Congress has adapted is by increasing its oversight capabilities. Consider oversight of the military. Congress conducts formal oversight of the military through the annual budget cycle. So-called regular order oversight takes place in multiple stages associated with the president's submission and congressional consideration of the defense budget. One facet of oversight is contained in the formal hearings associated with the defense budget request. Congressional committees can subpoena witnesses and compel their testimony under oath, with the exception of White House staff, and defense-related committees can hold classified hearings. Another facet of oversight is the frequent formal and informal briefings for members and congressional staff on specific defense programs. Members of Congress can submit formal questions for the record to the military.

Congress has significant staff resources at its disposal to assist in defense oversight. Each individual member of Congress will have at least one person on their personal staff that handles defense issues. Congressional committees have separate, large staffs that report to the chairperson and ranking minority party member on the committee. While all members of Congress have access to sensitive and classified material, as do some personal staff and most committee staff who work on national security–related issues, they do not always get the full picture. Personal office staff, for instance, may be cleared to the top secret level but are not permitted to have access to either sensitive compartmented information (SCI) or special access programs (SAP)—both clearance levels reserved exclusively for committee staff. And as the majority of key intelligence and programmatic data are held in either SCI or SAP channels, it means that rank-and-file members are denied the ability to have their personal staff briefed into these compartments, making those same rank-and-file members heavily dependent on cleared committee staff hired by—and thus loyal to—the chair or ranking member. Members of Congress also can ask any of three supporting agencies—the Congressional Research Service (CRS), the Government Accountability Office (GAO), and the Congressional Budget Office (CBO)—to engage in oversight on behalf of individual members of Congress or congressional committees. Together, these various forms of oversight provide Congress with a wealth of information as to what the military is doing.

The second way Congress has adapted is by (1) breaking up large program initiatives into smaller pieces and requiring executive branch reports at each milestone in the larger initiative and (2) forcing the president to declare intent before implementing a new initiative.[45] The Quadrennial Defense Review is one of the most well-known and largest examples of an executive branch report required by Congress. But note that it is simply one of the thousands of executive reports mandated each year.[46] Two of the best-known types of presidential statements of intent are national security waivers and presidential findings. Presidents have to sign national security waivers if they want to avoid imposing sanctions or to continue foreign assistance contrary to statutory intent. Before presidents can initiate covert activities, they must sign a presidential finding. Congress regularly requires executive branch reports and presidential declarations of intent in authorization and appropriations bills and, increasingly, in treaty ratification documents passed by the Senate.[47]

Frequent reports on administration actions allow Congress to unearth hidden information either possessed by the executive or available to it. The more frequent or comprehensive those reports, the more opportunity there is for Congress to halt initiatives before they escalate beyond the point of no return. Requiring prominent declarations of presidential intent and responsibility removes ambiguity about a politically salient executive branch position. Because public declarations of intent commit the president, and the public is unlikely to reward a president who breaks well-publicized promises, declarations are likely to be more than cheap talk. Both measures improve reporting.

Despite these oversight mechanisms, however, it seems that Congress cannot win. All too frequently, Congress is derided either for micromanaging defense policy in a way that advantages constituency interests at the expense of the national interest or for allowing the military (and the intelligence community) unfettered access to the nation's coffers. Both views are off the mark. There is a raft of issues—highly consequential for the US national security posture but engaging relatively few political interests outside the defense community—over which the defense committees have asserted themselves. These include everything from officer selection to military organization to veterans' care.[48] The defense authorizing committees are never going to be able to single-handedly dictate the size of the defense budget, as too many other members of Congress have a stake in that fight to defer to any one committee, but there are a host of other, important defense issues over which the Armed Services Committees have exercised significant influence.

CONCLUSION

Congress is often dubbed powerless to directly affect the national security enterprise. What is clear, pursuant to the Constitution, is that the underlying relationship between Congress and the executive in national security issues is one of shared control. Each branch has the power to affect US policy. While contemporary presidents generally direct this agenda during crises, control shifts toward Congress when structural policy issues arise and when a member's electoral and partisan incentives allow or even encourage congressional activism. Examples of such periods include congressionally mandated neutrality during the interwar period, limits on military interventions in the Balkans in the absence of consensus over American grand strategy in the aftermath of the Cold War, and periods of divided government or prolonged military conflicts, such as we witnessed after 2006 with regard to Iraq and Afghanistan.

Congress has the capability and at times the will to significantly influence national security policy. Yet it remains to be seen to what extent future congresses will be able to use all the powers of the institution to advance national security agendas through the House and Senate. After all, the personal motives, goals, and talents of the collection of individuals who serve in Congress at any given time have a direct impact on how the institution operates. Just as no two members of Congress perform their jobs in exactly the same manner, no one Congress interacts with the president in similar fashion, particularly with regard to controversial measures. History suggests that future Congresses will continue to devise innovative practices and fashion creative prerogatives in striving to secure the position of Congress as an influential first branch, capable of setting national security agendas and passing security-related legislation.

NOTES

The views expressed in this chapter are those of the authors and not the National Defense University, the Department of Defense, or any other entity of the US government.

1. Donald A. Ritchie, *The U.S. Congress: A Very Short Introduction* (New York: Oxford University Press, 2010), xv.

2. Thanks to an anonymous peer reviewer for this example.

3. Kate Phillips and Jeff Zeleny, "White House Blasts Shelby Hold on Nominees," *The Caucus* (blog), February 5, 2010, http://thecaucus.blogs.nytimes.com/2010/02/05/white-house-blasts-shelby -hold-on-nominees, accessed March 9, 2015. "Holds" are an informal senatorial custom that allow senators to request through party leadership that certain measures or matters be kept off the floor schedule.

4. Alex Byers and Seung Min Kim, "Paul Calls It a Night after 10 1/2 Hours: It's Not Clear Whether His Speech on the PATRIOT Act Had Any Real Effect on Mitch McConnell's Plans," *Politico*, May 21, 2015, www.politico.com/story/2015/05/rand-paul-filibuster-patriot-act-118141.

5. Woodrow Wilson, *Congressional Government: A Study in American Politics* (New Brunswick, NJ: Transaction Publishers, 2002), 79. First published 1885.

6. James M. Lindsay, *Congress and the Politics of U.S. Foreign Policy* (Baltimore: Johns Hopkins University Press, 1994); Roger Hilsman, *The Politics of Policy Making in Defense and Foreign Affairs* (Englewood Cliffs, NJ: Prentice-Hall, 1987); Stephen Krasner, *Defending the National Interest* (Princeton, NJ: Princeton University Press, 1978); and Robert Dahl, *Congress and Foreign Policy* (New York: Norton, 1950);

7. Jack Levy, "The Diversionary Theory of War: A Critique," in *Handbook of War Studies*, ed. Manus Midlarsky (Ann Arbor: University of Michigan Press, 1989); and Samuel Kernell, *Going Public: New Strategies of Presidential Leadership* (Washington, DC: Congressional Quarterly Press, 1986).

8. For examples, see James Sundquist, *The Decline and Resurgence of Congress* (Washington, DC: Brookings Institution, 1981); and Barbara Hinckley, *Less Than Meets the Eye: Foreign Policy Making and the Myth of the Assertive Congress* (Chicago: University of Chicago Press, 1994).

9. Van Alstyne, "Congress, the President, and the Power to Declare War: A Requiem for Vietnam," *University of Pennsylvania Law Review* 121 (1972): 1–28.

10. 147 Cong. Rec., S9948 (October 1, 2001).

11. Jeremy Rosner, *The New Tug of War* (Washington, DC: Carnegie Endowment for International Peace, 1995).

12. See Samuel Huntington, *The Common Defense* (New York: Columbia University Press, 1961); and Lindsay, *Congress and the Politics of U.S. Foreign Policy*, 3–5, 120–27, 147, 153–56.

13. Article II, section 3 of the Constitution states that the president "shall take care that the laws be faithfully executed."

14. The exception might be the early 2015 debate over President Obama's request for congressional authorization to use force against Daesh. For a review of the empirical record before and after passage of the War Powers Resolution, see David Auerswald and Peter Cowhey, "Ballotbox Diplomacy: The War Powers Resolution and the Use of Force," *International Studies Quarterly* 41 (1997): 505–28.

15. Russell Berman, "The War against ISIS Will Go Undeclared," *The Atlantic*, April 15, 2015, www.theatlantic.com/politics/archive/2015/04/the-war-against-isis-will-go-undeclared/390618/, accessed March 24, 2016.

16. Lindsay, *Congress and the Politics of U.S. Foreign Policy*, 151.

17. Kellerman and Barilleaux, *President as World Leader*; and Arthur Schlesinger, *The Imperial Presidency* (New York: Popular Library, 1973).

18. These entities include the Congressional Research Service (CRS), the Government Accountability Office (GAO), and the Congressional Budget Office (CBO). The CRS specializes in policy reviews. The GAO conducts audits of existing government programs. The CBO makes budget estimates of proposed government initiatives.

19. Hinckley, *Less Than Meets the Eye*; and Harold Koh, *The National Security Constitution* (New Haven, CT: Yale University Press, 1990).

20. Charles A. Stevenson, *Congress at War: The Politics of Conflict since 1789* (Washington, DC: Potomac Books, 2007); and Sundquist, *Decline and Resurgence of Congress*.

21. Norman J. Ornstein and Thomas E. Mann, "When Congress Checks Out," *Foreign Affairs* 85 (November/December 2006): 67–82; Andrew Rudalevige, *The New Imperial Presidency: Renewing Presidential Power after Watergate* (Ann Arbor: University of Michigan Press, 2006); and Louis Fisher, *Congressional Abdication on War and Spending* (College Station: Texas A&M University Press, 2000).

22. Brian Friel, "The Watchdog Growls," *National Journal*, March 2007, 20–29.

23. David R. Mayhew, *Congress: The Electoral Connection* (New Haven, CT: Yale University Press, 1974).

24. Eileen K. Burgin, "Representatives' Decisions on Participation in Foreign Policy Issues," *Legislative Studies Quarterly* 16 (November 1991): 521–46; and Aage R. Clausen, *How Congressmen Decide* (New York: St. Martin's, 1973).

25. Cecil V. Crabb Jr., "Foreign Policy," in *The Encyclopedia of the United States Congress*, vol. 2, ed. Donald C. Bacon, Roger H. Davidson, and Morton Keller (New York: Simon & Shuster, 1995).

26. Angus Campbell, Philip Converse, Warren Miller, and Donald Stokes, *The American Voter* (Chicago: University of Chicago Press, 1976).

27. Lindsay, *Congress and the Politics of U.S. Foreign Policy*; and Burgin, "Representatives' Decisions on Participation."

28. The Senate responded by passing (69–21) in 1951 a nonbinding Senate resolution (S. Res. 99) asking that future troop commitments to bilateral or multilateral treaty partners be subjected to a congressional vote before being undertaken (section 6). Consideration of this legislation became known as the Great Debate of 1951. For a legislative history, see *Congressional Quarterly Almanac, 1951*, 7:220–32. See also S. Rep. No. 175, at 2–3 (1951); and Fisher, *Congressional Abdication*, 97–101. President Truman's disdain for the resolution is apparent in "The President's News Conference of January 11, 1951," *Public Papers of the President, Harry S. Truman, 1951* (Washington, DC: Government Printing Office, 1965), 18–22.

29. Most Democratic congressional leaders spoke in favor of the president's actions. See *Foreign Relations of the United States, 1950*, 7:200–2; and Cong. Rec. 9154–60, 9268–69, 9319–29, 9537–40 (June 1950). Indeed, these same congressional leaders advised Truman against requesting a congressional vote on the intervention, warning that Republican members would use that opportunity to criticize the

administration. See Dean Acheson, *The Korean War* (New York: W. W. Norton, 1971), 32–33; and *Foreign Relations of the United States, 1950*, 7:286–91.

30. Julian E. Zelizer, *Arsenal of Democracy: The Politics of National Security—From World War II to the War on Terrorism* (New York: Basic Books, 2010); and Daniel Wirls, "Lap Dogs of War: Congress and National Security Policy" (presented at the Annual Meeting of the Western Political Science Association Annual Meeting, San Diego, 2008).

31. Susan Collins, "Congress Got Nasty: Here's How To Fix It," *Washington Post*, October 10, 2010.

32. 156 Cong. Rec. E705 (April 29, 2010).

33. Sunil Ahuja, *Congress Behaving Badly: The Rise of Partisanship and Incivility and the Death of Public Trust* (Westport, CT: Praeger, 2008).

34. Nicol C. Rae and Colton C. Campbell, "Party Politics and Ideology in the Contemporary Senate," in *The Contentious Senate: Partisanship, Ideology, and the Myth of Cool Judgment*, ed. Colton C. Campbell and Nicol C. Rae (Lanham, MD: Rowman & Littlefield, 2001).

35. Richard Fleisher and John R. Bond, "The Shrinking Middle in the U.S. Congress," *British Journal of Political Science* 34 (2004): 429–51; Sarah A. Binder, "Congress, the Executive, and the Production of Public Policy: United We Govern?" in *Congress Reconsidered*, 7th ed., ed. Lawrence C. Dodd and Bruce I. Oppenheimer (Washington, DC: CQ Press, 2001); and Thomas E. Mann and Norman J. Ornstein, *The Broken Branch: How Congress Is Failing America and How to Get It Back on Track* (New York: Oxford University Press, 2006).

36. Joseph Cooper and Garry Young, "Party and Preference in Congressional Decision Making: Roll Call Voting in the House of Representatives, 1889–1999," in *Party, Process, and Political Change in Congress: New Perspectives on the History of Congress*, ed. David W. Brady and Mathew D. McCubbins (Palo Alto, CA: Stanford University Press, 2002); and Robert S. Erickson and Gerald C. Wright, "Voters, Candidates, and Issues in Congressional Elections," in Dodd and Oppenheimer, *Congress Reconsidered*.

37. Barbara Sinclair, "Legislative Proposals to Change Senate Procedure" (testimony before the Senate Committee on Rules and Administration, Washington, DC, July 28, 2010), http://rules.senate .gov/public/index.cfm?p=CommitteeHearings&ContentRecord_id=2208a4dd-5e20-48bd-8f82-b2f75d 0cd21d&Statement_id=cc96ec80-03dd-43ba-8e3a-ba8bef5b2aec&ContentType_id=14f995b9-dfa5 -407a-9d35-56cc7152a7ed&Group_id=1983a2a8-4fc3-4062-a50e-7997351c154b&Month Display=7&YearDisplay=2010.

38. Michael F. Bennet, "Legislative Proposals to Change Senate Procedure" (testimony before the Senate Committee on Rules and Administration, Washington, DC, July 28, 2010), http://rules.senate .gov/public/?a=Files.Serve&File_id=847ae43d-3001-4073-bbab-f10f0fde1850.

39. Elizabeth Rybicki, "Filling the Amendment Tree in the Senate," *Extension of Remarks* 33 (January 2010): 1–10; and Steven S. Smith and Gerald Gamm, "The Dynamics of Party Government in Congress," in *Congress Reconsidered*, 9th ed., ed. Lawrence C. Dodd and Bruce I. Oppenheimer (Washington, DC: CQ Press, 2009).

40. Richard G. Forgette, *Congress, Parties, and Puzzles: Politics as a Team Sport* (New York: Peter Lang, 2004).

41. 151 Cong. Rec. 10547 (May 20, 2005).

42. House Select Committee on Benghazi, "Democrats Release Multiple Letters on Committee's Partisan Investigation," press release, January 27, 2015, http://democrats.benghazi.house.gov/news/ press-releases/democrats-release-multiple-letters-on-committee-s-partisan-investigation.

43. Ibid.

44. Jerry Markon, "Department of Homeland Security Has 120 Reasons to Want Streamlined Oversight," *Washington Post*, September 25, 2014, www.washingtonpost.com/news/federal-eye/ wp/2014/09/25/outsized-congressional-oversight-weighing-down-department-of-homeland-security/, accessed on March 24, 2016.

45. For an example of this logic applied to the American use of force, see David Auerswald and Peter Cowhey, "Ballotbox Diplomacy: The War Powers Resolution and the Use of Force," *International Studies Quarterly* 41, no. 3 (September 1997): 505–28.

46. For a *partial* list of executive branch annual reports to Congress, see "Reports Made to Congress," H. R. Doc. No. 113–85 (2014).

47. On the inclusion of reporting requirements in treaty ratification documents, see David Auerswald, "Senate Reservations to Security Treaties," *Foreign Policy Analysis* 2, no. 1 (January 2006): 83–100; and David Auerswald and Forrest Maltzman, "Policymaking through Advice and Consent: Treaty Consideration by the United States Senate," *Journal of Politics* 65, no. 4 (November 2003): 1097–110.

48. For detailed discussions of the congressional role in these and other defense-related issues, see Colton Campbell and David Auerswald, eds., *Congress and Civil–Military Relations* (Washington, DC: Georgetown University Press, 2015).

CHAPTER 14

The US Supreme Court

The Cult of the Robe in the National Security Enterprise

Harvey Rishikof

> There is hardly a political question in the United States that does not sooner or later turn into a judicial one.
>
> —Alexis de Tocqueville

> The absolute worst violation of the judge's oath is to decide a case based on a partisan political or philosophical basis, rather than what the law requires.
>
> —Associate Justice Antonin Scalia

> Some constitutional development comes about because judges evaluate significant facts differently from the way their predecessors viewed similar facts. The later judges discover some relevance to a constitutional rule where earlier judges saw none. Or they find an importance in some fact that once was thought trivial. In all sorts of ways the later judges see things that earlier judges did not see. Or they deal with facts that were not faced in earlier adjudication.
>
> —Associate Justice David Souter

It is now virtually impossible to discuss the national security enterprise without discussing the role of the US Supreme Court and the federal courts. Historically, the federal courts had shown deference to executive power and Congress in the carrying out of foreign policy, national security, and war. Over the last few years, however, federal courts have increasingly injected themselves into issues concerning detention of prisoners, interrogations, state secret protections, domestic surveillance, and the applicability of the Geneva Conventions. These legal incursions have not been without controversy and have often revealed deep jurisprudential divisions among the sitting justices. Regardless of one's view on these issues, what has become clear is that the federal judiciary is helping to shape the policy environment of the national security enterprise.

The constitutional framework, though, invites legal interpretations as a matter of text. Articles I and II assign overlapping functions; many clauses are general, as in the case of presidential authority; and the language fails to prescribe or allocate power in the area of national security, such as exactly when the writ of habeas corpus may be suspended.[1] Because of these overlapping and shared authorities and the formulation of the foreign policy powers of both the president and Congress, a leading constitutional scholar noted, the Constitution is "an invitation to struggle for the privilege of directing American foreign policy."[2] The modern national security arena has proved to be another invitation for struggle but this time including the federal courts as an active participant.

From the Supreme Court perspective, the two major precedents that previously established the power of the president and Congress in the national security enterprise were the *Curtiss-Wright* and Steel Seizure cases.[3] In *Curtiss-Wright* the Supreme Court announced that in foreign policy the president was "the plenary and exclusive power" and "the sole organ of the federal government in the field of international relations."[4] The Steel Seizure case is famous for the concurring opinion of Associate Justice Robert H. Jackson that established the continuum of the three categories of presidential authority: (1) when the president acts pursuant to expressed or implied authorizations of Congress, his authority is at its *maximum*; (2) when the president acts in absence of either a congressional grant or a denial of authority, he relies only on independent powers but is in a *zone of twilight* in which he and Congress may have concurrent authority, or in which the distribution of authority is uncertain; and finally, (3) when the president takes actions incompatible with the expressed or implied will of Congress, his power is at the *lowest ebb*, and he can rely only on his own constitutional powers.

In the recent war on terrorism, the Bush administration first asserted "sole organ" *Curtiss-Wright* authority in its view on legal interpretations of the Geneva Conventions and the law of armed conflict. When the Supreme Court rejected this view, the president then reasoned that according to the Steel Seizure doctrine, he enjoyed maximum power after Congress passed the Military Commission Act. Again the Court rejected this view under its interpretation of habeas corpus and allowed for the detainees to have access to the federal system. The extent of the power of the Court on habeas corpus remains unclear and will be determined by further litigation.

What explains this culture of judicial independence? This was not the role envisioned by the Founding Fathers. To appreciate this phenomenon of judicial independence, the chapter will trace the creation of the culture of independence that marks the US judiciary—its origins, budget, support organizations, rule making, remuneration, theories of representation, discipline/removal, and transparency. While to some these may seem to be merely bureaucratic or administrative issues, each critically reinforces an attitude of ideological independence. Part of the explanation of the ideological and constitutional independence of the federal judges rests on this unique historical organizational bureaucracy. To understand judicial independence, one must first appreciate the federal judicial bureaucratic culture. This analysis of the bureaucratic culture will be followed by discussion of how a majority of the Supreme Court assessed its role in the national security enterprise and required President Bush and Congress to moderate their assertions and interpretations of the law in the war on terrorism by finding the right of habeas corpus in the detention process.

A GENERAL CULTURAL HISTORY

The Inner Workings of the Court

The culture that the Supreme Court presents to the world is analytical—based on the written word—independent, apolitical, and detached. The method of interpreting the law is a case-by-case approach through the use of logical syllogisms both broad and narrow. Court debates and communications are formal and via memo. Each justice and his or her chambers approach a case independently. Cases are placed on the calendar when four justices vote to hear the case. The term runs from the first Monday in October to the last day in June.

The chambers are composed of two secretaries, a court aide, and three law clerks, though the chief justice (CJ) is allowed four clerks. The permanent staffs are lean, fiercely loyal, competent, and long serving. These public servants are loath to write kiss-and-tell memoirs. Though occasionally books such as *The Brethren*, *Closed Chambers*, or *The Nine* have been written to pierce the "black veil," these are the exceptions, not the rule.[5]

To most observers the inner workings of the Court in the magnificent building built by Cass Gilbert in 1928 have remained opaque. As Walter Bagehot once noted in describing the British Crown, "a little mystery is a good thing." But in another sense the Court is transparent; its decisions are published for all to read and comment on.

The law clerks, considered the "best and the brightest," have already clerked for a district or appellate court. They typically serve at the Supreme Court for only one term, after which many go on to significant government employment with the Department of Justice (DOJ) or Congress, teach, or more recently, join the most prestigious law firms in the nation.[6] The clerks from each justice's chambers form a "judicial family" that usually meets annually or biannually; the justices remain tied by keeping up with the marriages and births of their extended families. The "former clerk" culture is one of the key bases that have protected the independence of the judiciary. These clerks understand and promote the importance of an independent judiciary and can be counted on to support the institution whenever the concept of judicial independence is attacked.

The monastic-like imposed detachment of each justice is punctuated periodically by oral argument on a joined issue for usually one hour. The justices hold no press conferences; there are no lobbyists hanging around the chambers. Post argument the nine justices meet together to discuss the cases. Court protocol dictates that the CJ begins the discussion, and by tradition the justices then discuss the case in turn by seniority. At the conclusion of the discussion, if the CJ is in the majority, he chooses who shall be assigned to write the opinion. If the CJ is not in the majority, the most senior justice in the majority has the right to assign the opinion. In the most recent history, the Court has decided approximately eighty to ninety cases per term.

The opinions must be issued in the term in which the case was argued. If the opinion cannot be issued owing to lack of a majority, then the case will be slated for reargument for the next term. Rarely, the Court will determine that the decision to hear a case was "improvidently granted" and dismiss the case. In such circumstances the decision of the lower court will stand. In this culture there are no ties—someone must win and someone must lose.

There is a way to "duck" the case per constitutional design—namely, when the Court accepts the case but declines to decide on it on the grounds that the issues present a "political question." These cases have been brought at times to enjoin the president's military orders or to contest war taxing and spending, asserting the "unconstitutionality" of a particular military action, such as the Vietnam War. Explaining the political question doctrine, Associate Justice William J. Brennan in *Baker v. Carr* advised against the Court resolving cases that present "a textually demonstrable constitutional commitment of the issue to a coordinate political department; or a lack of judicially discoverable and manageable standards for resolving" the issue.[7] The jurisprudential debate among the justices focuses on which cases fall into this category.

Historic Origins

The place of the Court in our constitutional design begins with the US Constitution. As is well documented, the Constitution does not specify the size of the Supreme Court. The only justice mentioned is the CJ, who is mentioned in the context of impeachment proceedings in Article I. Article III of the Constitution gives Congress the power to fix the number of justices. Over the years the number has fluctuated. The first Judiciary Act of 1789 set the number at six justices. The Court was expanded to seven members in 1807, nine in 1837, and ten in 1863. Then the Judicial Circuits Act of 1866 set the number at seven to be reached by retirement and the eventual removal of seats. As a result, one seat was removed in 1866 and a second in 1867. Before the goal of seven was reached, however, the Judiciary Act of 1869 was passed, and the number of justices was again set at nine, where it has remained until this day. Under Article III the justices are the only actors that have life tenure and constitutionally protected salaries.

Although Article II contemplates removal by impeachment, no Supreme Court justice has ever been successfully impeached, though it was tried with Samuel Chase in 1804–5. The failure helped establish the principle that justices would not be removed for unpopular views or opinions. To understand this independence of mind, earlier in 1803 the paradigm-setting case of *Marbury v. Madison* established the Court's authority to rule a law passed by Congress unconstitutional, declaring, "[It] is empathically the province and duty of the judicial department to say what the law is." President Franklin Roosevelt's failure to "pack" the Supreme Court in the late 1930s cemented the concept of an independent court.[8] These three historic events—*Marbury*, the failed impeachment, and the discredited court packing—enshrined American commitment to an independent judiciary as a counter-majoritarian institution to pure democratic or political rule.[9]

As reflected by these three events, any discussion of the American judicial culture requires a deep appreciation of American political and legal history. Many of the cherished values and rights now enjoyed by the citizens of the United States were borne of intellectual and political struggles. The results of these debates became enshrined as part of our constitutional framework and have been passed down from generation to generation. This is not to say, however, that once an issue has been "settled" in the constitutional sense, it is no longer open to debate. In fact, the opposite may be more the order of the day, whereby a dissent of yesteryear resurrects itself to forge a majority for the next generation. The best example of this phenomenon are the early dissents by Associate Justices Oliver Wendell Holmes Jr. and Louis D. Brandeis in the 1920s concerning the right of privacy, which eventually became the law of the land forty years later under Chief Justice Earl Warren.[10]

Running the Courts

In the arena of judicial administration, there have similarly been decisions that have structured our legal system in a specific manner. In a sense, *all* legal systems must confront general bureaucratic questions and ultimately resolve them. But the answers are not fabricated in a vacuum and must reflect cultural experience. Nevertheless, all judicial systems must resolve questions of judicial independence, budgetary allocation, selection of the judiciary, and the administration of justice. The resolution of these "functions" will create a "structure" that possesses its own interlinking logic. For comparative purposes such a framework of analysis allows for a discussion of terms, but the answers will be informed by the cultural legacy of each country.

For the purposes of the general historic cultural discussion, the analysis will begin by looking on two essential "functions" that all systems must address: budget formulation and support organizations in civil society.[11] Budgets matter because courts can be neutralized by financial cuts, and support organizations also are essential so that an independent judiciary can weather unpopular decisions. Currently, the budget submission for the federal courts is approximately $7 billion. Often critical choices must be made to create of an independent administrative judiciary: the size of the judiciary, the method for legal rule making, compensation for judges, theories of judicial representation, discipline and removal, ethical codes, and transparency when dealing with the media. This is not meant to be an exhaustive list but rather an analytical rendering of the choices that have helped shape the American "judicial culture of independence."

Budget Submission

How a judiciary submits its budget for appropriations is a critical administrative decision. Before the 1930s the federal judicial budget, like many civil code jurisdictions, was submitted as part of the DOJ budget. In his biography the chief judge of the Second Circuit in New York City, Judge Learned Hand, expresses his sense of the humiliation and dependence of the judiciary, as he made requests for basic necessities. In fact, he becomes so dissatisfied with the thought of an administrative clique and judges involved in administrative matters that when a central organization was created in Washington and inquiries were made as to what the Second Circuit position was to be, he replied, "We have no organization, no offices and no standing committees."[12]

On a political level the budget's effect is more subtle. Representatives of the judiciary do not deal directly with the legislative branch but mediate the relationship through an executive agency, a department, or a ministry of justice. This allows the executive agency to "comment" on the submission and place the submission within the context of its own priorities, which may or may not be the priorities of the judiciary. The potential for mischief and petty penalization is great in such a system.

While insulating the judiciary from the legislative process does have some benefits, there are potential costs if the executive branch then substitutes its own judgments for the judiciary's. In the 1930s the judiciary won the right submit its budget to the Appropriations Committee with the executive playing only a minimal administrative role of including it in its general submission. However, could it be challenged? Under the Clinton administration, for example, the Office of Management and Budget (OMB), the executive agency charged with formulating the national budget, attempted to comment on and reduce some judicial categories. This continued for some months until the president himself intervened to end the ill-conceived attempt of bureaucratic "backdooring" and ordered the OMB to submit the judicial budget without comment.

This process of independent submission and judge-controlled budget has now become an accepted part of the constitutional framework. It is viewed as an important instrument by which the American federal judiciary asserts and maintains its reputation for independence. The courthouses and facilities of the federal judiciary are the envy not only of foreign judges but also of many American *state judiciaries* that look with awe at the resources controlled by the federal bench. Federal courthouses cost more per square foot than state courthouses, and federal judges and personnel are paid more than the average corresponding state judge or personnel. Although when these public sector salaries are compared with those of the private sector, the disparity is stark and the financial sacrifice of judicial service is clear.

Support Organizations: Internal and External

This complex machine of judicial administration could not work without the support of a number of critical internal support organizations all controlled by the judiciary. The Administrative Office of the United States (AO),[13] the Federal Judicial Center (FJC),[14] and the Office of the Chief Justice of the United States are composed of approximately 27,000 personnel, both in Washington and the thirteen circuits, who handle the day-to-day administrative and clerical tasks. What makes this administrative system distinctive is that ultimately all are reporting to and responsible to judges at all levels. At the end of the day, the Judicial Conference, a body composed only of federal judges, has the final word.

As a matter of constitutional law, the Judicial Conference has no authority over the administration of the Supreme Court of the United States.[15] The Court and its nine members are governed by their own rules, regulations, and traditions, and the CJ is understood to be "first among equals." As a matter of policy, the Court in the weekly conference meetings decides most significant questions. The Court's own budget of approximately $75 million is formulated by the Office of the Chief Justice and is presented separately, by two justices selected by the CJ, to the Appropriations Committees of Congress. This presentation occurs before the chair of the Judicial Conference Budget Committee presents the *total* federal judicial budget.[16]

The concept of having judges administratively *maître chez nous* (masters of their own house) is strongly endorsed by the relevant civil legal organizations that help form public opinion. The American Bar Association, the largest voluntary association in the United States, with a membership of nearly 400,000 attorneys and an influential political lobbying group, has stood by the federal judiciary in moments of crisis to protect this independence. In addition, the Center for State Courts, the American Judicature Society, the American Law Institute, and the American Association of Law Schools have helped develop an institutional network of public support for the judiciary. This support of civil society is a necessary condition for the American federal judiciary; its significance cannot be overestimated.

Selection and Number: "Size Matters"

A number of decisions over time have contributed to the independence of the American federal judiciary, as a matter of both jurisprudence and administration. The selection process of an Article III federal judge is a combination of local and national politics with both the president and Congress playing a vital role. The requirement of the advice and consent of the Senate bestows a national legitimacy not shared by state and local jurists. Moreover, the decision to keep the number of life-tenured Article III judges limited to approximately 1,000, of which 179 are appellate judges, has preserved the bench as a small elite with a high degree of esprit de corps.[17]

Needless to say, having life tenure insulates the judiciary from everyday politics. However, despite the limit on federal judges, there has been over the last thirty years a growth of "parajudicial" personnel who have helped shoulder the increasing burden of legal work. The increased jurisdiction and growth of such functionaries as magistrate judges, bankruptcy judges rather than referees, permanent law clerks, and *pro se* clerks reflect a new cadre of judicial officials. These officials are chosen by councils or individual Article III judges and are supervised by or report to Article III judges.[18]

Rule Making: "Internal or External"

The process of rule making has a critical impact on the courts in the areas of the allocation of burdens of proof, the introduction of evidence into the courtroom, and the manner by which appellate review takes place. Although the legislature retains ultimate authority for the approval of procedural rules, the judiciary controls the process. The Rules Enabling Act provides that the Supreme Court and all the courts established by an act of Congress may from time to time prescribe rules for the conduct of their business.[19] Through a series of specialized committees that report to a general Rules Committee, the federal system has constructed an intricate process that includes private practitioners, academics, government attorneys, and judges. The process requires an extensive public comment period including the holding of public hearings to solicit comments from the lay public. This is important because the internal rules for criminal, civil, and bankruptcy are controlled by the group charged with enforcing them. Although this may appear to be a rather technical point—and most of the points are technical in the rules area—it is significant. This is important because how burdens of proof, for example, are set affect the outcomes of cases over time. Rules over time tend to reward certain interests and a process overseen by neutral parties adds to the legitimacy of the court process.

Remuneration: "Money Always Counts"

A sensitive subject for most jurists is remuneration. Although as a matter of constitutional law, an Article III judge's salary cannot be diminished, the Founding Fathers failure to account for inflation has proved to be a point of aggravation for American jurists. Attempts have been made to create an automatic cost-of-living adjustment (COLA) that would be self-actuating. Owing to political reasons, salaries of legislators and judges are linked together for budgetary purposes, and all efforts to separate the salaries of federal judges from those of the legislators have failed. Under the current statutory regime, if the salaries of judges are to have a yearly COLA, or if the base salary is to be increased, the legislature must vote each time, and any increase must also be awarded to the legislature itself.[20] A lawsuit in 2009 by six federal judges for previously denied COLAs was finally resolved in 2013, when the DOJ agreed to no longer contest the case. As a result, all federal judges received a 14 percent pay raise. For political reasons legislators are reluctant to be seen as advocating for their own salary increases, and therefore, the salaries of both legislators and jurists have not kept pace with inflation.

In recent years, many believe, the salary issue has caused an increased number of jurists to leave the bench. Judicial compensation has not matched the increase in earnings afforded those in the private sector. Given their background and experience, federal judges could easily earn four to five times the government wage. Clearly, a sense of dedication to public service and the esteem afforded a federal judge help explain why many are willing to make the financial sacrifice, but for many this decision is becoming increasingly difficult even with the new raise.

Theories of Judicial Representation: "A Mixture of Systems to Avoid Oligarchy"

Since all federal judges have life tenure and each judge is independent following his nomination by the president and confirmation by the Senate, each is a "tall oak" that can stand alone. Administratively, the governing structure has combined leadership by statute with fixed terms of service. For example, the chief judge of a circuit or a trial court can serve for a maximum of seven years. The CJ of the United States, on the other hand, chairs for life the Judicial Conference, the AO, and the FJC. The CJ's administrative appointment is also for life and is concurrent with his judicial duties, unlike, for instance, the Lord Chancellor of England, who tenders his resignation with the change of power in Parliament, thereby aligning the head of the judiciary with the new administration. In addition, the Judicial Conference also has elected trial judges by the circuit and representation by proxy for magistrate and bankruptcy judges, who by theory are represented by the appellate and trial Article III judges who have selected them to serve.

By statute, though, magistrate and bankruptcy judges serve directly on the board of the FJC for a nonrenewable term of four years without any additional compensation.[21] In the continuing philosophy of not allowing for a permanent judicial administrative oligarchy, the director of the FJC must retire at the age of seventy.[22]

Discipline and Removal: "Independence Is Not Absolute"

As conditions of service and tenure, judges are required to be accountable in a variety of ways: publicly, personally, and intellectually.[23] To enforce the common law rule of serving "during good behavior," different countries have created specific judicial councils, tribunals, or panels allowing for the dismissal of a judge by the CJ. In the United States, along with Japan, Germany, and Brazil, an impeachment process that involves the political branch in a vote for removal has been incorporated into the constitutional framework for further protection.

Under Article III, federal judges "hold their offices during good behavior" and "receive for their services, a compensation, which shall not be diminished during their continuance in office." Removal from office is a drastic remedy, and until 1986 the last judge removed from office in the United States was in 1936, at which point in American history only four judges had ever been impeached. Unfortunately, the Senate removed from office three district court trial judges—Harry E. Claiborne (Nevada), Alice L. Hastings (Florida), and Walter L. Nixon (Mississippi)—in the short space of 1986 to 1989. Before 1986 twenty-two of the thirty-five federal judges charged with serious misbehavior had resigned from office rather than endure the strain of an impeachment trial. For lesser transgressions the power to discipline judges falls within the jurisdiction of the circuit judicial councils, but how far a council can go short of impeachment proceedings, owing to the independence of each individual judge, is still a question that contains legal gray areas.[24]

Removal for unpopular decisions is why most legal systems have put into place screening mechanisms to separate legitimate claims from those that are frivolous. Since, in every case, by its nature, one side must lose, in every case there is a potential disgruntled litigant ready to complain about the judge and the process. Criminal misbehavior, such as bribes, payoffs, and personal criminal violations, constitutes an act warranting removal. Needless to say, there is a range of moral turpitude that does not honor the office but does not demand removal; this behavior in the American system is handled by our ethical codes.

Ethics and Codes: "Maintaining Integrity with Self-Regulation"

The origins of judicial ethics in the United States stem from a variety of sources: the Code of Conduct for United States Judges; the requirement for disqualification for bias or prejudice;[25] the obligation of financial disclosure;[26] the restrictions on outside earnings, including gifts and honoraria;[27] and the judicial oath of office.[28] The Code of Conduct is composed of seven cannons focusing on (1) the integrity and independence of the judiciary; (2) impropriety and the appearance of impropriety; (3) impartiality and diligence; (4) extrajudicial activities to improve the law, the legal system, and the administration of justice; (5) extrajudicial activities creating the risk of conflict with judicial duties; (6) reports of compensation for law-related and extrajudicial activities; and (7) political activity. As one can readily appreciate, the code concentrates on both the appearance and the reality of conflict of interest and the subordination of impartiality for financial or political gain.[29] The American model combines both regimes of prohibiting certain activities and disqualifying for purposes of personal integrity.[30]

Transparency: "Media, Efficiency and Public Opinion"

A recurring complaint of most jurists is the failure of the press and media to appreciate the judicial functions. Periodically in an open and free society, a judge or court or opinion will be the subject of severe criticism in the press, or a president may attack a court decision in a State of the Union address. How should the judiciary as a whole and the judge as an individual respond to the attacks?

Because the federal judges have not created a specific press relations office to speak on behalf of the judiciary, there is no single organ to speak on behalf of the judiciary. Although the AO has a press office and a legislative office, the AO does not issue press releases dealing with the explanation of specific cases. The Canadian Supreme Court, for example, has an administrative assistant to the chief justice who works with the media and helps explain opinions when they are released. In the United States, although the Supreme Court does have a press officer, she does not comment on any cases, as the dominant dictum is "the opinion speaks for itself." From time to time proposals have been made to have regional press officers in each circuit or large district court, but each time the plan has been defeated.

First and foremost, a judge can point to his or her opinion to explain the reasons for the decision. The well-reasoned, albeit controversial decision is on the public record and can be read by all parties. Given the prevalence of electronic forms of communication in the United States, most opinions are easily accessible to the general public within minutes of publication. More recently, some justices have taken to writing biographies or general legal commentaries to express their judicial philosophy. On this question the external support organizations—the American Bar Association, American Association of Law Schools, and American Law Institute—are able to play an independent role in defending the judiciary or jurist unfairly criticized. By having a third party not directly involved in the dispute, the defense is more credible and should carry more weight with the general public.

As part of the accountability and transparency goal, however, the Civil Justice Reform Act of 1990 (the Biden Bill) was passed to have more open and explicit reporting of court workings.[31] By the terms of the act, each trial court is required to implement a civil justice expense and delay reduction plan that would "facilitate deliberative adjudication of civil cases on the merits, monitor discovery, improve litigation management, and ensure just, speedy, and inexpensive resolution of civil disputes."[32] Each court has to evaluate both the civil and criminal dockets, the trends in filing, the causes for cost and delay, suggestions for new legislation, and in addition to this case-specific reporting, the amount of time taken by individual judges to resolve specific motions.

This form of reporting makes it possible to evaluate the efficiency of individual courts, in particular in comparison to other courts in the nation. To some this has deprived judges of a degree of autonomy but with it has come a more open analysis of the internal operations of the courts and judicial docket management.

THE COURT: THE SHAPING OF A NATIONAL SECURITY LEGAL CULTURE

There are moments in the life of judiciaries that are "founding moments." Critical decisions affect the nature of the judicial function for long periods as a "legal culture" is created, recast, and nurtured by these outcomes. Paradoxically, although courts by and large are non-majoritarian institutions, they are essential for the smooth functioning of majoritarian or democratic systems.[33] A court's legitimacy turns on its perceived impartiality. Impartiality is achieved differently in continental regimes than in common law countries. Although there may be no life tenure, continental judges often directly control investigative teams and can conduct wide-ranging probes of governmental corruption. For Americans, judicial and administrative independence has been the chosen path. In fact administrative autonomy has helped support judicial independence. But what makes the American judicial system unique is that while other common law countries have created a constitutional structure permitting a simple majority of the legislature to overturn judicial decrees, in America a supermajority of two-thirds of the states is required to overturn a Supreme Court determination on constitutional matters under Article V.

When so much power is vested in one organ of government in order to adjudicate the constitutionality of the other branches, at times suspicion of motives becomes endemic to the process. Therefore, whatever institutional innovations can be made to ensure and foster impartiality can only strengthen the court system.

The Court's independence, though, rests on its legitimacy since, ultimately, the government must enforce the Court's judgments. Students of the judiciary often point out that in Federalist Paper No. 78, Alexander Hamilton underscored the fact that the judiciary would control neither the purse nor the sword, in order to reassure opponents to the creation of a national court system. Enforcement of judgments has been the essential criterion of an effective legal system. Both the state and the citizenry must have confidence in the process and the content of the order both to enforce and to obey the order. When this fragile social contract is breached, the system no longer enjoys voluntary compliance and moves away from democratic impulses.[34] The detainee and interrogation cases in the global war against terrorism during the George W. Bush administration demonstrate how the court has asserted its place in the national security enterprise and reformed the legal culture in the area of the laws of armed conflict.

After the 9/11 attack Congress passed the Authorization for the Use of Military Force (AUMF), which authorized the president "to use all necessary and appropriate force against those nations, organizations, or persons he determines planned, authorized, committed, or aided" the attacks and recognized the president's "authority under the Constitution to take action to deter and prevent acts of international terrorism against the United States."[35] The president declared a national emergency and, as commander in chief, dispatched armed forces to Afghanistan to seek out and destroy the al-Qaeda terrorist network and the Taliban regime that had supported and protected it.[36]

The Bush administration began by asserting a robust view of executive power, under a theory of the "unitary executive" in a time of war. Relying on the AUMF, the president asserted that he had the power to detain combatants captured anywhere in the world, to determine whether and how the Geneva Conventions applied to these detainees for treatment and interrogation, to establish military tribunals for adjudication, to decide not to follow the Foreign Intelligence Surveillance Act (FISA),[37] and finally to determine that the detention camp at the Guantanamo Bay Naval Base in Cuba was beyond judicial review. Over a period of fourteen years, the Supreme Court has rejected, modified, or reframed each of these claims of executive authority. The Court also became embroiled in debates with the executive branch and Congress over the definition of war, the due process owed to detainees, interpretations of the Geneva Conventions, and finally, the constitutional values that would shape the national security enterprise as it battles extremism both at home and abroad.

THE DETENTION PROCESS AND *HABEAS CORPUS*

In early January 2002 the first group of detainees arrived at Camp X-Ray in Guantanamo Bay and was housed in open-air cages.[38] The president determined the detainees were "unlawful combatants" and would not be afforded prisoner-of-war status under the Geneva Conventions, despite the objections of military Judge Advocate General (JAG) officers.[39] The choice of Guantanamo for detention was designed to avoid domestic US law under the legal theory that the base in Cuba was not within US territory, and therefore, the federal courts would have no jurisdiction. This legal theory was based on an earlier court decision, in the context of immigration law, in which the Supreme Court had ruled that Haitian "boat people" held at Guantanamo had no right to habeas corpus appeal to federal courts since the base was not US territory.

Shortly thereafter, offensive pictures of the detainees were released, and a habeas corpus lawsuit was filed, *Rasul v. Bush*.[40] Allegations concerning the harsh treatment of detainees in interrogations began to surface. The district trial court rejected the initial lawsuit, so the detainees responded with a hunger strike. Over the next six months, a new facility was constructed (Camp Delta), and another habeas suit was filed, *Hamdi v. Rumsfeld*, involving an American citizen.[41] By December 2002 the detainees had been transferred to this new facility.

In early March 2003, on appeal to federal appeals court, the Rasul habeas petition (which had been consolidated with other appeals—Habib and Al Odah Khaid) was rejected but appealed to the Supreme Court, as was the *Hamdi* case. But as a result of the appellate court denial, a number of detainees were scheduled for trial by military tribunals; one foreigner, an Australian, David Hicks, was the first detainee assigned an attorney, and the defense counsel argued that a number of the rules for the tribunals were unconstitutional.

In June 2004 the Supreme Court decided the two cases on appeal, *Rasul* and *Hamdi*. In *Rasul* the court rejected 6–3 the precedents of World War II prisoner-of-war cases, and the majority held that the federal courts have jurisdiction to determine the legality of the executive's potentially indefinite detention of individuals who claim to be wholly innocent of wrongdoing. This decision reversed the judgment of the Court of Appeals and remanded the cases to the District Court to consider in the first instance the merits of petitioners' claims.

In *Hamdi* the Court again rejected the administration's position, and eight of the nine justices of the Court agreed that the executive branch did not have the power to hold a US citizen indefinitely without basic due process protections enforceable through judicial review. In a plurality opinion Justice Sandra Day O'Connor (joined by Chief Justice William Rehnquist and Justices Stephen Breyer and Anthony Kennedy) argued that although Congress had expressly authorized the detention of unlawful combatants in its AUMF, due process required that Hamdi have a meaningful opportunity to challenge his detention. For Justice O'Connor, due process required notice of the charges and an opportunity to be heard. However, because of the ongoing military conflict, traditional procedural protections, such as placing the burden of proof on the government or the ban on hearsay, need not apply. In the opinion O'Connor suggested that the Department of Defense create fact-finding tribunals similar to the army rules for Article 5 hearings under the Geneva Conventions to determine a detainee's status. She concluded that Hamdi should have a right to counsel. The plurality held that judges need not be involved in reviewing these cases for status; rather, only an impartial decision maker would be required.

Justice David Souter, joined by Justice Ruth Bader Ginsburg, concurred with the plurality's judgment that due process protections must be available for Hamdi to challenge his status and detention but disagreed that AUMF established congressional authorization for the detention of unlawful combatants. In an ironic twist Justice Antonin Scalia, joined by Justice John Paul Stevens, dissented and, given Hamdi's US citizenship, reasoned that the government had only two options—either Congress must suspend the right to habeas corpus (a power provided under the Constitution only in times of "invasion" or "rebellion," which had not happened), or Hamdi must be tried under criminal law. For Justices Scalia and Stevens, the executive did not have the power to detain US citizens, and it was not the business of the Court to instruct the government on how to establish detention regimes. For these dissenting justices Hamdi's status as a US citizen afforded him special status. In the end, only Justice Clarence Thomas would have affirmed the lower court's ruling based on the AUMF and the president's war-making powers. The splits among the justices reflected the unsettled aspects of the law.

In July 2004, in response to the Supreme Court decisions, the administration established the Combatant Status Review Tribunals, consisting of three officers, to determine each detainee's "enemy combatant" status. Yet within five months a district court judge again challenged the administration. The judge, James Robertson, ruled in the case of Salim Ahmed Hamdan, Osama bin Laden's alleged driver, that his military commission trial was unconstitutional because, among other things, the accused could not be denied access to evidence; instead, the government should have held special hearings for detainees to determine whether they qualified as prisoners of war under the Geneva Conventions. Judge Robertson ordered that until the government provided the appropriate hearing, it could prosecute the detainees only in courts-martial as established by military law. On appeal in July 2005, the US Court of Appeals for the District of Columbia Circuit Court (included on the panel was Judge John G. Roberts, who would later be appointed CJ) unanimously affirmed the right of the president to create military commissions and overturned the Judge Robertson order.

Hamdan appealed the decision to the Supreme Court, asserting that the Geneva Conventions entitled him to an impartial hearing to determine whether he qualified as a prisoner of war and therefore should have a traditional court-martial—or whether he was an unlawful combatant. There was much speculation that the Court would refrain from imposing itself in this war powers and foreign policy arena, but the Court, to the surprise of many, accepted the case. Its decision to accept the case reflected the Court's view that it had a role to play since fundamental rights were involved.

In the meantime, Congress, which had been largely silent on these issues in December 2005, passed the Detainee Treatment Act (DTA), which restricts the interrogation techniques for the military and strips detainees such as Hamdan of the right to file habeas corpus petitions, apparently making the Hamdan appeal to the Supreme Court null and moot. Congress in the DTA made it clear that in its constitutional interpretation this matter of national security is for the executive and the legislature; the Supreme Court should have no say in the matter, in other words, no jurisdiction for habeas petitions.

In a clear rejection of the views of both the executive and legislative branches, the Supreme Court in June 2006, in *Hamdan v. Rumsfeld* (a 5–3 decision), not only agreed to hear the *Hamdan* case, rejecting the stripping of its jurisdiction, but further held that the military commissions at Guantanamo violated US and international law and that Common Article 3 (CA 3) of the Geneva Conventions applied to the detainees.[42] CA 3 of the Geneva Conventions is a provision that guarantees "minimum" protections for detainees.[43] Justice Stevens, writing for the majority, concluded that CA 3 applied to the war against al-Qaeda and was thus a part of the "law of war" as a matter of law. Military commissions, as constituted, did not meet the standard of CA 3 because they deprive defendants of protections that are basic to the courts-martial. Though the Bush administration had cited special dangers involved in fighting terrorism, Justice Stevens rejected the reasoning of the executive and concluded, "Nothing in the record before us demonstrates that it would be impracticable to apply court-martial rules in this case." For the majority, terrorism suspects fell under CA 3's prohibition against trials by anything other than "a regularly constituted court affording all the judicial guarantees which are recognized as indispensable by civilized peoples." Because the commissions were not properly authorized by Congress and did not match court-martial rules, the military commissions did not meet the requirements of CA 3.

In a scathing dissent Justice Scalia, joined by Justices Thomas and Samuel Alito, violently disagreed with the majority's decision to hear the case and asserted his views on the exercise of executive power and legislative jurisdictional authority:

> On December 30, 2005, Congress enacted the Detainee Treatment Act (DTA). It unambiguously provides that, as of that date, "no court, justice, or judge" shall have jurisdiction to consider the habeas application of a Guantanamo Bay detainee. Notwithstanding this plain directive, the Court today concludes that, on what it calls the statute's most natural reading, every "court, justice, or judge" before whom such a habeas application was pending on December 30 has jurisdiction to hear, consider, and render judgment on it. This conclusion is patently erroneous. And even if it were not, the jurisdiction supposedly retained should, in an exercise of sound equitable discretion, not be exercised.

As a cultural matter inside the national security enterprise, the Court's role could not have been clearer and more controversial. A majority of the Court had concluded that the Court had a role to play in the war on terrorism and was asserting its views under one of the great writs—the writ of habeas corpus—and under its authority to be the ultimate organ on the interpretation of domestic and international law. For the minority of the Court, however, the "extra-jurisdictional" exercise of judicial power in the war and foreign policy arena was a violation of the constitutional balance and an exercise of "judicial imperialism."

In the wake of the *Hamdan* decision, which had clearly stated that Congress had to be involved as a constitutional matter in the establishment of the military commission system and the interrogation process, Congress finally responded. Within four months of the decision in *Hamdan*, Congress passed the Military Commission Act (MCA) in September 2006. The new MCA is designed to legalize military commissions and to clarify interrogation techniques that CIA officers may use on hundreds of terrorism suspects considered "unlawful enemy combatants" being held at Guantanamo Bay and other locations. The new act, however, grants the executive branch authority in deciding how to comply with treaty obligations regulating actions that fall short of "grave breaches" of the conventions and again restricts the writ of habeas corpus.[44] The MCA bars military commissions from considering testimony obtained through interrogation techniques that involve "cruel, unusual or inhumane treatment or punishment," which the Constitution's Fifth, Eighth, and Fourteenth Amendments prohibit.[45]

But the Court's role in this unfolding drama of constitutional authority and the national security enterprise was not over. Again an appeal following the MCA made its way to the Court from a group of detainees in Guantanamo who asserted a writ of habeas corpus.

In June 2008 the Court yet again asserted itself in the detention process in the cases of *Boumediene v. Bush* and *Al Odah v. United States*.[46] Lakhdar Boumediene was an Algerian living in Bosnia at the time he was captured.[47] He was arrested on suspicion that he was involved in a plot to bomb the US embassy in Sarajevo. The Supreme Court of the Federation of Bosnia and Herzegovina—a court that the United States helped establish—released him because it could not find any evidence to justify his arrest. Despite the fact that the Bosnian court released him, the United States seized him and brought him to Guantanamo. This case is interesting because of the status of Lakhdar Boumediene. Boumediene is a non-US citizen, seized in a non-battlefield environment, and then placed under US authority.

As noted by the Court in *Boumediene*, this set of facts raises significant due process questions that must involve the Court. In yet another controversial 5–4 ruling, the Court held unconstitutional section 7(a) of the MCA and reasoned that both citizens and noncitizens in Guantanamo Bay should have a right to challenge their detention in US federal courts through habeas corpus petitions. Justice Kennedy, in his majority opinion, noted the unique nature of this war and its effects: "It is true that before today the Court has never held that noncitizens detained by our Government in territory over which another country maintains *de jure* sovereignty have any rights under our Constitution. But the cases before us lack any precise historical parallel. They involve individuals detained by executive order for the duration of a conflict that, if measured from September 11, 2001, to the present, is already among the largest wars in American history." He then cites the *Oxford Companion to American Military History* (1999): "The detainees, moreover, are held in a territory that, while technically not part of the United States, is under the complete and total control of our Government. Under these circumstances the lack of a precedent on point is no barrier to our holding." The majority was creating new law for the national security enterprise and was setting the values and norms for the executive and Congress when the United States would project force.

The dissenting justices bristled with attacks on the overreach of the majority. Justice Scalia was scathing in his response: "Today, for the first time in our Nation's history, the Court confers a constitutional right to *habeas corpus* on alien enemies detained abroad by our military forces in the course of ongoing war. The *writ of habeas corpus* does not, and never has, run in favor of aliens abroad; the Suspension Clause thus has no application, and the Court's intervention in this military matter is entirely *ultra vires*."[48]

For Justice Scalia this expansion of judicial reach through the use of the writ was an unconstitutional expansion of power at the expense of the executive. Chief Justice Roberts, joining Justice Scalia's dissent, nevertheless was compelled to write on his own to note the unprecedented intrusion of the Court in national security areas: "Today the Court strikes down as inadequate the most generous set of procedural protections ever afforded aliens detained by this country as enemy combatants [this is Congress's actions]. The Court rejects them today out of hand, without bothering to say what due process rights the detainees possess, without explaining how the statute fails to vindicate those rights, and before a single petitioner has even attempted to avail himself of the law's operation." For the dissenters the majority had generated shapeless procedures.

In the view of the dissenters in *Boumediene*, the DTA met the standards of *Hamdi* as set by Justice O'Connor. Then why did the majority disagree with this interpretation? The disagreement harkened back to an understanding of due process and rights retained by those under US jurisdiction detained against their will. In erasing the distinction between citizen and noncitizen, the majority forged a concept of justice with an international character. This power, in turn, then shaped the environment for both the executive and Congress when the Court acts in its national security capacity. By asserting its view as a matter of law, the Court by de jure and de facto became a critical institution in the national security enterprise. This was a prime example of the legal culture interacting with the national security enterprise and shaping the parameter of power and force.

As is the nature of legal disputes, post *Boumediene* the district courts of the District of Columbia held habeas hearings for scores of detainees from Guantanamo and slowly shaped the rules of evidence and judicial tests to determine, for example, what "membership" in al-Qaeda means. In essence, the legal skirmishing will continue both as a matter of law on the evidentiary level and as a matter of jurisdiction, as those being held under US custody in Afghanistan will surely sue for similar habeas corpus rights as those in Guantanamo. Moreover, the nature of the attack on the military commission process has called into question the legitimacy of military commissions, and as of the fall of 2016, the military commission process appears stalled in evidence motion practice with trials scheduled for 2017.

The Court in 2011 denied certiorari in *Kiyemba v. Obama* and left the question of whether a federal district court exercising its habeas corpus jurisdiction has the power to order the release of prisoners held under executive order at Guantanamo Bay into the United States unanswered. The issue was remanded to Circuit Court and what the law will be still remains to be litigated.

TECHNOLOGY AND THE COURT

The rate of technological change has meant that the law, owing to its more deliberative process, lags behind. Today smart phones, global positioning systems (GPS), iPads, Fitbits, and all other devices of technology generate terabytes of information. Who collects the information, how the information is collected, when the information is mined and analyzed, and what legal consequences flow from the exploitation of the data are the defining issues of our generation. How the courts and legislature define these issues will shape how we understand the relationship between security and privacy.

Surveillance issues have been dominant in the national security conversation since the actions of Bradley (Chelsea Elizabeth) Manning and Edward Snowden. Since those revelations trial courts in New York and Washington, DC, as well as appellate courts in New York and Washington have heard cases challenging the constitutionality of the decisions and statutes under a Fourth Amendment violation. A core issue involves how one views the protections regarding the telephone metadata being collected and how one interprets section 215 of the USA PATRIOT Act.[49] Increasingly, courts are confronted on how to structure the legal framework for "big data" in the national security and criminal context.

Courts need to evaluate the protections over data held by third parties and the continuing power of a 1979 precedent of *Smith v. Maryland*.[50] The *Smith* case held that the acquiring of a telephone number with a "pen register" was not a search under the Fourth Amendment and did not require a warrant since there was no "reasonable expectation of privacy." The Court reasoned that when individuals give the information to third parties, the numbers called are known to the telephone company, are recorded for billing purposes, and are not private. Similarly, metadata containing the "to" and "from" on emails, length of the email, and time of day are not private and are analogous to telephone "pen register" numbers for billing purposes. This metadata information, as interpreted by courts under section 215, was determined to be a "tangible thing" and was required to be turned over to law enforcement as long as the agency specified that it was for an authorized investigation of international terrorism or intelligence activities.

Critics contend that the telephone numbers and metadata are not analogous since more can be done with the data in the exploitation and that individuals' expectation of privacy is different now that technology has changed so radically. The government, along with some lower court judges, disagrees and contends the third-party doctrine remains a valid interpretation of the law. These issues will eventually reach the Supreme Court, and it will be up to the nine justices to determine if the analogies work or a new regime for law enforcement is required.

The other issue bedeviling the public debate concerns the 2008 amendments to section 702 of FISA, which critics contend granted the government unchecked power to monitor American citizens' international phone calls. The law has always distinguished between US citizens and non-US citizens. Under FISA the government must show probable cause that a person is an "agent" of a foreign power before a FISA investigation is pursued. Moreover, the technological issues of "place"—when is one outside the United States, given technological packet switches and how electronic bytes travel on the Internet, and what is a US number?—erased the historic domestic versus foreign distinction. In the most recent challenge to the FISA amendments, the Supreme Court dismissed the Amnesty International claim, agreeing with the government's argument that "the claims of the challengers that they were likely to be targets of surveillance were based too much on speculation and on a predicted chain of events that might never occur, so they could not satisfy the constitutional requirement for being allowed to sue."[51] Some Snowden revelations have rekindled the issue since it appears the litigants may have legal standing because their communications were swept up in the programs. In short, more litigation is expected, given the split in the circuits over the constitutionality of the programs

The Supreme Court, in addressing the issue of GPS, held that placing GPS on a vehicle and using the device to monitor the vehicle's movements constituted a search under the Fourth Amendment.[52] However, as mentioned by the dissent, law enforcement may use drones for surveillance, forgoing GPS, raising the issue of whether such technology is a "search" or whether one no longer has an expectation of privacy when leaving home given street cameras, trackers, sensors, and drones. What is "private"? and What is a "search"? are questions the courts will be defining for the next decade. For example, in a recent landmark "search incident to an arrest" cell phone case, *Riley v. California*, the Supreme Court ruled that cell phones cannot be searched without a warrant.[53] The lower circuits had been split on the issue of cell phone search cases, but the Court classified a cell phone as a minicomputer given its information storage capacity and required a warrant based on a reasonable expectation of privacy. But as Justice Alito noted in his concurrence, given the evolution of technology, new laws need to be drawn making reasonable distinctions based on categories of information or other variables given the blunt instrument of the Fourth Amendment. If not, courts will be the final arbiters of these issues.

CONCLUSION: THE INTERNAL BATTLE OF OUR JUDICIAL CULTURE IN THE NATIONAL SECURITY ENTERPRISE ARENA

This chapter has explored the independent culture of the Court, the way that culture is institutionally maintained, and the way the Court has participated in a constitutional dialogue with the executive and Congress in the national security arena. The preceding discussion of significant court actions on detainee measures makes it clear that the judiciary's independence has been very much on display as it continually rejected both executive and legislative exercises of power. Other contentious issues, such as wiretapping or leak investigations, also could have been chosen to illustrate the role of federal courts. The advantage of the detainee cases is that they strike at the heart of executive power while at war, demonstrate Congress's diffidence on the issue, and reveal the internal battle raging inside the Court on its appropriate role and on the judicial doctrine the majority argue should govern the detention process.

One legal commentator, Noah Feldman, characterizes the legal debate as reflecting the emergence of two schools. In Feldman's view one school

> begins with the observation that law, in the age of modern liberal democracy, derives its legitimacy from being enacted by elected representatives of the people. From this standpoint the Constitution is seen as facing *inward*, toward the Americans who made it, toward their rights and their security. For the most part, that is, the rights the Constitution provides are for citizens and provided only within the borders of the country. By these lights, any interpretation of the Constitution that restricts the nation's security or sovereignty—for example, by extending constitutional rights to noncitizens encountered on battlefields overseas—is misguided and even dangerous. . . .
>
> A competing view . . . defines the rule of law differently: law is conceived not as a quintessentially national phenomenon but rather as a global ideal. [This] position readily concedes that the Constitution specifies the law for the United States but stresses that a fuller, more complete conception of law demands that American law be pictured alongside international law and other (legitimate) national constitutions. The U.S. Constitution, in this cosmopolitan view, faces *outward*. It is a paradigm of the rule of law: rights similar to those it confers on Americans should protect all people everywhere, so that no one falls outside the reach of some legitimate legal order. What is most important about our Constitution . . . is not that it provides rights for us but that its vision of freedom ought to apply universally.[54]

This is the cultural struggle reflected in the pluralities, dissents, and majorities of the decisions as the Court struggles with its role and as a judicial beacon both domestically and internationally. But this debate is unfolding while the branches of government are engaged in funding and directing lethal force and capturing "detainees." The continuing "cultural" space of legal uncertainty undermines a coherent, logical, unified system of appropriate lethality, capture, interrogation, and detainment. Since the national security enterprise is engaged in a struggle that is part criminal law, law of armed conflict, and immigration law, both domestically and internationally, some intrusion of uncertainty is to be expected. The world is watching to see where the Court will draw the lines concerning security, privacy, and individual rights.

But for those charged with safeguarding national security, it is deeply troubling, and yet it is our legal culture. The Court, as it determines appropriate due process, the distinction between citizens and noncitizens, the interpretation and applicability of the Geneva Conventions, and the war powers of the presidency and Congress, has become a major force in the national security enterprise. As the chapter notes the courts are being dragged increasingly into technological issues that will redefine American notions of privacy. However, as noted by some members of the Court, these legal doctrines can sometimes be blunt instruments. Hence, despite not having the power of the sword or purse, the power of the Court pen has proved to be, at times, equally powerful.

NOTES

The author particularly would like to thank Trudi Rishikof and Roger George for their invaluable suggestions and assistance in writing the original chapter and Roger for the subsequent revisions.

1. Habeas corpus is Latin for "you have the body." Prisoners often seek release by filing a petition for a writ of habeas corpus. A writ of habeas corpus is a judicial mandate to a prison official ordering that an inmate be brought to the court so it can be determined whether or not that person is imprisoned lawfully and whether or not he or she should be released from custody. A habeas corpus petition is a petition filed with a court by a person who objects to his own or another's detention or imprisonment. The petition must show that the court ordering the detention or imprisonment made a legal or factual error. Habeas corpus petitions are usually filed by persons serving prison sentences. See '*Lectric Law Library*, s.v., "habeas corpus," www.lectlaw.com/def/h001.htm. For a discussion of the framework, see the discussion in Stephen Dycus, Arthur L. Berney, William C. Banks, and Peter Raven-Hansen, *National Security Law*, 4th ed. (New York: Aspen, 2006), chap. 2.

2. See Edward S. Corwin, *The President, Office and Powers, 1787–1984*, 5th ed. (New York: New York University Press, 1984), 171.

3. U.S. v. Curtiss-Wright Export Corp., 299 U.S. 304 (1936); Youngstown Sheet & Tube Co. v. Sawyer, 343 U.S. 579 (1952).

4. See *Curtiss-Wright Export Corp.*, 299 U.S. 304.

5. Bob Woodward and Scott Armstrong, *The Brethren* (New York: Simon & Schuster, 1979); Edward Lazarus, *Closed Chambers: The Rise, Fall, and Future of the Modern Supreme Court* (New York: Penguin Books, 1999); and Jeffrey Toobin, *The Nine: Inside the Secret World of the Supreme Court* (New York: Random House, 2007).

6. Bill Nelson, Harvey Rishikof, I. Scott Messinger, and Michael Jo, "The Liberal Tradition of the Supreme Court Clerkship: Its Rise, Fall, and Reincarnation," *Vanderbilt Law Review* 62, no. 6 (2009): 1749–1814.

7. See Baker v. Carr, 369 U.S. 186, 217 (1962).

8. When the court appeared to be rejecting his New Deal legislation, Roosevelt introduced legislation to add an additional justice, up to a maximum of six, for every justice then serving who was seventy years and six months old.

9. William H. Rehnquist, *The Supreme Court—How It Was How It Is* (New York: William Morrow, 1987); and William Rehnquist, *Grand Inquests: The Historic Impeachments of Justice Samuel Chase and President Andrew Johnson* (New York: William Morrow, 1992).

10. See dissent in Olmstead v. United States, 277 U.S. 438 (1928).

11. James G. Apple and Robert P. Deyling, *A Primer on the Civil-Law System* (Washington, DC: Federal Judicial Center, 1995).

12. Gerald Gunther, *Learned Hand* (New York: Knopf, 1994), 515.

13. Generally, 28 U.S.C. § 601 et seq.

14. Generally, 28 U.S.C. § 620 et seq.

15. Generally, 28 U.S.C. § 671–677 et seq.

16. Harvey Rishikof and Barbara A. Perry, "Separateness but Interdependence, Autonomy but Reciprocity: A First Look at Federal Judges' Appearances before Legislative Committees," *Mercer Law Review* 46 (1995): 667–95.

17. Gordon Bermant, William W. Schwarzer, Edward Sussman, and Russell R. Wheeler, *Imposing a Moratorium on the Number of Federal Judges* (Washington, DC: Federal Judicial Center, 1993).

18. Article III of the Constitution states that the judge enjoys life tenure, cannot have her salary diminished, and is confirmed by the Senate, as opposed to Article I judges or legislatively created judges who do not have the same constitutional protections.

19. 28 U.S.C. §2071.

20. See §140 of Pub. L. No. 97–92, 95 Stat. 1183, 1200.

21. See 28 U.S.C. § 621.

22. See 28 U.S.C. § 627.

23. The discussion for this section draws on the work of Kersi B. Shroff, "Judicial Tenure: The Removal and Discipline of Judges in Selected Countries," in *Research Papers of the National Commission on Judicial Discipline and Removal* (Washington, DC: National Commission on Judicial Discipline and Removal, 1993), 2:1461.

24. See Chandler v. Judicial Council of the Tenth Circuit, 398 U.S. 74 (1970), as the leading Supreme Court case in the area of judicial discipline.

25. 28 U.S.C. § 144; 28 U.S.C. § 455; and Code of Conduct.

26. 5 U.S.C. app. 6; Code of Conduct, Canon 5C.

27. 18 U.S.C. §§ 203, 205, 216; 5 U.S.C. app. 7; 5 U.S.C. §§ 7351, 7353.

28. 28 U.S.C. § 453.

29. This discussion draws on the work of Beth Nolan, "The Role of Judicial Ethics and the Discipline and Removal of Federal Judges," in *Research Papers of the National Commission on Judicial Discipline and Removal* (Washington, DC: National Commission on Judicial Discipline and Removal, 1993), 1:867–912.

30. The level of scrutiny of the code is reflected in the interpretation of canon 3C(1)(d)'s definition of "relative." A relative has been defined by the commentary that accompanies the code to include "a person related to either (the judge or judge's spouse) within the third degree of relationship, or the spouse of such a person. The degree of relationship is calculated according to the civil system and thus includes parents, grandparents, aunts, uncles, brothers, sisters, nieces, and nephews of the judge or the judge's spouse, or the spouses of any of those listed.

31. See 28 U.S.C. § 471 et. seq.; Pub. L. No. 101–650 (1990). Because Senator Joe Biden (D-DE), as chair of the Judiciary Committee in the Senate, sponsored the bill, it became known as the "Biden Bill."

32. See 28 U.S.C. § 471.

33. Ackerman has developed a theory of founding moments and counter-majoritarian courts in Bruce Ackerman, *We the People* (Cambridge, MA: Harvard University Press, 1993).

34. *Federalist 78* (Rossiter ed., 1961), 465.

35. Authorization for Use of Military Force, Pub. L. No. 107–40, 115 Stat. 224, 224 (2001).

36. Proclamation No. 7453, Declaration of a National Emergency by Reason of Certain Terrorist Attacks, 66 Fed. Reg. 48,199 (September 14, 2001).

37. See Pub. L. No. 95–511, 92 Stat. 1783. The FISA issue or the use of domestic surveillance for intelligence purposes is an area of the law not well researched or explored. How to balance security, emerging technologies, and individual liberty with the Fourth Amendment has been an ongoing struggle since the passage of the legislation in 1978. The discussion will focus on the detention issue since the Supreme Court has been so active in this area of the law but the legal issues involved in domestic electronic collection of foreign intelligence and its role in the national security enterprise is worth a chapter unto itself. Some of the FISA issues are discussed in chapter 11 on the Federal Bureau of Investigation.

38. The timeline and cases are drawn from the Guantanamo Bay Timeline found at www.washingtonpost.com/wp-srv/world/daily/graphics/guantanomotime_050104.htm.

39. See Lisa A. Turner, "The Detainee Interrogation Debate and the Legal-Policy Process," *Joint Force Quarterly* 54 (2009): 40–47.

40. Rasul v. Bush, 542 U.S. 466 (2004).

41. Hamdi v. Rumsfeld, 542 U.S. 507 (2004).

42. Hamdan v. Rumsfeld, 548 U.S. 557 (2006).

43. Article 3 has been called a "convention in miniature." It is an article of the Geneva Conventions that applies in non-international conflicts. It describes the protections that must be adhered to by all individuals within a signatory's territory during an "armed conflict not of an international character" (regardless of citizenship or lack thereof): Noncombatants, combatants who have laid down their arms, and combatants who are hors de combat (out of the fight) because of wounds, detention, or any other cause "shall in all circumstances be treated humanely," including prohibition of "outrages upon personal dignity, in particular humiliating and degrading treatment." The passing of sentences must also be "pronounced by a regularly constituted court, affording all the judicial guarantees which are recognized as indispensable by civilized peoples." Article 3's protections exist even if one is not classified as a prisoner of war. Article 3 also states that parties to the internal conflict should "endeavor to bring into force, by means of special agreements, all or part of the other provisions of Geneva Convention III."

44. See Charles Babington and Jonathan Weisman, "Senate Approves Detainee Bill Backed by Bush Constitutional Challenges Predicted," *Washington Post*, September 29, 2006, www.washingtonpost .com/wp-dyn/content/article/2006/09/28/AR2006092800824.html.

45. Ibid. The bar, though, is retroactive only to December 30, 2005—when Congress adopted the DTA—to protect Central Intelligence Agency operatives from possible prosecution over interrogation tactics used before that date.

46. Boumediene v. Bush, 553 U.S. 723 (2008).

47. Case descriptions and commentary drawn from Harvey Rishikof, "Powers, Distinctions, and the State in the Twenty-First Century: The New Paradigm of Force in Due Process," *Regent University Law Review* 21 (2009): 377.

48. *Ultra vires* is a Latin term meaning "beyond powers." The term is usually used to refer to acts taken by a corporation or officers of a corporation that are taken outside the powers or authority granted to them by law or under the corporate charter. *US Legal Definitions*, s.v., ultra vires, http:// definitions.uslegal.com/u/ultra-vires/.

49. 50 U.S.C. § 1861.

50. Smith v. Maryland, 442 U.S. 735 (1979).

51. Clapper v. Amnesty International USA, 132 S. Ct. 2431 (2012).

52. 132 S. Ct. 945.

53. 134 S. Ct. 2473 (2014).

54. See Noah Feldman, "When Judges Make Foreign Policy," *New York Times Magazine*, September 25, 2008.

PART V

The Outside Players

CHAPTER 15

Lobbyists

When US National Security and Special Interests Compete

Gerald Felix Warburg

> The activities of lobbies representing foreign interests have contributed to the gradual erosion of the United States' credibility and influence in the world. . . . The control of policy, once lost, may not be restored to capable, disinterested hands.
>
> —John Newhouse, "Diplomacy, Inc.: The Influence of Lobbies on U.S. Foreign Policy"

> Americans are a collection of special interests, and one person's special interest is another's job or moral crusade. If people can't organize to influence government, then democracy is dead. . . . The idea that the making of choices should occur in a vacuum—delegated to an all-knowing political elite—is profoundly undemocratic.
>
> —Robert J. Samuelson, "An Obama Gift for K Street"

Success in the national security enterprise (NSE) requires policymakers to anticipate and engage competing interests. International initiatives cannot be advanced effectively unless made sustainable through the development of support from voters and their elected representatives. In the American democratic system, this requires proponents to recruit allied factions and blunt the power of critics. Implementing tactics designed to promote desired policy options often leads to deployment of lobbyists to mobilize support and counter opposition.

This chapter explores the role lobbyists play in the NSE, both as advocates working full-time on behalf of a specific issue group and as lobbyists registered with Congress and the Department of Justice after they have been hired by a broad array of commercial or foreign government interests. First, it examines who these lobbyists are and how they work, including how they frame client desires as consistent with the US national interest. Second, it places the current lobbying environment in some historical context and looks at how lobbyists exploit divisions in the NSE bureaucracy while using Congress as a court of appeals. Third, the chapter weighs the effectiveness of foreign embassies and ethics requirements by analyzing some specific lobbying campaigns. These will include defense procurement, foreign aid, military base closure, and support for such US allies as Israel. The design throughout is to demystify the process by which lobbyists influence outcomes through interaction with NSE policymakers.

The purpose of this chapter is, thus, to explain how lobbying shapes national security policy options; it evaluates which strategies, tactics, and precedents are most effective. It also assesses the impact of money on policymaking. The chapter concludes by reinforcing the author's central thesis: lobbying on Washington's international policies is *inevitable*. Factional contests to shape policy were anticipated by—and altogether familiar to—the authors of the Constitution. As in James Madison's day, lobbying in the NSE risks distorting perceptions of the national interest. With ever more sophisticated techniques, NSE lobbying can elevate parochial concerns—commercial, bilateral, ethnic, and regional—on the US national agenda. Transparency, vigorous regulation, and law enforcement are therefore essential to ensure US national interests are clearly defined and pursued by government policymakers.

TYPES AND TECHNIQUES OF LOBBYISTS

The ranks of registered lobbyists in contemporary Washington include representatives of business, labor, and environmental interests. Lobbyists working national security issues represent organizations as diverse as Oxfam International and Boeing Corporation. They represent nongovernmental organizations (NGOs) as well as the broad array of ethnic American associations pushing for strengthened US bilateral ties with nations from Ireland to India. Some organizations, such as Heritage Action and the American-Israel Public Affairs Committee (AIPAC), seek to maximize influence by steering political contributions toward favored federal candidates who are scored on votes of greatest interest to organization members. Others, like the National Rifle Association (NRA) or MoveOn.org, rely heavily on members' strength at the polls to influence policies. The impact of such pressure groups on US international policies is significant; these groups shape outcomes on international issues as diverse as birth control assistance, defense spending, immigration reform, and climate change. For example, the NRA has thwarted efforts by the Mexican government to curb US assault weapons sales that officials believe fuel narcoterrorism. Moveon.org—an organization that grew from domestic supporters of President Bill Clinton during his impeachment trial in 1998—subsequently evolved into a group that led voter opposition to Iraq War funding. Such lobbying organizations help shape US national security policies in a complicated contest of ideas and money.

National security lobbyists develop their presentations through reliance on networks of contacts and targeted research on the positions of allies and adversaries. They cement situational alliances with champions in political parties, Congress, and the executive branch while trying to build coalitions. Favorable press commentary and public testimony are marshaled; third-party validation can affect possible outcomes. Lobbyists solicit emails and phone calls from grassroots supporters. Lobbyists draft bills and supportive statements for legislators. They promote caucuses of like-minded members of Congress, while coordinating with allies in the NSE. Lobbying teams produce issue briefs while soliciting third-party validation from research organizations.

This type of lobbyist involvement on national security policy has become routine. Post-Watergate reforms and the increasingly transnational nature of many heretofore domestic issues have led to extraordinary growth in federal lobbying. As of 2014 there are almost 13,000 registered lobbyists in Washington. This figure excludes both lawyers and consultants who engage in the process without registering, and large sums spent on advertising and public relations designed to influence the NSE. Lobbyists who seek to change federal policies must file quarterly reports with Congress under the Lobbying Disclosure Act (LDA). If they are paid by a foreign entity, they must file a Foreign Agent Registration Act (FARA) form. Table 15.1 is an illustrative list of some recent lobbying expenditures that affect national security issues.[1]

National security lobbyists are most often employed on one of four types of engagements. First, they build support for a specific commercial venture requiring federal approval, such as an energy pipeline or an air force procurement. Second, they advance proposed US policy initiatives, such as expanded trade with Cuba. Third, they promote sympathy for a particular bilateral relationship, such as US relations with Israel or China. Fourth, some lobbyists champion broad policy objectives, such as nuclear arms reductions or human rights, often on behalf of an NGO. Most offer clients insights into the bureaucratic politics of specific US government agencies, including the Departments of State, Energy, or Defense.

A further distinction can be made between lobbyists at not-for-profit organizations—who pursue the agenda of their board and members—and contract lobbyists from large government relations firms for hire. The latter often have specialty skills, and their prior government service can attract large fees. The former group tends to rely more on grassroots members to sway policymakers. The latter group often engages heavily in campaign fund-raising to influence policymakers. Both types include experienced professionals; these paid advocates employ similar tactics, using their knowledge of procedure and bureaucratic politics to influence policy. Under stringent Obama-era requirements, neither was allowed to move to executive branch service without White House waivers. Yet most corporate lobbyists have substantial fund-raising capabilities and thus possess built-in advantages over most NGO advocates.

National security lobbying is not a new phenomenon. American history offers ample precedents for lobbying international policies. President Washington was beset by Francophiles and Anglophiles; his farewell address condemned those who agitated for intervention overseas. The presidencies of John Adams and Thomas Jefferson were bedeviled by press attacks

Table 15.1. Annual Lobbying Expenditures on Select Domestic and International Issues

Organization	Principal National Security Issue	Expenditures ($)
Chamber of Commerce	International trade	124,080,000
Boeing	Defense procurement	16,800,000
AFL-CIO	Labor rights	3,320,000
Johnson & Johnson	International trade	7,647,500
Amnesty International	Human rights	195,525
Chevron	International trade	8,280,000
Sierra Club	Global climate change	360,000
AIPAC	US-Israel relations	3,060,000
Lockheed Martin	Defense procurement	14,581,800

Source: Center for Responsive Politics, based on data from the Senate Office of Public Records. Data downloaded January 22, 2015.
Note: Figures for expenditures cited include lobbying costs for both domestic and international issues. "Lobbying expenditures" means the total amount each organization claimed in lobbying disclosure forms filed with Congress in 2014, when the US Senate Office of Public Records reported total expenditures on registered lobbyists of $3.21 billion. Reported expenditures do not account at all for public relations and advertising campaigns designed to influence the policymaking environment, nor for the salaries and overhead for full-time support staff.

and street demonstrations by factions championing rival views regarding trade and foreign policies. In 1914 Woodrow Wilson narrowly avoided defeat in his reelection bid because of grassroots lobbying against US intervention in Europe. Enactment of FARA was prompted in the mid-1930s by fears that German–American groups sympathetic to Hitler's nationalist policies might promote isolationism. Heavy-handed lobbying by anticommunist backers of the Republic of China on Taiwan in the 1950s stalled US efforts to engage the People's Republic of China (PRC). The influence of international activists on US national interests remains a major preoccupation for some commentators. Critics lament the influence of special interest lobbying on pursuit of the national interest, often pointing to the outsized voice of pro-Israel groups. Journalist John Newhouse maintains that pervasive lobbying in Washington erodes American credibility and shifts control of policy away from the "capable, disinterested hands" of executive branch experts.[2]

As this volume illustrates, however, there are in reality few "disinterested hands" in the national security bureaucracy. However, greater transparency, a vigilant press, and an informed electorate can counter these dangers. The founders were driven by the express conviction that national security policy was too important to be left to an all-powerful executive or to a handful of experts removed from the political process. They sought to open government up and allow competing interests to shape America's role in the world. Like Newhouse, the authors of the *Federalist Papers* recognized the disharmony factions cause. They assumed the only practical solution was to counterbalance faction with faction. It would be undemocratic and impractical to insulate the public policymakers from such diverse interests.[3]

FOCUS ON THE US NATIONAL INTEREST

Most successful NSE lobbying campaigns advance a common theme: it is in the American interest to adopt the policy championed. For example, it is argued US aid to Israel is justified not because policymakers necessarily embrace Jerusalem's policies but rather because doing so advances Washington's security interests by supporting the only stable democratic US ally in the Middle East. Examples of lobbyists effectively pressing a foreign interest that stands in direct conflict with US national security priorities are rare.

To succeed in international lobbying campaigns, creative alliances often prove valuable. The PRC's lobbyists in Washington recruit and direct assistance from US companies seeking to expand market access in China. They argue that Beijing should not be assailed for policies that harm US interests or offend American sensibilities, including China's devalued currency or the PRC's suppression of democracy activists. Lobbyists claim such practices should not be sanctioned because China is working with the United States on other national security concerns. These include crucial financing of US debt and cooperation in efforts to contain North Korea's nuclear weapons program. Effective lobbyists frame arguments to emphasize mutual interests, maintaining theirs is a win–win option in which the US national interest and their client's objectives do not conflict.

The president's executive branch team of lobbyists seeks engagement with third-party allies to build support on issues as diverse as adoption of the North American Free Trade Agreement and the 2003 invasion of Iraq. Tactics resemble those used by registered lobbyists and NGO representatives. For example, the White House staff in 2006 enlisted domestic proponents of closer US–India ties before asking Congress to ratify a controversial nuclear trade accord. Bush administration allies included the American Nuclear Energy Council and Indian American groups. President George W. Bush publicly thanked Indian American community leaders when he signed the bilateral agreement lifting thirty-year-old US sanctions on nuclear commerce with India.[4] Similarly, President Barack Obama, during his early 2015 visit to India, coordinated closely with US commercial interests eager to enter the Indian market.

Lobbying campaigns directed by the executive branch sometimes take more subtle forms. When the Bush administration sought to make the case in 2002 for action against Iraq, executive branch strategists worked with pro-Israel lobbyists eager for US action against Saddam Hussein, an implacable foe. These alarms were then shared with wavering members of Congress, and excerpts from intelligence reports on an alleged weapon of mass destruction (WMD) program were fed to sympathetic reporters, who then helped justify a US attack on Baghdad.[5] Similarly, pro-Taiwan lobbyists benefit from executive branch sources concerned about China's growing military capabilities. Supportive members of Congress have been lobbied to require an annual public report on PRC military budgets and capabilities. This document has become an effective tool for highlighting threats the PRC might pose to US interests. Its annual release generates a cycle of news stories about the growing Chinese military capabilities that concern many in East Asia. It is also used, not coincidentally, to justify defense spending requests from both the Pentagon and certain Asian defense ministries.[6]

Money is a key element used in many effective NSE lobbying campaigns to frame proponents' goals as consistent with the national interest. The extraordinary expenditures in recent years on Washington lobbying of both domestic and international issues (illustrated in table 15.1) substantially influence outcomes. These expenditures are usually reinforced by significant funds spent on advertising and public relations designed to drive home lobbyists' messages. Money acts as a megaphone, skewing perceptions of the popular will and enabling lobbyists to project the notion that they have broad voter support. Funds advance preparation and placement of opinion pieces, as well as grassroots activities. Financial resources, however, are not always decisive.

Analysis of why certain policy outcomes occur needs also to factor in one's definition of the national interest, a question that remains entirely subjective. Should China have been permitted to buy the Conoco oil company and secure its energy assets? Did the Pentagon need to buy more F-22s? Determining which lobbying campaigns *should* have prevailed in such policy disputes is not an empirical exercise. Virtue does not always rest with the underfunded side. Maybe the winners had reason, logic, and precedent on their side, along with financial advantages in the lobbying contest. Yet in many battles, the preponderance of financial resources makes for a decidedly unfair fight and results in outcomes which distort definitions of the national interest to make it more compatible with those of special interests.

Congress and all but the most senior executive branch staff are relatively accessible. Members are usually open to new information and well-organized entreaties from groups of constituents and their representatives. Washington is regularly besieged by email campaigns, phone calls that inundate Capitol Hill receptionists, and door-knocking efforts of supporters bused and flown into the capital by competing lobbies. Here, again, money matters. Contract lobbyists active in campaign fund-raising are more likely to meet directly with elected officials, whereas an NGO representative may meet first with staff—unless representing a constituency important to the member of Congress. Past donations and the prospect of more campaign funding color debate on many national security issues, especially those involving defense procurement and sensitive bilateral relationships. However, the notion that money equals access and produces special-interest-backed policies can be overstated. More important than the size of lobbying fees or campaign contributions is usually the potential impact of policy options on voters. Representatives who ignore the will of voters to appease campaign contributors risk exposure and rejection on Election Day. Where organized interests have the most sustained success—for example, in the pro-Israel lobby—is when they make the case that voters will support champions of preferred policies and reject those who are unsympathetic. Politicians have strong survival instincts. Elected officials are remarkably sensitive to voter sentiment.

Effective lobbyists rely heavily on talking points—simply framed messages that become shorthand for policy. To prevail, lobbyists marshal information and build coalitions with like-minded groups to target pressure on executive branch and congressional decision makers. As former *Washington Post* reporter Jeffrey H. Birnbaum notes, "Lobbying is much more substantive and out in the open than its ugly caricature. Lobbyists primarily woo lawmakers with facts."[7] Lobbyists who frame issues effectively and who understand political imperatives confronting NSE policymakers are the most successful.

LOBBYING TACTIC: EXPLOITING DIVISIONS IN THE NSE BUREAUCRACY

Lobbying national security issues in Washington relies heavily on analysis of organizational behavior and differences in bureaucratic culture. Knowledge of recent precedents and fracture lines in the interagency process provides insights that guide lobbyists' strategies and tactics. The executive branch is far from monolithic on national security questions. The president can shape the initial terms of foreign policy debates by driving the interagency process, coordinating cabinet members' messages, and using the bully pulpit of the Oval Office. Yet, in many national security lobbying efforts, dissenters within the executive bureaucracy generate the key arguments employed by congressional opponents to contest policy proposals and insist on conditions. A further layer of complexity—affording lobbyists additional points of access—has been added by the creation of several policy "czars" in the White House. These presidential advisors oversee policy portfolios on issues as diverse as combating Ebola and addressing climate change. They create opportunities for lobbyists to influence formulation and implementation of policy by the executive branch.

Dissenters within the executive branch are sought out and exploited by lobbyists representing competing interests. Internal disagreements are often present between the Departments of State and Defense. Different interpretations of raw intelligence from within the intelligence community are subject to misrepresentation both by executive branch officials and NSE lobbyists—as in the case of Iraq's alleged WMD program in 2003. As basic a decision as whether the United States should wage war in Iraq was heavily influenced by pressures from Vice President Dick Cheney and his staff to selectively leak intelligence others found less than conclusive. Was an Iraqi government official present at a Prague meeting with an al-Qaeda recruiter? Did an Iraqi agent ask about buying uranium in Niger?[8]

Such tensions within the NSE bureaucracy create opportunities for lobbyists. NSE policy advocates often use dissenters within the executive branch process as the point of departure in making their case with Congress, the media, and the voting public. New facts and interpretations often emerge and are used to challenge the original basis for policy proposals. An executive branch consensus (e.g., the allegation that Russia acted virtually without provocation when it massed forces on the international border and invaded the Republic of Georgia in the summer 2008) can later become the subject of dispute as more accurate intelligence leaks out—in this case intelligence indicating Georgia had provoked Russia by shelling civilian areas for hours before Moscow responded.[9]

CONGRESS AS A COURT OF APPEALS

Lobbyists use Congress as a court of appeals, a public forum where advocates can enlist legislators to challenge White House execution of national security policies. Lobbyists' most effective tool is usually their substantial institutional memory. They have allies and former colleagues from previous executive–legislative policy fights. Veteran lobbyists often know the relevant procedural options, the legislative history and precedents, better than many of the executive branch's foreign policy and defense specialists. The latter are often technical experts operating at a distance from voters and the electoral process. Indeed, some foreign service officers—having spent the majority of their careers overseas—have limited exposure to the tumultuous American democracy. Lobbyists, by contrast, are armed with information of the constituencies and political sensitivities of members, often individuals with whom they served as staff on the armed services or international affairs committees of Congress. Lobbyists collect and disseminate information from numerous sources, often seeking compromise through congressional amendment of the original executive branch proposals. A good illustration can be found in the work of labor unions and environmental activists, who often push to alter the terms of free-trade accords, including requirements for labor standards and environmental protection, before acquiescing to the pact's ratification. Similarly, lobbyists for defense manufacturers facing Pentagon termination of a program may plead with Congress to extend procurement for one more year in order to live to fight another day.

In the wake of the Watergate scandal and the resignation of President Richard Nixon in 1974, congressional reforms dispersed concentrated power. Ironically, the creation of multiple legislative power centers and overlapping committee jurisdiction increased points of access for lobbyists. This diffusion of power has heightened the degree of difficulty for executing policy initiatives; there are now far more decision makers to convince. The dispersion of power also created opportunities for "panel shopping." This practice is similar to the way trial attorneys maneuver for the best judge or venue before which to present their client's case. For example, there are more than eighty separate committees or subcommittees of Congress with jurisdiction over aspects of homeland security. Lobbyists have also become more aggressive about using presidential transitions, the confirmation process, and fundraising as opportunities to press their case.

With the proliferation of think tanks and new media outlets, including blogs and websites, savvy lobbyists have refined techniques for making their case. Consider how effectively MoveOn.org was able over time to build voter opposition to the Iraq occupation.[10] Similarly, note the impact the US Chamber of Commerce and agribusiness lobbyists have had on efforts to pass climate change and energy policy legislation. Each effectively uses grassroots contact with stakeholders and voters, various Internet platforms, and both earned and paid media. In recent years even the most old-fashioned legislators have taken to such new communications platforms as YouTube and Twitter to reach voters and potential allies, ultimately shaping the congressional response.

Lobbyists use the specter of an assertive executive branch or the wounded pride of members of Congress to help shape outcomes to their clients' benefit. This is particularly true when pressing issues involving US defense contracts, an area where the survival instincts of Congress and the power of defense lobbyists often frustrate efforts to curb defense spending. "Keep the production line open" or "maintain the American defense-industrial base" are phrases that ably capture the essence of lobbying messages used to challenge Pentagon procurement decisions. There are few more powerful arguments to an elected official than the creation or protection of jobs in their districts or states. Legislators who advocate sharp reductions in defense spending usually make exceptions when weapons systems made in their home constituencies are imperiled.[11]

WASHINGTON EMBASSIES: OFTEN INEFFECTIVE LOBBYISTS

The least effective lobbyists on international security issues are, ironically, often the professionally trained diplomats posted to Washington's Embassy Row. Careerists from foreign embassies can become so concerned about protocol and hierarchy that they fail to demonstrate sufficient entrepreneurship. The risk-taking exceptions can both gather information and shape options. The British embassy has been particularly effective in gaining insights; British embassy personnel knew before many in the US executive branch that a White House decision to invade Iraq had been made early in 2002. In terms of individuals both Israeli prime minister Benjamin "Bibi" Netanyahu, as a deputy chief of mission at the embassy of Israel in the 1980s, and Prince Bandar, the longtime Saudi ambassador to the United States, developed extraordinary access to US politicians and decision makers during their Washington tenure, as did the late Soviet ambassador Anatoly Dobrynin. Such diplomats prove effective in shaping US options by cultivating extensive back-channel relationships while operating in an unorthodox, freelance manner to advance their nations' security interests.

Foreign embassies in the United States sometimes hire former US government officials to press a position that appears to conflict with elements of US policy. Such appeals face steep odds, unless they can be presented as consonant with US national interests. An unusual example of a foreign government thwarting an initiative in Congress occurred in 2007, when the Embassy of Turkey hired several prominent former members to help block the adoption of a congressional resolution it opposed. This effort to memorialize the deaths of Armenians expelled by Turkish authorities during World War I was long sought by Armenian Americans, who believe the US government should demonstrate solidarity with victims of genocide. House Democratic leaders at first committed to a vote. Then opponents argued successfully that the risk of alienating an important North Atlantic Treaty Organization (NATO) ally with a restive young Muslim population outweighed the symbolic benefits of adopting the resolution. Their case was bolstered by intense lobbying by the Bush administration and Turkey's lobbyists, who managed to get all living former US secretaries of state to publicly oppose adoption of the resolution.[12]

Similarly, in 1995 pro-Taiwan lobbyists overcame State Department restrictions preventing US travel by Taiwan's President Lee Teng-hui. The US interest in democracy promotion clashed here with the desire of State Department diplomats not to upset PRC officials working with the United States on issues of mutual interest. Proponents of President Lee's visit framed this dispute as a free speech issue. Lobbyists from a leading Washington firm, under contract with Lee supporters, argued that communist authorities in China should not be permitted to limit Americans' rights to hear a democratically elected leader. They pressed their argument over outspoken State Department objections by highlighting previous US visits of such controversial visitors as Irish Republican Army (IRA) leader Gerry Adams and Palestine Liberation Organization (PLO) head Yasser Arafat.[13]

The most effective Washington lobbyists engaged by foreign interests are often former US government policymakers. They take advantage of insights into executive branch divisions, the cleavages that separate political appointees from career bureaucrats. Some press their case without registering; they pose as legal counsel or "strategic consultants." They maintain they are simply working to "educate" policymakers and develop sympathy for their clients' perspectives. They insist that they do not lobby per se because they are not technically pressing for a specific legislative outcome and arguably not subject to registration with Congress or the Justice Department. This position should be viewed skeptically; these paid advocates often share information and talking points in sustained campaigns to influence policy. Such consultants maintain robust communications with senior American policymakers, shaping the diplomatic tactics of foreign clients while pressing US policymakers. Lucrative businesses developed by such retired government officials and respected national figures as former secretary of state Henry Kissinger and former Senate Republican leader Robert Dole have benefited from substantial consulting contracts through this type of engagement. Indeed, it is increasingly common for retiring members to go to work for lobbying firms advising foreign clients lobbying national security issues.

REGULATION OF FOREIGN LOBBYING

National security lobbyists are subject to an array of regulatory requirements. The LDA, FARA, and Foreign Corrupt Practices Act (FCPA) requirements promote some transparency and mark ethical boundaries. Some lobbyists on international security issues, frustrated in their efforts to penetrate decision-making circles with legitimate merit-based presentations, nevertheless become insensitive to ever-evolving ethics requirements. Washington has a long history of overzealous foreign businesspersons and defense contractors trying to corrupt US officials. In the 1950s and 1960s, supporters of Chiang Kai-shek and his anticommunist colleagues on Taiwan funneled money to those most outspoken against Mao's China. The Korea-gate influence peddling schemes of the 1970s and the Abscam scandal in the early 1980s produced modest reforms that curbed some abuses. More recent contracting scandals involving Boeing and air force officials appear also to have had a chilling effect on some corrupt practices.[14]

The most ethically challenged national security lobbyists rely heavily on money to curry favor. They not only recruit donors for direct campaign contributions but also steer donations to members' favorite charities and fund lavish foreign junkets. Among recent practices that crossed legal boundaries, the most notorious involved Paul Magliochetti Associates (PMA), an established lobbying firm of primarily defense appropriations specialists. The firm imploded in spring 2009 over evidence that its principals paid fake donors to make contributions to legislators who supported PMA clients' requests for earmarked appropriations. Criminal convictions ensued.[15] Still, enforcement of regulatory requirements is lax, and clumsy prosecutorial efforts, as in the 2008 trial of then-senator Ted Stevens of Alaska, make compliance problematic.

Abuses have also undermined some legitimate efforts to expose members of Congress to diverse international views. For example, foreign travel by congressional delegations appointed by the congressional leadership and parliamentary exchanges involve members in serious fact-finding missions that inform key policy decisions. Official travel to war zones and allied capitals increases understanding and builds long-term support. Other foreign travel, such as lobbyist-funded junkets to play golf in Scotland, are decidedly illegitimate and have resulted in several criminal prosecutions, as in the case of lobbyist Jack Abramoff and Congressman Ed Ney (R-OH).[16]

Members are warned by congressional ethics panels to avoid even the appearance of impropriety. Yet many rely heavily on lobbyists for funds. Scrupulously following evolving congressional ethics rules is essential for Washington lobbyists. They can retain their effectiveness only by staying abreast of changing ethics requirements designed to add transparency to the policymaking process. Members' pressure on lobbyists to contribute campaign funds creates troublesome appearances; this pressure will persist until meaningful election finance reforms are adopted.

RESEARCH EFFORTS TO PROMOTE LOBBYISTS' AGENDAS

Foreign governments have a long history of funding lobbying efforts to promote their interests in Washington, since domestic lobbyists have greater Washington knowledge than most diplomatic representatives from foreign governments. Foreign governments use third parties to validate the logic of their lobbying arguments. In recent years a new trend has arisen whereby foreign governments, as part of their lobbying campaigns, give substantial donations to widely respected US-based research and policy organizations, or think tanks. There are no laws explicitly prohibiting foreign money from flowing to such organizations. Concerns have arisen nevertheless about the potential bias contained in information flowing from some of Washington's most respected research institutions, including Brookings, the Atlantic Council, and the Center for Strategic and International Studies. Some NGOs that both conduct research and lobby have long been identified with one political party; the Chamber of Commerce and the Heritage Foundation are considered home base for Republicans, whereas the Center for American Progress and the American Civil Liberties Union are reliably supportive of most Democratic Party positions. Yet the flow of donations from foreign interests to certain Washington think tanks is clearly part of lobbying efforts.

These funds add a new and potentially troublesome dimension, requiring, at a minimum, far greater transparency regarding "expert" testimony and "independent" studies designed to support foreign lobbying efforts. Members of Congress and their committees have finite budgets for staff and research. While members' staff ranks have grown, legislators are spread thin across a variety of issues. In reality they have limited time to dedicate to complex international issues—many of which have limited immediate impact on their constituents. Owing to these time constraints and financial limitations, members have relied on witnesses from think tanks to gather supposedly unbiased information and provide expert testimony. The concern is that foreign governments and foreign commercial interests now have increased their capacity to influence the policymaking process in Washington and to do so with limited transparency. Numerous Washington think tanks have collectively received, and failed to disclose fully, millions of dollars of funding from foreign governments in recent years.

This is not a new issue. The French tried to influence the young American republic's views in the 1790s, just as Germany's and the Republic of China's governments did before and after World War II. Toward the end of the Cold War, Japanese economic influence was particularly pronounced in Washington. According to journalist Patrick Choate, an expert on Japanese government and business, in 1989 alone Japanese foundations and Japanese government officials spent more than $200 million in the United States trying to "win the hearts and minds" of the American people and curry favor for Japanese trade policies. This lobbying campaign included the hiring of numerous former congressional staffers to promote Japanese trade interests.[17] This issue of supposedly independent scholars being retained by lobbyists as third-party validators was not sufficiently publicized at the time. Thus, some members of Congress were shocked when the *New York Times* ran a detailed exposé of the phenomenon in September 2014. The *New York Times'* stories revealed that Washington-based think tanks receiving foreign funding have been pressured not only to pursue specific areas of research but also to arrive at certain conclusions. The *Times'* reports asserted that these donations could transform respected US think tanks from neutral and objective institutions into "muscular arms of foreign governments." As one friendly government stated, in a report commissioned by the Norwegian Foreign Affairs Ministry assessing its grant making: "In Washington, it is difficult for a small country to gain access to powerful politicians, bureaucrats and experts. . . . Funding powerful think tanks is one way to gain such access, and some think tanks in Washington are openly conveying that they can service only those foreign governments that provide funding."[18]

These donations primarily come from Europe, Asia, and oil-rich nations in the Middle East. Given the sensitivity of US commitments in the latter region and the fact that our military deployments place so many American lives at risk, policymakers have legitimate concerns about expert testimony for Congress on US national interests coming from sources colored by foreign influence. Some US allies—for example, Norway, eager to shape US policy on climate change—are using think tank donations as a means of engaging the policymaking process. For nations whose agendas have been traditionally received a lower priority in Washington, this may seem a sound means to advance their agenda.

Foreign funding has the potential to frame research in a specific way. Many think tanks are run by former US government officials who have seen and experienced firsthand the implications of foreign influence. In a *New York Times* interview, John Hamre, former deputy secretary of defense and president of the Center for Strategic International Studies, underlined the importance of maintaining institutional objectivity, insisting, "I don't represent anybody. . . . I never go into the government to say, 'I really want to talk to you about Morocco or about United Arab Emirates or Japan.' I have conversations about these places all the time with everybody, and I am never there representing them as a lobbyist to their interests."[19] Yet there is significant risk that such funding efforts directed by foreign lobbyists will harm the credibility of think tanks and ultimately hurt lobbyists' causes.

Since 2011 at least sixty-four foreign governments, state-controlled entities, or foreign government officials have donated a total of $92 million to more than two-dozen US-based research organizations, according to the *New York Times*. In the fall of 2014, in response to the exposé, Representative Jackie Speier (D-CA) proposed a rule in the House that would require testifying scholars to disclose any foreign support. Although some think tanks routinely disclose this information, others do not. Both Representative Rich Nugent (R-FL), chairman of a key House Rules subcommittee, and the ranking Democrat, Representative Jim McGovern (D-MA), joined other members in advocating adoption of such a rule.[20] Think-tank responses have varied. The Atlantic Council, which already discloses all of its donation sources, supports the rule. Other think tanks have proved more hesitant. Brookings representative David Nassar rejected the proposal, citing constraints on academic freedom and potential ripple effects internationally, which some maintain would in turn limit the influence of US interests on foreign governments. Nassar asserted that resolution of the issue requires greater transparency of research methods and methodology, not of the financial support of the research. Resolution of these tensions in the years ahead will have a significant impact on how foreign lobbying is conducted in Washington.

SPECIALIZED LOBBYING ON ENERGY, ENVIRONMENTAL PROTECTION, AND DEFENSE

Polices proposed by executive branch officials are often challenged by NGO lobbyists who coordinate grassroots campaigns. Opponents of a proposed US policy press their case via membership organizations, as MoveOn.org did on the Iraq War funding issue or the Natural Resources Defense Council (NRDC) and the Sierra Club do on global warming / climate change issues. For example, as the fight to legislate caps on carbon emissions escalated in 2009, more than 770 companies and interest groups engaging more than 2,300 lobbyists worked to influence US policies on energy production and climate change. Expenditures totaled more than $90 million in reported annual lobbying fees.[21] Interests as diverse as coal manufacturers and birding groups hired lobbyists, including such prominent figures as former Democratic House majority leader Richard Gephardt and former Appropriations Committee chairman Robert Livingston, a Republican.

The marshaling of such disparate forces increases the likelihood of delays in both energy production and efforts to combat climate change, especially troublesome to proponents of sweeping action. "The danger is that special interests will dilute and torque government policies," chief climate scientist of the National Aeronautics and Space Administration (NASA), James Hansen, lamented in 2009, "causing the climate to pass tipping points, with grave consequences for all life on the planet."[22] Similarly, protracted lobbying over routing of a single pipeline, the Keystone XL, occurred throughout much of the Obama presidency. This pipeline, designed to carry energy extracted from Canadian tar sands to Gulf Coast refineries and subsequent export overseas, attracted multimillion dollar campaigns by proponents and opponents who lobbied the executive branch and Congress, while mobilizing grassroots activists and pursuing extensive litigation for years.

Washington lobbying on international trade, security, and environmental issues is highly specialized. For example, when NRDC sought to block a project in an environmentally sensitive area of Belize, the leadership of this Washington-based advocacy group fielded a team that included experts in development policy (to deal with the World Bank) and Belizean contract law (to work locally), as well as lobbyists effective in dealing with members on key congressional committees (to press for enactment of restrictions via foreign aid– or trade-related legislation). Specialization is also required for lobbyists working with defense manufacturers. Defense lobbyists routinely encourage corporations to spread contracts widely to help secure local support from more legislators. Subcontracts for such big ticket items as the C-17 transport aircraft, the Stealth bomber, and the Seawolf submarine were secured in as many of the 435 congressional districts and 50 states as possible. This strategy broadens the base of support in Congress for continued funding. Indeed, in lobbying to continue funding defense procurement efforts—often after Pentagon officials have concluded it is time to shift priorities—NSE lobbyists have been most successful in altering government policymaking priorities.

Reforms designed to insulate policymaking from politics lag behind sophisticated lobbying efforts. Consider how a process explicitly designed to "take the politics out" of decisions to close military bases has become the focus of specialized lobbying campaigns. The BRAC process, named for the Base Realignment and Closure Commission, has evolved into a sophisticated and highly competitive lobbying specialty. What does a community do if it fears a major loss of local jobs and infrastructure investment because Pentagon officials propose closure of a long-standing military facility? Reliance on a single home-state champion in

Congress is unwise; members invariably argue that the most important issue in their reelection campaign is an effort to save a local military facility from the threat of BRAC closure. Members from the region will make the public case against a Pentagon closure recommendation. City leaders in such vulnerable communities as Portsmouth, New Hampshire, or San Diego, California, demand more, electing often to join with local business and labor leaders in a coordinated lobbying campaign to save local jobs. Communities heavily dependent on defense-related jobs now often hire BRAC lobbyists with specialized Washington practices.

BRAC cases expose the difficulty of putting national interests ahead of local concerns about jobs. Defense procurement issues have proved especially vulnerable to coordinated lobbying campaigns. For the post-Vietnam generation, especially in the left-leaning parts of the Democratic Party, elected politicians have feared being labeled "weak on defense." Post-9/11 events added the fear of being attacked as "soft on terrorism." This has made members reluctant to challenge budgets championed by officials in the NSE—unless to insist on amendments to increase spending. For example, when the Obama administration and its secretary of defense, Robert Gates, moved in 2009 to shut down the production line for several weapons systems, they were vulnerable to accusations from defense lobbyists. Program supporters enlisted lobbyists for local unions that cited the sharp economic recession as a reason for continuing military programs that Pentagon officials said were not cost effective: "It doesn't make sense that our government is looking to save or create jobs at the same time it's talking about cutting something like this [the F-22 fighter jet program]," the head of the Georgia machinists union, Jeff Goen, complained.[23]

BOX 15.1
State-of-the-Art Lobbying against Closing a Military Base

How does BRAC lobbying work? A good example can be found in the case of Los Angeles Air Force Base (LAAFB), an obscure California facility that plays a key role in procurement of communication and intelligence satellites used by scores of defense-related agencies of the US government, from the Weather Service to those tracking al-Qaeda. It was difficult for southern Californians to press the case for retaining LAAFB. An air force base without a runway, it remains a Cold War anomaly, an urban facility on highly valuable land. It was originally proposed by Pentagon staff as candidate for inclusion on the 2003 BRAC closure list. However, a bipartisan community coalition funded a targeted lobbying campaign. The team of lobbyists pored over Pentagon analysis, challenging data calls used to justify closure. Lobbyists developed a series of talking points, counterarguments emphasizing that the facility needed to remain close to California's high-tech and defense industrial base. They also enlisted the backing of then–House Appropriations Committee chairman Jerry Lewis (R-CA) and veteran Senate Appropriations Committee member Senator Dianne Feinstein (D-CA).

The ensuing process of public debate and private persuasion did not remove politics from the final decision. Indeed, powerful legislators from New Mexico eagerly sought to transfer the LAAFB functions to their home state. Other California political leaders held a series of rallies at the entrance to the Los Angeles base and requested Chairman Lewis's intervention. Proponents of the base retention effort believe Representative Lewis, who then played the lead House role in approving all Pentagon appropriations, argued the merits of their facility in direct conversation with Defense Secretary Donald Rumsfeld.[a] Although on the Pentagon's draft list of candidates for closure, the LAAFB was not on the final list of cuts the Pentagon sent to Congress for an up-or-down vote. Other survivors of BRAC rounds have employed similar lobbying strategies; politics most decidedly has remained a part of the base closure process.

[a]Jason Bates, "California Group Works to Shield Los Angeles Air Force Base," *Space News*, February 2, 2004. (Full disclosure: this author aided the California-based coalition as a senior partner of the Cassidy & Associates firm.)

The Obama administration's proposed Pentagon budget continued to grow at a rate of 4 percent in fiscal year 2010—and proposed procurement grew at 5.6 percent—even after liberal Democrats occupied the White House.[24] The threat of terrorists and nuclear proliferation justified much of the spending, to be sure, as did instability in Eastern Europe and the Middle East. Yet targeted lobbying increased the challenge of controlling defense spending increases. Indeed, it required a presidential veto threat against the Obama administration's first defense appropriations measure and an all-out coordinated lobbying campaign run by the White House—aided by arms control and taxpayer groups—for the administration to kill F-22 funding in a close Senate vote in July 2009.[25]

CONTROVERSIAL LOBBYING ON US MIDDLE EAST POLICY

Lobbying on foreign policy and security matters helps to shape and define the national interest. Yet passionate campaigns in support of particular US alliances have proved divisive and attracted sustained media commentary, from the days of Hamilton and Jefferson, when Francophiles and Anglophiles battled. No single US alliance in modern times has attracted as much lobbying activity as US support for Israel. Dating back to the 1940s, American backers of Israel have been a major political force in Washington. Prompt US recognition of Israel in 1948, when President Truman overrode nearly unanimous State Department opposition, became just the first success for this lobbying effort. Through the last decades of the twentieth century, the pro-Israel community in the United States, supported most visibly by AIPAC, argued that the United States had strong national security reasons for backing Israel against the threat of attack from hostile neighbors and such terrorist organizations as Hamas and Hezbollah. American interests cited by lobbyists included the promotion of an anticommunist democracy, the need to back a moderate ally in the unstable Middle East region, and the building of a bulwark against dangers from radical Islam and threats posed by the attainment of a nuclear weapons delivery capability by such implacable US foes as Iraq or Iran. AIPAC lobbyists have worked with supporters in Congress and the executive branch to resist arms sales to Israel's foes, most notably in a divisive effort through the 1980s to limit sales of sophisticated airborne warning and control system (AWACS) aircraft and weapons delivery systems to the Kingdom of Saudi Arabia.[26]

Pro-Israel lobbying campaigns have been countered for years by US diplomats, defense manufacturers, and oil company lobbyists, as well as some human rights organizations. These critics maintain that US support for Israel alienates Arab nations and Muslim leaders, while conflicting with US principles and perpetuating the Palestinian diaspora. Former Central Command commander David Petraeus, among others, has suggested that the US failure to press Israel and Arab leaders for a resolution of the Palestinian issue has put American soldiers and national interests at risk. In recent years breakaway groups within the pro-Israel community have alleged that AIPAC's unblinking support for positions taken by the most hard-line Israeli factions have harmed the interests of both the United States and Israel.

In early 2015 AIPAC's opposition to the negotiating stance taken by the Obama administration and its European allies toward Iran prompted efforts by supporters of Prime Minister Benjamin Netanyahu to circumvent the White House. Republican congressional leaders, without executive branch consent, invited the Israeli leader to address a joint session of US Congress just days before Israeli elections. This unprecedented breach of protocol brought into stark relief divisions within the pro-Israel lobbying community; it also revived highly charged commentary about "the Israel lobby." An earlier episode—the publication in 2007 of a study critical of AIPAC, authored by Professors John Mearsheimer and Stephen Walt—had sparked a series of bitter academic and press exchanges over the virtues of lobbying to promote US–Israel ties.[27] The conclusions of Mearsheimer and Walt remain highly controversial; they alleged that the power of money (campaign donations) and lobbyists' threats (to withhold same) have distorted US policy, caused the United States to abandon Palestinians, and encouraged anti-American violence in the Middle East and Europe.

Here, as on other emotionally charged national security issues, the key question to consider should be, Does the pro-Israel lobbying effort support or detract from the advancement of US national security interests? Critics of AIPAC's tactics maintain that US policy is so pro-Israel as to endanger other US security interests. Their conclusion—that nefarious lobbyists are to blame—is reflexive. The reality is that US policy has, but for a few incidents since the Truman presidency, been firmly supportive of Israel, regardless of which party controlled the White House and Congress or who was lobbying the issue. There remain tactical divisions among American supporters of Israel over how best to advance mutual interests through lobbying of the NSE.

CONCLUSION: CHECKING LOBBYISTS' POWERS BY TRANSPARENCY AND REGULATION

The US national security policymaking process affords lobbyists multiple points of access for influencing outcomes. The competition among executive branch agencies and the availability of Congress to serve as a court of appeals creates opportunities that lobbyists exploit. From career agency bureaucrats to Senate-confirmed administration appointees to White House and National Security Council staff, most decision-making layers of the executive branch bureaucracy are open to outside influence. In some cases political appointees are more malleable than career bureaucrats. Nevertheless, the complex system creates numerous pressure points. Similarly, with the diffusion of power in the post-Watergate Congress, lobbyists are provided a multitude of targets to attempt to persuade on the merits. The national security decision-making system in the United States is not, and never has been, a uniform process controlled by a single actor. It remains relatively open, subject to lobbying and most every step of the process of formulating and implementing policy.

Politics can no more be taken out of the NSE than lobbyists can be removed from the system American founders designed. Experience shows that hyperbolic appeals to "take politics out" of national security policymaking by curbing lobbying are unrealistic. Commentators like John Newhouse and Robert Samuelson have differing views on the desirability of lobbying to shape NSE efforts. The argument advanced in this chapter is that lobbying efforts remain a fact of life. These are inherently political disputes about national priorities. The notion advanced by such commentary as "Diplomacy, Inc."—that only an elite group of military and diplomatic professionals should define the national interest on war and peace issues—advances a Platonic ideal that obscures the reality of the imperfect American system. Sustained lobbying on war and peace issues—by both national security professionals and grassroots citizens—is the norm, not the exception.

Throughout US history, from "who lost China?" debates to divisions over Soviet relations to the bitter national divisions over Vietnam War policy, similar lobbying has occurred. During the second Obama term, debates on such sensitive matters as charting a new course for US–Cuba relations or making a risky multilateral effort to contain Iran's nuclear program sparked predictable battles over Washington's international policies. Only in rare moments of national crisis, as in the immediate wake of Pearl Harbor and 9/11, have partisan voices been silent and a bipartisan policy consensus briefly achieved. The old canard about Americans being united on international policy must be put to rest: politics, in fact, almost *never* stops at the water's edge.

The role lobbyists play in this competition to guide the NSE is increasingly transparent. In a regulated system registered lobbyists are not unlike lawyers in the judicial branch: they serve as both messengers and advocates. Frustration about national security lobbying is often made manifest as a desire to shoot the messenger. Understanding the tools available and mastering the policymaking process may prove more effective than lamenting lobbyists' influence. The power of money to distort policy, spin facts, and intimidate opposition can be countered. Democracy is imperfect. Nevertheless, transparent competition, voter mobilization, and timely presentation of facts can help level the playing field. A vigilant press, an engaged voting public, and a modicum of transparency can ameliorate much potential harm caused by lobbying campaigns that would compromise national objectives to advance those of special interests.

The Founding Fathers believed competition among factions was distasteful, but necessary, to ensure freedom in a democratic system. The pressure from competing lobbying interests influencing the contemporary US national security debate is consistent with what the architects of the American system anticipated. Opening the decision-making process in order to safeguard national interests—especially on issues of war and peace—was deemed the most efficient alternative. No one branch of government is the font of all wisdom, nor is any single individual or department empowered by the Constitution to define US national security interests. Washington today is a far cry from Plato's Republic; there are few of Newhouse's "disinterested hands" resident in the capital. Most parties to the NSE advance their particular interests. Specific departments from State to Defense and Homeland Security are subject to parochial perspectives and turf wars even as they pursue the national interest. Lobbyists from the private sector and NGOs thus find willing allies, even as they invariably argue that their commercial or ideological priorities are consistent with the national interest. Constitutional checks and balances enable lobbyists to compete with other factions to shape policy outcomes. They do so in a fashion not unlike how Madison envisioned in *Federalist 10*; factions can counterbalance one another. Well-funded interests are similar to mobilized electoral blocs. We can share the founders' distaste for factional lobbying even as we accept that such engagement is inevitable under the US democratic system. Factional lobbying mirrors how power is actually distributed in contemporary American society, if not how partisans might wish power to be allocated in a more perfect democracy. Lobbying to influence the national security policymaking process, like making sausage, is thus not pretty to observe. Nevertheless, it is the American way: inclusive, inelegant, and decidedly Darwinist. Participants in the NSE must compete vigorously, press for ever greater transparency, and then let the strong campaigns, advancing sound arguments, prevail.

NOTES

The author wishes to thank the University of Virginia's Frank Batten School of Leadership and Public Policy graduate Alexandra Hanway for research and editorial assistance in preparation of this chapter.

1. Congressional Quarterly, *CQ MoneyLine Lobby Database*; US Senate, Lobby Disclosure Act Database; and Federal Election Commission, *Campaign Finance Disclosure Database*, www.fec.gov/disclo sure.shtml. See also Carrie Dann, "K Street Thrives amid Economic Downturn," *Congress Daily*, January 30, 2009.

2. John Newhouse, "Diplomacy, Inc.: The Influence of Lobbies on US Foreign Policy," *Foreign Affairs*, May/June 2009.

3. In Federalist No. 10, James Madison (writing as "Publius") defined factions as "a number of citizens, whether amounting to a majority or minority of the whole, who are united and actuated by some common impulse of passion, or of interest, adverse to the rights of other citizens, or to the permanent and aggregate interests of the community." Madison observed that liberty fuels factions as surely as air fuels fire, concluding that regulation and competition can ameliorate their negative effects. Clinton Rossiter, ed., *The Federalist Papers* (New York: New American Library, 1961), 78.

4. Note there were two key congressional votes—one in 2006 to get conditions for the negotiations, a second in 2008 to approve the pact. Gerald Warburg, *Effective Foreign Lobbying in Washington: Ten Steps to Success* (Washington, DC: Brookings Institution, October 30, 2008); or Warburg, *Nonproliferation Policy Crossroads: The Strange Case of US-India Nuclear Cooperation* (Palo Alto, CA: Stanford Center for International Security and Cooperation, October 21, 2010).

5. There have been numerous studies on how this practice unfolded, particularly by the *New York Times*, whose editors reassessed in a series of public reexaminations of its own reporting. Many concluded the *Times* reporter Judith Miller had been used by White House officials to mischaracterize intelligence analysts' conclusions regarding the Iraq WMD program. (Miller was fired by the *Times*.) On the specific question of pro-Israel lobbyists being courted, see, for example, Craig Unger's "From the Wonderful Folks Who Brought You Iraq," *Vanity Fair*, March 2008. See also the controversial writings of John Mearsheimer and Stephen Walt, discussed later in this chapter.

6. Jay Chen and Sofia Wu, "Pentagon Required to Report on Taiwan Strait Security Annually," *CNA News*, May 28, 1999. Offered by the Republican leadership as an amendment to the FY 2000 annual Department of Defense spending bill, the provision (drafted by pro-Taiwan lobbyists at the firm of Cassidy & Associates) is sometimes referred to as "the [Senator Frank] Murkowski amendment." It generates a report officially titled "Military and Security Developments in the People's Republic of China."

7. As quoted in Robert J. Samuelson, "An Obama Gift for K Street," *Washington Post*, December 15, 2008.

8. For competing views on interagency disputes over Iraq War intelligence, see Tim Weiner, *Legacy of Ashes* (New York: Doubleday, 2007); or George Tenet, *At the Center of the Storm* (New York: Harper, 2007).

9. Nicholas D. Kristof, "Obama, Misha and the Bear," *New York Times*, November 20, 2008. The issue flared during the 2008 US presidential campaign, in part because senior advisors to Senator John McCain's campaign had recently served as lobbyists for the Republic of Georgia.

10. Efforts to rally a lobbying group's donors can backfire. For example, the left-leaning MoveOn .org provoked backlash with its 2007 *New York Times* ad impugning the integrity of General Petraeus, who directed US troops in Iraq. Juvenile wordplay questioning the respected general's patriotism (Petraeus rendered as "Betray-us") brought ridicule on the antiwar lobbyists and distracted from their efforts to curb US funding.

11. See *Congress Daily*, November 20, 2008. Note that in the 2009 F-22 funding debate, many liberal legislators who often oppose defense budget increase—such as Senator John Kerry (D-MA)—opposed Obama administration efforts to limit more production.

12. See account in Newhouse, "Diplomacy, Inc."

13. Jim Mann, "How Taipei Outwitted US Policy," *Los Angeles Times*, June 8, 1995. (Full disclosure: This author was involved, as Mann notes.)

14. See the excellent chronology in Reuters, "US Air Force Tanker Award Will Cap Long Saga," February 25, 2008.

15. Susan Crabtree, "Lobbyist to Serve 27 Months for Campaign Contribution Scheme," *The Hill*, January 8, 2011.

16. Neil A. Lewis, "Abramoff Gets 4 Years in Prison for Corruption," *New York Times*, September 4, 2008; and James V. Grimaldi, "Ney Chief of Staff Wore Wire, Was Key to Boss's Conviction," *Washington Post*, August 13, 2007.

17. John B. Judis, "Yen for Power," *New Republic*, January 22, 1990, 20–25.

18. Eric Lipton, Brooke Williams, and Nicholas Confessore, "Foreign Powers Buy Influence at Think Tanks," *New York Times*, September 6, 2014.

19. Ibid.

20. Ibid.

21. Marianne Lavelle, "Lobbyists Warm to Climate Change Debate," *Politico*, February 25, 2009.

22. Ibid.

23. Dan Eggen, "Plan to Cut Weapons Programs Disputed," *Washington Post*, April 28, 2009.

24. Megan Scully, "Obama Seeks 5.6 Percent Boost for Weapons Procurement," *Congress Daily*, May 8, 2009.

25. Christopher Drew, "Obama Wins Crucial Senate Vote on F-22," *New York Times*, July 21, 2009.

26. Full disclosure: The author played a role as a Senate leadership aide in a number of these battles, including opposition to Saudi arms sales, and continues to support strong ties between the United States and the people of Israel. In most of these Washington battles over Middle East policy, legislators who saw parallel interests between the United States and Israel worked in close concert with AIPAC. But in recent years AIPAC's strident criticism of American supporters of Israel who stray from the lobbying group's pro-Likud hard line have alienated moderate pro-Israel voices in Washington. Several of these lobbying campaigns are recounted in Gerald Warburg, *Dispatches from the Eastern Front: A Political Education from the Nixon Years to the Age of Obama* (Baltimore: Bancroft Press, 2014).

27. John J. Mearsheimer and Stephen M. Walt, *The Israel Lobby and U.S. Foreign Policy* (New York: Farrar, Strauss and Giroux, 2007).

CHAPTER 16

Think Tanks

Supporting Cast Players in the National Security Enterprise

Ellen Laipson

> Bureaucracies do not invent new ideas. They elaborate old ones. . . . But where do politicians get new ideas? Many sources, obviously, but certainly think tanks. Think tanks become important incubators of policy innovation.
>
> —John Hamre, former deputy secretary of defense, now president and CEO, Center for Strategic and International Studies

Think tanks are an important but unofficial part of the national security enterprise (NSE). Their contributions are indirect and informal. Think tanks do not make critical foreign policy decisions and face no public accountability, nor do they perform any inherently governmental functions. But they are increasingly integrated into the way the US government conceptualizes its national security interests and devises responses to the diverse challenges and opportunities of national and international security. They can be seen as an organic part of the way in which policy ideas are incubated, tested, promoted, and evaluated. Government officials vary in the degree to which they seek input from think tanks, but the frequency with which very senior officials launch new policy initiatives at think tanks, or working-level officers seek critical input and feedback from think-tank experts, suggests that think tanks are accepted as a normal and integral part of policy formulation and outreach.

Think tanks enjoy a different organizational culture from governmental agencies. They favor their independent status, cultivate individual expression, highlight personal achievement, and foster a work environment that supports intellectual productivity rather than programmatic teamwork and institutional process. The workforce of most US think tanks includes substantive experts with years of government experience alongside experts whose careers have been primarily in academia and think tanks, and these two groups can represent distinct subcultures within the think-tank environment. Some try to bring government-style methods into think tanks—memos to the president as think-tank advice to the new administration, for example—whereas others value scholarly articles and full-length books as the product that establishes value in the marketplace of ideas. For the most part American think tanks reside in an independent, nongovernment space; unlike their counterparts in Europe and Asia, they are less likely to be tied to political parties or funded by ministries of defense, intelligence, or foreign affairs. It is their independence that is the defining characteristic that provides them an ability to speak honestly about governance gaps, failures, or successes without being seen as political actors with a stake in the outcome.

The degree to which a think tank is associated with a worldview or political preference also defines it, although many think tanks get labeled as liberal or conservative by observers when their internal self-concept is more neutral or bipartisan. Some think tanks advocate a political philosophy that is in fact outside the US mainstream, and those organizations never find a politician who fully satisfies their ideal. Cato, for example, which advocates libertarian policies, can be seen as being to the right of the Republican Party, while the Institute for Policy Studies can be seen as being to the left of the Democratic Party.

Increasingly, some think tanks also aspire to being agents of change (sometimes giving themselves the description "do-tanks") and want to be seen as putting their ideas into action, rather than as detached observers. In some cases former officials who became disaffected by bureaucratic process want to continue to demonstrate how alternative policies could change conflict dynamics or build better relationships in key regions. Working with industry and with international nongovernmental organizations that have field operations, these think-do tankers have sometimes blurred the lines between research and its field applications; think tanks have successfully competed for government-funded peace-building activities in post-conflict situations, for example. This activism and deepening ties to governments and their policy objectives have generated new policy issues for the think-tank sector, among them a demand for more transparency and accountability.

The robustness of the think-tank world in the United States, larger by orders of magnitude than in other advanced democracies, is attributed to the relative weakness of American political parties, the developed philanthropic culture, and the public distrust of government.[1]

EVOLUTION OF THINK TANKS IN THE UNITED STATES

The history of think tanks in the United States goes back more than a century, when newly wealthy industrialists created a modern form of philanthropy, investing not in traditional charitable institutions but in the building of independent civil society. These Americans, including Henry Ford, Andrew Carnegie, and the Rockefeller family across generations, created the network of public libraries, research institutes on scientific topics, and the first think tanks: the Carnegie Endowment for International Peace (1910), the Brookings Institution (1916), the Hoover Institute at Stanford University (1919), and the Council on Foreign Relations (CFR, 1921).[2] These important institutions were initially funded by foundations that branded their family names and did so much to build American society as we know it.

By mid-century, think tanks competed with, or complemented, prestigious universities by providing intellectual talent for new presidential administrations and were becoming more and more "drawn into making political judgments as well."[3] Experts with professional ties to the Brookings Institution, the Center for Strategic and International Studies (CSIS), CFR, the Hoover Institution, and others can be easily found in the rosters of political appointees to presidents over the past sixty years. One assessment counts over fifty CFR scholars in the Carter administration, for example, and identifies the Reagan brain trust drawn from Hoover, the American Enterprise Institute (AEI), the Heritage Foundation, CSIS, and RAND.[4] The next milestone in the evolution of American think tanks was the emergence of ideologically driven institutions created to promote a coherent worldview and its associated policy ideas and to work politically to support candidates with similar views. The most prominent example is the Heritage Foundation, created in 1973, which was closely associated with the Reagan revolution regarding the role of government, the uses of American power, and conservative social values.

The success of ideological think tanks on the right created pressures on the liberal or centrist-oriented policy world, in part because of the business model: conservative think tanks were funded lavishly, often by individual donors who did not require the same formal review processes of the established foundations. This allowed the new think tanks to produce, and quickly, large volumes of polished and professional-looking publications targeted for a political audience. The older think tanks tended to follow a more academic model, with long gestation periods for the creation and publication of new policy ideas.

The end of the Cold War spawned a new generation of national security think tanks, pledging to take fresh approaches to public policy analysis based on a profoundly changed national security environment. This group included the Henry L. Stimson Center (1989), which was created to look at nuclear arms control issues with a fresh, post–Cold War perspective, and the Nixon Center (1994), created to promote the "strategic realism" of former president Nixon in a nonpartisan way.

By the late 1990s several new think tanks with a liberal or progressive orientation, or a single thematic focus, entered the scene, often funded by wealthy individuals. Donors, rather than large foundations, underwrote the establishment of the Washington Institute for Near East Policy (WINEP, 1987); the Center for Global Development (2001); and more recently, the Center for American Progress (CAP), founded in 2003 to provide the progressive movement with long-term leadership. Many observers think CAP represents yet another model for a think tank, the purpose of which is to provide a planning capacity for the Democratic Party when it is out of office.[5] CAP proved to be an indispensable part of the transition to the Obama administration; its president, former Clinton chief of staff John Podesta, served as the head of the Obama transition team and figured as a key advisor to the Hillary Clinton campaign and likely transition leader. America is still the superpower in terms of sheer numbers of think tanks focused on public policy issues. In Washington, DC, alone there are an estimated 400, and there are about 1,800 in the country as a whole, according to the University of Pennsylvania's 2014 Go To Think Tank Index. Just to name a few, Chicago has the Chicago Council on Global Affairs, Atlanta has the Carter Center, Los Angeles has the Pacific Council on International Policy, Boston has countless think tanks affiliated with its university community, and New York is home to CFR and other university-based think tanks.

OTHER VARIETIES

It is hard to know where to draw the line between think tanks and other kinds of public policy organizations. Some of these newer organizations may call themselves think tanks but are in fact advocacy groups. Others cross the line to lobbying, and law firms and corporations call their directed research units think tanks. There are two additional categories of research institutions that are less central to the discussion of this chapter: in-government think tanks and federally funded think tanks that enjoy degrees of autonomy from official policy and procedure. The Congressional Research Service (CRS) of the Library of Congress is a government think tank created to support analysis for the legislative branch. Formed in 1914 as the Legislative Reference Service, it was expanded and renamed in 1970 and currently employs 700 people with a budget of $100 million. CRS covers all issues of interest to Congress; only a subset of its staff works full-time on national security issues. CRS is also diligent in providing nonpartisan research on questions raised by both Democratic and Republican members; unlike a growing number of new think tanks that want to develop a policy agenda, CRS has only one agenda: what is on Congress's mind. In the executive branch the think tank most focused on the security agenda is the National Intelligence Council (NIC), which provides both classified and unclassified analysis, drawing on all the resources and agencies of the intelligence community (IC). The NIC also has the responsibility to connect the US IC with the outside worlds of academia and research regarding international affairs. The Office of Net Assessments in the Department of Defense can also be considered an inside think tank, as is the National Defense University's Institute for National Security Studies. Both of these institutions respond to taskings by senior defense officials and initiate their own research to support and inform the policy process.

The federal government also underwrites the core operating costs of several prestigious think tanks, including the Woodrow Wilson Center for Scholars and the US Institute of Peace (USIP), both of which have independent governance structures and have strong reputations for quality scholarly work, for fellowship programs, and in the case of USIP, for training and fieldwork. The defense community has also created a series of federally funded research and development centers (FFRDCs) such as RAND, the Institute of Defense Analyses, the Center for Naval Analysis, and Analytic Services (ANSER), which focuses on homeland security issues.

THE BUSINESS MODEL

Think tanks operate according to a range of business models. The large institutions formed in the early years of the twentieth century enjoy infrastructure and operating expense support from endowments, which they supplement through foundation grants for specific programmatic work, corporate donations, and individual contributions. Nongovernment think tanks vary enormously in size, from start-ups with annual budgets of less than a million dollars to a large cohort with budgets under $10 million per year to the largest institutions with budgets of $30 million and beyond.

Think tanks vary on the sensitive issue of government funding. Some eschew it entirely, whereas others accept US or other government funding when programmatic interests are well aligned and when they perceive no compromise to their reputation for independence. In the early years of the twenty-first century, many American think tanks branched out to collaborative relationships with prosperous countries in Europe and Asia, often through foreign ministry or development assistance channels. In 2014 investigative journalists reported on some of the foreign funding relationships with major think tanks, implying that the research and analysis produced with such funding was somehow tainted. Think-tank leaders pushed back, troubled by the one-sided media coverage. They have felt confident in defending internal policies and practices that govern such funding relationships and serve to protect the independence and integrity of the work product. The interactions between think tanks and governments may be driven by shared views of international problems that need analytic attention or by a middle power's desire to raise its profile as a useful player in Washington power circles.

In general, think tanks have diversified their funding, finding that grants from the large foundations (Carnegie Corporation, Ford Foundation, MacArthur Foundation, Hewlett Foundation, etc.) are no longer sufficient to cover the operating costs of organizations that have evolved from modest nonprofit organizations to more established parts of the mainstream urban economy, with long-term leases in business districts, competitive professional salaries, and modern infrastructure to provide global teleconferencing services and platforms for public–private engagement. Foreign think tanks with a Washington presence or foreign government–funded think tanks are also now part of the US landscape, creating an ever denser and complex think-tank community.

This expansion has generated new concerns about accountability and transparency. New watchdog nongovernmental institutions and journalists now monitor think-tank funding patterns, raising questions about "donor-driven" work that associates think tanks with forms of lobbying, advocacy, or consultancies. Think-tank leaders have pushed back, demonstrating their internal procedures to ensure objectivity and independence, but the reputational risk to think tanks remains an issue. The Think Tanks and Civil Societies Program at the University of Pennsylvania has been studying think tanks since the late 1980s and, for the past seven years, has produced an annual index, the Go To Think Tank Index, ranking over 6,000 think tanks around the world in various categories.[6] As a corollary to the annual index, the program, led by Dr. James McGann, has institutionalized think-tank summits, organized by region. In 2015 major think tanks in Washington hosted the second North American think-tank summit, gathering leaders from about seventy think tanks in Canada, Mexico, and the United States. The summits are forums in which to debate and pool information about a full suite of issues, from internal practices to public relations. Leaders debate concerns from think tanks' image problem related to funding sources to challenges of the information age, such as personal use of social media and the strategic relationships among think tanks, journalism, academia, and public policy institutions.

THE PRODUCT

Think tanks play an important role in the policy process, but that does not mean that they interact primarily with government. Think tanks have critical audiences in the scholarly community, the media, the private sector, and the general public. The products of think tanks, therefore, need to be appropriate for these different consumers.

Think tanks make their contributions at many points along the life cycle of policymaking:

- identifying needs, gaps;
- generating new ideas;
- building support, constituents;
- encouraging formal approval through legislation or executive authority;
- educating, informing, persuading;
- monitoring implementation; and
- determining when change is needed to refine, retool, rethink.

Some think tanks see their primary role as generators of big new ideas, and they aim to directly influence the strategic course of government policy. Think tanks that work on health care reform, for example, may work for years on complex policy initiatives that would have significant implications for government programs and would likely require legislative or executive action.

Others focus their energies on current policies, offering feedback, criticism, and suggestions for new directions. The role of think tanks during the presidential transition in 2008–9 provides a flavor for this kind of policy input from the think-tank world. Many think tanks offered policy advice on Iraq, Afghanistan, China, trade policy, and so forth that constituted course corrections on the roster of existing problems rather than radical new directions.[7]

From the national security world, the work done in the aftermath of the Cold War that came to be known as cooperative threat reduction is a compelling example of think-tank work at the beginning of a policy cycle. The end of the Soviet Union presented a dramatic challenge with respect to the Soviet nuclear arsenal; scholars at the Brookings Institution, working with colleagues at Harvard and Stanford Universities, were engaged in projects about the transition to the post–Cold War world that were first embraced by visionary members of Congress (Senators Sam Nunn and Richard Lugar, Congressmen Les Aspin and John Murtha) and later became executive branch policy. Their ideas can be credited with a number of policy initiatives, from programs to employ former weapons scientists in times of great economic stress in Russia to new systems to manage and reduce fissile and other dangerous weapons-related materials.[8]

Sometimes the greatest contribution of a think tank is in information gathering and analysis rather than policy recommendations. Think tanks can sometimes do field research that would be difficult for government analysts or action officers. Research on the activities of Islamic organizations in countries where the official US presence may be small or constrained by security conditions, for example, could play to the strengths of a nongovernment research organization with Arabic- or Dari-speaking staffers eager to embark on research trips on policy-relevant topics.

In some respects this information-gathering stage of the policy life cycle is comparable to intelligence work, and think tanks have learned to collaborate with analysts in agencies of the IC. The tasks of collecting and interpreting data and analytic work in general are core to think-tank work, as they are to intelligence. The exchange of information and assessments of key national security topics can be rewarding for both parties. Government analysts are often constrained by large bureaucratic structures and by the press of producing daily reporting from collaborating across regional and functional areas; think tanks, by virtue of their smaller size, have a natural advantage in synthesizing across domains and producing more strategic outlooks. Think-tank experts may feel rewarded by knowing that their research and analysis is valued by government analysts and may contribute in some way to the NSE.

But think tanks tread carefully in these relationships, to protect their reputations and images as independent organizations and to avoid any associations that could present risk to the researchers themselves, particularly those who do field research in places that may be hostile to official Americans. It is also inappropriate for intelligence agencies to engage nongovernment experts to collect data for intelligence purposes; these protocols are well established and serve all parties' interests.

As part of the post-9/11 reforms of the IC, most intelligence agencies are eager to show that they have learned to engage in productive relationships with nongovernment experts.[9] The State Department's Bureau of Intelligence and Research (INR) and the NIC, which produces national intelligence estimates and unclassified strategic analysis and which reports to the director of national intelligence, are two components that have resources for regularized collaboration with think tanks. In the case of the NIC, the quadrennial Global Trends report, which provides each new presidential term with assessments of major transnational developments that could affect US interests, is now heavily based on inputs from think tanks around the world.[10]

Later in the life cycle of a policy, think tanks play a useful role in monitoring the implementation of policies and offering ideas about improving the effectiveness of policies. The US campaign to respond to the HIV/AIDS crisis, not purely as a humanitarian or health policy issue but as one with security implications for US allies or other US interests such as in Africa, led to some creative work monitoring existing programs and providing useful input from target countries so that an ongoing and high-profile policy could be improved and increase its ability to save lives and reach the targeted populations.[11]

American think tanks provide new ideas and critical feedback to government actors other than the United States. The UN Department of Peacekeeping Operations (DPKO) and the newer Peacebuilding Support Office (PBSO), for example, have formed close research partnerships with American think tanks in New York and Washington, with goals of increasing awareness of UN activities in American constituencies and working hard on the problems faced by UN experts on challenges related to deployments in post-conflict or conflict-ridden countries.[12]

IMPACT OF THINK TANKS' CONTRIBUTION
TO SECURITY DEBATES

Iraq, 2003–10

The US decision to go to war to oust Saddam Hussein, made by the Bush administration in 2002 and executed in 2003, is a disturbing case with respect to the role of think tanks and serves as a warning that think tanks can be marginal or irrelevant players when an administration has strongly held views or solicits input only from like-minded thinkers. This case could weaken the argument of this chapter, that think tanks are often an integral part of national security policymaking, or it could be seen as an outlier or exception.

The Bush administration took power in 2001 with a clearly articulated worldview and confident beliefs in American power as a force for transformation in the world. Bush had a national security agenda prepared by prominent defense intellectuals who advised his campaign, and Iraq was high on the list of problems that needed attention. The administration believed that Saddam Hussein's continued defiance of international norms, his probable continued work on nonconventional weapons, and his dismal domestic record constituted a threat to US credibility and authority. Removing Saddam Hussein's regime would benefit the Iraqi people, create prospects for a new regional political culture, and accrue important advantages to US prestige worldwide.

Mainstream and conservative think tanks helped validate this thinking and provided additional documentation on conditions in Iraq, the dangers of an Iraq with WMDs, and the potential benefits to the Middle East region once Saddam Hussein was removed. Titles from the Brookings website in early 2003, for example, are "The Dangers of Delaying an Attack on Iraq," "Why Iraq Can't Be Deterred," and "A Last Chance to Stop Iraq." From AEI, "The False Allure of Stability."

More avowedly liberal-leaning think tanks raised a number of issues about Iraq, including doubts about its weapons status and the downsides of a policy to remove Saddam Hussein by force. Of special note was the Carnegie Endowment for International Peace. With deep expertise on WMD, the Carnegie team developed alternative approaches for ridding Iraq of any possible WMDs. Its main proposal was for coercive inspections, building on UN capabilities established in 1991 to detect, monitor, and eliminate Iraqi weapons programs. But its message was strategic: there are alternatives to war, and war will accrue terrible costs to the United States in human and reputational terms. No other well-established Washington think tank took as clear an antiwar position as Carnegie did.

Others addressed the larger, indirect costs of war and questioned how Iraqi society would respond to an abrupt change of fortune. But many of these analytic pieces accepted the inevitability of the Bush administration's decision to go to war, with reluctance or satisfaction, and their purpose was to add value to that decision on the margins, not to assess the fundamental soundness of the decision.

Some think tanks are deeply interested in questions of governance, and for some Iraq was a "test lab" for trying out their ideological ideas on a submissive subject. Accordingly, some think tanks willingly helped staff the US occupation of Iraq; dozens of young enthusiasts for the policy made their way to Baghdad for positions that were often intended for experienced civil servants.[13] In many cases these proved to be failed missions. And overall, the Iraq case seems to have been a missed opportunity to analyze and draw lessons from how the United States dealt with questions of decision making, authorities, and process. In general, journalists showed more interest in these important challenges and issues than think tanks did.

Once the war began, think tanks displayed their impressive capacity for data collection and analysis, often presenting the picture on the ground in Iraq in more articulate and compelling forms than government bureaucrats did, at least in the public domain. Some new and creative partnerships were formed: the *New York Times* commissioned Brookings's Michael O'Hanlon to offer periodic graphic assessments of the costs of the war, measuring discrete categories of the war effort as well as casualties, both American and Iraqi.

A large set of secondary effects of the Iraq War were studied: Brookings contributed important work on Iraqi internally displaced and refugee populations, as well as analysis of the potential UN role in a post-occupation Iraq; CSIS offered deep analysis of the impact of the war on US military readiness; AEI, WINEP, and USIP became venues for the new Iraqi political class to engage with Washington pundits and researchers.

USIP, in a special category of think tank as a federally funded but independently governed research institute, provided perhaps the most significant platform for bipartisan, cross-disciplinary work on Iraq after the fall of Saddam. At the request of Congress and with the reluctant acquiescence of the Bush White House, USIP convened, with three other think tanks as cohosts, what came to be known as the Iraq Study Group (ISG). Cochaired by former congressman Lee Hamilton and Republican Party statesman James Baker, the ISG spent much of 2006 grappling with how to improve the effectiveness of the US intervention in the face of spiraling violence in Iraq and political anguish at home. Its mission was to identify some new directions for US policy without labeling the entire Iraq effort a devastating failure. The Bush administration, in the fall 2006 election period, seemed to dismiss the study's findings but later quietly began implementing some of the ideas, including its recommendations related to engaging with Iraq's neighbors.[14] The expert groups that advised the study group continued to meet informally and address Iraq's political and security developments through occasional publications and in a politically inclusive way.

Some US think tanks, irrespective of their position on the decision to go to war, have tried to help the new Iraq build its own think-tank culture. USIP, Brookings, AEI, WINEP, and Stimson, among others, have hosted new civil society leaders in Iraq, traveling on US embassy and State Department programs. In some cases US think tanks conducted capacity-building workshops as a way to strengthen democratic practice and culture in Iraq. In these different fashions think tanks accommodated themselves to Iraq as a government priority during the Bush years and found diverse ways to contribute to stability in Iraq as an American interest, irrespective of their views on the decisions of 2002 and 2003. It could be argued that with very few exceptions, think tanks demonstrated that they are only supporting cast players in a national security play whose heroes or villains are government officials. Think tanks can bring some color and texture to the performance but are unlikely to drive the plot.

Iran and Ukraine

Two more cases demonstrate how think tanks provide a platform for informed debate of major foreign policy challenges and how think tanks create ad hoc coalitions to collaborate on vital issues. On Iran the think-tank community has reflected the shifting policy concerns, examining Iran as a source of regional and international terrorism, as a failed democracy and human rights case, as a virtual adversary of the United States with respect to most Middle East regional problems, and increasingly, as a challenge to the nonproliferation regime over its nuclear activities. Think tanks active on arms control issues as their main or major focus, such as the Arms Control Association (ACA), the Institute for Science and International Security (ISIS), and the Carnegie Endowment for International Peace, have given significant attention to the Iran issue over the past decade; ISIS developed a supplemental website to track and monitor the issue. As the nuclear talks led by the UN's Permanent Five members plus Germany picked up steam and seriousness of purpose in the Obama administration, think tanks have been active players in evaluating the details of the negotiating positions, gaming out the geopolitical consequences of a deal or a failure to achieve one and dissecting the seemingly irreconcilable positions of US and Middle Eastern interests and politics over the negotiations. In 2014, as a negotiated outcome appeared more likely, USIP organized a coalition of seven think tanks of diverse profiles (and one foundation, the Ploughshares Fund) to work together to provide independent analysis and information to inform the public, and in particular congressional staff who might be tasked with supporting a formal congressional debate over an agreement.

The Russia–Ukraine crisis has been another acute foreign policy challenge in which think tanks have offered rich analysis and policy options for public debate. Think tanks benefit from having former American diplomats as staff or adjunct fellows, and this brings an additional dimension of authority and credibility to the deliberations. A winter 2015 coalition of Brookings, the Atlantic Council, the Center for New American Security, and the Chicago Council on Global Affairs worked quickly to generate a very specific policy recommendation on arming the Ukrainian military; the think-tank team included former ambassadors to Ukraine and former senior Russia policy officials.[15] To date their recommendations in support of a dramatic increase in US lethal support for Ukraine has not led to a shift in US policy but has sharpened the terms of the domestic debate over US options.

IDENTITY ISSUES

For the twenty-first-century think tank, a new set of issues arises: Are American think tanks only American? Many think tanks approach the foreign policy landscape from the globalization paradigm and increasingly see themselves as part of a global community.[16] The US Carnegie Endowment launched a new initiative of rebranding when it opened offices in Moscow, Beijing, Brussels, Beirut, and eventually Delhi and pronounced that Carnegie was the "first global think tank."[17] The Brookings Institution has an office in Doha, Qatar, from which it manages a range of activities in the Middle East region, including an annual Islamic World Forum, and newer offices in India and China. Other think tanks are increasingly part of a global network, through collaborative relationships with non-US think tanks, through funding relationships, and through the reach of their publications and ideas in the information age. Think tanks are beginning to formalize their relationships, through consortia that cross-publish and promote each other's work, work jointly to seek funding for collaborative work, and host international meetings at which individual and joint work can be featured. In some cases leading organizations are the sponsors of annual international conferences that serve as major policy forums and opportunities for consultations. For example, the Carnegie Endowment's annual nuclear conference has become an essential global platform for intergovernmental consultations on nuclear nonproliferation. Other institutions, like Brookings, CSIS, and the German Marshall Fund (GMF), host a variety of annual conventions that allow a mixing of academics, think-tank experts, and policymakers to exchange views at senior levels.

Identity issues are not limited to the global versus national issue. Political labeling is also a challenging identity issue. Think tanks' internal culture, which often values individual positions more than institutional ones and often perceives itself as nonpartisan or bipartisan, can be injured by a facile press reference to the presumed political preferences of the entire organization. Think tanks are often labeled by outsiders as liberal or Democratic, even when a quick study of their boards or their governing principles would suggest a more neutral identity.

Think tanks may also bristle at the ease with which universities, law firms, lobbyists, corporations, and governments refer to their own activities as think tanks. These entities often serve a more directed purpose: to analyze a political situation from the perspective of a client or a weapons system from the perspective of a market player, for example. They are often not intended to promulgate knowledge for knowledge's sake or for a public policy purpose.

One scholar sees harm to think tanks from this pressure to market their products and see their work as a commodity and from the need to mimic the tactics and methods of interest groups. In this view the "research" done in think tanks has come to resemble "polemical commentary" rather than empirical truths or objective analysis.[18] But a quick review of think tanks' websites would dispute this critique; think tanks are generally competent at providing accessible data and information, as well as interpretation and policy recommendations.

Think tanks are also often associated with different types of nongovernmental organizations, such as human rights or democracy-promoting groups, when their analysis is critical of a particular government. Officials in nondemocratic countries in the Middle East or Asia may view think-tank analysis as part of a larger agenda to change the political culture and to promote American values. In that way foreign officials may suspect that a think tank is actually an extension or a tool of US policy. The environment for think tanks to conduct research or to operate in nondemocratic settings has become more fraught with these political sensitivities in recent years.

THINK TANKS FROM THE POLICYMAKERS' POINT OF VIEW

Policymakers do not share a single view about the utility or value of think tanks; just as government officials vary in their use of information and their strategies to master the issues for which they are responsible, so too do they differ in how they value the contribution of nongovernment expertise in their work. What is clear is that increasingly, government officials consider it normal and constructive to perform their official duties by carefully following what think-tank experts are writing and saying and by engaging directly with think tanks to solicit their input on key policy issues. It has long been common for government officials to engage informally with experts they know, from graduate school or through social networks. It is particularly true of political appointees, who often bring information-gathering practices established in other professional settings to their work in government. But it appears increasingly common for government officials to make overtures to think tanks, as they familiarize themselves with a new account, begin a new policy initiative, or consider ways to change an existing policy.

Some in government may harbor the view that think tank work is superficial or is not informed by deep inside truths. Think tanks for the most part have no access to intelligence or other insider information, and their analysis and recommendations may suffer from this lack. But the challenge is for actors in the NSE to appropriately and effectively use the knowledge and judgment of think-tank experts in the interest of wiser policymaking and policy implementation. Think tanks are not intended to substitute for the insider policy deliberations or to compete with work done in government teams and interagency meetings. Yet think tanks can provide unique data in some cases and deep wisdom and judgment in others that cannot be acquired inside the bureaucracy.

NOTES

1. James McGann, *Think Tanks and Policy Advice in the United States: Academics, Advisors and Advocates* (New York: Routledge, 2007), 8.

2. CFR is also a membership organization, funded by member dues. It has functioned as both an elite club and a think tank. The Pacific Council on International Policy is also a membership organization.

3. Andrew Rich, *Think Tanks, Public Policy and the Politics of Expertise* (Cambridge, UK: Cambridge University Press, 2004), 41.

4. Donald E. Abelson, "Changing Minds, Changing Course: Obama, Think Tanks and American Foreign Policy," in *Obama and the World: New Directions in US Foreign Policy*, ed. Inderjeet Parmar, Linda B. Miller, and Mark Ledwidge (London: Routledge, 2014), 107–14. See also his longer work, *Do Think Tanks Matter? Assessing the Impact of Public Policy Institutes* (Montreal: McGill-Queen's University Press, 2002); and Andrew Selee, *What Should Think Tanks Do? A Strategic Guide to Policy Impact* (Stanford, CA: Stanford University Press, 2013).

5. CAP describes itself as nonpartisan. The planning function is also identified by CSIS as a core mission. President John Hamre wrote, "CSIS is committed to undertake strategic planning for the US government." In McGann, *Think Tanks and Policy Advice*, 90.

6. The repository of material from the Think Tanks and Civil Societies Program, which in 2015 released its seventh index of think tanks worldwide, is available online at http://gotothinktank.com.

7. Think-tank advice on the Obama transition includes "A Better Deal: Twelve Suggestions for the New US President" (RAND); "Advice to President Obama" (MIT Center for International Studies); "Foreign Policy for the Next President" (Carnegie Endowment for International Peace); "Presidential Inbox 2009" (Stimson Center).

8. I am grateful to Laura Holgate of the Nuclear Threat Initiative for her recollections of the early intellectual churning that led to the cooperative threat reduction programs.

9. See in particular Commission on the Intelligence Capabilities of the United States Regarding Weapons of Mass Destruction, *Report to the President of the United States* (Washington, DC: Government Printing Office, March 31, 2005), 387–429.

10. See the Office of the Director of National Intelligence's Global Trends series at www.dni.gov/index.php/about/organization/national-intelligence-council-global-trends. The net Global Trends 2035 is in process now and likely to be very different from its predecessors.

11. In January 2003 a delegation of health leaders formed by CSIS under the umbrella of its Task Force on HIV/AIDS visited China "to examine [its] approach to HIV/AIDS and to explore the possibility of expanded U.S.-Chinese collaboration." Drawing explicitly on the findings of this delegation, the Presidential Advisory Council on HIV/AIDS (PACHA) passed a resolution on August 8, 2003, calling for "the President, the Secretary of Health and Human Services, and the U.S. Congress to provide

strong international leadership and technical assistance to China, India, Russia and other nations to fight the HIV/AIDS pandemic."

12. The DC-based Better World Fund, for example, hosts high-ranking UN officials in meetings with the Washington community and makes a case for the UN on Capitol Hill. The Stimson Center has worked both directly with the UN and through government grants to supply lessons-learned research to DPKO's Security Sector Reform Team, analysis and doctrine development support to its Police Division, and field research for its Best Practices Section. Stimson has reviewed drafts of major UN policy statements on peacekeeping doctrine, security sector reform strategy, and the best way to benchmark peace-building activities, the latter for PBSO. The New York–based International Peace Institute has seconded personnel to help draft the secretary general's 2009 report on peace building, and the Center on International Cooperation at New York University publishes an annual compendium of peacekeeping activities in collaboration with DPKO.

13. Rajiv Chandrasekaran, "Ties to GOP Trumped Know-How among Staff Sent to Rebuild Iraq," *Washington Post*, September 17, 2006. Adapted from Rajiv Chandrasekaran, *Imperial Life in the Emerald City* (New York: Knopf, 2006).

14. James A. Baker III and Lee H. Hamilton, cochairs, *The Iraq Study Group Report: The Way Forward—A New Approach* (New York: Vintage Books, 2006).

15. For information about the Ukraine in Europe initiative, see www.atlanticcouncil.org/ukraine. For the text of the report, see Strobe Talbott, Michèle Flournoy, Jan Lodal, Steven Pifer, Ivo Daalder, John Herbst, James Stavridis, and Charles Wald, *Preserving Ukraine Independence, Resisting Russian Aggression: What the United States and NATO Must Do* (Washington, DC: Atlantic Council, 2015), www.brookings.edu/research/reports/2015/02/ukraine-independence-russian-aggression. The Carnegie Endowment has also offered analysis of the crisis from both its Washington and Moscow offices.

16. James G. McGann and R. Kent Weaver, *Think Tanks and Civil Societies: Catalysts for Ideas and Action* (New Brunswick, NJ: Transaction Publishers, 2002). This book and other online surveys by Mr. McGann are useful catalogues of the global network of think tanks.

17. One could easily call the International Crisis Group, created with an international board and offices in sixty countries, the first global think tank. It was initially conceived with an activist mission as its primary function—pressing foreign ministries to engage to prevent or resolve conflicts—but it has become best known for its research and analysis work.

18. Rich, *Think Tanks*.

CHAPTER 17

The Media

Witness to the National Security Enterprise

John M. Diamond

> I hate newspapermen. They come into camp and pick up their camp rumors and print them as facts. I regard them as spies, which in truth, they are. If I killed them all there would be news from Hell before breakfast.
> —Gen. William Tecumseh Sherman

> To the ordinary guy, all this is a bunch of gobbledygook. But out of the gobbledygook comes a very clear thing: . . . You can't trust the government; you can't believe what they say; and you can't rely on their judgment; and the . . . implicit infallibility of presidents, which has been an accepted thing in America is badly hurt by this, because it shows that people do things the president wants to do even though it's wrong, and the president is wrong.
> —"Bob" H. R. Haldeman, advisor to President Nixon on Pentagon Papers Release

In today's information age asserting that the media has an impact on national security decision making is almost akin to saying that geography has an impact on national security decision making. The ways in which the dynamics of mass communication influence the military and national security leadership are countless and as complex as the influences of geography, politics, logistics, or any number of other factors beyond the balance of forces at the scene of conflict. As with any of these other influences, each situation in which media dynamics play a role in the development, execution, and outcome of national security strategies must be regarded as unique, making broad academic generalizations or principles difficult to propound with any confidence. What is useful, however, is examining how the media–national security dynamic works by looking at situations in which media influence is pronounced and by understanding how the relationship changes with the times and the technology. As Michael Massing has noted, the Internet's properties—speed, immediacy, interactivity, boundless capacity, global reach—provide tremendous new opportunities for the gathering and presentation of news and information.[1]

The aim of this chapter is to draw on the author's experience as a journalist, most of it covering national security affairs, in identifying and describing important themes in the media and national security dynamic. Overriding principles may be elusive in a field in which the contributing factors are so numerous and, at times, random. Instead, the author examines a number of themes or dynamics that can inform national security decision making under media scrutiny.

There can be little doubt that the media can influence events in international relations and national security, sometimes by design, sometimes by accident. New studies on the end of the Cold War have brought out vivid examples of how even when the media gets the story wrong it can change the course of history. In November 1989, for example, a widely viewed West German news broadcaster reported that the Berlin Wall had been opened. The report was erroneous, or as it turned out, premature; the report itself helped spark a flood of East Berliners who had seen the news broadcast to the wall.[2]

The years since the 9/11 attacks have been marked by extremes in national security journalism. In the aftermath of the terrorist attacks, saturation media coverage focused on the ultimately unanswerable question of whether the attacks were avoidable. Then, the run-up to the US-led 2003 invasion of Iraq wound up putting US media under intense public scrutiny for having been too ready to buy the Bush administration's allegations about Iraq's supposed arsenal of weapons of mass destruction (WMDs). Under assault for missing the story, elite US media rebounded in the ensuing years with exposés on torture, secret Central Intelligence Agency (CIA) prisons, decrepit housing for wounded veterans of the Iraq War, a secret program to conduct warrantless domestic wiretapping, and most recently, extensive electronic surveillance of allies as well as adversaries by the National Security Agency (NSA). As of this writing, with multiple wars ongoing, the American newspaper industry is coping with a financial crisis of unprecedented severity, struggling simply to keep reporters in the field, let alone influence world-changing events.[3] Even as the mainstream media is being challenged by a business model that is no longer profitable and by competition from social media, its own national security reporting has ignited an aggressive US government crackdown on leaks, aimed not just at the leakers but also at those journalists whose sources have been increasingly "insiders" to the national security enterprise.

This chapter, then, examines aspects of these and other media episodes. First, though, it is important to discuss national security media in more general terms to give readers unfamiliar with this arena a sense of the landscape. It is important to keep in mind that some of the dynamics between the media and US national security could just as easily apply in civilian contexts. Among the aspects of the media–national security relationship that stand out are the importance to the information flow of relationships of trust between reporter and source, the highly sensitive nature of some of the information and the reasons for sharing it, and the often compressed time frame of crisis, decision making, and result.

THE TRIBES OF NATIONAL SECURITY MEDIA

US media coverage of national security breaks down into four broad types: correspondents based in Washington and focused on diplomatic and military policymaking; foreign correspondents based in foreign capitals and focused on world news, but with an emphasis on news of interest to US audiences; war correspondents assigned to a combat area who may at times be embedded with US forces; and US-based regional journalists who work near major military installations in places such as San Diego; Norfolk, Virginia; and Tampa. Added to this list, of course, is the endless variety of online outlets, blogs, social media outlets, interest group websites, and postings by principal actors, whether they be governments, corporations, refugee organizations, terrorist groups, whistleblowers, or any number of other key players.

Washington Reporters

Washington-based correspondents include journalists with extensive experience and a deep base of sources. Reporters such as David Martin of CBS News, Eric Schmidt and David Sanger of the *New York Times*, Barbara Starr of CNN, and Tony Capaccio of Bloomberg News have been covering their beats for years—in some cases, decades. It is not uncommon for journalists such as these to develop sources of mid-level civilian or military rank and then stick with those sources for years, through promotion to increasingly senior positions.

These reporters have been on the job so long that, at times, they may know the political and policy landscape better than the colonels and one-stars and assistant secretaries they cover. At times this can make things easier for official Washington because such reporters do not need an elementary-level education in the issues, policies, and operations they cover. They start with a broad and deep base of knowledge so the national security officials dealing with them need not fear some gross distortion of reality based on ignorance of the way things work, nor do they have to spend precious time walking these reporters through the basics.

On the other hand, these reporters can pose a significant challenge to officials because they know the right questions to ask. It is a basic reality of official Washington that bureaucracies are fairly willing to share information but quite often will do so only if asked. It therefore takes a reporter of some experience to know the right questions and to drill past the surface to gain a deeper understanding of what is going on. This class of national security journalist has access to trusted sources that will provide unofficial and sometimes contrasting perspectives on the story line that an administration or cabinet office is trying to disseminate. They report in a milieu filled with contrasting opinions and perspectives, whether it is the ranking minority-party member of the Senate Armed Services Committee, a former cabinet secretary now out of government at a think tank, a retired intelligence officer, or an executive at a defense contractor embroiled in heated competition for a new weapons program. Finally, these reporters work in an environment where official self-examination and criticism are standard procedure. The military and intelligence community, more than most other government institutions, engage in lessons-learned exercises. These combined with congressional oversight reports, blue-ribbon commission studies, and after-action reviews form a steady stream of critical (if not uniformly negative) information available to the national security beat reporter.

The environment in which these reporters work may vary from assignment to assignment. Pentagon correspondents go through a clearance process to get a building pass. The clearance does not provide them access to classified information, but it does give them freedom to roam all but the most secure corridors of the vast building, a great asset for bumping into senior officials at coffee stands or in cafeteria lines and for dropping in on various offices where a face-to-face conversation (whether authorized or not) may elicit information more quickly than a phone call or email. Because the State Department press corps includes a large contingent of foreign reporters, a State Department press pass limits reporters' access to the first two floors, far below the senior executive suites where the key decision makers work. The casual drop-by is not an option at State; reporters must hustle from photo opportunities to briefings to the occasional public ceremony to get access to principals. Select members of the Pentagon and State Department press corps travel with the secretaries of state and defense on official trips.

This is an expensive proposition and not all news organizations can afford to pay the hotel bills and airfare (equivalent to a first-class ticket) on weeklong trips making multiple stops in world capitals. But the payoff is considerable, for unlike the restricted access typical in Washington, an international trip can afford journalists extensive access to senior officials, including the cabinet secretary, whether in in-flight briefings, in casual conversations en route, or over hotel meals during the trip. Being in the bubble does not always mean being first to get the news.

Unlike the Pentagon, State Department, and White House, the CIA provides no filing center for reporters, though journalists who cover the agency can make the occasional appointment to come to CIA Headquarters for a carefully monitored deep-background interview. The CIA, like the White House, is often best covered from the outside in. Rather than trying to get a reticent organization to yield closely held information, it is better to go to those who are the CIA's overseers—the House and Senate Intelligence Committees—or its customers, the many people across the US government with regular access to intelligence reports. Reporters with long experience covering US intelligence, such as the *New York Times*'s James Risen or the *Washington Post*'s David Ignatius, have learned the value of developing sources among the large community of CIA retirees, many of whom continue to do sensitive work for the government long after they have handed in their agency badges.

Foreign Correspondents

Foreign correspondents are sometimes quite senior in rank but not always, particularly in recent years. For much of the twentieth century, foreign postings were the capstone on a career. In his account of the *New York Times*, Gay Talese tells the story of A. M. Rosenthal's long-delayed quest to become a foreign correspondent. Rosenthal, who would go on to become the paper's executive editor, slogged through years of domestic assignments before finally getting a foreign posting.[4] Today, a young reporter with ability in a difficult foreign language or a willingness to go to dangerous places can jump ahead in line. Thomas Friedman's early career experience in Lebanon for United Press International and then for the *New York Times* in the late 1970s and 1980s and Richard Engel's reporting on the Iraq War for ABC News and then NBC News are examples of this phenomenon.[5]

In the nineteenth and twentieth centuries, a typical foreign correspondent did well to locate near a major foreign capital. These days it is, perhaps, more important for a foreign correspondent to locate near a major international airport. As the ranks of foreign correspondents have dwindled, the job of the foreign correspondent has had less to do with covering the goings-on of the government of the country in which the correspondent is based than it does with using the overseas posting as a base of operations for covering stories within a much larger geographic base than any one country.

Generalizations on the output of US correspondents reporting from overseas are much harder to make than for Washington-based national security correspondents because the type of story and circumstances of assignment vary so widely. It is safe to say that a foreign correspondent will have ample opportunity to find officials and prominent citizens willing to criticize the policies of the United States. A foreign correspondent will often be well positioned to produce stories that suggest that the reality on the ground or the impact of a policy forged in Washington differs greatly from the view of events at the White House or State Department. There is generally no shortage of opportunities to report on the views of foreign officials who believe Washington's aims or demands to be unreasonable. Foreign correspondents may, at times, be able to draw attention to crises or developments—famine, ethnic cleansing, corruption in a foreign government—that have been ignored or overlooked by official Washington. In a breaking news context, the reality is that a single foreign correspondent, even one who happens to be close to the scene of the crisis, often has to rely heavily on local or regional media coverage to put together a complete story.

The decline of media budgets—particularly for large newspapers—has dramatically reduced the ranks of foreign correspondents for US news organizations. Staffing levels, the numbers of reporters assigned to overseas bureaus and war zones, and the ability of news organizations to dedicate multiple beat reporters to diplomacy, defense, and intelligence organizations have all succumbed to the sea change in readership habits and advertising economics (see box 17.1).

BOX 17.1
State of the News Media

Journalism is under stress. Numerous studies document the decline in media coverage of international issues. Between 1998 and 2011 the *American Journalism Review* counted eighteen American newspapers and two newspaper chains that had shut down all their foreign bureaus, with most of the closures coming after 2003, the year US forces invaded and occupied Iraq.[a] In 2011, as the ten-year anniversary of the US war in Afghanistan approached, veteran investigative reporter John Hanrahan found, "The American print press is almost totally absent from Afghanistan, leaving the reporting to a handful of news organizations."[b] The shuttered bureaus and vanishing reporters were reflected in the quantity of news coverage of US military operations. A Pew Research Center survey found that in 2010 only 4 percent of news coverage was devoted to the war in Afghanistan, a low level that held steady except for brief spikes in coverage over the firing of Gen. Stanley McCrystal, the US commander in Afghanistan, and the disclosure of classified documents by WikiLeaks. About 1 percent of news coverage that year was devoted to events in Iraq. Major news dailies like the *Baltimore Sun* and the *Philadelphia Inquirer* now have no foreign bureaus.[c]

While CNN, NPR, the *New York Times*, and the *Washington Post* continue to send reporters out to cover the world or to hire local reporters in foreign countries, other major news outlets are cutting back on foreign bureaus and resorting to wire service coverage or, when absolutely necessary, to "parachute reporters"—that is, nationally based reporters who are dropped into foreign countries as breaking news happens. Although more cost effective, this trend, according to some experienced journalists, sets up news stories that lack the historical context, miss comparisons with other events, and encourage clichés and stereotypes.

Cost issues have hit newspapers—traditional mainstays of international and national security reporting—particularly hard. US newspaper revenue fell 59 percent between 2004 and 2014, from $48.2 billion to $19.9 billion, Pew reported. Digital media revenue for newspapers increased 133 percent during that time but in 2014 still represented only 17.5 percent of newspaper revenue.[d]

Other studies of American newspapers conclude that "coverage of international events is declining more than any other subject."[e] Some attribute this trend to the clash among news, profits, and technologies that transformed news outlets into "profit centers" that had to make money or face reductions and staff cuts. As papers literally become smaller, even major news dailies like the *Los Angeles Times* experience staff cuts and a recurring battle between editorial staffs and corporate management over whether newspapers should become local or try to remain national news providers. Citizen reporting—via blogs and the Internet—also challenged traditional media outlets in providing trusted as well as easily accessible and cheap forms of current news.

[a] Jodi Enda, "Retreating from the World," *American Journalism Review*, December/January 2011.
[b] John Hanrahan, "The War without End Is a War with Hardly Any News Coverage," *Nieman Watchdog*, August 10, 2011, www.niemanwatchdog.org/index.cfm?fuseaction=background.view&bac kgroundid=5 69.
[c] Pew Research Center, "Press Coverage and Public Interest: Matches and Mismatches," January 11, 2011, www .people-press.org/2011/01/11/press-coverage-and-public-interest-matches-and-mismatches/. See also Pamela Constable, "Demise of the Foreign Correspondent," *Washington Post*, February 18, 2007, www.washingtonpost.com/ wp-dyn/content/article/2007/02/16/AR2007021601713.html.
[d] Amy Mitchell, "State of the News Media 2015," Pew Research Center, www.journalism.org/2015/04/29/state-of-the-news-media-2015/.
[e] Tricia Sartor and Dana Page, "Foreign Coverage Shrinking, Not Gone," Pew Project for Excellence in Journalism, July 23, 2008, www.journalism.org/node/12042.

News organizations are under economic pressure from multiple directions: newspapers facing the flight of classified advertising to the Internet, networks facing increasing loss of viewership to cable, or cable stations confronting the rising cost of maintaining round-the-clock operations. They have responded by cutting back on foreign correspondents. The added costs of providing security, drivers, translators, and guarded living and office space in Iraq and Afghanistan have only accelerated the trend.[6] Wire services and local hires have filled the void only up to a point. The ability of a foreign editor at a major US metropolitan daily to spot an interesting trend overlooked by other news organizations and to deploy reporting resources to get the story is waning.[7]

Citizen digital journalists with cell phone cameras are becoming the first recorders of history. It is a grim fact that the declining ranks of journalists working overseas are partly attributable to their deaths covering conflict or at the hands of extremists, both in terms of absolute losses and in the growing reluctance of news organizations to put their reporters into harm's way. The Committee to Protect Journalists, in an annual survey on the hazards of reporting from conflict zones and other unstable regions, found that sixty-one reporters were killed while on the job, down slightly from seventy killed in 2013. These included Anja Niedringhaus, a German photographer shot and killed in Afghanistan while she was covering the presidential elections, and freelance American journalist James Foley and American-Israeli journalist Steven J. Sotloff, both taken hostage by the Islamic State and later executed.[8] Gone are the swashbuckling days of foreign reporting when, as the late and legendary correspondent Arnaud de Borchgrave told a friend, all one needed to pack for a foreign assignment was a tuxedo and a safari suit.[9] The increasing risk level associated with foreign reporting has multiplied the costs, as news organizations with bureaus in Baghdad, Kabul, and other dangerous environments pay for body armor, helmets, security guards, drivers, and translators.

The kidnapping of journalists has confronted news organizations with a dilemma. Security experts have advised news managers to withhold news reports on these cases to avoid creating further incentive for militants to kidnap more journalists. The resulting instances of blacked-out coverage have led to charges that newsrooms are according their own with a privilege of withheld coverage that would not be extended to non-journalist hostages. Commenting on a media-wide agreement to hold stories about the kidnapping of a *New York Times* reporter in Afghanistan, Associated Press senior editor John Daniszewski said, "Your instinct is to publish what you know. But we felt there was just too high a risk that something would happen to him." But there is skepticism about whether the blackout strategy works. By keeping the hostage takings secret, the media kept the public unaware of, and therefore unable to support action on, a problem that too often surfaced with the release of videotaped executions.[10]

The decline of dedicated foreign bureaus and correspondents has left the field open for new media, or nontraditional media coverage. A public furor in the summer of 2010 over disparaging remarks by army general Stanley McChrystal, then the commander of US forces in Afghanistan, and by his staff—remarks directed at President Barack Obama, Vice President Joe Biden, and other senior civilian officials—stemmed not from a major media outlet's reporting but from an article in *Rolling Stone* magazine.[11] Weeks later, major media outlets in the United States, Britain, and Germany published accounts of some 92,000 pages of classified documents unearthed not through their own sleuthing but by a website called WikiLeaks, an episode to be discussed later.[12]

Creative ideas are emerging for finding new ways to finance foreign coverage. And in the information age, torrents of information unavailable from any source even a decade ago have altered the dynamic of the way information is collected around the globe.[13] The wide circulation of mobile phone images of civilian casualties in Syria and the reposting on social media of news photos of a drowned Syrian child whose family was fleeing the conflict are among the most recent examples.[14] But new business models at mainstream media organizations have not fully emerged. Hiring foreign nationals to provide coverage has the advantage of providing a US news organization with deep local knowledge and language skills, but with the corresponding absence of familiarity with the US readership or viewership or of US sensibilities and priorities. An election in Pakistan, for example, might present innumerable interesting local angles as factions and well-known personalities vie for advantage. But to the US audience, the only thing likely to matter much is which candidate or slate is deemed most desirable for US interests and which most threatening.[15]

War Correspondents

War correspondents may come from the ranks of Washington national security reporters, foreign correspondents, or regional writers focused on the military; from nonmilitary beat assignments; or in a few cases, straight from school. For news organizations big enough to maintain foreign bureaus, war correspondents are often drawn from the ranks of foreign correspondents. Typically, a Mideast correspondent based in Cairo or Jerusalem would be deployed to conflict in the Mideast. Correspondents based in Berlin, Rome, or Paris were often called on to cover the Balkan wars of the 1990s. Correspondents based in Nairobi or Johannesburg might be called on to cover any one of the seemingly endless African wars virtually anywhere on the continent. Under this model the image of the foreign correspondent as an urbane figure hobnobbing with diplomats in elegant foreign capitals gives way to the reality of dangerous assignments, months away from family and home, and few creature comforts. World geography and time zones mean that in most cases foreign reporting entails extremely long hours, as a full workday of reporting typically would end in Europe, Africa, or much of Asia at about the time editors are arriving at work at US news organizations. This then requires long evenings and nights of interaction with headquarters before stories (and reporters) are put to bed.

The issue of embedded journalists has been chronicled extensively, and a detailed treatment is beyond the scope of this chapter. The concept of attaching reporters to military units, placing them under their care and protection, and to varying degrees, limiting or controlling what they can report goes back generations. The term "embedded" took on a sort of official status, however, in connection with the US-led invasion of Iraq in March 2003. Some 800 reporters from scores of US news organizations signed contracts with the military giving those reporters the ability to travel with advancing troops but also limiting what and when certain information could be reported. The Pentagon was particularly concerned about reports that would pinpoint the location of US troops. As a result, there were a number of "Somewhere in Southern Iraq" datelines on stories during the invasion phase of the conflict. This concern was not necessarily the result of a new anti–press freedom attitude at the Department of Defense so much as recognition of the instantaneous nature of today's journalism. Not only wire services and broadcast and cable outlets but daily papers and even weekly news magazines now have online outlets that can disseminate information about troops' dispositions in real time.

What turned out to be far more restrictive and controlled was the choice available to news organizations as to which units they could cover.[16] During the Vietnam War correspondents made their own decisions, hopping choppers out of Saigon to frontline operations in any one of a number of locations. In Iraq the Pentagon decided which reporters went with which units, the result being that news outlets spending exorbitant sums of money to cover the conflict sometimes found their correspondent in the field assigned to a unit far removed from the most important action.[17] The Pentagon also proved understandably sensitive on reporting about the details of enemy attacks, particularly attacks that succeeded in destroying or damaging their targets, so as not to give Iraqi forces or insurgents valuable information. And there was a consciousness at the Pentagon of the impact of reporting on public opinion that drove some restrictions, such as photographs of damaged or destroyed US military vehicles or of coffins of US war dead returning to the United States.[18]

Generally, policy restrictions on media lost out to the pressure of information. The army could try to control or limit the release of a photo of a damaged tank, for example, to prevent the enemy from learning the points of vulnerability on a tank's armor. But there was no way to stop the avalanche of video and photographic information flowing from Iraq, whether from media cameras, civilian cell phone images, insurgent reports posted online, or video clips exchanged via email between US soldiers.

The restrictions placed on embedded reporters in the field due to operational security, however, contrast with the information-gathering and source-building opportunities that go along with spending extended periods forward-deployed with the troops. As a reporter covering the first two years of the Iraq War, the author reported on developments from a desk in Washington, DC, during the invasion phase, combining field dispatches with whatever could be squeezed out of officials at the Pentagon and the White House who often had their own struggles collecting good information about what was going on in Iraq. The circumstances for reporters in Iraq were markedly different—provided they had the time and freedom to get out of Baghdad and visit forward-operating bases. In early 2005, when the war was transitioning from a relative lull to the most violent phase of the insurgency, the author had the opportunity to deploy with troops and was amazed at how much more freely information flowed at combat outposts and in convoys. There the exchange of sensitive information did not depend on carefully cultivated sources and long-standing relationships of trust but on proximity to the action. Troops going through the day-to-day business of fighting an insurgent war are too busy coping with the threats coming at them every day to bother thinking up phony stories or spin to tell reporters.

Regional Reporters

The fourth group of US national security correspondents—those based at regional news organizations in areas with heavy military representation—can be a vitally important source of news and quite often beat Washington journalists to important developing stories. Gregory Vistica, reporting for the *San Diego Union-Tribune*, uncovered the US Navy "Tailhook" scandal in the 1990s, and the *Birmingham News* broke many of the important Gulf War syndrome stories in the 1990s, to name just two examples. Local and regional journalists also have been instrumental in telling the stories of veterans returning from the long wars in Iraq and Afghanistan, dealing with debilitating injuries, issues of suicide and post-traumatic stress, difficulty finding work, and challenges reintegrating with family and civilian life.

What's not captured in any of these four tribes is the new feature of self-anointed "whistleblowers" that disclose classified information, either by posting it themselves on a variety of websites or by offering their information to mainstream media in order to guarantee broader distribution as well as greater national and international attention to it. In this new social media environment, the mainstream press tribes are placed less in the role of developing trusted sources as they are competing for offering the best platform for "insider" leakers to get their stories out. This poses a challenge to traditional media outlets, which like to develop sources and also to hold themselves out as more responsible in their use and release of government secrets, compared to the new class of Internet media outlets. As will be described later, the advent of Julian Assange's WikiLeaks, along with the massive disclosures of army private Manning and NSA contractor Edward Snowden, has not only altered the media–national security dynamic but also shifted the way the traditional media is operating.

THE MEDIA CULTURE AND MYTHS OF ANONYMITY

The non-journalist is sometimes overly impressed by the aura of anonymity that often surrounds media stories. The concept of an unnamed source brings to mind Woodward and Bernstein and their Deep Throat source meeting via potted geranium signal in a downtown Washington parking garage. Without question, important stories burst on the scene on occasion as a result of courageous risk taking by a source or, as some would undoubtedly view it, reckless disregard for national security. Far more often, however, the reasons for anonymity are prosaic rather than profound. Perhaps the most common explanation stems from a combination of haste and a preference for the somewhat more frank information that can be conveyed on background as compared to the polished, not to say canned, rhetoric that would flow from an on-the-record statement. A reporter speaking to a mid-level officer or civilian in a military or intelligence public affairs office might call wanting to know the agency's view on a congressional report, a think-tank study, a piece of pending legislation, or a remark made that day on the Senate floor. Given enough time, an on-the-record answer could be obtainable. In that case the staffer taking the call would have to take the question up the chain of command, probably propose an answer, and get the most readily available principal figure to sign off on having his or her name attached to the statement. Depending on the subject matter, such a process could take anywhere from a few hours to days. Far better, then, journalists usually conclude, to get the information on background and get it out on the wire, or into the paper, or on the air, and spare a lot of waiting around. The source agency might prefer it that way as well—the better to get a more pointed response in circulation without having to stand by it in case it provoked a harsh reaction. Of course, this method has two major faults: It enables the bureaucracy to disavow the content of the on-background response if, for some reason, changing circumstances or political miscalculation make it no longer the appropriate answer. This method forfeits the opportunity to hold the agency accountable later on for its position. The other, far more important fault is that readers, viewers, or listeners are deprived of the elemental ability of being able to, as the saying goes, consider the source.[19]

Reporters often prefer keeping sources anonymous to prevent other reporters from knowing who is talking. Perhaps journalists like to think they build sources by dogged hard work, painstaking development of relationships of trust—and perhaps sometimes they do. But quite often journalists build sources by paying attention to who is being quoted by competing media outlets and calling up the same people. This is one of the main reasons why it often seems that the same names keep cropping up as talking heads on cable television or in daily coverage of a long-running story such as a presidential campaign. To prevent this kind of source creep, journalists will try to horde their sources by keeping them anonymous for as long as possible.

In recent years media organizations, in the wake of newsroom scandals involving journalistic fabricators and in response to increasingly strident reader objections, have instituted policies strictly limiting the use of anonymous sources.[20] Because the national security arena remains the place in American journalism where anonymity continues—of necessity—in frequent use, journalists and sources have developed new methods for getting on-the-record material into circulation. One method is for a reporter to conduct an interview on background, pull together the story, select those quotes from the interview that seem most useful, and then run the quotes by the source for permission to use those selected remarks on the record.

As an alternative to veiled sourcing, this method may be preferable. But it has problems as well. One problem with this approach relates to the issue of special treatment for people of high rank. When reporters run to cover a fire or a flood, or to interview the neighbors of a person who has suddenly become notorious, the people the reporter questions do not get the benefit of a later callback or email from the reporter seeking permission to use selected quotes. The reporter gets a name and runs to file. The kind of special treatment involved in allowing a source to review quotes before they go to press is a privilege offered only to those of high rank who are able to negotiate this special treatment by holding out the threat of providing the reporter with nothing. This, it seems to the author, is a serious concession by the journalist.

Digital journalism—blogs—is potentially changing the landscape and beat. The *Huffington Post*, the *Drudge Report*, *Slate*, *Salon*, the *Daily Beast*, *The Dish*, *Politico*, *The Intercept*, *BuzzFeed*, and *ProPublica*, just to mention a few, are poaching journalists, creating new media stars, and creating a new incentive to bring news to the marketplace. One effect is the fragmentation of the audience as readers turn to the blogs of interest for specialized information, the way lawyers in national security do for *Lawfare* or *Just Security*. There is an emerging market for this specialized information; *BuzzFeed*, for example, claimed its revenues in 2014 surpassed $100 million.[21]

How this will affect the historic institutions of the media remains to be seen, as both the *Washington Post* and *New York Times*, for example, played important roles in the defining media events concerning national security disclosures. The past decade of major national security media events, however, has focused less on anonymity and more on the sensational release of actual classified documents by so-called insiders who have personal reasons to become a focus of media attention. They have declared themselves to be "whistleblowers" aimed at uncovering alleged government wrongdoing. In some cases they claim they have tried more traditional channels of dissent, or they simply believe the US government will not alter its policies without exposure of its secret activities.[22]

THE MEDIA–NATIONAL SECURITY ENVIRONMENT

Reporting on the national security enterprise occurs within a particular media environment. What is apparent in the post-9/11 world is that several changes have made the government's ability to keep secrets more difficult. At the same time, however, the government has responded with what appears to the press to be an all-out campaign to punish not only those who "leak" but those who publish those leaks. This has led to a far more adversarial relationship between the press and the American government, largely because of the changed nature of the information environment in which we now operate. On the one hand, the twenty-first century is now driven, if not dominated, by the expanding scale and speed of information creation, management, and retrieval. On the other hand, the US government's "need to share" principle in the post-9/11 world has expanded the number of people with access to sensitive information—in effect breaking down the long-standing "need to know" practice of compartmentation—resulting in the government's growing vulnerability to the "insider" threat.[23]

WikiLeaks: When Is Information Really Sensitive?

The difference between news and sensitive information came into sharp relief in July 2010 with the online posting of some 92,000 classified US government documents relating to the war in Afghanistan. The website WikiLeaks obtained and posted the documents but allowed three media organizations—the *New York Times*, the British newspaper the *Guardian*, and the German magazine *Der Spiegel*—advance access to the material so they could analyze and put into context, not to mention confirm as legitimate, the material. A consensus emerged quickly that the documents, despite their volume, did not convey much about the war that was not already generally known. Although commentators drew many a comparison to the leak of the Pentagon Papers in 1971, there was a key difference in that the WikiLeaks material tended to confirm that the Obama administration had been telling the truth about the war, or at least not hiding it, while the Pentagon Papers pointed up the false optimism that attended the US effort in Vietnam and especially the Johnson administration's systematic concealment of the war's aims, strategy, and cost.

Despite the absence of startling news content in so large a volume of material, the Obama administration was at pains to point out that the documents' public disclosure represented a serious breach of national security. Claims by WikiLeaks founder Julian Assange to the contrary, the Pentagon maintained that the material posted online had not been fully scrubbed of references to sensitive sources inside Afghanistan who were risking their lives by cooperating with US and allied forces. Adm. Michael Mullen, in a Pentagon briefing, had the most vivid comment:

> Mr. Assange can say whatever he likes about the greater good he and his source are doing, but the truth is they might already have on their hands the blood of some young soldier or that of an Afghan family. Disagree with the war all you want, take issue with the policy, challenge me or our ground commanders on the decisions we make to accomplish the mission we've been given, but don't put those who willingly go into harm's way even further in harm's way just to satisfy your need to make a point.[24]

The message was clear: The reading public in the United States might not be poring over the memos, cables, and field reports, bereft as they were of new perspectives on America's longest war, but the enemy was, and in great detail. Publication of such details as the home village and occupation of an otherwise unnamed source was as good as putting the source's name up in lights, the Pentagon maintained. Not only did it jeopardize the life of a source, as if that were not enough; it also made it much more difficult for the Pentagon and other US intelligence branches to recruit sources.

Although some regarded the WikiLeaks case as an example of the future of media, with new online sources working in coordination with mainstream media, *New York Times* executive editor Bill Keller told NPR that he regarded WikiLeaks not as a collaborating news organization but as a source. The only difference was that in the past sources leaked to the press and the press had exclusive control over what was made public; today's online culture enabled individuals to self-publish.[25] WikiLeaks had no control over how the *Times* handled the material, nor did the *Times* have any say over what WikiLeaks decided to post. The *Times* went to lengths to contrast its handling of the classified documents with WikiLeaks' handling, noting that it consulted at length with multiple US government agencies, including the Pentagon, over what could be safely published. WikiLeaks withheld some 15,000 documents but did not directly engage with the Pentagon over publication.[26]

The episode points up an emerging problem that goes along with the new media forms available in the online world. More and more information can now be related without any filter to readers and viewers. While this sometimes, perhaps most times, brings with it benefits of getting more material out to a wider audience, it can short-circuit the journalist's role of assessing, weighing, reviewing, and contextualizing material before publishing or broadcasting it. However one may want to praise full, rather than filtered, availability of information, the practical reality is that very few Americans are going to sit down and plow through 92,000 documents, but many will hear about the story through the filter of brief—sometimes extremely brief—media reports. To be sure, critics in the national security community are hardly satisfied with the job the mainstream media does at filtering. At about the same time as the WikiLeaks controversy, the *Washington Post* published an extensive series on the vast expansion of the US intelligence community since the September 11, 2001, terrorist attacks. Both in print and, in greater detail, online, the *Post* showed how, largely outside public view, an immense network of public and private contractor organizations had sprung up around Washington and across the country doing intelligence work wholly outside public scrutiny. As did the *Times* in the WikiLeaks case, the *Post* consulted extensively with the US government over what to publish and what to withhold. Still, there were complaints that some of the material amounted to a road map to potential terrorists who might wish to attack or attempt to penetrate US intelligence installations.[27]

The problem the Pentagon encountered in the WikiLeaks episode was not entirely the result of an online organization with no compunction about publishing classified material nor of an insider source (a twenty-two-year-old private convicted of leaking and now serving a long prison term) seeking to expose government secrets.[28] Indeed, the WikiLeaks story and the *Post* series on the intelligence community had a connection beyond the publication of sensitive information. Because, as then–defense secretary Robert Gates acknowledged, the extensive detail in the 92,000 documents on the war in Afghanistan and their wide distribution (and with it the increased risk of a leak) stemmed from a lesson learned in the Persian Gulf War and reinforced in the wake of the 9/11 attacks. The lesson was that intelligence needed to be shared and, in the case of military intelligence, needed to be pushed forward to the warfighter and given the widest distribution possible.

Said Gates,

> The interesting thing is, and it really was one of the lessons learned from the first Gulf War in 1991, was how little useful intelligence information was being received by battalion and company commanders in the field. And so there has been an effort over the last 15 or so years in the military, and I would say really accelerated during the wars in Iraq and Afghanistan, to push as much information as far forward as possible, which means putting it in a secret channel that almost everybody has access to in uniform.

The publication of the war documents not only exposed past communications, some of them containing sensitive information; it also carried the risk of denying war-fighters future communications. Because, as a result of the leak, Gates said, the high command was "going to have to look at . . . should we change the way we approach that, or do we continue to take the risk?"[29]

Bowman H. Miller, a former senior State Department intelligence officer, took the argument further, arguing that the leak would have a chilling effect on reporting by US diplomats and intelligence officers overseas. They would now be inclined to hold back their more frank assessments in dispatches to headquarters for fear the words would emerge in public, complicating relations with other countries. Miller suggested that WikiLeaks stemmed in part from an overreaction to the main conclusion of the 9/11 investigations, namely, that a failure to share intelligence across agencies had been a key factor in the failure to detect the terrorist plot. The post-9/11 solution was to make much more intelligence easily available to more individuals with security clearances; however, this ran the risk not only of leaks but of massive leaks. WikiLeaks, Miller wrote, was "an aberrant manifestation of transparency advocacy" resulting from well-intentioned reforms that followed the 9/11 attacks.[30]

NSA REVELATIONS: MEDIA AS POLICY CHANGE AGENT

The simplest process by which media coverage can play a role in shaping governmental decision making is one in which coverage draws attention to a hitherto overlooked issue; the outrage or shock or interest generated by the coverage then spawns political action. This impulse to appear responsive to a problem raised by media attention can stem from a sincere desire to address the problem or from a cynical play on the part of elected officials to draw media attention to themselves. A familiar sequence of events ensues: enterprising journalism draws public attention to an issue; public attention spurs political action to address that issue; resulting reform efforts help generate a journalism award. A journalist can often claim his or her reporting led to a special commission investigation, the passage or reconsideration of legislation, or a presidential decision to alter current policies. In the case of Edward Snowden's release of NSA classified information, all three occurred.

On June 5, 2013, Britain's *Guardian* newspaper published a story on a top secret US court order requiring the telephone giant Verizon to provide the US National Security Agency with vast quantities of telephone calling data on the communications activities of millions of US customers and to continue doing so daily for a period covering just over three months. "The document shows for the first time that under the Obama administration, communication records of millions of US citizens are being collected indiscriminately and in bulk—regardless of whether they are suspected of any wrongdoing," the newspaper reported.[31]

For followers of news coverage about US national security, two things were startling about the *Guardian* report: first, the classified document it cited was less than two months old; second, the document itself was reproduced in the article. The newspaper wasn't just writing about a secret decision, it wasn't relating the contents of a secret document according to a description of the document by someone who had seen it, nor was it reporting on the contents of a document it had been allowed to read but not keep. In this case, the newspaper had the underlying document in its possession.[32]

The next day the *Washington Post* revealed the existence of a top secret US and British program, code-named Prism, used for the bulk extraction of audio and video chats, photographs, emails, documents, and connection logs from Internet-based communications traffic involving foreign parties. The article explained that NSA accessed the foreign communications data in cases when foreign-to-foreign Internet contacts passed through servers based in the United States. As with the *Guardian* article a day earlier, the *Post* story not only discussed but actually disclosed top secret documents that had been produced recently, in this instance, top secret NSA briefing slides dated April 2013.[33] According to the article, the Prism program, though unknown to the public until the *Post* disclosed it, traced its origins to an earlier major media coup involving reporting on highly classified information. Prism, the *Post* reported, "was launched from the ashes of President George W. Bush's secret program of warrantless domestic surveillance in 2007, after news media disclosures, lawsuits, and the Foreign Intelligence Surveillance Court forced the president to look for new authority."[34]

The *Post* and *Guardian* stories delivered considerably extra punch because, as they pointed out, the secret programs being disclosed appeared to completely undermine repeated official assurances that the private communications of US citizens were *not* the subject of bulk collection of communications metadata by the NSA. On March 20, 2012, for example, just over a year before the Snowden story broke, Gen. Keith Alexander, director of the NSA, was asked directly in a House subcommittee hearing if the NSA had the capability to sift through the emails of US citizens looking for individuals criticizing former vice president Dick Cheney. "NSA does not have the ability to do that in the United States," Alexander said. "No no, we don't have the technical insights in the United States. In other words, you have to have something to intercept or some way of doing that either by going to a service provider with a warrant or you have to be collecting in that area. We're not authorized to do that nor do we have the equipment in the United States to collect that kind of information."[35]

A year later, in an even higher-profile statement in March 2013—in other words, at about the same time that the NSA was producing the top secret briefing slides shortly to be revealed by Snowden—James Clapper, the director of national intelligence (DNI), was questioned in open session by Senator Ron Wyden (D-OR). Wyden, who, as a member of the Senate Select Committee on Intelligence, had already been briefed in classified settings on NSA surveillance programs, asked Clapper, "Does the NSA collect any type of data at all on millions or hundreds of millions of Americans?" Clearly uncomfortable discussing the topic in open session, Clapper, rubbing his forehead and looking down, replied, "No, sir." Wyden, looking quite surprised, pressed, "It does not?" "Not wittingly," Clapper continued. "There are cases where they could, inadvertently perhaps, collect, but not wittingly."[36]

General Clapper could not have known it at the time, but his attempt to protect the secrecy of a sensitive program would have precisely the opposite effect. In January 2014, in his first broadcast interview after he had disclosed the NSA secrets the previous spring, Snowden told German television that the "breaking point" in his decision to leak the surveillance files came when he heard Clapper denying the existence of bulk collection in response to Wyden's question:

> There's no saving an intelligence agency that believes it can lie to the public, and the legislators who need to be able to trust it and regulate its actions. Seeing that really meant for me there was no going back. Beyond that, it was the creeping realization that no one else was going to do this. The public had a right to know about these programs. The public had a right to know that which the government was doing in its name, and that which the government was doing against the public.[37]

After the leaks General Clapper acknowledged the evasiveness of his answer to Wyden, but President Obama defended him, saying the intelligence chief had been put in an impossible situation in which a refusal to respond in public would have been tantamount to confirming a highly classified program, something Clapper was not authorized to do.

Once the secrets were out, the administration, its hand forced by the Snowden disclosures, declassified the existence of the metadata program. But regardless of one's view of General Clapper's testimony, the important point, in terms of information security for US intelligence, is that a wide gap, or perceived gap, between the public statements of an administration and the internal programs, decisions, and deliberations of that administration can be a significant factor in motivating insiders to disclose secrets.

While many people viewed the Snowden revelations as a continuation of a pattern established in the WikiLeaks case, the reproduction of top secret documents in the *Guardian* and *Post* articles was highly unusual (the WikiLeaks documents were classified at lower "secret" or "confidential" levels). Media reports citing classified information are fairly common in Washington; disclosure of classified documents—especially at the top secret level—is exceedingly rare. The Snowden material marked the first time since the Pentagon Papers story broke in 1971 that a comprehensive collection of documents still classified top secret had been published in news media.[38] And Snowden's secrets were in some cases no more than a few months old, whereas the Pentagon Papers were leaked during the Nixon presidency but compiled during the Johnson administration and consisted of a secret history of US involvement in Vietnam going back decades. There had been a few leaks of small quantities of top secret documents—notably some twenty-three confidential, secret, and top secret documents published in the appendix of a book by *Washington Times* reporter Bill Gertz, some less than a year old. But most of the Gertz material concerned North Korea and contained nothing that other news organizations considered particularly explosive.[39]

The impact of the Snowden affair was almost immediate. A few weeks following the first reports, Congress reacted. Senator Wyden, a longtime critic of NSA's surveillance programs, joined with twenty-five other senators (in all, twenty-one Democrats, four Republicans, and one Independent) in writing to DNI Clapper that bulk collection of calling data, even without the content, represents a significant intrusion into Americans' privacy. "These records can reveal personal relationships, family medical issues, political and religious affiliations, and a variety of other private, personal information," the lawmakers wrote.[40]

The publication of the Snowden documents also forced the president to act. He ordered increased judicial oversight over the surveillance program and convened a presidential commission to examine the issue of NSA surveillance and propose any changes that might be needed. As of this writing, the US Court of Appeals for the Second Circuit has also ruled that the NSA bulk collection of Americans' domestic phone records is illegal, coming just at a time when Congress was on the verge of replacing the "overreach" contained in the USA PATRIOT Act with new legislation that would prevent such programs and require that NSA seek warrants to gain access to such records held by US companies.[41]

In reviewing the relative impact on intelligence community activity that the judicial branch, Congress, and the media have had on this issue, at least one legal expert concluded that the media has been by far the most effective check on executive power in the domestic intelligence arena. Until recently, to some the federal courts have proved to be too compliant to government requests for permission to collect against domestic intelligence targets; Congress is hampered by its total reliance on the intelligence community for information about what it does and is constrained from discussing much if any of that information in public. At times the media has exercised perhaps too much power, this expert writes, noting that once a media organization obtains a top secret document, decisions about what can safely be disclosed to the public migrate from an elected government to a private company.[42] But overall, media disclosure of NSA surveillance has been a powerful catalyst for debate and a definite move toward a more carefully monitored intelligence collection effort.

President Obama may have indirectly acknowledged the media's impact via the Snowden revelations when he told the press, "I think we're getting better at it. I think we're striking the balance better." The bottom-line issue was public confidence—confidence the government was doing all it could to protect the homeland but with the assurance "that our governments are not going around phishing into whatever text you might be sending on your smartphone." Public fears of Big Brother, the president said, were exaggerated and overlooked extensive safeguards put in place to protect privacy. Still, Obama acknowledged, "There are times where law enforcement and those of us whose job it is to protect the public aren't thinking about those problems because we're trying to track and prevent a particular terrorist threat from happening. And it's useful to have civil libertarians and others tapping us on the shoulder in the midst of this process and reminding us that there are values at stake as well." This, presumably, in the president's view, was one of those times.[43]

With the rise of Daesh and the resurgence of terrorist attacks on the West, the debate over security versus privacy, or secrecy versus a free press, seems unlikely to resolve itself any time soon. On Friday, November 13, 2015, Daesh launched a coordinated, simultaneous attack on several targets in Paris—a soccer stadium, cafés and restaurants, and a crowded concert hall. The attacks left at least 129 dead and hundreds wounded, in the most lethal attack on French soil since World War II. The same media outlets that had been asking whether intrusive US intelligence collection violated privacy rights were now asking how a complicated terrorist plot went undetected by Western intelligence and law enforcement. French law gave police considerable leeway to penetrate terrorist cells, and a number of the participants in the assault were already on terrorist watch lists. NSA, meanwhile, was unconstrained in its ability to collect intelligence against targets on foreign soil, so the debate over bulk data collection against American citizens was inapplicable to the terrorist threat in Europe and elsewhere. Still, the plot remained undetected. Days later, CIA director John Brennan, speaking to an audience at the Center for Strategic and International Studies in Washington, suggested that media leaks had helped terrorists learn how to keep their plans from being discovered:

> There has been a significant increase in the operational security of a number of these operatives and terrorist networks as they have gone to school on what it is they need to do in order to keep their activities concealed from the authorities. In the past several years, because of a number of unauthorized disclosures and a lot of hand-wringing over the government's role in the effort to try to uncover these terrorists, there have been some policy and legal and other actions taken that make our ability collectively to find these terrorists much more challenging.[44]

Public appearances by senior national security officials must be cleared by the White House, and it is unlikely that Brennan's comments, which were bound to draw media attention, had not been prescreened by Obama's staff. At any rate the president did not distance himself from what Brennan said.

Civil libertarians were not accepting Brennan's interpretation of events. "As far as I know, there's no evidence the French lacked some kind of surveillance authority that would have made a difference," said Jameel Jaffer, deputy legal director of the American Civil Liberties Union. "When we've invested new powers in the government in response to events like the Paris attacks, they have often been abused."[45] Clearly, the debate is cyclical, and the cycles oscillate depending on events and media coverage of those events. The cycle shows no sign of stopping.

MEDIA AS ADVERSARY:
GOVERNMENT LEAKS INVESTIGATIONS

During the Obama administration more journalists and alleged leakers have been investigated in connection with leak cases than in all previous administrations combined (see table 17.1). The Obama administration, as of early 2015, had filed criminal charges under the 1917 Espionage Act in eight media leak investigations; in all previous administrations combined, there had been three such cases.[46] A number of factors contributed to this policy shift. While candidate Obama seemed skeptical of the national security establishment and supportive of an open press, President Obama said he came to see the value of aggressive counterterrorism intelligence collection and the damage done by leaks. In 2009 the intelligence community complained to the new administration that it had referred 153 national security leaks in crime reports to the Justice Department, only 24 were investigated by the FBI, and none of those investigations had led to a prosecution.

The Obama administration's legal efforts to thwart or discourage leaks of classified information, it is important to note, predated the Snowden disclosures. If the stepped-up prosecutions were intended to deter disclosure of classified information, Snowden's actions rendered that strategy a resounding failure. But a closer look reveals that the tension in at least two of these cases was not primarily between the administration and the media but between the intelligence community and the White House, with some partisan presidential politics thrown in for good measure. In May 2012, just over a year before the Snowden leaks, the Associated Press reported that the CIA had thwarted a second al-Qaeda attempt to down a US airliner with an underwear bomb.[47] The next month, the *New York Times* reported on a secret operation ordered by President Obama to disrupt the computer systems related to Iran's suspected nuclear weapons program. The Iran story cited, among other anonymous sources, "members of the President's national security team." The Associated Press dispatch cited "U.S. officials who were briefed on the program."[48] Republicans charged the White House with leaking classified information for the sake of burnishing the president's tough-on-terrorism image. The CIA, then headed by retired army general David Petraeus, filed criminal referrals with the Justice Department in response to the leaks. In response then–attorney general Eric Holder appointed two US attorneys to lead separate investigations. Opinion varied on whether the administration was making good on the president's "zero tolerance" policy on classified leaks, trying to have it both ways—by leaking favorable material and then appearing to get tough on leaks—or merely carrying over a number of investigations that had begun under the previous administration.[49] The CIA's motivations in filing criminal referrals were not at all ambiguous, nor was there anything symbolic about the investigations and prosecutions that followed.

The reporting about the cyber attack on Iran's nuclear systems led to two prosecutions. In May 2015 CIA intelligence officer Jeffrey Sterling was found guilty of providing the *New York Times* with information on the operation.[50] In October 2016 retired US Marine Corps general James E. Cartwright, former vice chairman of the Joint Chiefs of Staff and a confidant of President Obama's, pleaded guilty to making false statements to the FBI in connection with the investigation into the leaks.[51] Shortly after Petraeus instigated the Iran leak probe in 2012, he found himself swept up in a leak prosecution stemming from his sharing of classi-

Table 17.1. Key Media Leak Cases

Leaker	Government Claims	Date	Outcome
Shamai K. Leibowitz, FBI linguist[a]	Leibowitz leaked classified information about Israel to an unknown blogger. The court records say the documents concerned "communication intelligence activities."	May 25, 2010	Leibowitz pleaded guilty and was sentenced to twenty months in prison for a violation of the 1917 Espionage Act.
Thomas Drake, senior executive at NSA[b]	Drake intentionally logged into a system called NSANet, obtained official NSA information, and provided it orally and in writing to Siobhan Gorman, a reporter for the *Baltimore Sun*.	June 10, 2011	Drake pleaded guilty to exceeding authorized use of a computer, a misdemeanor, and the government dropped the ten felony counts under the Espionage Act.
John Kiriakou, CIA officer[c]	Kiriakou discussed a covert CIA agent with Matthew Cole, who, in turn, discussed the agent with a researcher for defense lawyers for al-Qaeda suspects detained at Guantanamo Bay.	October 23, 2012	Kiriakou pleaded guilty to violating the Intelligence Identities Protection Act and was sentenced to thirty months in prison.
Chelsea Manning, army intelligence analyst[d]	Manning, while in Baghdad, downloaded a colossal amount of classified information and gave it to the antisecrecy group WikiLeaks. News media outlets throughout the world published stories based on the documents obtained through WikiLeaks. This is the most voluminous leak of classified documents in US history, as the amount of information leaked by Edward Snowden is still not known.	August 21, 2013	Manning was eventually charged in a military court with twenty-two offenses, including violations of the Espionage Act, and pleaded guilty in February 2013 to ten of the lesser charges of accessing and communicating classified information. Manning was convicted by a military judge in July 2013 and sentenced to thirty-five years in prison. Manning was acquitted on aiding the enemy.

Leaker	Government Claims	Date	Outcome
Donald J. Sachtleben, FBI contractor and former FBI bomb technician[e]	Sachtleben was charged with disclosing national defense information relating to a disrupted terrorist plot on a US-bound airliner to a news organization not entitled to receive it.	November 14, 2013	He was sentenced to 140 months (11 years, 8 months) in federal prison after he plead guilty to possessing and distributing child pornography, as well as unlawfully disclosing national defense information relating to a disrupted terrorist plot.
Stephen Jin-Woo Kim, State Department contract analyst[f]	Kim was charged for sharing classified information from an intelligence report on North Korea with reporter James Rosen, Fox's chief Washington correspondent.	April 2, 2014	Kim entered a guilty plea and was sentenced to thirteen months in prison.
Jeffrey Sterling, CIA intelligence officer[g]	Sterling was charged with espionage for providing *New York Times* reporter James Risen with extensive information about a failed CIA effort to sabotage Iran's nuclear program.	May 11, 2015	Sterling was found guilty and sentenced to three and a half years in prison.

[a] Maria Glod, "Former FBI Employee Sentenced for Leaking Classified Papers," *Washington Post*, May 25, 2010, www.washingtonpost.com/wp-dyn/content/article/2010/05/24/AR2010052403795.html.

[b] Douglas Birch and Pete Yost, "Thomas Drake Gets Plea Deal in NSA Classified Leaks Case," *Huffington Post*, July 9, 2011, www.huffingtonpost.com/2011/06/09/thomas-drake-nsa-whistleblower_n_873740.html.

[c] Charlie Savage, "Former C.I.A. Operative Pleads Guilty in Leak of Colleague's Name," *New York Times*, October 23, 2012, www.nytimes.com/2012/10/24/us/former-cia-officer-pleads-guilty-in-leak-case.html.

[d] Julie Tate, "Bradley Manning Sentenced to 35 Years in WikiLeaks Case," *Washington Post*, August 21, 2013, www.washingtonpost.com/world/national-security/judge-to-sentence-bradley-manning-today/2013/08/20/85bee184-09d0-11e3-b87c-476db8ac34cd_story.html.

[e] Department of Justice, "Former Federal Contractor Petitions to Plead Guilty to Unlawfully Disclosing National Defense Information and to Distributing Child Pornography," press release, September 23, 2013.

[f] Ann E. Marimow, "Ex-State Department Adviser Stephen J. Kim Sentenced to 13 Months in Leak Case," *Washington Post*, April 2, 2014, www.washingtonpost.com/world/national-security/ex-state-dept-adviser-stephen-j-kim-sentenced-to-13-months-in-leak-case/2014/04/02/f877be54-b9dd-11e3-96ae-f2c36d2b1245_story.html.

[g] Matt Apuzzo, "Ex-C.I.A. Officer Sentenced in Leak Case Tied to Times Reporter," *New York Times*, May, 11, 2015, www.nytimes.com/2015/05/12/us/ex-cia-officer-sentenced-in-leak-case-tied-to-times-reporter.html?_r=0.

fied information with a woman who was his biographer and his mistress, a scandal that cost the revered former army general his CIA post. In April 2015, a month before the conclusion of the Sterling case, Petraeus pleaded guilty to a misdemeanor charge of mishandling classified information.[52] The plea deal drew criticism from some quarters that Petraeus was being treated more leniently than lower-ranking leakers. But whatever the political undercurrents of the Cartwright and Petraeus cases, the message was unmistakable: neither superstar military status nor a close relationship with the president would spare an official from leak prosecution if the evidence was there.

As the investigation, indictment, and prosecution count has climbed in leaker cases, Columbia Law School professor David E. Pozen has tried to inject some perspective into the debate, pointing out in an extensive study published by the *Harvard Law Review* that the number of recent leak prosecutions, though unprecedented, is "still statistically meager." Obama may have countenanced investigations of highly respected figures and former top advisors such as Petraeus and Cartwright not as part of an aggressive antileak campaign run out of the Oval Office but as a result of a hands-off attitude in which the president has allowed the Justice Department to pursue leaks even when the investigations focus on his own senior aides. Even in the Snowden era, Pozen argues, leaks, even unauthorized ones, serve a purpose that senior policymakers understand but are reluctant to articulate.

The status quo, although ritualistically condemned by those in power, has served a wide variety of governmental ends at the same time as it has efficiently kept most disclosures within tolerable bounds. The leak laws are so rarely enforced not only because it is difficult to punish violators but also because key institutional players share overlapping interests in vilifying leakers while maintaining a permissive culture of classified information disclosures.[53]

Increasingly, the political fallout from these events seemed to be coming from all directions. Republicans accused the president of leaking secrets to enhance his image. Confronted with that charge, Obama oversaw the most aggressive legal effort to investigate and prosecute media leaks in US history. Critics of the torture policy were asking why the Justice Department was pursuing mid-level career intelligence officers for leaks while taking no action against the senior officials and former officials who had authorized torture. Defenders of enhanced interrogation techniques were accusing Democrats of releasing secrets about interrogation methods for a partisan attack on the previous (Republican) administration. Navy SEALs were complaining about White House leaks containing details on the bin Laden raid only to see some of their own comrades come under investigation for the same offense. And journalists were saying that the antileak investigations were creating a chilling effect that was preventing them from doing their jobs even as publication of stories based on leaks of sensitive information continued unabated.

One unexpected consequence of the revelations, as noted in a 2014 Human Rights Watch report, was that NSA metadata collection made it extremely difficult for would-be government whistleblowers to communicate with journalists:

> An increase in the frequency of leak prosecutions, as well as the government's implementations of programs—such as the Insider Threat Program—aimed at discouraging officials from sharing information outside the government, have raised the stakes for officials who might consider even talking to journalists. Large-scale surveillance dramatically exacerbates those concerns by largely cutting away at the ability of government officials to remain anonymous in their interactions with the press, as any

interaction—any email, any phone call—risks leaving a digital trace that could subsequently be used against them.[54]

Human Rights Watch interviewed forty-six journalists who cover national security issues and found that most detected a sharp drop-off in the willingness of sources to provide information. Even long-established and trusted source–reporter relationships were drying up. The report cited no direct proof that metadata collection was being used to expose leakers, but the digital trails left by phone calls and emails, and the awareness on the part of reporters and their sources of the government's power to access those trails, all combined with the aggressive posture toward prosecuting leakers, had made the day-to-day job of reporting on national security issues much more difficult. If this "chilling effect" on coverage of national security issues was real, then–White House press secretary Jay Carney, for one, wanted to know why so much classified information continued to show up in the press.[55] Not everyone on the government side of the debate was unhappy to learn about this supposed chilling effect. "Leaking is against the law," Robert Deitz, who served as NSA general counsel from 1998 to 2006, told Human Rights Watch. As for the chilling effect, he said, "Good! I want criminals to be deterred."[56]

In the wake of the WikiLeaks disclosures, the Obama administration in October 2011 implemented a new Insider Threat Program to be implemented by the National Insider Threat Task Force. Although the executive order did not explicitly mention the news media or leaks, it was widely understood as part of a broader administration effort to safeguard classified information from unauthorized disclosure.[57] Journalists, meanwhile, were also taking defensive measures, increasingly resorting to in-person meetings reminiscent of the parking garage meetings of Watergate fame and to surveillance-resistant technology such as air-gapped computers, throwaway mobile phones, and encryption devices. Tools such as SecureDrop were increasingly used by journalists to receive sensitive documents from sources who wished to remain anonymous. How effective such technology could be against the formidable surveillance, collection, and decryption systems used by NSA is a matter of speculation. Suffice it to say that neither reporters nor their sources were behaving in ways that suggested they fully trusted these techniques.[58]

In 2016 WikiLeaks was back in the news in a way that suggested that chilling effects and anti-snooping software were no match for determined effort by a sophisticated intelligence agency to penetrate supposedly secure systems. This time the leaks concerned not classified national security information but gossipy insider email exchanges from members of Hillary Clinton's presidential campaign staff. From the national security point of view, the main concern was not the content of the leaked material but its source. The US intelligence community concluded that Russian intelligence, authorized by the highest levels of the Kremlin, had hacked into the Clinton campaign staffer and Democratic National Committee emails with the intent of making the material public through WikiLeaks to disrupt the US election process.[59]

These most recent disclosures suggest that the earlier WikiLeaks and Snowden cases represented a trend rather than rare breaches of mass classified information. Either way, the media is in a new era in which disclosure of large volumes of classified or confidential information has been matched by aggressive government efforts to staunch the flow of secrets. Journalists are alarmed about the government crackdown on leakers and about investigations and prosecutions focused on reporters. Americans appear more focused on intrusion into their lives, weighing the balance between security and liberty; whereas the media–government tension over leaks boils down to security versus a free press. As an example of this divide, a Pew Research

Center poll found that 54 percent of Americans disapprove of the government's bulk collection of telephone and Internet data as part of counterterrorism efforts; 74 percent said they should not have to give up privacy and freedom for the sake of security. A separate poll done around the same time by KRC Research for the American Civil Liberties Union, however, showed that 64 percent of Americans hold a negative opinion of Snowden.[60]

ETHICS, WAR, AND THE REPORTING PROFESSION

During the North Africa campaign in World War II, US commanders struggled with operational security issues created by American correspondents trying to outdo one another in getting a bead on where the next offensive or battle was likely to occur. Eventually, Gen. Dwight Eisenhower hit on an approach that worked better than he could have hoped. It served as a model for at least some press dealings in the European theater for the rest of the war. With the war correspondents speculating—increasingly accurately—that the next Allied move would be toward Sicily, Eisenhower decided to neutralize the security threat by bringing the journalists into the fold. One month before the invasion, American correspondents assigned to cover the US forces campaigning in North Africa were briefed on the broad outlines of the planned assault on Sicily. The correspondents got the briefing on the promise they would not publish anything about it until given the go-ahead by army press handlers. The idea was that reporters made privy to what was going on would cooperate in holding the information, while reporters kept on the outside would struggle constantly to break stories and would inevitably succeed. The results of this approach exceeded expectations. Not only did the speculative reporting about an assault on Sicily halt, the reporters actually policed one another, imposing an effective form of peer pressure on any correspondent in the inner circle who violated the bond of trust with the Allied high command.[61]

The episode adds some perspective to the later deterioration of relations between the military and the media, particularly during and after the Vietnam War. One offshoot of the deterioration is a hypothetical question journalists who cover the Pentagon are asked frequently by military officers, particularly junior and mid-level officers. The question goes like this: You, the correspondent, have managed to insert yourself into the confidence of an enemy insurgent force and are traveling with them as they go about planning attacks on US forces. You become aware that the insurgents, tomorrow, will mount what is sure to be a lethal attack on a US convoy moving through the area. You know where, when, and how the attack will unfold. Do you keep quiet and let the attack unfold or do you somehow try to get word back to US forces so they can evade or repel the attack?

To this reporter's knowledge, no scenario of this type involving an American journalist accompanying guerrilla fighters has ever occurred. This is an urban myth, a tale that has taken on real form through multiple retellings. Military worries along these lines trace their origins to an article in the *Atlantic Monthly* that described a conference involving former military officers and prominent journalists in which a hypothetical scenario of this sort was proposed. In the panel discussion CBS News correspondent Mike Wallace defended the proposition that the hypothetical reporter's response should be to report the ambush on the US forces "simply as another story."[62]

In this case the hypothetical question was not well thought through. A reporter running with the insurgents, once having been told about plans to mount an ambush on US forces, would not likely be allowed by Internet-savvy guerrillas to file a story about this impending attack. If the insurgents were remarkably clumsy, a reporter could, at great risk, try to sneak away and convey the information back to his or her domestic bureau to be broadcast or put on the wire or online. Such a reporter might well convey the information directly to a US military official hoping not only to save lives but to build goodwill that would help the reporter on future stories. Journalistic excursions with insurgents—in those rare instances in which they occur—usually take place under extremely tightly controlled circumstances. In the unlikely event that an attack set for the next day on soldiers of the same nationality as the journalist was disclosed to that journalist, the disclosure would almost certainly take place under strict controls—the reporter's communications equipment confiscated, the information kept sufficiently vague as to conceal the key details, and so forth.

The scenario depicts a reporter suddenly in a deeply uncomfortable situation upon realizing an attack on US forces is about to occur. Well, if you are covering the enemy, isn't that to be expected? The CNN reporters who found themselves in the middle of a US air attack on Baghdad at the outset of the Persian Gulf War never faced criticism for failing to notify the Pentagon that Iraqi antiaircraft guns were about to open fire on US warplanes; the Pentagon was perfectly aware of that fact and did not need CNN's warning; it could simply watch the action unfold on television like everyone else.

The reality is that in the wars in Iraq and Afghanistan, such access to frontline enemy insurgents has been virtually nonexistent. What little reporting has surfaced usually originates from foreign reporters or, far more likely, is produced and posted online by the insurgents or terrorists themselves. Reporting by US correspondents from within the enemy camp has tended to be confined to those much-celebrated instances like CNN reporting from Baghdad or cable news coverage of the first attacks on Baghdad in 2003.

The scenario laid out in this frequently asked question is thus highly unlikely, bordering on unheard of. Moreover, there was another element missing from the equation, namely, any recognition that if an American correspondent was able to spend a few weeks traveling with insurgents, the reporting would be of keen interest to US intelligence as a rare inside look at the operating methods of the enemy.

WHEN "NEGATIVE" NEWS DOES GOOD

Over the past several years, national security reporting has detailed delivery delays of armored vehicles to the combat theater in Iraq, squalid conditions at Walter Reed Army Medical Center for injured veterans, army investigations into prisoner abuses at Abu Ghraib, the CIA's extreme interrogation techniques at secret detention centers, and the secret and warrantless domestic surveillance program begun after the 9/11 attacks. These kinds of stories are often seen within national security organizations as negative in media terms. But like the old saying about it being an ill wind that blows no good, it is the rare story that has no upside, at least for someone. To the extent that critical stories about the army's sluggish response to the urgent need for body armor and more heavily armored vehicles accelerated the efforts by the Pentagon and industry to get better protective equipment into the field, then those stories benefited the troops in need. If a few generals and acquisition officers were embarrassed, so what? Within days, if not hours, of the *Washington Post*'s publication of the problems at Walter Reed, living conditions started to improve. What, precisely, is negative about that? The debate rages on about whether coverage of the Abu Ghraib abuses and the CIA's interrogation program harmed national security by serving as a recruiting tool for Islamic extremists. To Americans who actually care about what is being done around the world and at home in their name, the Abu Ghraib and secret CIA prison stories cleared the way to halting deeply objectionable policies.[63] In the case of the surveillance story, the disclosure opened the way to reining in what many viewed was an imperial executive branch—not to mention galvanizing the legislative branch into performing its oversight responsibilities—that had stepped far beyond legal and constitutional boundaries in the name of domestic security and the international war on terrorism.[64]

For purposes of better understanding what can drive or elevate a story, it would be well to examine briefly some of the characteristics of these stories. The Water Reed housing story was a classic media exposé. An enterprising reporter found the problem and reported on it at a time when, in official circles, the decrepit housing in which recuperating soldiers were living had been entirely overlooked. The Abu Ghraib story brought to light an ongoing internal investigation. That is to say, the government had already discovered the scandal and was investigating—but in secret—and the news media brought before the public what was going on, most especially the photographs of abusive treatment. The other major contribution of the Abu Ghraib coverage was in taking the story beyond the initial investigation and up the chain of command, bringing to light links as high as the White House to official backing for some harsh interrogation methods. The existence of secret detention centers exposed secret policy, as did the disclosure of warrantless domestic wiretapping as part of the larger war on terrorism. Both raised questions of legality, inviting greater court and congressional involvement to ensure that the American constitutional system was not being undermined on grounds of national security.

In addition to the simple power to expose and to draw public attention and sometimes condemnation of officials and policies, these stories illustrated the media's power to accelerate events. At Walter Reed top officials were fired and repair work began with stunning speed as a result of the news coverage, while the problem had languished, entirely ignored, before the media became involved. Abu Ghraib, and the complex issues surrounding secret detention, overseas prisons, and harsh interrogation techniques, showed the media's ability to spark immediate and intense public debate, whereas the actual machinery of government—investigation, legislation, court action, and elections—moved on a much slower time scale. The surveillance story is an interesting exception because the *New York Times* chose to hold the story for a year at the request of the Bush administration. In that case the *Times* moved with a deliberateness that mirrored that of government. Publication in the newspaper may ultimately have been driven not by a change in the fact set but by a simple matter of competitive advantage: James Risen, the reporter who broke the story, was also writing a soon-to-be-released book that, as a result of the *Times'* hold on its story, risked scooping the newspaper.[65]

CONCLUSION: REPORTERS ARE ACTORS, NOT JUST OBSERVERS

The foregoing discussion of the national security journalist's environment, culture, and dynamics suggests that more than anything else, a reporter is not just an observer but an action player in the national security enterprise. If one needed any proof of this, consider the experience this reporter had in the 1990s when covering the CIA and being asked to lecture to a National Defense University class of mid-career military officers and civilians involved in national security and intelligence matters. A CIA careerist from the Directorate of Operations—the clandestine service—taught this course. Imagine addressing a group that included many who regarded journalists with a mixture of horror and disdain: horror that the media sometimes published classified information and disdain that journalists had any notion of the

damage they might be causing. The talk tried to methodically walk the class through a journalist's day-to-day working life. As a beat reporter assigned to cover national security and
intelligence matters, source building was a key job requirement, and the key to source building lay in developing relationships of trust with people who could responsibly and accurately
share sensitive, though not necessarily classified, information. These sources were placing
their careers in the reporter's hands. If the story came out wrong or information was mishan-
dled, or if it was made too obvious who had provided the information, the consequences
could be dire—at the very least for the sources, and potentially for the country. Journalists
needed to know that their sources possessed access to the information; they, in turn, needed
to know that the journalist had the depth of background needed to understand and handle
the information appropriately.

Every word in the phrase "developing relationships of trust" is operative. "Developing,"
because valuable reporter–source relationships take time to build. They might get off to a
decent start by a reporter demonstrating that he was not just assigned to cover a defense or
intelligence story on a random Tuesday but was devoting all working hours to the national
security beat. The source might become familiar with the reporter's work by reading or hearing his reports, and might, in some cases, be able to test the reporter's handling of a complex
story with his own understanding of what had happened. "Relationship," because the best
sources work with a given reporter for months, even years, at a time. Officials in sensitive
positions do not share closely held information with reporters they do not know or will not
be seeing again. They do not leak to reporters who are parachuting in to cover a single crisis
(the McChrystal case being a notable exception). In a constructive reporter–source relationship, the reporter might get to know a source on an official trip or on a battle front—where
there is enough time to establish a rapport and discover common interests. "Trust," because
neither the reporter nor the source has a great deal of leverage over the other and because the
consequences of a miscommunication or betrayal are so severe.

At the end of the presentation, the professor, a career intelligence officer with years of
experience overseas in sensitive CIA assignments, said to the class, "Well, as you can see,
what Mr. Diamond does in his day-to-day work is remarkably similar to what we do in the
Directorate of Operations." And in a sense, the journalist is every much a part of the national
security enterprise as is the case officer, the diplomat, or the warrior, although his culture and
world are very different.

As often as not, the issue of the media's influence on national security could just as well be
described in terms of national security's influence on the media. Even in this era of bloggers
and online media, national security journalism is a source-intensive business in which the
desire for the scoop or exposé is at least somewhat tempered by the journalist's realization that
there will be other stories to write tomorrow, stories that may well require the same sources.

At certain times and in certain places, there is no small amount of hostility between the
media and military and national security decision makers. But we would probably do well to
assume that given the generally long-standing tenure of reporters who cover the military,
well-established relationships of trust are developed between source and reporter that are the
driving force behind the new information the media is able to bring to light.

Public criticism of the media in the WMD case underscores the point that whether or not
the media can be said to influence military and national security affairs, there is a widespread
belief that this is so. That belief, then, becomes the dynamic that drives the cycle of reporting,
leaking, reacting, and re-reporting that makes this system go. But as there is a fog of war, so
there is a fog of journalism; stories emerge not fully formed, sometimes based on wrong

assumptions, occasionally warped by bias or politics, and often shaped in an environment of decision making that is far from unified within the government. Stories can and do take on a life of their own and get out of the control of their original sources, reporters, or subjects. That, more than anything, may be what can make them at times so powerful.

NOTES

The author would like to state that the facts, opinions, and analysis are entirely his and do not reflect in any way the views of the World Bank, its board of directors, or any of the governments they represent.

1. Michael Massing, "How Good Is Digital Journalism?" *New York Review of Books*, June 4, 2015, 43.

2. Timothy Garton Ash, "1989," *New York Review of Books*, November 5, 2009, 4.

3. See, for example, Marisa Guthrie, "Cover Story: Networks Face Grim Cost of War: Budgets Are Trimmed, Coverage Is More Perilous—and Ratings Are Falling," *Broadcasting and Cable*, August 13, 2007, www.broadcastingcable.com/news/news-articles/cover-story-networks-face-grim-cost-war/ 83526. For more on the newspaper industry crisis, see David J. Collins, Peter W. Olson, and Mary Furey, "The Newspaper Industry in Crisis," *Harvard Business Publishing*, March 11, 2009.

4. Gay Talese, *The Kingdom and the Power: The Story of the Men Who Influence the Institution That Influences the World, New York Times* (New York: NAL, 1969), 280–81.

5. See Thomas L. Friedman, *From Beirut to Jerusalem* (New York: Farrar, Straus and Giroux, 1989), 3–18; and Richard Engel, *A Fist in the Hornet's Nest: On the Ground in Baghdad Before, During and After the War* (New York: Hyperion, 2004).

6. In a specific case the *Washington Post* in 2009 explained that its Baghdad bureau was costing roughly $1.5 million a year, as it had sent nearly eighty reporters to cover the war. According to the *Post*, a foreign bureau might run from $5 to $10 million annually to cover salaries, travel, war zone insurance, relocation expenses, cost-of-living adjustments, security personnel, and local support staff. Andrew Alexander, "A Changing Future for Foreign Coverage," *Washington Post*, December 13, 2009.

7. For an overview, see John Maxwell Hamilton, *Journalism's Roving Eye: A History of American Foreign Reporting* (Baton Rouge: Louisiana State University Press, 2009).

8. Rick Gladstone, "Conflict Coverage Proves Deadly Job for Journalists," *New York Times*, December 23, 2014, www.nytimes.com/2014/12/23/world/conflict-coverage-proves-deadly-job-for -journalists-.html. The Committee to Protect Journalists survey is available at https://www.cpj.org/ killed/.

9. Sam Roberts, "Arnaud de Borchgrave, Journalist Whose Life Was a Tale Itself, Dies at 88," *New York Times*, February 16, 2015, www.nytimes.com/2015/02/17/business/media/arnaud-de-borchgrave -a-journalist-whose-life-was-a-tale-itself-dies-at-88.html?_r=0.

10. Howard Kurtz, "Media Agreed to Stay Silent on Kidnapping of Reporter David Rohde," *Washington Post*, June 21, 2009, www.washingtonpost.com/wp-dyn/content/article/2009/06/20/AR 2009062001745.html. See also David Rohde, "An Epidemic of Journalist Kidnappings," *Reuters*, November 15, 2013, blogs.reuters.com/david-rohde/2013/11/15/an-epidemic-of-journalist-kidnapping/. Rohde himself was captured in Afghanistan while reporting for the *New York Times*, which kept the kidnapping secret and appealed to other news organizations to do the same. See David Rohde, "Held by the Taliban: 7 Months, 10 Days in Captivity," *New York Times*, October 17, 2009, www.nytimes .com/2009/10/18/world/asia/18hostage.html.

11. Michael Hastings, "The Runaway General: Stanley McChrystal, Obama's Top Commander in Afghanistan, Has Seized Control of the War by Never Taking His Eye off the Real Enemy: The Wimps in the White House," *Rolling Stone*, June 22, 2010.

12. C. J. Chivers, Carlotta Gall, Andrew W. Lehren, Mark Mazzetti, Jane Perlez, and Eric Schmitt, "The War Logs. Inside the Fog of War: Reports from the Ground in Afghanistan," *New York Times*, July 26, 2010.

13. John Maxwell Hamilton and Eric Jenner, "The New Foreign Correspondence," *Foreign Affairs*, September/October 2003, 131–38.

14. NBC News, "Syria Battle Lines: Social Media Sites Show Fierce Fighting in the North as Syrian Government Forces and Rebels Clash in Sahl al-Ghab," August 21, 2015, www.nbcnews.com/video/nbc-news/57764694#57764694; Ishaan Tharoor, "A Dead Baby Becomes the Most Tragic Symbol Yet of the Mediterranean Refugee Crisis," *Washington Post*, September 2, 2015, www.washingtonpost.com/news/worldviews/wp/2015/09/02/a-dead-baby-becomes-the-most-tragic-symbol-yet-of-the-mediterranean-refugee-crisis/.

15. Mark Glaser, "GlobalPost Aims to Resuscitate Foreign Correspondents Online," *MediaShift*, January 8, 2009, www.pbs.org/mediashift/2009/01/globalpost-aims-to-resuscitate-foreign-correspondents-online008.html.

16. For an example of the media criticism of the embed policy, see Ameen Izzadeen, "Embedded: Prostituting Journalism and Producing Bastardized News," *Daily Mirror*, March 28, 2003. For a different perspective, see Albert Eisele, "Embed Cavallaro Sees War from the Inside," *The Hill*, March 31, 2005.

17. Victoria Clarke, meeting with news bureau chiefs, transcript, Department of Defense, January 14, 2003, http://archive.defense.gov/Transcripts/Transcript.aspx?TranscriptD=1259

18. See, for example, Joe Strupp, "MRE Criticizes Expelling of Embeds over Pix of Shot-up Humvee," *Editor and Publisher*, December 15, 2005.

19. For references on the well-chronicled subject of anonymous sourcing in journalism, see the Poynter Institute, "Anonymous Sources," *Poynter*, www.poynter.org/tag/anonymous-sources/.

20. For an account of *USA Today*'s tough policy on anonymous sourcing, see David Folkenflik, "USA Today Cuts Use of Anonymous Sources," *Morning Edition*, NPR, August 29, 2005, www.npr.org/templates/story/story.php?storyId=4815420.

21. Michael Massing, "Digital Journalism: The Next Generation," *New York Review of Books*, June 24, 2015, 42.

22. See Paul Rosenzweig, Timothy J. McNulty, and Ellen Shearer, eds., *Whistleblowers, Leaks, and the Media: The First Amendment and National Security* (Chicago: ABA Press, 2014).

23. See Dina Temple-Raston and Harvey Rishikof, "Keeping Secrets: How the Government and the Press Adapt in a World Awash in Information," in ibid., 189.

24. Robert Gates and Mike Mullen, briefing, transcript, Department of Defense, July 29, 2010, http://archive.defense.gov/Transcripts/Transcript.aspx?TranscriptID=4666.

25. David Folkenflik, "WikiLeaks: An Editor-in-Chief or Prolific Source?" *Weekend Edition*, NPR, July 31, 2010, www.npr.org/templates/transcript/transcript.php?storyId=128870288.

26. See Eric Schmitt, "In Disclosing Secret Documents, WikiLeaks Seeks 'Transparency,'" *New York Times*, July 26, 2010; and *New York Times* staff, "Piecing Together the Reports, and Deciding What to Publish," *New York Times*, July 26, 2010.

27. Dana Priest and William Arkin, "Top Secret America: A Hidden World, Growing Beyond Control," *Washington Post*, July 19, 2010.

28. Voice of America News, "Army Private in WikiLeaks Case Transferred to U.S. Military Jail," *GlobalSecurity.org*, July 20, 2010, www.globalsecurity.org/military/library/news/2010/07/mil-100730-voa07.htm.

29. Gates and Mullen briefing.

30. Bowman H. Miller, "The Death of Secrecy: Need to Know . . . with Whom to Share," *Studies in Intelligence* 55, no. 3 (September 2011), www.cia.gov/library/center-for-the-study-of-intelligence/csi-publications/csi-studies/studies/vol.-55-no.-3/the-death-of-secrecy-need-to-know . . . with-whom-to-share.html

31. Glenn Greenwald, "NSA Collecting Phone Records of Millions of Verizon Customers Daily," *Guardian*, July 5, 2013, www.theguardian.com/world/2013/jun/06/nsa-phone-records-verizon-court-order.

32. US Foreign Intelligence Surveillance Court, Secondary Order: In re application of the Federal Bureau of Investigation for an order requiring the production of tangible things from Verizon Business Network Services Inc., on Behalf of MCI Communication Services Inc. D/B/A Verizon Business Services, Docket No. 13–80 (classified Top Secret/SI/NOFORN), signed April 25, 2013, by Judge Roger Vinson.

33. Barton Gellman and Laura Poitras, "U.S., British Intelligence Mining Data from Nine U.S. Internet Companies in Broad Secret Program," *Washington Post*, July 6, 2013, www.washingtonpost.com/investigations/us-intelligence-mining-data-from-nine-us-internet-companies-in-broad-secret-program/2013/06/06/3a0c0da8-cebf-11e2-8845-d970ccb04497_story.html.

34. Ibid.

35. *Hearing on National Defense Authorization Act for Fiscal Year 2013 and Oversight of Previously Authorized Programs Before the Committee on Armed Services, House of Representatives,* 112th Cong. (2012) (Keith Alexander, NSA director, questioned by Representative Hank Johnson). The passage is quoted in Andy Greenberg, "NSA Chief Denies *Wired*'s Domestic Spying Story (Fourteen Times) in Congressional Hearing," *Forbes,* March 20, 2012.

36. *Current and Projected National Security Threats to the United States: Hearing Before the Select Comm. on Intelligence of the US Senate,* 113th Cong. (2013). C-SPAN video of the entire hearing is available at www.c-span.org/video/?311436-1/senate-intelligence-cmte-hearing-worldwide-threats -us. The quoted exchange begins at 1:46:12 of the video.

37. Edward Snowden, interview by German TV channel NDR, January 26, 2014. The full conversation (without the German translation over the audio) was posted by LiveLeak: www.liveleak.com/ view?i=f93_1390833151. The quoted passage starts at 4:52.

38. Nicky Woolf, "How *The Guardian* Broke the Snowden Story . . . and What It Says about the British Media Company's Emerging Threat to *The New York Times*," *Atlantic,* July 5, 2013.

39. Bill Gertz, *Betrayal: How the Clinton Administration Undermined American Security* (Washington, DC: Regnery, 1999), Appendix.

40. Ron Wyden et al., letter to James R. Clapper, June 27, 2013, www.wyden.senate.gov/download/?id=87b45794-0fa4-4b1a-b3a6-e659a91a5042&download=1. The letter is signed by Wyden and Senators Mark Udall (D-CO), Lisa Murkowski (R-AK), Patrick Leahy (D-VT), Mark Kirk (R-IL), Dick Durbin (D-IL), Tom Udall (D-NM), Brian Schatz (D-HI), Jon Tester (D-MT), Jeanne Shaheen (D-NJ), Dean Heller (R-NV), Mark Begich (D-AK), Bernie Sanders (I-VT), Patty Murray (D-WA), Jeff Merkley (D-OR), Mazie Hirono (D-HI), Al Franken (D-MN), Tom Harkin (D-IA), Chris Coons (D-DE), Maria Cantwell (D-WA), Richard Blumenthal (D-CO), Max Baucus (D-MT), Elizabeth Warren (D-MA), Martin Heinrich (D-NM), Tammy Baldwin (D-WI), and Mike Lee (R-UT).

41. Ellen Nakashima, "NSA Collection of Phone Data Ruled Unlawful," *Washington Post,* May 8, 2015.

42. Rahul Sagar, *Secrets and Leaks: The Dilemma of State Secrecy* (Princeton, NJ: Princeton University Press, 2014), 73–76, 90–91, 114.

43. Barack Obama and David Cameron, joint news conference on US–UK relations, January 16, 2015, White House, Washington, DC. C-SPAN video of the entire news conference accessed at www .c-span.org/video/?323842-1/news-conference-president-obama-british-prime-minister-david -cameron. The quoted passage begins at 56:53 of the video.

44. Ryan Teague Beckwith, "Read the CIA Director's Thoughts on the Paris Attacks," *Time,* November 16, 2015, http://time.com/4114870/paris-attacks-cia-john-brennan/. (The CIA website posted Brennan's prepared remarks but not the question-and-answer session in which the cited statements were made.)

45. Scott Shane, "After Paris Attacks, CIA Director Rekindles Debate over Surveillance," *New York Times,* November 16, 2015, www.nytimes.com/2015/11/17/us/after-paris-attacks-cia-director -rekindles-debate-over-surveillance.html.

46. See Rosenzweig, McNulty, and Shearer, *Whistleblowers.* A description of all eight cases can be found in a special report by the Committee to Protect Journalists. See Leonard Downie, *The Obama Administration and the Press: Leak Investigations and Surveillance in Post-9/11 America,* with Sara Rafsky (Washington, DC: Committee to Protect Journalists, October 10, 2013), www .cpj.org/reports/us2013-english.pdf. See also Cora Currier, "Charting Obama's Crackdown on National Security Leaks," *ProPublica,* July 30, 2013, www.propublica.org/special/sealing-loose-lips -charting-obamas-crackdown-on-national-security-leaks. Currier's article cites seven prosecutions under Obama; the eighth case, still under investigation, involves alleged leaks by former CIA director David H. Petraeus.

47. Adam Goldman and Matt Apuzzo, "US: CIA Thwarts New al-Qaida Underwear Bomb Plot," *Yahoo! News,* May 7, 2012, http://news.yahoo.com/us-cia-thwarts-al-qaida-underwear-bomb-plot -200836835.html.

48. David Sanger, "Obama Order Sped Up Wave of Cyberattacks against Iran," *New York Times,* June 1, 2012, www.nytimes.com/2012/06/01/world/middleeast/obama-ordered-wave-of-cyberattacks -against-iran.html?ref=stuxnet.

49. See, for example, Scott Shane and Charlie Savage, "Administration Took Accidental Path to Setting Record for Leak Cases," *New York Times*, June 19, 2012, www.nytimes.com/2012/06/20/us/politics/accidental-path-to-record-leak-cases-under-obama.html?pagewanted=all; Associated Press, "Barack Obama's Record on Terrorism, National Security Gives Republicans Little to Criticize," *Cleveland.com*, June 19, 2012, www.cleveland.com/nation/index.ssf/2012/06/barack_obamas_record_on_terror.html; and Cora Currier, "Classified Confusion: What Leaks Are Being Investigated, and What's the Law on Leaks," *ProPublica*, July 2, 2012, www.propublica.org/article/classified-confusion-what-leaks-are-being-investigated-and-whats-the-law-on.

50. Matt Apuzzo, "Ex-C.I.A. Officer Sentenced in Leak Case Tied to Times Reporter," *New York Times*, May, 11, 2015, www.nytimes.com/2015/05/12/us/ex-cia-officer-sentenced-in-leak-case-tied-to-times-reporter.html?_r=0.

51. Charlie Savage, "James Cartwright, Ex-General, Pleads Guilty in Leak Case," *New York Times*, October 18, 2016, www.nytimes.com/2016/10/18/us/marine-general-james-cartwright-leak-fbi.html.

52. Adam Goldman, "Petraeus Pleads Guilty to Mishandling Classified Material, Will Face Probation," *Washington Post*, April 23, 2015, www.washingtonpost.com/world/national-security/petraeus-set-to-plead-guilty-to-mishandling-classified-materials/2015/04/22/3e6dbf20-e8f5-11e4-aae1-d642717d8afa_story.html.

53. David E. Pozen, "The Leaky Leviathan: Why the Government Condemns and Condones Unlawful Disclosures of Information," *Harvard Law Review* 127 (December 20, 2013): 517 and 629, http://harvardlawreview.org/2013/12/the-leaky-leviathan-why-the-government-condemns-and-condones-unlawful-disclosures-of-information/.

54. Human Rights Watch, *With Liberty to Monitor All: How Large-Scale U.S. Surveillance Is Harming Journalism, Law and American Democracy* (Washington, DC, July 2014), 3, www.hrw.org/sites/default/files/reports/usnsa0714_ForUPload_0.pdf.

55. Downie, *Obama Administration and the Press*, 4.

56. Human Rights Watch, *With Liberty to Monitor All*, 72.

57. Barack Obama, "Structural Reforms to Improve the Security of Classified Networks and Responsible Sharing and Safeguarding of Classified Information," Executive Order 13587, October 7, 2011, www.whitehouse.gov/the-press-office/2011/10/07/executive-order-13587-structural-reforms-improve-security-classified-net.

58. Sarah Laskow, "Is Communications Security for Reporters Improving? A New Tool Makes Encrypted Phone Calls Easy; No One Can Keep Information Safe," *Columbia Journalism Review*, August 11, 2014, www.cjr.org/behind_the_news/is_communications_security_for.php.

59. David E. Sanger and Charlie Savage, "U.S. Says Russia Directed Hacks to Influence Elections," *New York Times*, October 7, 2016, www.nytimes.com/2016/10/08/us/politics/us-formally-accuses-russia-of-stealing-dnc-emails.html?_r=0.

60. George Gao, "What Americans Think about NSA Surveillance, National Security and Privacy," *Fact Tank*, Pew Research Center, May 29, 2015, www.pewresearch.org/fact-tank/2015/05/29/what-americans-think-about-nsa-surveillance-national-security-and-privacy/; and Steven Nelson, "Edward Snowden Unpopular at Home, a Hero Abroad, Poll Finds," *US News and World Report*, April 21, 2015, www.usnews.com/news/articles/2015/04/21/edward-snowden-unpopular-at-home-a-hero-abroad-poll-finds.

61. Dwight D. Eisenhower, *Crusade in Europe, A Personal Account of World War II* (New York: Doubleday, 1948), 169–70.

62. James Fallows, "Why Americans Hate the Media," *Atlantic Monthly* 277, no. 2 (February 1996): 45–64.

63. Dana Priest, "CIA Holds Terror Suspects in Secret Prisons: Debate Is Growing within Agency about Legality and Morality of Overseas System Set Up after 9/11," *Washington Post*, November 2, 2005.

64. See, for example, Blake Morrison and John Diamond, "Pressure at Iraqi Prison Detailed," *USA Today*, June 17, 2004.

65. James Risen and Eric Lichtblau, "Bush Lets U.S. Spy on Callers without Courts," *New York Times*, December 16, 2005.

Navigating the Labyrinth of the National Security Enterprise

Harvey Rishikof and Roger Z. George

> To put it bluntly, we are trying to face 21st century threats with . . . a bureaucracy that sometimes seems designed for the Byzantine Empire, which, as you recall, didn't end well. We are still often too rigid when we need to be flexible, too clumsy when we need to be agile, slow when we need to be fast, too focused on individual agency equities, when we need to be focused on the broader whole of government mission.
>
> —Under Secretary of Defense Michele Flournoy, 2010

This book examines the key organizations and institutions that make up the national security enterprise (NSE). As its title suggests, navigating the labyrinth of this enterprise is a daunting challenge. Even our collective effort to describe and analyze the process is incomplete and subject to some oversimplification. For example, this book uses an inside-the-beltway perspective to elucidate a bureaucratic cultural viewpoint of how US national security policy works. One could write another volume on many organizations' field activities and operations—be they embassies, commands, or news bureaus—that provide even more insight into the workings of these national security players. Moreover, other agencies must be considered part of the NSE deserving their own treatment. This second edition goes part of the way in expanding the readers' understanding by including important players like USAID and the Treasury Department. Yet, the NSE is even broader than that. Just as one example, we see the Obama administration's negotiation of the Iran nuclear deal involved other important players, including the Department of Energy, whose Secretary Ernest Moniz played a key role. One could go further, if space permitted, as many national security issues—from climate change to pandemics to foreign cyber manipulation of US domestic politics—will involve other parts of the executive branch.

The NSE has proved to be a very resilient and evolving set of organizations, institutions, cultures, and processes. For the past seven decades, the American system has functioned well enough to successfully avert a major nuclear war with the Soviet Union and contain its influence to bring an end to the Cold War. That was a monumental achievement. On one level the national security system has adapted, weathered the legislative and court battles against executive power, and endured and perhaps benefited from the intervention of outside lobbyists, pressure groups, and think tanks. That is the American system of checks and balances. A conventional view suggests that whatever changes need to be made to confront new issues facing the United States can be managed through the traditional pulling and hauling of those interagency and political processes.

We, however, respectfully dissent. For more than two decades, major commissions and outside studies have been arguing that a more fundamental set of changes is required.[1] First, the world is far different than anything that the creators of the 1947 National Security Act could have imagined. The range of issues, their complexity, and their global dimension simply are far more diverse than what the Trumans or Achesons imagined. The international system is being transformed and will be unrecognizable by 2025. Such changes are being driven by economic, climate, information, demographic, energy, and social shifts that were hard to imagine only a few years ago. Moreover, the multiplicity of actors, the rise of Asia as well as nongovernment players, and the shift of economic power suggest the United States will be a much less influential player, although not without considerable leverage.[2] The events of this second decade of the twenty-first century—Russia's resurgence to the national stage, the Syrian crisis, the rise and possible fall of Daesh, immigration and terrorism fears in Europe, nuclear tests of North Korea, and cyber threats—have posed yet a new set of challenges for American foreign policy.

Second, the growth of the NSE itself has now reached a point where complex interactions among agencies and organizations are particularly bewildering. The day is past when a single government agency or organization—even one as large as the Department of Defense (DOD)—can manage a key foreign policy issue. This was true to some extent even in the late 1940s, but today there are no clear agency lanes in the road for twenty-first-century problems. When the Clinton administration talked about complex contingency operations in the 1990s, it was only beginning to appreciate what that would entail. The failure of the Bush administration to handle Iraq's post-conflict reconstruction and stability operations was a perfect storm of unanticipated problems, poor planning, and the obsolete notion that a single-agency approach could handle all the issues. Moreover, the Obama administration's over-centralization of power in the White House and a huge National Security Council (NSC) staff has received criticisms for lack of agility and vision.[3] Another example is the complexity of today's proliferation problems and the way many elements of the US government are struggling to map out what is needed to counter the spread of dangerous weapons and technologies. As figure C.1 highlights, the pieces of government involved—only the executive branch in this case—can barely be put on a single chart or comprehended without a magnifying glass.

Third, the once clear line between domestic and foreign security threats has now almost completely dissolved in regard to counterterrorism as well as other transnational issues like climate, immigration, and health. As the Department of Homeland Security (DHS) has discovered, coordinating aspects of global terrorism, emergency responses to natural disasters, and border control involves agencies and authorities that range from the federal to the state to the local levels. Separating out these responsibilities is nearly impossible. A key role for the NSE is ensuring that these levels of government can exchange information, share responsibilities, and collaborate to avert or at least minimize damage to US foreign and domestic interests.

This complex picture has been laid out in numerous studies. As far back as the 2001 Hart–Rudman Commission, there was an appreciation of the new twenty-first-century challenges facing the NSE. The report, presented to the George W. Bush administration only a few weeks after it began its term, warned that the new century would require agencies to adjust their portfolios and achieve a level of interagency cooperation and partnering with nongovernment

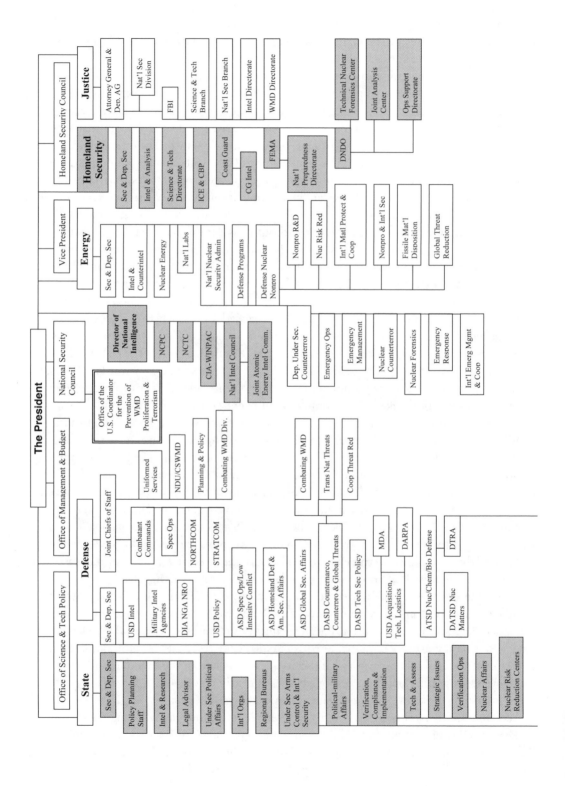

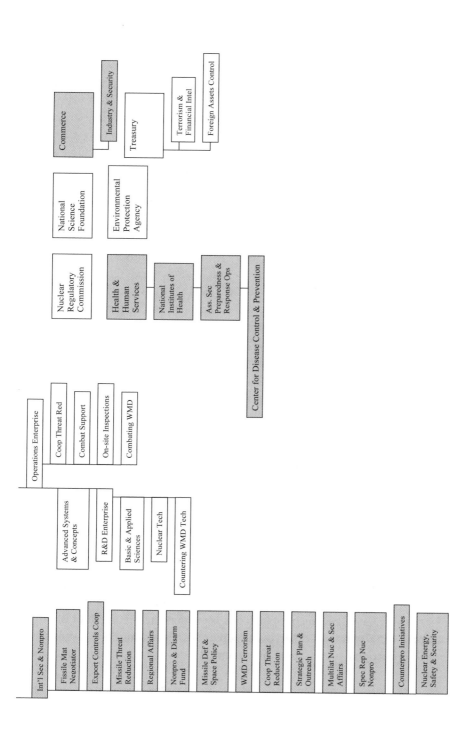

Figure C.1. Principal US Government Agencies Combating Nuclear Proliferation

Source: Leonard S. Spector, Director, James Martin Center for Nonproliferation Studies and Anya Loukianova for the illustration.

organizations as well as allies to a degree not anticipated during the Cold War. A decade later, many of the same recommendations are to be found in the Project on National Security Reform (PNSR). Like the seven-volume 2001 Hart–Rudman report that preceded it, the PNSR displayed in copious detail and in multiple volumes the tasks ahead in redesigning the NSE. Like Hart–Rudman, the PNSR saw the necessity of whole-of-government approaches that integrated the operations of very different organizations and developed mechanisms for overcoming many of the organizational and bureaucratic obstacles that stood in the way of effective interagency national security planning and implementation. The PNSR noted, "U.S. national security missions are shifting, broadening, and becoming increasingly interdisciplinary." In 2017, as this volume is being completed, efforts at reform remain stymied by a combination of political and substantive factors, but also by bureaucratic ones.[4] Time will tell if President Trump and his administration can produce meaningful reform of the NSE. According to one study, presidents are partly to blame because they lack the experience to know what kinds of reforms to push, but also Congress can be turf conscious, not wishing to give up their prerogatives over significant parts of the NSE, and of course, the feasibility of some suggested reforms can be challenged on the grounds of costs or practicality. But one cannot forget, according to this study, that the agencies themselves often resist these reforms for their narrow organizational reasons.[5]

Most recommendations for improving the NSE seem to take as a given that various organizations, agencies, and institutions of government will be able to adapt their own unique cultures to work better with other parts of the US government in the pursuit of effective national security policies. These same studies routinely complain that more agile and innovative policies typically run afoul of narrow and parochial organizational interests. Often, organizations and institutions prefer to operate using their well-developed processes and traditional missions, rather than adapt to new conditions or surrender control to other agencies. How can such diverse organizations and their cultures effectively adapt and yet maintain this uniqueness? To a large extent, this is the conundrum on which this book is focused.

Reform efforts must, at a minimum, consider a number of unavoidable truths. First, no one agency or institution is capable of designing grand strategy. And American grand strategy confronts a complicated myriad of organizations, institutions, and cultures that attempt to reshape or bend the strategy in their own images. Describing these "organizational" or "professional" cultures for the practitioners and students of national security is a first step to understanding the expanding NSE. Second, these cultures are not all bad nor all good. Appropriate evaluation of a culture turns on the context: what new goal or new mission is the organization challenged to meet as its critical priority? Third, the National Security Council staff, while often charged with orchestrating national security strategy, is incapable by itself of achieving this goal. For one thing, it is far too small a staff with far too limited an institutional memory to be saddled with the function of drafting grand strategy; for another, it lacks any real strategic planning element, which has been a constant complaint of numerous studies of national security reform. Moreover, there is strong institutional prejudice that the NSC staff not be operational, in the sense of running day-to-day operations, and coordinate as best it can.

Indeed, as more and more interagency functions are added to the NSC staff's set of tasks, it will tend to become more of a traffic cop, scheduler of meetings, and mediator rather than a grand strategic planner. Yet, it is instinctive to recommend more directorates for the NSCS to coordinate, as a 2009 Council on Foreign Relations report does for Prevention / Stabilization / Reconstruction and Development / Governance.[6] These added duties, including coordinating the response to Ebola, will be successful only if one envisions a very much more expanded NSC staff of 2,500 or so—a combat command so to speak. As has been noted by analysts, the size of the NSC has grown over the years and then been cut back; however, this growth has been, even at its zenith, modest in comparison to that of other agencies or combat commands.[7] For many the "Scowcroft" solution of an NSCS of fifty—fifty true experts who act as mini–national security advisors and who truly run the interagency process—would be a more effective and manageable approach. Whether this is even thinkable, there has been a more recent effort to pare back the current size. This is a trend that a new president might wish to consider.

Both Congress and department secretaries have always resisted a large NSC staff. One think-tank report has suggested that the executive and legislative branches jointly establish a standing independent strategic review panel of experienced and senior experts to review the strategic environment over the next twenty years and provide prioritized goal and risk-assessment recommendations for use by the US government for each new administration.[8] This report would become the basis for a new administration to implement. Such suggestions point to the urgent need to define a clear set of national interests and establish an organization with the authorities to implement the necessary strategy to achieve them. So-called organizational fixes—that is, adding new units on top of existing ones or realigning agencies or their elements—are not sufficient to address the new boundary-crossing issues. If one needs proof of this, the creation of DHS makes it clear that placing twenty-two different agencies under a single secretary for homeland security did not ensure common purpose or clear missions; rather, it multiplied the challenges of creating a common culture and the number of missions for which the department was responsible. Similarly, the creation of the director of national intelligence (DNI) has not ended the interagency disputes within the intelligence community (IC) or integrated its functions smoothly. Rather, new turf battles seem to have cropped up between the DNI and the Central Intelligence Agency (CIA) over who serves the president and who represents the IC overseas. So, organizational changes are only part of the solution and may be part of the problem if cultures do not adapt and shift along with the line charts and reporting responsibilities (see box C.1).

We believe that organizational cultures can change, but they will do so only if the incentives for change are stronger than the incentives to remain the same. At the same time, care should be taken to preserve what is best in the existing cultures so that the proposed changes do not undermine what needs to be preserved. The 9/11 shock produced substantial reforms in priorities within the FBI, the CIA, and other national security agencies. The promotions and recognition coming from those who worked counterterrorism were suddenly much more obvious to those working inside these agencies, and the need to share became the dominant mantra over the need to know. But those incentives might weaken over time as new demands on those agencies arise and agencies' priorities shift again. As we know, DHS has been buffeted by emerging crises, causing its focus to zigzag from counterterrorism to emergency management (Hurricane Katrina) and then to border controls (immigration). Likewise, the tendency of most agencies is to allow their organizations to return to business as usual, be that arresting criminals, recruiting agents, or preparing for traditional war operations. The failed Detroit Christmas bombing plot of December 2009 reinvigorated the debate about core DHS counterterrorism functions but did not resolve its responsibility for its other missions. Similarly, in the cyber realm, despite 2016 legislation to give DHS primacy in the public–private sharing effort, questions concerning capacity still exist. Hence, there will be a

---

BOX C.1
Crafting an Intelligence Community Culture

The 2004 intelligence reforms that created the DNI were based on the presumption that the sixteen federal agencies performing intelligence functions are in fact a community. As many practitioners and critics will acknowledge the concept of community is a work in progress. Instead, a loose confederation of agencies operates with different missions and organizational cultures, competing for attention, personnel, and dollars. Agencies only superficially like the idea of a DNI who is charged with integrating and directing them. These agencies, the CIA especially, guard their special relationships with other foreign intelligence services with territorial vigilance.

The DNI-CIA disagreement over selection of the senior officer in overseas missions to represent the IC's interests illustrates the challenge. These days, those interests touch on the missions of agencies far beyond the CIA to include the National Security Agency (NSA), the Defense Intelligence Agency (DIA), the Federal Bureau of Investigation (FBI), the Drug Enforcement Administration (DEA), and DHS, suggesting the DNI should select the representative. On the other side, the CIA insists it is the agency with the deepest ties and most critical missions overseas, namely, clandestine collection and covert action. Hence a CIA officer must be the senior-most officer in country, commonly called the chief of station. Anything less would undermine the CIA's ability to conduct its clandestine mission and the long-established bilateral relations between the United States and host country intelligence services.

The national security advisor's decision in favor of the CIA does not settle the question of whether the CIA can truly represent the entire IC because the IC lacks officers trained in and knowledgeable about the IC. Agencies continue to train, direct, and promote career professionals entirely separately from each other. Creating a "jointness" equivalent to the military is a necessary step if an IC culture is to emerge.

All intelligence officers must have more opportunities to train together and get to know each other's cultures. To do this, the purported National Intelligence University—at the moment a virtual, on-paper institution—needs to become a bricks-and-mortar facility where officers from across the community are educated about each other and their professions.

Intelligence professionals must serve together. There are limited opportunities for officers now, largely in the centers focused on counter-proliferation and counterterrorism. To many, the best example of "jointness" may occur overseas, where different intelligence agencies are collocated under the direction of the ambassador as chief of mission. The DNI has made a start at this by instituting a joint duty-assignments list that places aspiring officers in each other's agencies for broadening experiences. This must become a serious professional requirement for senior responsibilities—with no waivers—if the IC is to create a multiagency perspective among the few leaders of the IC. This "jointness," which the military has been working on for decades, is only a baby step at this point in the IC.

Finally, when officers within the community are about to be promoted into the senior ranks—"flag equivalents" or the civilian senior executive service—a joint promotion board of the sixteen agencies should be convened to pass on candidates. Individuals who have demonstrated an unwillingness to be community players should not be promoted. In addition, there should be a required course that throws these future executives from the CIA, NSA, DIA, etc., into a monthlong training experience to develop their sensitivity to other parts of the IC, build personal networks, and give them a broader sense of community than currently is inculcated in the agency-specific training they have received throughout their careers.

---

tendency to regress or drift back to traditional core missions over time unless new incentive structures are put in place that outlast the current set of presidential advisors and agency leaders.

Various models of orchestrating the NSE—NSC-centric, single-agency-led, or special-envoy-driven—all require that issue leaders understand the organizations and the cultures they represent. As Marc Grossman noted, when Henry Kissinger came into the State Department, he had little idea what constituted a foreign service "ethos." Kissinger came to admire many career diplomats, but he also realized that the best diplomats did not necessarily make the best strategists. The vision thing was not what the State Department did, and generally speaking, Kissinger was not going to be able to rely on careerists to produce new approaches to foreign policy problems. By the same token the NSC-centric model seldom produces comprehensive policies, unless of course the national security advisor is a Henry Kissinger who carries strategy inside his head and has a special relationship with the president. More than most national security advisors, Kissinger disdained the interagency process and sought to develop overarching policies on his own with presidential support and approval.

Launching a strategy development process inside the NSC staff was one objective of the Obama administration. As the second Obama administration came to an end, there was already an effort to assess the president's "legacy." Many pundits complained that Obama's 2010 and 2015 National Security Strategies fell short of true vision. However, other senior participants in the administration's national security decision making claimed that the president was playing a "long game." As Derek Chollet argues, Obama ultimately shifted America's role in the world to reflect new realities of the diffusion of power and the need to rebalance its use of instruments, prioritize US interests, and show more strategic restraint in order to develop sustainable foreign policies in the future.[9] Whether this proves to be the case remains to be seen, but one thing is for sure: the next president will deal with a world no less complex and challenging than the one Obama inherited, meaning the next president will have face some of the same dilemmas of coordinating a diverse set of organizations to address twenty-first-century problems.

ORGANIZATIONS ARE "US"

As mentioned in the introduction to this book, national security studies devote little attention to the specific dynamics or underlying organizational cultures that often drive the bureaucratic politics of American foreign policy. Scholars who do are more the exception than the rule. In 2009, for example, Peter Hall and Michele Lamont focused on how institutional and cultural structures affect societies that are successful in providing health care for their citizens.[10] Drawing on the literature of organizations, Hall and Lamont conceptualized institutions as sets of regularized practices with a rule-like quality that vary according to how expectations are established, whether by formalized sanctions or by informal mechanisms that create perceptions to serve mutual interests and shape appropriate behavior.[11] A similar analytical approach was pioneered in the 1970s for national security issues. For example, Morton Halperin's work on bureaucratic politics touched on the organizational essence that drove defense decision making. Likewise, Graham Allison's early work and later collaboration with Philip Zelikow reexamined the bureaucratic and organizational behavior evident in the Cuban Missile Crisis. Both efforts remain the basis for serious thinking about the organizational dimension of security.[12] These works tend to focus on explaining policy outcomes that are the result of the pulling and hauling of organizations and of effective bureaucratic entrepreneurs. They do not pretend to be in-depth studies of the individual organizations, although they do rely on key organizational behaviors that social scientists have discovered in examining many other government and private sector organizations. Amy Zegart, though, has focused on the organizational behaviors of the CIA and FBI, noting how dysfunctional these organizations became when asked to take on new tasks or work with other organizations in new ways.[13] She too, however, focuses on generalities in laying out how these organizations operate given her questions and does not explore the subcultures of the structures. Finally, Richard Haass has written about the "bureaucratic entrepreneur" and the way ambitious bureaucrats must assess their own organization's operational style and that of others if they are to flourish in the national security organization.[14] While laying out important traits of the successful organizational man or woman, this useful contribution makes no attempt to analyze the radically different organizational perspectives found inside the executive branch, which are laid out here.

This book argues that a more systematic and detailed understanding of the various organizations and cultures will help scholars and practitioners to navigate the NSE. It has focused on three key aspects to this enterprise. First, the key executive branch agencies—including the NSC, the State and Defense Departments, the CIA, the Office of Management and Budget, the Treasury, and the broader IC and domestic / law enforcement agencies (chiefly, the FBI and DHS)—that make up the formal interagency process can lead policy development and implementation. Second, we have discussed the operation of the two other branches of government. Congress, with its unique cultures and operating styles, has the ability to frustrate or redirect policy in ways not intended or desired by the executive branch, but also the Supreme Court, with its seemingly remote and detached view of policy, has lately become a more prominent feature of the NSE. And third, the book examined the important role of outside actors and their agendas. In particular, the media, the think-tank world, and lobbyists influence and inform but also can amplify or distort the development of foreign policies. Our concluding thoughts will address each of these three levels in turn.

THE INTERAGENCY PROCESS

The interagency process today is far more than the NSC, the State and Defense Departments, the military, and the CIA as envisaged by the 1947 National Security Act. New players like the Treasury, the FBI, and DHS are increasingly being drawn into high politics as lines blur between purely foreign and domestic policies. The combining of the NSC with the Homeland Security Council staff by the Obama administration reflects the desire to integrate these spheres. This interagency process has become the target of much of the criticism for ineffective policy formation and implementation. But more attention needs to be placed on the clash of cultures that often lies underneath the lack of cooperation or information exchange.

Rebalancing the Special State–Defense Relationship

Some rebalancing is required in terms of raising priorities on nondefense resources for national security. However, simply giving the State Department more people and funding will not solve the problem. Ultimately, the solution lies in changing the mission and necessarily the culture of the State Department, whereby foreign service officers (FSOs) see their role as problem solvers as much as negotiators; likewise, DOD civilians and military officers alike will also need to accept that military operations other than war are now part of their skill set until such time as the rebalancing of defense and nondefense resources is accomplished. But this new relationship will also require Congress to fully fund a civilian foreign office with a budgetary training mandate that has been hitherto avoided. Historically, the approach has been to use local talent and not FSOs to maintain a small diplomatic footprint for practical foreign policy reasons. As one would expect, the 2015 study *American Diplomacy at Risk* recommends the reduction of political appointees, more career professional development, and more resources—these recommendations have continually been made over the decade.[15]

Understanding the subcultures of these departments and harmonizing them better is also required. One internal coordination mechanism for the military, for example, is the US Army tribes built around weapons systems: armor versus artillery versus special forces. Comparable tribes exist in the US Air Force and US Navy. Added to this set of subcultures is the grooming of senior officers that takes place.[16] While the diplomat is the poster child for the State Department, there are many varieties depending on the bureau or region in which an FSO serves. Its subcultures, driven by political, economic, public, or consular affairs career tracks, make a difference in their outlook and loyalties. Sometimes these loyalties can produce internal governmental interests that act as single-issue nongovernment organizations. One bureau committed to human rights will veto agreements being negotiated by other bureaus and sabotage programs if those programs do not comport with views of the prevailing approach on human rights. This can result in a battle between different careerist factions. Or the State Department, like DOD and some other institutions, can be divided between the careerist and political appointee cultures. Getting the career subcultures as well as the political appointees to agree on a policy is often difficult. NSC frustrations, as related in the chapter focused on that institution, often stem from its impatience with the State Department's inability to formulate its own internal policy, much less coordinate with other agencies.

A recent trend toward appointing special envoys who can carry both a department and White House imprimatur seems aimed at giving State more clout and an ability to overcome internal State Department wrangling. The Obama administration became full of special envoys from Afghanistan-Pakistan to Arab-Israeli to Sudan.[17] Is this reliance on envoys an admission of failure on the part of career ambassadors and assistant secretaries to implement policies? Does this solution only serve to accentuate the careerist–political appointee tensions, or can it help make the careerists more effective and galvanize them? To be sure, the appointment of envoys avoids a congressional confirmation process. Much will depend on whether this strategy of bringing in powerful outsiders is seen as intended to discipline a bureaucracy or to advocate for it. Overall most of the bureaucracies appeared to be sidelined.

The Pentagon, however, suffers from exactly the opposite problem. Well resourced compared to other agencies, with plenty of personnel and hardware, it has become the interagency's 911 for doing anything hard or rapidly. More than many other organizations, DOD has acknowledged the existence of its separate military and civilian cultures, as civilian–military relations have long been recognized as a major flashpoint historically. Similarly, though, it has internalized "jointness" in a way other agencies can only envy: it has not solved all the problems of unique service cultures scrambling for resources and mission relevance. Likewise, DOD's battles to hammer out a joint policy between the military services—represented by the Joint Staff—and the civilian leadership found in the Office of the Secretary of Defense (OSD) can be time consuming; moreover, after the Goldwater–Nichols reforms, the Pentagon now is allowed to come to the table with separate Joint Staff and OSD positions, which further complicates the integration of separate agency perspectives. In fact, authors Michael Meese and Isaiah Wilson also point out that the effectiveness of the Pentagon is still undercut by its sheer size and power; the multiple competing organizational structures and internal bureaucratic cultures make change within DOD exceptionally problematic; and finally, extraordinary management structures needed to ensure that its tremendous budgets and personnel lists do not encourage waste and inefficiency also limit its agility and innovation. One strategic analyst, Eliot A. Cohen, in testimony before Congress, has argued that to meet the new challenges confronting DOD, the department needs the following bureaucratic cultural reforms: remake the system for selecting and promoting general officers so more junior and innovative officers can skip the rigid process of promotions to find the next Adm. Hyman Rickover; overhaul the current system for producing strategic documents and move to a white paper system of commissions for speed and innovation; reform recruitment and mobilization of civilians for particular expertise such as in state building or cyber; and finally, renew processional military education to promote a true joint general staff to overcome the tendency of producing tactical and unit leaders through a tougher and smaller selection process of thirty to fifty officers.[18] Needless to say, such reforms would be controversial but would help build a new culture for innovation for the department.

Redefining the Lanes

The twenty-first century has forever blurred the distinctions formerly recognized as the domestic–foreign policy divide and the law enforcement–security divide. As the chapters on the FBI, DHS, the Treasury, the CIA, and the DNI highlight, there are no clear lanes anymore in the realms of terrorism, proliferation, and other global threats to American citizens. The 9/11 case illustrates how both the CIA and FBI were tracking parts of this threat. The importance of interdependence among agencies is reflected in the Detroit Christmas bombing plot of 2009. Or consider the rising significance to US counterterrorism and counter-proliferation goals of the Treasury's financial tools in starving Daesh as well as nuclear proliferators of the resources to conduct their dangerous activities. Today, agencies must acknowledge this interconnection if they are to fulfill their own missions. Moreover, they must examine where their own cultural norms prevent or hinder them from playing well with others. So the FBI faces the challenge of adapting its special-agent-in-charge culture of prosecutions and arrests into something closer to the CIA's analytical-operator culture, but in a domestic context. Similarly, the CIA needs to remake its current self-image of the detached analytic provider of information to the policy process or the clandestine solo operator conducting covert action into more of a team player who straddles the line between intelligence and policy. As the chapter on the CIA notes, there is a gray area in which the CIA must be both an intelligence agency and a policy implementer. This gray zone is precisely where the CIA runs the risk of being accused of politicizing its intelligence, or at least allowing itself and its analysis to become politicized by the decision makers pushing a certain agenda. Or in the case of unmanned armed vehicles operated by CIA employees, where questions arise as to whether their actions are covered by the protections of the Geneva Conventions.

In the field of counterterrorism, however, the model of the National Counterterrorism Center (NCTC) has been offered as the best practice so far in terms of melding together the diverse cultures and organizations fighting global terrorism to create a fusion center. The NCTC, although it was at first a creation of a presidential order as a follow-on to the previously executively created Terrorist Threat Integration Center, became congressionally mandated and lodged in the Office of the Director of National Intelligence under the 2004 Intelligence Reform Act.[19] The NCTC was unique in how it blended both its intelligence and policy functions but also in how it joined the law enforcement and intelligence organizations together. Not only was NCTC tasked to develop intelligence on terrorism threats, both foreign and domestic, it also had the responsibility to develop counterterrorism strategies and operations. Moreover, the position of the NCTC director, a Senate-confirmed office, was unique in government. For analyzing and integrating information pertaining to terrorism (except domestic terrorism), budget, and programs, the NCTC director reports to the DNI. However, for planning and progress of joint counterterrorism operation (other than intelligence operations), the director reports directly to the president. Operationally, the director works through the NSC and White House staff.[20]

The goal was to bring together law enforcement, military, and intelligence organizations in one place. The assignment of more than thirty intelligence, military, law enforcement, and homeland security networks, including the FBI, DHS, DOD, and IC officers, to this center was envisioned to create more "jointness" among the diverse organizational cultures. However, the failure of the NCTC to coordinate and analyze critical information in two cases in late 2009 called into question the effectiveness of the center in forging information sharing. The November shootings at Fort Hood army base in Texas by Maj. Nidal M. Hassan and the failed December Detroit bomb attempt by Umar Farouk Abdulmutallab caused President Obama to characterize the bombing attempt as a systematic failure. The immediate response, as one would expect, was a call for better technology to help analysts connect information, better technology at airports, wider and faster distribution of intelligence data, smarter guidelines for watch lists, and a clearer responsibility for the chain of command to investigate leads of plots to harm the United States. But even with such reforms, organizational cultural questions remain for Congress to consider, in addition to the perennial distinction between analysts versus operators. What were the consequences of the dual-reporting scheme for the director to both the president and DNI, how did the NCTC interact with the CIA's Counterterrorism Center and State Department's immigration bureaus, and finally, how did the NCTC interact with the NSCS over policy proposals? In addition, how can counterterrorism officials overcome the resistance of the military to share personnel files with law enforcement, as in the Fort Hood incident, and the rights of US citizens to protect sensitive medical information?[21]

The 2009 Detroit Christmas airplane bomber incident, however, reflects a deeper cross-cultural challenge on two levels. First, one 2010 study found that the counterterrorism arena was still a spider web of overlapping missions and ambiguous lines of authority and that the different departments and agencies also continued to interpret their responsibilities on the basis of their own statutes, histories, and bureaucratic cultures. In short, these entities were not accountable to NCTC's Directorate of Strategic Operations (DSOP), and there were insufficient bureaucratic incentives to fully support the interagency integration process of the DSOP. The Paris terrorist attacks in January and November 2015 have reinvigorated the US debate on how to use surveillance assets and share information among agencies—a round two of post-Snowden issues.

Second, even within the field of law enforcement, national and cultural differences could complicate cooperation. When US and European Union authorities attempted to exchange law enforcement information for travel while ensuring the protection of personal data and privacy, they discovered their different interpretations of the definition of law enforcement purposes. The United States defines law enforcement purposes as the use "for the prevention, detection, suppression, investigation, or prosecution of any criminal offense or violation of law related to border enforcement, public security, and national security, as well as for noncriminal judicial or administrative proceedings related directly to such offenses or violations." In contrast, the European Union defines it more narrowly as the use "for the prevention, detection, investigation, or prosecution of any criminal offense."[22] Such different definitions of "law enforcement" are significant as they implicate different actors, agencies, processes, and types of information that need to be coordinated and involved in the different countries.[23] While fusion centers such as the NCTC may be the way to attack the domestic and international coordination of transnational travel issues, successfully bridging these different organizational and national cultures requires a full understanding of them. Securing movement of people for travel, migration, and the management of borders will require a new mindset that reorganizes the bureaucracies and approaches information with a twenty-first-century understanding of data mining and analytics.[24] Since the Paris terrorist attacks of the past several years, how information will be shared between Europe and the United States may be up for review as well.

Needed: Coordinators and Integrators

Responding to new transnational threats has led to the need to break down traditional jurisdictional boundaries and integrate disparate parts of the government. In many cases the creation of new organizational structures has met with confusion if not conflict. In the case of DHS, this step toward horizontal coordination of federal, state, and municipal authorities to deal with homeland security issues has been a step forward. Yet an American legal and constitutional framework that separates domestic and international arenas hampers the coordination of authorities at all these levels. Unity of command is fractured by congressional oversight involving eighty-six subcommittees of Congress. The recommendation of the Hart–Rudman Commission to consolidate these committees remains unheeded. Whether DHS can ever overcome the legacy of several dozen diverse cultures and be capable of responding to a range of transnational issues (terrorism and immigration) as well as natural emergencies remains to be seen.

The DNI, now a decade and a half old, has already had four directors—and most likely its fifth by the time this volume is published. Reforms introduced in the midst of wars in Afghanistan and Iraq also have to be measured carefully. But the DNI, along with the creation of the NCTC and the National Counterproliferation Center, has added to the organizational complexity and cultures of the IC. The intent for having a DNI appears pretty clear. The job was designed to turn a collection of sixteen specialized agencies into a more integrated, single enterprise; at the same time, the legislation also aimed at correcting the specific problems that contributed to the September 2001 strategic surprise and the 2003 flawed Iraq weapons of mass destruction estimate. Arguably, President Obama's DNI, James Clapper, has done better than his predecessors in establishing the role of the DNI as the spokesperson if not the "leader" of the IC. On the issue of whether the DNI has reduced the prospects of future intelligence failures, the jury is still out, as there continue to be "surprises," whether they be the emergence of Daesh and its terrorist strategy, Russian hacking or meddling in the Middle East, or intelligence leaks of enormous portions that have undermined public confidence in its intelligence services and weakened its capabilities.

THE INSTITUTIONAL PROCESS—
CONGRESS AND THE COURTS

Neither the constitution nor existing statutes dictate any precise internal structure to the legislative–executive management of the NSE, and so it has remained an invitation to struggle as a number of the authors have noted. But the playing field is a crowded space with an often divided executive confronting Congress (itself divided between the House and Senate), the medley of media outlets, think tanks ranging from conservative to liberal, and assorted lobbyists working both ends of Pennsylvania Avenue for contending interest groups. One of our claims for the book is that to fully grasp the NSE, one needs to understand that more than just the government is a player. As detailed in a number of the chapters, the actions of the media, lobbyists, and think tanks affect power relations as different institutional players jockey for advantage in the policy process. Moreover, the professionalism of the agencies shapes the cultures of the organizations. A culture of professionalism becomes the behavior pattern in which individual employees and their organizations approach the interagency process. Talented professionals roam the corridors of power using all the elements of the playing field to influence and shape policy.

The Constitution lays out the battlefield of overlapping national security powers. As the chapter on Congress makes clear, this was more by design than most people wish to acknowledge. The constitution grants shared power between Congress and the executive, and different contexts favor power concentration in one or the other. War, for example, tends to concentrate power into the hand of the executive and reinforce its tendency for secrecy, while Congress's ability to shape national security tends to be reactive, personality driven, and most assertive on large ideological issues in times when external threats seem to be diminished.

Owing to the different structural and cultural settings of the House and the Senate, Congress tends to pursue broad ideological objectives, such as human rights or nonproliferation, and not view national interests with the nuanced lens required by the executive branch. The Senate will extract concessions by withholding confirmation of appointments to the executive branch, and both the House and Senate will attach amendments to legislation reflecting specific interests, such as the Boland amendments during the Iran-Contra affair. Whether war financing, genocide resolutions, Supreme Court nominations, or free trade agreements, Congress will find ways to assert their ideological views that can be at loggerheads with the administration. The House is marked by hyper-partisan top-down leadership, while the overlapping committee jurisdiction structure of the Senate can create arenas for struggle against the administration that bestow powerful influence on individual senators. Further complicating the executive–legislative management of lawmaking is the fact that the House, the Senate, and the president each have weapons to stall the process: the Rules Committee, the filibuster, and the veto, respectively. In other words, the president and 34 senators can stop 66 senators and 435 House members.[25] The tendency is toward deliberative deadlock and incremental change until a crisis supports more sweeping change.

While oversight of the NSE through jurisdictional and appropriations committees is a fundamental function of Congress, Congress has been sporadic in its effectiveness. In the intelligence arena it has tended to act after the fact and legislated reform, but then it returns to a passive role, especially during times when the same party controls Congress and the executive branch. While in the military appropriations arena, the military-industrial-congressional complex has rarely lost battles and has usually been able to override the proposed termination of weapons systems. Nonetheless, when the stars are aligned, some weapons systems can be terminated, or at least cut back, as in the example of the F-22 aircraft.[26]

On the issue of self-reform, for example, to create a more coherent oversight system for new departments like DHS, Congress has been an abysmal failure. In short, the congressional cultures and structure favor the status quo, leaving coalitions in the House and powerful senators in the Senate to extract concessions on particular NSE issues, depending on the nature of the issue involved and the will of the executive to respond.

As underscored in chapter 14, it is now virtually impossible to discuss the NSE without discussing the role of the US Supreme Court and the federal courts. Historically, the federal courts had shown deference to executive power and Congress in the carrying out of foreign policy, national security, and war. Over the last few years, however, federal courts have increasingly injected themselves into issues of executive power concerning detention of prisoners, interrogations, state secret protections, domestic surveillance, and the applicability of the Geneva Conventions. Using the doctrine of habeas corpus, the courts have demonstrated to both the president and Congress that when it comes to the protection of rights and the applicability of international conventions, the Court will have the last word.

The *Boumediene* case, which eroded the legal distinction between citizens and noncitizens held in custody outside the United States, is a watershed precedent whose effects await further adjudication. The DC district courts will now be setting the policy on who can be detained as a member of al-Qaeda based on the legal tests the courts establish. In addition, many have lamented the legalization of armed conflict and the new role "juridical warfare" or "lawfare" plays in the projections of force.[27] As the distinctions between domestic and international spheres continue to erode owing to the nature of transnational threats, more and more the issues of privacy and state needs will come into conflict over appropriate surveillance technologies. The federal courts, given their capacity for independent action, will continue to shape the NSE in potentially unexpected ways. It is hard to imagine the courts now retreating from this expanded role in the NSE process. The court culture of doctrinal independence, grounded in administrative autonomy, has been supported by the domestic political culture regardless of the nature of the decisions. To paraphrase Tocqueville, all national security enterprise issues will sooner or later turn into legal ones.

OUTSIDE PLAYERS: SETTING THE AGENDA

Think tanks, lobbyists, and the media all influence and shape the political environment for the national security debates. Some individuals rotate among these professions at different times in their careers. Although one cannot quantify their influence, the cultures of outside players are pervasive and significant in the policy process.

As described by Ellen Laipson in chapter 16, the think-tank culture has become increasingly integrated into the way the US government understands its national security interests and formulates policies and solutions. These organizations have become accepted as a normal and integral part of the policy-formulation process. The different institutes have become convenient locations for government officials to launch new policy initiatives and attract the media. Think tanks not only have critical audiences in the scholarly community but specific connections with the press, the private sector, and the general public. Policy ideas are "incubated, tested, promoted, and evaluated" in these organizations. The recently retired, aspiring to be, or seasoned veterans of the government who populate think tanks have extensive indexes of contacts and influence.

Think tanks can make their contributions at many points along the cycle of policymaking: identifying needs and gaps in policy, generating new ideas and approaches, building support for announced policies among constituents, assisting in gaining formal approval of ideas through legislation or executive authority, and monitoring implementation and issuing reports. In short, think tanks educate, inform, and persuade and are a transmission belt of ideas and information between government and the governed.

As noted by Laipson, in the national security world the work done in the aftermath of the Cold War that became known as cooperative threat reduction was a perfect example of how think tanks can influence policy. The collapse of the Soviet Union presented a dramatic challenge with respect to the Soviet nuclear arsenal. Scholars at the Brookings Institution, working with colleagues at Harvard and Stanford, were engaged in projects about the transition to the post–Cold War world that were first embraced by concerned members of Congress and later became executive branch policy. The ideas from this working group helped launch a number of policy initiatives, from programs to employ former weapons scientists in times of great economic stress in Russia, to new systems to manage and reduce fissile and other dangerous weapons-related materials. Today, some of these same think tanks are working on how to contain or at least manage the possibility of Iranian and North Korean nuclear programs.

This role of influencing current policy took an unprecedented leap in January 2010, when Maj. Gen. Michael T. Flynn, then deputy chief of staff for intelligence for the International Security Assistance Force in Afghanistan and presumptive National Security Advisor for President Trump, chose the think tank Center for a New American Security to publish a scathing critique of the US IC's performance in counterinsurgency in Afghanistan.[28] To many it was curious that a think tank and not the Pentagon was the vehicle for such a report by an active-duty officer. Only time will tell if this approach of collaboration between the administration and think tanks will become an accepted way to provide policy analysis.

What explains the robustness of the think-tank world in the United States? As Laipson notes, some attribute it to the relative weakness of American political parties, the developed philanthropic culture, and the public distrust of government.[29] Whatever the explanation, they are here to stay and will continue to be a force with which to be reckoned.

If think tanks approach the NSE as a battle of ideas, lobbyists are the critical implementers of the warring ideas and play a significant role advocating interests in the struggle over the political agenda. As insightfully stated by Gerald Warburg, politics can no more be taken out of the policymaking process than lobbyists can be removed from the system designed by America's founders to shape US laws.

To be successful, lobbying campaigns create an alliance of interests securing access to decision makers and energizing voters. The role lobbyists play in this competition to guide the NSE is readily apparent. Lobbyists are expert in navigating the national security labyrinth because they understand the access points, the interests of the major players, and the way to cobble together the necessary coalitions of interest groups. In a regulated system registered lobbyists are not unlike lawyers in the judicial branch: they are both messengers and advocates. Frustration about lobbying designed to influence US international policy often appears as a desire to shoot the messenger. Lobbyists, money, and access are all part of the executive and congressional branches. To some this use of money and access can distort the process and undermine what is best for the national interest. For Warburg, however, understanding the tools available and mastering the policymaking process is more effective than railing against the allegedly excessive influence of lobbyists. Many come to the NSE with the view to solve the lobbyist problem; the so-called problem, though, is embedded in the enterprise itself. There have been recent efforts to change the process around the edges, such as the calls to eliminate all earmarking involving for-profit entities. Looking forward, we see that foreign governments may well take a different route—not through lobbyists in Washington, but through the Internet—to influence US politics and elections through disclosures designed to weaken US policies or personalities, and institutions.

In many senses the media is like the culture of lobbying. Students of the NSE may rail against its influence, but for practitioners, like the tides and the moon, the media is a force of nature. There is little doubt that the media can influence events in international relations and national security and set the agenda, sometimes by design and sometimes by accident. As explored in chapter 17, anonymity plays a crucial role for both the media and government officials. The critical issues are when is information sensitive, and when can the strategic leak be used to affect policy? For the profession of the media, a key debate centers on when the story trumps national interests. Will a reporter compromise an exclusive story and disclose the potential whereabouts of Osama bin Laden to assist the US military or, for professional reasons, not pass on the information until after the interview? Regardless of the answer to this question, as John Diamond explains, even negative stories can have positive results as when incompetence or dereliction is exposed and legitimate grievances are heard and remedied. Owing to its nature, the media is a controversial player in the NSE, but owing to our values, it is a critical and necessary one for our culture of governmental accountability. The emerging impact of "fake news" will only add to the unpredictability of the media's impact on the NSE.

John Diamond catalogues how historically the different correspondent cultures—whether Washington-based, foreign, war, or regional—place a premium on being on site and interpreting the story or getting the scoop. Increasingly, though, given the competition from the other new technologies, reporters add value by being able to provide in-depth analysis that places events in context. It is clear that the media is undergoing a revolution as traditional papers and television networks struggle to adapt to the information revolution and the new emerging technologies. From a business perspective with two wars ongoing, the American newspaper industry is coping with a financial crisis of unprecedented severity and laboring simply to keep reporters in the field. Television networks are in a desperate effort to transform themselves from a static medium to one linked to home pages, the Internet, and 24-7 live coverage. This internal business struggle within the media will affect how the NSE is covered in the future. Media concentration combined with a democratization of forums paradoxically restricts and expands points of view at the same time. Increasingly, it is becoming harder to keep secrets as individuals with cell phone cameras, global tracking technology, and access to massive databases become private investigative reporters with blog pages. Leaks have come to dominate the news cycles and have helped caused reforms on how the IC conducts surveillance.

The 2010 series in the *Washington Post* on Top Secret America—based on open-source documents—was an extensive exposé of the IC's growth since 9/11.[30] The three-part reporting series asserted that the government had built a national security and intelligence system so big, so complex, and so hard to manage that it is questionable whether anyone knows if it is fulfilling its primary purpose of keeping us safe. In the process the series revealed facts previously not generally known to the pubic concerning the size of the community, locations of facilities, and a number of programs. At about the same time, the news organization WikiLeaks released on its dedicated web page 92,000 classified reports covering the war in Afghanistan from 2004 to 2010, titled *Afghan War Diary*. This was an extraordinary set of reports written by soldiers and intelligence officers describing lethal military actions involving the US military; however, it also is alleged to include intelligence information, reports of meetings with political figures, and other details. The release of some 15,000 additional reports that were to be redacted to protect certain information also troubled senior defense officials for fear it might endanger lives.[31]

The *Washington Post* story became possible in part because of the ability of technology and data banks to be cross-referenced from public sources and public electronic reports—the electronic risk of public data storage. There was no leaker per se; it was an investigation of public electronic databases. WikiLeaks was a bit different. A few observers have compared the WikiLeaks business model to the Pentagon Paper leaks during the Vietnam War. Yet what made this latest disclosure different was that all the original material could be stored electronically on a public website that then could be instantly accessed, searched, and downloaded by friend and foe for information on US approaches to the war in Afghanistan. This reflects the new age of computer technology. In addition, the latest WikiLeaks disclosure of hacked Democratic Party officials' and advisors' emails illustrates how media can be exploited by foreign governments to influence American politics. The future national security media environment promises to become ever more disruptive, diverse, and potentially destructive as a source of solid facts.

THE FUTURE FOR THE NATIONAL SECURITY ENTERPRISE

We have detailed in the book why it is hard to navigate and reform the current institutions and cultures of the NSE. Why coordination and reform is so difficult stems in part from one of the central tenets of the Washington bureaucracy—the mandarin algorithm of power:

$$J = FTEs + \$.$$

(Translated as follows: Legal jurisdiction over function or task [J] = Full-time equivalents or employees [FTEs] plus Money [$].)

Bureaucratic entrepreneurs know that if they can acquire statutory jurisdiction for a problem or issue, they will eventually acquire FTEs or hiring authority and funding from Congress. This is one reason why turf battles are so pitched inside the beltway: what appear to be parochial concerns of statutory jurisdiction are really about people and money—the lifeblood of power. So how does the NSE overcome this combined problem of the culture of organizations and the algorithm of the culture of power given the challenges of the future?

To create more of a unity of effort among the senior career managers, much more must be done to coordinate interagency career paths, provide pay incentive programs, and combine training and joint educational opportunities. To some these suggestions may appear to support an antidemocratic proposal for the creation of an elite set of career managers. To be accurate, we already have a managerial elite, the senior executive service, and over the last few years, some have become the gorillas in the cylinders of excellence that have undermined collective efforts. This reform, though, even if successful, may not eliminate the deep cultural and organizational rivalries. Goldwater–Nichols, the model of reform for "jointness," has not been the panacea for the military, as highlighted in a number of our chapters.

Unfortunately, we believe that if all the innovations fail, or are not even tried, significant change will come only with different scenarios of institutional failure. A massive physical or even virtual attack on the continental United States will be understood as a critical domestic crisis. The ripple effects would be felt through the entire structure. The US Northern Command (NORTHCOM), Cyber Command (CYBERCOM), and the National Security Agency (NSA) would be scrutinized to reevaluate their effectiveness and missions. It is predictable that the domestic departments and agencies charged with protecting the homeland—DHS, NSA, the FBI, the CIA, NORTHCOM, and DOD—would come under severe political attack, and once again there would be pressure to create a domestic intelligence agency. Potentially, a new domestic agency would be proposed to house all of the component parts for domestic intelligence currently scattered in the different departments. At the very least, a major effort will be launched to review and assess the allocation of authorities. A reflection of this tension is present in the debate over encryption and the extent of the government's right to access information without undermining due process.

Whether such a failure would also spur internal congressional reform of our present fractured oversight structure remains unclear. Presidential power would be strengthened in the short term as cries for action and executive response would be made. The environment would be supportive for massive institutional change; for us, effective change would require a full understanding of the cultures of the NSE. One reason we have written this book is to precipitate change before such a domestic crisis occurs.

Internationally, failure in overseas military operations would similarly cause soul-searching on whether the current balance of resources between the military and all the other agencies charged with political, economic, and social development is the proper mix. Yet again, debates would occur over how to define our vital interests and when we should venture abroad with the projection of force. Much ink will be spilled on how to deploy smart power with new and improved national security structures, empowered and well-resourced state departments, and effective modern development plans for fragile states and ungoverned spaces. To be sure, there would be support from some for a return to neo-isolationist policies and a withdrawal or cutback of overseas commitments without allied support. Reform of the NSE process would again be part of the debate, particularly if there was a consensus that the United States needed to be more involved in an international duty to protect vulnerable minority populations in failing states. Again, we contend reforms will not be effective unless the cultures of the agencies are understood.

Our book is being published in the wake of the terrorist attacks in France as well as the United States, along with escalating conflict in Syria. More than ever the NSE is being pressured for a strategy and not a set of reactive uncoordinated responses. In a 2015 study on blinders, blunders, and wars in the international system, the experts noted that the following eight factors are often part of poor decision making:[32]

- information is ignored, filtered, misconstrued, or manipulated to fit predispositions;
- decision makers rely too much on intuition and experience;
- arrogance, egotism, or hubris causes unwarranted confidence;
- a rigid but wrong strategic concept or vision prevails;
- contingencies are not part of the decision-making process;
- the enemy will or capabilities are underestimated;
- operational difficulty or duration is underestimated; and
- dissent and debate are stifled.

To respond to these factors, the authors recommend organizational cultural fixes such as more independent policy advice, better standards for analytical objectivity, and more use of technology. Again, it is always hard to institutionalize judgment, so any reform that contributes to building judgment, we support. Historically, the United States has proved to be resilient. The Cold War NSE served us well. We now confront global climate change, a weakening US dollar, failing or fragile states, rising economic powers, an information revolution, the potential spread of nuclear and biological weapons, increasing transnational terrorism, destabilizing migration, and an evolving hybrid for warfare. Creating new institutions and navigating a new labyrinth of power is fraught with risk and is not for the fainthearted or those with wobbly integrity. We are hopeful that our generation, like the generations before us, will craft policies that will appeal to our better angels and overcome the tendency of the triumph of parochialism and turf. It is our goal that this book will assist in the conversation needed to promote reform of the NSE.

NOTES

1. For an excellent summary of the efforts, benefits, and failures of such reforms, see Christopher J. Lamb and Joseph C. Bond, "National Security Reform and the 2016 Election," *Strategic Forum*, no. 293 (March 2016): 1–15, http://inss.ndu.edu/Portals/68/Documents/stratforum/SF-293.pdf.

2. See National Intelligence Council, *Global Trends 2025: A Transformed World* (Washington, DC, November 2008), vii–xi; or US Institute of Peace, *The QDR in Perspective: Meeting America's National Security Needs in the 21st Century: The Final Report of the Quadrennial Defense Review Independent Panel* (Washington, DC, July 2010), www.usip.org/files/qdr/qdrreport.pdf. (Five key global trends: radical Islamist extremism and the threat of terrorism; the rise of new global great powers in Asia; continued struggle for power in the Persian Gulf and the greater Middle East; an accelerating global competition for resources; and persistent problems from failed and failing states.)

3. Former secretary of defense Robert Gates made such complaints in his *Washington Post* interview in April 2016. See David Ignatius, "Bob Gates Unpacks Obama's Foreign Policy," *Washington Post*, April 14, 2016, www.washingtonpost.com/opinions/bob-gates-unpacks-obamas-foreign-policy-and-offers-advice-to-the-next-president/2016/04/14/1c4904c8–0275–11e6–9d36–33d198ea26c5_story.html?utm_term=.855148c36edb.

4. Lamb and Bond, "National Security Reform," 3.

5. Ibid, 10–11. The authors cite the State Department and CIA as perhaps the most recalcitrant, more so than DOD.

6. Paul B. Stares and Micah Zenko, *Enhancing U.S. Preventive Action*, Special Report No. 48 (New York: Council on Foreign Relations, October 2009).

7. David Rothkopf, *Running the World* (New York: Public Affairs, 2004).

8. US Institute of Peace, *QDR in Perspective*.

9. See Derek Chollet, *The Long Game: How Obama Defied Washington and Redefined America's Role in the World* (New York: Perseus Books, 2016).

10. Peter A. Hall and Michele Lamont, eds., *Successful Societies: How Institutions and Culture Affect Health* (New York: Cambridge University Press, 2009).

11. Ibid., 14.

12. See Graham T. Allison and Philip Zelikow, *Essence of Decision: Explaining the Cuban Missile Crisis*, 2nd ed. (New York: Longman, 1999); and Morton Halperin, Priscilla Clapp, and Arnold Kanter, *Bureaucratic Politics and Foreign Policy* (Washington, DC: Brookings Institution Press, 2007).

13. See Amy B. Zegart, *Spying Blind: The CIA, the FBI and the Origins of 9/11* (Princeton, NJ: Princeton University Press, 2007); and Amy B. Zegart, *Flawed by Design: The Evolution of the CIA, JCS, and NSC* (Palo Alto, CA: Stanford University Press, 1999).

14. Richard Haass, *The Bureaucratic Entrepreneur: How to Be Effective in Any Unruly Organization* (Washington, DC: Brookings Institution, 1999). Haass argues that an individual must develop his or her compass to navigate among the North, South, East, and West poles that shape the national security field.

15. This phenomenon found in the army is recently detailed in *The Fourth Star*, a book about the Department of Social Sciences (Sosh) at West Point. The department attracts both generals-in-waiting and dissidents, from Gen. Peter Chiarelli to Gen. David Petraeus. At Sosh intellectual ties and relations are forged that can follow and assist rising general officers until they are finally awarded the fourth star of command. See David Cloud and Greg Jaffe, *The Fourth Star* (New York: Crown Publishers, 2009), 54–60.

16. As of the time this book was completed, the Obama administration had already established special envoys for Afghanistan-Pakistan (Richard Holbrooke), Arab-Israeli (George Mitchell), Sudan (Gen. Scott Gration), and climate change (Todd Stern).

17. See Richard A. Best Jr., *The National Counterterrorism Center (NCTC)—Responsibilities and Potential Congressional Concerns* (Washington, DC: Congressional Research Service, January 15, 2010).

18. Eliot A. Cohen, Testimony Before the Senate Armed Services Committee, October 22, 2015.

19. Best, *National Counterterrorism Center*.

20. Ibid.

21. Ibid.

22. Hiroyuki Tanaka, Rocco Bellanova, Susan Ginsburg, and Paul De Hert, *Transatlantic Information Sharing: At a Crossroads* (Washington, DC: Migration Policy Institute, January 2010), 3–4, www.migrationpolicy.org/pubs/infosharing-Jan2010.pdf.

23. Ibid.

24. See Susan Ginsburg, *Securing Human Mobility in the Age of Risk: New Challenges for Travel, Migration, and Borders* (Washington, DC: Migration Policy Institute, 2010).

25. See W. Lee Rawls, *In Praise of Deadlock—How Partisan Struggle Makes Better Laws* (Washington, DC: Woodrow Wilson Center, 2009), 25.

26. See CNN, "Gates Announces Major Pentagon Priority Shifts," April 6, 2009, www.cnn.com/2009/POLITICS/04/06/gates.budget.cuts/index.html.

27. See Charles J. Dunlap Jr., "Lawfare amid Warfare," *Washington Times*, August 3, 2007; and Harvey Rishikof, "Juridical Warfare: The Neglected Legal Instrument," *Joint Force Quarterly*, no. 48 (1st Quarter 2008).

28. Michael T. Flynn, Matt Pottinger, and Paul D. Batchelor, *Fixing Intel: A Blueprint for Making Intelligence Relevant in Afghanistan* (Washington, DC: Center for New American Security, January 2010). The report opined that the "vast intelligence apparatus is unable to answer fundamental questions about the environment in which the US and allied forces operate and the people they seek to persuade. Ignorant of local economies and landowners, hazy about who the powerbrokers are and how they might be influenced, incurious about the correlations between various development projects and levels of cooperation among villagers, and disengaged from people in the best position to find answers."

29. James McGann, *Think Tanks and Policy Advice in the United States: Academics Advisors and Advocates* (New York: Routledge, 2007), 8.

30. See Dana Priest and William M. Arkin, "Top Secret America," *Washington Post*, July 19–21, 2010, projects.washingtonpost.com/top-secret-america.

31. Greg Jaffe and Joshua Partlow, "Joint Chiefs Chairman Mullen: WikiLeaks Release Endangers Troops, Afghans," *Washington Post*, July 30, 2010, www.washingtonpost.com/wp-dyn/content/article/2010/07/29/AR2010072904900.html.

32. David C. Gompert, Hans Binnendijk, and Bonny Lin, *Blinders, Blunders and Wars: What American and China Can Learn* (Santa Monica, CA: RAND, 2015); and Franklin D. Kramer, review of *Blinders, Blunders and Wars* by David C. Gompert, Hans Binnendijk, and Bonny Lin, *Prism* 5, no. 3 (2015).

Contributors

Gordon Adams is professor emeritus at the School of International Service at American University and is a distinguished fellow at the Stimson Center. From 1993 to 1997 he was the senior White House official on national security budgets as associate director for national security and international affairs at the Office of Management and Budget. He has written widely on defense and foreign policy budgeting. His book on national security and foreign policy planning and budgeting—*Buying National Security* (coauthored with Cindy Williams)—was published in 2009.

Brittany Albaugh has been serving as a law clerk for the American Bar Association's Standing Committee on Law and National Security since 2014. She will assume the position of federal law clerk in the Central District of Illinois in 2017. She holds an LL.M. degree in national security and foreign relations from the George Washington University and a JD from Hofstra Law School.

David P. Auerswald is professor of security studies at the National War College in Washington, DC, where he teaches courses on the national security policy process and has previously served as acting dean of faculty and associate dean of academic programs. He has worked as a congressional staff member on three separate occasions. His recent books include *Congress and Civil-Military Relations*, *NATO in Afghanistan: Fighting Together, Fighting Alone*, and *Congress and the Politics of National Security*.

Rodney Bent served as an international economist at the US Treasury Department and as a project financier in a New York bank, followed by twenty years at OMB, where his final position was as a deputy associate director for international affairs. He was a senior advisor to the Iraqi ministers of finance and planning. He returned to Washington in 2004 to work at the House Appropriations Committee, with subsequent positions at the Millennium Challenge Corporation, Booz Allen Hamilton, the State Department, and the United Nations.

Colton C. Campbell is professor of national security strategy at the National War College. Before joining the National War College, he worked as a legislative aide in the House of Representatives and the US Senate and as an analyst at the Congressional Research Service. Before his government service, he was an associate professor of political science at Florida International University. He has authored or contributed to numerous books and articles on Congress and the legislative process, most recently, *Congress and Civil-Military Relations* (Georgetown University Press, 2015).

John M. Diamond spent twenty-five years as a daily journalist and covered defense, foreign policy, and intelligence issues from 1989 to 2006 for the Associated Press, *Chicago Tribune*, and *USA Today*. He is the author of *The CIA and the Culture of Failure: U.S. Intelligence* *from the End of the Cold War to the Invasion of Iraq*, published in 2008 by Stanford University Press. He is currently a senior communications officer at the World Bank Group.

Thomas Fingar is the Oksenberg-Rohlen Distinguished Fellow and a senior scholar at Stanford's Freeman Spogli Institute for International Studies. He served as the first deputy director of national intelligence for analysis and chairman of the National Intelligence Council from 2005 through 2008, after nearly two decades at the State Department's Bureau of Intelligence and Research. His books include *Reducing Uncertainty: Intelligence Analysis and National Security.*

Roger Z. George is the professor of national security practice at Occidental College and formerly professor of national security studies at the National War College from 2009 to 2015. He was also previously an adjunct professor for Georgetown University's Security Studies Program. During a thirty-year career as a CIA analyst, he also served at the State and Defense Departments and was the national intelligence officer for Europe. He is coeditor with James B. Bruce of *Analyzing Intelligence: National Security Practitioners' Perspectives*, 2nd edition, published in 2011.

Susan Ginsburg is a member of the ABA Standing Committee on Law and National Security Advisory Committee. She served on the first Quadrennial Homeland Security Review Advisory Committee and as a senior counsel at the National Commissioner of Terrorist Attacks upon the United States (9/11 Commission). Her prior government service includes senior staff roles at the Treasury and State Departments. She is the author of *Securing Human Mobility in the Age of Risk* and *Countering Terrorist Mobility, Shaping an Operational Strategy.*

Marc Grossman is a vice chairman of the Cohen Group and teaches at the Georgetown University Edmund Walsh School of Foreign Service. He was a career foreign service officer from 1976 to 2005, having held numerous senior positions, including under secretary of state for political affairs, director general of the foreign service, assistant secretary of state for European affairs, and US ambassador to Turkey. He was recalled to the State Department from 2011 to 2012 to serve as the US special representative for Afghanistan and Pakistan.

Ellen Laipson has been president and CEO of the Stimson Center since leaving government service in 2002. Before assuming her responsibilities at the Stimson Center, she was the vice chairman of the National Intelligence Council. She began her career serving as a Middle East analyst at the Congressional Research Service, the State Department's Policy Planning Staff, and the National Intelligence Council. She has also served as the director of Near East and South Asian affairs at the NSC and at the US Mission to the UN. Since joining the Stimson Center, she has served on the President's Intelligence Advisory Board (2009–13) and the Secretary of State's Foreign Affairs Policy Board (2011–14).

Joseph McMillan served as principal deputy assistant secretary of defense for international security affairs from 2009 to 2012, capping a thirty-four-year career as a Department of Defense civil servant. He had previously been an acting deputy assistant secretary and senior research fellow at the Institute for National Strategic Studies. He has authored book chapters and policy papers on the Middle East, South Asia, terrorism, and radical Islam and was the editor of *In the Same Light as Slavery: Building a Global Antiterrorist Con-*

sensus (2007). He is now a principal with the Beaconsfield Strategy Group, an independent consulting firm.

Michael J. Meese is the chief operating officer of the American Armed Forces Mutual Aid Association (AAFMAA). He concluded his thirty-two-year army career as professor and head of the Social Sciences Department at West Point, having previously taught at the National War College and Princeton University. He has served as an advisor for senior military and civilian leaders in Afghanistan, Iraq, and Bosnia, on the Army Staff, and on the Defense Science Board and Defense Policy Board. He is a member of the Council on Foreign Relations and is an adjunct professor at Georgetown University. His books include *American National Security* and the *Armed Forces Guide to Personal Financial Planning*.

Franklin C. Miller is a principal at the Scowcroft Group. During thirty-one years of government service he was a senior policy official in the Office of the Secretary of Defense from 1979 until 2005, rising through the ranks to office director, deputy assistant secretary, principal deputy assistant secretary, and acting assistant secretary. From 2001 to 2005 he was seconded from DOD to become the senior director for defense policy on the National Security Council and special assistant to President George W. Bush.

Desaix Myers has been professor of national security studies at the National War College since 2010, after more than thirty years with the US Agency for International Development in a variety of assignments, including mission director in Russia and Indonesia. Before joining USAID, he had worked for the Investor Responsibility Research Center, reporting on corporate social responsibility and authoring books on South Africa and the debate over the nuclear power industry in the United States.

Kathleen Peroff is the head of the consulting firm Peroff and Associates, LLC. She served for twenty-nine years in the Office of Management and Budget, where she oversaw domestic, energy, and defense budget issues. From 2000 to 2013 she was deputy director of OMB's National Security Division. She has taught at the University of Maryland and holds advanced degrees from the University of Wisconsin.

Harvey Rishikof was formerly the dean of faculty and professor of law and national security at the National War College. He has written and lectured widely in the areas of national security, civil and military courts, terrorism, international law, civil liberties, and constitutional law. He has held senior positions in the federal judiciary, the Office of the Director of National Intelligence, and the FBI. He has been the chairman of the ABA's standing committee on law and national security.

Jon J. Rosenwasser has been a professional staff member of the US Senate Select Committee on Intelligence since 2013, serving as majority and minority budget director. He also has held positions at the CIA, the National Intelligence Council, and the Office of the Director of National Intelligence. Earlier in his career he was on the professional staff for the US Senate Budget Committee, a fellow at the Council on Foreign Relations and the Brookings Institution, and a consultant to the Defense Department. He has also been adjunct professor at George Mason University's Graduate School of Public Policy.

Dina Temple-Raston is the counterterrorism correspondent for National Public Radio, where she reports on terrorism at home and abroad for the network's news magazines. She previously was a reporter for both Bloomberg's financial wire and its radio operations in Asia. She has written four books, including *A Death in Texas* and *The Jihad Next Door*, on radicalization in America. She recently completed a Nieman Fellowship at Harvard University focused on the intersection of Big Data and intelligence.

Gerald Felix Warburg is assistant dean at the University of Virginia's Frank Batten School of Leadership and Public Policy, where he teaches courses on legislative strategy and the national security policymaking process. He previously served as legislative assistant to members of the House and Senate leadership and with Cassidy & Associates. He is author of *Conflict and Consensus: The Struggle between Congress and the President over Foreign Policymaking* and *Dispatches from the Eastern Front: A Political Education from the Nixon Years to the Age of Obama*.

Michael Warner is a historian for the Department of Defense and is also adjunct professor at Johns Hopkins University and American University. He has written widely on intelligence history, theory, and reform. His most recent book *The Rise and Fall of Intelligence: An International Security* was published by Georgetown University in 2014.

Isaiah (Ike) Wilson III is the chief of the Commander's Initiatives Group (CIG) at US Central Command. Previously, he was a professor of political science and the director of the American politics, policy, and strategy program at West Point and has taught at the National War College and Yale University. He is a member of the Council on Foreign Relations and has been an adjunct professor at Columbia University and George Washington University. He was chief of plans of the 101st Air Assault Division in Mosul, Iraq; contributed to the army's first assessment of Operation Iraqi Freedom; served as an advisor and planner in Afghanistan on civil–military integration; and is the author of numerous articles and books, including *Thinking Beyond War*.

Index

Boxes, figures, notes, and tables are indicated by b, f, n, *and* t *following the page number.*